John's Transformation of Mark

John's Transformation of Mark

Edited by

Eve-Marie Becker
Helen K. Bond
Catrin H. Williams

LONDON • NEW YORK • OXFORD • NEW DELHI • SYDNEY

T&T CLARK
Bloomsbury Publishing Plc
50 Bedford Square, London, WC1B 3DP, UK
1385 Broadway, New York, NY 10018, USA

BLOOMSBURY, T&T CLARK and the T&T Clark logo are trademarks of Bloomsbury Publishing Plc

First published in Great Britain 2021

Copyright © Eve-Marie Becker, Helen K. Bond, Catrin H. Williams and contributors, 2021

Eve-Marie Becker, Helen K. Bond and Catrin H. Williams have asserted their right under the Copyright, Designs and Patents Act, 1988, to be identified as Editors of this work.

All rights reserved. No part of this publication may be reproduced or transmitted in any form or by any means, electronic or mechanical, including photocopying, recording, or any information storage or retrieval system, without prior permission in writing from the publishers.

Bloomsbury Publishing Plc does not have any control over, or responsibility for, any third-party websites referred to or in this book. All internet addresses given in this book were correct at the time of going to press. The author and publisher regret any inconvenience caused if addresses have changed or sites have ceased to exist, but can accept no responsibility for any such changes.

A catalogue record for this book is available from the British Library.

Library of Congress Cataloging-in-Publication Data
Names: Becker, Eve-Marie, editor. | Bond, Helen K. (Helen Katharine), editor. | Williams, Catrin H., 1964- editor.
Title: John's transformation of Mark / edited by Eve-Marie Becker, Helen K. Bond, Catrin H. Williams.
Description: London ; New York : T&T Clark, 2021. | Includes bibliographical references and index. | Summary: "John's Transformation of Mark brings together a cast of internationally recognised biblical scholars to investigate the relationship between the gospels of Mark and John. In a significant break with the prevailing view that the two gospels represent independent traditions, the contributors all argue that John both knew and used the earlier gospel. Drawing on recent analytical categories such as social memory, 'secondary orality,' or 'relecture,' and ancient literary genres such as 'rewritten Bible' and bioi, the central questions that drive this volume focus on how John used Mark, whether we should speak of 'dependence,' 'familiarity with,' or 'reception,' and whether John intended his work to be a supplement or a replacement of Mark. Together these chapters mount a strong case for a reassessment of one of the key tenets of modern biblical criticism, and open up significant new avenues for further research"—Provided by publisher.
Identifiers: LCCN 2020032744 (print) | LCCN 2020032745 (ebook) | ISBN 9780567691897 (pb) | ISBN 9780567691934 (hb) | ISBN 9780567691903 (epdf) | ISBN 9780567691910 (epub)
Subjects: LCSH: Bible. John—Criticism, interpretation, etc. | Bible. Mark—Criticism, interpretation, etc.
Classification: LCC BS2615.52 .J656 2021 (print) | LCC BS2615.52 (ebook) | DDC 226.5/066—dc23
LC record available at https://lccn.loc.gov/2020032744
LC ebook record available at https://lccn.loc.gov/2020032745

ISBN:	HB:	978-0-5676-9193-4
	PB:	978-0-5676-9189-7
	ePDF:	978-0-5676-9190-3
	ePUB:	978-0-5676-9191-0

Typeset by RefineCatch Limited, Bungay, Suffolk

To find out more about our authors and books visit www.bloomsbury.com and sign up for our newsletters.

Contents

Notes on Contributors		vii
Acknowledgements		xi
1	John's Transformation of Mark: Introduction *Eve-Marie Becker, Helen K. Bond and Catrin H. Williams*	1
2	John and Mark in the History of Research *Harold W. Attridge*	9
3	The Johannine 'Relecture' of Mark *Jean Zumstein*	23
4	'If John Knew Mark': Critical Inheritance and Johannine Disagreements with Mark *Chris Keith*	31
5	John's 'Rewriting' of Mark: Some Insights from Ancient Jewish Analogues *Catrin H. Williams*	51
6	Defining and Debating Divine Identity in Mark and John: The Influence of Classical Language and Literature *George Parsenios*	67
7	Parallel Traditions or Parallel Gospels? John's Gospel as a Re-Imagining of Mark *Mark Goodacre*	77
8	Beyond History: How John Transcends Mark and Ancient Historiography *Eve-Marie Becker*	91
9	The Beginnings of Mark and John: What Exactly Should Be Compared? Some Hermeneutical Questions and Observations *Christina Hoegen-Rohls*	101
10	Jesus in Sharper Relief: Making Sense of the Fourth Gospel's Use of Mark 1.2–8 in John 1.19–34 *Steve A. Hunt*	121
11	John the Baptist in Mark and John: An Exercise in Comparison *Troels Engberg-Pedersen*	135
12	How John 'Rewrites' Mark as Seen in John 5.1–18 *Gilbert Van Belle*	149
13	From the Expectation of the Imminent Kingdom to the Presence of Eternal Life: Eschatology in Mark and John *Jörg Frey*	169
14	Ethical Concepts in Mark and John: A Comparative Approach *Oda Wischmeyer*	187
15	The 'Speeches' in Mark and John: Comparative Readings *Susanne Luther*	203

16　The Lost Temptation of Christ? John's Philosophical Rewriting of Markan
　　Temptation Scenes　*Kasper Bro Larsen*　　215
17　The Plot to Kill Jesus in Mark and John: Reflections on the
　　Literary Relationship between Two Early Christian Theological
　　Biographies of Jesus on the Basis of a Detail in Their Storytelling
　　Michael Labahn　　229
18　The Triumph of the King: John's Transformation of Mark's
　　Account of the Passion　*Helen K. Bond*　　251

Bibliography　　269
Index Ancient Sources　　299
General Index　　315

Contributors

Harold W. Attridge is the Sterling Professor of Divinity at Yale University Divinity School. He has engaged in research on Hellenistic Judaism, the Epistle to the Hebrews, Nag Hammadi texts and the Gospel according to John. Among his many publications are *First-Century Cynicism in the Epistles of Heraclitus* (Scholars Press, 1976), *The Interpretation of Biblical History in the* Antiquitates Judaicae *of Flavius Josephus* (Scholars Press, 1976), *Hebrews: A Commentary on the Epistle to the Hebrews* (Fortress, 1989), *The Acts of Thomas* (Polebridge, 2010) and *Essays on John and Hebrews* (Mohr Siebeck, 2010). He was elected to be a Fellow of the American Academy of Arts and Sciences in 2015.

Eve-Marie Becker is Professor of New Testament at the Westfälische Wilhelms-Universität Münster and was previously Professor of New Testament exegesis at Aarhus University. She is the author of a number of monographs on Paul and Mark and (early Christian) literary history, including *Der Begriff der Demut bei Paulus/Paul on Humility* (Mohr Siebeck, 2015/Baylor, 2020), *Der Philipperbrief des Paulus* (Narr Francke, 2020), *Das Markus-Evangelium im Rahmen der antiken Historiographie* (Mohr Siebeck, 2006), *Der früheste Evangelist* (Mohr Siebeck, 2017) and *The Birth of Christian History* (Yale University Press, 2017). She is currently working on a *Frühchristliche Literaturgeschichte* (de Gruyter) and a commentary on *Philippians* (Meyers KEK series).

Helen K. Bond is Professor of Christian Origins and Head of the School of Divinity at the University of Edinburgh. Her research focuses on the social and political history of Judaea under Roman rule, the historical Jesus, and the canonical gospels. She is the author of a number of books, including *Pontius Pilate in History and Interpretation* (Cambridge University Press, 1998), *Caiaphas: Friend of Rome and Judge of Jesus?* (Westminster John Knox, 2004), *The Historical Jesus: A Guide for the Perplexed* (Bloomsbury, 2012) and *The First Biography of Jesus: Genre and Meaning in Mark's Gospel* (Eerdmans, 2020). She is presently writing a commentary on Mark's Gospel for the Oxford Bible Commentary.

Troels Engberg-Pedersen was educated in Classics (Copenhagen, 1974) and ancient and modern philosophy (Oxford, 1974–76). His first doctoral dissertation (DPhil) addressed Aristotle's ethics (1982); he then wrote on Stoic ethics (1990), and his second doctoral dissertation (DTheol) addressed Paul and Stoicism (2000). Until his retirement in 2016 he was Professor of New Testament at the University of Copenhagen. His research focuses on ancient philosophy, not least Stoicism, and the New Testament, particularly Paul and John. Among his most recent publications are *From Stoicism to Platonism: The Development of Philosophy, 100 BCE–100 CE* (editor, Cambridge

University Press, 2017) and *John and Philosophy: A New Reading of the Fourth Gospel* (Oxford University Press, 2017).

Jörg Frey is Professor of New Testament Interpretation with special focus on Ancient Judaism and Hermeneutics in the Faculty of Theology at the University of Zürich, and Research Fellow in the Department of Old and New Testament Studies at the University of the Free State, Bloemfontein, South Africa. He is the author of several works, including *Die johanneische Eschatologie* (3 vols; Mohr Siebeck, 1997–2000), *Die Herrlichkeit des Gekreuzigten / The Glory of the Crucified One: Christology and Theology in the Gospel of John* (Mohr Siebeck, 2013; Baylor University Press, 2018) and *Theology and History in the Fourth Gospel: Tradition and Narration* (Baylor University Press, 2018).

Mark Goodacre is the Frances Hill Fox Professor of Religious Studies at Duke University, North Carolina. He earned his MA, MPhil and DPhil at the University of Oxford. His research interests include the Gospels, the Apocryphal New Testament, and the Historical Jesus. Goodacre is the author of four books, including *Goulder and the Gospels: An Examination of a New Paradigm* (T&T Clark, 1996), *The Case Against Q: Studies in Markan Priority and the Synoptic Problem* (Trinity Press International, 2002) and *Thomas and the Gospels: The Case for Thomas's Familiarity with the Synoptics* (Eerdmans, 2012). He is currently working on a book on John's knowledge of the Synoptic Gospels.

Christina Hoegen-Rohls studied Protestant theology, German studies and comparative education in Munich and Zürich and is currently Professor for Biblical Studies (Old and New Testaments) and their didactics at Westfälische Wilhelms-Universität Münster. Her main research areas are the Johannine Writings and Paul's Letters, and the history of the reception of the Bible in literature and arts. She is Area Editor (Literature) of the *Encyclopedia of the Bible and its Reception* and is currently working on a commentary on the Pastoral Letters (KEK; Vandenhoeck and Ruprecht). She is a Research Fellow in the Department of Old and New Testament Studies at the University of the Free State, Bloemfontein, South Africa.

Steven A. Hunt has a PhD from the University of Sheffield and is Professor of New Testament at Gordon College in Wenham, Massachusetts. In addition to a number of professional articles and his technical work, *Rewriting the Feeding of Five Thousand: John 6.1–15 as a Test Case for Johannine Dependence on the Synoptic Gospels* (Peter Lang, 2011), he also edited *Perspectives on Our Father Abraham* (Eerdmans, 2010) and co-edited and contributed several chapters to the volume *Character Studies in the Fourth Gospel: Narrative Approaches to Seventy Figures in John* (Mohr Siebeck/Eerdmans, 2016). He is presently co-writing a commentary on John's Gospel for the Oxford Bible Commentary.

Chris Keith is Research Professor of New Testament and Christian Origins at St Mary's University, Twickenham, where he also serves as the Director of the Centre for the

Social-Scientific Study of the Bible. His research focuses on the book cultures of Second Temple Judaism and early Christianity, sociological approaches to memory and historiography, the Gospels, and the historical Jesus. He was a winner of the 2010 John Templeton Award for Theological Promise and his publications include *The Pericope Adulterae, the Gospel of John, and the Literacy of Jesus* (Brill, 2009), *Jesus against the Scribal Elite: The Origins of the Conflict* (rev. ed. T&T Clark, 2020) and *The Gospel as Manuscript: An Early History of the Jesus Tradition as Material Artifact* (Oxford University Press, 2020).

Michael Labahn is Extraordinary Professor at Martin-Luther-University in Halle-Wittenberg, and Extraordinary Associate Professor at North-West University (Potchefstroom Campus), South Africa. His primary research interests include Q, the Johannine literature, the Book of Revelation, and the religious and cultural context of early Christianity, early Christian ethics, and the reception of the Old Testament in the New. He is the author of *Jesus als Lebensspender: Untersuchungen zu einer Geschichte der johanneischen Tradition anhand ihrer Wundergeschichten* (de Gruyter, 1999), *Der Gekommene als Wiederkommender: Die Logienquelle als erzählte Geschichte* (Evangelische Verlagsanstalt, 2010), and a selection of his essays on John have been published in *Ausgewählte Studien zum Johannesevangelium: Selected Studies in the Gospel of John* (ed. Antje Labahn; Peeters, 2017).

Kasper Bro Larsen is Professor of New Testament Studies at Aarhus University, Denmark, and Research Fellow in the Department of Old and New Testament Studies at the University of the Free State, Bloemfontein, South Africa. He has published widely in Johannine studies, especially on the relationship between John's Gospel and similar motifs in the wider Graeco-Roman literature. His publications include *Recognizing the Stranger: Recognition Scenes in the Gospel of John* (Brill, 2008, repr. 2012) and *The Gospel of John as Genre Mosaic* (ed., Vandenhoeck & Ruprecht, 2015).

Susanne Luther, Dr. habil., is Assistant Professor of New Testament, Faculty of Theology and Religious Studies, University of Groningen. Her main research interests include speech ethics, ancient miracle stories, and the debate on fictionality and factuality in early Christian literature. She is the author of *Sprachethik im Neuen Testament: Eine Analyse des frühchristlichen Diskurses im Matthäusevangelium, im Jakobusbrief und im 1. Petrusbrief* (Mohr Siebeck, 2015) and *Die Authentifizierung der Vergangenheit: Literarische Geschichtsdarstellung im Johannesevangelium* (Mohr Siebeck, 2020).

George Parsenios is Professor of New Testament at Princeton Theological Seminary, and Research Fellow in the Department Old and New Testament Studies of the University of the Free State, Bloemfontein, South Africa. His research explores the interaction of early Christianity with classical literature, as well as the interpretation of the New Testament in the early church. He is the author of *Departure and Consolation: The Johannine Farewell Discourses in Light of Greco-Roman Literature* (Brill, 2005),

Rhetoric and Drama in the Johannine Lawsuit Motif (Mohr Siebeck, 2010) and *First, Second, and Third John* (Paideia Commentaries on the New Testament; Baker Academic, 2014).

Gilbert Van Belle is Emeritus Professor with formal duties in the Research Unit Biblical Studies (New Testament) at the Faculty of Theology and Religious Studies (KU Leuven). His research focuses on the Fourth Gospel, especially its style, Christology, soteriology, theology and history of research. As a proponent of the 'Louvain School', he defends the literary unity of the Fourth Gospel and accepts that the author of the Fourth Evangelist used the Synoptic Gospels. Recently he published 'The Two Johannine Colophons and John's Rereading of Mark 1.7-8' in *Reading the Gospel of Mark in the Twenty-First Century: Method and Meaning*, ed. G. Van Oyen, 781–98 (BETL, 301; Leuven, Peeters, 2019).

Catrin H. Williams is Reader in New Testament Studies at the University of Wales Trinity Saint David, Lampeter, and Research Fellow in the Department Old and New Testament Studies at the University of the Free State, Bloemfontein, South Africa. She is the author of *I am He: The Interpretation of 'Anî Hû' in Jewish and Early Christian Literature* (Mohr Siebeck, 2000) and has edited various volumes on John's Gospel, including *John's Gospel and Intimations of Apocalyptic* (Bloomsbury, 2013), *Engaging with C.H. Dodd on the Gospel of John* (Cambridge University Press, 2013) and *Discovering John* (Cascade Press, 2020).

Oda Wischmeyer was, until her retirement, Professor of New Testament Studies and Ancient Judaism at the Friedrich-Alexander Universität Erlangen-Nürnberg (1993–2009). She has an honorary doctorate from the University of Lund (2015) and was Guest Professor at the Pontificio Istituto Biblico in Rome (2019–20). Among her numerous publications are *Von Ben Sira zu Paulus: Gesammelte Aufsätze* (Mohr Siebeck, 2002), *Die Kultur des Buches Jesus Sirach* (de Gruyter, 2012) and *Liebe als Agape: Das frühchristliche Konzept und der moderne Diskurs/Love as Agape* (Mohr Siebeck, 2015/Baylor University Press, 2021). She is currently working on a commentary on *James* (Meyers KEK series).

Jean Zumstein is Professor Emeritus at the Faculty of Theology of the University of Zürich, and Research Fellow in the Department of Old and New Testament Studies of the University of the Free State, Bloemfontein, South Africa. His areas of specialization are hermeneutics, the Gospel of Matthew and the Johannine Literature. He is the author of *Kreative Erinnerung: Relecture und Auslegung im Johannesevangelium* (2nd edition; Theologischer Verlag, 2004) and *L'Evangile selon Saint Jean* (2nd edition; Labor et Fides, 2016).

Acknowledgements

We are grateful to Aarhus University for partial funding towards the conference in Athens at which most of the essays in this volume were first presented; to *cand. theol. et phil.* Leonie Best (Münster) for assistance with some of the copy-editing; and to Dominic Mattos and Sarah Blake at Bloomsbury T&T Clark for accepting this volume for publication and for seeing it through the editorial process. Last but not least we would like to thank all participants at the Athens conference and the contributors to this volume for being such reliable collaborators from start to finish.

Münster, Edinburgh, Lampeter
May 2020

1

John's Transformation of Mark: Introduction

Eve-Marie Becker, Helen K. Bond and Catrin H. Williams

John and Mark – Mark and John: two gospel narratives, somehow related yet at the same time distinct, endlessly prompting questions about their relationship. Which author has built on whom, when, why and how? The present volume seeks to address these questions by presenting a proposal resulting from a multi-perspective reading of Mark in relation to John, namely *John's* transformation of *Mark*.

Scholarly debates about the relationship between the canonical gospels have a long history. Since at least the time of Tatian's *Diatessaron* and patristic exegesis, various attempts have been made to find meaning in the fourfold gospel canon. New Testament interpreters have sought ever since to relate the four gospel narratives to each other and to establish plausible explanations for how, why and in which order the gospel writings were composed. New Testament scholarship has, in this respect, directed significant attention to the question of the relationship between Matthew, Mark and Luke. Various attempts have been made at solving the so-called 'Synoptic problem', although most of the proposed hypotheses about Synoptic relationships – in whatever configuration – are underpinned by theories of literary dependence.

The precise relationship between John and Mark also has an extensive history of scholarly attention. Long regarded as a spiritual interpretation of the earlier three canonical Gospels, a broad scholarly consensus (at least in North America) has, throughout most of the second half of the twentieth century, tended to regard John's Gospel as quite independent of the other gospels and related to them only on the level of prior tradition (whether oral, written or some combination of both). However, the idea that there exists some kind of a *literary* connection between John and the others never completely went away, and it is even enjoying a resurgence in much recent scholarship. It is these issues, with reference specifically to *Mark* (rather than the Synoptic Gospels more generally), that are the focus of this particular collection of essays.

The majority of papers in this volume were first aired at a conference held in the Titania Hotel, Athens, Greece, 4–6 August 2018, prior to the SNTS meeting at the same venue.

Although two of the conference organizers were already convinced that the author of John's Gospel had not only known Mark's Gospel but had reflected deeply upon it, the aims of the conference were more modest. Contributors – all of them internationally recognized experts in the Gospels of either John or Mark (or both) – were asked simply to compare various themes and motifs across the two works, taking a view on any possible relationship between them only if they felt so disposed. Our expectation was that the group would include several scholars wishing to maintain the view that the two gospels represent independent traditions, and we were anxious to include as broad a range of perspectives as possible.

As paper after paper was delivered, however, in a mercifully air-conditioned room overlooking the Parthenon, a curious thing began to emerge. Every contributor, without exception, expressed the considered opinion that John had reworked the earlier gospel in some way or another, and the conversation quickly began to focus on recent analytical categories such as social memory, 'secondary orality', or 'relecture', on ancient literary genres such as 'rewritten Bible', historiography and *bioi*, on whether we should speak of 'dependence', 'familiarity with', or 'reception', and on whether John intended his work to be a supplement or a replacement of Mark. As we pulled together the various threads at the end of the conference, there was a general desire to be rather bolder in the published version of the essays. The conference's rather diffident original title – 'John and Mark: Is There a Connection?' – became the much more confident current title – *John's Transformation of Mark*.

As already noted, the 'independent tradition' theory has been the dominant hypothesis in Johannine studies for several decades, but it is important to remember that it is only that – a hypothesis. It took hold in a very different scholarly climate when form criticism with its emphasis on oral traditions and community transmission shaped the agenda, with little appreciation of the Gospels as literary works crafted by creative authors in control of their sources. Added to this is the scholarly assumption that any discussion of the relationship between John and Mark has to be conducted along the same lines as Synoptic relationships, that is, the close, almost scribal, editing of Mark by Matthew and Luke. The last decade has seen a much greater recognition of the strategies and techniques applied by ancient authors in their use of sources, relying much more on paraphrase and selective use of material rather than close verbatim reproduction of earlier texts. In this respect, the way in which Matthew and Luke use Mark is anomalous rather than John's use of his predecessor. The recognition that Mark and John both share the same genre, both start and finish in broadly the same place, and both are preoccupied with the death of Jesus are further important arguments for why readers should have confidence that John did not compose his gospel in total isolation from Mark.

The essays in this volume are exploratory in nature and we have not attempted to come to any consensus on exactly *how*, *why* or *when* John used Mark. Was John drawing on the written text, recasting his recollection of an oral reading of the earlier gospel, or a combination of the two? Did he intend to supplement, replace or complement the earlier work? Some contributors to this volume come to firm conclusions on these matters, others take as their starting point the assumption that John has used Mark and then test the explanatory power of this new hypothesis on various passages and themes.

The collection begins with a survey of earlier scholarship. Harry Attridge helpfully leads us through the data and provides an overview of the various positions regarding the parallels between the Gospels of Mark and John. He demonstrates how the view that John knew and used the Synoptics generally and Mark in particular was widely accepted from patristic times through to the nineteenth century, though the opinion that the two gospels represented independent traditions dominated much twentieth-century scholarship. Many scholars explained the common elements by appealing to a written source, often described as a 'Signs Gospel', or to common oral tradition. Some recent scholars have argued that the gospels mutually influenced each other during the process of their gradual composition. The evidence, he suggests, particularly in the details of passages that seem to be built on elements derived from deconstructed Markan pericopes, supports the judgment that there was substantial, but very creative, use of Mark by the Fourth Evangelist.

The next few essays consider various creative ways and fresh methodological paradigms in which we might think about the relationship between John and Mark. Jean Zumstein hypothesizes that *the relationship is a typical case of hypertextuality*. He argues that John wrote his work based on a previous generic model, namely Mark. But the Gospel of John is not a simple repetition of Mark, it is a *derived* text that bears the hallmark of a process of *transformation*. Various key texts, he argues – the Temple incident, the miracle of the loaves, the walking on water, Gethsemane, the footwashing – are classical examples of this process.

Chris Keith's essay supports theories for Johannine knowledge of the Gospel of Mark by engaging critically with Percival Gardner-Smith's influential argument for Johannine independence. Gardner-Smith focused heavily upon Johannine disagreements with Mark's Gospel and argued that such disagreements indicate that the author of John's Gospel could not have known Mark's Gospel. Employing the concept of 'critical inheritance' from social memory theory, Keith argues instead that the reception of inherited tradition consists of simultaneous acceptance of some aspects of the prior tradition and rejection of other aspects of it. Thus, and contra Gardner-Smith, disagreement with a prior tradition can function as an indicator of knowledge of that prior tradition.

Catrin Williams adds the concept of 'rewritten Bible' and other Jewish forms of 'rewriting' to the discussion. Authoritative texts, she notes, were often subjected to a process of rewriting in late Second Temple Judaism, a phenomenon that has received considerable attention in recent debates about the category of 'rewritten Bible' or 'rewritten Scripture'. Her essay examines some of the compositional features attested in early Jewish rewritten texts (such as *Jubilees,* the *Genesis Apocryphon,* and *4 Maccabees*) in order to determine how the points of contact between such features and John's Gospel can inform the discussion of John's familiarity with, or even its 'reworking' of, the Gospel of Mark. She considers various ancient Jewish 'rewriting' techniques and strategies, including the issue of how authority is understood in rewritten compositions with reference to their underlying base text.

Addressing the topic from a rather different angle, George Parsenios argues that John develops and expands material from Mark by recourse to classical literature. Mark, for instance, places in the mouth of Jesus the phrase 'I am' (ἐγώ εἰμι). John follows suit, but he develops this phrase even further by placing it within the context of the categories of 'being' and 'becoming' common to Plato and a Platonist like Philo. The same happens on a narrative level with the use of models from classical literature.

Recent scholarship has argued that Mark relies on the mode of tragic narrative to present the life of Jesus, but these dramatic devices are deployed in an embryonic or rudimentary fashion. One of these is the dramatic interest in scenes of recognition (*anagnôrisis*). Mark introduces this device into the life of Jesus in a basic fashion, and John develops it more fully. In both cases, classical literature provides the scaffolding for John to build on material in Mark.

Those who consider John to be independent of the Synoptic Gospels tend to explain the agreements between them by appeal to ever fluid 'tradition'. However, John's literary familiarity with the Synoptics is more plausible than independence because there are literary parallels at every point, from the minutiae of verbal agreements in individual verses, to whole pericopae, like the Anointing (where John becomes a fourth Synoptic gospel), to the entire structure of the gospel (which, like Mark, is a 'passion narrative with an extended introduction'). Moreover, John shares Mark's fundamental literary conceit, writing a gospel of a hidden Messiah who is only retrospectively understood after the resurrection. This is not a question of individual parallel traditions but – as Mark Goodacre argues in his contribution – of overall parallel literary concepts. The idea that John independently hit on exactly the same project as Mark assumes that Mark's Gospel is somehow normative and that its way of telling Jesus' story is inevitable. John is more plausibly understood as a creative re-imagination of Mark, inspired by his project, but critically reinterpreting it.

Eve-Marie Becker turns her attention to the relation of both Mark and John to ancient historiography. She argues that the Gospel of John shares some elementary narrative patterns that characterize the Synoptic approach to history-writing. However, at various crucial points John intentionally leaves the history-oriented view of the gospel story. This becomes particularly evident in a passage like John 11. Primarily for reasons of re-conceptualizing time and history, Becker maintains, John thus aims to 'transcend' the model of ancient history-writing and instead prepares the ground for a type of early Christian literature that is 'revelatory'.

The remaining chapters in the volume focus attention on particular passages or themes, arranged broadly in the sequential order in which they first emerge or become prominent in the text of John's Gospel. Christina Hoegen-Rohls begins at the very start of the gospels, with their opening verses. But what exactly, she asks, should be compared when comparing the *beginnings* of the Gospels of Mark and John? The opening sentences (Mk 1.1; Jn 1.1), the opening sections (Mk 1.1-3; Jn 1.1-5), the beginnings of the narratives (Mk 1.4-8; Jn 1.7, 15, 19-26), or the very first segments marked by the so-called *kephalaia* (Mk 1.1-22; Jn 1.1-51)? More provocatively, she asks whether Mark 16.7-8 is to be seen as the real beginning of Mark's Gospel. On the basis of all these comparisons, Hoegen-Rohls concludes that the observable similarities and differences suggest that John knew the beginning of Mark and deliberately transformed it.

Steve Hunt's essay focuses on John the Baptist as he appears in Mark 1.2-8 and John 1.19-34. At its most basic level, he argues, the Fourth Gospel tells the story of Jesus, the one sent by God in order to reveal Godself to the world. Because this beloved yet estranged world had never fully seen God, John's Gospel says implicitly throughout: if you want to see God, take a look at Jesus. But how is this revelation communicated by the narrative? John's Jesus stands in sharper relief when understood in light of Mark's

Gospel than when he stands alone. Thus, the essay attempts to demonstrate that the Fourth Gospel is – at least in part – a *relecture* of Mark. The essay offers a plausible, coherent reading showing how the author of the Fourth Gospel may have used (that is, may have rewritten and transformed) the story of John the Baptist in Mark in the pursuit of his own theological agenda.

Distinguishing between 'parallel comparison', 'heuristic comparison' and 'genealogical comparison', Troels Engberg-Pedersen's essay pushes a little further at the John the Baptist material *if* we take it that John knew and used the earlier work. At the end of the essay it is suggested that if the 'heuristic' comparison is illuminating and convincing, then one may also draw a 'genealogical' conclusion: that John knew Mark. In terms of substance, the essay argues that where Mark has described the Baptist in relation to Jesus as both a *Vorläufer*, *Vorbild*, and *Zeuge*, John transforms all of Mark's material so that it falls under seeing the Baptist as a *Zeuge*, only. However, *as* a witness to Jesus, John's Baptist also becomes the author's mouthpiece for his own understanding of the *full* meaning of the story about Jesus. This pertains specifically to the role of the *pneuma*, both in making Jesus the Elect and Son of God and also in incorporating believers into Christ. In both cases, the Baptist's witness is directed to the special role of the *pneuma* in baptism (or 'baptism' in the case of God in relation to Jesus). In this way, John has extracted a highly specific, substantial picture of the Baptist from the much more sprawling account given of him by Mark.

In the 1970s, 'the Leuven school' rejected the prevailing views of the relationship between Mark and John, and defended both John's dependence on the Synoptics and the literary unity of the Fourth Gospel. In our next chapter, Gilbert Van Belle (himself a prominent member of the Leuven school) recounts a dialogue that took place between Peder Borgen and Frans Neirynck at the Jerusalem Symposium of 1984. This dialogue has been brought back into the spotlight again, thirty years later, by Borgen himself. After looking back at the history of research and especially this dialogue, Van Belle defends the Leuven hypothesis in three steps. First, the methods and criteria used to determine John's dependence or independence are analysed. Secondly, based on the Borgen-Neirynck dialogue, and taking John 5.1–18 as an example, the arguments for dependence or independence regarding Mark 2.1–12 are considered. Thirdly, an evaluation of the Leuven method is given in light of recent research on oral tradition, media culture and social memory. In his conclusion, Van Belle emphasizes that the combination of two arguments are very important in the discussion of John's dependence on the Synoptics. That is, the striking verbal agreements should be considered in combination with the order of the texts. Moreover, through an intertextual comparison of the written documents, he deduces that we can see how John rewrites Mark. He thus determines that it is easier to understand the redaction of the Fourth Evangelist without taking oral tradition into account *a priori*.

In the next contribution to the volume Jörg Frey builds on his influential 2003 article – where he argues that John presupposes that his readers were already familiar with Mark – by undertaking a close comparison of eschatological concepts in both gospels. After highlighting the apocalyptic orientation of much of Mark's eschatology, he examines how John's Gospel parts company with its predecessor. Cosmic and future-oriented aspects become more internalized in John's eschatology, which focuses not so much on future events but on the here and the now. Some conceptual points of contact with Mark can be identified, such as John's use of 'the hour' and a few references to the core eschatological concept of 'the kingdom', although for John these are now centred on Jesus and the present gift of life that comes through believing in him. All in all, argues Frey, there are only a few close connections between Mark and John in their understanding of eschatology; where there are conceptual parallels, they have been creatively transformed by John in light of its Christology.

Oda Wischmeyer analyses ethical themes and concepts in John and Mark by engaging, first of all, with questions about their authors, intended audiences, as well as the norms and values underpinning the two texts. Her essay, moreover, provides important methodological reflections on the study of *comparison*, noting how motif-critical, tradition-critical and intertextual approaches can shed new light on the foundations of Markan and Johannine ethics. Mark presents Jesus as the authoritative teacher of Torah, but also as one who establishes a form of discipleship characterized by humility and service. In the light of recent significant developments in the study of Johannine ethics, Wischmeyer argues towards the end of her essay that John draws out more emotional and personal dimensions in relation to Mark's two ethical 'pillars' – the double love commandment and understanding of discipleship – in order to highlight a love-centred connection between the life and mission of the Johannine Jesus and that of his disciples.

Susanne Luther undertakes a comparative reading of the longer speech-compositions in the Gospels of Mark and John. These differ considerably in terms of their themes, structure, language and style and also in their reception of sources and traditions. However, both present themselves as factual narratives that report events of the past with a claim to historical referentiality and which construct authenticity through literary strategies such as the speeches of the literary characters. Read from the perspective of ancient historiography, a comparison of the function and impact of the speeches in John and Mark leads to the inference that John knew and used early Christian traditions and genre conventions, either through knowledge of Mark's Gospel or through knowledge of Mark's reception in other early Christian gospels.

Scholars have often noticed that the Johannine Jesus acts more actively, more independently and more determinedly than the Markan Jesus in the face of temptation. If John knew Mark's Gospel, argues Kasper Bro Larsen, then he creatively rewrote Markan temptation scenes by the use of omission, reuse, and dispersion, while also contributing new temptation scenes. His essay argues that John's recasting of Jesus is philosophical in the sense that it associates Jesus with the values ascribed, ever since Socrates, to the wise and temptation-resistant sage. John erases some of Mark's unphilosophical ambiguities, but retains an image, inherited from tradition, of Jesus as moved by emotions. John, argues Larsen, thus navigates between philosophical values and tradition, just as Philo and Josephus do in their Hellenistic-Jewish reframing of Moses as both philosophical and emotional. In short, John's high Christology is in fact philosophical Christology.

For both Mark and John, the plot to kill Jesus serves as an important transitional link between Jesus' public ministry and his death and resurrection. Michael Labahn's essay provides a detailed analysis of the function of this episode in both gospels, arguing that although the motif of an early plot or decision to kill Jesus is not integral to the genre of a biographical or historical gospel, it does fit well in narratives oriented towards the death of Jesus. A comparison of both texts discloses some small but significant similarities between them, including Jesus' Sabbath healing as the catalyst for the plot, the forgiveness of sins motif, the depiction of central characters, and also some verbal paralls. The nature of the resemblances does not, however, establish John's *literary dependence* on Mark's version of this episode nor can it be argued that both accounts stem from independent oral tradition. Rather, with the aid of the concept of 'secondary orality' or 're-oralization', Labahn proposes that John's knowledge of Mark is best understood as filtered through oral memory and as the result of the aural reception of Mark by the Johannine readers and/or narrator.

Helen Bond's essay compares the trial scenes in Mark and John. Starting with an overview of the death of Jesus in both gospels which highlights their distinctive presentations and interests, she goes on to consider Mark's carefully structured double trial scenes, in which the Jewish and Roman proceedings parallel one another, before assessing John's creative and thoughtful rewriting of this material. John's presentation of Jesus' earlier ministry as his Jewish 'trial', it is proposed, leads to a considerable reduction of the Jewish proceedings in this gospel, leaving an enlarged Roman trial to function as the centre-piece of John's entire passion account. Careful exegesis, however, reveals the many links that still remain between the two accounts, both in terms of vocabulary and concepts. While John might alter the earlier gospel for a variety of reasons – apologetic, theological, or to align his work with traditions current in his own setting – a frequently overlooked feature of his work, she argues, is his ability to draw out the dramatic quality of features that are already implicit in Mark, most notably themes of kingship and triumph.

These essays are, for many of the contributors, a first attempt at investigating John's relationship with Mark through a new paradigm. We join the voices of a growing body of other scholars who are similarly seeing links between the two gospels in new ways and through different lenses. We recognize that there is still much work to be done in this important and exciting area. Nevertheless, together these essays mount a strong case for John's reception of the earlier gospel and, therefore, for a reassessment of one of the key tenets of modern biblical criticism.

2

John and Mark in the History of Research

Harold W. Attridge

Discussion of the relationship between John and Mark, and the larger issue of the relationship of John and the Synoptics, has had a long history, usefully surveyed by several scholars in recent decades.[1] Dwight Moody Smith summarizes the basic facts: 'John taken as a whole seems to be a significant commentary on the synoptic Gospels, or the Synoptic tradition. But when compared more closely with these other Gospels, the differences, and even the contradictions, are striking.'[2] The similarities suggest a connection, the differences point toward independence or, in more recent scholarship, a radical hermeneutical programme.

The first section of the following chart, adapted from the summary of Udo Schnelle,[3] contains a roster of passages where there is at least a thematic connection between John and one or more of the Synoptics. The second section contains a roster of passages where there is some verbal similarity. These charts provide a useful framework for discussions in this volume.

---

[1] D. Moody Smith, *John Among the Gospels* (Minneapolis, MN: Fortress, 1992; 2nd edn Columbia, SC: University of South Carolina Press, 2001), summarized in D. Moody Smith, *John* (ANTC; Nashville, TN: Abingdon, 1999), 29–33; Manfred Lang, *Johannes und die Synoptiker: Eine redaktionsgeschichtliche Analyse von Joh 18–20 vor dem markinischen und lukanischen Hintergrund* (FRLANT, 182; Göttingen: Vandenhoeck & Ruprecht, 1999), 14–56; Frans Neirynck, 'John and the Synoptics: 1975–1990', in Frans Neirynck, *Evangelica III: 1992–2000: Collected Essays* (BETL, 150 Leuven: Leuven University Press; Leuven, Paris, Sterling, VA: Peeters, 2001), 3–64; Michael Labahn and Manfred Lang, 'Johannes und die Synoptiker: Positionen und Impulse seit 1990', in *Kontexte des Johannesevangeliums: Das vierte Evangelium in religions- und traditionsgeschichtlicher Perspektive*, ed. Jörg Frey and Udo Schnelle (WUNT, 175; Tübingen: Mohr Siebeck, 2004), 443–515; Ian D. Mackay, *John's Relationship with Mark: An Analysis of John 6 in the Light of Mark 6–8* (WUNT, 2/182 Tübingen: Mohr Siebeck, 2004); Steven A. Hunt, *Rewriting the Feeding of Five Thousand: John 6.1–15 as a Test Case for Johannine Dependence on the Synoptic Gospels* (Studies in Biblical Literature, 125; New York: Peter Lang, 2011); Jörg Frey, 'Das vierte Evangelium auf dem Hintergrund der älteren Evangelientradition: Zum Problem: Johannes und die Synoptiker', in *Das Johannesevangelium – Mitte oder Rand des Kanons? Neue Standortbestimmungen*, ed. Thomas Söding (QD, 203; Freiburg: Herder, 2003), 60–118; Harold W. Attridge, 'John and Other Gospels', in *The Oxford Handbook of Johannine Studies*, ed. Judith M. Lieu and Martinus C. de Boer (Oxford: Oxford University Press, 2018), 44–62.
[2] Smith, *John*, ANTC, 31.
[3] Udo Schnelle, *Einleitung in das Neue Testament* (6th edn; Göttingen: Vandenhoeck & Ruprecht, 2007), 525–34, esp. 529–31; ET of the 1994 edn: *The History and Theology of the New Testament Writings* (London: SCM, 1998), 492–504.

Chart Ia: Synoptic narrative parallels

	John	Mark	Matthew	Luke
The Baptist[4]	1.19–34	1.2–11	3.1–17	3.2–22
First Disciples	1.35–42	1.16–20	4.18–22	5.1–11
Temple cleansing[5]	2.14–22	11.15–17	21.12–13	19.45–46
Ministry in Galilee	4.43–46	1.14b–15	4.13–17	4.14–15
Healing a boy	4.46–54		8.5–13	7.1–10
Healing a paralytic[6]	5.8, 9	2.11, 12	9.6b–8	5.24b, 25
Feeding 5,000[7]	6.1–15	6.32–44	14.13–21	9.10b–17
Walking on Water (or the Sea)	6.16–21	6.45–52	14.22–33	
Crossing	6.22–25	6.53–54	8.18	14.34–35
Demand for sign	6.26	8.11–13	12.38–39	11.16, 29
			16.1–4	12.54–56
Peter's confession	6.66–71	8.27–30	16.13–20	9.18–21
Healing the blind	9.1–7	8.22–26		

---

[4] Étienne Trocmé, 'Jean et les Synoptiques: L'example de Jn 1:15–34', in *The Four Gospels, 1992: Festschrift Frans Neirynck*, ed. Frans Van Segbroeck, Christopher M. Tuckett, Gilbert Van Belle and Joseph Verheyden (BETL, 100; 3 vols; Leuven: Leuven University Press and Peeters, 1992), 3:1935–41; E. D. Freed, 'Jn 1,19–27 in Light of Related Passages in John, the Synoptics and Acts', in Van Segbroeck *et al.* (ed.), *The Four Gospels*, 3:1943–61; D.-A. Koch, 'Der Täufer als Zeuge des Offenbarers: Das Täuferbild von Joh 1,19–34 auf dem Hintergrund von Mk 1,2–11', in Van Segbroeck *et al.* (ed.), *The Four Gospels*, 3:1963–84; Ismo Dunderberg, *Johannes und die Synoptiker: Studien zu Joh 1–9* (AASF, Dissertationes Humanarum Litterarum, 69; Helsinki: Suomalainen Tiedeakatemia, 1994); Frey, 'Das vierte Evangelium', 93–100.

[5] Maurits Sabbe, 'The Cleansing of the Temple and the Temple Logion', *CBG* 2 (1956): 289–99, 466–80, repr. in Maurits Sabbe, *Studia Neotestamentica: Collected Essays* (BETL, 98; Leuven: Leuven University Press, 1991), 331–54; Udo Schnelle, 'Die Tempelreinigung und die Christologie des Johannesevangeliums', *NTS* 42 (1996): 359–73; Jean Zumstein, 'Johannes 2:13–22 im Plot und in der Theologie des vierten Evangeliums', in *The Opening of John's Narrative (John 1:19–22)*, ed. R. Alan Culpepper and Jörg Frey (WUNT, 385; Tübingen: Mohr Siebeck, 2017), 275–87.

[6] Frans Neirynck, 'John 5,1–18 and the Gospel of Mark: A Response to P. Borgen', in *The Interrelations of the Gospels: A Symposium Led by M. É. Boismard – W. R. Farmer – F. S. Neirynck, Jerusalem 1984*, ed. David L. Dungan (BETL, 95; Leuven: Leuven University Press and Peeters, 1990), 438–50; repr. in Frans Neirynck, *Evangelica II: 1982–91: Collected Essays* (BETL, 99; Leuven: University Press and Peeters, 1991), 699–712.

[7] Favouring dependence on Mark: François Vouga, 'Le quatrième évangile comme interprète de la tradition synoptique: Jean 6', in *John and the Synoptics*, ed. Adelbert Denaux (BETL, 101; Leuven: University Press and Peeters, 1992), 261–79; Johan Konings, 'The Dialogue of Jesus, Philip and Andrew in John 6,5–9', in Denaux (ed.), *John and the Synoptics*, 523–34; Dunderberg, *Johannes und die Synoptiker*, 126–56; Hunt, *Rewriting*; Eugen Ruckstuhl, 'Die Speisung des Volkes durch Jesus und die Seeüberfahrt der Jünger nach Joh 6,1–25 im Vergleich zu den synoptischen Parallelen', in Van Segbroeck *et al.* (ed.), *The Four Gospels*, 3:2001–19; Manfred Lang, 'Andersheit und Musterwissen: Beobachtungen zum Verhältnis Johannes und die Synoptiker anhand von Johannes 6,1–71', in *Studies in the Gospel of John and Its Christology: Festschrift Gilbert Van Belle*, ed. Joseph Verheyden, et al. (BETL, 265; Leuven, Paris, Walpole: Peeters, 2014), 189–204; Mackay, *John's Relationship*; Christian Riniker, 'Jean 6,1–21 et les évangiles synoptiques', in *La Communauté johannique et son histoire: La trajectoire de l'évangile de Jean aux deux premiers siècles*, ed. Jean-Daniel Kaestli, Jean-Michel Poffet and Jean Zumstein (MoBi, 20; Genève: Labor et Fides, 1990), 41–52. Favouring independence: Paul N. Anderson, *The Christology of the Fourth Gospel: Its Unity and Disunity in the Light of John 6* (WUNT, 2/78; Tübingen: Mohr Siebeck, 1996; 2nd edn, Valley Forge: Trinity Press International, 1997; 3rd edn, Eugene, OR: Cascade, 2010). Favouring a Synoptic-like source, see John Painter, 'Tradition and Interpretation in John 6', *NTS* 35 (1989): 421–50.

	John	Mark	Matthew	Luke
Raising the dead[8]	11.1–44	5.35–43	9.23–26	8.49–56
				7.11–17
Anointing[9]	12.1–8	14.3–9	26.6–13	7.36–50
Entry	12.12–19	11.1–10	21.1–9	19.28–40
Arrest[10]	18.3–12	14.43–50	26.47–56	22.47–53
Peter's denial[11]	18.25–27	14.66–72	26.69–75	22.56–62
Trial before Pilate[12]	18.29–38	15.2–5	27.11–14	23.3
Barabbas	18.39–40	15.6–14	27.15–23	23.17–23
Mocking	19.1–3	15.16–20a	27.27–31a	
Crucifixion[13]	19.16b–19	15.20b–26	37:31–37	23.33–34
Witnesses	19.24b–27	15.40–41	27.55–56	23.49
Burial	19.38–42	15.42–46	27.57–60	23.50–54
Empty tomb[14]	20.1–10	16.1–8	28.1–8	24.1–8, 12
Appears to 11	20.19–20			24.36–49
Fish fry	21.1–19			5.1–11

Chart Ib: Sayings parallels[15]

	John	Mark	Matthew	Luke
One who comes	1.27	1.7	3.11b, c	3.16c, d
Baptize w HS	1.33b	1.8	3.11d	3.16e
Voice	1.34	1.11	3.17	3.22

[8] Hartwig Thyen, 'Die Erzählung von den bethanischen Geschwistern (Joh 11,1–12,19) als "Palimpsest" über synoptischen Texten', in Van Segbroeck et al. (ed.), *The Four Gospels*, 3:2021–50. The detail of Jesus' spit in both Mark and John is striking.

[9] Ismo Dunderberg, 'Zur Literarkritik von Joh 12,1–11', in Adelbert Denaux (ed.), *John and the Synoptics*, 558–70.

[10] Maurits Sabbe, 'The Arrest of Jesus in Jn 18,1–11 and Its Relation to the Synoptic Gospels: A Critical Evaluation of A. Dauer's Hypothesis', in *L'Évangile de Jean: Sources, redaction, théologie*, ed. Marinus de Jonge (BETL, 44; Leuven: University Press, 1977), 203–34; Lang, *Johannes und die Synoptiker*, 61–86.

[11] John R. Donahue, *'Are you the Christ?' The Trial Narrative in the Gospel of Mark* (SBLDS, 10; Missoula, MT: Scholars, 1973), 58–63.

[12] Maurits Sabbe, 'The Trial of Jesus before Pilate in John and Its Relation to the Synoptic Gospels', in Denaux (ed.), *John and the Synoptics*, 341–85; repr. in Sabbe, *Studia*, 467–513; Lang, *Johannes und die Synoptiker*, 115–205.

[13] Maurits Sabbe, 'The Johannine Account of the Death of Jesus and Its Synoptic Parallels (Jn 19,16b–42)', *ETL* 70 (1994): 34–64; Lang, *Johannes und die Synoptiker*, 207–38.

[14] For dependence: Frans Neirynck, 'John and the Synoptics: The Empty Tomb Stories', *NTS* 30 (1984): 161–87; repr. in Frans Neirynck, *Evangelica II*, 571–97; Wendy E. S. North, 'Points and Stars: John and the Synoptics', in *John, Jesus, and History*, Vol. 3: *Glimpses of Jesus through the Johannine Lens*, ed. Paul N. Anderson, Felix Just, S. J. and Tom Thatcher (ECL, 18; Atlanta, GA: Society of Biblical Literature, 2016), 3:119–32, repr. in Wendy E. S. North, *A Journey Round John: Tradition, Interpretation, and Context in the Fourth Gospel* (LNTS, 534; London: T&T; Clark, 2015), here 215–16; Lang, *Johannes und die Synoptiker*, 259–94. For common tradition: Barnabas Lindars, 'The Composition of John XX', *NTS* 7 (1960–61): 142–47, repr. in Barnabas Lindars, *Essays on John*, ed. Christopher M. Tuckett (Studiorum Novi Testamenti Auxilia, 17; Leuven: University Press and Peeters, 1992), 1–8; and William L. Craig, 'The Disciples' Inspection of the Empty Tomb (Lk 24,12.24; Jn 20,2–10)', in Denaux (ed.), *John and the Synoptics*, 614–19.

[15] Michael Theobald, *Herrenworte im Johannesevangelium* (HBS, 34; Freiburg: Herder, 2002), 647–58, provides a convenient table of sayings. Cf. Schnelle, *Einleitung*, 530–31.

Chart Ib: *continued.*

	John	Mark	Matthew	Luke
Simon's name	1.42	3.16b	16.17	6.14a
Hour has come	2.4; 13.1	14.35, 41		
Temple logion	2.19	14.58	26.61	
		15.29	27.40	Acts 6.14
Entering the Kingdom[16]	3.3, 5	10.15	18.3	18.17
Son of Man raised[17]	3.13	8.31	16.21	9.22
Prophet[18]	4.44	6.4	13.57	4.24
Whoever denies	5.23b			10.16b
It is I, fear not	6.20	6.50	14.27	
Parents	6.42	6.3	13.55	4.22
Father and Son	10.15		11.27	10.22
Christ, Son of God	11.27		16.16	
Loving/hating life[19]	12.25	8.35	16.25	9.24
Soul troubled	12.27	14.34ff	26.38ff	22.42
Blindness (Isa 6.10)[20]	12.38–41	4.12		
Servant/master	13.16	15.20	10.24	6.40
Whoever receives	13.20	9.37b	10.40	9.48b/10.16
Prediction of betrayal	13.21–30	14.18–21	26.21–23	22.21
Prediction of denial[21]	13.36–38	14.26–31	26.30–35	22.31–34
Ask and receive[22]	14.13–14	11.24	21.22	
	15.7; 16.23			
Let's depart[23]	14.31	14.42	26.46	
For sake of name	15.21	13.13	10.22a; 24.9	21.17
Scattering	16.32	14.27	26.31	
Binding/loosing	20.23		18.18	
Some won't die[24]	21.23	9.1		

Chart Ic: Miscellaneous Parallels

	John	Mark	Matthew	Luke
Holy One of God	6.69	1.34		
Mary and Martha	11.1			10.38–39
Martha serves	12.2			10.40
Leaders condemn	11.47, 53		26.3–4	
Voice from heaven	12.28–30	9.7	17.5	9.35
Servant at supper[25]	13.1–11	[14.12–25]		22.26
Jesus sends Spirit	14.16			24.49
	20.22			

[16] Theobald, *Herrenworte*, 61–96.
[17] Theobald, *Herrenworte*, 201–23.
[18] Barnabas Lindars, 'Capernaum Revisited: Jn 4,46–53 and the Synoptics', in Van Segbroeck *et al.* (ed.), *Four Gospels*, 3:1985–2000; Frans Neirynck, 'John 4,46–54: Signs Source and/or Synoptic Gospels', *ETL* 60 (1984): 367–75, repr. in *Evangelica II*, 679–88.
[19] Theobald, *Herrenworte*, 97–129.
[20] Craig A. Evans, 'The Function of Isaiah 6:9–10 in Mark and John', *NovT* 24 (1982): 124–38.
[21] Mark Jennings, 'The Fourth Gospel's Reversal of Mark in John 13,31–14,3', *Bib* 94 (2013): 210–36.
[22] Theobald, *Herrenworte*, 152–73.
[23] Ulrich Busse, 'Joh 14,31 und sein Kontext', *ETL* 94 (2018): 27–75.
[24] Theobald, *Herrenworte*, 232–43.
[25] Maurits Sabbe, 'The Footwashing in Jn 13 and its Relation to the Synoptic Gospels', *ETL* 58 (1982): 279–308, repr. in Sabbe, *Studia*, 409–41.

The case for independence

As Smith reports, Church fathers assumed that the Fourth Evangelist knew and supplemented the Synoptics, producing a more 'spiritual gospel'.[26] Twentieth-century critics by contrast, following Percival Gardner-Smith,[27] grew sceptical of a relationship between Mark and John, arguing that the Fourth Evangelist used oral traditions or written sources but not the gospels that became canonical. Prominent among those holding this position was C. H. Dodd in Britain[28] and, in Germany, Rudolf Schnackenburg and Ernst Haenchen, whose commentaries were translated into English.[29] In North America, the landmark commentary by Raymond Brown followed Gardner-Smith and Dodd.[30] Exploring the general development of gospels, Helmut Koester also argued for the independence of John.[31] The position of these influential scholars has been reflected in more popular commentaries such as that of Alan Culpepper.[32] On a more technical level scholars such as Peder Borgen[33] and Stanley Porter[34] have continued to defend Johannine independence.

The case for dependence

Like the Church fathers, most nineteenth-century scholars held that John depended on the Synoptics in general and Mark in particular. They also argued that John attempted to supplement the earlier gospels. Hans Windisch[35] argued instead that the Fourth Evangelist aimed to supplant, not supplement, the Synoptics.

---

[26] Clement of Alexandria, *Hypotyposes*, cited in Eusebius, *Hist. eccl.* 6.14.7.
[27] Percival Gardner-Smith, *Saint John and the Synoptic Gospels* (Cambridge: University Press, 1938).
[28] C. H. Dodd, *The Interpretation of the Fourth Gospel* (Cambridge: Cambridge University Press, 1953), 196–221.
[29] Rudolf Schnackenburg, *Das Johannesevangelium* (4 vols, HThKNT, 4,1–4; Freiburg: Herder, 1965–84); ET: *The Gospel According to St. John*, trans. Kevin Smyth (3 vols; London: Burns & Oates; New York: Crossroad, 1968–82); Ernst Haenchen, *Das Johannesevangelium*, ed. Ulrich Busse (Tübingen: Mohr Siebeck, 1980), ET: *A Commentary on the Gospel of John*, trans. Robert W. Funk (2 vols, Hermeneia; Philadelphia, PA: Fortress, 1984).
[30] Raymond E. Brown, 'John and the Synoptic Gospels: A Comparison', in Raymond E. Brown, *New Testament Essays* (Garden City, NY: Doubleday, 1965), 192–213; Raymond E. Brown, *The Gospel According to John* (2 vols, Anchor Bible, 29–29a; Garden City, NY: Doubleday, 1966, 1970), on John 6: 1.236–39, 252–54.
[31] Helmut Koester, *Ancient Christian Gospels: Their History and Development* (Philadelphia, PA: Trinity Press International; London: SCM, 1990), 244–72.
[32] R. Alan Culpepper, *The Gospel and Letters of John* (Interpreting Biblical Texts; Nashville, TN: Abingdon, 1998), 39–41.
[33] Peder Borgen, *Bread from Heaven: An Exegetical Study of the Concept of Manna in the Gospel of John and the Writings of Philo* (NovTSup, 10; Leiden: Brill, 1965); Peder Borgen, 'The Independence of the Gospel of John: Some Observations', in Van Segbroeck et al. (ed.), *The Four Gospels*, 3:1815–1833; Peder Borgen, *The Gospel of John: More Light from Philo, Paul and Archaeology: The Scriptures, Tradition, Exposition, Settings, Meaning* (NovTSup, 154; Leiden, Boston: Brill, 2014).
[34] Stanley E. Porter, *John, His Gospel and Jesus: In Pursuit of the Johannine Voice* (Grand Rapids, MI: Wm. B. Eerdmans, 2015).
[35] Hans Windisch, *Johannes und die Synoptiker: Wollte der vierte Evangelist die älteren Evangelien ergänzen oder ersetzen?* (UNT, 12; Leipzig: Hinrichs, 1926).

While Gardner-Smith persuaded most twentieth-century scholars, some continued to note the similarities between John and the Synoptics in overall structure and in specific details. In Britain, Edwin Hoskyns argued that John knew the Synoptics but used them freely;[36] C. K. Barrett continued to maintain that John knew and used Mark.[37] Others agreed with varying degrees of nuance.[38] The position that John knew and used Mark gathered new momentum through the work of Frans Neirynck[39] and other members of the Louvain school, including Adelbert Denaux[40] and Maurits Sabbe.[41] More recent German scholars, Udo Schnelle,[42] Jörg Frey,[43] Michael Labahn and Manfred Lang,[44] have followed suit.

Scholars exploring the complexities of intertextuality have renewed the position that John knew and used Mark. Hartwig Thyen, celebrating a 'paradigm shift' (*Paradigmenwechsel*),[45] robustly defended the dependence of John on Mark and the other Synoptics, in essays[46] and in his commentary.[47] Thyen calls for a more nuanced theory of intertextual relations, arguing that the Fourth Evangelist use the Synoptics as 'pretexts' (*Prätexten*) and reworked them throughout his gospel. Similarly Jean Zumstein, acknowledging Thyen's innovative work, argued that the Fourth Evangelist is engaged in a process of 'relecture' of other gospels,[48] definitely Mark, perhaps Luke,

---

[36] Edwin Clement Hoskyns, *The Fourth Gospel*, ed. Francis Noel Davey (2nd edn; London: Faber & Faber, 1947, repr. 1967), 82: 'That the author of the Fourth Gospel had the three synoptic gospels before him when he composed his gospel is most improbable .... But that he was familiar with the synoptic material, and even with its form, is certain.' See also Edward F. Siegman, 'St. John's Use of the Synoptic Material', *CBQ* 30 (1968): 183–98.

[37] C. K. Barrett, 'John and the Synoptic Gospels', *ExpT* 85 (1974): 228–33; C. K. Barrett, *The Gospel According to St. John: An Introduction with Commentary and Notes on the Greek Text* (2nd edn; Philadelphia, PA: Westminster; London: SPCK, 1978), 42–54.

[38] R. H. Lightfoot, *St. John's Gospel: A Commentary* (Oxford: Clarendon, 1956, repr. 1983; London: Oxford University Press, 1960), 155–56, on John 6. John Ashton, *Understanding the Fourth Gospel* (Oxford: Clarendon, 1993), 81, acknowledges the differences.

[39] Frans Neirynck, *Jean et les Synoptiques: Examen critique de l'exégèse de M.-E. Boismard* (BETL, 49; Leuven: University Press, 1979), as well as his several collected essays: Frans Neirynck, *Evangelica: Gospel Studies – Études d'évangile: Collected Essays*, ed. Frans Van Segbroeck (BETL, 60; Leuven: University Press, 1982); Frans Neirynck, *Evangelica II*, and Frans Neirynck, *Evangelica III*.

[40] Denaux (ed.), *John and the Synoptics*.

[41] Sabbe, *Studia*, contains articles on individual pericopes, noted above.

[42] Schnelle, 'Johannes und die Synoptiker', in Van Segbroeck et al. (ed.), *Four Gospels*, 3:1799–1814, summarized in Schnelle, *Einleitung*, 525–34; *History and Theology*, 492–504.

[43] Frey, 'Das vierte Evangelium'.

[44] Labahn and Lang, 'Johannes und die Synoptiker', 443–516.

[45] See also Lang, *Johannes und die Synoptiker*, 41.

[46] Hartwig Thyen, 'Johannes und die Synoptiker: Auf der Suche nach einem neuen Paradigma zur Beschreibung ihrer Beziehungen anhand von Beobachtungen an Passions- und Ostererzählungen', in Denaux (ed.), *John and the Synoptics*, 81–107; Hartwig Thyen, 'Die Erzählung von den bethanischen Geschwistern (Joh 11,1–12,19)', in Van Segbroeck et al. (ed.), *The Four Gospels*, 3:2021–50.

[47] Hartwig Thyen, *Das Johannesevangelium* (HNT, 6; Tübingen: Mohr Siebeck, 2005), 4, summarizes his position: 'Es erscheint mir nämlich sehr viel wahrscheinlicher, daß Johannes außer der jüdischen Bibel nicht nur eine anonyme, ihm womoglich nur mündlich überlieferte, den Synoptikern ähnlichen Tradition kennt und sie als Quelle benutzt hätte, sondern daß er vielmehr intertextuell mit den alttestamentlichen Texten ebenso wie mit den synoptischen Evangelien in ihren überlieferten redaktionellen Gestalten spielt; und zwar nicht allein mit dem Markusevangelium sondern auch mit den Evangelien nach Matthäus und nach Lukas.'

[48] For an earlier presentation, see Jean Zumstein, 'Ein gewachsenes Evangelium: Der Relecture-Prozess bei Johannes', in *Johannesevangelium – Mitte oder Rand des Kanons? Neue Standortbestimmungen,*

though not Matthew.[49] This 'rereading' did not involve the kind of literary redaction represented by Matthew and Luke's use of Mark,[50] exemplifying instead what Gérard Genette labelled 'hypertextuality'.[51] Thyen and Zumstein offer a more nuanced version of the position of scholars who argued for Johannine dependence on Mark.

Also relevant to the topic under investigation is the claim by Richard Bauckham that the Fourth Gospel assumes that its readers know the Synoptic accounts.[52] This assumption appears in the reference to Andrew, the brother of Simon Peter (Jn 1.40), when neither has been named; the note of John the Baptist's imprisonment (3.24), nowhere recounted in the gospel; and the anointing of Jesus by Mary of Bethany, mentioned at 11.2, but not described until 12.1–8. Knowledge of stories in the Synoptics does indeed seem to be evident in the Fourth Gospel, but it does not guarantee that John was using the Synoptics as sources.

While some defend a more robust version of dependence,[53] other scholars argue for a more limited version, finding evidence of dependence only at a particular redactional stage of the Fourth Gospel. These include the Finnish scholar Ismo Dunderberg[54] and the American Urban von Wahlde, who posits three editions of John, only the third of which incorporated the Synoptics.[55] More recently Dennis R. MacDonald argues that the Fourth Gospel's earliest stratum is a 'Dionysian Gospel', a 'mimesis' of Euripides' *Bacchae*,[56] which only later received an orthodox veneer with added Synoptic details.

ed. Thomas Söding (QD, 203; Freiburg: Herder, 2003), 9–37. On 'relecture', see Zumstein, *L'Évangile selon St. Jean* (2 vols; CNT, IV; Genève: Labor et Fides, 2007, 2014), 1.31: 'A notre avis, cependant, il n'est plus possible d'aborder cette question sous la forme d'une simple alternative entre des deux hypothèses (scil. indépendance et direct littéraire dépendance). Il est préférable de supposer que l'école joh avait connaissance de l'évangile de Mc, peut-être de celui de Lc, mais probablement pas de celui de Mt.' See also Frans Van Segbroeck, 'Theologie als kreative Sinnbildung: Johannes als Weiterbildung von Paulus und Markus', in Thomas Söding (ed.), *Johannesevangelium*, 119–45.

[49] On John's possible relationship to Matthew, see Gilbert Van Belle and David R. M. Godecharle, 'C. H. Dodd on John 13:16 (and 15:20): St. John's Knowledge of Matthew Revisited', in *Engaging with C. H. Dodd on the Gospel of John: Sixty Years of Tradition and Interpretation*, ed. Tom Thatcher and Catrin H. Williams (Cambridge: University Press, 2013), 86–106.

[50] Zumstein notes Stephan Landis, *Das Verhältnis des Johannesevangeliums zu den Synoptikern: Am Beispiel von Mt 8,5–13, Lk 7,1–10, Joh 4,46–54* (BZNW, 74; Berlin: de Gruyter, 1992), and Riniker, 'Jean 6,1–21'.

[51] Zumstein, *L'Évangile*, 32, n. 33, cites Gérard Genette, *Palimpsestes: La littérature au second degré* (Collection Poétique; Paris: Éditions du Seuil, 1982), 11–12: L'hypertextualité désigne 'toute relation unissant un texte B (que j'appellerai *hypertexte*) à un texte antérieur A (que) j'appellerai bien sûr hypotexte) sur lequel il se greffe d'une manière qui n'est pas celle du commentaire'.

[52] Richard Bauckham, 'John for Readers of Mark', in Richard Bauckham, *The Gospels for All Christians. Rethinking the Gospel Audiences* (Edinburgh: T&T Clark, 1998), 147–71, critiqued in Wendy E. S. North, 'John for Readers of Mark? A Response to Richard Bauckham's Proposal', *JSNT* 25 (2003): 449–68.

[53] Thomas Brodie, *The Quest for the Origin of John's Gospel: A Source-Oriented Approach* (Oxford: Oxford University Press, 1993), 30–31: 'The fourth evangelist . . . sought to produce a new theological synthesis, and . . . in doing so used a diverse range of sources – some non-canonical material, the OT, at least one epistle (Ephesians), and, above all, the synoptics, especially Mark. . . . In simplified terms, Mark supplied the fundamental ingredients of John's *narrative framework*, and Matthew the fundamental ingredients of his *discourses*.'

[54] Dunderberg, *Johannes und die Synoptiker*, summarized on pp. 190–92.

[55] Urban C. von Wahlde, *The Gospel and Letters of John* (3 vols, Eerdmans Critical Commentary; Grand Rapids, MI: Wm. B. Eerdmans, 2010), 1:22.

[56] Dennis R. MacDonald, *The Dionysian Gospel: The Fourth Gospel and Euripides* (Minneapolis, MN: Fortress, 2017).

An alternative source-critical theory sees Mark using John. This position, proposed by John A. T. Robinson,[57] echoed in Germany by Peter Hofrichter,[58] as well as by English language scholars,[59] has not won wide support. A related theory is the hypothesis that Luke, at least in its final form, depends on John.[60]

Various arguments support the dependence of John on Mark. Some focus on the overall structure. Both gospels begin with Jesus encountering John the Baptizer; both recount Jesus' deeds and teaching, highlighting a miraculous feeding of 5,000, and both end reporting on the last days of Jesus in Jerusalem, including dramatic entry, anointing, last supper with disciples, one of whom betrays Jesus, trials before high-priestly authorities and Pontius Pilate, crucifixion, death, and empty tomb. It would be remarkable if John developed such a structure independent of the Synoptics. Yet at every point in that structure there are notable differences. In the Fourth Gospel John does not baptize Jesus, nor does Jesus institute the Eucharist at the last supper. While some reported deeds of Jesus overlap in a generic way, they lack detailed parallels, what Jesus teaches in John has points of contact with Mark but in style and focus is quite distinctive. Such differences require some explanation.

In tracing possible connections, some scholars pursue a particular theme, such as that of 'witnessing',[61] or the relationship between the 'kingdom of God' in Mark and 'eternal life' in John.[62] Others focus on particular passages, such as the citation of Isaiah 6.9–10 in Mark 4.12 // John 12.40.[63] In an important essay Jörg Frey offers a detailed analysis of specific passages with significant parallels between Mark and John, such as the echo of Mark's Gethsemane account (Mk 14.42) in John 14.31,[64] the references to the 'hour' of Jesus in Mark 14.41 and John 12.23, combined with the reference to the 'cup' (Mk 14.35 and Jn 12.27),[65] or the treatment of the role of the Baptist in Mark 1 and John 1. In each case, John's version involves creative reinterpretation of a Markan or Synoptic element.[66]

One frequently discussed issue is whether the parallels between Mark and John involve redactional elements of the Synoptics. Some find precisely such details in the mention of 200 denarii in the feeding miracle (Mk 6.37; Jn 6.7), while John 6.3 seems

---

[57] John A. T. Robinson, *The Priority of John*, ed. J. F. Coakley (London: SCM, 1985; Oak Park, IL: Meyer-Stone, 1987). See also Erwin R. Goodenough, 'John a Primitive Gospel', *JBL* 64 (1945): 145–82; more recently, Klaus Berger, *Im Anfang war Johannes: Datierung und Theologie des vierten Evangeliums* (Stuttgart: Quell, 1997), and Klaus Berger, 'Das Evangelium nach Johannes und die Jesustradition', in Thomas Söding (ed.), *Johannesevangelium*, 38–59.

[58] Peter L. Hofrichter, *Modell und Vorlage der Synoptiker – Das vorredaktionelle 'Johannesevangelium'* (TTS, 6; Hildesheim: Olms, 1997); and Peter L. Hofrichter, *Für und Wider die Priorität des Johannesevangeliums* (TTS, 9; Hildesheim: Olms, 2002).

[59] J. F. Coakley, 'The Anointing at Bethany and the Priority of John', *JBL* 107 (1988): 241–56.

[60] Mark A. Matson, *In Dialogue with Another Gospel? The Influence of the Fourth Gospel on the Passion Narrative of the Gospel of Luke* (SBLDS, 178; Atlanta, GA: Society of Biblical Literature, 2001).

[61] Roland Bergmeier, 'Die Bedeutung der Synoptiker für das johanneische Zeugnisthema: Mit einem Anhang zum Perfekt-Gebrauch im vierten Evangelium', *NTS* 52 (2006): 458–83.

[62] Jörg Frey, 'From the "Kingdom of God" to "Eternal Life": The Transformation of Theological Language in the Fourth Gospel', in Paul N. Anderson *et al.* (ed.), *John, Jesus, and History*, 3:439–58.

[63] Evans, 'The Function of Isaiah 6:9–10'.

[64] Frey, 'Das vierte Evangelium', 86–88.

[65] Frey, 'Das vierte Evangelium', 88–90.

[66] Frey, 'Das vierte Evangelium', 93–100.

to depend on the redactional introduction to the second feeding miracle in Matt 15.29. Similarly, the concluding scene of the episode, John 6.66-71, echoes redactional elements of Mark 8.27-33.

Independent but sharing common sources

The 'Signs[67] Gospel'

The combination of similarities and differences between John and the Synoptics in general, and Mark in particular, led to an alternative to the thesis of a direct relationship, the hypothesis of a 'signs source'. This hypothetical document comprised at least a collection of miracle stories detected in the two numbered 'signs' (Jn 2.11 and 4.54). Prominent in Rudolf Bultmann's commentary,[68] this theory was elaborated systematically in North America by Robert Fortna,[69] who expanded the source to include a passion narrative, also by W. Nicol,[70] and in Germany by Folker Siegert[71] and Siegfried Bergler.[72] It was also subjected to vigorous criticism by the Louvain school, particularly by Gerhard Van Belle.[73]

The Passion narrative

The fact that parallels between John and Mark abound in the passion narratives has produced complex theories about the relationship between the two gospels, either directly, through a common source, i.e., an early Passion narrative, or through oral

---

[67] Frans Neirynck, 'The Signs Source in the Fourth Gospel: A Critique of the Hypothesis', ET of 'De semeia-bron in het vierde Evangelie: Kritiek von een hypothese', *Academiae Analecta* (1983): 1-28, in Frans Neirynck, *Evangelica II*, 651-78.
[68] Rudolf Bultmann, *Das Evangelium des Johannes* (KEK; Göttingen: Vandenhoeck & Ruprecht; with the supplement of 1966, repr. 1950-1986), ET: *The Gospel of John* (Philadelphia, PA: Westminster; Oxford: Blackwell, 1971).
[69] Robert Fortna, *The Gospel of Signs: A Reconstruction of the Narrative Source Underlying the Fourth Gospel* (SNTSMS, 11; Cambridge: Cambridge University Press, 1970); Robert Fortna, *The Fourth Gospel and Its Predecessor: From Narrative Source to Present Gospel* (Studies in the New Testament and its World; Philadelphia, PA: Fortress, 1988; Edinburgh: T&T Clark, 1989), and Robert Fortna, 'The Gospel of John and the Signs Gospel', in *What We Have Heard from the Beginning: The Past, Present and Future of Johannine Studies*, ed. Tom Thatcher (Waco, TX: Baylor University Press, 2007), 149-58.
[70] W. Nicol, *The Semeia in the Fourth Gospel: Tradition and Redaction* (NovTSup, 32; Leiden: Brill, 1972).
[71] Folker Siegert, *Der Erstentwurf des Johannes: Das ursprüngliche, judenchristliche Johannesevangelium in deutscher Übersetzung vorgestellt, nebst Nachrichten über Verfasser und zwei Briefen von ihm (2./3. Joh.)* (Münsteraner Judaistische Studien; Wissenschaftliche Beiträge zur christlich-jüdischen Begegnung, 16; Münster: LIT, 2004), idem, *Das Evangelium des Johannes in seiner ursprünglichen Gestalt: Wiederherstellung und Kommentar* (SIJD, 7; Göttingen: Vandenhoeck & Ruprecht, 2008).
[72] Folker Siegert and Siegfried Bergler, *Synopse der vorkanonischen Jesusüberlieferungen: Zeichenquelle und Passionsbericht, die Logienquelle und der Grundbestand des Markusevangeliums in deutscher Übersetzung gegenübergestellt von Folker Siegert. Rekonstruktion der Zeichenquelle von Siegfried Bergler* (SIJD, 8/1; Göttingen: Vandenhoeck & Ruprecht, 2010).
[73] Gilbert Van Belle, *The Signs Source in the Fourth Gospel: Historical Survey and Critical Evaluation of the Semeia Hypothesis* (BETL, 116; Leuven: Leuven University Press and Peeters, 1994). Fortna, 'The Gospel of John and the Signs Gospel', responds.

tradition. The hypothesis of an early Passion narrative,[74] initially developed by Karl Ludwig Schmidt[75] and Martin Dibelius,[76] played a major role in Bultmann's source analysis, and was adopted in a modified form by Vincent Taylor.[77]

For Bultmann, this passion narrative was independent of the 'Signs Gospel'. Others, such as Fortna, argued that the 'Signs Gospel' included a passion account. Anton Dauer argued instead that Markan motifs came to John through oral tradition.[78] Matti Myllykoski argued that a short form of a passion narrative was later expanded to a passion gospel of which Mark and John used similar forms. While John knew Mark, he preferred the alternative.[79] Till Arend Mohr[80] developed a more complex hypothesis: Mark used a primitive passion narrative; John then used the Synoptics and a separate source. Wolfgang Reinbold[81] developed a theory of a primitive passion gospel, which told of Jesus' entry to Jerusalem but did not include a Temple event. The account also told of the supper, arrest, interrogation by the High Priest, Peter's denial, the interrogation by Pilate, and Jesus' scourging, mocking, crucifixion, death and burial. This account lies behind both the Markan and Johannine versions of the Passion, but Mark and John are not directly connected, although some details may have been transmitted to John 'by memory'. Most recently Frank Scheritt continues to make a case for an early passion narrative.[82]

The hypothetical character and complexity of these reconstructions has prevented their wide acceptance and prompted a return to finding the Synoptics, supplemented by some other tradition, oral or written, as the foundation of the Johannine passion narrative.[83] This is the position of Manfred Lang, who sketches an intricate array of interconnections involving elements from both Mark and Luke in the Johannine tapestry.

---

[74] Summarized in Adela Yarbro Collins, *Mark: A Commentary* (Hermeneia; Minneapolis, MN: Fortress, 2007), 620–39.

[75] Karl Ludwig Schmidt, 'Die literarische Eigenart der Leidensgeschichte Jesu', *Die Christliche Welt* 32 (1918): 114–16, repr. in *Redaktion und Theologie des Passionsberichtes nach den Synoptikern*, ed. Meinrad Limbeck (Wege der Forschung, 481; Darmstadt: Wissenschaftliche Buchgesellschaft, 1981), 17–20.

[76] Martin Dibelius, *From Tradition to Gospel* (London: Nicholson and Watson, 1934; New York: Scribner, 1965; repr. Cambridge: James Clarke, 1971).

[77] Vincent Taylor, *The Gospel According to St. Mark: The Greek Text with Introduction, Notes, and Indexes* (2nd edn; Grand Rapids, MI: Baker, 1966), 654.

[78] Anton Dauer, *Die Passionsgeschichte im Johannesevangelium: Eine traditionsgeschichtliche und theologische Untersuchung zu Joh 18,1–19,30* (SANT, 30; München: Kösel-Verlag, 1972), 335–36: 'written texts were reabsorbed into oral tradition', cf. Yarbro Collins, *Mark*, 622.

[79] Matti Myllykoski, *Die letzten Tagen Jesu: Markus und Johannes, ihre Traditionen und die historische Frage*, 2 vols (Annales Academiae Scientiarum Fennicae, Series B 256/272; Helsinki: Suomalainen Tiedeakatemia 1991/1994).

[80] Till Arend Mohr, *Markus- und Johannespassion: Redaktions- und traditionsgeschichtliche Untersuchung der markinischen und johanneischen* Passionstradition (AThANT, 70; Zürich: Theologischer Verlag, 1982).

[81] Wolfgang Reinbold, *Der älteste Bericht über den Tod Jesu: Literarische Analyse und historische Kritik der Passionsdarstellungen der Evangelien* (BZNW, 69; Berlin: de Gruyter, 1994).

[82] Frank Schleritt, *Der vorjohanneische Passionsbericht: Eine historisch-kritische und theologische Untersuchung zu Joh 2,13–22; 11,47–14,31 und 18,1–20,29* (BZNW, 154; Berlin: de Gruyter, 2007).

[83] Lang, *Johannes und die Synoptiker*.

Mark, John and orality

While the differences between Mark and John persuade many scholars that there is no direct dependence, an appeal to oral tradition explains many parallels of wording.[84]

Common oral tradition

Michael Theobald, while finding that some sayings in Mark are useful 'metatexts' to the sayings in John, generally appeals to shared oral traditions to explain parallels.[85] Thus, for example, in the case of the Son of Man saying in John 3.14, paralleled in Mark 8.31; 9.31; 10.33–34, Theobald maintains that the Markan sayings 'are based on an oral *Urfassung* that is utilized by Mark in three variant forms, the oldest of which is probably preserved in Mark 8.31. The saying was known in the pre-Johannine tradition and was there transformed into the new saying in John 3:14–15'.[86] Each evangelist used his common tradition in different ways.

> While the oldest version employed the *passio-iusti* tradition, which Mark strengthened by adding line 4 (with an allusion to Ps 118:22), the pre-Johannine tradition chose the path of a typological comparison of the exaltation of the Son of Man and the lifting up of the serpent in the wilderness by Moses (Num 2:14–19). Mark and John here reflect different biblical theologies, and these very differences support the independence of the Fourth from the Second Evangelist.
>
> ibid. 398–99

In a similar example, Theobald finds a common oral tradition behind the saying on petitionary prayer in Mark 11.24 and John 14.13–14, a saying paralleled in several other Johannine contexts.[87] What Theobald finds striking about this use of a common oral source is the creativity of the Fourth Evangelist: 'The creativity of this Johannine *Fortschreibung* is astounding. Though the aphorism from Jesus does indeed remain the nucleus, it is elaborated upon and made to be an entirely new saying of Jesus and one of significant theological moment' (ibid. 400). With his judgement on that point, almost all who have addressed the problem of the relationship of Mark and John would agree.

---

[84] James D. G. Dunn, 'John's Gospel and the Oral Gospel Tradition', in *Jesus and the Oral Gospel Tradition*, ed. Henry Wansbrough (JSNTSup, 64; Sheffield: JSOT, 1991), 351–79, repr. in *The Fourth Gospel in First-Century Media Culture*, ed. Anthony Le Donne and Tom Thatcher (ESCO/LNTS, 426; London: T&T Clark, 2011), 157–85.

[85] Theobald, *Herrenworte*, 200–43, explored possible connections between John 3.14–15 and Mark 8.31; John 12.28a and Mark 6.9c, but also Luke 11.2c; and John 21.22 and Mark 9.1.

[86] Michael Theobald, 'Johannine Dominical Sayings as Metatexts of Synoptic Sayings of Jesus: Reflections on a New Category within Reception History', in Paul N. Anderson *et al.* (ed.), *John, Jesus and History*, 3:398.

[87] John 15.7–8, 16; 16.23–24, 26–27; 1 John 3.21–22; 5.14–15.

Secondary orality

Another widely cited possibility involving oral tradition is to imagine that the written versions of the Synoptics were read, taught and served as the basis for homilies in Christian communities. Familiar elements from those stories entered the Johannine story through 'secondary orality'. Adela Yarbro Collins favours this approach to explain similarities between John and Mark in the Passion Narrative.[88] The principle has also been invoked by Ian D. Mackay, in connection with the feeding story.[89]

Interdependence

Theories invoking oral tradition generally see the sequence of gospel development along conventional lines, with the Synoptics, or at least Mark, preceding John. An alternative is to see mutual influence between the oral traditions lying behind the written gospels. So argues Paul Anderson, labelling the relationship as 'interfluential'.[90] His position has evolved over time. Initially sure that John and the Synoptics were independent,[91] Anderson proposed that John and Mark had equally valid status as records of Jesus. Thus, any attempt to give an account of Jesus should pay attention to data from both gospels, which provide a 'bi-optic' lens. This hypothesis generated the 'John, Jesus, and History' project of the Society of Biblical Literature.[92]

While maintaining the language of 'bi-optic' sources, Anderson, developing a theory of Barnabas Lindars, more recently acknowledges John's dependence on Mark. The theory posits a first edition of John, lacking chapters 6, 15–17 and 21, in 80–85 CE, a decade after Mark appeared; a second edition, around 100 CE, perhaps by the author of the Johannine epistles, and a final edition with chapter 21, material about the Beloved Disciple, and the theme of eyewitnesses. Mark influenced each stage of the Johannine tradition and John constantly 'engaged in an intertextual dialogue with other Gospel traditions, and in particular, Mark'.[93]

---

[88] Yarbro Collins, *Mark*, 625, n. 46, appeals to 'reoralization' in folklore studies, citing Margaret A. Mills, 'Domains of Folkloristic Concern: The Interpretation of Scriptures', in *Text and Tradition: The Hebrew Bible and Folklore*, ed. Susan Niditch (Semeia Studies, 32; Atlanta, GA: Scholars Press, 1990), 231–41, and William A. Graham, *Beyond the Written Word: Oral Aspects of Scripture in the History of Religion* (Cambridge: Cambridge University Press, 1987).

[89] Mackay, *John's Relationship*.

[90] Paul Anderson, 'John and Mark – the Bi-Optic Gospels', in *Jesus in Johannine Tradition*, ed. Robert T. Fortna and Tom Thatcher (Louisville, KY: Westminster John Knox, 2001), 175–88; Paul Anderson, 'Interfluential, Formative, and Dialectical – A Theory of John's Relation to the Synoptics', in Peter Hofrichter (ed.), *Für und wider die Priorität des Johannesevangeliums*, 19–58; Paul Anderson, 'Aspects of Interfluentiality between John and the Synoptics: John 18–19 as a Case Study', in *The Death of Jesus in the Fourth Gospel*, ed. Gilbert Van Belle (BETL, 200; Leuven: Leuven University Press and Peeters, 2007), 711–28; Paul Anderson, 'Mark, John, and Answerability: Interfluentiality and Dialectic between the Second and Fourth Gospels', *Liber Annuus* 63 (2013): 197–245.

[91] Anderson, *Christology*, 102: 'Markan dependence is highly improbable – nay, absolutely so.'

[92] Paul Anderson, Felix Just, S.J., Tom Thatcher, *John, Jesus and History*, Vol. 1: *Critical Appraisals of Critical Views* (SBLSymS, 44; Atlanta, GA: Society of Biblical Literature, 2007); Vol. 2: *Aspects of Historicity in the Fourth Gospel* (ECL, 2; Atlanta, GA: Society of Biblical Literature, 2009); Vol. 3: *Glimpses of Jesus Through the Johannine Lens* (ECL, 18; Atlanta, GA: Society of Biblical Literature, 2016).

[93] Anderson, 'Mark, John and Answerability', 205–206.

According to Anderson, John's relationship to Mark was 'interfluential, augmentative, and corrective'.[94] He finds oral 'interfluentiality' in references to Isa. 40.3 in Mk 1.2–3 and John 1.23 or Isa. 6.9–10 in Mark 8.17–18 and John 12.39–40, as well as many of the details about the encounter of Jesus and the Baptist (Mk 1 and Jn 1). Oral tradition provided graphic details, such as, in the feeding miracle, the 200 denarii (Mk 6.37; Jn 6.7), the number of loaves and fish (Mk 6.38; Jn 6.9), the grass (Mk 6.39; Jn 6.10). Yet it is not the details, but the overall pattern, the similar beginnings and endings and the structure of episodes along the way, that convince him that the first edition 'appears to have been crafted – at least to some degree – with Mark in mind'.[95] The Fourth Evangelist also adds material to the Markan framework, including five non-Markan miracles and debates with Jewish leaders, while omitting prominent Markan elements: the agrarian parables, the call of the Twelve, exorcisms, apocalyptic predictions and the institution of the Eucharist.

Examples of 'corrections' of Mark appear in John's 'dialectic' relationship to Markan affirmations, e.g., comparisons with Moses (5.45–46; 6.32) and Elijah, exalting Jesus' exalted status; replacing 'Kingdom of God' (3.3, 5) with 'eternal life' (3.15); the reversal of the Markan 'Messianic secret', where the Johannine Jesus does nothing secretly (18.20); and the characterization of miracles as revelatory 'signs' (2.11; 4.54). Specific corrections appear in the gospel's final edition, on small points such as the satisfaction of the crowds (Jn 6.26, vs Mk 6.42) and on larger issues such as the egalitarian character of the Johannine community. Such a 'dialectical' relationship echoes what Windisch long ago maintained.

As examples of 'interfluentiality', Anderson notes[96] the Johannine motifs in the longer Markan ending, the appearance to Mary Magdalene (Mk 16.9–10); the disciples' unbelief (Mk 16.11–13, recalling Thomas); the fact that Jesus dined with his disciples (Mk 16.14); and the confirmatory function of signs (Mk 16.16–20). Such evidence of Johannine influence is not so clear apart from the longer ending of Mark.

Conclusion

The most interesting development in recent scholarship has been the appreciation of a more complex 'intertextuality' than earlier analysis assumed. Authors can play with texts and innovate much more freely than Matthew and Luke did in using Mark.

The character of the texts in question remains to be explored. Debates continue about the Fourth Gospel's 'genre',[97] but most agree that it is a complex work that uses intertexts in subtle ways. The literary dynamics of Mark continue to intrigue scholars. As Matthew Larsen[98] has recently argued, it seems clear that Mark was treated by at

---

[94] Anderson, 'Mark, John and Answerability', 208.
[95] Anderson, 'Mark, John and Answerability', 227.
[96] Anderson, 'Mark, John and Answerability', 228.
[97] See Harold W. Attridge, 'Genre', in *How John Works: Storytelling in the Fourth Gospel*, ed. Douglas Estes and Ruth Sheridan (Atlanta, GA: Scholars Press, 2016), 9–22.
[98] Matthew D.C. Larsen, *Gospels Before the Book* (New York: Oxford University Press, 2018).

least two of its readers as an 'unfinished' text. If Mark was or was perceived to be such a simple collection, it will hardly be surprising that the author(s) of the Fourth Gospel used it, however they knew it, with creative freedom.

In general, then, scholars have come to recognize a substantial relationship between Mark (and perhaps some other Synoptics) and John. The extent of that relationship and its dynamics are open to the kind of conversation evident in this collection of essays.

3

The Johannine 'Relecture' of Mark

Jean Zumstein

In the long and intense discussions on the relationship between the Gospel of John and the Gospel of Mark, two main theories come into contention.[1] The first, and much older, theory of *literary dependence* is today enjoying a revival.[2] It postulates that John knew one or more of the Synoptic Gospels and that he used these as a source. The second theory argues for John's *literary independence* from the Synoptic Gospels.[3] This approach has enjoyed the support of Bultmann and Dodd, as well as, more recently, that of Becker and Theobald.[4] It postulates that John neither knew nor used the Synoptics in their literary form, but rather was drawing from a pool of traditions that are pre-Johannine and also pre-Synoptic (an example is the story of the passion of Jesus). Neither of the theories, be it that which employs methods of literary criticism

---

[1] See Jörg Frey, 'Das vierte Evangelium auf dem Hintergrund der älteren Evangelientradition: Zum Problem: Johannes und die Synoptiker', in *Die Herrlichkeit des Gekreuzigten: Studien zu den Johanneischen Schriften I*, ed. Juliane Schlegel (WUNT, 307; Tübingen: Mohr Siebeck, 2013), 239–94, here 240–55; D. Moody Smith, *Johannine Christianity: Essays on its Setting, Sources, and Theology* (Columbia: University of South Carolina Press, 1984), 39–61.
[2] Charles Kingsley Barrett, *The Gospel According to St John: An Introduction with Commentary and Notes on the Greek Text* (2nd edn; Philadelphia, PA: Westminster Press, 1978), 42–54; Frans Neirynck, 'John and the Synoptics 1975-1990', in *John and the Synoptics*, ed. Adelbert Denaux (BETL, 101; Leuven: Leuven University Press and Peeters, 1992), 3–62; Udo Schnelle, *Einleitung in das Neue Testament* (3rd edn, UTB, 1830; Göttingen: Vandenhoeck & Ruprecht, 1999), 506–11; D. Moody Smith, *John among the Gospels* (Minneapolis, MN: Fortress, 1992).
[3] Percival Gardner-Smith, *Saint John and the Synoptic Gospels* (Cambridge: Cambridge University Press, 1938).
[4] Rudolf Bultmann, art. 'Johannesevangelium', in *Religion in Geschichte und Gegenwart* (3rd edn; Tübingen: Mohr Siebeck, 1959), 3:845–46; C. H. Dodd, *Historical Tradition in the Fourth Gospel* (Cambridge: Cambridge University Press, 1963), 423–32; Jürgen Becker, *Das Evangelium nach Johannes: Kapitel 1–10* (3rd edn, ÖTBK, 4/1; Gütersloh/Würzburg: Gütersloher Verlagshaus Gerd Mohn, Echter Verlag, 1991), 41–45; Michael Theobald, *Das Evangelium nach Johannes: Kapitel 1–12* (RNT; Regensburg: Friedrich Pustet, 2009), 81.
[5] The relationship between John and Mark is one characterized by distance and freedom. Recent research has shown that the type of intertextuality evident between the Synoptics (cf. the two-source theory) is not present in John. The decisive argument is as follows: in the case of parallel narratives (Jn 4 and 6), the Johannine version never contains editorial elements, which are, however, characteristic of the Synoptic versions. This shows that John does not depend on the Synoptics in the same way that, for example, Matthew depends on Mark. This argument, although it excludes a relationship of literary dependence of the 'Synoptic type', does not mean that John was ignorant of the Synoptics, but only that he used them in a different way.

(*Literarkritik*),⁵ or that which depends primarily on tradition history,⁶ has established itself as the uncontested model.

In order to renew this discussion, we need to adopt a different perspective, a fresh methodological paradigm. As Thyen rightly sensed, the theory of intertextuality presents us with such an opportunity.⁷ To define the relationship between John and the Synoptic Gospels, Thyen places the notion of 'play' (*Spiel*) at the centre of his intertextual model. This notion needs some clarification, however, in order to avoid arbitrariness; we should thus review the analysis of the intertextual paradigm and its applicability to John.

My analysis falls into two parts. In the first, I summarise my presuppositions and some elements of the theory of intertextuality. In the second, I will show how the theory applies to the relationship between the Gospels of John and Mark. Finally, in the conclusion, I discuss the implications of my analysis.

Presuppositions and the intertextual model

Let me, first of all, lay out the presuppositions that will guide this analysis:

1. The Fourth Gospel (as Clement of Alexandria recognized) was composed later than the Gospel of Mark, and its author knew of the earlier work.⁸ The historical context speaks in favour of this chronological order.⁹ In terms of intertextuality, Mark is therefore the *hypotext* (source text) and John the *hypertext* (derived text).¹⁰
2. I leave aside the question of which form of Mark was known to John (direct or indirect? total or partial? canonical or pre-canonical?).¹¹
3. The Gospel of Mark was not the only pre-text available to the Johannine school (others include the Jewish Bible, early Christian traditions etc.).

---

⁶ Theobald, *Johannes*, 77: 'Was die Frage der Synoptiker*kenntnis* durch den vierten Evangelisten angeht, ist einzuräumen, dass sie weder positiv noch negativ entscheidbar ist, ja dass Verifikationsmöglichkeiten in der einen oder anderen Richtung fehlen.'
⁷ Hartwig Thyen, *Das Johannesevangelium* (HNT, 6; Tübingen: Mohr Siebeck, 2005), 4; Hartwig Thyen, 'Johannes und die Synoptiker: Auf der Suche nach einem neuen Paradigma zur Beschreibung ihrer Beziehungen anhand von Beobachtungen an Passions- und Ostererzählungen', in *John and the Synoptics*, ed. Adelbert Denaux (BETL, 101; Leuven: Leuven University Press and Peeters, 1992), 81–107.
⁸ Eusebius, *Hist. eccl.* 6.14.7, citing Clement of Alexandria: 'John, last of all, realising that bodily things (σωματικά) had been set forth in the gospels, encouraged by his disciples and divinely inspired, wrote a spiritual gospel (πνευματικόν ... εὐαγγέλιον)'.
⁹ John's knowledge of Mark and, perhaps, of Luke (cf. the Passion narrative) is a matter of historical plausibility. If John is indeed the most recent of the canonical gospels, and if one accepts that he was working in Syria or Ephesus, then it seems unlikely that the Johannine school was not aware of the existence of the gospels that circulated in the first Christian communities of those regions, and in a sense thus re-invented the gospel genre (thus, e.g., Becker, *Das Evangelium nach Johannes*, I:45–47: 'Er war also ein zweiter Mk' [47]). See also Frey, *Herrlichkeit*, 257.
¹⁰ The terminology here draws on Gérard Genette, *Palimpsestes: La littérature au second degré* (Collection Poétique; Paris: Seuil, 1982).
¹¹ Frey, *Herrlichkeit*, 257–60, critically examines the notions of *Abhängigkeit* (dependence) and *Unabhängigkeit* (independence).

4. Not only the Johannine school, but also the first readers of the Fourth Gospel had knowledge of the Gospel of Mark,[12] which means that their reading was a 'relational reading', that is, where the hypertext is read in relation to the hypotext, as well as *vice versa*.[13]

It is now necessary to determine what type of intertextuality we are dealing with. Genette distinguishes at least four types of trans-textual relationships.[14] First, there is *intertextuality* in the strictest sense, which is defined as 'a relationship of co-presence between two or more texts or, ideally and most often, by the actual presence of one text in the other'. The two-source hypothesis for the Synoptic Gospels is a good example of this process. Second, *paratextuality* refers to 'the relationship [...] that the text has with what can be called its paratext: title, [...], preface, postscript [...]'.[15] The title, prologue and epilogue of the Fourth Gospel are classic examples of a paratext. Third, mention should be made of *metatextuality*, which 'is the relationship [...] between a text and another text of which it speaks, but without necessarily quoting it'.[16] Here we might think of the many explicit comments that appear throughout the Gospel of John. Finally, we have *hypertextuality*, which is 'any relationship linking a text B ([...] *hypertext*) to an earlier text A ([...] *hypotext*) to which it is grafted in a manner other than that of a commentary'.[17] In other words, a 'hypertext [is] any text derived from an earlier text by transformation'.[18] In this case, we are dealing with a new text based on a pre-existing, generic model. To my mind – and this is my hypothesis[19] – *the relationship between Mark and John is a typical case of hypertextuality*. John wrote his work based on a previous generic model, namely Mark. But the Gospel of John is not a simple repetition of Mark; it is a *derived* text that bears the hallmark of a process of *transformation*.

How can we describe, in more concrete terms, this process of transformation? It occurs on several levels:

1. First, there is clear *stylistic transformation* – the Johannine language differs profoundly from that of Mark. This leads to the introduction of a new semantics that, in turn, leads to a new interpretation of Jesus' life.
2. A *quantitative transformation* occurs by increasing (e.g., the farewell speeches), decreasing (e.g., the trial before Jewish authorities), or substituting (e.g., the foot

---

[12] The implicit author of the gospel seems to assume that his intended reader knows the Gospel of Mark. The hypothesis of an intertextual play between John and Mark is supported by the presentation of the Baptist in the Fourth Gospel, the transposition of the Temple incident to the beginning of the narrative, and the Johannine version of Gethsemane. Cf. Frey, *Herrlichkeit*, 290.
[13] Genette, *Palimpsestes*, 452; similarly, Thyen, *Johannesevangelium*, 4.
[14] Genette, *Palimpsestes*, 11.
[15] For further details, see Gérard Genette, *Seuils* (Collection Poétique; Paris: Seuil, 1987).
[16] Genette, *Palimpsestes*, 10.
[17] Genette, *Palimpsestes*, 11–12.
[18] Genette, *Palimpsestes*, 14. Classic examples of hypertexts based on Homer's *Odyssey* are Virgil's *Aeneid* and Joyce's *Ulysses*.
[19] I first suggested this in my commentary: Jean Zumstein, *L'Évangile selon Saint Jean (1–12)* (CNT, IVa; Genève: Labor et Fides, 2014; 2nd edn. 2016), 30–22 (= Jean Zumstein, *Das Johannesevangelium* [KEK, 2; Göttingen: Vandenhoeck & Ruprecht, 2016], 44–47).

washing) narrative material. Entire scenes are also rewritten (e.g., the sign of abundant bread).
3. The *narrative mode* is also different. The temporal order, the frequency, and the length of the narrative are significantly altered when compared with Mark.
4. A *diegetic transformation* leads to the establishment of a new space–time universe when compared to Mark. This transformation of the story's universe is accompanied by a transformation of the hero's action (the Johannine Jesus no longer acts in the same way as Mark's Jesus).
5. Finally, the *point of view* that guides the narrative is also different.

Let us look at some examples of this process.

Some examples of hypertextuality

The *Temple incident* provides us with a first example of the Johannine reinterpretation of the Synoptic tradition.[20] Two well-known differences distinguish the Johannine version (2.13–22) from that of Mark (11.15–17). The first regards the location of the incident in the narrative. The order is different. While Mark, followed by Matthew and Luke, situates this episode during the last week of Jesus' ministry in Jerusalem, John places it at the beginning of Jesus' activity, just after the first sign at Cana. It would be wrong to think that John was misinformed, or that he had access to another tradition evoking a different purification of the Temple. In fact, John uses a technique that is dear to him in that he shifts elements into the first part of the Gospel that, in the Synoptic tradition, belong to the cycle of the Passion.[21] In doing so, John wants to show that all of Jesus' activity is placed under the sign of the cross.

The second difference supports this observation. It consists of a process of amplification and displacement. The Johannine school does not give one interpretation of the purification of the Temple, but rather two. The first, which is the traditional interpretation, belongs to the wider tradition, prophetically arguing against a mercantile instrumentalization of the Temple. The second, found only in John, is a controversy story that contains two *logia* that, in the Synoptics, belong to the cycle of the Passion: the demand for a sign (Mk 11.27–33) and the saying about rebuilding the Temple (Mk 14.58 and 15.29). This difference results in an important interpretative gesture, namely that the motif of the Temple is given a christological significance. The destruction and

---

[20] See Udo Schnelle, 'Die Tempelreinigung und die Christologie des Johannesevangeliums', NTS 42 (1996), 359–73; Jean Zumstein, '"Und wir wissen, dass sein Zeugnis wahr ist": Fiktion und Geschichte in der johanneischen Vita Jesu', in *Wahrheit und Geschichte: Exegetische und hermeneutische Studien zu einer dialektischen Konstellation*, ed. Eva Ebel and Samuel Vollenweider (AThANT, 102; Zürich: Theologischer Verlag, 2012), 33–52, here 42–45; Jean Zumstein, 'Johannes 2:13–22 im Plot und in der Theologie des vierten Evangeliums', in *The Opening of John's Narrative (John 1:19 – 2:22)*, ed. R. Alan Culpepper and Jörg Frey (WUNT, 385; Tübingen: Mohr Siebeck, 2017), 275–87.

[21] Hans-Josef Klauck, 'Geschrieben, erfüllt, vollendet: Die Schriftzitate in der Johannespassion', in *Israel und seine Heilstraditionen im Johannesevangelium: Festgabe für Johannes Beutler SJ zum 70. Geburtstag*, ed. Michael Labahn, Klaus Scholtissek and Angelika Strotmann (Paderborn: Schöningh, 2004), 140–57.

reconstruction of the Temple is the object of a metaphorical transfer; it is the body of Jesus that is now the place of God's presence, thanks to the Nazarene's death and resurrection. The re-contextualisation and reinterpretation of the Temple incident are, in this manner, placed at the service of Johannine theology.

In both the Synoptic tradition and the Fourth Gospel, we find the sequence: *miracle of the loaves – walking on water*.[22] I present this as my second example. Without going into the details, it should be noted that the Johannine school provides the miracle of the loaves with a conclusion (6.14–15) that does not appear in Mark. The supplement interprets the sign of the loaves (6.14b: οὗτός ἐστιν ἀληθῶς ὁ προφήτης ὁ ἐρχόμενος εἰς τὸν κόσμον), even if this confession of faith is immediately distorted by the plan to make Jesus a messianic king on earth (6.15). The story of walking on water, which follows, is a corrective to this. In effect, the story is rewritten in John and becomes an epiphany narrative. Jesus reveals his true identity to his disciples – he is not a messianic king in the earthly sense, but he does possess the authority of God (as his mastery over nature demonstrates). In the Fourth Gospel, Jesus' walking on water is intended to remove the misunderstanding that resulted from the miracle of the loaves and to reveal to the disciples the true identity of Christ.

The clarification does not end there. For the Johannine school there is more to say about the miracle of the loaves. There is also a process of amplification. Five exchanges between Jesus and his interlocutors follow in the continuation of chapter 6, exploring the different possible meanings of the miracle (6.22–29). Through intertextual play with the episode of manna in the desert, a link is made with the tradition of Israel. The christological reading moves, step by step, toward its famous culmination (ἐγώ εἰμι ὁ ἄρτος τῆς ζωῆς), which is the correct interpretation of the sign. Finally, the Eucharistic turn (6.52–58), which concludes the exchanges between Jesus and his interlocutors, links the theme of bread to that of Jesus' death. Chapter 6 thus shows, in an exemplary manner, how two familiar elements of the tradition – the miracle of the loaves and the walking on water – can trigger an interpretative process far beyond that found in the Synoptics.

My third example is the well-known episode from Gethsemane (Mk 14.32–42; cf. Jn 12.27–28),[23] so important in the Synoptic tradition, but missing from John. In Mark, it takes place between the last meal and Jesus' arrest, but it disappears from John, who instead has farewell speeches. There is, to be sure, an allusion to Gethsemane at John 12. Once again, a classic element of the Passion narrative is moved to the first part of the gospel, and its meaning is completely altered.

---

[22] Cf. Michael Labahn, *Offenbarung in Zeichen und Wort: Untersuchungen zur Vorgeschichte von John 6,1–25a und seiner Rezeption in der Brotrede* (WUNT, 2/117; Tübingen: Mohr Siebeck, 2000); Jean Zumstein, '"Ich bin das Brot des Lebens": Wiederholung und Variation eines johanneischen Ego-Eimi-Wortes in Joh 6', in *Repetitions and Variations in the Fourth Gospel: Style, Text, Interpretation*, ed. Gilbert Van Belle, Michael Labahn and Petrus Maritz (BETL, 223; Leuven: Leuven University Press and Peeters, 2009), 435–52; Jean Zumstein, *Johannesevangelium*, 249–52.

[23] Dodd, *Historical Tradition*, 69–72; Frey, *Herrlichkeit*, 265–71; Jean Zumstein, 'Au seuil de la passion (Jean 12)', in *Studies in the Gospel of John, and its Christology: Festschrift Gilbert Van Belle*, ed. Joseph Verheyden, Gilbert van Oyen, Michael Labahn and Reimund Bieringer (BETL, 265; Leuven: Leuven University Press and Peeters, 2014), 275–88; Jean Zumstein, *Johannesevangelium*, 457–59.

While Mark insists on the trial and the struggle experienced by Jesus in the face of his imminent death (v. 34: περίλυπός ἐστιν δυνατά ἡ ψυχή μου ἕως θανάτου), then v. 36 (αββα ὁ πατήρ, πάντα δυνατά σοι· παρένεγκε τὸ ποτήριον τοῦτο ἀπ᾽ ἐμοῦ· ἀλλ᾽ οὐ τί ἐγὼ θέλω ἀλλὰ τί σύ), John proposes a very different reading, one which eliminates fear and anguish. Admittedly, 'Jesus' soul is troubled' in the face of imminent death (v. 27a: ἡ ψυχή μου τετάρακται). But how should the Johannine Jesus react in this situation (v. 27a: καὶ τί εἴπω;)? The natural response, which recalls both the psalmist's request (Ps. 6.5b) and Mark's version, would be: πάτερ, σῶσόν με ἐκ τῆς ὥρας ταύτης ('Father, save me from this hour'). And yet, the Johannine Jesus excludes this possibility and responds as follows: ἀλλὰ διὰ τοῦτο ἦλθον εἰς τὴν ὥραν ταύτην ('but for this cause I came unto this hour'). Jesus' mission is not to avoid death, but rather to transform it into the heart of his action, since it is on the cross that God's presence finds its full expression. Gethsemane is thus reinterpreted according to the Christology of the Fourth Gospel.

A fourth, and particularly interesting, example is that of the Johannine version of Jesus' last meal.[24] The Pauline and Synoptic traditions are unanimous in stating that this last meal culminated in the institution of the Eucharist. But there is nothing of the sort in John. To be sure, the last meal of Jesus is described in detail, but at its core is the washing of the feet, which replaces the Eucharist. Again, it is wrong to assume that John was unaware of the Eucharistic tradition (which interprets Jesus' death and demonstrates its significance). John 6.52–59 clearly shows that the Johannine school knows of the Eucharistic practice and that it took place in Johannine churches. But by substituting the Lord's Supper with the washing of the feet, John wants to introduce an interpretation of the now imminent cross: the death of Jesus is presented as a service of love that cleans and purifies those who are its beneficiaries. And John does not stop there. To explore the event of the cross, in all its dimensions, he adds two farewell speeches (13.31–16.33) as well as the priestly prayer (ch. 17).

A final example is provided by what Michael Theobald calls the 'sayings of the Lord' (*Herrenworte*) as metatexts of the Synoptic tradition'.[25] According to Theobald, the author of the Fourth Gospel used certain *logia* of the Synoptic tradition as 'basic texts' (*hypotexts*), which he then reinterpreted either by deepening or adapting them to fit his own perspective (*hypertext*). The most interesting aspect of this hypothesis is the transformation process from hypotext to hypertext. Among the examples given by Theobald is the word of Jesus, quoted at 21.22: ἐὰν αὐτὸν θέλω μένειν ἕως ἔρχομαι, τί πρὸς σέ.[26] This is supposed to be a metatext of Mk 9.1 (ἀμὴν λέγω ὑμῖν ὅτι εἰσίν τινες ὧδε τῶν ἑστηκότων οἵτινες οὐ μὴ γεύσωνται θανάτου ἕως ἂν ἴδωσιν τὴν βασιλείαν τοῦ θεοῦ ἐληλυθυῖαν ἐν δυνάμει). One would then have to assume that the Johannine community considered the Beloved Disciple to be one of Jesus' witnesses, destined to live up to the Parousia. According to this hypothesis, the logion of Mark 9.1 was adapted to suit the situation of the Johannine community. However, the death of the

---

[24] Jean Zumstein, 'Story, Plot, and History in the Johannine Passion Narrative', in *John, Jesus, and History*, Vol. 3: *Glimpses Through the Johannine Lens*, ed. Paul N. Anderson, Felix Just, S. J. and Tom Thatcher (ECL, 18; Atlanta, GA: Society of Biblical Literature, 2016), 109–18.
[25] Cf. Michael Theobald, *Herrenworte im Johannesevangelium* (HBS, 34; Freiburg: Herder, 2002), 200–43.
[26] On Jn 21.22, see Theobald, *Herrenworte*, 232–37.

disciple, mentioned indirectly in verse 23, seems to invalidate the promise made by the Risen One, so that the author of the gospel is forced to add a correction: the Beloved Disciple did die, but would live until the Parousia via his written testimony. Here we have an exemplary illustration of a hypertext, a free and creative transposition of a known hypotext.

Conclusions

Classical literary criticism (*Literarkritik*), especially when applied to the relationship between Mark and John, was driven by a desire to identify the oldest form of the tradition, in order to go back, as far as possible, to the historical Jesus. By observing the various transformations of the traditions that fed into the gospels, scholars sought to find the original version. This aim, however legitimate it might be, has been strongly qualified by recent historical research. Each expression of a tradition is in fact already a construction, and authenticity is not necessarily linked to age. The Gospel of Mark, which is the oldest that has come down to us, is itself based on traces found in numerous earlier traditions; it is simultaneously a construction and a reconstruction of Jesus' life. Even if the Gospel of John is the most recent of the New Testament gospels, it has, from a methodological point of view, the same status as that of Mark and should not be discredited from the outset by resorting to arguments about documentary reliability.

By adopting the theory of intertextuality to articulate the possible relationship between Mark and John, we alter the paradigm. We are no longer engaged in a quest for origins, nor does documentary authenticity stand at the centre of the investigation, but rather the type of relationship between two completed literary works that succeed each other in time. Choosing the category of hypertextuality to characterize this relationship presents an obvious heuristic interest. We are no longer dealing with a relationship of direct dependence (as assumed by the Synoptic question), but rather a much freer relationship that presupposes a process of both literary and theological transformation. Focusing our attention on this transformation has two main implications. On the one hand, it allows us better to characterise the work of the authorial instance at the various stages of its intervention. On the other hand, it shows how the first recipients were engaged in the act of reading (which can be characterized as a 'relational reading').

Comparison between the Gospel of Mark and the Gospel of John and, in particular, analysis of their intertextual relationship, highlights the connection between history and fiction that is typical of ancient historiography. The selecting of events from the life of Jesus, their contextualization in a plot, and the desire to interpret them is not a betrayal of the truth (as a positivist view of history might argue), but simply a way of writing history. The Johannine school, when compared with the Synoptic literature, took very seriously its role as an interpreter, attempting to give meaning to the story of Jesus. The question that arises when reading the Fourth Gospel is, therefore, not whether John, from a documentary point of view, betrays Jesus, but rather: did he properly understand the history of the Nazarene?

4

'If John Knew Mark': Critical Inheritance and Johannine Disagreements with Mark

Chris Keith

Introduction

This essay will address the question of the Fourth Gospel's familiarity with[1] the Gospel of Mark from the perspective of social memory theory. I draw upon a specific concept within the wider discourse of social memory theory – critical inheritance. My application of this concept to the question of Johannine familiarity with Mark's Gospel is narrowly focused, so I need to be clear at the outset about what social memory theory can – and cannot – contribute to an answer. I affirm that John's Gospel shows familiarity with Mark's Gospel.[2] Social memory theory in and of itself, however, does not prove this matter one way or another. As I and others have stated elsewhere,[3] one of social memory theory's most significant contributions to New Testament studies relates to how scholars think 'tradition' – that vague and elusive but omnipresent and thus unavoidable concept – works, both in terms of how it worked in the ancient world and how it works in our own scholarly historiographies.[4] This contribution emerges from the fact that social memory theory focuses upon the roles of the present and the past when an individual or group holds up an image of the past from the position of, and for the sake of, the present. Social memory theory remains fundamentally a *theory*

---

[1] Following Mark Goodacre, *Thomas and the Gospels: The Case for Thomas's Familiarity with the Synoptics* (Grand Rapids, MI: Wm. B. Eerdmans, 2012), 5–7, I prefer to speak of a later tradition's 'familiarity with' prior tradition, or 'knowledge of' prior tradition, rather than 'dependence upon'.

[2] In addition to some of the discussion below, see generally Chris Keith, 'The Competitive Textualization of the Jesus Tradition in John 20:30–31 and 21:24–25', *CBQ* 78 (2016): 321–37.

[3] Chris Keith, 'Social Memory Theory and Gospels Scholarship: The First Decade (Part One)', *EC* 6.3 (2015): 354–76; 'Social Memory Theory and Gospels Scholarship: The First Decade (Part Two)', *EC* 6.4 (2015): 517–42. See also Alan Kirk, 'Memory and Media: Towards a New History of the Jesus Tradition', in *Memory and the Jesus Tradition* (RJFTC, 2; London: Bloomsbury T&T Clark, 2018), 1–8; Alan Kirk and Tom Thatcher, 'Jesus Tradition as Social Memory', in *Memory, Tradition, and Text: Uses of the Past in Early Christianity*, ed. Alan Kirk and Tom Thatcher (Semeia Studies, 52; Atlanta, GA: Society of Biblical Literature, 2005), 31–42.

[4] Foundational for the relationship between the present and the past on the part of both the ancients and modern scholars are the essays in Jens Schröter, *From Jesus to the New Testament: Early Christian Theology and the Origin of the New Testament Canon*, trans. Wayne C. Coppins (BMSEC; Waco, TX: Baylor University Press, 2013), 9–132.

about the interaction between the present and the past, though. As such, it is not, strictly speaking, a *method*: it is not a quasi-mechanical or scientific process that produces for the scholar an assured result. It tells us that good historiography accounts for the images of the past that persist, but it does not tell us how to account for them, and thus does not write the past for us.[5] Therefore, although I affirm Johannine familiarity with Mark's Gospel and this essay will support that position, the theory is equally relevant for a scholar taking the opposite position.

That being said, this essay will use social memory theory in support of a theory of Johannine familiarity with Mark's Gospel by challenging the idea that disagreement with a prior tradition favours a later tradent's independence from that tradition. I will argue that Johannine disagreement with the Gospel of Mark lends itself just as readily to a theory of familiarity as it does to a theory of independence.

I will first briefly discuss how assumptions about the potential disagreement of John with Mark[6] functioned within the thinking of Gardner-Smith's landmark *Saint John and the Synoptic Gospels*.[7] I will then introduce the concept of critical inheritance as an alternative to this approach. This concept aligns with Thyen's theory of John's 'intertextuelle Spiel' with the Synoptics and with Zumstein's intertextual theory (via Genette) of John's 'relecture' of the Synoptics.[8] Like these theories, critical inheritance embraces a greater range of complexity in the transmission of tradition. I will then finish with an application of the concept of critical inheritance to the identification of Jesus' πατρίς in John 4.44 and Mark 6.4.[9]

Disagreement and independence in P. Gardner-Smith

Gardner-Smith's *Saint John and the Synoptic Gospels* disrupted a previously dominant scholarly *communis opinio* that the Fourth Gospel was dependent upon the Synoptic Gospels. Thatcher evens speaks of Gardner-Smith's slim volume 'dismantl[ing]' the state of the field.[10] One can hardly disagree about its impact, and Smith has shown

---

[5] Jens Schröter, 'The Criteria of Authenticity in Jesus Research and Historiographical Method', in *Jesus, Criteria, and the Demise of Authenticity*, ed. Chris Keith and Anthony Le Donne (London: T&T Clark, 2012), 59–65.
[6] I will use the traditional names 'John' and 'Mark' for the authors of the Gospels of John and Mark respectively with no further assumptions about the identity of the authors.
[7] P. Gardner-Smith, *Saint John and the Synoptic Gospels* (Cambridge: Cambridge University Press, 1938).
[8] Hartwig Thyen, *Das Johannesevangelium* (HNT, 6; Tübingen: Mohr Siebeck, 2005), 101, and throughout; Jean Zumstein, *Kreative Erinnerung: Relecture und Auslegung im Johannesevangelium* (2nd edn, AThANT, 84; Zürich: TVZ, 2004), 15–30 and throughout, respectively. As Zumstein makes clear (*Kreative*, 15 n.3), he uses the term 'relecture' for what Genette calls 'transtextuality' (Gérard Genette, *Palimpsests: Literature in the Second Degree*, trans. Channa Newman and Claude Doubinsky [Stages, 8; Lincoln: University of Nebraska Press, 1982], 1).
[9] This final section will build upon ideas first expressed in Chris Keith, 'Jesus the Galilean in the Gospel of John: The Significance of Earthly Origins in the Fourth Gospel', in *Portraits of Jesus in the Gospel of John: A Christological Spectrum*, ed. Craig Koester (LNTS, 589; London: Bloomsbury T&T Clark, 2018), 45–59.
[10] Tom Thatcher, 'The New Current through John: The Old "New Look" and the New Critical Orthodoxy', in *New Currents through John: A Global Perspective*, ed. Francisco Lozada Jr. and Tom Thatcher (RBS, 54; Atlanta, GA: Society of Biblical Literature, 2006), 3.

clearly how Gardner-Smith's argument, especially once spoken through the megaphone of C. H. Dodd, created a new consensus.[11] Gardner-Smith published his study in 1938, but returning to his ideas is helpful not only because of his considerable influence, but also because he gives particularly clear expression to the idea that disagreement between John and Mark favours a theory of independence.

Disagreements between Mark's Gospel and John's Gospel

In numerous places, the Johannine narrative displays a difference of opinion with Mark and the Synoptics. These instances constitute not just stylistic differences, but contradictions of detail. There are major and obvious examples, such as Mark's placement of the Temple Incident at the end of Jesus' ministry (Mk 11.11–21) and John's placement of it at the beginning of Jesus' ministry (Jn 2.13–22), or Mark's placement of the crucifixion on Passover proper, following the eating of the Passover meal the prior evening (Mk 14.12–25; 15.25–39), and John's placement of the crucifixion on the Day of Preparation, prior to the eating of the Passover meal (19.14, 31, 42). There are also less-obvious examples that do not always get as much attention but are perhaps even more interesting. For example, whereas the Markan narrator states that Jesus prayed that 'the hour (ἡ ὥρα) might pass from him' (Mk 14.35),[12] the Johannine Jesus scoffs at even the idea of responding to 'the hour' in this manner: 'Now my soul is troubled. And what should I say? 'Father, save me from this hour (τῆς ὥραν ταύτης)'? But for this I have come for this hour (τὴν ὥραν ταύτην)' (Jn 12.27). Likewise, whereas Mark claims that Simon of Cyrene carried Jesus' cross for him (Mk 15.21), John specifies that Jesus carried his cross himself (Jn 19.17).

To these we can add several more possible disagreements with other Synoptic Gospels. In contrast to the Matthean and Lukan infancy narratives, wherein Jesus is born of a virgin in Bethlehem (Mt. 1.18–2.1; Lk. 1.26–2.40), the Johannine Jesus receives no narrated birth, virgin or otherwise, and is never in Bethlehem (cf. Jn 7.42). In the account of the miraculous haul of fish, Luke 5.6 claims that there were so many fish that 'their nets were being torn' (διερρήσσετο ... τὰ δίκτυα αὐτῶν) whereas John 21.11 states that, despite there being exactly 153 fish, 'the net was not ripped' (οὐκ ἐσχίσθη τὸ δίκτυον).

Disagreement and independence

These differences and others have played an important role in scholarly discussion of the relationship between John and the Synoptics.[13] Gardner-Smith launched his attack

---

[11] D. Moody Smith, *John among the Gospels* (2nd edn; Columbia, SC: University of South Carolina Press, 2001), 37–84, 199. For Dodd's comments on Gardner-Smith, see C. H. Dodd, *The Interpretation of the Fourth Gospel* (Cambridge: Cambridge University Press, 1953), 449, 449 n.2; C. H. Dodd, *Historical Tradition in the Fourth Gospel* (Cambridge: Cambridge University Press, 1963), 8, 8 n.2.
[12] All translations are those of the author.
[13] See Smith, *John*.

on the theory of Johannine dependence upon Mark by foregrounding such 'differences which require to be explained'.[14] This procedure was strategic, as he viewed the then-dominant view of Johannnine knowledge of the Synoptics as overly reliant upon agreements.[15] His volume proceeds sequentially through the Johannine narrative by presenting each disagreement as it arises and discussing whether a theory of dependence or independence best accounts for it, concluding ultimately in favour of a theory of independence.

A core aspect of what needed 'to be explained', for Gardner-Smith, is how John could possibly say what he does in an ecclesial context where Mark's Gospel is revered. Already on page five of his book, this issue arises in relation to the Johannine dismissal of the Markan and Matthean identifications of John the Baptist as Elijah (Jn 1.24–34). Gardner-Smith says,

> It is hard to believe that the author had the written work of Mark or Luke in mind.... Most significant for our present enquiry is the explicit denial that John is to be identified with Elijah.... Mark put the plain words into the Lord's mouth, 'I say unto you that Elijah has come' (Mk. ix. 13), and Matthew adds, 'Then the disciples understood that he spake concerning John the Baptist' (Mt. xvii. 13). St John will allow the Baptist no such distinction; he was 'the burning and shining light', but even so his witness was almost superfluous: 'I have a greater witness than John's the works of which my Father hath given me' (Jn. v. 35, 36). It is easy to see that the Fourth Evangelist, writing for readers who were not greatly interested in the claim that Jesus was the Messiah of Jewish expectation, may have considered the theory that John was Elijah unimportant, or even absurd; *but if he had been writing in a Church in which the Gospel according to St Mark was known and esteemed it is most improbable that he would have brushed aside Mark's important contention without a word of argument*.... It is easier to think that the Fourth Evangelist wrote at a time when traditions about John had not yet been fixed by *the acceptance of the written Gospels*; indeed, some of the synoptic traditions had not yet been developed.[16]

This lengthy quotation is characteristic for Gardner-Smith's volume as a whole. He identifies a disagreement between the Johannine and Markan or Synoptic narratives and proceeds, on its basis, to affirm a remarkably early date for the composition of the Gospel of John, prior even to the 'development' of some Synoptic traditions. As the italicizations indicate, what makes it 'easier' for Gardner-Smith to affirm an early and independent Gospel of John is his conviction that John could not or would not have voiced such a disagreement with Mark once Mark's Gospel had already risen to a position of 'esteem' and 'acceptance' – *if* John was in the Christ community that read Mark's Gospel, that is.

---

[14] Gardner-Smith, *Saint John*, xi.
[15] Gardner-Smith, *Saint John*, xi: 'Critics who have discussed the relationship of St John to the synoptic writings have exhibited a curious tendency to concentrate their attention solely on those points on which agreement is manifest, and to ignore the much greater and surely no less significant differences which require to be explained.'
[16] Gardner-Smith, *Saint John*, 5–6 (emphases added).

The combination of narrative disagreements and Gardner-Smith's inability to imagine a John in disagreement with an authoritative Mark virtually necessitates an early and independent stream of Johannine tradition as well as a separate Johannine community, and these two matters collide consistently in his discussion. In another example, Gardner-Smith generates leverage for his argument for an early, independent Gospel of John from the (for him) unlikely scenario that John would contradict the Gospel of Mark once it was already recognized in the Christ assembly.

> The whole passage describing the call of the first disciples is irreconcilable with the synoptic accounts ... *If St John had heard any such story as that contained in Mk. i*, he set it aside, and substituted for it an account more in keeping with his own ideas. But it is more likely that he would have done so if he was acquainted with oral traditions than that he would have contradicted a written Gospel *that had already gained currency in the Church.*[17]

And yet again:

> *If the Fourth Evangelist had read St Mark's Gospel* its general scheme must have seemed to him entirely unsatisfactory, for he presents an irreconcilable alternative.... *If he knew Mark* he can hardly have been unaware that he was contradicting him. The possibility should at least be considered that he was composing an original account, the product of his own faith working on the floating traditions of the Christian Church and uninfluenced by other *accounts which gained currency* simultaneously in quite different circles of believers.... His intention here may be to put Jesus and John side by side, but he certainly contradicts St Mark, who dates the beginning of the ministry of Jesus from the time that John was imprisoned by Herod (Mk. i. 14). Surely the simplest explanation is that the Fourth Evangelist was writing at a time when the *acceptance of St Mark's Gospel* had not yet fixed his tradition on the Church.[18]

I have not yet moved beyond the first eight pages of Gardner-Smith's main text. The remainder of the volume is similarly rife with arguments that a certain interpretive scenario is essentially impossible 'if John knew Mark', and if followers of Jesus already revered Mark's Gospel. Although working through numerous matters of detail in the text, Gardner-Smith closes his first chapter with an 'if' statement that states explicitly perhaps *the* foundational issue for him, what he 'finds hard to believe'[19] and 'most improbable:'[20] 'If he had read them, he held them in very low esteem.'[21]

There are several assumptions on the part of Gardner-Smith that the evidence does not support. One is the assumption that followers of Jesus at the time of the composition of the Gospel of John already esteemed the Gospel of Mark to the extent that John

---

[17] Gardner-Smith, *Saint John*, 7 (emphases added).
[18] Gardner-Smith, *Saint John*, 7–8 (emphases added).
[19] Gardner-Smith, *Saint John*, 5.
[20] Gardner-Smith, *Saint John*, 5.
[21] Gardner-Smith, *Saint John*, 10.

would have not contradicted it. The degree to which John or any other follower of Jesus venerated Mark's Gospel if he or she knew it is unknown for this period. If he knew it, John presumably appreciated Mark's contribution to the transmission of the Jesus tradition enough to replicate it. Mark's Gospel was read among Jesus followers from its inception (Mk 13.14).[22] According to Eusebius in the early fourth century, Papias claimed in the early second century that the Roman church in the late first century venerated Mark's Gospel as the written teachings of Peter.[23] Clement of Alexandria claims similarly in the late second/early third century, also according to Eusebius in the fourth century.[24] But we have no evidence of Jesus followers reading it *liturgically* in an *ecclesia* and with a *scriptural* status – the scenario that Gardner-Smith posits – until Justin Martyr describes the public reading of the gospels (presumably including Mark's Gospel) with the prophets at the church in Rome *c.* 150 CE.[25] Irenaeus does not explicitly articulate a fully authoritative status for Mark's Gospel alongside John's Gospel (as well as Matthew's and Luke's) until *c.* 180 CE.[26] In the late first or early second century, however – that is, around the traditional dating of the composition of John's Gospel – we do not know exactly to what extent Jesus' followers granted Mark's Gospel an authoritative status, and thus also do not know whether it would have precluded John's disagreement with it.

A related assumption in Gardner-Smith's theory is that disagreement necessarily amounts to disparagement. Gardner-Smith never seriously entertains whether John's attempts at improvement upon Mark's Gospel might have sprung ultimately from appreciation for Mark's work, or whether some degree of disparagement could have co-existed with some degree of respect. His approach to the disagreements rules out any possibility other than disparagement for a theory that John knew Mark.

I isolate these matters because it is on the basis of such things – the conceptualization of how an individual or group appropriated the past from the position of, and on behalf of, their present – that social memory can make a contribution to this discourse. Gardner-Smith wrote long before social memory theory broke into Gospels research (though not before its inception).[27] It is nevertheless easy to see the theory's main foci as operative in his thinking since his theory hinges upon how John, in his present circumstances, would or would not have received an image of the past from Mark.

Critical inheritance

Social memory theory concerns the past, the present, and the complex relationship between the two in commemorative activity. The foundational insight of Maurice

---

[22] For an argument that Mark 13.14 refers to the public reading of the Gospel of Mark, likely, though not necessarily, in assembly, see Chris Keith, *The Gospel as Manuscript: An Early History of the Jesus Tradition as Material Artifact* (New York: Oxford University Press, 2020), 176–81.
[23] Eusebius, *Hist. eccl.* 3.39.15.
[24] Eusebius, *Hist. eccl.* 2.15.1; 6.14.6.
[25] Justin Martyr, *1 Apol.* 67.3–4. For further discussion, see Keith, *Gospel*, 182–89.
[26] Irenaeus, *Adv. haer.* 3.11.8.
[27] For a brief history of research, see Keith, 'Social Memory Theory (Part One)', 354–56.

Halbwachs, the founder of social memory theory, was that the past is always constructed from the perspective of the present, and thus 'memory' is always affected by the social circumstances in which someone(s) perform(s) the remembering.[28] To address a common misconception, the phrase 'social memory' does not refer to a 'thing' so much as it refers to a process. 'Social memory' is not the same as 'group memory'; it does not refer to a form of groupthink that excludes the agency of individuals.[29] Although social memory theory does theorize group memory, it does not do so on those terms. It theorizes how individuals and groups alike appropriate the past from the perspective of the present by employing 'social frameworks' to structure the commemorative activity.[30] 'Social memory' is 'social' because even individuals appropriate the past in their present on the basis of their social contexts.

With regard to the impact of those social frameworks upon the shape of memory, a central debate among social memory theorists concerns the degree to which the present can rewrite the past and, reciprocally, the degree to which the past can force itself upon the present. Over the past several decades, sociologist Barry Schwartz has advocated a 'continuity perspective',[31] insisting that, although the past is malleable, its malleability has limits: 'To conceive of memory as a mirror of reality is to conceive a fiction.... To conceive the meaning of the past as fixed and steady is likewise meaningless, since any event must appear differently as perceptual circumstances change.'[32]

As part of his overall arguments that the past, in most cases, is 'neither totally precarious nor immutable',[33] in 1997 Schwartz published an article with Tong Zhang wherein they introduced to collective memory theory the concept of 'critical inheritance', which they describe as 'a form of collective memory that has no close Western counterpart'.[34] They define critical inheritance as 'a deliberative process wherein both positive and negative aspects of historic figures are recognized'.[35] Their case study was the reception of Confucius in China, particularly during the Chinese Cultural Revolution. Through a lengthy discussion of how various political and social forces have appropriated Confucius, they show that 'the Chinese people's reverence for Confucius has varied from generation to generation, but they have never felt free to

---

[28] See, for example, Maurice Halbwachs, *The Social Frameworks of Memory*, in his *On Collective Memory*, ed. and trans. Lewis A. Coser (Chicago, IL: University of Chicago Press, 1992). For a brief overview of his work as it relates to Biblical Studies, see Keith, 'Social Memory Theory (Part One)', 359–64. More broadly, see Sarah Gensburger, 'Halbwachs' Studies in Collective Memory: A Founding Text for "Memory Studies"?' *JCS* 16.4 (2016): 396–413.

[29] Lewis A. Coser, Introduction to *On Collective Memory*, by Maurice Halbwachs (Chicago, IL: University of Chicago Press, 1992), 22: 'Nor is [collective memory] some mystical group mind.'

[30] Halbwachs, 'Social Frameworks', 38, 48, 51, 182.

[31] I first used this term for Schwartz's position in Chris Keith, 'Memory and Authenticity: Jesus Tradition and What Really Happened', *ZNW* 102 (2011): 169.

[32] Barry Schwartz, *Abraham Lincoln and the Forge of National Memory* (Chicago, IL: University of Chicago Press, 2000), 7. He applied these thoughts, and even words, to historical Jesus studies in Barry Schwartz, 'Christian Origins: Historical Truth and Social Memory', in Alan Kirk and Tom Thatcher (ed.), *Memory, Tradition, and Text*, 53.

[33] Schwartz, *Abraham Lincoln*, 125.

[34] Tong Zhang and Barry Schwartz, 'Confucius and the Cultural Revolution: A Study in Collective Memory', *IJPCS* 11.2 (1997): 194.

[35] Zhang and Schwartz, 'Confucius', 194.

reconstitute his life and teachings'.[36] The inherited Confucius is too culturally significant and thus too stubborn an image to be reconstructed entirely anew in every unfolding present. This is not to claim that the image of Confucius never changed, however. It did, but not by means of wholesale reconstruction. Rather, it changed by each receiving context selectively emphasizing or de-emphasizing aspects of the inherited image. Cultural stakeholders could find both positive and negative resonances with their current identity. Thus, for example, 'The communist establishment, assuming power in 1949, was simultaneously drawn to Confucius because his memory legitimated its hegemony and repelled by Confucius because his ideals opposed its revolution.'[37] Confucius was too important to ignore entirely,[38] so an anti-Confucius campaign was launched. Even here, the altered image of Confucius they offered was not a complete reconstruction but a shifting placement of emphasis upon information already known.[39]

Zhang and Schwartz's concept of critical inheritance is relevant for scholars of Second Temple Judaism and early Christianity. It applies concepts of collective memory theory to a non-Western culture, and does so in order to diagnose a Western bias in the field of research. They position their argument squarely against the predominant trend in social memory studies of focusing upon instances in which the past is constantly remade – or 'constructed' – in the present. They argue that this research focus has an inherently Western bent,[40] and that more traditional societies show how collective memory can also remain stable despite substantial political changes: 'Construction of the past, although deemed universal, is least pronounced among cultures in which innovation, libertarianism, cognitive and moral flexibility are least valued.'[41] More succinctly, 'the less traditional the cultural, the more that can be done with the past interpretively'.[42] Such an approach fits with Schwartz's opinion voiced elsewhere that the field of social memory theory is geared toward memory's pathologies because they are more interesting.[43]

Zhang and Schwartz have already applied their concept of critical inheritance to the cultural reception of Jesus. In their original article, and citing Jaroslav Pelikan's *Jesus through the Centuries*, they discuss the changing images of Jesus in the eighteenth and nineteenth centuries:

---

[36] Zhang and Schwartz, 'Confucius', 191.
[37] Zhang and Schwartz, 'Confucius', 194.
[38] Zhang and Schwartz, 'Confucius', 194: 'Confucius can be revered – must be revered – by the institutions and individuals that reject his political convictions.'
[39] Zhang and Schwartz, 'Confucius', 201: 'Since the Cultural Revolution's characterization of Confucius conveys no information about him that was unknown in previous years, it cannot be a "reconstruction".'
[40] Zhang and Schwartz, 'Confucius', 189.
[41] Zhang and Schwartz, 'Confucius', 191. It is important to recognize that Zhang and Schwartz do not equate the stability of the past with the truthfulness of a particular image of it: 'Stable images of the past are not always demonstrably true images. Sometimes false ideas are transferred across generations and accepted as if they were true. And sometimes we do not know whether an account of the past is true or not. Truth value and its resistance to revision is plainly not the only source of the past's stability.'
[42] Zhang and Schwartz, 'Confucius', 205.
[43] Schwartz, 'Christian Origins', 43–47.

Benjamin Franklin and Thomas Jefferson, like many if not most enlightened men of the late eighteenth century, considered Jesus a nondivine epitome of reason and author of revolutionary ethical codes. By mid nineteenth century, however, Jesus had become the Great Liberator – divine champion of the oppressed and enslaved.[44]

Subsequently, Schwartz has applied social memory to the ancient context, arguing the same point he pursued with Zhang: 'Social memory functions differently in traditional and modern societies.'[45] He even applies some of the language from his earlier study to Jesus, ending with a rhetorical question:

> 'Critical inheritance' is a deliberative process whereby positive aspects of historical figures are embraced; negative ones recognized but rejected. Thus, Confucius can be revered – must be revered – by the very institutions and individuals that find his political convictions inconvenient. Might the malleability of Jesus have been similarly, if not identically, limited?[46]

Despite this relevance and a growing profile for sociological approaches to memory in Gospels research, critical inheritance has made essentially no impact. I noted this lack of engagement in a 2013 overview of the first decade of applications of social memory theory in Gospels research, and nothing has changed since then.[47]

'Critical inheritance' nevertheless remains relevant for Gospels studies due to its articulation of a relationship between the inheritors of the past and the past they inherit that is multifaceted and able to accommodate diverse transmission processes. Whereas Gardner-Smith eliminates disagreement with a prior source from the start, critical inheritance acknowledges a variety of possible postures of tradents toward prior tradition in non-mutually exclusive terms. Zhang and Schwartz acknowledge that inheriting the past in the context of the present can consist of both embrace and rejection of that past, stability and malleability, recognition of positive and negative aspects. Tradents do not always eliminate entirely aspects of the past that do not resonate with present identity construction; rather they can neutralize them with a narrative that shifts hermeneutical emphasis upon aspects that are more conducive to the present's agenda(s). Critical inheritance is therefore a model for reception of the past in the present that consists of selective emphasis and de-emphasis, not wholesale reconstruction, and a model where the strictures of the received coexist with the innovations of those receiving. Scholars should not, therefore, think of the receivers of tradition as robots who function only in modes of full acceptance or full rejection, but

---

[44] Zhang and Schwartz, 'Confucius', 196.
[45] Schwartz, 'Christian Origins', 46. See also Barry Schwartz, 'What Difference Does the Medium Make?', in *The Fourth Gospel in First-Century Media Culture*, ed. Anthony Le Donne and Tom Thatcher (ESCO/LNTS, 426; London: T&T Clark, 2011), 225–38; Barry Schwartz, 'Where There's Smoke, There's Fire: Memory and History', in *Memory and Identity in Ancient Judaism and Early Christianity: A Conversation with Barry Schwartz*, ed. Tom Thatcher (Semeia Studies, 78; Atlanta, GA: Society of Biblical Literature, 2014), 7–37.
[46] Schwartz, 'Christian Origins', 56.
[47] Keith, 'Social (Part One)', 370.

as culturally conditioned human beings who emphasize what resonates with their current agenda and de-emphasize what does not, even while acknowledging it. 'This is the essence of critical inheritance: the past serves the present interests not by unwitting reconstruction but deliberately selective appreciation and condemnation.'[48]

Although scholars may quibble with details of Zhang and Schwartz's proposal, question whether critical inheritance truly has 'no Western counterpart', and issue predictable cautions about applying dynamics of one cultural setting to another cultural setting, Zhang and Schartz's insistence that appropriation of the past cannot be boiled down to choices between full approval or full disapproval is correct and applicable to the critical study of the texts and traditions of ancient Judaism and early Christianity. The author of 2 Samuel commemorates David with a narrative that nevertheless includes criticism of him. He includes the account of David's sin with Bathsheba, commencing it by observing that David was not where he was supposed to be as king (2 Sam. 11.1). He is similarly critical when he notes that David moved to build the deity a house only once he completed his own house (2 Sam. 7.1–2). As another example of creative reception of prior tradition, the Gospel of Thomas eliminates the contextualizing narrative for Jesus' sayings in order to reproduce a Jesus who is simultaneously similar to and dissimilar to the Synoptic Jesus.[49] These examples exhibit what it means to inherit the past critically. They rewrite the pasts they receive not by unthrottled denial or rejection, even if those remain options, but by strategic realignment of the past with a present agenda.

The concept of critical inheritance does not directly answer the question of what a tradent knew. It cannot – again, in and of itself – answer *whether* John knew Mark. It does, however, show that rejection of an image of the past that is disfavoured in a present cultural moment can function, under some circumstances, as simply one aspect of a multifaceted act of reception. Rejection of one part of an inherited past may be surrounded immediately by acceptance of other aspects of an inherited past. In such a scenario, disagreement with that image of the past is simply one part of an overall process of a mutable but stable image of the past moving forward.

This tradition model is fatal for Gardner-Smith's approach to the relationship between John and Mark. It demonstrates the falsity of a strict disagreement/agreement binary. If reception of the past can – and sometimes must – involve 'selective appreciation and condemnation', it means that disagreement with that received tradition cannot function as an index for independence or unfamiliarity. On the contrary, it *can* function as an index for familiarity. Thus, Gardner-Smith's inability to imagine a scenario in which John could or would disagree with Mark owes more to the limitations of his historical imagination than it does to a theorized approach to the transmission of tradition in antiquity. If John critically inherited Mark's Gospel, selectively emphasizing some aspects of that prior tradition when he re-deploys it under his own authorial control, while simultaneously de-emphasizing and

---

[48] Zhang and Schwartz, 'Confucius', 206.
[49] See further Goodacre, *Thomas*, 172–92, especially 192: '*The Gospel of Thomas*'s genius is that it conveys its radical difference from the Synoptic Gospels by hiding its theology in words and images it derives from them.'

condemning other aspects of it, we should expect to find points of agreement and disagreement with the tradition he inherits.

The critical inheritance of Jesus' πατρίς

Critical inheritance therefore provides a helpful way of explaining both the agreements and disagreements that John has with Mark. I am conscious that I am replacing Gardner-Smith's 'If John knew Mark' scenario that implies that he did not know Mark with an 'If John knew Mark' scenario that implies that he did know Mark. But the crucial question that either of these hypothetical scenarios must answer is which theory best accounts for the agreements and disagreements alike, not just one or the other. Does a theory of Johannine familiarity with the Gospel of Mark that can accommodate both acceptance and rejection of aspects of Mark's narrative better account for the narrative details of the Gospel of John? Or does Gardner-Smith's theory of an early, independent Gospel of John better account for those details?

These are not necessarily the only two options for a global theory, but the present essay is concerned specifically with the role that disagreements between the narratives play within larger theories. In that light, what follows is a proposal for how scholars can apply the concept of critical inheritance to a theory of the reception of Markan tradition in John's Gospel, focusing upon the tradition of Jesus' rejection by his πατρίς or 'hometown' in John 4.43–44 and Mark 6.1–6. These texts contain both disagreement and agreement. They show, I suggest, how John has reproduced a Markan perspective in some matters while rejecting a Markan perspective in others.

The prophet without honour

In John 4.44 and Mark 6.4, Jesus utters a saying about a prophet not receiving honour in his hometown that also appears in Matthew's Gospel, Luke's Gospel, and the Gospel of Thomas.

Mk 6.4:	'A prophet is not dishonoured (ἄτιμος) except in his hometown (πατρίδι αὐτοῦ) and his relatives and his house (οἰκίᾳ).'
Mt. 13.57:	'A prophet is not dishonoured (ἄτιμος) except in his hometown (πατρίδι . . . αὐτοῦ) and house (οἰκίᾳ).'
Lk. 4.24:	'No prophet is accepted (δεκτός) in his hometown (πατρίδι αὐτοῦ).'
Jn 4.44:	'A prophet has no honour (τιμὴν) in (his) own hometown (ἰδίᾳ πατρίδι).'
Gos Thom 31:	'A prophet is not accepted (δεκτὸς) in his hometown (πατρίδι αὐτοῦ).'

There are some minor differences in how Mark and John receive this tradition. Some of these differences consist of wording. Examples are 'is not dishonoured' (οὐκ ἔστιν ἄτιμος) in Mark versus 'has no honour' (τιμὴν οὐκ ἔχει) in John, 'his hometown' (πατρίδι αὐτοῦ) in Mark versus '(his) own hometown' (ἰδίᾳ πατρίδι) in John, or inclusion of the reference to relatives and a 'house' (οἰκία) in Mark. There is also a difference in the presentation of the saying. The words appear on the lips of Jesus in Mark's Gospel. In John's Gospel, they appear as a narratorial report that Jesus, at some non-narrated point, had previously 'testified' about a prophet and his hometown. Nevertheless, Mark 6.4 and John 4.44 attest the same teaching of Jesus, in which he self-referentially states that a prophet is rejected by his πατρίς.[50]

The 'hometown' – Nazareth? Jerusalem? Elsewhere?

The rest of this essay concerns another difference between Mark and John. In Mark's Gospel, Jesus' 'hometown' is seemingly Nazareth. Mark does not name Nazareth explicitly in Mark 6, and there is room for some debate. Mark 1.9 states that Jesus came from Nazareth to receive the baptism of John the Baptist. The Markan Jesus also seems to have made Capernaum a hub in his early Galilean ministry. Mark 2.1 describes a 'house' or 'home' (οἶκος) in which he dwelled there (cf. also the οἰκία in Capernaum in Mk 9.33). Mark 3.20 then states that Jesus went to his οἶκος after appointing the twelve on a mountain, but does not specify whether that home was in Nazareth or Capernaum. The only clue is that his mother and brothers are understood to be close by since they hear about his activities (3.21) and go to see him (3.31). The prior reference to Jesus' οἶκος in Capernaum at Mark 2.1 may suggest that the οἶκος in 3.20 is also in Capernaum, though the presence of his family may suggest Nazareth as the location. It is also possible that the narrator imagines his family travelling to Capernaum from Nazareth upon rumours of Jesus reaching them.

Jesus' statement about the rejection of the prophet in Mark 6.4 refers to rejection by the πατρίς, relatives and his οἰκία. The distinctions are possibly intended to render the prophet's rejection emphatic – his place of origin as well as his current place of residence, and his kinfolk all reject him. One could also, however, read Mark 6.4 as claiming that the 'hometown', 'home' and relatives are in the same place, which would shed no light on whether that place is understood to be Nazareth, from which Jesus came (Mk 1.9), or Capernaum, in which he often stayed in a house (Mk 2.1; 9.33). Most scholars have favoured viewing the πατρίς in Mark 6.4 as Nazareth, however, not least because that is how Luke understood Mark (Lk. 4.16). Regardless, in Mark's Gospel, Jesus' πατρίς is unquestionably in Galilee.

In the immediate context of the Johannine narrative, however, such a location makes little sense, and this is only the beginning of things not making sense in John 4.44.[51] Whatever one takes as Jesus' πατρίς, John 4.43 states that Jesus left it after

---

[50] Πατρίς can refer to a 'hometown' (Mk 6.1; Mt. 13.54; Lk. 4.24; Josephus, *Ant.* 11.165; Philo, *Legat.* 278) or 'homeland' (Heb. 11.14). See further U. Hutter, 'πατρίς, ίδος, ἡ', *EDNT* 3:58; 'πατρίς, ιδος', *LSJ* 1349.

[51] Francis J. Moloney, *The Gospel of John* (SP, 4; Collegeville, MN: Liturgical Press, 1998), 151: 'But in v. 44 a notorious problem emerges.'

two days in order to go to Galilee, and thus does not place the πατρίς in Galilee. John 4.45 confirms this element of Johannine geography, stating that Jesus 'came to Galilee' from the πατρίς, and that the Galileans welcomed him, which stands in contrast to the rejection he experienced before going to Galilee.

Brown nevertheless maintains a Galilean identification for the πατρίς by arguing that a redactor added 4.44 and that the narrative presents this seemingly positive reception as actually a rejection: 'The welcome given to Jesus in Galilee (vs. 45) is just as shallow as the reaction that greeted Jesus in Jerusalem (ii 23–25). Therefore, the insertion of vs. 44 does not contradict 45 once we understand that a superficial welcome based on enthusiasm for miracles is no real *honor*.'[52] More recently, Williams continues this interpretation:

> It is increasingly agreed that the πατρίς in question must be Galilee. The explanation (γάρ) about a prophet lacking honor in his own country is not retrospective but anticipatory, pointing to the less than adequate reception that Jesus actually receives from Galileans: they welcome him, but it is a signs-based faith (Jn 4.45) which is then criticized by Jesus (4.48; cf. 2.23–25).[53]

Despite my great respect for Brown and Williams, this reading of the text is less clear than they indicate. Where one assumes the rejection of the prophet takes place determines how the γάρ of John 4.44 relates to the rejection, so it does not settle the matter so much as extend the question about the location of that place. And even if one takes the γάρ as anticipatory rather than retrospective, Jerusalem/Judea would still be an interpretive possibility in light of Jesus' death in Jerusalem that is forthcoming in the Johannine narrative. The γάρ of John 4.44 is only anticipatory of 4.45–48 specifically if 4.45 refers to a rejection in Galilee rather than a welcome, which is the very matter under discussion in the first place.

As a result, it is not clear that Jesus' reception in Galilee in John 4.45 is 'less than adequate' on the basis of Jesus' response to the official in 4.48. Jesus states to the royal official, 'Unless you see signs (σημεῖα) and wonders you will not believe (πιστεύσητε)' (4.48), and Brown and Williams both read this as a criticism of the official. I question whether this is necessarily a critical response from Jesus for three reasons. First, *requests* for signs appear in a negative light (2.18; 6.30–32) but the royal official to whom Jesus speaks in 4.48 did not request a sign. He requested that Jesus save his son's life (4.47) and Jesus did (4.49).

Second, the Gospel of John does not present signs-based faith *in toto* as inadequate. It is possible to read Jesus' statement, 'Unless you see signs (σημεῖα) and wonders you will not believe (πιστεύσητε)' (4.48) in a more positive sense of signs potentially leading to belief, which is why Jesus performs this sign. Williams cites John 2.23–25 to support the notion that Jesus' words in 4.48 are critical, but 2.23 claims that 'many' in Jerusalem 'believed (ἐπίστευσαν) in his name because they saw the signs (σημεῖα) he

---

[52] Raymond E. Brown, *Gospel According to John* (2 vols, Anchor Bible, 29–29A; Garden City, NY: Doubleday, 1966–1970), 1:187 (emphasis original).
[53] Catrin H. Williams, 'Jesus the Prophet: Crossing the Boundaries of Prophetic Beliefs and Expectations in the Gospel of John', in Craig R. Koester (ed.), *Portraits of Jesus*, 99.

was doing'. The narrator goes on to say that Jesus did not trust himself to them because he 'knew what was in man' (2.24–25), which is less than laudatory, but this seemingly is in reference to his eventual rejection. When the narrator wants to state explicitly that signs-based faith was inadequate, he does so. For example, in John 12.37 the narrator says of 'the crowd', 'Although he performed so many signs (σημεῖα) before them, they were not believing (οὐκ ἐπίστευον) in him'. No such statement accompanies John 2.23 or 4.48, and so it is not a foregone conclusion that these texts are necessarily critical of the immediate responses of the believers they narrate.

Third, a more positive reading of Jesus's reception in Galilee and words to the royal official in 4.48 accords with other aspects of the Johannine narrative. The narrator is still counting signs for the reader at 2.11 and 4.54, the latter of which closes this pericope by referring to the healing of the official's child as Jesus' 'second sign' after traveling from Judea to Galilee. Following 4.48, 4.54 has the narrative effect of ensuring that the reader not miss that which just occurred, a 'sign' that contributes to belief. A more positive reading of Jesus' welcome in Galilee in 4.45 and statement in 4.48 also accords with John 11, which similarly links Jesus' performance of signs with belief. In the midst of raising Lazarus, which the Jewish leadership immediately refers to as one of Jesus' 'many signs (πολλὰ ... σημεῖα)' (11.47), Jesus speaks to God in front of the crowd 'in order that they might believe (πιστεύσωσιν) that you sent me' (11.42). This reading of 4.48 also accords with the fundamental purpose statement of the gospel, which similarly and explicitly connects 'signs' written in the Gospel of John with saving 'belief': 'Jesus thus did many other signs (σημεῖα) before his disciples, which are not written in this book; but these are written in order that you believe (πιστεύ[σ]ητε)[54] that Jesus is the Christ, the son of God, and that by believing (πιστεύοντες) you might have life in his name' (Jn 20.30–31).

In short, the Gospel of John does not present signs-based faith as monolithically insufficient. On the contrary, it frequently refers to the presentation of signs before an audience – including the audience reading the Gospel of John itself – as faith-enabling. The royal official in Capernaum is therefore not clearly an instance of someone displaying inadequate faith in Jesus and thus also not clearly evidence of Galilean rejection of Jesus rather than the explicitly narrated 'welcome' of 4.45. Meeks is correct that 'only by a very strange logic can such language be supposed to describe a rejection of Jesus'.[55] The case for a Galilean rejection in 4.45, and thus a Galilean πατρίς in 4.44, is therefore not as strong as some have claimed, despite the facts that the Synoptics demonstrably place the πατρίς in Galilee and the Gospel of John otherwise refers to Jesus consistently as a Galilean (Jn 1.45–46; 7.41; 18.7–8; 19.19; cf. 6.42).

Based on the immediate context of John 4, stronger cases for Jesus' πατρίς can be made for Sychar in Samaria or Jerusalem in Judea. Sychar is undoubtedly 'that place' (ἐκεῖθεν) that the narrator identifies as Jesus' πατρίς in John 4.43–44. In addition to Jesus having just been in Sychar in the previous story (Jn 4.1–42), and thus being his

---

[54] On whether to read the aorist or present subjunctive, see Bruce Metzger, *A Textual Commentary on the Greek New Testament* (2nd edn, reprint; Stuttgart: Deutsche Bibelgesellschaft, 2000), 219–20.
[55] Wayne A. Meeks, *The Prophet-King: Moses Traditions and the Johannine Christology* (NovTSup, 14; Leiden: Brill, 1967), 30.

most recent locale prior to travelling to Galilee, John 4.40 offers the narrative detail that the 'two days' after which Jesus went to his πατρίς in 4.43–44 were spent in Sychar. Furthermore, the γάρ of 4.44 links Sychar directly with the πατρίς since it explains that Jesus left 'that place' *because* he had testified that a prophet has no honour in his πατρίς.

Despite these points of clarity, no scholar of whom I am aware affirms Sychar as Jesus' πατρίς in the Gospel of John, and for good reason. The Gospel of John never describes him as having come from Sychar, and the only time he is identified as a Samaritan is when 'the Jews' use the term as an ethnic slur (8.48).[56] The Samaritan woman refers to Jesus as a 'Jew' (4.9) and an outsider to Samaria. Furthermore, Jesus is ultimately accepted in Sychar, not rejected. The seemingly clear identification of Jesus' πατρίς with Sychar in John 4.40, 43–45 thus remains an oddity of the text.

In terms of the Johannine narrative as a whole, one can make an even stronger case for Jerusalem and Judea as the πατρίς that rejects Jesus in the Gospel of John, and numerous Johannine scholars have opted for this solution.[57] Prior to the account of the Samaritan woman, John 4.3 claimed that Jesus 'left Judea and went again into Galilee'. John 4.4 then claims that he had to go through Samaria in order to do so, and after the events in Samaria both 4.47 and 4.54 state once more that Jesus went from Judea to Galilee. The itinerary outlined in John 4.3, 47, 54 thus suggests that 4.44–45 contrasts the welcome reception in Galilee with the rejection of his location prior to the Samaritan interlude, which would be Judea. Strengthening the identification of Jesus' πατρίς in 4.44 with Judea and Jerusalem is the Johannine modification of the term with 'own' (ἴδιος). The rejection by Jesus' 'own' hometown coheres with John 1.11's description of Jesus' rejection by his 'own' (ἴδιος). 'He came to what was his own (ἴδια), and his own people (οἱ ἴδιοι) did not accept him.' Over the course of the Gospel of John, Jesus typically meets rejection in Jerusalem/Judea and acceptance outside it, so it would be natural to conclude that Jesus' 'own' who reject him are the Judeans/Jews in and around Jerusalem.[58] This rejection is likely prefigured in 2.24–25 and finds its fullest expression in Jesus' crucifixion in Jerusalem, which means that the γάρ of 4.44 could be retrospective, anticipatory, or both. Also supporting Jerusalem/Judea as the πατρίς is John 4.45. This verse specifies that Galileans welcomed Jesus on the basis of what happened *in Jerusalem* when they too were there for the festival (cf. 2.13, 23–25),[59] and thus reinforces that John places Galilean welcome within the broader narrative geography of Jesus' transition from Jerusalem to Galilee. That is, even when Galileans are spectators of events in Jerusalem, John narrates a specifically Galilean welcome for Jesus only once he leaves Jerusalem and enters Galilee.

---

[56] On this passage, see Stewart Penwell, *Jesus the Samaritan: Ethnic Labeling in the Gospel of John* (BibInt, 170; Leiden: Brill, 2019).

[57] Most prominently, Wayne A. Meeks, 'Galilee and Judea in the Fourth Gospel', *JBL* 85 (1966): 164; Wayne A. Meeks, *Prophet-King*, 39. See also Jo-Ann A. Brant, *John* (Paideia; Grand Rapids, MI: Baker Academic, 2011), 89; F. F. Bruce, *The Gospel of John* (Grand Rapids, MI: Wm. B. Eerdmans, 1983), 116; Dodd, *Interpretation*, 352; Edwyn Clement Hoskyns, *The Fourth Gospel*, ed. Francis Noel Davey (2nd rev. edn; London: Faber & Faber, 1947), 260–61; Craig S. Keener, *The Gospel of John: A Commentary* (2 vols; Grand Rapids, MI: Baker Academic, 2003), 1:629.

[58] Dodd, *Interpretation*, 351–52.

[59] One can thus read John 2.23–25 as Jesus' anticipation of rejection in Jerusalem despite the acceptance of Galileans who were, at the time, also in Jerusalem.

None of these solutions is without blemishes.[60] Scholars arguing for any of them can marshal various aspects of the narrative to support their cause, while other aspects of the narrative do not fit easily with it. To a certain extent, preferring one solution over another is a matter of choosing the rock upon which one would like their exegetical ship to crash. If one posits a Galilean πατρίς, it is difficult to explain how the narrative assumes rejection and welcome there simultaneously. The Sychar solution makes lots of sense in the context of John 4.40–43 and no sense whatsoever in the rest of the gospel. If one posits a Judean πατρίς, it is difficult to explain why the narrative throughout presents Jesus as a Galilean and nowhere asserts that he came from Judea.

Jerusalem/Judea nevertheless has the strongest case for the πατρίς in John 4.44, even if its case is not so strong that one can conclusively rule out alternative solutions. It makes the most sense in the context of Jesus's Judea-to-Galilee travel itinerary in John 4, the Galilean welcoming Jesus receives in John 4.45, and the broader narrative theme of Jesus' rejection in Jerusalem. If this solution is affirmed on exegetical grounds under the assumption that John knew Mark's Gospel, it introduces a tradition-historical problem. Mark claims Jesus's πατρίς rejected him and places the πατρίς in Galilee. John claims Jesus's πατρίς rejected him but places the πατρίς in Judea. John disagrees with Mark over the locale of the πατρίς that rejected Jesus while agreeing with him that the πατρίς did reject him.

John 4.44 as reception of Mark 6.4?

The real crux of the present discussion is not whether one agrees with me that Jerusalem/Judea is the most likely identification of Jesus' πατρίς in John 4.44. The important matter is how the relationship between John's Gospel and Mark's Gospel factors into scholarly attempts to offer a solution to this problem. One solution is to assert that when the Johannine narrator claims that Jesus had previously testified that a prophet is not honoured in his hometown in John 4.44, he refers not to a previous occurrence in the narrative world of John's Gospel, but to an earlier tradition that the reader is expected to know. This solution thus assumes the familiarity of John with Mark's Gospel. Thyen, for example, suggests that the aorist tense of ἐμαρτύρησεν ('he testified') is an instance of the author's 'Spiel … mit den synoptischen Prätexten'.[61] Similarly, while identifying Nazareth as the πατρίς, Lagrange proposed that that 4.44 is unintelligible in itself, but intelligible on the basis of the reader's knowledge of the Synoptics. For Lagrange, the γάρ in that verse refers not to 'a logical causality' (*une causalité logique*) but to 'a literary causality' (*une causalité littéraire*).[62] That is, the evangelist has Jesus go to Galilee because readers otherwise know from the Synoptics that this is where he made this statement.[63] Under this solution, not only is John 4.44

---

[60] Cf. J. Ramsey Michaels, *The Gospel of John* (NICNT; Grand Rapids, MI: Wm. B. Eerdmans, 2010), 272–73, who concludes: 'A precise identification is not the point' (273).
[61] Thyen, *Johannesevangelium*, 284; cf. also 286.
[62] M.-J. Lagrange, *Évangile selon Saint Jean* (EBib; Paris: J. Gabalda, 1925), 124.
[63] Lagrange, *Évangile*, 124. For main text, see also Andrew T. Lincoln, *The Gospel According to St John* (BNTC, 4; London: Continuum, 2005), 184–85.

evidence of Johannine familiarity with the Synoptics, it is evidence that is needed to make sense of the Johannine narrative in the first place.

Predictably taking the exact opposite point of view is Gardner-Smith: 'Here, we are told, is a clear case of John's quoting from Mark. On the contrary, it is very nearly a clear proof that he did not know our Second Gospel.'[64] Identifying Nazareth as the Markan πατρίς and Judea as the Johannine πατρίς, he claims, 'There is no reason for supposing that the evangelist had read Mk. vi. 4. Even the "quotation" is not accurate.'[65] One may well wonder what standard Gardner-Smith is using to measure accuracy, but such a matter receives no explanation. Rather, Gardner-Smith once more appeals to a potential contradiction between John and Mark – if John knew Mark – as a rhetorical supplement to his argument:

> This conclusion is supposed in the next verse where we read that the Galileans received Him because they had seen what He had done at Jerusalem at the feast. Is it credible that the writer can have had at the back of his mind any such picture as that presented by Mark and Luke, who place the ministry of Jesus almost wholly in Galilee? If John knew our Second and Third Gospels then he contradicted them deliberately for dogmatic reasons, but it is much more probable that he did not know them.[66]

Once more, Gardner-Smith's conclusion that John did not know his predecessors' work grows out of his assumption that John would not 'dogmatically contradict' his predecessors. Gardner-Smith has not provided an actual argument for Johannine independence. He has instead provided a conclusion of Johannine independence on the basis of his inability to conceptualize an alternative solution.

The critical inheritance of Mark 6.4 in John 4.44

I propose instead that a more economical solution is that John has critically inherited Mark 6.4 in John 4.44. To answer Gardner-Smith's rhetorical questions in a manner he did not intend, then, yes, it is credible to think that John knew Mark and contradicted him. Not only is it credible, it is what we should expect. This solution has the advantage of accounting for both the similarities and differences between the Markan and Johannine πατρίς sayings. In receiving this Synoptic tradition, John has selectively emphasized the connection between rejection and Jesus' πατρίς. He has selectively de-emphasized, however, the connection between rejection and Galilee. Elsewhere, I have suggested a possible reason why: namely, his interest in creating a north–south axis in the symbolic geography of his gospel, wherein Jesus is typically rejected in Jerusalem in anticipation of his final rejection, and typically accepted in Galilee in accordance

---

[64] Gardner-Smith, *Saint John*, 21.
[65] Gardner-Smith, *Saint John*, 21.
[66] Gardner-Smith, *Saint John*, 21–22.

with his identity as the 'light' (φῶς) (Jn 1.4-9; 3.19-21; 8.12; 9.5; 11.9-10; 12.35-36, 46) that Isa 9.1 LXX promised to Galilee.[67] Under this proposal, John's present narrative agenda leads him to reuse prior tradition in a manner that agrees with some aspects of that tradition and disagrees with others. John as an Evangelist was in control of the image of Jesus that he is offering, influenced by inherited tradition but not in a slavish way.

As noted earlier in this essay, this proposal does not prove that John knew Mark. But it does prove that such a theory is thoroughly compatible with the fact that John disagreed with Mark on some points. Disagreement can function as an index of familiarity rather than an index of independence, contra Gardner-Smith. In this sense, a theory of John's critical inheritance of Mark supports the earlier arguments of Thyen and Zumstein that the Fourth Evangelist was not bound to the hermeneutical casting of the tradition he inherited, but could and did use tradition creatively in different ways from how it was used in the contexts from which he inherited it.[68]

Conclusion

Neither social memory theory nor critical inheritance demonstrates conclusively that the author of John's Gospel was familiar with Mark's Gospel. Yet, if scholars have other reasons to think that this scenario was historically possible or plausible, the concept of critical inheritance can provide a theoretical framework for familiarity with Mark's Gospel that accounts for points of continuity and discontinuity. It can do so because it asserts that both the received past and the present that receives it influence the tradent simultaneously. Critical inheritance demonstrates that disagreement with a prior tradition cannot serve unequivocally as evidence for a tradent's independence from that tradition. Contrary to Gardner-Smith, John's points of disagreement with Mark's Gospel can serve just as strongly as evidence for his familiarity with the Markan image of Jesus.

Social memory theory and the concept of critical inheritance can, therefore, help us formulate an answer to the question of whether John's reception of the tradition of Jesus' rejection in his πατρίς in John 4.44 is plausible as a reception of Mark's Gospel by providing a theoretical framework within which scholars recognize the force of both the inherited past and the context in which it is inherited, and without predetermining what a tradent's hermeneutical options would or would not have been. I do not pretend, much less assert, that such a framework provides an answer to every question related to Johannine reception of prior sources. As an example, the curious instance of John 7.42 continues to perplex me, and I am uncertain whether to read this as a case of Johannine irony, a case of Johannine ignorance of prior tradition, or a case of Johannine

---

[67] Keith, 'Jesus the Galilean', 56-58, building upon Sean Freyne, 'Locality and Doctrine: Mark and John Revisited', in *Galilee and Gospel: Collected Essays* (WUNT, 125; Tübingen: Mohr Siebeck, 2000), 289-92.

[68] Thyen, *Johannesevangelium*, 286; Zumstein, *Kreative Erinnerung*, throughout.

familiarity with, but rejection of, prior tradition. This observation brings me back to the above point and the one with which I began this essay, however: social memory theory is a helpful tool for scholars because it articulates a relationship between the present and the past that is dynamic rather than restrictive. It encourages us to embrace the fact that the Gospel authors were creative artists in their own rights who were influenced by the past, but not slaves to it.

5

John's 'Rewriting' of Mark: Some Insights from Ancient Jewish Analogues

Catrin H. Williams

Introduction

In his discussion of John 19.38–42 in *Saint John and the Synoptic Gospels*, Percival Gardner-Smith argued that if John had known Mark he would not have introduced the episode about Joseph of Arimathea and Nicodemus binding Jesus' body in linen cloths, since it contradicts the Markan (and Lukan) account that Jesus was 'hastily buried without the usual spices'.[1] 'It is of course possible', he remarked, 'that John wished to correct the synoptic account, either from motives of reverence, or to put the death of Jesus still further beyond the possibility of doubt; but if he had known *and respected* the Second and Third Gospels he could hardly have introduced his account of the elaborate embalming by Joseph and Nicodemus'.[2] Such sentiments are expressed by Gardner-Smith with striking regularity throughout the work because, in his estimation, there could only be two possible scenarios: either John was familiar with, even literarily dependent on, one or more of the Synoptic Gospels, or the evangelist had access to, and drew from, independent (oral) tradition. He claimed, moreover, that if John did know the Synoptic Gospels, clearly 'he had no regard for their authority'.[3] And since only 'an active, uncontrolled, imagination' can 'see in the Johannine account a conscious rewriting of [Mark's] plain narrative',[4] Gardner-Smith opted decisively for John's independence of the Synoptics – to form what was to become the dominant hypothesis about John's relationship with the Synoptics during the second half of the twentieth century.

Notwithstanding the obvious fact that Mark and the other Synoptic Gospels did not yet possess canonical status at the time of the composition of John's Gospel,[5] some

---

[1] Percival Gardner-Smith, *Saint John and the Synoptic Gospels* (Cambridge: Cambridge University Press, 1938), 72.
[2] Gardner-Smith, *Saint John*, 72 (emphasis mine).
[3] Gardner-Smith, *Saint John*, 36 (with reference to Jn 7.1–13).
[4] Gardner-Smith, *Saint John*, 25.
[5] For discussion of this issue with particular reference to Gardner-Smith's arguments and assumptions, see Chris Keith, '"If John Knew Mark": Critical Inheritance and Johannine Disagreements with Mark' (Chapter 4 in this volume).

recent evaluations of John's relationship with the other gospels, particularly Mark, have noted that authoritative texts – as broadly defined – were in fact frequently subjected to a process of *rewriting* in the first-century Mediterranean world. There is growing recognition, particularly in discussions of Synoptic relationships,[6] that ancient Greek and Roman authors did not practice verbatim reproduction of antecedent texts but engaged in free paraphrase, consciously rewriting and reconfiguring their sources for the purpose of interpretation and the careful (stylistic) integration of source material into their own compositions. Graeco-Roman biographies and histories whose underlying sources are still available for comparison can be shown to have made use of several compositional devices, including the displacement of narrated events, the conflation of two or more elements, compressed narration of events or figures, and also simplification through the omission or revision of details from earlier source(s).[7] Training in such textual techniques was also an essential part of elementary education; children, for example, were to be taught how to recount Aesop's fables in simple language and then, in their own written versions, to adopt 'bolder paraphrase' (*tum paraphrasi audacius vertere*) that could include abridgement as well as embellishment, as long as the intended meaning of the original text remained intact (Quintilian, *Institutio Oratoria* 1.9.2).[8]

Whatever the precise nature of John's relationship with Mark's Gospel, the compositional techniques attested in a range of Greek and Roman sources may be able to shed some light on why John's engagement with Synoptic source(s) differs so significantly from the way in which Matthew and Luke appropriated Mark. The Matthean and Lukan redaction models do indeed continue to function in some studies as a kind of methodological template for assessing whether John is dependent on or independent of Mark,[9] but without offering clear criteria for determining what level of

---

[6] See especially F. Gerald Downing, 'Redaction Criticism: Josephus' *Antiquities* and the Synoptic Gospels I and II', *JSNT* 8 (1980): 46–65; 9 (1980): 29–48; F. Gerald Downing, 'Compositional Conventions and the Synoptic Problem', *JBL* 107 (1988): 69–85; Robert A. Derrenbacker, *Ancient Compositional Practices and the Synoptic Problem* (BETL, 186; Leuven: Leuven University Press, 2005), 52–76. With reference to John's relationship to Mark, see especially Richard Bauckham, 'The Gospel of John and the Synoptic Problem', in *New Studies in the Synoptic Problem: Oxford Conference, April 2008: Essays in Honour of Christopher M. Tuckett*, ed. Paul Foster, Andrew Gregory, John S. Kloppenborg and Joseph Verheyden (BETL, 239; Leuven: Peeters, 2011), 657–88, especially 660–62. In the same 2011 volume, see the articles by Robert A. Derrenbacker, 'The "External and Psychological Conditions Under Which the Synoptic Gospels Were Written": Ancient Compositional Practices and the Synoptic Problem' (435–57) and F. Gerald Downing, 'Writers' Use or Abuse of Written Sources' (523–48).

[7] For the application of these (and other devices) in Plutarch's *Lives*, see Michael R. Licona, *Why Are There Differences in the Gospels? What We Can Learn from Ancient Biography* (Oxford: Oxford University Press, 2017).

[8] Cf. Downing, 'Writers' Use or Abuse', 529. On verbal transformation through the practice of paraphrastic 'emulation' (*aemulatio*) in Greek and Roman sources, see John S. Kloppenborg, 'The Reception of the Jesus Tradition in James', in *The Catholic Epistles and Apostolic Tradition: A New Perspective on James to Jude*, ed. Karl-Wilhelm Niebuhr and Robert W. Wall (Waco, TX: Baylor University Press, 2009), 84–88.

[9] As noted, for example, by Jörg Frey, 'Das vierte Evangelium auf dem Hintergrund der älteren Evangelientradition: Zum Problem: Johannes und die Synoptiker', in *Johannesevangelium – Mitte oder Rand des Kanons? Neue Standortbestimmungen*, ed. Thomas Söding (QD, 203; Freiburg: Herder, 2003), 80–81. See also Jean Zumstein, *L'Évangile selon Saint Jean (1–12)* (CNT, IVa; Genève: Labor et Fides, 2014), 31–32, who describes John's (different) relationship with Mark as an example of 'hypertextuality'.

agreement is required to make a strong case one way or another. What is still not widely acknowledged, moreover, is that the character of the Matthean/Lukan reworking of Mark is in fact something of an anomaly in comparison with the 'rewriting' processes of contemporary Greek and Roman biographers and historians.[10] John's evidently flexible and creative engagement with sources is actually more in line with known compositional conventions,[11] and, for that reason, cannot necessarily be taken as evidence of John's reliance on related, and yet divergent, oral traditions.

The phenomenon of rewriting in ancient Judaism

The search for possible analogues to the ways in which the gospels rework their source material has, to date, largely focused on Graeco-Roman practices and their concomitant low levels of lexical adherence to textual predecessors. Some comparisons have, admittedly, been made with Josephus' rewriting strategies in his *Jewish Antiquities*, where he similarly adopts devices like paraphrase, expansion, omission and rearrangement.[12] When he uses the *Letter of Aristeas*, for example, close verbal agreements are limited to a small number of words in sequence,[13] and, strikingly, the same applies to Josephus' retelling of the Jewish Scriptures in *Antiquities* 1–11.[14] Thus, even in his summary paraphrase of the Decalogue, only four of its 'cited' words are identical to those found in the Septuagintal versions of Exodus 20 and Deuteronomy 5 (*Ant.* 3.91–92), prefaced by Josephus' clarification that what follows is a reworded outline rather than a faithful reproduction of the text: 'These words we are not permitted to state explicitly, to the letter (πρὸς λέξιν), but we will indicate their general import' (3.90). No explanation is given as to the motivation, theological or otherwise, for Josephus' tightly rephrased adaptation of Scripture, but there is no doubt that, compositionally, it amounts to a clear-cut case of paraphrastic speech.

What has not so far been explored, however, is whether the positioning of Josephus' rewriting techniques specifically within a *Jewish* context – that is, instead of aligning them primarily with Graeco-Roman conventions – can inform the discussion of John's familiarity with or even reworking of Mark. Extending the scope of the investigation to

---

[10] Cf. Downing, 'Redaction Criticism: II', 33; Bauckham, 'The Gospel of John and the Synoptic Problem', 661–62. Nevertheless, John S. Kloppenborg, 'Variation in the Reproduction of the Double Tradition and an Oral Q?', *ETL* 83 (2007): 74–77, notes some examples of 'high agreement' copying, especially in legal and regulatory texts (cf., e.g., 1QS and 4QS^{h,d}), that are closer to the Matthean and Lukan method of using sources.
[11] Cf. Marianne M. Thompson, *John: A Commentary* (New Testament Library; Louisville, KY: Westminster John Knox, 2015), 8: 'John's interpretive freedom in selecting and ordering events, expanding or contracting material, especially discourses, in order to give an account of what Jesus did and said and how one should understand their significance – all this is exactly what one would expect of an ancient biography'.
[12] Downing, 'Redaction Criticism: I', 46–65; Derrenbacker, *Ancient Compositional Practices*, 92–116.
[13] See further Kloppenborg, 'Variation in the Reproduction of the Double Tradition', 67–70.
[14] On Josephus' use of Scriptures, particularly with reference to *Ant.* 1.17, see Louis H. Feldman, *Josephus's Interpretation of the Bible* (Berkeley, CA: University of California Press, 1998), 37–46; Steve Mason, 'Josephus and His Twenty-Two Book Canon', in *The Canon Debate*, ed. Lee Martin McDonald and James A. Sanders (Peabody, MA: Hendrickson, 2002), 121–24.

take into account the practices of rewriting within late Second Temple Judaism has the clear advantage of increasing the number of ancient compositions at one's disposal for comparative purposes. It provides access to multiple examples of reworked texts whose central source, the Jewish Scriptures – whether in Hebrew or in Greek – can be directly consulted to assess the method and scope of literary dependence. It also raises the possibility that additional, distinctively Jewish, compositional factors and features are brought to light so that John's methods of reworking earlier sources can be regarded as part and parcel of its connectedness to first-century Judaism. This can hopefully lead to the sharpening of questions and proposals about the nature of John's relationship with Mark, as well as clarifying likely connections between John and Jewish interpretative methods in the first century CE.[15] The aim, then, is not necessarily to search for fresh evidence or new examples of literary connections between John and Mark but to mark out some of the mechanics of a possible relationship through comparison with the phenomenon of rewriting within a Jewish milieu. This essay will therefore proceed by examining various textual techniques and strategies as applied by late Second Temple Jewish authors in their recasting of earlier sources. I will focus initially on texts widely classified as belonging to the category of 'rewritten Bible' or 'rewritten Scripture' – interpretative rewritings of authoritative scriptural texts – before broadening the discussion to include other evidence that 'rewrittenness' was a well-established form of literary production in Jewish texts roughly contemporaneous with the Gospel of John.

Rewritten Bible/Scripture

Much of the relevant discussion during the past few decades has focused on the nature and extent of the Jewish category labelled as 'rewritten Bible',[16] particularly as to whether it amounts to a literary genre or should be defined as an interpretative strategy and process of rewriting. In an influential essay published in 1988 Philip Alexander proposed that four Jewish texts – *Jubilees*, the *Genesis Apocryphon*, Pseudo-Philo's *Biblical Antiquities* and books 1–11 of Josephus' *Antiquities* – belong to the generic classification of 'rewritten Bible', based on the formal literary characteristics that they all share.[17] In all four texts lengthy portions of scriptural material, particularly from the Pentateuch, are retold in sequence through a combination of elaboration, omission, conflation and rearrangement – that is, broadly speaking, the same rewriting techniques as those encountered in certain Greek and Roman texts. The possible significance of these characteristics for the study of John's relationship with Mark will be examined

---

[15] See also Catrin H. Williams, 'John, Judaism, and "Searching the Scriptures"', in *John and Judaism: A Contested Relationship in Context*, ed. R. Alan Culpepper and Paul N. Anderson (RBS, 87; Atlanta, GA: Society of Biblical Literature, 2017), 77–100.
[16] Geza Vermes was responsible for coining this term. See Geza Vermes, *Scripture and Tradition in Judaism: Haggadic Studies* (Leiden: Brill, 1961; 2nd rev. edn 1973), 67–126.
[17] Philip S. Alexander, 'Retelling the Old Testament', in *It Is Written: Scripture Citing Scripture. Essays in Honour of Barnabas Lindars*, ed. D. A. Carson and H. G. M. Williamson (Cambridge: Cambridge University Press, 1988), 99–121, including 119 n. 11: 'Any text admitted to the genre must display *all* the characteristics'. For Alexander's criteria, see 'Retelling the Old Testament', 116–18.

later in the essay, but – from a methodological perspective – this kind of 'generic' approach has been questioned on the basis that the listed features are 'to some extent predetermined by the selection and demarcation of those compositions' said to belong to this particular classification of texts.[18]

The centrality of texts like *Jubilees* and the *Genesis Apocryphon* cannot be disputed in any analysis of the phenomenon of 'rewritten Bible', although many of their literary features are in fact attested in a range of additional works that are of divergent form, content and perspective and which exhibit varying degrees of reliance on a scriptural base text. The emphasis then falls on 'rewriting' as a textual strategy, with the net cast much more widely to include Jewish texts belonging to different genres,[19] including narrative blocks in a non-narrative composition (such as the accounts of the flood in *I Enoch* 6–11) and poetic presentations of scriptural stories in epic form (e.g., *Ezekiel the Tragedian*). Furthermore, after the publication of all the extant Dead Sea Scrolls, the category is now widely regarded as including legal compositions like the *Temple Scroll*. Qumran scholarship is also primarily responsible for shifting the category's labelling from 'rewritten Bible' to 'rewritten Scripture' because it can no longer be assumed that Second Temple Jews had a canonically recognizable 'Bible' at the turn of the Common Era; 'Scripture', in this respect, is a more apposite term for describing religiously authoritative texts that have not yet been subjected to delimitation in a closed collection of compositions.[20]

There is no doubt that a substantial number, if not the majority, of writings in late Second Temple Judaism interacted closely with existing scriptural texts through expansion, paraphrase and implicit commentary. But if tight generic classifications can be overly restrictive, the consequence of subsuming a much wider range of compositions under the rubric of rewritten Bible/Scripture is that it can become a description of phenomena that are observable in several loosely related compositions, thereby losing focus on those writings that have a recognizably *sustained* and *sequential* attachment to a scriptural base text.

Some clarity emerges when works of rewritten Scripture are assessed as a category distinct from, and yet closely linked to, other examples of interpretative scriptural

---

[18] George J. Brooke, 'Memory, Cultural Memory, and Rewriting Scripture', in George J. Brooke, *Reading the Dead Sea Scrolls: Essays in Method* (Atlanta, GA: Society of Biblical Literature, 2013), 52. See also Jonathan G. Campbell, 'Rewritten Bible: A Terminological Reassessment', in *Rewritten Bible after Fifty Years: Texts, Terms, or Techniques? A Last Dialogue with Geza Vermes*, ed. József Zsengellér (SuppJSJ, 166; Leiden: Brill, 2014), 56.

[19] George W. E. Nickelsburg, 'The Bible Rewritten and Expanded', in *Jewish Writings of the Second Temple Period: Apocrypha, Pseudepigrapha, Qumran Sectarian Writings, Philo, Josephus*, ed. Michael E. Stone (CRINT, II/2; Assen: van Gorcum, 1984), 89–156; Daniel J. Harrington, 'Palestinian Adaptations of Biblical Narratives and Prophecies: The Bible Rewritten (Narratives)', in *Early Judaism and its Modern Interpreters*, ed. Robert A. Kraft and George W. E. Nickelsburg (Minneapolis, MN: Fortress, 1986), 239–47. Harrington also includes the *Testament of Moses, Life of Adam and Eve* and the *Ascension of Isaiah* (among other texts).

[20] See Eugene Ulrich, 'The Notion and Definition of Canon', in *The Canon Debate*, ed. Lee Martin McDonald and James A. Sanders (Peabody, MA: Hendrickson, 2002), 21–35, especially 29–30. Cf. Jesper Høgenhaven, 'Fortschreibung und Kanonisierung in der Bibliothek von Qumran: Bemerkungen mit besonderem Hinblick auf Genesis-Kommentar A (4Q252)', in *Rewriting and Reception in and of the Bible*, ed. Jesper Høgenhaven, Jesper Tang Nielsen and Heike Omerzu (WUNT, 396; Tübingen: Mohr Siebeck, 2018), 14–15.

reworking. Molly Zahn thus helpfully identifies three core elements in what she describes as a 'prototypical' group of rewritten texts in which the structure and flow of their principal source remains recognizable, even if they differ from each other in terms of individual literary features.[21] First, those responsible for producing 'rewritten Scripture' viewed their compositions as constituting distinctly new works, and these authors regarded themselves as '*doing* something different' from scribes who produced new editions or copies of a scriptural text.[22] Second, works of rewritten Scripture are concerned with the sustained interpretation of a succession of specific scriptural passages; the aim is not simply to supplement or expand prior tradition but to interact with it through improvement and/or correction. Third, the authors of rewritten Scripture intended their works to be seen as the same 'kind of text', positioned within the same 'discourse' as the text forming the basis of rewriting.[23] And so, from a rhetorical perspective, reworked texts of this nature produce a 'version of past tradition that better reflects the concerns and ideology of their community', thus enabling authoritative tradition to be of significance in the present.[24]

Other Jewish rewritten texts

The category of 'rewritten Scripture' can, as a result, allow sufficient flexibility for texts like the *Genesis Apocryphon* and *Jubilees* to act as a template for assessing the nature and function of a much wider range of Jewish rewritten texts. What binds together the examples of Jewish rewriting so far considered in the 'genre versus process' debate is that they all display adherence, albeit with varying degrees, to a *scriptural* predecessor. In other words, rewriting constitutes the retelling of sacred and authoritative texts, while in the case of a text like *Jubilees* even the rewritten product was, at least in some circles, regarded as possessing 'scriptural' status as a divinely mediated text (CD 16.3-4; 4Q225-28). However, if the focus shifts to compositional matters, there is ample evidence that the same methods and techniques were applied in texts where the basis of the recasting was not a scriptural source.[25] To cite one particularly instructive example that I mentioned earlier in this study: when Josephus, in *Antiquities* 12-13, rewrites the *Letter of Aristeas* (*Ant.* 12.1-118) and I Maccabees

---

[21] Molly Zahn, *Rethinking Rewritten Scripture: Composition and Exegesis in the 4Q Reworked Pentateuch Manuscripts* (STDJ, 95; Leiden: Brill, 2011); Molly Zahn, 'Genre and Rewritten Scripture: A Reassessment', *JBL* 131 (2012): 271-88.

[22] Zahn, 'Genre and Rewritten Scripture', 282.

[23] Zahn, 'Genre and Rewritten Scripture', 284. Zahn defines 'rewritten Scripture' as follows: '[It is] a genre that functions interpretively to renew (update, correct) specific earlier traditions by recasting a substantial portion of those traditions in the context of a new work that locates itself in the same discourse as the scriptural work it rewrites' (p. 286).

[24] Zahn, 'Genre and Rewritten Scripture', 286. See also Molly Zahn, 'Rewritten Scripture', in *The Oxford Handbook of the Dead Sea Scrolls*, ed. Timothy H. Lim and John J. Collins (Oxford: Oxford University Press, 2010), 323-36.

[25] Campbell, 'Rewritten Bible: A Terminological Reassessment', 70, helpfully distinguishes between 'rewrittenness' and 'scripturality'. Cf. Molly M. Zahn, 'Talking about Rewritten Texts: Some Reflections on Terminology', in *Changes in Scripture: Rewriting and Interpreting Authoritative Traditions in the Second Temple Period,* ed. Hanne von Weissenberg, Juha Pakkala and Marko Marttila (BZAW, 419; Göttingen: de Gruyter, 2011), 110 n. 58.

1-13 (*Ant.* 12.241-13.214), he handles them in the same way as he treats scriptural material in *Ant.* 1-11: the structure and flow of the base texts are kept intact, but they are interpretatively rewritten to create a new literary composition using paraphrase combined with techniques like omissions, adjustments, expansions and additions.[26] Similar conclusions can be drawn, as we shall see, regarding the relationship between 2 Maccabees and *4 Maccabees*. The reasons for rewriting may be different, but they share striking affinities when it comes to textual processes. This also widens further the scope of the analogical base for comparisons with John's Gospel and its relationship with Mark, demonstrating that the phenomenon of rewriting was far more widespread in late Second Temple Judaism than is often assumed.

John's gospel and 'rewriting'

The scholarly debate about 'rewritten Scripture' has led to the identification of important questions for investigating how and why ancient Jewish authors produced compositions that preserved the structural outline of existing texts and yet recast those texts with varying degrees of innovation. In terms of using that debate as a platform for assessing the appropriateness of classifying John's Gospel as a 'rewriting' of Mark, it remains to be investigated how works of 'rewritten Scripture', and Jewish rewriting more generally, can be brought into fruitful dialogue with the question of John's relationship with Mark.[27] In what ways, therefore, can a study of the compositional techniques, processes and strategies of Jewish rewritten texts, as well as points of contact between such features and John's Gospel, inform the discussion of the character of John's engagement with Mark?

Before addressing these questions with reference to specific Johannine/Jewish analogues, three issues of methodological relevance need to be clarified. First, as far as generic classifications are concerned, John – and, for that matter, Matthew and Luke as well – does not meet the criteria of 'rewritten Scripture' as an ancient literary genre. Even a fairly broad definition, such as the one provided by George Brooke, demonstrates some of the clear obstacles in this regard: '[It] refers to any representation of an authoritative scriptural text that implicitly incorporates interpretative elements, large or small, in the retelling itself.'[28] If the rewriting of *Scripture* is adopted as the key characteristic of this generic category and/or literary phenomenon, John's relationship with Mark cannot, by definition, be described as the recasting of an earlier scriptural work. This point needs to be emphasized in view of recent attempts at presenting John's

---

[26] See especially Downing, 'Redaction Criticism: I', 162-65; Campbell, 'Rewritten Bible: A Terminological Reassessment', 70-72.

[27] Bauckham, 'The Gospel of John and the Synoptic Problem', 661 n. 6: 'Further study of the Jewish examples of the genre of "rewritten Bible" might prove profitable'. One of the few references to Jewish 'rewriting' in connection with John's use of (Synoptic) sources can be found in Ruth B. Edwards, *Discovering John: Content, Interpretation, Reception* (2nd edn; London: SPCK, 2014), 36. See also nn. 29-31 below. For a recent analysis of Matthew's relationship with Mark through the interpretative lens of 'rewriting' and 'rewritten Bible/Scripture', see Garrick V. Allen, 'Rewriting and the Gospels', *JSNT* 41 (2018): 58-69.

[28] George J. Brooke, 'Rewritten Bible', in *Encyclopaedia of the Dead Sea Scrolls*, ed. Lawrence H. Schiffman and James C. VanderKam (Oxford: Oxford University Press, 2000), 777.

reworking of the Synoptic tradition as a case of 'rewritten Scripture', with 'Scripture' interpreted as a designation for 'any writing or book that is attributed a particular authoritative status'.[29] This definition is in fact so broad that it can be applied to compositions regardless of how 'authority' is defined.[30] The same applies to Mogens Müller's proposal that John functions as a radical and creative 'biblical rewriting' of Mark, which manifests itself as a 'biblical' book because 'its Jesus story perceives itself as a continuation of the biblical history contained in the sacred books of Judaism'.[31] While it may be possible, from an analogical perspective, to align the New Testament gospels – as rewriting projects – with ancient Jewish texts categorized as 'rewritten Scripture', this exercise must not be confused with how John engages in the creative redrafting and reinterpretation of a text (in this case Mark) that was only later attributed canonical status.

Having said that, if the 'rewritten Scripture' debate is examined for what it discloses about ancient Jewish 'rewriting' procedures more generally, a number of the core elements identified in 'prototypical' texts, such as *Jubilees* and *Genesis Apocryphon*, resemble – and help to delineate – the affinities between John and Mark, that is, if John is understood as a new composition locating itself within the same discourse as the text it reworks and, to some degree, rewrites. The comparative value of drawing on actual examples of Jewish rewritten texts is that it affords specific cases of analogous interpretative strategies and that it prevents the notion of 'rewriting' from becoming unhelpfully vague when applied to the study of John's appropriation of Mark.[32] Understood in this way, investigating the compositional techniques and aims of Jewish rewritten texts, particularly in relation to their base text, can be heuristically valuable for the study of John in relation to Mark.

Second, the term 'rewriting' can evidently be employed to cover a large spectrum of 'rewrittenness' in Second Temple Jewish texts. Even within the category of 'rewritten

---

[29] Anders Klostergaard Petersen, 'Rewritten Bible as a Borderline Phenomenon – Genre, Textual Strategy, or Canonical Anachronism?', in *Flores Florentino: Dead Sea Scrolls and Other Early Jewish Studies in Honour of Florentino García Martínez*, ed. Anthony Hilhorst, Émile Puech and Eibert Tigchelaar (SuppJSJ, 122; Leiden: Brill, 2007), 285–306, here 287–88.

[30] This is even more so the case in Anders Klostergaard Petersen, 'Textual Fidelity, Elaboration, Supersession or Encroachment? Typological Reflections on the Phenomenon of Rewritten Scripture', in *Rewritten Bible after Fifty Years: Texts, Terms, or Techniques? A Last Dialogue with Geza Vermes*, ed. József Zsengellér (SuppJSJ, 166; Leiden: Brill, 2014), 13–48, where he locates the category of 'rewritten Scripture' 'in the wider context of rewriting authoritative texts, which is a far more prevalent phenomenon found not only in literature but in arts in general' (13 n. 3). See also Anders Klostergaard Petersen, 'The Riverrun of Rewriting Scripture: From Textual Cannibalism to Scriptural Completion', *JSJ* 43 (2012): 475–96.

[31] Mogens Müller, 'The New Testament Gospels as Biblical Rewritings: On the Question of Referentiality', *Studia Theologica* 68 (2014): 21–40, here 29, 31–32. See also his essays in *Luke's Literary Creativity*, ed. Mogens Müller and Jesper Tang Nielsen (LNTS, 550; London: T&T Clark, 2016), as well as pages xxi–xxiv.

[32] For valuable methodological reflections on using the category of 'rewritten Bible/Scripture' for interpreting early Christian texts, see Heike Omerzu, 'Das Petrusevangelium als "rewritten Gospel"? Eine forschungsgeschichtliche Erörterung der Rezeption der Kategorie "rewritten Bible" in Bezug auf frühchristliche Texte', in *Rewriting and Reception in and of the Bible*, ed. Jesper Høgenhaven, Jesper Tang Nielsen and Heike Omerzu (WUNT, 396; Tübingen: Mohr Siebeck, 2018), 235–51, especially 245–51.

Scripture' the sliding scale can extend from close paraphrase of the content of a single source text to a process of substantial reworking in which large blocks of material from other sources are incorporated into the rewritten text.[33] There are clear limitations to describing John's Gospel as a rewritten form of Mark if the designation is understood in a narrow or literal sense. Nevertheless, it can be a meaningful description if it is used more flexibly to denote the characteristic features of rewriting techniques that are also identifiable in John's engagement with Mark. This relates in some respects to discussions as to whether one speaks of John's acquaintance with or rather dependence on Mark. The more limited evidence of a close connection between the two gospels does not, in the light of known Jewish rewriting conventions, provide a firm argument against positing John's 'reliance' on Mark in favour of a more at-a-distance familiarity with the text. Rewriting, in other words, can embrace close adherence to a base text in terms of structure and sequence as well as extensive literary and theological creativity.

Third, to speak of an ancient author 'rewriting' a core source does not necessarily assume an exclusively visual mode of contact with a written text. Given the complex oral-textual matrix from which first-century CE compositions emerged, ancient rewriting practices could accommodate indirect as well as direct use of sources. Accentuating the prominence of literary conventions may point in the direction of John's visual knowledge of the written text of Mark at some stage in the reception process, but it does not rule out the possibility that John was (also) mnemonically and aurally acquainted with oral recitations of Mark.[34]

Having outlined some important considerations and certain caveats with regard to methodological and definitional matters, I will now examine three aspects in particular that point to the explanatory power of 'rewriting' conventions in ancient Judaism for investigating John's relationship to Mark.

Preservation of outline and 'rewriting' of content

The core Jewish compositional rewriting technique, as I have already noted, is to retain the structural outline of the antecedent text, but at the same time to make

---

[33] On this wide spectrum of 'rewriting', see, for example, Sidnie White Crawford, *Rewriting Scripture in Second Temple Times* (Grand Rapids, MI: Wm. B. Eerdmans, 2008), 13–14. See also Michael Segal, 'Between Bible and Rewritten Bible', in *Biblical Interpretation at Qumran*, ed. Matthias Henze (Grand Rapids, MI: Wm. B. Eerdmans, 2005), 16; Brooke, 'Memory, Cultural Memory, and Rewriting Scripture', 53–65.

[34] On re-oralization processes, see especially Michael Labahn, '"Secondary Orality" in the Gospel of John: A "Post-Gutenberg" Paradigm for Understanding the Relationship between Written Gospel Texts', in *The Origins of John's Gospel*, ed. Stanley E. Porter and Hughson T. Ong (Johannine Studies, 2; Leiden: Brill, 2016), 53–80. See also Michael Labahn, 'The Plot to Kill Jesus in Mark and John: Reflections on the Literary Relationship Between Two Early Christian Theological Biographies of Jesus on the Basis of a Detail in their Storytelling' (Chapter 17 in this volume); Andrew Gregory, 'What is Literary Dependence?', in *New Studies in the Synoptic Problem: Oxford Conference, April 2008: Essays in Honour of Christopher M. Tuckett*, ed. Paul Foster, Andrew Gregory, John S. Kloppenborg and Joseph Verheyden (BETL, 239; Leuven: Peeters, 2011), 90–95.

additions, omissions, abbreviations, conflations, rearrangements and other changes that can be positioned along a continuum of minor to major revisions, from close equivalence to innovative modification. Therefore, even if Matthew and Luke are to be placed on the less expansive end of the rewriting spectrum, certainly in comparison with John, all three gospels display the same strategy of keeping Mark's framework intact and preserving the basic Markan order. After the prologue, John's narrative focuses on the relationship between Jesus and John the Baptist, and then on Jesus' miracles and conflicts with the Jewish authorities and a Roman trial, before culminating with an account of Jesus' death, burial and resurrection. Indeed, the framing of John's actual narrative with an opening and ending evocative of Mark's points to a conscious attempt by John to position his account within an overarching Markan framework.

The broad spectrum of 'rewrittenness' in the New Testament gospels is analogous, moreover, to the varying degrees of reworking attested in Jewish texts betraying the hallmarks of 'rewritten Scripture'. John's Gospel includes a significant amount of non-Markan material as well as appearing to work closely with known Markan material in blocks (Jn 1, 5–6, 12),[35] including some striking verbal agreements (e.g., Mk 5.11 and Jn 5.8; Mk 6.37 and Jn 6.7; Mk 6.50 and Jn 6.20; Mk 14.3, 5 and Jn 12.3, 5). It is therefore noteworthy that many of the prototypical Jewish rewritten compositions similarly incorporate lengthy additions that contain no evident interaction with their underlying *Vorlage*. Rewritten texts can also be highly selective, overlooking entire sections of the base text, such as the omission of I Samuel from the reworking of the books of Samuel and Kings in Chronicles. *Jubilees* is the work of 'rewritten Scripture' that follows its scriptural base most closely, but even here some scriptural sections are significantly condensed or omitted altogether (e.g., Gen. 10.8–12), while in other places it incorporates a substantial body of new material such as its expansions of the story of Abraham (*Jub.* 11–12, 20–22). Pseudo-Philo's *Biblical Antiquities* presents history from Adam to the death of Saul, and yet omits large portions of Genesis (chs 1–3, 12–50) and Exodus (chs 3–13), while offering an expansive rewriting of the period of the Judges and, strikingly, a number of new speeches ascribed to Israel's leaders. The same expansiveness can be found in many of the earlier columns of the *Genesis Apocryphon*, where lengthy additions possessing no scriptural parallels are interwoven into what is essentially an interpretative compilation of Israel's story from the birth of Noah to God's promise of a son to Abraham, although it follows the Genesis account much more closely in the final section of the scroll (21.23–22.34).

Since 'rewritten Scripture' compositions belong to the much broader phenomenon of rewriting in Second Temple Judaism, yet another illuminating example in this respect is *4 Maccabees*, whose detailed account of the martyrdom of the seven brothers and their mother offers an interpretative rewriting of the earlier, much briefer, narrative

---

[35] For the view that ancient authors tended to follow one source at a time, see Downing, 'Compositional Conventions', 71; Derrenbacker, *Ancient Compositional Practices*, 440–41. See, however, James W. Barker, 'Ancient Compositional Practices and the Gospels: A Reassessment', *JBL* 135 (2016): 109–21, for examples of compositions that simultaneously access (and reorder) multiple sources.

in 2 Maccabees 3–7. In line with its distinct philosophical aims, *4 Maccabees* recasts many of the literary features of 2 Maccabees,[36] but it also clearly follows the same sequence and structure as its base text:[37]

2 Maccabees	Content	4 Maccabees
2.32	Introduction	3.19
3.1–3	Favourable conditions under Seleucus IV	3.20–21
3.4–40	Attack on the temple treasury	4.1–14
4.7–17	Change of government	4.15–20
5.1–26	Conquest of Jerusalem	4.21–23
6.1–11	Suppression of Judaism by Antiochus	4.24–26
6.18–31	Eleazar's martyrdom	5.1–7.23
7.1–41	Martyrdom of the seven brothers and their mother	8.1–17.6

Within this same outline *4 Maccabees* conflates certain characters and overlooks a number of events/developments to offer no more than a sketch of key episodes that accord with its own outlook and purpose.[38] *4 Maccabees* condenses the historical context of the martyrdoms (cf. 2 Macc. 3.1–6.17) to the bare minimum, trimming down eighty-eight verses to just twenty-eight, but greatly embellishing the descriptions of the actual martyrdoms. This particular example demonstrates how Jewish texts in the late Second Temple period could display great freedom towards their underlying texts, both when the precursor is scripturally authoritative and, more broadly, when it is regarded as constitutive for the rewritten composition.

The fact that such a vast range of rewriting strategies – from close running paraphrases to expansive reworking – is attested in late Second Temple Jewish texts warns against rejecting John's appropriation of Mark on the grounds that its engagement with the Markan text is far less overt and less consistently sustained than is the case in the Matthean and Lukan texts. The compositional techniques encountered in Jewish rewritten texts, especially the inclusion of significant additional material, also lends support to the view that the question of whether John is interacting with Mark is independent of the question whether he (also) makes use of distinctively Johannine tradition.

---

[36] See M. Gilbert, 'Wisdom Literature', in *Jewish Writings of the Second Temple Period: Apocrypha, Pseudepigrapha, Qumran Sectarian Writings, Philo, Josephus*, ed. Michael E. Stone (CRINT, II/2; Assen: van Gorcum, 1984), 317; David A. deSilva, *4 Maccabees: Introduction and Commentary on the Greek Text in Codex Sinaiticus* (Septuagint Commentary Series; Leiden: Brill, 2006), xxxi: 'If it should be objected that the author played fast and loose with 2 Maccabees, if that was his source, the author's freedom in retelling the story of King David's thirst (2 Sam 23:13–17; 1 Chron. 11:15–19) – a biblical narrative – should provide sufficient evidence to suggest that the author's treatment of 2 Maccabees is consistent with his *modus operandi* elsewhere'. One may add: it is also consistent with known Jewish rewriting practices during the period in question.

[37] For the table, see David A. deSilva, *4 Maccabees* (Sheffield: Sheffield Academic Press, 1998), 29; a modified version can be found in Campbell, 'Rewritten Bible', 71.

[38] See further deSilva, *4 Maccabees: Introduction*, xxx–xxxi; Christian Blumenthal, *Allweiser Schöpfer und durchsetzungsstarker Gesetzgeber: Eine Studie zur erzählerischen Entfaltung des Gottesbildes im 4. Makkabäerbuch* (Deuterocanonical and Cognate Literature Studies, 35; Berlin: de Gruyter, 2016), 47–49.

Interpretative frames

What often separates Jewish rewritten texts from other Jewish exegetical compositions is not so much the extent to which they part company from the scriptural base text but the fact that some of their innovative modifications accentuate the identity of these cases of 'rewriting' as the *same-but-new* literary entities. One such feature is the fact that several rewritten texts open with an interpretative frame that differs significantly from that of their predecessor.[39] As in the Johannine prologue, whose cosmic context acts as an interpretative filter for the 'inherited' earthly setting of the subsequent account of Jesus' ministry, new literary opening frames place the composition in a different setting and offer a new lens through which to interpret the underlying text. The rewriting of the martyrdom narrative in *4 Maccabees*, for example, is preceded by an exordium (1.1–12) and extended philosophical treatise (1.13–3.18) outlining the importance of reason and the virtues of prudence and courage. The martyrdom accounts that follow the lengthy introduction serve as historical illustrations of this principle of 'pious reason', as exemplified by the praise given to Eleazar's courage: 'only a wise and courageous person is lord of emotions' (7.23).

Similarly, the elaborate retelling of Genesis 1 to Exodus 16 in *Jubilees* is prefaced by an introduction (1.1–4) constituting a new literary frame: the text opens with verses from Exodus 24.12–18 before stating that the angel of the presence – acting on God's express instructions ('through the word of the Lord') – dictates the contents of the heavenly tablets to Moses during the forty days he was on Mount Sinai to receive the law (1.27, 29; 2.1), namely, what has happened and what will happen 'from the beginning of creation … through the ages of eternity' (1.27). This recasting of Scripture is presented as divine revelation, as a 'primordial writing' existing before the revelation that gave rise to the Pentateuch; its interpretative frame shapes the narrative that follows by signposting frequent interventions from the angel that are addressed to Moses.

Issues of authority

The literary framing of *Jubilees* leads, seamlessly, to the question of how authority is recognized and created by rewritten texts, particularly – though not exclusively – by compositions that form rewritings of scriptural texts. How do their compositional techniques relate to the authors' motivation or goals for recasting the base text and also to the status of the rewritten product? Does the strategy of rewriting constitute a claim to authority on the part of the new text? And what can be said about the relative authority of the rewritten text in relation to the text it rewrites? Such questions are important when seeking to determine the nature of the relationship between John and Mark, particularly if John's audience had already come to view Mark's Gospel as an authoritative account of Jesus' life and ministry.

---

[39] See Segal, 'Between Bible and Rewritten Bible', 21–22.

There is much debate as to how a text's authoritative status was understood, acquired or even lost in late Second Temple Judaism.[40] Not every rewritten version of a text was regarded as authoritative, and it cannot be assumed that their authors all understood what they set out to do in the same way. The author of a narrative retelling of Scripture, like the one offered by Josephus in *Antiquities* 1–11, no doubt understood the task of that retelling differently from a rewritten text claiming for itself the status of divinely mediated revelation or 'Scripture'.

Jewish rewritten texts may – or may not – attempt to replace or usurp the works they rewrite. The connection between them could be understood in reciprocal terms, in the sense that the rewritten text acknowledges,[41] even enhances, the established authority of the underlying work through the act of rewriting and, at the same time, claims authoritative status for itself.[42] But the relationship between them can also be quite paradoxical: the rewritten text may rely upon the authority of the *Vorlage* for its own legitimacy but (only) according to the rewritten text's interpretation of it.[43] This applies in particular to interpretations of legal material in the Pentateuch.[44] *Jubilees* affirms the validity of the laws written in Genesis-Exodus, referring to them as the 'first law' (2.24; 6.22; cf. 30.21; 50.6), although it does claim to be the authoritative interpretation of those laws, namely, as 'immediate revelation to Moses, not an interpretation of a prior one'.[45] Similarly, the *Temple Scroll* presents itself as unmediated divine revelation whereby God speaks directly to Moses; no reference is made to the 'first law' and it claims for itself the status of Torah (56.20–21: 'this law'). In both cases, but especially in *Jubilees*, the aim of the rewriting is not so much to replace the scriptural text, without which it lacks purpose; however, by offering what it regards as the 'correct' interpretation of Scripture, it does in some sense surpass it.

Molly Zahn helpfully distinguishes in this respect between *literal or physical replacement*, on the one hand, and *functional replacement*, on the other.[46] For most rewritten texts, especially those based on the Pentateuch, it seems unlikely that their aim was to displace the underlying scriptural text in the sense that it could be literally/physically cast aside and forgotten as though it had never existed. From a functional perspective, however, certain Jewish works of rewritten Scripture could present themselves as *replacing* their predecessors in terms of authority by providing what was

---

[40] Hanne von Weissenberg, Juha Pakkala and Marko Marttila, 'Introducing Changes in Scripture', in *Changes in Scripture: Rewriting and Interpreting Authoritative Traditions in the Second Temple Period* (BZAW, 419; Göttingen: de Gruyter, 2011), 5.

[41] John J. Collins, 'Changing Scripture', in Hanne von Weissenberg et al. (ed.), *Changes in Scripture*, 32–33. Cf. Hindy Najman, *Seconding Sinai: The Development of Mosaic Discourse in Second Temple Judaism* (SuppJSJ, 77; Leiden: Brill, 2003), 46: works like *Jubilees* and the *Temple Scroll* attempt to provide 'the interpretive context within which scriptural traditions already acknowledged as authoritative can be properly understood'.

[42] Brooke, 'Rewritten Bible', 780. See further George J. Brooke, 'Hypertextuality and the "Parabiblical" Dead Sea Scrolls', *Reading the Dead Sea Scrolls: Essays in Method* (Atlanta, GA: Society of Biblical Literature, 2013), 73–76.

[43] Segal, 'Between Bible and Rewritten Bible', 11–12.

[44] See Collins, 'Changing Scripture', 33.

[45] Eva Mroczek, *The Literary Imagination in Jewish Antiquity* (New York: Oxford University Press, 2016), 140. See also Hindy Najman, 'Interpretation as Primordial Writing: *Jubilees* and Its Authority Conferring Strategies', *JSJ* 30 (1999): 379–410, especially 408.

[46] Zahn, 'Rewritten Scripture', 331.

deemed to be their true meaning, even though the rewritings would have been intended for audiences who heard or read the retelling with the antecedent scriptural text very much in mind.[47] They were, in other words, to be read or heard 'side by side'.

This kind of distinction, I suggest, is valuable for assessing whether and in what sense John's Gospel can be viewed as a 'rewriting' of Mark. Matthew virtually absorbs Mark,[48] arguably making it more or less redundant by incorporating and yet adapting so much of the Markan text.[49] The much more sparing use of Mark in the Gospel of John arguably points in the other direction, away from any attempt at literal replacement. This envisaged scenario is lent additional support if John's relationship with Mark is assessed through a more audience-oriented lens, with John interpreted as a text presupposing that its audience already has knowledge of Mark.[50] John can then be read in conjunction with the Markan text: it shares the same narrative outline, it sometimes assumes Mark's content (e.g., Jn 1.32-33; 6.67-71; 12.27), and in places it even attempts to dovetail the two accounts.[51] This would signify that, different from Matthew and probably also Luke (1.1-4), the Markan text is not absorbed in John's Gospel so that it can be set aside and forgotten, but it rather works symbiotically with the Johannine text.

From a *functional* perspective, however – and this is where some of the Jewish analogues are particularly instructive – John's Gospel presents itself as *the* authoritative, and written,[52] interpretation of Jesus' identity and mission (20.30-31; 21.24-25).[53] The superior status of John's Gospel over alternative Jesus narratives is further heightened if the purpose of its two endings (20.31; 21.25) is deliberately to contrast John's βιβλίον (δέ is used in both cases) with literary predecessors that, in all likelihood, include Mark's Gospel.[54] For that reason the Johannine account, it can be argued, does more than supplement or complement the understanding of Jesus provided by its Markan

---

[47] Cf. Alexander, 'Retelling the Old Testament', 108: Pseudo-Philo refers to the *Aqedah* on three different occasions (*LAB* 18.5; 32.1-4; 40.2) but does not narrate the event at the point where its actual retelling would be expected.

[48] For this language of 'absorption', see Eric Eve, *Writing the Gospels: Composition and Memory* (London: SPCK, 2016), 130. Cf. Petersen, 'The Riverrun of Rewriting Scripture', 490-93; and also Petersen, 'Textual Fidelity', 39, where he refers to Matthew's 'loyal textual engulfment of Mark'.

[49] Cf. David C. Sim, 'Matthew's Use of Mark: Did Matthew Intend to Supplement or to Replace His Primary Source?', *NTS* 57 (2011): 183. See also page 182: 'What role could Mark have possibly played in the Matthean community once Matthew had published his own corrected, revised, enlarged, improved and updated edition of Mark?'.

[50] Cf. Frey, 'Das vierte Evangelium auf dem Hintergrund der älteren Evangelientradition', 114.

[51] E.g., the explanatory aside in John 3.24 fills the 'gap' between Mark 1.13 and 1.14; cf. John 7.1; 18.24-28.

[52] Note the repeated use of γράφω in John 20.30-31 and 21.24-25 to denote the (authoritative) *content* of the gospel. On the emphasis on 'scripture/writing' as an authority-conferring device in Second Temple Jewish text, see, e.g., Hans Debel, 'Anchoring Revelations in the Authority of Sinai: A Comparison of the Rewritings of "Scripture" in *Jubilees* and in the P Stratum of Exodus', *JSJ* 45 (2014): 473.

[53] See, most recently, Chris Keith, 'The Competitive Textualization of the Jesus Tradition in John 20:30-31 and 21:24-25', *CBQ* 78 (2016): 324-27, 329. Keith uses the colophons to support the argument that John knew the Synoptic Gospels but does not pursue in any detail how John understood its authoritative status in relation to them.

[54] Keith, 'The Competitive Textualization of the Jesus Tradition', 325-26. See also D. Moody Smith, *John* (ANTC; Nashville, TN: Abingdon, 1999), 401.

forerunner. The Fourth Evangelist rather seeks to demonstrate that the interpretative key to Jesus' true identity and significance lies within the Johannine text. That key cannot to be located in, or wholly derived from, Mark's Gospel, and, in that respect, John's aim, ultimately, must be to replace it.

Conclusion

The overarching aim of this chapter has been to demonstrate that ancient compositional techniques, as attested in Jewish rewritten texts from the late Second Temple period, have much to contribute to the debate as to how and why John's Gospel engages with Mark's Gospel in the way that it does. The creative freedom exhibited by John in its interaction with Mark is undeniably in line with the rewriting methods and strategies adopted by a wide range of Jewish authors in and around the first century CE, who, like John, drew upon their precursors to varying degrees but without necessarily making explicit reference to them. Focusing analogically on the ways in which predecessor texts were appropriated in late Second Temple Judaism may, admittedly, not establish conclusively that John made use of Mark as a literary source, but it does situate John's procedures within known rewriting practices and, as with several of its other textual features, indicates that the Fourth Evangelist breathed the same compositional and interpretative air as contemporaneous Jewish authors who invariably entered into dialogue with those that preceded them. Aligning John with Jewish rewritten texts can, consequently, provide a plausible explanation for the curious combination of significant points of similarity between John and Mark – the same general outline, some overlapping material, even occasionally striking verbal agreements – coupled with the many discrepancies, disagreements and even contradictions that exist between them.

6

Defining and Debating Divine Identity in Mark and John: The Influence of Classical Language and Literature

George L. Parsenios

The Gospel of John tells us why it was composed. As the narrative draws to a close at the end of chapter 20, we read that the book was written so that we 'may come to believe that Jesus is the Messiah, the Son of God' (20.31).[1] Its purpose is to clarify the identity of Jesus. The Gospel of Mark is the same. At the climactic turning point in the middle of Mark, Jesus turns to his disciples and asks, 'Who do people say that I am?' (8.27). 'The question of Jesus' true significance and identity', says Hurtado, 'pulses through the whole of Mark'.[2] But, if John and Mark focus together on the identity of Jesus, I will explore in this essay two ways in which John extends and expands on the portrait of Jesus in Mark. I will argue that, at least in some cases, the mechanism by which John develops the Markan material is by recourse to material from classical authors. The first example will build on Greek philosophy. Mark places in the mouth of Jesus the phrase 'I am' (ἐγώ εἰμι). John follows suit, but he develops this phrase even further by placing it within the context of the categories of 'being' and 'becoming' common to Plato and a Platonist like Philo. The second example comes from Greek drama. Recent scholarship has argued that Mark relies on the mode of tragic narrative to present the life of Jesus, but these dramatic devices are deployed in an embryonic or rudimentary fashion. One of these is the dramatic interest in scenes of recognition (*anagnôrisis*).[3] I will argue that Mark introduces this device into the life of Jesus in a basic fashion, and John develops it more fully.

A point of clarification is in order before the argument can proceed. First, I do not intend to show in minute detail that John has read and consciously altered Mark. That may be the case, but I will not try to show this. My concern is simply comparison. By placing the two texts next to one another, I will show that a tradition present in

---

[1] All translations are from the New Revised Standard Version.
[2] Larry W. Hurtado, *Lord Jesus Christ: Devotion to Jesus in Earliest Christianity* (Grand Rapids, MI: Wm. B. Eerdmans, 2005), 288.
[3] See Jeff Jay, *The Tragic in Mark: A Literary-Historical Interpretation* (Hermeneutische Untersuchungen zur Theologie, 66; Tübingen: Mohr Siebeck, 2014), 87–89, 190–93, 239–42.

Mark is also present in John, but it is present in John in a way that shows further elaboration from classical literature. Another way of saying this is to employ the language of Nils Dahl, who said that John makes explicit things that the Synoptic Gospels leave implicit.[4]

The argument can begin by recognizing that both Mark and John present the life of Jesus in paradoxical fashion.[5] The point seems obvious, but bears repeating. Mark's image of Jesus reflects a dialectical tension between knowledge and ignorance, power and weakness, as well as divinity and humanity. As Boring says, Jesus is presented as both 'fully human' and 'fully divine'.[6] For example, Jesus heals a woman who touches his garments, but he does not know who touched him (Mk 5.30). The language from the psalms (Pss. 29.3; 46.3; 65.8) regarding God's victory over violent seas applies to Jesus (Mk 4.35–41), and yet Jesus cannot decide who will sit at his right hand (Mk 10.40). In the same way, only the Father, and not Jesus, knows the time of the end (Mk 13.32). Jesus, finally, can drive out demons and walk upon the water, but he also dies a painful death on the cross.

John is similar, but even more emphatic in presenting the paradoxical quality of Jesus' identity. Where Mark will call Jesus Lord (1.3) in order to underscore his association with God, John goes so far as to call Jesus God (1.1, 18; 20.28). Even so, just like Mark, John emphasizes together the two poles of humanity and divinity, as Frey has recently shown.[7] The key dilemma is 'to regard as divine a human being who lived and acted in the "flesh"'.[8] When he praises the Gospel of John, Origen writes that, if the four gospels represent the first fruit of the New Testament, then John is the first fruit of the gospels (*Comm. Jo.*1.6). He justifies this declaration with the claim that no one else illuminates so clearly the divinity of Jesus. John indeed emphasizes the divinity of Jesus, who is explicitly called God in the opening prologue and is recognized as Lord and God by Thomas as the gospel draws to a close (1.18; 20.28). Jesus himself says that seeing him is equivalent to seeing the Father (14.7, 9), and that he and the Father are one (10.30). Jesus' divinity is, thus, clear from the beginning of John to the end. His humanity, however, is no less clear. If Jesus says that he and the Father are one, he also says that the Father is greater than he is (14.28). If Jesus is called both God and the Son of God repeatedly, he is also called a merely human Jew, whose earthly parents are known (4.9; 6.42). He famously weeps and is brutally beaten and painfully executed (11.35; 19.1–3). If Jesus is divine, he is just as fully human. But there is more. Not only does John balance divinity and humanity. Even more profound, the divinity is most fully recognized in Jesus' most human moment. Thomas identifies Jesus as God, not in his pre-incarnate state, but precisely when he appears with the marks in his hands as the crucified one.[9] He is most clearly divine when he is most human.

---

[4] Nils Dahl, 'Anamnesis: Memory and Commemoration in Early Christianity', in Nils Dahl, *Jesus in the Memory of the Early Church* (Minneapolis, MN: Augsburg, 1976), especially 28–29.
[5] The language of paradox is from Hurtado, *Lord Jesus Christ*, 288. See also M. E. Boring, 'Markan Christology: God Language for Jesus?', *NTS* 45 (1999): 451–71.
[6] Boring, 'Markan Christology', 451.
[7] Jörg Frey, *Theology and History in the Fourth Gospel: Tradition and Narration* (Waco, TX: Baylor University Press, 2018).
[8] Frey, *Theology and History*, 19.
[9] Frey, *Theology and History*, 17.

Both John and Mark, therefore, stress the paradox of Jesus' identity, balancing in delicate ways his link with humanity and his link with divinity. But as we have just seen, John is more explicit on Jesus' divinity, which makes the paradox even more profound. Mark has Jesus called 'Lord' (*Kyrios*), which evokes the divine identity of Jesus, but only John calls him explicitly God.[10] What Mark leaves implicit, John makes explicit. This is the kind of development I would like to trace, to show how John has deepened the paradoxical character of Jesus by reliance on classical models.

The first example of this phenomenon appears in the very famous words of Jesus, which appear in both John and Mark, where Jesus identifies himself with the phrase, 'I am' (ἐγώ εἰμι). Jesus utters this phrase three times in Mark: 6.50, 13.6 and 14.62.[11] In the first instance, Jesus is walking on the water toward the disciples in a boat, in the midst of a heavy wind (6.50). As he walks toward them, the disciples believe that Jesus is a ghost. But Jesus says to them, 'Take heart, it is I (ἐγώ εἰμι); do not be afraid.' In the second instance, Jesus is in the midst of delivering his eschatological discourse in Mark 13. As he warns the disciples against false prophets coming in his name to deceive them, he says, 'Many will come in my name and say, "I am he!" (ἐγώ εἰμι) and they will lead many astray' (13.6). Finally, in the trial before the Sanhedrin just prior to the crucifixion, the High Priest asks Jesus, 'Are you the Messiah, the Son of the Blessed One?' Jesus says to him in response, 'I am' (ἐγώ εἰμι; 14.62).

Each of these three passages has been investigated to see whether the identification of Jesus by the phrase 'I am' is meant merely as a casual identification where he is simply saying, 'It is me.'[12] The phrase can certainly mean this. But it can also have what Brown has called 'a solemn and sacral use'.[13] This more profound meaning of the phrase is based on the way that God identifies himself in the Old Testament, beginning in Exodus 3.14, where God says to Moses, 'I am He who is' (LXX: ἐγώ εἰμι ὁ ὤν). Making any connection between this precise phrase and the phrase in any of the New Testament gospels is hard to do on the basis of the Greek text of Exodus alone, however, since the New Testament texts say only ἐγώ εἰμι, and not ἐγώ εἰμι ὁ ὤν. But the absolute phrase is used in several other places in the LXX, such as at Deuteronomy 32.39 where God says, 'Behold, behold that I am' (ἴδετε ἴδετε ὅτι ἐγώ εἰμι). The same phrase appears in Isaiah several times (41.4; 43.10–11; 47.8, 10). Richard Bauckham has said that this phrase is 'extremely significant', because, 'it is a divine self-declaration, which encapsulates Yahweh's claim to unique and exclusive divinity'.[14]

The question is, does the Markan Jesus imply this profundity and sacred sense of the phrase when he uses it? Interpreters are divided. Some see it as possibly meaning,

---

[10] For ways in which the title 'Lord' identifies Jesus with God, see C. Kavin Rowe, *Early Narrative Christology: The Lord in the Gospel of Luke* (Grand Rapids, MI: Baker Academic, 2009).

[11] For discussion of the passages and their Old Testament background, see Catrin H. Williams, *I Am He: The Interpretation of 'Anî Hû' in Jewish and Early Christian Literature* (WUNT 2/113; Tübingen: Mohr Siebeck, 2000). For the Markan passages in particular, see pp. 214–54.

[12] See Joel Marcus, *Mark 1–8: A New Translation with Introduction and Commentary* (Anchor Bible, 27; New York: Doubleday, 1999), 427.

[13] Raymond E. Brown, *The Gospel According to John* (2 vols, Anchor Bible, 29–29A; Garden City, NY: Doubleday, 1966), 1.533.

[14] Richard Bauckham, 'Monotheism and Christology in the Gospel of John', in Richard Bauckham, *The Testimony of the Beloved Disciple* (Grand Rapids, MI: Baker Academic, 2007), 158.

'It is me'. Adela Yarbro Collins recognizes the possible profundity of the phrase, but writes, 'Jesus' words "It is I" ... serve primarily to let the disciples know that it is Jesus whom they have seen'.[15] While she recognizes that the phrase can have an association with divine identity, as signified above in the comments of Bauckham, she adds that human beings could use the designation as well.[16]

But Collins also recognizes that Jesus is assimilated to God in this passage in a variety of ways. For instance, Jesus wanted to pass the disciples by as he walked on the water, and this mention of his 'passing by' (παρελθεῖν) evokes the same activity of God in Exodus 34.5-6 LXX, when God passed by Moses (παρῆλθεν), and in 3 Kgdms 19.11 LXX in the theophany to Elijah, where God will pass by (παρελεύσεται). Likewise, the ability to walk on water demonstrates that Jesus has the power and might of God from the Old Testament.[17] Marcus sees even more symbolism in the walking on the sea. To him, it is part of the typology that has characterized this section of the Gospel of Mark, linking Jesus to Moses, and Exodus and Passover.[18] Thus, the miraculous sea crossing evokes the crossing of the Red Sea by the people of Israel. Even more significant, several Old Testament texts speak of God walking on the waters, showing his surpassing divinity (Job 9.8; Hab. 3.15; Ps. 77.19; Isa. 43.16; 51.9-10; Sir. 24.5-6). In this context, the mention of Jesus saying 'I am' seems to carry profound significance.

Less obviously profound are the other two uses of the phrase in Mark. Although he saw the statement in 6.50 as an expression of divine identity, in 13.6, Marcus says, 'Lacking the epiphanic context and the OT echoes present in Mark 6.45-52 ... , the declaration ascribed to the deceivers in the present instance is probably not meant to be understood in this way'.[19] But Williams suggests that the two are not separate. In the use of the phrase in 6.50 Jesus is disclosing his identity, and in 13.6 he is referring to those who would falsely claim that identity. This reference to the identity of Jesus links the two passages.[20] And the statements in both chapter 6 and chapter 14, in the trial, are linked in the same fashion. Williams says that when Jesus says 'I am' before the High Priest, he is affirming his identity, as it has just been spelled out by the High Priest, which is an elaboration of everything that has preceded in the narrative, especially the disclosure of his identity in chapters 6 and 13.[21] To sum up, then, the context and the function of the Markan 'I am' sayings makes it very reasonable, even likely, to read them as identifying Jesus with God in a profound way.

John does the same, but in a far more developed fashion.[22] Like in Mark, Jesus in John says 'I am' as he identifies himself while he walks on the water (6.20). But Jesus

---

[15] Adela Yarbro Collins, *Mark: A Commentary* (Hermeneia; Minneapolis, MN: Fortress, 2007), 335.
[16] Judges 5.3 (twice); 11.35, 37. Ruth 4.4. Cf. Yarbro Collins, *Mark*, 335.
[17] Yarbro Collins, *Mark*, 332-34.
[18] Marcus, *Mark*, 427.
[19] Marcus, *Mark*, 879.
[20] Williams, *I Am He*, 253.
[21] Williams, *I Am He*, 253-54.
[22] This discussion of the phrase 'I am' in John is dependent on Bauckham, 'Monotheism and Christology'.

uses this phrase many, many other times, and the sayings are of two broad types. The first type of 'I am' sayings are followed by a predicate, as follows:

I am the bread of life (6.35, 41, 48)
I am the light of the world (8.12; cf. 9:5)
I am the gate for the sheep (10.7, 9)
I am the good shepherd (10.11, 14)
I am the resurrection and the life (11.25)
I am the way, the truth, and the life (14.6)
I am the true vine (15.1)

These sayings are thought to be at least loosely connected to the absolute versions of the saying, with no predicate, but scholarly opinion varies on this point.[23]

The second type of sayings has no predicate. These absolute 'I am' sayings are scattered throughout the gospel, and, like the sayings with a predicate, the absolute sayings are also seven in number. Like with the Gospel of Mark, some of these seven absolute sayings are not immediately obviously to be read as references to the divine identity of Jesus. For instance, when Jesus talks to the Samaritan Woman, she mentions the Messiah to him, and so, when he replies by saying 'I am', it is reasonable to see him as merely responding to her question (4.26). He is saying, essentially, 'I am the Messiah'. The same could reasonably be happening at John 6.20, when Jesus walks on water and identifies himself to the disciples, or in chapter 18, when he identifies himself to the arresting officers (18.5, 6, 8). In each of these cases, it appears that Jesus is simply saying 'I am he' in order to identify himself to people who wonder about his identity. But these sayings do not appear in a vacuum. I would suggest that, while they might appear at first to be mundane statements, they derive their full meaning from those places where Jesus seems clearly to be evoking the divine use of the phrase from the Old Testament. The same is true of the 7 'I am' sayings with a predicate.

Jesus seems quite clearly to be using the phrase in the sense of the divine name that identified Yahweh in the LXX in three places in John. He does so first in John 8.24, where he says to his opponents, 'I told you that you would die in your sins, for you will die in your sins unless you believe that I am'. Unlike the other occasions, Jesus is not referring back to some antecedent question or figure, as he did with the Samaritan Woman who has asked him about the Messiah. He is using the phrase exactly as it is used in Deuteronomy 32.39. Proof of this is in the response of his interlocutors, who ask him, 'Who are you?' (8.25). The same occurs a few verses later in John 8.28, where Jesus says, 'When you have lifted up the Son of Man, then you will realize that I am'. As in the previous example, there is no referent to which the phrase 'I am' is pointing or referring.[24] The most extreme and obvious example of this use of the phrase comes at the end of chapter 8, where Jesus says, 'Very truly, I tell you, before Abraham was, I am' (8.58). His interlocutors realize what he is saying, and they try to stone him for

---

[23] See Brown, *John*, 1.533–35. I believe that these sayings with a predicate are elaborations on the saying without a predicate, but will return to this matter below.

[24] Although, see C. K. Barrett, 'Christocentric or Theocentric: Observations on the Theological Method of the Fourth Gospel', in C.K. Barrett, *Essays on John* (London: SPCK, 1982), 12–13.

blasphemy (8.59). These last three examples all appear to be evocations of the name of Yahweh as expressed in the LXX, and it is reasonable, as many argue, to read all of the other examples, which may or may not be so profound, through the prism of these three examples. Bauckham writes,

> So in 8.58, which serves to cap the whole presentation of Jesus' climactic declaration of his identity, his affirmation 'I am' is understood by the Jewish leaders as blasphemous. The fuller meaning implicit in the earlier occurrences can now be recognized by hindsight. And when in ch. 18 this phrase on the lips of Jesus provokes the soldiers to fall prostrate on the ground before him, attentive readers will not, with ch. 8 as background, be surprised.[25]

It would seem that John has followed Mark in using this phrase to identify Jesus with God. When the opponents of Jesus try to stone him for using this phrase, they certainly seem to confirm this reading. But John has used the phrase more broadly, widely and has more closely identified Jesus with God.

But John also goes further by connecting this phrase to Greek philosophical categories in the Platonic tradition. John connects the idea of God's eternal 'being' (εἶναι) with the idea of Jesus' temporary 'becoming' (γίνεσθαι). This is most clear in the passage just cited from John 8.58, which can be translated slightly differently as follows: 'Truly, truly I say to you, before Abraham became (γενέσθαι), I am (ἐγώ εἰμι).' In other words, before Abraham entered the realm of flux and 'becoming', I exist in the realm of eternal 'being'. This linkage of 'being' and 'becoming' occurs elsewhere, especially in the prologue. Of the Word in his pre-existence, we apply the verb 'to be' (εἶναι), as follows: 'In the beginning was (ἦν) the Word, and the Word was (ἦν) with God, and the Word was (ἦν) God. He was (ἦν) in the beginning with God.' But, of the production of the world, we read the term γίνεσθαι, as follows: 'All things became (ἐγένετο) through him, and without him not one thing became (ἐγένετο) which has become (γέγονεν).' The pre-existence of the Word is described as 'being', while the creation of the world is described as 'becoming'. Then, when Jesus enters the world, it is said of him that he, too, participates in the process of 'becoming' as follows: 'And the Word became (ἐγένετο) flesh and lived among us...' Finally, in a passage that anticipates the alternation of 'being' of Jesus and the 'becoming' of Abraham in John 8.58, the Baptist says, 'He who becomes (γέγονεν) after me ranks ahead of me because he was (ἦν) before me' (1.18). There is a play on the contrast between 'being' and 'becoming' in 1.18 just like there is in John 8.58.

To understand the significance of this language, we have to understand the Platonic background of the distinction between 'being' and 'becoming' that is indicated by the pairing of these two terms. The realm of the physical, material world is a world of flux and change, where things 'become' for a while, but exist in a world of impermanence and sense-perception. The realm of the 'Forms', by contrast, is a world of permanence and perfection, where things do not 'become' only for a while, but they always 'are'.[26] The difference is the difference between true and perfect 'being' (εἶναι)

---

[25] Bauckham, 'Monotheism and Christology', 157.
[26] An excellent and brief summary of Plato's philosophy on these issues is contained in K.J. Dover (ed.), *Plato, Symposium* (Cambridge: Cambridge University, 1980), 5–8.

and mere 'becoming' (γίνεσθαι). Plato speaks of these two realities in the *Timaeus* as follows (27d–28a):

> Now first of all we must, in my judgement, make the following distinction. What is that which is Existent (τὸ ὄν) always and has no Becoming (γένεσιν)? And what is that which is Becoming (τὸ γιγνόμενον) always and never is Existent (ὄν)? Now the one of these is apprehensible by thought with the aid of reasoning, since it is ever uniformly existent (ὄν); whereas the other is an object of opinion with the aid of unreasoning sensation, since it becomes (γιγνόμενον) and perishes and is never really existent (ὄν).[27]

These speculations of Plato are taken up in the writings of Philo, and they do so in regard to precisely the passages under discussion in this essay. When God describes himself with the verb 'to be' (εἶναι) by saying ἐγώ εἰμι ὁ ὤν in Exodus 3.14, Philo writes as follows: 'He says, "I am that I Am", which is equivalent to saying, "It is my nature to be, not to be described by names."'

If it is in the nature of God to 'be' and not to be named or to be visible, the physical world is a world, not of permanent 'being', but of temporary 'becoming'. In his *On the Creation of the World*, Philo expands on the relation between 'being' and 'becoming' when he writes,

> But the great Moses considered that what is ungenerated was of a totally different order from that which was visible, for the entire sense-perceptible realm is in a process of becoming and change and never remains in the same state. So to what is invisible and intelligible he assigned eternity as being akin and related to it, whereas on what is sense-perceptible he ascribed the appropriate name becoming (*genesis*). Since therefore this cosmos is both visible and sense-perceptible, it must necessarily also be generated.
>
> 2.12[28]

Thus, the Platonic language of 'being' and 'becoming' is scriptural language to Philo, separating the invisible, intelligible God from the visible, sense-perceptible world.

The Gospel of John operates under this same paradigm. Thus, in his pre-existence, the Word is spoken of with the language of 'being', while the created order is spoken of in the language of 'becoming'. When Jesus enters the realm of becoming, the language of John signals this by saying that the Word 'became' flesh.

And yet, even as John relies on the language of Plato and Philo, he also deviates from it. He uses their language, but he subverts it. For Plato and Philo, the language of 'being' and 'becoming' describes separate realms that are separated by an impassable ontological divide. For John, this language underscores precisely that Jesus has passed

---

[27] Translation from Plato in Twelve Volumes, Vol. 9, trans. W.R.M. Lamb (Cambridge, MA: Harvard University Press; London: William Heinemann Ltd., 1925).
[28] Translation from David Runia, *Philo of Alexandria: On the Creation of the Cosmos According to Moses* (Philo of Alexandria Commentary Series, 1; Leiden: Brill, 2002).

through this ontological divide. This language does not separate Jesus from the created order, but emphasizes precisely the opposite, that he is from the realm of pure being, and yet has entered the world of flux and of change, the world of 'becoming'. This is why, even after he has 'become' flesh, he can still say, 'I am' in 8.58. This use of philosophical vocabulary does not mean, therefore, that John is 'platonizing'. If he were Platonizing, he would be saying that being and becoming cannot mix. He uses Platonic language precisely to break Platonic boundaries, and to underscore the scandal of the Incarnation.

So, John has ploughed the same furrow as Mark. He wishes to underscore the paradoxical quality of Jesus' earthly existence. And he has also taken a start from Mark's language, by repeating the phrase 'I am'. But he has heightened the profundity of this paradox by recourse to philosophical vocabulary. Mark uses the phrase 'I am' as a way to present the paradoxical identity of Jesus, who is a human being, but also identified with God. John has also used this same phrase to underscore the paradoxical identity of Jesus, but he has taken what is implicit in this Markan phrase, and he has developed it further by recourse to Platonic categories. John is not doing something different from Mark, but he takes something that has one dimension in Mark, and he adds another dimension to it by relying on classical literature.

John does the same in the next area of inquiry under review in this essay, the area of dramatic recognition (*anagnôrisis*). Recognition scenes occur when long lost intimates (typically family members) recognize one another after a period of separation. A recognition scene is, in the words of Aristotle, 'a change from ignorance to knowledge, producing either friendship or hatred' (*Poetics* 11.4).[29] The paradigmatic recognition in Greek literature is that of the long-lost Odysseus (*Poetics* 16.4), who is recognized by his family and friends when he returns to Ithaca after twenty years of war and wandering.[30] But perhaps the most famous recognition scene is that in *Oedipus Rex* (*Poetics* 11.5–6), when Oedipus, in an instant, recognizes that he has murdered his father and married his mother.

It has been recently shown that the Gospel of Mark operates in a dramatic mode as it plays on the need to 'recognize' the identity of Jesus. Mark, of course, is not a drama, but the prose literature of the early Roman Empire regularly turned to dramatic models for inspiration. Easterling has dubbed this influence the 'theatricalization of ancient culture'.[31] Easterling relies on this phrase to explain the influence of Greek tragedy far beyond the chronological and geographical boundaries of classical Athens. This influence is not so obvious in the sparse evidence about the production of plays, but is indeed evident in the ripples of influence in various other social and literary contexts, especially in the prose authors of the Roman Empire.[32] Greek prose authors like

---

[29] Translation slightly modified from the translation of Hamilton Fyfe, trans. *Aristotle: Poetics, Longinus: On the Sublime; Demetrius: On Style* (LCL; Cambridge: Harvard University Press, 1973).

[30] On recognition in Homer's *Odyssey*, see Sheila Murnaghan, *Disguise and Recognition in the Odyssey* (Princeton, NJ: Princeton University Press, 1987).

[31] Patricia E. Easterling, 'From Repertoire to Canon', in *The Cambridge Companion to Greek Tragedy*, ed. Patricia E. Easterling (Cambridge: Cambridge University Press, 1997), 226.

[32] The dramatization of Roman social life is reflected in the grisly practice of staging public executions and punishments in the form of dramatic productions. See, for instance, Kathleen M. Coleman, 'Fatal Charades: Roman Executions Staged as Mythological Enactments', *JRS* 80 (1990): 44–73.

Thucydides and Herodotus, of course, had earlier steeped their histories in tragic motifs, and Polybius was also indebted to tragic models.[33] But closer in time and place to the Gospel of John, Josephus relies on dramatic models at great length for character development and the staging of scenes in the production of his *Bellum Judaicum*.[34] Greek and Roman novels also borrow heavily from dramatic patterns.[35] Finally, Lucian and Plutarch refer as well to tragic performances or themes, and often write with dramatic models in mind.[36]

Jeff Jay has recently tried to capture the influence of dramatic models on the Gospel of Mark, and he has done so by means of what he calls the tragic 'mode' of writing. Jay borrows the term 'mode' from Alastair Fowler. For Fowler, 'mode' is distinct from 'genre'. 'Mode is to genre as an adjective is to a noun.'[37] To write in the tragic genre means to write in meter, and to write a work of a certain length, etc. But to write in the tragic mode means to focus on tragic features like reversal of fortune or revenge or lamentation. When prose writers, from Thucydides to Lucian, draw on the dramatic 'mode', they evoke drama, without actually writing a drama. Recognition is one of the modal characteristics of drama that Jay believes is operative in Mark.

But if it is operative, it is operative in a very basic and underdeveloped way. Characters are certainly focused on the identity of Jesus, which evokes recognition motifs. Characters regularly ask, 'Who is this man?' (see Mk 1.27; 2.7; 4.41; 6.2–3). The disciples are repeatedly unable to recognize Jesus, though. Even though Peter can say that Jesus is the Messiah (8.29), he does not recognize the profundity of what this means regarding the need to suffer and to die.[38] Like the Ephesian Tale of Xenophon, the Gospel of Mark closes in chapters 14–15 with a series of recognition scenes, in which the identity of Jesus is debated with great enthusiasm, both in the trial and the crucifixion, culminating in the statement of the centurion at the cross, 'This man was

---

[33] Charles W. Fornara, *The Nature of History in Ancient Greece and Rome* (Berkeley, CA: University of California Press, 1983). On Polybius, see F. W. Walbank, 'History and Tragedy', *Historia* 9 (1960): 216–34.

[34] Jonathan Price, 'Drama and History in Josephus', *Scripta Classica Israelica* 21 (2002): 97-111; Louis Feldman, 'The Influence of the Greek Tragedians on Josephus', in *Hellenic and Jewish Arts: Interaction, Tradition and Renewal*, ed. A. Ovadiah (Tel Aviv: Ramot Publ. House, Tel Aviv University, 1998), 51–80.

[35] See the following, for instance, in regard to the *Satyricon* of Petronius: Gerald N. Sandy, 'Scaenica Petroniana', *TAPA* 104 (1974): 329–46; Gianpiero Rosati, 'Trimalchio on Stage', in *Oxford Readings in the Roman Novel*, ed. S. J. Harrison (Oxford: Oxford University Press, 1999), 85–104.

[36] For the study of Lucian's writings, with an eye toward using them to determine theatre productions occurring in the second century AD, see M. Kokolakis, 'Lucian and the Tragic Performances in his Time', *Platon* 12 (1960): 67–106. See also for attention to the dramatic character of Lucian's writing, Diskin Clay, 'Lucian of Samosata: Four Philosophical Lives (Nigrinus, Demonax, Peregrinus, Alexander Pseudomantis)', in *ANRW* II. 36.5, ed. Wolfgang Haase (Berlin: de Gruyter: 1992), especially 3414, where Clay begins to speak of 'The Mime of Philosophy'. For an analysis of Plutarch's condemnation of tragedy, as well as the nevertheless very full use of tragic elements in the *Demetrios*, see Phillip de Lacy, 'Biography and Tragedy in Plutarch', *AJP* 73 (1952): 159–71. More recently, see Judith M. Mossman, 'Tragedy and Epic in Plutarch's *Alexander*', in *Essays on Plutarch's Lives*, ed. Barbara Scardigli (Oxford: Clarendon Press, 1995), 209–28, as well as G. Zanetto, 'Plutarch's Dialogues as Comic Dramas', in *Rhetorical Theory and Praxis in Plutarch: Acta of the IVth International Congress of the International Plutarch Society, Leuven, July 3-6, 1996*, ed. L. Van der Stock (Collection d'Etudes Classiques, 11; Leuven: Leuven University Press and Peeters, 2000), 533–41.

[37] Jay, *The Tragic in Mark*, 13.

[38] Jay, *The Tragic in Mark*, 190–92.

the Son of God' (15.39). He, indeed, recognizes Jesus in a dramatic mode, but the scene is underdeveloped, at least in comparison to what is seen in John.

Larsen has carefully described the microgenre of the recognition scene in ancient literature, and has shown just how useful the recognition scenes in ancient literature are for interpreting the Gospel of John. In his taxonomy of the recognition type-scene, the following elements narrate the various stages in which people go from ignorance to knowledge in a recognition scene:[39]

1. the meeting, which determines the economy of knowledge in the scene to follow;
2. the move of cognitive resistance, which contains expressions of doubt, requests for proof, suggestions of alternative identification, judicial investigation, or sheer rejection;
3. the display of the recognition token;
4. the moment of recognition; and
5. the move of attendant reaction and physical (re)union.

These five phases occur not only in classical literature, but in John in various places. For instance, in the climactic recognition scene where Thomas calls Jesus 'My Lord and my God' (20.28), these five stages are very much in play. Phase 1, the meeting, occurs when the disciples tell Jesus that they have seen the Lord (20.25). Phase 2, the cognitive resistance is embodied in Thomas' refusal to believe that it was Jesus (20.25). Phase 3, the display of a token comes when Jesus displays his body for proof (20.27), and this is followed by Phase 4, the moment of recognition (20.28). Jesus then responds and reacts to Thomas, Phase 5, in 20.29. Compared to this close adherence to the phases of a recognition scene, the Markan scene is fairly spare and underdeveloped. Such scenes are regularly developed in this detail throughout John, with equal adherence to the techniques of recognition.

In the two areas of inquiry surveyed in this essay, we have seen that John and Mark both carefully develop a paradoxical presentation of the identity of Jesus. He is fully God and fully human, and each of the gospels in its own way comes to grips with this reality. But John seems to take material that was used in a more rudimentary and more primitive way in Mark, and develop it in a more nuanced and elaborate fashion. In the base of both the language of 'I am' and of the dramatic recognition scene, John has developed Mark by adding a thicker layer of classical influence to the portrayal of Jesus. He is chasing the same goal in his presentation of Jesus, but adds layers of nuance that Mark does not possess by delving more fully into classical language and classical models.

---

[39] Kasper Bro Larsen, *Recognizing the Stranger: Recognition Scenes in the Gospel of John* (Biblical Interpretation Series, 93; Leiden, Brill, 2008), 219–20. For more on recognition scenes in John, see also George L. Parsenios, *Rhetoric and Drama in the Johannine Lawsuit Motif* (WUNT, 258; Tübingen: Mohr Siebeck, 2010), chapter 3.

7

Parallel Traditions or Parallel Gospels? John's Gospel as a Re-Imagining of Mark

Mark Goodacre

Introduction: 'I believe in Dodd'

The idea that John knew the Synoptic Gospels is that rare thing in scholarship on Christian origins – a view that has extraordinary historical pedigree. Unlike consensus jewels in the scholar's crown such as Markan Priority, it is a view that has been held by the vast majority of scholars for the vast majority of the common era. The view was still so widespread in the middle of the twentieth century that C.H. Dodd could characterize it 'almost as a dogma'.[1] The remarkable rise of the view that John was independent of the Synoptics, which almost became a consensus in the second half of the twentieth century,[2] and which has many adherents today, has a range of interlocking causes and contexts. The popularity of the two-source theory provided an essential backdrop. If two literary works as similar in structure, content and vocabulary as Matthew and Luke were independent of one another, how could John, with all its differences, have known either of them, or Mark? Moreover, an independent John offered an additional route back to the historical Jesus at a moment when the quest was getting some new life, and the theological impetus for the view is clear in Dodd's work, and in the reaction to it. Realized eschatology, which was at the heart of so much of

---

[1] C. H. Dodd, *The Interpretation of the Fourth Gospel* (Cambridge: Cambridge University Press, 1953), 449: 'A majority of critics, for many years past, held the opinion, almost as a dogma, that he did so use them – or Mark at least – altering them in accordance with special motives of his own.' The tide was turning within a decade. In 1963, Dodd wrote, 'Recently there has been a certain trend away from this position'; see C. H. Dodd, *Historical Tradition in the Fourth Gospel* (Cambridge: Cambridge University Press, 1963), 8.

[2] It is commonly claimed that a new consensus emerged in the second half of the twentieth century; e.g., among many, Gail R. O'Day, 'The Johannine Literature', in Mark Allan Powell (ed.), *The New Testament Today* (Louisville: Westminister John Knox, 1999), 70–85 (72–73). But the view can only be sustained by ignoring major players like C. K. Barrett, *The Gospel According to St John: An Introduction with Commentary and Notes on the Greek Text* (2nd edn; Philadelphia, PA: Westminster Press, 1978), Werner G. Kümmel, *Introduction to the New Testament* (rev. edn, Nashville, TN: Abingdon, 1975), 200–4, and Frans Neirynck's multiple articles on the topic. A useful beginning point for the latter and for others in the Leuven school is found in Adelbert Denaux (ed.), *John and the Synoptics* (BETL, 101; Leuven: Leuven University Press and Peeters, 1992).

Dodd's thinking about Christian origins, can become mainstream when its most famous witness, the Gospel of John, finds it not in his own creative reflections on the Synoptics, but rooted instead in the earliest Jesus tradition. This takes place in a context where form criticism is still dominant, and all similarities between the Synoptics and John can straightforwardly be projected onto the ever general, ever vague 'tradition'. 'It is now widely recognized', Dodd wrote in 1953, 'that the main factor in perpetuating and propagating the Christian faith and the Gospel story was oral tradition in its various forms'.[3]

Although form criticism is now no longer dominant, its love of 'tradition' is still alive and well, and it is thriving in Johannine scholarship. The strength of the appeal to tradition is clear. It has the potential to explain every parallel between John and the Synoptics at the same time as guaranteeing some kind of historical pedigree. The similarities are attributed to common traditions, while the differences are allowed to be diagnostic of ignorance. Since oral traditions are by their nature lost, except in so far as they are later crystallized in texts, there is an innate plausibility in appealing to them. It is not like theorizing hypothetical literary sources, though those too have had their attractions. Who would want to deny the existence of shared oral traditions about Jesus? Moreover, the appeal to unseen 'traditions' rather than attested literary works like the Synoptics gives interpreters a certain freedom in their analysis and exegesis, as well as the opportunity to rescind from the kind of work that many scholars find tedious, and best relegated to the introductory lectures.

In spite of the utility of the 'parallel traditions' model, the imagery that scholars use when they invoke it should give us pause. Oral tradition is a 'reservoir'. It is a 'pool'. It has 'channels'. It is a 'living spring'. The use of water imagery is endemic and continues even in recent scholarship that has a greater degree of sophistication in its discussions of orality. The use of this water imagery suggests a studied vagueness in what is being imagined. It is infinitely flexible. It is literally 'fluid'. As a sole explanatory factor, it is allowed great malleability. There is nothing tangible, and 'fluidity' gives freedom to the interpreter. Unseen sources provide untold explanatory power.

It is not, of course, a problem to recognize the role played by oral tradition in gospel origins and interrelations. It is beyond reasonable doubt that oral traditions were influential, and it is difficult to imagine life in antiquity without storytelling and the sharing of traditions. The Synoptics and John themselves take the phenomenon for granted (Lk. 1.2; Mt. 28.15; Jn 21.25). Any discussion of the origins of John must surely take this seriously. The problem with the appeal to oral tradition is not what it affirms but what it denies. The unnecessary elevation of oral tradition to become the sole means of explanation for John's links with the Synoptics, and so to question the influence of one gospel upon another, is unfortunate and unnecessary. In this chapter I would like to propose that John's literary familiarity with the Synoptics explains the data far more successfully than the view that the connections between them are due to swirling pools of parallel traditions that somehow flowed into two independent gospel streams, and I would like to explore this thesis by progressing from the minutiae to the grand plan, beginning with small agreements that show direct connections, expanding

---

[3] Dodd, *Interpretation*, 449.

to whole pericopae where John becomes a fourth Synoptic gospel, and concluding with the fundamental literary, theological, and conceptual similarity that suggests that it is time to change our focus 'from tradition to gospel'.

Minor verbal agreements

Given the number of scholars who affirm John's independence of the Synoptics, it is worth remembering that there are, in fact, a lot of close verbal agreements between the Synoptics and John. The difficulty is that in simplifying the data in our introductory courses, and attempting to underline the manifold differences between the Synoptics and John, we have begun to believe our own propaganda. It is of course the case that John's agreements with the Synoptics are vastly different in volume from the agreements among Matthew, Mark and Luke, but the excessively high levels of verbatim agreement among the Synoptics are outliers in antiquity, when paraphrase was the norm.[4]

Three examples here illustrate the kind of agreement that one often finds between John and the Synoptics.

(a) Prediction of Judas's betrayal (Mt. 26.21 // Mk 14.18 // Jn 13.21)

Mt. 26.21	Mk 14.18	Jn 13.21
καὶ ἐσθιόντων αὐτῶν εἶπεν· Ἀμὴν λέγω ὑμῖν ὅτι εἷς ἐξ ὑμῶν παραδώσει με.	καὶ ἀνακειμένων αὐτῶν καὶ ἐσθιόντων ὁ Ἰησοῦς εἶπεν· Ἀμὴν λέγω ὑμῖν ὅτι εἷς ἐξ ὑμῶν παραδώσει με ὁ ἐσθίων μετ' ἐμοῦ.	Ταῦτα εἰπὼν ὁ Ἰησοῦς ἐταράχθη τῷ πνεύματι καὶ ἐμαρτύρησεν καὶ εἶπεν· Ἀμὴν ἀμὴν λέγω ὑμῖν ὅτι εἷς ἐξ ὑμῶν παραδώσει με.
And while they were eating, he said, 'Amen I say to you, one of you will betray me'.	And when they had taken their places and were eating, Jesus said, 'Amen I say to you, one of you will betray me, one who is eating with me'.	After saying this Jesus was troubled in spirit, and testified and said, 'Amen Amen I say to you, one of you will betray me'.

The underlined words here (Ἀμὴν λέγω ὑμῖν ὅτι εἷς ἐξ ὑμῶν παραδώσει με) provide a nine-word verbatim string with Mark and Matthew, the kind of agreement that is diagnostic of literary familiarity. When one has several words in a verbatim string in a specific narrative context, in cases where one cannot appeal to 'free floating' traditional aphorisms of Jesus, one has good evidence of a literary connection.

---

[4] On the distorting effect that intra-Synoptic agreement has on our appreciation of other literary relationships, see Mark Goodacre, *Thomas and the Gospels: The Making of an Apocryphal Text* (London: SPCK, 2012), 44–48. For a helpful contrast between high verbatim agreement in the Synoptics and the norm of paraphrasing sources, see John S. Kloppenborg, 'Variation in the Reproduction of the Double Tradition and an Oral Q?', *ETL* 83 (2007): 49–79.

(b) The walking on the water (Mt. 14.22-33 // Mk 6.45-52 // Jn 6.16-21)

Mk 6.50	Jn 6.20
ὁ δὲ εὐθὺς ἐλάλησεν μετ' αὐτῶν, καὶ λέγει αὐτοῖς· Θαρσεῖτε, ἐγώ εἰμι, μὴ φοβεῖσθε.	ὁ δὲ λέγει αὐτοῖς· ἐγώ εἰμι· μὴ φοβεῖσθε.
But immediately he spoke with them, and he says to them: 'Take heart, I am; do not fear!'	But he says to them: 'I am; do not fear!'

John's familiarity with Mark's Gospel makes sense of this kind of agreement. John never elsewhere has this construction, ὁ δὲ + λέγει + αὐτοῖς ('but he is saying to them'), but it is at home in Mark (6.38, here, 9.19, 10.24; it also occurs twice in Matthew – 17.20 and 21.16, i.e. it has figures of 2/4/0/1[5]).

(c) The crown of thorns (Mt. 27.27-29 // Mk 15.16-18 // Jn 19.1-3)

Mt. 27	Mk 15	Jn 19
27 Τότε		Τότε οὖν ἔλαβεν ὁ Πιλᾶτος τὸν Ἰησοῦν καὶ ἐμαστίγωσεν. 2 καὶ
οἱ στρατιῶται τοῦ ἡγεμόνος παραλαβόντες τὸν Ἰησοῦν εἰς τὸ πραιτώριον συνήγαγον ἐπ' αὐτὸν ὅλην τὴν σπεῖραν. 28 καὶ ἐκδύσαντες αὐτὸν χλαμύδα κοκκίνην περιέθηκαν αὐτῷ, 29 καὶ πλέξαντες στέφανον ἐξ ἀκανθῶν ἐπέθηκαν ἐπὶ τῆς κεφαλῆς αὐτοῦ καὶ κάλαμον ἐν τῇ δεξιᾷ αὐτοῦ, καὶ γονυπετήσαντες ἔμπροσθεν αὐτοῦ ἐνέπαιξαν αὐτῷ λέγοντες· Χαῖρε, βασιλεῦ τῶν Ἰουδαίων.	16 Οἱ δὲ στρατιῶται ἀπήγαγον αὐτὸν ἔσω τῆς αὐλῆς, ὅ ἐστιν πραιτώριον, καὶ συγκαλοῦσιν ὅλην τὴν σπεῖραν. 17 καὶ ἐνδιδύσκουσιν αὐτὸν πορφύραν καὶ περιτιθέασιν αὐτῷ πλέξαντες ἀκάνθινον στέφανον· 18 καὶ ἤρξαντο ἀσπάζεσθαι αὐτόν· Χαῖρε, βασιλεῦ τῶν Ἰουδαίων·	οἱ στρατιῶται πλέξαντες στέφανον ἐξ ἀκανθῶν ἐπέθηκαν αὐτοῦ τῇ κεφαλῇ, καὶ ἱμάτιον πορφυροῦν περιέβαλον αὐτόν, 3 καὶ ἤρχοντο πρὸς αὐτὸν καὶ ἔλεγον· Χαῖρε, ὁ βασιλεὺς τῶν Ἰουδαίων·
²⁷Then the soldiers of the governor took Jesus into the governor's headquarters, and they gathered the whole cohort around him. ²⁸They stripped	¹⁶And the soldiers led him into the courtyard of the palace (that is, the governor's headquarters); and they called together the whole cohort. ¹⁷And they	Then Pilate took Jesus and scourged him. ²And the soldiers,

---

[5] Figures in this format stand for number of instances in Matthew/Mark/Luke/John.

him and put a scarlet robe on him, ²⁹and <u>after twisting a crown from thorns, they put it on his head</u>. They put a reed in his right hand and knelt before him and mocked him, saying, 'Hail, King of the Jews!'	clothed him in a purple cloak; and after twisting some thorns into a crown, they put it on him. ¹⁸And they began saluting him, 'Hail, King of the Jews!'	<u>after twisting a crown from thorns,</u> put <u>it on his head</u>, and they dressed him in a purple robe. ³They kept coming up to him, saying, 'Hail, King of the Jews!' and striking him on the face.

Here, John's agreements with Matthew against Mark are telling, and there is little difficulty in representing the similarities and differences straightforwardly in a Synopsis. There are twenty-seven words in John 19.2–3a, and fifteen of them are parallel with Matthew. Where agreement like this occurs in the Synoptics, scholars do not hesitate to conclude in favour of a literary connection between them. πλέκω ('twist') is found only here in the Gospels and Acts (1/1/0/1+0), and ἄκανθα ('thorns') is found only in this context in John (19.2, 5), while it is common in the Synoptics. Matthew and John agree, against Mark, in their sentence structure, πλέξαντες στέφανον ἐξ ἀκανθῶν ἐπέθηκαν ('after twisting a crown from thorns, they put …'). Both Matthew and John have the same redundancy, whereby the crown of thorns is placed upon his head (αὐτοῦ τῇ κεφαλῇ),[6] and this stress on parts of the body is somewhat typical of Matthew. He has a similar redundant clarificatory addition to Mark 7.14–15 involving a part of the body when he talks about words that proceed from 'the mouth' (Mt. 15.10–11).[7]

The parallel here between Matthew and John is telling because it occurs at a point where Matthew is rewriting Mark in minor, subtle ways. Matthean commentators do not need to appeal to fresh traditional material here. It is just a standard case of Matthew re-casting his Markan source in his own words. What is striking is that it is Matthew's re-wording of Mark that finds its way also into John. Moreover, in cases like this, John effectively becomes a fourth Synoptic gospel. The very thing that causes us to name three of the gospels 'Synoptic' is that it is straightforward to place them in synopsis. And here, placing John in synopsis is easy, and the verbatim agreement clear. Nor is this an isolated example. John's version of the Anointing provides a particularly striking case of the phenomenon.

Where John is a fourth Synoptic Gospel

The clearest example of John becoming a fourth Synoptic is in the Anointing pericope (Mt. 26.6–13 // Mk 14.3–9 // Jn 12.1–8). Here, John is remarkably close to both Mark and Matthew. Indeed, he is far closer to Mark and Matthew in this pericope than is

---

[6] Robert H. Stein, 'The Matthew–Luke Agreements against Mark: Insight from John', *CBQ* 54 (1992): 482–502 (490 n. 27) asks, 'Is this due to an independent logical assumption? (Where else would they put a crown?) More likely is the view that another tradition, with which John was familiar, specified this'. This kind of recursion – not Matthew but Matthew's source – is endemic among those who maintain John's independence. It is not clear why it is preferable to project agreements onto hypothetical prior sources except that it helps one to avoid the obvious.

[7] On this example, see further Goodacre, *Thomas and the Gospels*, 70–71.

Luke in his rather different version of the Anointing (Lk. 7.36–50), a version on which John also seems to draw.[8] John shares with Mark and Matthew a cluster of motifs in a similarly structured pericope that features close verbatim similarities:

1. The incident takes place in Bethany,
2. just before Passover,
3. at a dinner where a woman has a jar of very expensive perfume of pure nard (Mk 14.3, ἀλάβαστρον μύρου νάρδου πιστικῆς πολυτελοῦς; John 12.3, λίτραν μύρου νάρδου πιστικῆς πολυτίμου),
4. which she uses to anoint Jesus;
5. there are complaints about the costliness of the perfume (τριακοσίων δηναρίων), which could have been given to the poor (καὶ ἐδόθη πτωχοῖς, Jn 12.5; καὶ δοθῆναι τοῖς πτωχοῖς, Mk 14.5);
6. Jesus says 'Leave her ... The poor you will always have with you ... But you will not always have me' (ἄφες αὐτήν ... τοὺς πτωχοὺς γὰρ πάντοτε ἔχετε μεθ' ἑαυτῶν ἐμὲ δὲ οὐ πάντοτε ἔχετε, Jn 12.7-8; ἄφετε αὐτήν ... πάντοτε γὰρ τοὺς πτωχοὺς ἔχετε μεθ' ἑαυτῶν καὶ ὅταν θέλητε δύνασθε αὐτοῖς εὖ ποιῆσαι ἐμὲ δὲ οὐ πάντοτε ἔχετε, Mk 14.6-7);
7. Jesus interprets the anointing in connection with his burial (Jn 12.7, Mk 14.8).

Looking at a Gospel synopsis for this passage is instructive, but even a segment of it will help to draw attention to several of these connections with clarity:

Mk 14	Jn 12
⁴ἦσαν δέ τινες ἀγανακτοῦντες πρὸς ἑαυτούς· Εἰς τί ἡ ἀπώλεια αὕτη τοῦ μύρου γέγονεν; ⁵ἠδύνατο γὰρ τοῦτο τὸ μύρον <u>πραθῆναι</u> ἐπάνω <u>δηναρίων</u> <u>τριακοσίων</u> <u>καὶ</u> <u>δοθῆναι</u> <u>τοῖς</u> <u>πτωχοῖς</u>·	⁴λέγει δὲ Ἰούδας ὁ Ἰσκαριώτης εἷς τῶν μαθητῶν αὐτοῦ, ὁ μέλλων αὐτὸν παραδιδόναι· ⁵Διὰ τί τοῦτο τὸ μύρον οὐκ <u>ἐπράθη</u> <u>τριακοσίων</u> <u>δηναρίων</u> <u>καὶ</u> <u>ἐδόθη</u> <u>πτωχοῖς</u>; ⁶εἶπεν δὲ τοῦτο οὐχ ὅτι περὶ τῶν πτωχῶν ἔμελεν αὐτῷ, ἀλλ' ὅτι κλέπτης ἦν καὶ τὸ γλωσσόκομον ἔχων τὰ βαλλόμενα ἐβάσταζεν.
καὶ ἐνεβριμῶντο αὐτῇ. ⁶<u>ὁ δὲ Ἰησοῦς εἶπεν· Ἄφετε αὐτήν·</u> τί αὐτῇ κόπους παρέχετε; καλὸν ἔργον ἠργάσατο ἐν ἐμοί· ⁷<u>πάντοτε γὰρ τοὺς πτωχοὺς ἔχετε</u> <u>μεθ' ἑαυτῶν</u>, καὶ ὅταν θέλητε δύνασθε αὐτοῖς εὖ ποιῆσαι, <u>ἐμὲ δὲ οὐ</u> <u>πάντοτε ἔχετε</u>·	⁷<u>εἶπεν</u> οὖν <u>ὁ Ἰησοῦς· Ἄφες αὐτήν,</u> ἵνα εἰς τὴν ἡμέραν τοῦ ἐνταφιασμοῦ μου τηρήσῃ αὐτό· ⁸<u>τοὺς πτωχοὺς</u> γὰρ <u>πάντοτε ἔχετε</u> <u>μεθ' ἑαυτῶν</u>, <u>ἐμὲ δὲ οὐ</u> <u>πάντοτε ἔχετε</u>.

---

[8] Streeter's discussion of John's familiarity with Luke is still a classic: Burnett H. Streeter, *The Four Gospels: A Study of Origins* (London: MacMillan, 1924), 401–8; see 402–3 on the Anointing.

But some were there who said to one another in anger, 'Why was the ointment wasted in this way? 5 For this ointment could have been <u>sold</u> for more than <u>three hundred denarii, and</u> the money <u>given to the poor.</u>'	But Judas Iscariot, one of his disciples (the one who was about to betray him), said, 5 'Why was this perfume not <u>sold</u> for <u>three hundred denarii and</u> the money <u>given to the poor?</u>' 6 (He said this not because he cared about the poor, but because he was a thief; he kept the common purse and used to steal what was put into it.)
And they scolded her. 6 But <u>Jesus said, 'Leave her alone</u>; why do you trouble her? She has performed a good service for me. 7 For <u>you always have the poor with you</u>, and you can show kindness to them whenever you wish; <u>but you</u> will <u>not always have me.</u>'	7 <u>Jesus said, 'Leave her alone.</u> She bought it so that she might keep it for the day of my burial. 8 <u>You always have the poor with you, but you do not always have me.</u>'

Such close agreement in structure and wording naturally raises the question of the direction of dependence. There are those who have suggested Johannine priority in different forms,[9] but there are indications here that John is secondary. John appears to have crafted this account on the basis of the Markan/Matthean narrative. The story, the structure, and the wording are substantially similar. The only major fresh elements in John are the naming of the woman as Mary, contextually determined by his resetting of the account as a postlude to the Lazarus story, and the naming of the one who complains as Judas. This element itself may be derived from Mark 14.10–11, which comes straight after the anointing, and links Judas with an unhealthy interest in money.[10] But there is one element in John that is not to be found in Mark or Matthew, Mary's wiping Jesus' feet with her hair (καὶ ἐξέμαξεν ταῖς θριξὶν αὐτῆς τοὺς πόδας αὐτοῦ, Jn 12.3; cf. 11.2). This detail appears to come from Luke 7.38 (καὶ ταῖς θριξὶν τῆς κεφαλῆς αὐτῆς ἐξέμασσεν . . .), where it forms part of Luke's story of the anointing (Lk. 7.36–50). As in Mark and Matthew, it is an anointing by an anonymous woman in the house of a man called Simon, though Luke relocates it at an earlier point in the narrative, as often (cf. the Rejection at Nazareth, brought forward to Lk. 4.16–30; Paul's first visit to Jerusalem, brought forward to Acts 9.25–26 and the Jerusalem Council, brought forward to Acts 15 from its 'true' location in Acts 18.22), a move that necessitates some reworking of the details, especially the stress on the forthcoming death and burial. It is now a story about a 'sinner', whose hair hangs loose.

The anointing in each of the Synoptic accounts makes sense. In Mark and Matthew, Jesus' head is anointed with perfume. No hair is mentioned; no feet are mentioned. In

---

[9] For the argument for Johannine Priority from this pericope, see especially J. F. Coakley, 'The Anointing at Bethany and the Priority of John', *JBL* 107 (1988): 241–56.

[10] For other examples of John naming unnamed Synoptic characters, see Mk 14.47 // Jn 18.10–11 (Jesus' arrest) where the 'one who stood near' becomes Peter, and the 'slave of the high priest' becomes Malchus; and Mt. 28.17 // Lk. 24.37 // Jn 20.24–28 where Matthew's and Luke's doubting disciples become Thomas.

Luke, the woman wets Jesus' feet with her tears, an act of repentance, and she wipes them with her loose 'sinner's' hair before she anoints them with perfume. But John's reminiscence of the Lucan detail about the wiping of Jesus' feet with her hair creates an anomaly. First, there is no reason for Mary, in John, to be wearing her hair like Luke's 'sinner', which is the point of the Lucan story. Second, because there are no tears in John, Mary's wiping of Jesus' feet with her hair means that the perfume ends up on her hair and not on Jesus. Jesus is the one who is supposed to be being anointed.[11] The most plausible explanation here is that John has drawn a favourite Lukan detail into a narrative in which it no longer makes sense.

'A Passion narrative with an extended introduction'

If, though, there are places where John appears to carry over Synoptic minutiae, as well as occasions when the gospel effectively becomes a fourth Synoptic, the question might still be asked about whether agreements of this kind are sufficient to draw a direct line from the Synoptics to John. After all, parallel structuring in one passage like the Anointing will be attributed by some to good-old form-critical chriae, according to which the structural parallels are there in the text because they were already there in the tradition. In order to move more decisively beyond parallel traditions, we need something more. We need some attention to the macro-similarities between the Synoptics and John, similarities like the structuring of their entire gospels as literary works.

The substantial differences in content between the Synoptics and John have provided the kind of misdirection that has made it easy to ignore the fundamental structural similarities between Mark and John. Who told Mark and John, independently of one another, to begin their works with John the Baptist's testimony to Jesus, to go on with the calling of the disciples, and to devote half of their gospels to the Passion Narrative? This is not a question of individual 'traditions' but of narrative direction and overall literary structure. The generic constraints of writing a *bios* do not account for this specific way of configuring the Jesus story. Our failure to find the similarities striking may say more about our innate canonical bias than anything else; our presumption of the normativity of telling the story in this way not only ignores countless other 'non-canonical' ways of telling Jesus' story, but it assumes that there is something inevitable about the Synoptic and Johannine constructions.

It is amazing how often Martin Kähler's description of 'a Passion Narrative with an extended introduction' is applied to Mark when it is equally applicable to John. Indeed Kähler himself was talking about all four canonical gospels.[12] If anything, John out-Marks Mark by devoting the whole of the last half of the gospel to the last week of Jesus'

---

[11] See Michael D. Goulder, *Luke: A New Paradigm* (JSNTSup, 20; Sheffield: Sheffield Academic Press, 1989), 403.

[12] Martin Kähler, *The So-Called Historical Jesus and the Historic Biblical Christ* (trans. by Carl E. Braaten; Philadelphia, PA: Fortress, 1964), 80 n. 11.

life, much of it to one evening (Jn 13–17), so that Jesus' teaching is thoroughly immersed in a crucifixion context. Moreover, just as Mark early on signals the coming conflict (Mk 2.1–3.6), so too John foreshadows the Passion by sending Jesus to Jerusalem at Passover, immediately after the narration of the first sign (Jn 2.1–12), audaciously drawing forward the telling of the temple incident (Jn 2.13–22) to this remarkably early moment. There are, of course, those who would argue for the historicity of the Johannine placement of the incident, but to press an uncertain point about historicity would be to miss the certain point that John's Gospel uses the incident to begin the foreshadowing of the Passion story, explicitly evoking Jesus' death and resurrection (Jn 2.19–22).

The structural similarities between Mark and John are in fact much closer than is commonly perceived, even by those arguing for literary contact between them. It is possible roughly to quantify the extent of the 'extended introduction' in each work, and on the assumption that the Triumphal Entry begins the Passion Narrative proper, it is striking to see how similar its position is in each gospel:

Mk 1.1–10.52 425 verses[13] **63.8%**	Jn 1.1–12.11 535 verses **61.7%**
Mk 11.1–11: Triumphal Entry	Jn 12.12–19: Triumphal Entry
Mk 11.1–16.8 241 verses **36.2%**	Jn 12.12–21.25 332 verses **38.3%**

In other words, the 'Extended Introduction' in both of the gospels occupies just over 60% of the whole, and the Passion Narrative begins at a very similar moment. If one thinks of the Passion Narrative proper as beginning later, with Jesus' arrest, the same point can still be made:

Mk 1.1–14.43 581 verses **87.2%**	Jn 1.1–17.26 729 verses **84.1%**
Mk 14.43–52: Arrest	Jn 18.1–14: Arrest
Mk 14.43–16.8 85 verses **12.8%**	Jn 18.1–21.25 138 verses **15.9%**

We should not imagine, of course, that the evangelist has precisely measured his Markan scroll, with a view to introducing his own Passion Narrative at a similar point. But the parallels in the structuring of the two books are noteworthy, and literary influence of the one work on another, especially given the strikingly similar openings to the two works, is preferable to the idea that this is coincidence.

---

[13] The figures here are based on Mark having 666 verses, omitting Mk 16.9–20, and John having 867 verses, omitting Jn 7.53–8.11.

The revelation of the hidden Messiah

In this chapter, I have attempted to argue that John's familiarity with the Synoptics makes better sense than the idea of mutually shared traditions by giving examples of literary influence beginning with words and sentences, moving then to entire pericopae, and ultimately to whole gospels.[14] There is, however, something still more fundamental. John shares Mark's basic literary conceit that the story is one in which Jesus' identity is hidden only to be retrospectively understood after the resurrection. Just as Kähler's 'passion narrative with an extended introduction' gets forgotten when it comes to John, so too William Wrede's *Messianic Secret* is all too often focused solely on Mark.[15] In some ways, this is unsurprising given the boldness of Jesus' public pronouncements in John, which we rightly stress in our introductory lectures in a bid to make sure that our students have grasped the differences between the Synoptics and John. But once again we are in danger of taking our own propaganda too seriously. Despite the apparently public revelations in John, the evangelist repeatedly depicts Jesus as a hidden Messiah. There are three elements to the way that John configures this: (a) There are insiders who understand and outsiders who do not; (b) Jesus hides himself from the crowds; and these are resolved by (c) the hermeneutical key of the resurrection.

(a) Insiders and outsiders

John divides Jesus' audience into two. There are those who believe – who perceive Jesus' identity and for whom Jesus' speeches make sense – and there are others who are hostile to Jesus – who fail to understand his speeches, thinking him either blasphemous or incomprehensible. Examples are manifold, but John 10.24–27 illustrates the two groups effectively:

> So the Judeans gathered around him and said to him, 'How long will you keep us in suspense? If you are the Messiah, tell us plainly.' 25 Jesus answered, 'I have told you, and you do not believe. The works that I do in my Father's name testify to me; 26 but you do not believe, because you do not belong to my sheep. 27 My sheep hear my voice. I know them, and they follow me.'

---

[14] One of the strengths of Andrew T. Lincoln, *The Gospel According to St John* (BNTC, 4; London: Continuum, 2005), is that as well as word, verse and pericope level comparisons, he looks at larger motifs; see, for example, his summary comment, 'While there are some instances of similarities with Synoptic material, where an equally strong case for John's use of Synoptic-like independent tradition might be made, this commentary argues that the much stronger case is that John knows the Synoptic Gospels themselves. The case becomes even stronger when not simply isolated pericopes are compared, as is frequently done, but when whole units of material or whole motifs are also taken into account, as will be indicated below' (p. 32).

[15] William Wrede, *Das Messiasgeheimnis in den Evangelien: Zugleich ein Beitrag zum Verständnis des Markusevangeliums* (Göttingen: Vandenhoeck & Ruprecht, 1901); English edn: William Wrede, *The Messianic Secret* (Cambridge: James Clarke and Co, 1971). But for exceptions, see John Ashton, *Understanding the Fourth Gospel* (2nd edn; Oxford: Oxford University Press, 2007), 207–11, Troels Engberg-Pedersen, *John and Philosophy: A New Reading of the Fourth Gospel* (Oxford: Oxford University Press, 2017), 315–20, and works cited in notes 16 and 18 below. Wrede himself did not, of course, see the Messianic Secret motif as Mark's literary creation (*Messiasgeheimnis*, 145).

In other words, in spite of Jesus' bold declarations, many of his hearers simply cannot hear what he is saying. This functions in a way similar to the 'parable secret' in Mark 4.10–12: 'To you has been given the secret . . . but to those outside, everything comes in parables'. Indeed, John shares with Mark (and the other Synoptists) the quotation of Isa. 6.10, about those whose hearts have been hardened (Jn 12.39–40; cf. Mk 4.11–13), in a very similar context. It could be argued that John's Gospel not only uses but also improves on the way that Mark configures the secrecy theme. Whereas Mark's disciples all appear to remain ignorant, and are still absent at the end of the gospel, John's disciples ultimately do understand who Jesus is. John's insiders/outsiders motif improves on Mark's by properly contrasting the understanding disciples with the confused outsiders.

(b) The hidden Messiah

Just as Jesus often withdraws himself in Mark, so too Jesus frequently hides himself in John:[16]

> But after his brothers had gone to the festival, then he also went, not publicly but as it were in secret. The Judeans were looking for him at the festival and saying, 'Where is he?'
>
> John 7.10–11

> After Jesus had said this, he departed and hid from them. Although he had performed so many signs in their presence, they did not believe in him.
>
> John 12.36b–37[17]

In the latter case, the passage combines the hidden Messiah motif with the insiders/outsiders motif – Jesus hides himself (12.36), and while hidden, the narrator steps forward to expound Isaiah 53.1 and Isaiah 6.10 (12.37–43). In other words, these are aspects of the same phenomenon, according to which Jesus' identity is revealed only to those he chooses, and only when the time is right.[18]

---

[16] On the hidden Messiah motif, see especially the helpful discussion in Susan Miller, '"Among You Stands One Whom You Do Not Know" (John 1:26): The Use of the Tradition of the Hidden Messiah in John's Gospel', in *The Ways That Often Parted: Essays in Honor of Joel Marcus*, ed. Lori Baron, Jill Hicks-Keeton and Matthew Thiessen (Atlanta, GA: Society of Biblical Literature, 2018), 243–63, and literature cited there. Although the feature is occasionally noted in Johannine scholarship, it is rarely seen as deriving from Mark's redactional presentation of the motif. See also note 18 below.

[17] See also 7.25–31, 8.59, 10.6, 11.54, and 12.36.

[18] Cf. Mark W. G. Stibbe, 'The Elusive Christ: A New Reading of the Fourth Gospel', *JSNT* 44 (1991): 19–37, especially 25: 'The constant emphasis in Johannine scholarship on Jesus the revealer needs challenging precisely for this reason. The Jesus of John's story is just as much the concealer as the revealer; just as much the one who conceals truth as the one who discloses it.' Stibbe hints that John's 'elusive Christ' may have been influenced by Mark's characterization of Jesus (pp. 32–33).

(c) The hermeneutical key: The Resurrection

In John, just as in the Synoptics, the resurrection marks the turning point for the full revelation of Jesus' identity, the hermeneutical key to the gospel, which the readers already possess, without which the characters in the drama are doomed to confusion. The key passage in Mark famously occurs at the conclusion of the Transfiguration story (Mk 9.9–10), where 'resurrection' is defined as the key turning point, but the same idea is developed in Luke, who adds the element of 'remembering' that now becomes important in John:

> 'Why are you looking for the living among the dead? 6 He is not here, but has been raised! <u>Remember</u> how he spoke to you while he was still in Galilee, 7 saying that the Son of Man must be delivered into the hands of men who are sinners, and be crucified, and on the third day rise?' 8 <u>And they remembered his words</u> …
>
> Luke 24.5–8

> After he was raised from the dead, <u>his disciples remembered</u> that he had said this; and they believed the scripture and the word that Jesus had spoken.
>
> John 2.22

> His disciples did not understand these things at first; but when Jesus was glorified, then <u>they remembered</u> that these things had been written of him and had been done to him.
>
> John 12.16

Like Luke, John makes the Markan motif more coherent, with disciples who do succeed, ultimately, in understanding Jesus' identity and mission, as they interpret through 'remembering', in the new light of the resurrection.

Hans Conzelmann once said that the Messianic Secret was the hermeneutical presupposition of the gospel genre.[19] Whether or not one accepts Conzelmann's assumption that the canonical gospels are *sui generis*, his insight makes sense of the very nature of the Synoptics and John, gospels that are obsessed with Jesus' death while explaining his life by focusing on the resurrection, and taking it as the reader's key to the whole.[20]

---

[19] Hans Conzelmann, 'Present and Future in the Synoptic Tradition', *Journal for Theology and the Church* 5 (1968): 26–44 (43).

[20] Cf. Engberg-Pedersen, *John as Philosophy*, 319, 'If one believes (as one should) that John must have taken over (and developed) from Mark the whole genre of the gospel narrative as this had been created by the latter, one must surely also agree that John has taken over and developed the much more specific theme of the Messianic secret that constitutes the "inner form" in Mark of the genre of the gospel narrative, the theme that drives the story to its conclusion.'

Conclusion: From tradition to gospel

I have attempted to suggest that the significant literary parallels between the Synoptics and John are sufficient to awaken us to the possibility that Dodd, and the greats who followed in his wake, like Raymond Brown, J. Louis Martyn, Ernst Haenchen and John Ashton, who would only ever go as far as to say that John must have used 'Synoptic-like' traditions, may have underestimated the extent of John's familiarity with Matthew, Mark and Luke. The key word here is 'literary'. The most striking parallels between John and the Synoptics occur at the literary level, from sentences in verbatim agreement, to words in redactional reworkings of Mark, to parallel pericope forms where John becomes a fourth Synoptic gospel, to the very structure of the Fourth Gospel, and all this in addition to John sharing Mark's fundamental literary conceit, of the hidden Messiah whose identity is only understood retrospectively through the hermeneutic of the resurrection.

To maintain John's independence from the Synoptics, one has to maintain that there were a surprising number of coincidences, floating on the swirling seas of oral tradition. At the same time, it requires the emergence of John's Gospel to be without clear literary precedent, regarding Mark's way of telling the Jesus story not as an innovation but as normative and inevitable. This is not to play down John's profound differences from the Synoptics but to suggest, instead, that differences are not diagnostic of independence but of the extent of John's creative, dramatic, christological transformation of the Synoptic source material that is at the root of his project.

8

Beyond History: How John Transcends Mark and Ancient Historiography[1]

Eve-Marie Becker

Mark, Luke and John in light of ancient historiography

In various ways, Mark and Luke match the conceptual and literary demands of ancient historiography.[2] As the inventor of the 'gospel genre', Mark defines its outline as follows: he chooses prose style for his composition; he provides a coherent narrative about events that are situated in the past; he uses and re-arranges historical (e.g., passion narrative) and documentary (Mk 15.26) sources; he oscillates in his narrative between myth and history, proclamation and narration (see already Mk 1.1, 14–15); he provides meta-historical explanations (e.g., Mk 8.31); he applies a wide range of literary elements and rhetorical strategies that are known from or that are even typical of ancient history-writing, such as: *brevitas*, *prosopopoiia*, prosopography, emotions, fictionalization and so forth; he includes speeches (Mk 4; 13) in order to interpret the story in retrospective and prospective terms (esp. Mk 13); and he invents a concept of spatiality (Galilee, Jerusalem) that allows for the configuration of a specific *chronotope*.

Luke, one of the earliest successors of Mark (see Lk. 1.1–4), continues and further develops the narrative outline he finds in Mark: he chooses prose style; he provides a coherent narrative about events that are situated in the past; he uses and re-arranges historical and documentary sources; he provides a range of synchronisms by which he connects his story to world history (Lk. 1.5; 2.1; 3.1); he provides even more meta-historical explanations than Mark on various levels of the narrative (e.g., Lk. 1.1–4; 16.16; Acts 1.8); he enriches the set of historiographical elements known from Mark with further elements from ancient literature, such as: *diegesis*, *prosopopoiia*, prosopography, emotions, fictionalization and so forth; he includes speeches (Lk. 6.20ff.; speeches in Acts), delivered by various protagonists in order continuously to

---

[1] The article was originally published as 'Beyond History: How the Fourth Gospel Transcends Ancient Historiography', in *Biblische Notizen* 182 (2019): 111–21. The version of the article in this volume is slightly expanded and revised. The editors of *Biblische Notizen* are to be thanked for allowing the reissuing of the article.
[2] See the following: Eve-Marie Becker, *The Birth of Christian History: Memory and Time from Mark to Luke-Acts* (New Haven, CT: Yale University Press, 2017), especially chapter 2.

interpret the story in retrospective and prospective terms; and he invents a concept of spatiality (Galilee, Jerusalem, Rome) that is forcefully implemented by itineraries (Lk. 9.51ff.; Acts 13ff.).

Two observations of how Mark shapes the gospel genre and how Luke adopts and further develops it are important. First, when counting Mark and Luke–Acts among historiographical literature in a broader sense, this classification does not imply that Mark or Luke–Acts are seen as *bruta facta* accounts. The literary concept of historiography and the historical concept of 'historicity' in a modern sense have to be kept distinct. Second, it seems evident that Luke, in his two-volume project, takes up Mark's pre-historiographical outline intentionally and aims at improving it.[3] Mark's early reception history, as reflected in Luke, thus gives some indication of how the earliest gospel narrative *could* have been understood: as a (pre-)historiographical account that allows for, from Luke's point of view, further reworking according to historiography. We have to keep both observations in mind when moving on now to the Fourth Gospel.

How does John fit into the picture of the birth of historiography in early Christianity? The Fourth Gospel also follows the basic patterns of history-writing as defined by Mark and further developed by Luke: John provides a prose narrative that contains a story line (1.19ff.), told mainly in past tense(s); the story consists of a more or less cohesive sequence of narrative units, which are – at least on the level of the macro-structure – put in a chronological and causal order; in arranging his narrative and dialogic materials, John keeps the crucial structure of Mark and Luke's plot: during Jesus' powerful ministry of teaching and performing signs, the Son of God critically interferes with the Jewish authorities of his time so that he is finally sentenced to death (esp. 11.47ff.). Thus, in several ways, John follows the narrative concept of how to write an *event*-based and *person*-centered account of history – as found in Mark and Luke. As it is the case in Mark and Luke, also the Johannine narrative serves both to memorialize the past and to orientate it to the present and future needs of Christ-believing communities.

It is only reasonable then that in more recent years the scholarly interest in relating John to the Synoptic Gospels and ancient historiography has significantly grown – after a period of time where the Fourth Gospel was treated rather differently, either in a conceptual distance to the Synoptic Gospels (Rudolf Bultmann), or – even because of its huge affinity to Mark – as a piece of rather fictitious literature (William Wrede).[4]

---

[3] In the monograph I show how the concept of early Christian history writing evolved especially from Mark to Luke. Matthew, as a recipient of Mark and a contemporary of Luke, is mainly considered to offer a narrative outline whose conceptual interests are less historiography-oriented, and in that respect differs from Luke-Acts (e.g., Becker, *Birth of Christian History*, 83–85).

[4] In earlier scholarship, John was mostly separated from the Synoptic Gospels (Rudolf Bultmann), and thus from historiography; and even when it was related closely to the Synoptics, especially to Mark, scholars basically wanted to reveal the fictitious character of both gospel writings (William Wrede): 'Man betrachte Markus durch ein starkes Vergrösserungsglas, und man hat etwa eine Schriftstellerei, wie sie Johannes zeigt': W. Wrede, *Das Messiasgeheimnis in den Evangelien: Zugleich ein Beitrag zum Verständnis des Markusevangeliums* (Göttingen: Vandenhoeck & Ruprecht, 1901), 145. 'Natürlich denke ich nicht daran, den Unterschied zwischen ihm [= Markus] und Johannes zu verwischen... er steht, was den realen Boden der Geschichte Jesu... betrifft, ganz anders da, er hat ein wesentlich anderes Verhältnis zur Tradition als Johannes' (p. 144). The results for reading John in light of

The contemporary, more explicit, interest in relating John to the Synoptic Gospels [5] *and* to the field of ancient historiography[6] also profits from the narrative and the linguistic turn in that it helps us to overcome simple distinctions between ancient (fictitious) literature on the one side and historiography on the other. We have learned to see how even in the field of ancient historiography fact and fiction interfere (G. W. Bowersock et al.).[7] According to Jean Zumstein the tension between history and fiction in the Fourth Gospel is caused by the concept of a '*nachösterliche(r) Anamnese*', where three types of storylines – Jesus-story, story about the pre-existent *logos*, and history of the addressees – are conflated.[8] While the conflation of various narrative perspectives might in general be a typical element of ancient historiography, the programmatic concept of 'melting the temporal horizons' ('Verschmelzung der Zeithorizonte zwischen vorösterlicher und nachösterlicher Zeit')[9] of the narrative outline has to be seen as a rather specific Johannine feature. It seems, thus, as if John draws on historiography-like conceptual features – which he possibly knew from earlier Synoptic Gospel accounts – by 'fissuring' or breaking open the concept of history-writing at the same time.

As is evident from these preliminary remarks, the multifaceted scholarly discourse about 'John and history'[10] is still a complex one – especially when discussed from the point of view of Synoptic Gospel studies: it can neither be resolved by strictly separating the Fourth Gospel from Mark and Luke, nor by reading it as a continuation of the Synoptic gospel outline. In this paper, I shall explore how John, by basically upholding the gospel concept, transforms it at the same time, and how and why this re-shaping challenges the concept of ancient historiography.

We shall see *how* and *why* John 11 in particular provides a perception of time and history that transcends the narrative concept of gospel writing as historiography and

---

ancient history-writing were pretty much the same: John was either – because of its conceptual distance to the Synoptics (R. Bultmann) – distinguished generically from the early Christian concept of historiography; or – because of its literary affinity to Mark, understood as a piece of rather fictitious literature (W. Wrede) – it was likewise treated as fictitious literature, in any case not as a piece of historiography.

[5] Cf., e.g., Michael Labahn and Manfred Lang, 'Johannes und die Synoptiker: Positionen und Impulse seit 1990', in *Kontexte des Johannesevangeliums: Das vierte Evangelium in religions- und traditionsgeschichtlicher Perspektive*, ed. Jörg Frey and Udo Schnelle (WUNT, 175; Tübingen: Mohr Siebeck, 2004), 443–515.

[6] Cf. also Eve-Marie Becker, 'John 13 as Counter-Memory: How the Fourth Gospel Revises Early Christian Historiography', in *The Gospel of John as Genre Mosaic*, ed. by Kasper Bro Larsen (SANt, 3; Göttingen: Vandenhoeck & Ruprecht, 2015), 269–81.

[7] Glen W. Bowersock, *Fiction as History: Nero to Julian* (Berkeley, CA: University of California Press, 1994). Cf. Jean Zumstein, *Das Johannesevangelium* (KEK, 3; Göttingen: Vandenhoeck & Ruprecht, 2016), 37: 'Eine historische Darstellung, die immer ein Konstrukt ist, kommt nicht umhin, Geschichte und Fiktion miteinander zu verflechten. Im Gebiet der Geschichtsschreibung entstammt die Fiktion also nicht primär der Phantasie, sondern gehört in den Bereich der Interpretation.'

[8] Zumstein, *Johannesevangelium*, 37.

[9] Zumstein, *Johannesevangelium*, 37.

[10] The 'John and history'-discourse entails questions about the historicity of the Fourth Gospel and/or the image of the historical Jesus as provided herein (e.g., James H. Charlesworth, 'The Historical Jesus in the Fourth Gospel: A Paradigm Shift?', *JSHJ* 8 [2010]: 3–46; Paul Foster, 'Memory, Orality, and the Fourth Gospel', *JSHJ* 12 [2014]: 165–83) or quests about John's literary outline and genre (e.g., Richard Bauckham, 'Historiographical Characteristics of the Gospel of John', *NTS* 53 [2007]: 17–36).

notions of time as implemented herein. However, John 11 is more than a simple test case for investigating John's approach to history and time: in John 11 the gospel story reaches its actual peak.

John 11 as the turning point of the narrative

John 11.1–44/57 is to be understood as one of the most important passages in the Fourth Gospel since it has a crucial function for the overall gospel outline and its construction of time.[11] Accordingly, scholars describe the passage as: 'der Höhepunkt des öffentlichen Wirkens Jesu und zugleich der Anlaß des endgültigen Todesbeschlusses der Juden (Jn 11.53). Bewußt wurde das größte Wunder im Neuen Testament von Johannes an diesen Ort gestellt'.[12] John 11 builds many interconnections, or narrative links, to the rest of the gospel narrative: (1) in terms of its macro-context, John 11 can be seen as the climax of Jesus' public ministry, and hereby, it basically sums up chapters 1–10; (2) in John 11, vv. 4, 8, 16, 25, 40 refer to the passion story,[13] and thus prepare the reader for chapters 18–19; (3) John 11.25–26 appears to be the climax of ἐγώ εἰμι-words in John; and together with (4) the miracle story, more specifically: the topic of resurrection in John 11 points to the Easter stories in John 20; (5) the raising of Lazarus alludes to discourses about resurrection in John 5–6;[14] (6) especially a verse like John 11.2 – if it is not simply understood as a 'späte Leserglosse..., die erst durch Abschreibertätigkeit in den Text geriet',[15] – calls for special attention: John obviously writes retrospectively;[16] in chapter 11 he anticipates the narrative of chapter 12 by either presupposing the knowledge of the tradition among his readers (Mk 14.3–9; Mt. 26.6–13) or simply by preparing his audience already for the later reading of chapter 12.[17]

Despite the variety of narrative links between John 11 and the rest of the gospel narrative, the textual interpretation soon uncovers many obstacles. We have to deal with a comparatively long textual unit in which – basically – three types of literary forms are mixed up: a miracle story (11.38–44), revelatory words (esp. vv. 25–26; 40) or dialogic scenes (esp. vv. 21–27), and various narrative elements (e.g., vv. 1–2; 19). The complexity of the overall narrative, which is mirrored by various literary

---

[11] Cf. Klaus Wengst, *Das Johannesevangelium: 2. Teilband: Kapitel 11–21* (ThKNT, 4.2; Stuttgart: Kohlhammer, 2001), 11: 'Kap. 11 hat einen wichtigen Platz in der Gesamtkonzeption des Evangeliums'. On the concept of time in John 11, see now Olivia L. Rahmsdorf, *Zeit und Ethik im Johannesvangelium: Theoretische, methodische und exegetische Annäherungen an die Gunst der Stunde* (WUNT, 2/488; Tübingen: Mohr Siebeck, 2019), 279ff.
[12] Udo Schnelle, *Das Evangelium nach Johannes* (3rd edn, ThHNT, 4; Leipzig: Evang. Verl.-Anst., 2004), 208.
[13] Cf. Schnelle, *Evangelium nach Johannes*, 208.
[14] Cf. Yoshimi Azuma, 'Reading John 11:1–12:11 through the Lens of the Resurrection in 1 Enoch' (PhD dissertation, Emory University, Atlanta, GA, 2015).
[15] Jürgen Becker, *Das Evangelium nach Johannes: Kapitel 11–21* (2nd edn, ÖTBK, 4/2; Gütersloh, Würzburg: Gütersloher Verl.-Haus Mohn, 1984), 345.
[16] Cf. Wengst, *Johannesevangelium*, 14.
[17] Cf. Wengst, *Johannesevangelium*, 14.

tensions,[18] therefore has inspired various theories on *Literar- und Quellenkritik*[19] that aim to reconstruct the tentative initial tradition behind the textual unit.[20] Even though scholars do not necessarily hold any longer to earlier source theories in which the miracle story is placed within the *Semeia*-source (SQ), there still seems to be a tendency to consider the resurrection story as the initial part – the nucleus – of the tradition behind John 11.[21]

However, chapter 11 does not only provide interconnection to the rest of the gospel narrative, and it does not only give reason to engage in source criticism. The chapter also raises literary issues of intertextuality since it alludes most evidently to the Synoptic Gospels in multiple ways. Hartwig Thyen suggests that John 11 should be read as a 'Palimpsest über synoptischen Texten'.[22] In other words, John 11 is composed of a variety of intertextual relations, especially to Mark and Luke. I will only mention four of the most important of these relations:

a. By referring to concretely named figures – Lazarus, Mary and Martha – John 11 is reminiscent of two different kinds of stories that the evangelist knew from the Lukan Gospel (Lk. 16.19-31; 10.38-42).
b. The special character of the miracle story in John 11 – the raising of the dead Lazarus – reminds us of similar stories that we find in Mk 5.21 par. (Mt. 9.18ff.; Lk. 8.40ff.), Lk. 7.11-17 and Acts 9.36-42; 20.7-12.[23] However, we will see in a short while that John 11 by far exceeds the revivification stories told in the Synoptic Gospels and Acts. John in fact intends to allude to those stories by surpassing them.
c. If we take into account the close connection between John 11 and 12, we have to name further recourses to the Synoptic Gospels: the anointing story (Jn 12.3ff.) then can be seen as overlapping with Mk 14.3-9 par., Mt. 26.6-13 or Lk. 7.36-50.
d. On a more abstract level, we can finally see how John in chapter 11 further develops the motif of incomprehension or misunderstanding (cf. Mary and

---

[18] According to Jürgen Becker, there are three types of tensions: (a) tension between vv. 25-26 and the general topic of resurrection stories; (b) breaks within the narrative: vv. 2, 4, 16, 24-26, 40; (c) divergent information, e.g., about Lazarus (v.1 versus vv. 2, 19, 21, 23, 32, 39); references to Mary and Martha (v.1 versus vv. 20-27; 5, 19); v.17 versus v. 30, 38: Becker, *Evangelium nach Johannes*, 344.

[19] Cf. on this, e.g., Michael Labahn, *Jesus als Lebensspender: Untersuchungen zu einer Geschichte der johanneischen Tradition anhand ihrer Wundergeschichten* (BZNW, 98; Berlin: de Gruyter, 1999), 395ff.

[20] Jürgen Becker tries to distinguish between different layers behind the textual composition: Cf. Becker, *Evangelium nach Johannes*, 344-46. Becker reconstructs a miracle story as the '*Basistext*': vv. 1, 3, 17, 38-39, 41, 43-44 (345). He works with a model of a 'dreifachen Schichtung des Textes...: der Vorlage für die SQ aus der mündlichen Tradition, der Stufe der SQ und der Ebene von E' (p. 344). Udo Schnelle separates tradition and redaction throughout the chapter: Cf. Schnelle, *Evangelium nach Johannes*, 208-10. He distinguishes in detail between tradition (e.g., vv. 1, 2, 3), and redaction (e.g., in v. 4).

[21] Cf. Becker, *Evangelium nach Johannes*, 345; Labahn, *Jesus als Lebensspender*, 434ff.

[22] Cf. Hartwig Thyen, 'Die Erzählung' von den bethanischen Geschwistern (Joh 11,1-12,9) als "Palimpsest" über synoptischen Texten', in Hartwig Thyen, *Studien zum Corpus Iohanneum* (WUNT, 214; Tübingen: Mohr Siebeck, 2007), 182-212.

[23] Cf. Labahn, *Jesus als Lebensspender*, 437ff. Cf., more comprehensively, Stephanie M. Fischbach, *Totenerweckungen: Zur Geschichte einer Gattung* (FzB, 69; Würzburg: Echter, 1992).

Martha figures) which we find already in Mark in various forms (e.g., Mk 8.32–33).

What do we conclude from these observations?

1. The narrative complexity of John 11 obviously reflects the wide-ranging narrative function of this chapter for the overall gospel outline (Jn 1–20).
2. The variety of textual interrelations and interlinkages to the so-called Synoptic Gospels[24] shows how John wants to palimpsest Mark and Luke. Having said this, we have to go one step further.
3. We have to expose the narrative characteristics of John 11 in order to see how far John's composition follows the Synoptic molding of historiography. The motif of delay in John 11 will be of specific significance since it reflects John's particular notion of time and history.

The motif of delay in John 11

In narrative terms, the story about the raising of Lazarus in John 11 is not presented stringently. Jesus accomplishes the *semeion* of a supposed healing with huge delay (11.4, 14; cf. also 11.21, 32). Meanwhile, his friend Lazarus who was mortally ill has died. Instead of healing Lazarus, Jesus has to raise him from the dead. What role does the motif of delay thus play in the narrative?

Some scholars offer an explanation based on narratology with its impact on the conceptual interrelation of narrative and narrated time: Jesus' delay then appears to be a tactic (*Verzögerungstaktik*) reflecting John's intentional narrative strategy,[25] probably created by the evangelist himself. Other scholars tackle the question about the motif of delay on the basis of form criticism: by separating the Lazarus story from healing accounts (*Heilungsgeschichte*), John 11 is defined more specifically as a resurrection story (*Auferweckungswunder*).[26] When assuming the latter, the so-called *Verzögerungsmotiv* is seen as an initial part of the miracle story,[27] which can supposedly even be traced back to Mark (Mk 5.21–43). It is argued, then, that Mark would already

---

[24] From here further questions arise: In which way does John compile various motifs or traditions, or allude to them? How does he adhere to the general narrative outline he might have found especially in Mark and Luke? How much does his way of perceiving and transforming the gospel concept lead to its re-shape, which consequently brings about a transcendence of the historiography-oriented gospel outline as defined by Mark and further developed by Luke?

[25] It is understood as a 'bewusste Erzählstrategie..., bei der Erzählzeit und erzählte Zeit in ein spezifisches Verhältnis gebracht werden': Ruben Zimmermann, 'Narrative Ethik im Johannesevangelium am Beispiel der Lazarus-Perikope Joh 11', in *Narrativität und Theologie im Johannesevangelium*, ed. Jörg Frey and Uta Poplutz (BThSt, 130; Neukirchen-Vluyn: Neukirchener Verlag, 2012), 133–70, especially 159–160: 'Während der sensationslustige... Leser nur auf das Ziel, auf das Nachher... ausgerichtet ist, zwingt die retardierende Erzählweise immer mehr im Augenblick zu verharren' (p. 160).

[26] Cf. discussion in Labahn, *Jesus als Lebensspender*, 441–42.

[27] So Labahn, *Jesus als Lebensspender*, 442.

be operating with the motif of delay since the request to heal Jairus' daughter (5.23) likewise becomes an issue of resurrection; because Jesus is detained on the way (5.25ff.) he will find the girl already deceased (5.35).

However, the form-critical based interpretation of the motif of delay in John 11 falls too short for two reasons. First, form criticism assumes that there existed a specific type of resurrection miracle in ancient literature. But if we look at all texts usually related to such a type of miracle narrative, we see that these texts only tell *revivification* stories, not resurrection stories. This demarcation applies to the Hebrew Bible/Septuagint and early Jewish stories (1 Kings 17.17–24; 2 Kings 4.18–37; 13.20–21; *4 Ezra* 9.38–10.4) as much to revivification narratives in the Greco-Roman literature (Iamblichus, *Bab.* 2.700; Philostratus, *Vit.* 4.45; Apuleius, *Flor.* 19; *Met.* 2.21–30)[28] and in early Christian texts (see above),[29] including Mk 5.35ff.[30] In contrast to all these stories, John 11 tells an actual resurrection narrative, since Lazarus was already in the tomb for four days (Jn 11.17, 39). Therefore, we cannot understand the motif of delay in John 11 against the background of revivification stories; we must relate it to a different area of discourse.

Second, the motif of delay itself is not at all an issue in Mk 5.21ff. The claim that Jesus would have come 'too late' is not explicated; the fact that he is detained on his way to Jairus' house is basically caused by Mark's technique of 'sandwiching': Mark includes the healing of the woman suffering from haemorrhages (5.25) as an interruption to the previous narrative. In terms of literary techniques John might have been stimulated by Mark's narrative style without finding the motif of delay as such in the Markan story.

To sum up: the motif of delay in John 11 can neither be traced back to an inventory of motifs inherited from ancient resurrection miracles – since such a group of a narrative/text-type does not exist; nor is this motif shaped by Mark 5. Rather, John creates this motif himself in order to refer to another area of discourse: Mary and Martha's explicit statement about Jesus' delay – 'if you had been here, my brother would not have died' (Jn 11.21, 32) – can be seen not only as John's attempt to deal with Jesus' absence,[31] but rather as his reply to the famous early Christian debate about the delay of the *parousia* (e.g., 1 Thess. 4.13; Mk 13.13ff.; 2 Pet. 3.8–9; 1 Jn 2.28).[32]

Within the frame of discussing the destiny of those Christ-believers who (will) have died *before* Christ returns, John argues that the earthly Jesus – as the incarnated *logos* – has already conquered death by raising Lazarus. In order to achieve this, Jesus must intentionally delay his arrival. Otherwise he could not have accomplished the *semeion* of raising the dead. As a consequence, speculations about time and the coming of the *parousia* (1 Thess. 5.2; Mk 13.33) are useless. It is only by having faith in Christ (Jn 11.25–26) that the Christ-believer will instead fully participate in the eschatological gift of eternal life.

---

[28] *PGM* IV 155–285 does not contain a story at all, but gives instruction for an evocation ritual.
[29] *GMk* frgm. 1–2 might be an exception.
[30] Accordingly, in classical contributions to New Testament form history (Klaus Berger; Gerd Theißen) John 11 is typically not considered when it comes to miracle stories – the chapter is rather left out.
[31] Cf. Wendy E. S. North '"Lord, if you had been here…" (John 11.21): The Absence of Jesus and Strategies of Consolation in the Fourth Gospel', *JSNT* 36 (2013): 39–52.
[32] On the motif of delay in the frame of the early Christian discourse about *parousia*, see, more comprehensively, Eve-Marie Becker, *Der verspätete Jesus: Joh 11 als Parusieerzählung?* (in preparation).

John's narrative about the miracle of raising Lazarus from the dead – a miracle accomplished in the past – provides no less than eschatological salvation for present believers (see also Jn 20.30–31). John 11 thus is reaching beyond the aim of providing consolation to present readers:[33] the story is a good, if not the best, example of how the Fourth Gospel – by merging past, present and future time – denies the concept of a history-oriented gospel narrative as we find it in Mark and Luke. The story about Jesus' ministry (past) is conflated with the current need to make sense of the delay of the *parousia* (present) in order not to give up faith in Jesus' life-giving eschatological ministry (future).

John 11 and the transcendence of history and time

In many ways the Fourth Gospel continues the narrative gospel outline as defined by Mark and further developed by Luke (and Acts).[34] Hereby, John confirms the idea that the gospel story – as an account of Jesus' earthly ministry – has to be put in a historical framing that is re-told in historiographical-like terms. Comparable to Mark and Luke, a miracle story also functions for John as a historiographical element of an event-based and person-centred narrative about Jesus' ministry. Evidently, John is persuaded by the basic narrative outline he finds in Mark and Luke. In John 11 he even goes so far as to palimpsest both gospels far beyond simply adopting a single narrative like Mk 5.21ff. (see above).

However, in many ways John also fissures the Markan and Lukan gospel concept as a history-oriented account. This becomes clear not only in John 13, but also in chapters 14–16: elsewhere I have argued how John – according to Foucault[35] – in the story about the foot washing 'applies a paradigm of counter-memory' to a historiographical narrative (cf. Jn 13 in contrast to Mk 14par. Lk. 22). Later, especially in the farewell speeches (Jn 14–16), we even 'encounter a dissolution of temporality': the speeches are 'illustrative in that the temporal setting oscillates between "now-then-again"' (e.g., Jn 16.16). In chapters 14–16, John basically 'abrogates a perception of time based on linearity and causality ... he replaces history with Christology – John may in fact deploy a revelatory concept of Christology as a counter-memorial attack on Lukan historiography'.[36]

As this essay has sought to demonstrate, what can be said about John 13 and 14–16 is also supported by a more detailed analysis of John 11. Even though John in chapter 11 deliberately alludes to the Synoptic Gospels in multiple ways (see above), he goes further and, as a consequence, counteracts the Synoptic concept of a historiography-oriented gospel account: by presenting a *resurrection* story as an event that happened in the past, John places the eschatological time awaited by Christ-believers to Jesus'

---

[33] So North, '"Lord, if you had been here"', 39–43.
[34] On Matthew, see note 1 above.
[35] Cf. M. Foucault, 'Counter-Memory: The Philosophy of Difference', in *Language, Counter-Memory, Practice: Selected Essays and Interviews*, ed. D. F. Bouchard and S. Simon (Ithaca, NY: Cornell University Press, 1977), 113–96.
[36] All quotations taken from Becker, *Birth of Christian History*, 145–46.

earthly ministry; in that John views belief (πιστεύειν) to be the sufficient and ultimate attitude of anticipating God's salvation in Christ, he envisages full participation in eschatological existence already now for the readers of his book. Consequently, time, temporality and history are once again dissolved. By dismantling the narrative principles of linearity and causality in and beyond chapter 11, John in fact counteracts the Markan and Lukan gospel concept and develops a counter-concept of early Christian memory.[37]

It might well be that Mark, Luke and John are equally challenged by the early Christian eschatological discourse about the delay of the *parousia* and the fate of the dead (cf. also Mk 9.1 par. Lk. 9.27). Nevertheless, all three authors differ significantly in how they respond to these questions: while Mark is primarily eager to narrate the past by perceiving the acceleration of time (e.g., Mk 1.14–15), Luke intends to map out the gospel story as a certain period of a *historia continua*. John is the sole author to discuss explicitly the issue of delay. Jesus' delay is shown to be a prospect for faith rather than a contestation of it: it allows for a miracle story (Jn 11) in which the *future* eschatological expectation of the resurrection of the dead – a question most urgently relevant to *present* readers – becomes a story about the *past*.

At first sight, it may seem that by doing so, John enriches the narrative patterns of a historiography-like gospel account: future hope is transformed into a past tense miracle story. What the evangelist finally achieves, however, is quite the opposite: by merging past, future and present time(s) as he does in chapter 11, he in fact once more fissures the concept of gospel writing as a historiography that proceeds linearly *within* time and history. Rather, in chapter 11, John gives up linearity as the basic principle of historiography and departs from the Synoptic route of gospel writing. As a result, the Fourth Gospel paves the way for the genre of revelatory literature.

---

[37] On counter-memory cf. in general, Becker, *Birth of Christian History*, 19–20.

9

The Beginnings of Mark and John: What Exactly Should Be Compared? Some Hermeneutical Questions and Observations

Christina Hoegen-Rohls

Reading the beginnings of Mark and John may spontaneously provoke two opposing reactions: 'How many differences!', some will say. 'What similarities!', others will object. One may assume that both are correct. A closer look reveals that differences and similarities cannot be sharply distinguished. Looking for similarities, one also discovers differences within them. By highlighting differences, one finds in them analogies as well. In methodological terms, this shows that a close comparative reading of Mark and John requires both contrastive reading and combined reading – as Eve-Marie Becker and Anders Runesson have pointed out with regard to a comparative reading of Mark and Matthew.[1]

But to find sharp or fine distinctions between the beginnings of the Gospels of Mark and John, or to find similarities and analogies, we have to identify where the gospels actually begin. This is indeed my guiding question in the present chapter: where do the Gospels of Mark and John begin? In other words, what exactly should be compared when comparing their beginnings? I will examine some ways at answering this question. First, I will simply compare the opening sentences of both Mark and John as they are found in our text-critical editions of the Novum Testamentum Graece,[2] in order to ask what insights emerge from a comparison of this narrow text-base. Second, I will provocatively ask, as an interlude, whether the beginning of Mark's ἀρχὴ τοῦ εὐαγγελίου Ἰησοῦ Χριστοῦ is also present at the end of the text (Mk 16.7–8)? Suggesting a hermeneutical understanding of what is meant by a 'beginning', I will then ask: is there a hermeneutical *pendant* in John? Third, I will consider what insights we gain by comparing Mark 1.1–3 with John 1.1–5. Does Mark depict a heavenly scene

---

[1] Eve-Marie Becker and Anders Runesson (eds), *Mark and Matthew I: Comparative Readings: Understanding the Earliest Gospels in their First-Century Settings* (WUNT, 271; Tübingen: Mohr Siebeck, 2011), 2.
[2] Nestle-Aland, *Novum Testamentum Graece*. Based on the work of Eberhard and Erwin Nestle. Edited by Barbara and Kurt Aland, Johannes Karavidoppulos, Carlo M. Martini, Bruce M. Metzger; 28th edn. Edited by the Institute for New Testament Textual Research Münster/Westphalia under the direction of Holger Strutwolf, Stuttgart: Deutsche Bibelgesellschaft, 2012.

and the pre-existence of Jesus in his opening section? And what about the interpretation of the opening verses in John? Fourth, I will ask what results emerge when comparing the beginning of the gospel narratives, and so, for that purpose, it is important to clarify where the narratives of Mark and John do actually begin. And finally, with reference to this, I would like to ask what '*kephalaia*' might contribute to the question of where the beginnings of Mark and John are to be seen.

In the interest of the present volume, I will – with each of my five questions – try to observe how John's agreements with Mark and its deviations from Mark can be described and evaluated. What is John doing with Mark? A conclusion will bring together my observations, which may stimulate further discussion.

Comparing the first sentences of Mark and John (Mk 1.1; Jn 1.1)

Mk 1.1 Ἀρχὴ τοῦ εὐαγγελίου Ἰησοῦ Χριστοῦ [υἱοῦ θεοῦ].
The beginning of the gospel of Jesus Christ, the Son of God.[3]

Jn 1.1a Ἐν ἀρχῇ ἦν ὁ λόγος,
In the beginning was the Word,
1b καὶ ὁ λόγος ἦν πρὸς τὸν θεόν,
and the Word was with God,
1c καὶ θεὸς ἦν ὁ λόγος.
and the Word was God.

The first sentences of Mark and John offer an interesting analogy in their use of the term ἀρχή. The beginnings of both gospels begin with 'the beginning'. But what is meant by 'beginning' (ἀρχή) in Mark, and what is meant by 'beginning' (ἀρχή) in John? What, in each case, is the focus? In order to offer comparative observations on Mark and John, it is helpful to look at the way in which Harold Attridge approaches the comparison of the shepherd imagery in John and the Synoptics. He chooses an example from art history, saying: 'Both Renoir and Picasso created paintings, and did so using similar materials, in the same general cultural setting within a few years of one another, but the former's *Après le bain* (of 1910) and the latter's *Sitting Nude* (of 1908) display radically different visions of how to paint the female form. There is as much difference between John's Noble Shepherd (...) and the searching shepherd of Matthew and Luke as there is between impressionism and cubism.'[4] Building on this, it can be said: Mark and John create the beginnings of their gospels by using the same term ἀρχή, within the same general cultural setting, and yet they offer radically different visions of how to paint the beginning of the gospel form or the gospel genre. Mark paints the beginning of the gospel genre by highlighting the fact, that now – at the very moment, when the

---

[3] The English translations follow the New Revised Standard Version.
[4] Harold W. Attridge, 'Genre Bending in the Fourth Gospel' [first published in *JBL* 121 (2002): 3–21], in Harold W. Attridge, *Essays on John and Hebrews* (WUNT, 264; Tübingen: Mohr Siebeck, 2010), 61–78 (here 73).

writer begins to present his text and the readers begin to read it – the proclamation starts, that Jesus is the Christ, the Son of God. With his first sentence, even with his first word, Mark heightens his audience's awareness of never having been confronted before with such a proclamation. And John? John paints the beginning of the gospel genre by telling of the origin of the Logos. With special emphasis he brings his audience face to face with an outstanding sort of 'beginning', in which the Word was, was with God, and was God. With his first two sentences, even with his first two words, John makes clear that there is nothing that precedes this extraordinary beginning. And he makes it clear that '[t]here can be no speculation about how the Word came to be, for the Word simply was'.[5]

In comparing both models of gospel beginnings I will highlight four aspects. First, both Mark and John use the term ἀρχή without the definite article. Mark presents the term ἀρχή in the nominative, John in the dative case, linked with the preposition ἐν. A noun in the nominative case, used without the definite article, is located in 'the beginnings of Hosea, Proverbs, and Song of Solomon in the LXX and of Matthew and Revelation in NT',[6] acting as the title of a book. So 'Mark begins his work with a title',[7] specified by two attributive genitives in order to present the specific topic of his book: Jesus Christ.[8] And John? John begins his work not with a book-title, but with a new title for Jesus Christ himself: Logos.

Second, both Mark and John use the term ἀρχή in a temporal way.[9] With ἀρχή Mark indicates not only the title of his book, but also the very beginning of his book, that tells the story of Jesus. By doing so he possibly reflects on the fact that he is the first to tell that story in a literary form, and that he is interested in composing an original micro-genre related to the historiographical 'macro-genre' of '*Geschichtsdeutung*'.[10] So Mark, the initiator of a *genre sui generis*, reflects both the historical beginning of this new genre and the historical beginning of the good news, which began in the books of the prophets, was continued by the voice of John the Baptist, and fulfilled in the voice and person of Jesus. And John? John – to borrow from Harold Attridge's approach of genre bending[11] – bends the beginning of Mark's Gospel by signifying that the beginning of his book speaks about a beginning that lies beyond a book's beginning and also beyond any historical beginning of proclaiming good news. For the beginning – in which the Word was and was with God and was God – lies beyond the beginning of the world,

---

[5] Raymond E. Brown, *The Gospel According to John (I–XII)* (Anchor Bible, 29; Garden City, NY: Doubleday, 1966), 4.
[6] Joel Marcus, *Mark 1–8: A New Translation with Introduction and Commentary* (Anchor Bible, 27; New Haven, CT: Doubleday, 2000), 141.
[7] Marcus, *Mark 1–8*, 143.
[8] An overview over the possible meanings and functions of the expression ἀρχὴ τοῦ εὐαγγελίου is offered by Eve-Marie Becker in *Das Markus-Evangelium im Rahmen antiker Historiographie* (WUNT, 194; Tübingen: Mohr Siebeck, 2006), 105, 112. She emphasizes that, against the background of Israelite-Jewish and Graeco-Roman historiography, the expression in the context of Mark 1.1 acts as the beginning of the book ('Buchanfang'), the title of the book ('Buchtitel'), and the beginning (*initium*) of the presentation of events ('Beginn der Ereignisdarstellung').
[9] See also Becker, *Markus-Evangelium*, 112.
[10] See Eve-Marie Becker, *Der früheste Evangelist: Studien zum Markusevangelium* (WUNT, 380; Tübingen: Mohr Siebeck, 2017), 3–4.
[11] See note 4.

that means beyond history. In that beginning nothing exists except God and the Word. We usually call that Johannine beginning/ἀρχή *Ur-Anfang*, the very beginning, the first beginning, the primordial beginning. So John's ἀρχή surpasses Mark's ἀρχή.

Third, Mark, 'der früheste Evangelist', to quote Eve-Marie Becker,[12] designs and characterizes the gospel literature as a kerygmatic genre, creating an event-based narrative of good news. The main topic of this narrative is the close proximity of the Kingdom of God, the βασιλεία τοῦ θεοῦ, announced by the prophets and then by John the Baptist and proclaimed in and through Jesus' appearance and kerygma, culminating in the events of Easter morning. In Jesus' appearance and kerygma the Kingdom of God acquires physical closeness and earthly proximity of time and space. And John? John (in accordance with a broad consensus in Johannine scholarship regarding 'der späteste Evangelist') agrees with Mark's emphasis on the kerygmatic character of the gospel genre and he knows – like Mark – the importance of the beginning for this genre. But he is bending the beginning of this genre (as far as I can see) by changing its emphasis. He wants to tell of a different beginning from Mark, because he wants to tell another story of Jesus.[13] He does not want to present Jesus as messianic proclaimer of the Kingdom of God. Rather, his interest is in depicting him as God. John thus shifts his attention from Mark's beginning on earth[14] – precisely located in the region of Judaea at the Jordan river – to a beginning in heaven beyond any geographical location. This creates a sharp distinction between them. John exhibits interest in the divinity and eternity of the Logos, his pre-existence and eternal union with the eternal God, and in the fact that encountering the Word incarnate changes the relationship between heaven and earth. John's transformation of Mark is an effort to confront the gospel readers, from the beginning, not only with God's salutary words but with God as the Word himself.[15]

Fourth, I want to refer to a contrastive reading of John 1.1 that does not accept a distinction between the Markan and Johannine beginning. For the 16th-century Socinians – Lelio Sozzini and his nephew Fausto Sozzini, Italian humanists from Siena – the Johannine beginning means exactly the same as Mark's beginning. The Socinians understood the sentence ἐν ἀρχῇ ἦν ὁ λόγος, *in the beginning was the Word*, as the beginning of the gospel according to John and as the beginning of the events told in that gospel. The Johannine ἀρχή, with its connotations of Christ's divinity and even eternity, was a serious problem for Socinianism and its arguments against the divine trinity and Christ's divinity.[16] While orthodoxy correlated the expression ἐν ἀρχῇ to the

---

[12] See Becker, *Der früheste Evangelist*.
[13] Cf. Attridge, 'Genre Bending', 75: The 'fourth evangelist knew other ways of telling the story of Jesus. But the creation of this Gospel is not simply an extension of other narratives'.
[14] For further discussion of whether Mark's Gospel begins on earth or in heaven, see section 3 below of the present essay.
[15] Cf. Attridge, 'Genre Bending', 78: 'John's genre bending is an effort to force its audience away from words to an encounter with the Word himself'.
[16] See Otto Fock, *Der Sozinianismus: Nach seiner Stellung in der Gesamtentwicklung des christlichen Geistes, nach seinem historischen Verlauf und nach seinem Lehrbegriff dargestellt* (Kiel: Carl Schröder, 1847; Neudruck Aalen: Scientia, 1970), 519: 'Ganz besondere Schwierigkeiten mussten [...] dem Socinianismus eine Reihe von Schriftstellen darbieten, in denen Christus als ein wenn auch nicht gerade ewiges, so doch wenigstens präexistentes Wesen erscheint, woraus denn die Orthodoxie auf

pre-mundane being of the Logos with God, Socinianism maintained that the Bible always uses ἀρχή in a temporal sense for intra-mundane subjects. So the Socinians, arguing for that on the basis of John 15.27 (ὅτι ἀπ' ἀρχῆς μετ' ἐμοῦ ἐστε) and John 16.4 (Ταῦτα δὲ ὑμῖν ἐξ ἀρχῆς οὐκ εἶπον), also relate the ἀρχή of John 1.1 not to a pre-mundane beginning but to the beginning of the literary gospel and exactly to those events narrated in it: '*In loco citato nihil habetur de ista praeeterniate, quum hic principii mentio fiat, quod praeaeternitati opponitur. Principii vero vox in Scriptura fere semper ad subjectam refertur materiam, ut videre est Dan. 8,1. Joh. 15,27. 16,4. Act. 11,25. Quum igitur hic subjecta sit materia Evangelium, cujus descriptionem suscepit Joannes, sine dubio per vocem hanc Principii, principium Evangelii Joannis intellexit*.'[17]

Is the beginning of the ἀρχὴ τοῦ εὐαγγελίου Ἰησοῦ Χριστοῦ (Mk 1.1) present at the end of Mark's Gospel (Mk 16.7–8)? Is there a hermeneutical pendant in John?

Mk 16.7–8

7a ἀλλ' ὑπάγετε
    But go,
7b εἴπατε τοῖς μαθηταῖς αὐτοῦ καὶ τῷ Πέτρῳ
    tell his disciples and Peter
7c ὅτι προάγει ὑμᾶς εἰς τὴν Γαλιλαίαν·
    that he is going ahead of you to Galilee;
7d ἐκεῖ αὐτὸν ὄψεσθε,
    there you will see him,
7e καθὼς εἶπεν ὑμῖν.
    just as he told you.[18]
8a Καὶ ἐξελθοῦσαι ἔφυγον ἀπὸ τοῦ μνημείου,
    So they went out and fled from the tomb,
8b εἶχεν γὰρ αὐτὰς τρόμος καὶ ἔκστασις·
    for terror and amazement had seized them;
8c καὶ οὐδενὶ οὐδὲν εἶπαν·
    and they said nothing to anyone,
8d ἐφοβοῦντο γάρ.
    for they were afraid.

---

seine Ewigkeit, und daraus auf seine göttliche Natur schloss. Hierher [sc. zu diesen Schriftstellen] gehört vor Allem der Anfang des vierten Evangeliums, im Anfang war das Wort u. s. w. Bezog die Orthodoxie das *im Anfang* auf das vorweltliche Sein des Logos bei Gott, so glaubte der Socinianismus den Begriff des Anfangs nach dem vorliegenden Gegenstande [sc. dem Evangelienbuch] bestimmen zu müssen und bezog es daher auf den Anfang des Evangeliums, dessen Abfassung Johannes unternahm, d.h. auf den Anfang derjenigen Ereignisse, welche den Inhalt des Evangeliums ausmachen sollten.'

[17] Quoted from Fock, *Sozinianismus*, 519 (with reference to F. Socin. Explic. Primi cap. Joann. B. F. P. I, p. 78).

[18] Cf. Mark 14.28: 'But after I am raised up, I will go before you to Galilee.'

Some Markan scholars argue that, in a hermeneutical or text-pragmatic sense, the abrupt end of Mark's Gospel is not the end – but the beginning: 'Since Mark does not wrap up all the loose ends, we have no alternative but to return to the inception of his narrative (...) and to start to read it again as *our* story'.[19] Not only does this seem to be an appropriate reading of 16.8 but, as Norman Petersen has pointed out, '[c]onsiderations of the closural qualities of the ending to Mark's narrative will help us to determine whether it is an incompetent ending or a competent one when "rightly interpreted"'.[20] 'The criterion for this determination is the closural congruity between textually generated expectations and satisfactions.'[21] 'Dissatisfaction with the textual closure in 16.8' may derive from the juxtaposition of 16.7 and 8.[22] In v. 7 the young man, sitting in the empty tomb, telling the women that Jesus has risen, 'continues his speech by directing the women to go to the disciples and Peter and tell them that [the risen] Jesus is going before them to Galilee where they will see him, as he told them earlier (14:28)'.[23] But the women, as the narrator notes, 'went out and fled from the tomb [...] and they said nothing to anyone, for they were afraid' (16.8). In alignment with the expectations generated by the very beginning of Mark's Gospel, the readers may understand that the women's silence is not the last word of the gospel. The readers may realize that it is their turn now.

> The text ends. However, the narrator's unexpected withdrawal from communication with the reader is such that the reader is compelled by the narrator to respond. The juxtaposition of the expectation introduced in 16:7 with the terminal frustration of it in 16:8 requires the reader to review what he has read in order to comprehend this apparent incongruity and its meaning for the narrator's message. The text ends, but the readerly work, and perhaps even the literary work itself, goes on. The end of a text is not the end of the work when the narrator leaves unfinished business for the reader to complete, thoughtfully and imaginatively, not textually.[24]

So Mark 16.8 may signify that readers not only need to start reading the εὐαγγέλιον again but must begin with their own proclamation of the good news. The text ends. But the readers have to continue the ἀρχὴ τοῦ εὐαγγελίου Ἰησοῦ Χριστοῦ.[25]

---

[19] Joel Marcus, *Mark 8–16: A New Translation with Introduction and Commentary* (Anchor Bible, 27A; New York: Doubleday, 2000), 1096.
[20] Norman R. Petersen, 'When is the End not the End? Literary Reflections on the Ending of Mark's Narrative', *Interpretation* 34 (1980), 151–66 (here 152).
[21] Petersen, 'Ending of Mark's Narrative', 152.
[22] Petersen, 'Ending of Mark's Narrative', 152.
[23] Petersen, 'Ending of Mark's Narrative', 153.
[24] Petersen, 'Ending of Mark's Narrative', 153.
[25] Cf. Marcus, *Mark 8–16*, 1096: 'Mark's Gospel is just the *beginning* of the good news, because Jesus' story has become ours, and we take it up where Mark leaves off.' See also Marcus, *Mark 1–8*, 146, interpreting Mark 1.1: 'Interpreting 1.1 as the title of the book (...) helps make sense of the abrupt ending at 16.8 – the beginning of the good news is over Easter morning; after that "the good news of Jesus" will continue through the life of the church.' Cf. also Becker, *Der früheste Evangelist*, 9: 'Das Ziel der Evangeliumsverkündigung wird im Markusevangelium erkennbar weiterverfolgt (z.B. Mk 16,7f.)'.

Perhaps we may find a modified and much more obvious hermeneutical counterpart in John when we read 1.14, 14.26, 17.20 and 20.30 together, in combination, as a cluster:

Jn 1.14
a Καὶ ὁ λόγος σὰρξ ἐγένετο
   And the word became flesh
b καὶ ἐσκήνωσεν ἐν ἡμῖν,
   and lived among us,
c καὶ ἐθεασάμεθα τὴν δόξαν αὐτοῦ [...].
   and we have seen his glory [...].

Jn 14.26
a ὁ δὲ παράκλητος, [...]
   But the Advocate [...]
d ἐκεῖνος ὑμᾶς διδάξει πάντα
   will teach you everything
e καὶ ὑπομνήσει ὑμᾶς πάντα
   and remind you of all
f ἃ εἶπον ὑμῖν [ἐγώ].
   that I have said to you.

Jn 17.20
a Οὐ περὶ τούτων δὲ ἐρωτῶ μόνον,
   I ask not only on behalf of these,
b ἀλλὰ καὶ περὶ τῶν πιστευόντων διὰ τοῦ λόγου αὐτῶν εἰς ἐμέ, [..].
   but also on behalf of those who will believe in me through their word [...].

Jn 20.31
a ταῦτα δὲ γέγραπται
   But these are written
b ἵνα πιστεύ[σ]ητε
   so that you may come to believe
c ὅτι Ἰησοῦς ἐστιν ὁ χριστὸς ὁ υἱὸς τοῦ θεοῦ, [...].
   that Jesus is the Messiah, the Son of God [...].

The 'we' of John 1.14a make it clear that, taught by the Paraclete (Jn 14.26d), they did understand the significance of Jesus' death and resurrection: the manifestation of his divine glory (that is, to see him as the Word, which came from God and returns to God). The 'we' in question are those who continue the revelation of God, given by the Logos, by retaining and proclaiming his words to further generations – as implicitly predicted in John 17.20 and enabled by the Paraclete's teaching and anamnesis (Jn 14.26de). Furthermore, they are those who wrote down and delivered the gospel's words, intending that all who read it come to faith (Jn 20.31ab). The end of the gospel's first epilogue – 'that Jesus is the Messiah, the Son of God' (Jn 20.31c) – cites the beginning of Mark's Gospel more or less verbatim. Surveying the evidence gleaned from this Johannine cluster, it seems likely that John – in his literary beginning, the Farewell Discourses, and the first epilogue – reflects upon Mark's open-ended 'hermeneutical beginning'.

Comparing the opening sections of Mark and John
(Mk 1.1–3; Jn 1.1–5)

Mk 1.1–3

1 Ἀρχὴ τοῦ εὐαγγελίου Ἰησοῦ Χριστοῦ [υἱοῦ θεοῦ].
   The beginning of the gospel of Jesus Christ, the Son of God.
2a Καθὼς γέγραπται ἐν τῷ Ἠσαΐᾳ τῷ προφήτῃ·
   As it is written in the prophet Isaiah,
2b ἰδοὺ
   'See,
2c ἀποστέλλω τὸν ἄγγελόν μου πρὸ προσώπου σου,
   I am sending my messenger ahead of you,
2d ὃς κατασκευάσει τὴν ὁδόν σου·
   who will prepare your way;
3a φωνὴ βοῶντος ἐν τῇ ἐρήμῳ·
   the voice of one crying out in the wilderness:
3b ἑτοιμάσατε τὴν ὁδὸν κυρίου,
   "Prepare the way of the Lord,
3c εὐθείας ποιεῖτε τὰς τρίβους αὐτοῦ,
   make his paths straight,"
[4a ἐγένετο Ἰωάννης [ὁ] βαπτίζων ἐν τῇ ἐρήμῳ]
[4b ...].[26]

Inspired by Lohmeyer's dictum that the beginning of Mark's Gospel is 'wie ein Prolog vom Himmel her' (like a prologue from heaven),[27] Hans-Josef Klauck asked in 1997 whether Mark's beginning should be called a 'Vorspiel im Himmel' (a prelude in heaven) – as in Goethe's *Faust*.[28] In the end, Klauck notes that the question mark must remain: a transcript of a heavenly dialogue between God, the Father, and Son cannot strictly be seen in verses 2 and 3 of Mark's beginning.[29] But Bärbel Bosenius posed the same question in 2015,[30] and this time answered in the affirmative: she argues that Mark 1.2b–3c represents a heavenly scene, showing God the Father addressing his Son ('you') in a heavenly throne-room. The Father tells the Son that he will send Elijah ahead of him to earth as John the Baptist (v. 2c: 'ahead of you'/'before your face'[31]), so that John the Baptist – as a voice in the wilderness may prepare the Son's way (v. 2d: 'your way'). Bosenius first bases her argument on punctuation, maintaining that there

---

[26] Nestle-Aland, *Novum Testamentum Graece*, sets the full stop of the sentence starting with Καθὼς γέγραπται only after verse 4b.
[27] Hans-Josef Klauck, *Vorspiel im Himmel? Erzähltechnik und Theologie im Markusprolog* (BThS, 32; Neukirchen-Vluyn: Neukirchener Verlagsgesellschaft, 1997), 16.
[28] Klauck, *Vorspiel im Himmel?*, 13–15.
[29] Klauck, *Vorspiel im Himmel?*, 113.
[30] Bärbel Bosenius. *Der literarische Raum im Markusevangelium* (WMANT, 140; Neukirchen-Vluyn: Neukirchener Verlagsgesellschaft, 2015).
[31] Marcus, *Mark 1–8*, 3, 141.

should be a comma rather than a full stop between vv. 1 and 2.³² Mark 1.1–2a, she claims, forms one coherent sentence that should be translated as: 'Anfang des Evangeliums Jesu Christi, [des Sohnes Gottes,] wie es im Buch des Propheten Jesaja geschrieben ist'.³³ Her other argument is that Mark ascribes the following verses (vv. 2b–3c) to Isaiah, intending that the Prophet speaks with God's voice. Since Mark 1.2b–3c should be understood as the 'wörtliche Rede Gottes',³⁴ she argues that the figure addressed as 'you' must be a character who has already been mentioned in the text. This can only be Jesus Christ, mentioned in Mark 1.1 (Ἰησοῦ Χριστοῦ [υἱοῦ θεοῦ]).

Like Klauck, Bosenius has been inspired by Lohmeyer.³⁵ However, I think she misunderstands his arguments. With regard to Mark 1.2b–3, Lohmeyer does not in any way envisage a scene that is situated in heaven. For Lohmeyer, 'Prolog vom Himmel her' signifies that the story told in Mark 1.4–13 testifies to the divine will. This divine will is expressed by means of the composite Old Testament quotation in Mark 1.2b–3.³⁶ Lohmeyer points out that this prophecy is commented upon line by line in Mark 1.4–8.³⁷ The purpose of the quotation is to demonstrate that God's will is fulfilled in the narrated events. This also applies to the sections that follow in 1.9–11 and 1.12–13. These sections likewise belong to what Lohmeyer calls 'Prolog vom Himmel her', although they certainly do not take place in heaven but in the desert and at the Jordan.³⁸ Finally, for Lohmeyer, Mark 1.1–2a – as part of verses 1–8 – belongs to the 'Prolog vom Himmel her'.³⁹ All three sections belong to it because they show 'wie Gott den "Anfang des Evangeliums" gesetzt hat: Er erfüllte im Täufer ein altes verheißenes, sprach über Jesus sein eschatologisch vollendendes Wort und dieser widerstand dem eschatologischen Widersacher Gottes'.⁴⁰ The citation of prophetic words from the Old Testament suggest that it is God who performs his eschatological work through the coming of the Baptist, in Jesus' baptism, and in Jesus' resistance to the devil's temptation.⁴¹

It is therefore correct, in my opinion, that Klauck understands Mark 1.2b–3 as a *Motto* or heading for what is subsequently narrated.⁴² I would like to emphasize that understanding Mark 1.2b–3 as a 'heading' should not be overstated, given the syntactic form and function of the introduction to the quotation (2a: καθὼς γέγραπται) and its syntactic relation to the finite verb ἐγένετο in verse 4a.⁴³ That is, the introductory

---

³² Bosenius, *Der literarische Raum*, 21–2. On this much discussed problem, cf. also Klauck, *Vorspiel im Himmel?*, 27–9. Bosenius shares the same view as Klauck on the punctuation issue, but they do not draw the same conclusions.
³³ Bosenius, *Der literarische Raum*, 22 n. 3.
³⁴ Bosenius, *Der literarische Raum*, 23.
³⁵ See Bosenius, *Der literarische Raum*, 21.
³⁶ The quotations uniformly attributed to Isaiah are from Isaiah 40.3, Exodus 23.20, and Malachi 3.1. See further Marcus, *Mark 1–8*, 144.
³⁷ Ernst Lohmeyer, *Das Evangelium des Markus* (16th edn; KEK, I/2; Göttingen, 1963), 9–10.
³⁸ See Lohmeyer, *Das Evangelium des Markus*, 19–28.
³⁹ See Lohmeyer, *Das Evangelium des Markus*, 9–11.
⁴⁰ Lohmeyer, *Das Evangelium des Markus*, 9.
⁴¹ See Lohmeyer, *Markus*, 9, 26, 28.
⁴² Klauck, *Vorspiel im Himmel?*, 22, 27–30.
⁴³ For discussion, see Klauck, *Vorspiel im Himmel?*, 27; Bosenius, *Der literarische Raum*, 22; Robert A. Guelich, 'The Gospel Genre', in *Das Evangelium und die Evangelien: Vorträge vom Tübinger Symposium 1982*, ed. Peter Stuhlmacher (WUNT, 28; Tübingen: Mohr Siebeck, 1983), 183–220 (here 205).

citation formula καθὼς γέγραπται (1.2a) does not introduce a sentence that only finds its main verb in ἐγένετο.[44] Rather, καθὼς γέγραπται begins a sentence that is constructed as an ellipse to highlight the function of the prophetic quotation as the hermeneutical key to the gospel's narrative. This function remains valid even if a comma rather than a full stop is placed between verse 1 and verse 2 (as in the reading of the Greek text offered by Lohmeyer, Klauck and Bosenius). The explanatory heading, introduced by the formula καθὼς γέγραπται, is then even more strongly linked to the title ἀρχὴ τοῦ εὐαγγελίου Ἰησοῦ Χριστοῦ [υἱοῦ θεοῦ]. Both syntactical solutions enable the opening section of Mark's Gospel to emphasize that God is fulfilling his promises and thereby setting a new beginning in and through Jesus Christ. Through this new beginning, God's previous dealings in history – with his created beings and his beloved people Israel – do continue. At the same time, these earlier beginnings are transformed into one that brings the Kingdom of God into a completely new proximity (see Mk 1.15).

Jn 1.1–5

1a Ἐν ἀρχῇ ἦν ὁ λόγος,
    In the beginning was the Word,
1b καὶ ὁ λόγος ἦν πρὸς τὸν θεόν,
    and the Word was with God,
1c καὶ θεὸς ἦν ὁ λόγος.
    and the Word was God.
2   οὗτος ἦν ἐν ἀρχῇ πρὸς τὸν θεόν.
    He was in the beginning with God.
3a πάντα δι' αὐτοῦ ἐγένετο,
    All things came into being through him
3b καὶ χωρὶς αὐτοῦ ἐγένετο οὐδὲ ἕν.
    and without him not one thing came into being.
3c ὃ γέγονεν
    What has come into being
4a ἐν αὐτῷ ζωὴ ἦν,
    in him was life.
4b καὶ ἡ ζωὴ ἦν τὸ φῶς τῶν ἀνθρώπων·
    And the life was the light of all people.
5a καὶ τὸ φῶς ἐν τῇ σκοτίᾳ φαίνει,
    The light shines in the darkness,
5b καὶ ἡ σκοτία αὐτὸ οὐ κατέλαβεν.
    and the darkness did not overcome it.

The opening section of John's Gospel, as already indicated above, speaks of a very different beginning in comparison with Mark.[45] And yet, in the first five verses, John

---

[44] Klauck, *Vorspiel im Himmel?*, 27, points out that the syntactic equivalent of καθὼς γέγραπται must be not simply ἐγένετο but οὕτως ἐγένετο.

[45] See section 1 of the present essay.

also sets an explanatory 'heading' for his gospel. He does not do this with the aid of Old Testament prophetic quotations, but rather by alluding to the beginning of the Old Testament itself (Gen. 1.1). John's main interest is not to underline, as Mark does, that God eschatologically fulfills his promises and that he surpasses all previous beginnings by means of a new beginning created through the work of his Son. John's main interest lies in emphasizing that the Son, the Logos, is himself the Creator and that he was creating in God's sphere before all things came into being. The difficult syntactic transition from verse 3c to verse 4a[46] probably reflects John's intention to claim that the whole creation is not only created *through* the Logos, but owes its life to that life that is *in* the Logos and *is* the Logos (Jn 11.25, 14.6; cf. 6.35, 51). Verse 4a, in my view, seeks to claim that the Logos is the epitome of life.[47] He is the origin of all – 'die Lebendigkeit der ganzen Schöpfung hat im Logos ihren Ursprung'.[48] Not only the vitality, but also the salvation of the world has its origin in the Logos insofar as he is 'the light' of humankind. The soteriological metaphor of 'light', used to describe the function of the Logos (Jn 1.4b–5) and his being (cf. Jn 8.12), signifies that the creative power of the Logos gives that human life enlightened by faith.[49]

With the explanatory heading in vv. 1–5, John thus shifts Mark's emphasis. He does not focus on God acting in history, as revealed by his promises and their fulfillment. He focuses rather on the eternal being and inner worldly activity of the divine Word. In christological terms, he goes further than Mark, who does not refer to the pre-existence of Jesus Christ in his introductory section (unless one follows Bosenius' view that the Gospel of Mark begins with God's direct speech in heaven, addressed to his Son Jesus Christ, which thus implies his pre-existence).[50] What John shares with Mark, however, is that he traces the beginning of his gospel to God. He makes this even more explicit than Mark, who does so by quoting prophetic words. John places God at the beginning of his gospel by binding the Logos back to God.

Comparing the beginning of Mark's and John's narratives: Where do the narratives of Mark and John begin?

Mk 1.4–8

4a ἐγένετο Ἰωάννης [ὁ] βαπτίζων ἐν τῇ ἐρήμῳ
    John the baptizer appeared in the wilderness
4b καὶ [sc. ἐγένετο Ἰωάννης] κηρύσσων βάπτισμα μετανοίας εἰς ἄφεσιν ἁμαρτιῶν.

---

[46] For a text-critical discussion, see Brown, *John*, 6; Michael Theobald, *Das Evangelium nach Johannes: Kapitel 1–12* (RNT; Regensburg: Friedrich Pustet, 2009), 112–15.
[47] Cf. Christina Hoegen-Rohls, 'Ewigkeit und Leben: Der bibische Vorstellungskreis III: Johannes', in *Das Leben: Historisch-systematische Studien zur Geschichte eines Begriffs*, edited by Petra Bahr and Stephan Schaede (RuA, 17; Tübingen: Mohr Siebeck, 2009), 1:135–37.
[48] Rudolf Bultmann, *Das Evangelium des Johannes* (16th edn, KEK, 2; Göttingen: Vandenhoeck und Ruprecht), 20; see also Rudolf Bultmann, *The Gospel of John: A Commentary*, trans. George R. Beasley-Murray (Oxford: Blackwell, 1971).
[49] Hoegen-Rohls, 'Ewigkeit und Leben', 137–39.
[50] Cf. Bosenius, *Der literarische Raum*, 21 n. 1.

	proclaiming a baptism of repentance for the forgiveness of sins.
5a	καὶ ἐξεπορεύετο πρὸς αὐτὸν πᾶσα ἡ Ἰουδαία χώρα καὶ οἱ Ἱεροσολυμῖται πάντες,
	And people from the whole Judean countryside and all the people of Jerusalem were going out to him,
5b	καὶ ἐβαπτίζοντο ὑπ' αὐτοῦ ἐν τῷ Ἰορδάνῃ ποταμῷ ἐξομολογούμενοι τὰς ἁμαρτίας αὐτῶν.
	and were baptized by him in the river Jordan, confessing their sins.
[6	...]
7a	<u>Καὶ ἐκήρυσσεν λέγων·</u>
	He proclaimed,
7b	ἔρχεται ὁ ἰσχυρότερός μου ὀπίσω μου,
	'The one who is more powerful than I is coming after me;
7c	οὗ οὐκ εἰμὶ ἱκανὸς κύψας λῦσαι τὸν ἱμάντα τῶν ὑποδημάτων αὐτοῦ.
	I am not worthy to stoop down and untie the thong of his sandals.
8a	ἐγὼ ἐβάπτισα ὑμᾶς ὕδατι,
	I have baptized you with water;
8b	αὐτὸς δὲ βαπτίσει ὑμᾶς ἐν πνεύματι ἁγίῳ.
	but he will baptize you with the Holy Spirit.

If we do not adopt Bosenius' view that the characters already introduced in Mark 1.2–3 are the only actors (God, Jesus Christ, God's angel = the voice in the wilderness), Mark's narrative plot begins in Mark 1.4 with the lead actors of John the Baptist, people from the whole Judean countryside, and people from Jerusalem. Where does the narrative plot start in John? Usually the beginning of John's narrative is located in 1.19. But if we examine the two gospels comparatively, we discover that there are much earlier similarities between the passages introducing 'John the Baptist' as the predecessor of Jesus (Mark)/the Logos incarnate (John): Mark's narrative beginning, ἐγένετο Ἰωάννης (Mk 1.4), can already be found in John 1.6ac:[51]

Jn 1.6

6a	Ἐγένετο ἄνθρωπος,
	There was a man
6b	ἀπεσταλμένος παρὰ θεοῦ,
	sent from God,
6c	ὄνομα αὐτῷ Ἰωάννης·
	whose name was John.

Also the κηρύσσειν of Mark 1.7a is already present in John 1.15b:

---

[51] Cf. Theobald, *Johannes*, 120, with regard to John 1.6: 'Wir haben einen klassischen Erzählanfang vor uns.'

Jn 1.15

15a	Ἰωάννης μαρτυρεῖ περὶ αὐτοῦ	
	(John testified to him	
15b	<u>καὶ κέκραγεν λέγων·</u>	
	and cried out,	
15c	οὗτος ἦν	
	'This was he	
15d	<u>ὃν εἶπον·</u>	
	of whom I said,	
15e		ὁ ὀπίσω μου ἐρχόμενος ἔμπροσθέν μου γέγονεν,
		"He who comes after me ranks ahead of me
15f		ὅτι πρῶτός μου ἦν.
		because he was before me."'

Both the Markan and the Johannine Baptist speak about themselves with an emphatic ἐγώ. The Markan Baptist introduces himself by clarifying that 'the one stronger than me' (cf. Mk 1.7) will baptize with the Holy Spirit – in contrast to himself who baptizes with water:[52]

Mk 1.8a

8a ἐγὼ ἐβάπτισα ὑμᾶς ὕδατι,
    I have baptized you with water;[53]

Also the Johannine John the Baptist points out, with his 'superfluous' 'I', that he is to be contrasted with the one who is the Messiah (Jn 1.20d) and who baptizes with the Holy Spirit (cf. Jn 1.33). He himself is the prophetic voice proclaiming the coming of the Lord, but not the Lord himself (Jn 1.23b.c):

Jn 1.19a, 20d, 23a-d, 26

19a	Καὶ αὕτη ἐστὶν ἡ μαρτυρία τοῦ Ἰωάννου,
	This is the testimony given by John
20d	ἐγὼ οὐκ εἰμὶ ὁ χριστός.
	I am not the Messiah.
23a	ἔφη·
	He said,
23b	<u>ἐγὼ φωνὴ βοῶντος ἐν τῇ ἐρήμῳ·</u>
	'I am the voice of one crying out in the wilderness,
23c	εὐθύνατε τὴν ὁδὸν κυρίου,
	"Make straight the way of the Lord"',
23d	καθὼς εἶπεν Ἠσαΐας ὁ προφήτης.
	as the prophet Isaiah said.

---

[52] Cf. Marcus, *Mark 1–8*, 154.
[53] Marcus, *Mark 1–8*, 152, elucidates as follows: 'The *egō* (= 'I') is superfluous, and probably emphatic'. His translation is: 'I myself have baptized you with water' (p. 149).

26   ἀπεκρίθη αὐτοῖς ὁ Ἰωάννης λέγων·
     John answered them:
         ἐγὼ βαπτίζω ἐν ὕδατι·
         I baptize with water;

But there are striking differences as well. Mark initiates the beginning of the gospel genre by introducing John explicitly as the Baptist (Mk 1.4a, b, 5b). For Mark, it is baptism that characterizes the relationship between John the Baptist, who baptizes with water, and Jesus, who baptizes with πνεῦμα (Mk 1.8ab). It is with John's baptizing activity that Mark's narrative world begins. John bends the genre created by Mark by modifying the role of 'John the Baptist'. The Johannine Baptist is not so much the one who baptizes Jesus but the witness to the pre-existent and incarnate Logos (Jn 1.7, 15), who emphatically identifies himself with the voice in the desert calling for the straightening of the Lord's way (Jn 1.23bc).

That John's Gospel integrates the Baptist into the prologue about the origins of the Logos may demonstrate that he is familiar with the beginning of Mark's narrative (Mk 1.4–8), understands its close connection with the Markan explanatory heading (1.2–3), and recognizes the ambiguous role of the beginning of the text as a heading and as a reference to the new action of God in Jesus Christ (Mk 1.1). If, as stated above, John 1.1–5 is an explanatory heading analogous to Mark 1.2–3, then there is an interesting congruence between them in the continuation of the heading through the immediate reference to John the Baptist (Mark)/John the Witness (John). With regard to this, John follows Mark very closely, recognizing that the earthly beginning of Jesus' ministry must be linked directly to the 'Baptist'. However, he transforms the Baptist into a witness and also strengthens this role in vv. 19–23. Furthermore, he does not mention John's clothing and food (cf. Mk 1.6), but instead highlights the importance of his mission. By witnessing to the identity of the Logos as the light, John the witness opens up the opportunity for *all* (πάντες) – not only the people of the Judean countryside and of Jerusalem (cf. Mk 1.5a) – to come to believe:

7a   οὗτος ἦλθεν εἰς μαρτυρίαν
     He came as a witness
7b   ἵνα μαρτυρήσῃ περὶ τοῦ φωτός,
     to testify to the light,
7c   ἵνα πάντες πιστεύσωσιν δι' αὐτοῦ.
     so that all might believe through him.

What can 'kephalaia' contribute to the question of the beginnings of Mark and John?

In some threads of the Greek manuscript tradition for Mark and John, there are markers to indicate the division of the texts into segments. In Nestle Aland these markers, the so-called 'kephalaia', are written as marginal notes in Arabic numbers in a larger type size, located at the inner edge of the pages.[54] Counting usually starts with the second segment of the text, so that everything before number 1 is regarded as the text's first segment – in other words, its beginning. The manuscripts of Mark and John display the number one at Mark 1.23 and John 2.1, which means that most manuscripts regarded 1.1-22 the beginning of Mark as 1.1-22 and 1.1-51 as the beginning of John. These beginnings include:

Mk 1.1-22
1.1   The heading Ἀρχὴ τοῦ εὐαγγελίου Ἰησοῦ Χριστοῦ [υἱοῦ θεοῦ].
1.2-3   The explanatory heading: the collection of transformed scriptural citations (Mal. 3.1/Ex. 23.20/Isa. 40.3 LXX) ['composite quotation']
1.4-8   The ministry of John the Baptist
1.9-11   The baptism of Jesus
1.12-13   Jesus in the wilderness, being tested by Satan
1.14-15   Jesus' inaugural preaching
1.16-20   The call of the first disciples (1.16-18: Peter and Andrew; 1.19-20: James and John)
1.21-22   The first specific location (1.21: the synagogue in Capernaum)
          The first summary of Jesus' authoritative synagogue teaching (1.22)
          The first reaction of amazement to Jesus' powerful teaching (1.22)

Jn 1.1-51
1.1-5   The explanatory heading Ἐν ἀρχῇ ἦν ὁ λόγος
1.6-18   The ongoing prologue, introduced by the reference to John the witness
1.19-28   John's testimony to the Logos
1.29-31   John, for the first time, describes Jesus as 'the Lamb of God' (1.29)
1.32-34   John acclaims Jesus 'the Son of God' (1.34)
1.35-51   John (not called 'the baptizer') describes Jesus for the second time as 'the Lamb of God' (1.36); John's disciples come to Jesus/Jesus calls the first disciples (1.35-42: Andrew, an unnamed disciple, and Peter; 1.43-51: Philip and Nathanael)

Both the beginning of Mark's Gospel and the beginning of John's Gospel are marked by a first *kephalaion*, which includes the following: the explanatory heading, the appearance of John the Baptist, the scene in which Jesus makes his Markan and Johannine narrative debut by being baptized or witnessed, and the scene in which the first disciples are called by Jesus. In both gospels this sets the stage for Jesus' further ministry. The first *kephalaion* in the ancient Greek manuscripts of Mark's Gospel reflects the interpretative insight that the narrative of Jesus' life and ministry begins with his baptism, the calling of his disciples, and Jesus' appearance in the Capernaum synagogue. What about the first *kephalaion* in John's Gospel? To answer this question, striking differences between Mark 1.1-22 and John 1.1-51 must be noted.

---

[54] See NA28, Einführung IV.2, 42*.

First, John's explanatory heading is embedded in a passage whose literary form can be classified as a hymn prologue that, with the aid of mythical language, praises the coming of the divine Word into the world (Jn 1.1–18).[55] This genre and its poetic character have no counterpart in Mark, even if some scholars describe Mark 1.1–3 or 1.1–13 or 1.1–15 as the 'prologue' to Mark's Gospel on the analogy of the prologue to John's Gospel.[56]

Second, even if both Mark's heading (1.1) and John's conclusion to the prologue (1.18, as the climax to the explanatory heading of 1.1–5) are echoed in the narrative of Jesus' baptism (cf. Mk 1.11) and in the narrative of the Baptist's testimony to Jesus (cf. Jn 1.34), it seems that John wants to transform the Markan keywords, 'Jesus Christ (Son of God)' (Mk 1.1), and the direct address, 'You are my Son, the Beloved' (Mk 1.11), into an elaborate theological description of the relationship between God and his Logos (Jn 1.1–5, 14, 18). John can significantly modify Mark's baptism scene because he has already emphasized the deity of Jesus in the prologue. He does not need the divine voice (Mk 1.11) or the story of Jesus' temptation by the devil (Mk 1.12–13).

Third, in Mark, Jesus proclaims that God's Kingdom is near and in his inaugural preaching calls people to repentance and faith (Mk 1.15). In John, no initial preaching by Jesus addressed to future believers is recounted; rather the post-Easter believers, speaking as 'we' in the prologue, bear witness to the Logos' incarnation and glory (Jn 1.14, 16). In this way, John ensures the inclusion of believers in the relationship between God and the Logos (Jn 1.12–13). The Johannine presentation of the relationship between God, the Logos and believers, as introduced in the prologue and disclosed in the Farewell Discourses (Jn 13.1–17.26) as being founded in the Spirit-Paraclete (cf. 13.31–16.33), goes beyond the Markan concept of the Kingdom of God: believers receive a share in God and Christ, they 'are in' God and his Logos (cf. Jn 17.21: ἵνα καὶ αὐτοὶ ἐν ἡμῖν ὦσιν / may they also be in us). Therefore, John breaks away from traditional speech about ἡ βασιλεία τοῦ θεοῦ. The soteriological pivot of John's concept of a triple relationship, as shown in the prologue, is the possibility of becoming children of God. John, unlike Mark, wants to emphasize this from the very outset to make clear that this is exactly the experience that led to the writing of his gospel.

Fourth, the Baptist's testimony that Jesus is the Son of God (Jn 1.34) is framed by his testimony that Jesus is the Lamb of God (Jn 1.29: ἴδε ὁ ἀμνὸς τοῦ θεοῦ ὁ αἴρων τὴν ἁμαρτίαν τοῦ κόσμου; Jn 1.36: ἴδε ὁ ἀμνὸς τοῦ θεοῦ). In contrast to Mark, John integrates the death of Jesus into the beginning of his gospel. When John's first disciples are addressed, it is already clear that Jesus – the Lamb of God who takes away the sin of the world – will die. The motif of Jesus' death is thus highlighted from the beginning of the narrative.

Fifth, in Mark the first disciples are called directly by Jesus' voice (Mk 1.17). In John the first disciples are called indirectly in two ways, by the Baptist's voice proclaiming Jesus as the Lamb of God (1.36) and by Jesus' turning around, seeing the Baptist's disciples following him, and asking them what they are looking for (Jn 1.38: στραφεὶς

---

[55] Cf. Jean Zumstein, *Das Johannesevangelium* (KEK, 2; Göttingen: Vandenhoeck und Ruprecht, 2016), 66.

[56] For discussion, see Klauck, *Vorspiel im Himmel?*

δὲ ὁ Ἰησοῦς καὶ θεασάμενος αὐτοὺς ἀκολουθοῦντας λέγει αὐτοῖς· τί ζητεῖτε;). As with the 'we' speakers in the prologue, this indirect calling of disciples reflects the perspective of post-Easter believers.[57] They were not called directly and personally by Jesus, but through the word and proclamation of his followers (cf. Jn 17.20). Taking this crucial difference into account, John transforms Mark's chronological narrative by creating a narrative on two levels, a chronological and, simultaneously, a hermeneutical level upon which post-Easter knowledge is superimposed.

Sixth, in Mark the narration of the calling of the disciples by the Sea of Galilee proceeds with an initial summary that reports on Jesus' public teaching in the synagogue of Capernaum and the astonished reaction of the audience at his authority (Mk 1.21–22). In John the calling of the first disciples[58] culminates in a promise that applies exclusively to them: 'You will see greater things than these' (Jn 1.50b). What will they see? The image of the ladder with ascending and descending angels illustrates the ongoing communion between God and the Logos. This represents the 'greater things' to be seen by the disciples. Unlike the gospel's readers, who have already been made aware of the unique relationship between God and the Logos through the prologue, the disciples have not been informed until the present point in the narrative. The metaphorical promise in 1.51 provides them with this insight. It seems as if the first *kephalaion* in the ancient Greek manuscript of John's Gospel reflects the fact that, with John 1.51, a first unit, that is, the beginning of the gospel, has been completed insofar as the knowledge of the post-Easter community – already expressed on the hermeneutical level in the prologue – is now made available on the chronological level of the narrative: the disciples grasp the communication between Jesus and his Father, God. As a result, the narration of the ministry of the Logos incarnate can now continue.

Conclusions

Various questions about the precise 'beginnings' that can be compared between Mark and John have demonstrated that, regardless of the extent of these passages, it is possible to observe both similarities and differences. In the interest of the present volume, I will end by highlighting six aspects of how John transforms Mark:

1. John bends the beginning of Mark's Gospel by indicating that the opening of his own book speaks about a beginning that lies beyond any historical beginning of proclaiming good news. The beginning in which the Word was and was with God and was God extends back beyond the beginning of the world, that is, beyond history.
2. John does agree with Mark about the kerygmatic character of the gospel genre and, like Mark, recognizes the importance of a beginning for this genre. However, John

---

[57] Cf. Zumstein, *Johannesevangelium*, 105.
[58] Cf. Francis J. Moloney, 'The First Days of Jesus and the Role of the Disciples: A Study of John 1:19–51', in Francis J. Moloney, *Johannine Studies 1975–2017* (WUNT, 372; Tübingen: Mohr Siebeck, 2017), 307–30.

bends the beginning by changing its emphasis. He wants to include a beginning that is different from Mark's; he wants to tell another story of Jesus. His interest lies not in portraying Jesus as messianic proclaimer of the Kingdom of God but rather to present him *as* God. Thus, John shifts his attention from Mark's narrative opening on earth – precisely located in the region of Judaea at the Jordan river – to heaven, to what is beyond any earthly location. John's transformation of Mark is an effort to confront readers, from the outset, not only with God's salutary words but with God as the Word himself.

3. (a) With his first five verses (1.1–5), John sets out an explanatory heading for his gospel ('Prolog im Prolog'[59]). Different from Mark, he does not do so with the aid of Old Testament prophetic quotations, but rather through scriptural allusion to the beginning itself (Gen. 1.1). John's main interest is not to prove, like Mark, that God eschatologically fulfills his promises and surpasses all previous beginnings with a new one created through his Son's work. He emphasizes, rather, that the Son, the Logos, is himself the Creator and that he was before all things, creating in the sphere of God.

(b) Through the explanatory heading (Jn 1.1–5) John shifts from Mark's focus on God acting in history, as revealed by his promises and their fulfillment, to the eternal being of the divine Word. In christological terms, he goes further than Mark, who does not refer to the pre-existence of Jesus Christ in his introductory section. Both place God at the beginning of their gospel; Mark does so by citing prophetic words, John does so by associating the Logos with God.

(c) John's explanatory heading (1.1–5) is embedded in a text whose literary form can be classified as a hymnic prologue (1.1–18). This has no generic counterpart in Mark 1.1–15. John therefore transfers the Markan keywords, 'Jesus Christ (Son of God)' (Mk 1.1), and the direct address, 'You are my Son, the Beloved' (Mk 1.11), into an elaborate theological description of the relationship between God and his Logos (Jn 1.1–5, 14, 18) – a relationship which also involves believers (1.12–13). John, unlike Mark, highlights this from the outset to emphasize that it is this experience that led to the writing of his gospel.

(d) John's explanatory heading (1.1–5) exhibits an interesting congruence with Mark's in that it leads directly to a reference to John the Baptist (Mark)/'John the Witness' (John). John follows Mark closely at this point, recognizing that the beginning of Jesus' earthly ministry must be linked to the 'Baptist'. However, the Baptist is transformed into a witness (1.6–8, 15; cf. 1.19–23), and, by testifying to the Logos as the light, opens up the opportunity for *all* (πάντες) to come to believe.

4. In contrast to Mark's beginning, John integrates the death of Jesus into the beginning of his gospel. When John address his own disciples, it is already clear that Jesus, the Lamb of God who takes away the sin of the world, will die. The motif of Jesus' death is thus highlighted from the beginning of the narrative.

---

[59] Cf. Zumstein, *Johannesevangelium*, 73–74.

5. John transforms Mark's chronological narrative by creating a two-level narrative. This is demonstrated by the 'we' statements of the post-Easter community in John 1.14, 16 (hermeneutical level) and by the metaphorical promise addressed to the disciples as characters in John 1.51 (chronological level).
6. It is precisely this last observation that suggests that John wanted to deepen the gospel genre as prescribed by Mark. All other observations also indicate that John knew Mark and consciously transformed his gospel.

10

Jesus in Sharper Relief: Making Sense of the Fourth Gospel's Use of Mark 1.2–8 in John 1.19–34

Steven A. Hunt

Introduction – theory, defence, agenda

At its most basic level, the Fourth Gospel tells the story of Jesus, the one sent by God to reveal Godself to the world. Because this beloved (3.16) yet estranged and inhospitable world (1.10–11) had never fully seen God (1.18; 5.37; 6.46; cf. 14.17), the Fourth Gospel says explicitly in passages like 12.45 and 14.7–9 (cf. 11.40; 15.24) and implicitly virtually everywhere else: if you want to see God, take a look at Jesus.[1] Doubling down on that line of thought, the narrative pushes readers further: if you really want to see God, take a look at Jesus on the cross.[2]

But how is this story told? Or more precisely, how is this revelation communicated by the narrative? At least *part* of the answer to that question is to assert this: the Fourth Gospel's Jesus stands in sharper relief when understood in light of Mark's Gospel than when he stands alone. For those having already read Mark, the colours around Jesus when reading John are more vibrant, the details more textured. And in those places where the parallels between Mark and the Fourth Gospel are most obvious

---

[1] While modern scholars largely reject Bultmann's understanding of the Gnostic origins of the Fourth Gospel's presentation of Jesus' revelatory mission, many would still affirm his view of its primacy as the *Leitmotiv* of John (Rudolf Bultmann, *The Gospel of John: A Commentary* [Philadelphia, PA: Westminster, 1971], esp. 45–83; see also Oscar Cullmann's pointed observation that in Johannine thought, 'Jesus not only brings revelation, but in his person is revelation' (*The Christology of the New Testament*, rev. edn, trans. by Shirley C. Guthrie and Charles A.M. Hall [Philadelphia, PA: Westminster, 1963], 258); C. K. Barrett writes, 'So completely does he reflect the Father's character that to see Jesus is to see the Father' (*The Gospel According to St John: An Introduction with Commentary and Notes on the Greek Text* [2nd edn; Philadelphia, PA: Westminster, 1978], 72). See further, B. F. Westcott, *The Revelation of the Father: Short Lectures on the Titles of the Lord in the Gospel of St John* (London: MacMillan and Co, 1884), esp. 133–44.

[2] Richard Bauckham makes this point about the Fourth Gospel's theology concisely in *Jesus and the God of Israel: God Crucified and Other Studies on the New Testament's Christology of Divine Identity* (Grand Rapids, MI: Wm. B. Eerdmans, 2009), esp. 46–50. Theologically speaking, there is no finer treatment of this important concept than Jürgen Moltmann's *The Crucified God* (40th Anniversary edn; Minneapolis, MN: Fortress, 2015).

and compelling, one central feature stands out: in nearly every scene, the Fourth Gospel's Jesus becomes more central to the narrative. The Fourth Gospel throws a spotlight on Jesus.

Following in the wake of others, this paper attempts to demonstrate that the Fourth Gospel is – *at least in part* – a *relecture* of Mark.[3] Thus, the Fourth Gospel offers a thoughtful rewriting, a complete refashioning, a deliberate retooling of various Markan narratives. These have, of course, several twists and turns, but there is one overarching theological agenda – the revelation of God. The author of the Fourth Gospel intends neither to supplement Mark's story by simply adding detail that Mark has omitted (although he obviously does some of that), nor to supplant Mark by changing details which, from his perspective, need to be corrected (although he appears to do some of that as well); instead, at one basic level, the Fourth Gospel repurposes Mark's narrative to focus the story more clearly on Jesus, the one who reveals God.[4]

I can prove none of this, of course. It could very well be that Mark and the Fourth Gospel are both relying on independent or overlapping oral traditions. But I cannot prove any of those theories either. Indeed, such theories appear to me to be nothing more than 'hermeneutical black holes', as Dennis MacDonald aptly described them.[5] Attempting to demonstrate any of these positions, much less to use them heuristically in the interpretation of John, seems like chasing after the wind. But, to quote legal theorists, 'it takes a theory to beat a theory'.[6] So I have laid out mine. For all of its shortcomings,[7] at least it can be evaluated by others, since it simply compares one known text to another in order to explain how the latter text made use of the former and to what end.[8]

---

[3] As it relates to the use of this term in Johannine studies, see especially the work of Jean Zumstein; see, e.g., his 'Intratextuality and Intertextuality in the Gospel of John', in *Anatomies of Narrative Criticism: The Past, Present, and Futures of the Fourth Gospel as Literature*, ed. Tom Thatcher and Stephen D. Moore (RBS, 55; Atlanta, GA: Society of Biblical Literature, 2008), 121–35. The scholarly language as it relates to this concept is quite varied. For example, some refer to 'transformative imitation', others to 'intertextual reconfigurations' etc. On 'other' ways in which the narrative communicates its story, see the recent volume, *How John Works: Storytelling in the Fourth Gospel*, ed. Douglas Estes and Ruth Sheridan (RBS, 86; Atlanta, GA: Society of Biblical Literature, 2016).

[4] This is what C. K. Barrett was suggesting when he wrote (referring specifically to the Fourth Gospel's use of Mark in the composition of the Passion narrative), 'Every one of the differences between John and Mark is at least connected with a dogmatic motive' (*John*, 547).

[5] Dennis R. MacDonald, *My Turn: A Critique of Critics of 'Mimesis Criticism'* (The Institute for Antiquity and Christianity Occasional Papers, 53; Claremont, CA: Institute for Antiquity and Christianity, 2009), 4.

[6] The common aphorism is often attributed to the law professor Richard A. Epstein (see, e.g., his 'Common Law, Labor Law, and Reality: A Rejoinder to Professors Getman and Kohler', *Yale Law Journal* 92 [1983]: 1435–41; quotation on p. 1435).

[7] I am mindful that once one has landed on a working hypothesis, the resulting work all too often becomes nothing more than an exercise in confirmation bias. Consider, for example, the circular relationship between presuppositions and conclusions so routinely on display in Historical Jesus studies.

[8] I have addressed my views on these subjects more fully in *Rewriting the Feeding of Five Thousand: John 6.1–15 as a Test Case for Johannine Dependence on the Synoptic Gospels* (Studies in Biblical Literature, 125; New York: Peter Lang, 2011). I continue to maintain that 'If a compelling case can be made for John's literary dependence on the Synoptics based on literary-critical, historical, and philological arguments, and the differences between them can be understood as intelligible within the broad sweep of the Evangelist's thinking and presentation, we should then understand our author to be attempting what so many others in antiquity attempted – the transformative imitation of another written text' (p. 64).

The following chapter, therefore, intends to offer nothing more than a plausible, coherent reading, one which attempts to show how the author of the Fourth Gospel may have used (that is, may have rewritten and transformed) the story in Mark, specifically the story of John the Baptist in Mark 1.2–8, in the pursuit of his own theological agenda. This reading of the Fourth Gospel's use of Mark should at least be able to stand alongside other readings since it accounts for the similarities by positing direct dependence and the differences by insisting that the author of the Fourth Gospel was in fact an author, not just a copyist.

In any case, we need different approaches, multiple readings. The more the merrier, I say. Given that most of what we see is behind our eyes, that our minds have an endless capacity to generate the meanings we seek to find, especially those meanings that are in keeping with our own presuppositions and biases, we should not expect to land on the *correct* reading of John, much less the one that will finally convince everyone else.[9] Moreover, a generous, open-ended approach seems especially fitting for a slippery work like the Fourth Gospel anyway. As noted elsewhere, if Jesus would not ride in his disciples' boat in John, I am quite sure he will not ride in any of ours as modern readers either.[10]

Four illustrative examples of the Fourth Gospel's rewriting of Mark

Before proceeding with my specific topic, let me briefly draw attention to a few rather obvious examples in order to illustrate my point. Long before entering the garden in John 18, where in Mark's Gospel Jesus prays to the Father to be saved from the hour (14.35), in John 12 Jesus has already explicitly rejected the notion that he should ask the Father to be saved from the hour (v. 27).[11] This shift in Jesus' perspective in the Fourth Gospel suggests Jesus' determination to complete what he has been sent to do. To avoid the hour is to abort the mission. But God cannot be revealed in his fullness if Jesus does not go to the cross. And in keeping with this Johannine understanding of his mission, when Jesus finally does enter the garden in the Fourth Gospel, he does not pray at all.[12]

Second, the garden scene in Mark is filled with a profound sense of Jesus' mental anguish. He is 'distressed and agitated' (14.33). He says to three of his disciples, 'I am deeply grieved, even to death' (14.34). The narrator then records that Jesus 'threw

---

[9] Of course, the ambiguity does not pertain to readers alone, it begins with an author's use of words, as Tennyson rightly observed a long time ago, 'Words, like Nature, half reveal and half conceal the Soul within' (*In Memoriam A.H.H.*, 5).

[10] Steven A. Hunt, D. Francois Tolmie and Ruben Zimmermann, 'Foreword' in *Character Studies in the Fourth Gospel: Narrative Approaches to Seventy Figures in John*, ed. Steven A. Hunt, D. Francois Tolmie and Ruben Zimmermann (Grand Rapids, MI: Wm. B. Eerdmans, 2016), xii.

[11] So also, Andrew T. Lincoln, *The Gospel According to St John* (BNTC, 4; London: Continuum, 2005), 351.

[12] John 18.1–12; note also that in Mark 'the hour' arrives when Judas comes with the arresting party (14.41–43). In the Fourth Gospel, 'the hour', anticipated since 2.4 when Jesus first spoke about it while at a wedding, is not about betrayal but about revelation, not to mention the positive impact that revelation will have on all people (cf. 12.23, 32).

himself down on the ground to pray' (14.35). The Fourth Gospel, of course, omits all of this in the garden. Instead, 'knowing all that was to happen to him' (18.4), Jesus went out to meet those who had come to arrest him and then initiated the arrest itself: 'Whom are you looking for?', he says twice in 18.4 and 7. And, most poignantly, instead of Jesus throwing himself on the ground in prayer (as in Mark), it is the entire arresting party who fall to the ground when Jesus says, ἐγώ εἰμι ('I AM') in 18.6. Jesus' pathos in Mark's garden scene is replaced by Jesus' victorious Christophany in the Fourth Gospel's rewritten account.[13]

Third, in the garden at Jesus' arrest in the Fourth Gospel, when Peter attacks one of the arresting party, Jesus tells him to put the sword away, since he has come specifically to 'drink the cup that the Father has given' (18.11). The language in this scene clearly echoes the language of Jesus' petition in the garden in Mark's Gospel, when he asks the Father repeatedly to take the cup from him (14.36, 39).[14] Again, the arrest scene in the Fourth Gospel shows Jesus' resolve to drink the cup; there is not even a hint of Jesus' desire to avoid this outcome. As we have said, it is for this reason he has been sent.

Finally, in Mark's Gospel, Simon of Cyrene, 'the father of Alexander and Rufus', carries the cross for Jesus to the place of execution (15.21). In the Fourth Gospel, after Pilate hands Jesus over for crucifixion, Jesus carries the cross to the place of execution, specifically and quite emphatically, 'by himself' (19.17). There is no room for Simon of Cyrene, much less reference to his children, in the Fourth Gospel's account. While there is much more that could be drawn out from this detail,[15] if nothing else, the reader remains focused on Jesus in this most critical scene. Since Jesus will fully reveal the Father on the cross, readers dare not take their eyes off him even as he makes his way.[16]

All of this rewriting of the broader Markan account follows a consistent trajectory: Jesus, sent to reveal God to the world, is fully committed to his mission, a mission that is his alone.[17] The changes to Mark are not merely supplemental; nor are they simply corrections. Rather, the refashioning of source material in each of these examples sets Jesus' determination in sharper relief in the Fourth Gospel, precisely when it is understood in light of Mark's narrative, a narrative where Jesus sincerely desires to avoid the cross if at all possible. What does all of this reveal about God? At the very least it suggests this: if Jesus is utterly determined to save, so is God who sent him.[18]

---

[13] Whatever else Jesus' twice-repeated 'my soul is troubled' (12.27; 13.31) is communicating, it also serves to anticipate his twice-repeated instruction that his disciples not allow such trouble (14.1; 14.25), as well as to contrast with themes in the final discourse relative to courage (cf. 16.33), peace (cf. 14.27), mutual love (cf. 13.34; 15.12–13), etc.

[14] Cf. J. Ramsey Michaels, *The Gospel of John* (NICNT; Grand Rapids, MI: Wm. B. Eerdmans, 2010), 895–96.

[15] See further, Chelsea N. Revell and Steven A. Hunt, 'The Co-Crucified Men: Shadows by His Cross' in Hunt, Tolmie and Zimmerman (eds), *Character Studies in the Fourth Gospel*, 607–17.

[16] Francis J. Moloney notes that an 'awareness of [the Synoptic] tradition heightens the impression that in the Johannine Gospel even on his way to Golgotha Jesus is master of his own situation' (*The Gospel of John* [SP, 4; Collegeville, MN: Liturgical Press, 1998], 506).

[17] On the programmatic importance of Jesus' being 'sent' in the Fourth Gospel, see especially the helpful essay, 'The Mission of the Son of God' by G. R. Beasley-Murray in his *Gospel of Life: Theology in the Fourth Gospel* (Peabody, MA: Hendrickson, 1991), 15–33.

[18] While beyond the scope of the present work, the Fourth Gospel appears to be making use of Matthew and/or Luke similarly, since one could argue that, at least in some instances, there is a

The identity and ministry of John (the Baptist or Prince?) in John 1.19–34

It is not at all obvious or necessary that a story about Jesus should start with a story about John the Baptist. That it does in Mark's Gospel is noteworthy. That it does similarly in Matthew and Luke becomes just part of the mass of evidence suggesting that those gospels depend on Mark in one way or another.[19] Since the Fourth Gospel's opening narrative also begins with John, one should probably be forgiven for seeing that as just another piece of evidence that suggests the author's use of Mark as well.

Indeed, in the Fourth Gospel, after an initial prologue celebrating the Word (1.1–18), the first two days in the narrative world in 1.19–34 can well be understood as a completely rewritten version of the basic Markan story about John the Baptist. Following the agenda laid out so clearly in the prologue, the Fourth Gospel's story focuses completely on Jesus, the Word made flesh.

Put quite simply, Mark's opening narrative in 1.1–8 is a story entirely about John. We read about his appearance in the wilderness, his ministry, his popularity. He is even referred to as 'the baptizer' (1.4), a designation of sorts that functions something like a working title, since it describes the essence of his ministry. Given Herod's glorious temple in nearby Jerusalem, readers are all but required to marvel at John's 'out-in-the-middle-of-nowhere' call to repentance in baptism and to the consequent forgiveness of sins available therein. Readers should be stunned to read about the overwhelming response to this call when 'people from the whole Judean countryside and all the people of Jerusalem were going out to him' and 'confessing their sins' (1.5). And readers will no doubt puzzle over John's strange clothing and odd diet (1.6). Even in Mark 1.7–8, when

---

logical trajectory from Mark, moving through Matthew and Luke, and proceeding into the Fourth Gospel: briefly, Mark begins his story when Jesus is an adult. The author appears to know nothing of Jesus' divine conception. Alternatively, Matthew and Luke begin their stories earlier, evidently believing that the story of Jesus is better understood in light of his birth. Despite their profound differences, the birth narratives emphasize, among other things, Jesus' divine conception, his parents (Joseph and Mary), his descent from King David, his birth in Bethlehem, and his being brought up in Nazareth. True to the Matthean and Lukan idea of starting the story earlier, the author of the Fourth Gospel begins with the Word who was with God and was God 'in the beginning' (1.1). Even though the Fourth Gospel does not speak of Jesus' divine conception, the basic building blocks of Matthew's and Luke's infancy stories are still written into the narrative in interesting ways. So, for example, Jesus is still God's son (1.18; *passim*); he is also understood to be the son of Joseph (1.45; 6.42); Jesus' mother figures prominently (2.1–12; 19.25–27); Jesus is from Nazareth (1.45; 18.5, 7; 19.19); interestingly, in keeping with the author's basic motif related to opponents of Jesus speaking unwitting truths about him, Jesus' descent from David and connection to Bethlehem are hinted at in 7.42. More importantly, however, while Matthew and Luke begin their stories with Jesus' divine conception, the Fourth Gospel's prologue emphasizes that those who receive Jesus are 'children of God'; indeed, they are 'born not of blood or of the will of the flesh or of the will of man, but of God' (1.12–13). Thus, the Fourth Gospel's prologue gives the impression of being written in light of Matthew's and Luke's opening birth narratives, with an eye not only on Jesus as the only begotten son of God, but on the 'divine conception' of all those who will receive him. See also in this regard, Barrett, *John*, 51–53.

[19] On John the Baptist and the Synoptic problem, see especially Mark Goodacre, 'The Synoptic Problem: John the Baptist and Jesus', in *Method and Meaning: Essays on New Testament Interpretation in Honor of Harold W. Attridge*, ed. Andrew B. McGowan and Kent Harold Richards (RBS, 67; Atlanta, GA: Society of Biblical Literature Press, 2011), 177–92.

John the Baptist is drawing attention to the *one* who is coming after him, that aspect of the story is still *also* about John's proclamation, his power vis-à-vis the one who is more powerful, his baptistic ministry, etc. All of this to say, before Jesus ever gets to centre stage in Mark 1.9, the first story in Mark is simply a story about who John *is*.[20]

In the Fourth Gospel, however, the first story about John is primarily a story about who he is *not*.[21] Indeed, the lone negation in Mark (i.e., when John says, 'I am *not* worthy to stoop down and untie the thong of his sandals' in 1.8) is effectively repeated in John 1.27. But the *idea* of negation goes on to get written into the Fourth Gospel so thoroughly that it becomes a primary motif with respect to John.[22] Almost immediately upon his introduction, the narrator begins to describe John in negative terms: 'He himself was *not* the light' (1.8). And when John himself speaks for the first time he also begins negatively: 'I am *not* the Messiah', he says in 1.20.[23] This particular statement is especially odd when one considers that it is in response to the simple and rather straightforward question, 'Who are you?', in 1.19. In other words, he could have said more simply, 'My name is John.' Then, when pressed further by the delegation sent from Jerusalem, he goes on to deny being Elijah, and then the prophet as well (1.21).[24]

Clearly showing some frustration at these denials, the questions come again, rapid fire: 'Who are you? Let us have an answer for those who sent us. What do you say about yourself?' (1.22). At this point, unlike in Mark 1.3 (and Matthew 3.3 and Luke 3.4 for that matter) where the narrator quotes Isaiah 40.3 about John, in the Fourth Gospel, John now quotes in direct speech a shortened form of that verse about himself: 'I am the voice of one crying out in the wilderness. Make straight the way of the Lord.'[25]

---

[20] On John the Baptist in Mark, see further Walter Wink, *John the Baptist in the Gospel Tradition* (SNTSMS, 7; Cambridge: Cambridge University Press, 1968), 1–17; Willi Marxsen, *Mark the Evangelist: Studies on the Redaction History of the Gospel*, trans. James Boyce, et al. (Nashville, TN: Abingdon, 1969), 30–53.

[21] On John in the Fourth Gospel, see especially Cornelis Bennema, *Encountering Jesus: Character Studies in the Gospel of John* (2nd edn; Minneapolis, MN: Fortress, 2014), 61–73; and Catrin H. Williams, 'John (the Baptist): The Witness on the Threshold', in Hunt, Tolmie and Zimmerman (eds), *Character Studies in the Fourth Gospel*, 46–60.

[22] On the reasons for this motif in the Fourth Gospel more broadly, see the discussion related to John the Baptist in Raymond E. Brown, *The Community of the Beloved Disciple* (New York: Paulist Press, 1979), 69–71. Rudolf Schnackenburg (*The Gospel According to St. John*, trans. Kevin Smyth [New York: Crossroad, 1968], 1.167) states flatly that the Fourth Gospel 'had the polemical and apologetical intention of combatting the disciples of John the Baptist, who still existed and competed with Christianity in the time of the evangelist'. While 'it is certainly not the main intention of the Gospel . . . it is definitely there'. A number of scholars attribute the discovery of this motif in the Gospel to the 1898 publication of W. Baldensperger, *Der Prolog des vierten Evangeliums, sein polemisch-apologetischer Zweck* (Tübingen: J. C. B. Mohr, 1898).

[23] John's testimony in the timeless prologue in v. 15 is proleptic, anticipating his declaration in the narrative world in 1.30.

[24] On John's three denials, note how in the Greek text they *decrease* in length (anticipating 3.30?), from five words in v. 20, to two words in v. 21a, to one word in v. 21b. Also, in view of the careful use of the important phrase ἐγώ εἰμι throughout the Fourth Gospel specifically in relation to Jesus (cf. 4.26, 6.20, 35, 48, 51; 8.12, 24, 28, 58; 10.7, 9, 11, 14; 11.25; 13.19; 14.6; 15.1, 5; 18.5, 6, 8; save the important exception in 9.9 in relation to the blind man), note the deliberate structure of the Greek phrase in the first denial: Ἐγὼ οὐκ εἰμί.

[25] Some have suggested that this is exactly the kind of evidence that shows the Fourth Gospel's use of independent traditions. The discussion often turns on whether or not the historical John ever applied Isa. 40.3 to himself. See, for example, the discussion of this very point in Craig S. Keener, *The*

Finally, we can say something concrete about John, right? Not so fast. The investigators, unmoved by his use of Isaiah and obviously unsatisfied, proceed as if he did not say anything at all. They simply return to the previous line of questioning which, following the narrator's agenda to minimize John, only serves to press his earlier denials home: 'Why then are you baptizing if you are *neither* the Messiah, *nor* Elijah, *nor* the Prophet?' (1.25). Isaiah 40.3, and whatever it meant about John in the Fourth Gospel, drops from view immediately in the narrative, its Markan (and Matthean and Lukan) import notwithstanding.

Given their back and forth so far, John's response now – 'I baptize with water' – must have been truly maddening. Either John misunderstood their simple question (*'Why are you baptizing?'* Did he perhaps think they had asked, 'With what are you baptizing?'), or, more likely, he was being deliberately enigmatic.[26] It is rather amusing to imagine that John had to shout his equally cryptic follow-up – 'Among you stands one whom you do not know, the one who is coming after me; I am not worthy to untie the thong of his sandal' (1.26b–27) – because the delegates from Jerusalem, realizing they were getting nowhere with John, had already turned their backs on him to go.[27] If so, then off they went, trudging all the way back up to the city without an answer to either question. One can only imagine their frustration when, utterly exhausted by their journey, they had to give this report in Jerusalem: 'We don't know who he is. And we don't know why he's baptizing.'

It is surely noteworthy that while John will never answer their first question – who are you? – with anything remotely like a concrete answer, he answers the second – why are you baptizing? – by offering a straightforward reply 'on the next day' (1.29): 'I came baptizing with water *for this reason*, that he might be revealed to Israel' (1.31). In other words, from his perspective and that of the narrator's, John's identity was irrelevant; he came only in order to identify another whose identity was everything.[28] This presumably simple task was more difficult than it might have appeared since, as John observes twice in direct speech, 'I myself did not know him' (1.31, 33), that is, the one he came to identify. What is this all about? And how does it play into the Fourth Gospel's rewriting of the Markan account?

Readers already know from the Fourth Gospel's prologue that 'there was a man sent from God, whose name was John' (1.6) and that this man 'came as a witness to testify to

---

Gospel of John: A Commentary (Peabody, MA: Hendrickson, 2003), 1.437–40. But similar types of transformation of Mark occur elsewhere in the Fourth Gospel. For example, note how at Jesus' trial in Mark 'false' witnesses testify that they heard Jesus say 'I will destroy this temple that is made with hands, and in three days I will build another, not made with hands' (14.58). In this instance, the Fourth Gospel moves the saying (from the trial to the 'temple cleansing', which he also relocates), abbreviates it (fourteen words in the Greek text of Mark, compared to ten in John) and, as with Isa. 40.3 and John the Baptist, transforms it into direct speech, this time on the lips of Jesus: 'Destroy this temple, and in three days I will raise it up' (2.19).

[26] John F. McHugh notes that here 'the Baptist does not in fact answer their question. Instead he replies by changing the subject', *John 1–4* (ICC; London: T&T Clark, 2009), 122.

[27] As with others in the gospel, the delegates simply disappear from the scene, so it is impossible to say when they departed (cf. Nicodemus in ch. 3; the brothers of Jesus in ch. 7; the Blind Man in chs 9–10, etc.).

[28] Keener (*John*, 1.447) observes rightly, 'To the Johannine community ... the critical fact of John's baptismal mission was that he came to reveal Israel's king to Israel'.

the light' (1.7). Considering that grand introduction, it is rather strange that this John is consistently denied any identity marker such as 'the Baptist' or 'the baptizer' in the Fourth Gospel. And in the gospel traditionally attributed to another John, the son of Zebedee, some sort of designation that would distinguish one from the other would be most welcome. Its absence then, especially in this gospel, is doubly odd. More to the point, however, in a gospel replete – indeed, seemingly obsessed – with various titles for Jesus,[29] the absence of Mark's traditional designation for John is telling. To understand this omission one could suggest that the Fourth Gospel's author believed that referring to John with anything like a title would only distract readers from the important titles given to Jesus. Since these titles serve to reveal Jesus to the world, John's typical identity marker in Mark has been dropped from the Fourth Gospel.[30]

Perhaps in keeping with that major omission is the notion that the Fourth Gospel also deliberately refuses to refer to the great crowds coming out to John from Jerusalem and the Judean countryside. In fact, there are no *explicit* references to John's broad popularity among the people at all in the Fourth Gospel. The closest one gets to this idea is in 3.22–30, where, despite John's continuing baptistic ministry (3.23), John's disciples complain that 'all' are now going to Jesus for baptism (3.26), even though the water available there was abundant (3.23) and, presumably, could have accommodated both of their ministries. Even so, no one is going to John. Demonstrating remarkable equanimity, John suggests that this is exactly as it should be since Jesus 'must increase, but I must decrease' (3.30).[31] While his disciples' complaint *implies* that many were coming at one point to John for baptism, the Fourth Gospel never speaks explicitly about John's popular ministry. The Fourth Gospel's rewriting suggests the author's interest in maintaining the focus on Jesus, the Markan motif with respect to John's remarkable crowds notwithstanding.

Still, John's ministry did get the attention of some in Jerusalem, as evidenced by those sent to inquire about his identity and the nature of his ministry; he must have been doing something worthy of the questions put to him on that first day. What then was he doing? Well, John was obviously baptizing (1.25, 26, 28 make that perfectly clear). But in what is a most telling omission from Mark's story, the Fourth Gospel studiously avoids any sense that John's baptism was linked to repentance, much less to the forgiveness of sins. Since this is so, obviously no one is confessing their sins in the Fourth Gospel as a result of John's proclamation either.[32]

So why is John baptizing? Returning to our point above, John's 'ministry', if it can properly be called that, is presented in the Fourth Gospel as something akin to a role

---

[29] Indeed, Schnackenburg devotes an entire excursus to the eleven 'titles' and four 'descriptions' of Jesus that appear already in John 1 (*John*, 1.507–14).

[30] Interestingly, while the author of the Fourth Gospel refuses to add any identity marker to John's name such as 'the baptizer' (employing the participle; cf. Mk 1.4; 6.14, 24) or 'the Baptist' (employing the noun; cf. Mk 6.25; 8.28), in the Fourth Gospel, it is actually John who will refer to Jesus as 'the baptizer' in 1.33.

[31] Compare John's reaction to this news with the authorities' very different sentiment in Jn 11.48 and 12.19.

[32] There is some sense that John's baptistic ministry is associated with Jewish purification in 3.25, although the referent there is notoriously difficult. See further, Mark Appold, '"A Jew": A Search for the Identity and Role of an Anonymous Judean', in Hunt, Tolmie and Zimmerman (eds), *Character Studies in the Fourth Gospel*, 260–67.

the Prince plays in the popular seventeenth-century French version of the story of Cinderella (by the author Charles Perrault). Since the Prince did not know Cinderella aside from her fairy god-mother's magic at the ball, and since all that remained of their magical evening together was her glass slipper, the Prince was forced to try that slipper on all of the maidens in the kingdom until it finally fit on the one for whom it was made – Cinderella. The presentation of John's mission in the Fourth Gospel is similar. Since he does not know the one he is to identify, as both 1.30 and 1.33 make abundantly clear, he seems to be portrayed in the Fourth Gospel as baptizing anyone and everyone indiscriminately, hoping *only* to see the Spirit descend and remain on 'the one' to be revealed to Israel. When Jesus finally showed up, the Spirit descended and remained (1.33) – hence, the Spirit fit, just like Cinderella's slipper.[33]

Given John's stated understanding of *this* baptistic ministry, it really is quite interesting that his personal understanding of God's plan to reveal 'the one' gets short-circuited by the narrator. On that second day, when John 'saw Jesus coming toward him' (1.29), he was able immediately to identify him. In other words, the narrative suggests that before Jesus could even get to John, much less be baptized by John, the Spirit had already descended and stayed on Jesus. All that remained for John was to testify to what he had seen, which he does in various ways in the verses that follow. We will explore what John says about Jesus more fully below. Suffice it to say that while John evidently believed 'the one' would be identified by the Spirit's descent *during* the baptism, the baptism itself never took place.[34] John was able to testify to the Sprit's descent nevertheless.

Before turning our attention to John's important testimony about Jesus, we need to attend to one more feature of John's ministry as it is described in the Fourth Gospel. The narrator never offers any explanation for why John's ministry appears to continue, since that ministry, by his own account, consisted only in identifying the one to come. Returning to the Cinderella story, once she had been found, the Prince obviously stopped trying the slipper on other maidens. John's search, like the Prince's search, should have been over. To put the matter plainly, if Jesus is identified already in chapter 1, why is John still attempting to baptize in chapter 3? On a related note, given that at least two of John's disciples have left him to follow Jesus in chapter 1, why does John have any remaining disciples left in chapter 3? Should not John, who baptizes with water, have sent all of his disciples to Jesus, who baptizes with the Holy Spirit, once the latter has been identified? Whatever else this awkward story in John 3 is doing, it should be understood as evidence of the author's knowledge of John the Baptist's

---

[33] On the Cinderella story, its history, and the multiple variants related to it, see Paul Fleischman, *Glass Slipper, Gold Sandal: A World-Wide Cinderella* (New York: Henry Holt, 2007). For those interested in such things, I happened upon this comparison while working on this paper and simultaneously watching the recent Disney film 'Cinderella' with my (then) six-year old and three-year old sons, Parker and Anders.

[34] Most scholars agree that the Fourth Gospel omits Jesus' actual baptism. Lincoln is representative of the typical view: 'In contrast with the accounts in Matthew and Mark, this narrative does not actually relate Jesus' baptism. That Jesus was baptized by John is suppressed (again to avoid any suggestion that Jesus could be considered subordinate to John in some sense), and only if readers were familiar with this event through other accounts would they find here an allusion to it through John's testimony' (*John*, 113–14).

ministry as it is described more broadly in Mark. And if this true, it should also be understood as evidence of how thoroughly the author has rewritten this story in order to pursue his own agenda related to Jesus in chapter 1.

The testimony of John 'the Witness/Confessor' in John 1.19–34

It is the nature of John's testimony in the Fourth Gospel, however, that gets at the heart of this rewritten story. To review, in Mark, John the Baptist's sweeping call to 'a baptism of repentance for the forgiveness of sins' (1.4) is met by a massive response from the people who come for baptism and to confess their sins (1.5). John's effectiveness in Mark relates, no doubt, to the fact that he is presented as an Elijah-like character whose own proclamation and baptistic ministry anticipates that of another who will be even more powerful than he is (see Mk 9.11–13).

While many aspects of this Markan story about John drop from view in the Fourth Gospel, there are still some important overlapping ideas in both narratives. Though they are few, they are most informative. In Mark, John said, 'the one who is more powerful than I *is coming after me*' (1.7a). There is not even a hint of John the Baptist's knowledge of Jesus' pre-existence in the saying in Mark. From John's perspective, his ministry simply precedes Jesus' ministry. In the Fourth Gospel, John begins by suggesting essentially the same thing. Responding to the investigators from Jerusalem, he says: 'Among you stands one whom you do not know, *the one who is coming after me*'. With respect to the timing of their ministries, the Fourth Gospel's John – at least on this first day – is saying nothing beyond what Mark's John said. The ministry of the one to come is subsequent to John's ministry.

The uniquely Johannine notion that the one who is coming is *unknown* to those asking John the questions, only serves to concretize the prologue's point that although the world came into being through the Word, it nevertheless 'did not know him' (1.10). Of course, it also serves to anticipate John's own lack of knowledge about the one to come in 1.30 and 33.

Given that John's testimony about Jesus 'the next day' (1.29) is more theologically profound, one could easily understand this in light of the way that characters in the Fourth Gospel routinely develop in their understanding of Jesus, particularly when they have encountered him themselves. See the Samaritan Woman in John 4 or the Blind Man in John 9 as classic examples of this narrative contrivance.[35]

Incidentally, having made the basic point about Jesus' ministry coming after John's, both Mark and the Fourth Gospel immediately offer notably similar versions of John's statement of unworthiness:

Mark 1.7b: οὗ οὐκ εἰμὶ ἱκανὸς κύψας λῦσαι τὸν ἱμάντα τῶν ὑποδημάτων αὐτοῦ ('I am not worthy to stoop down and untie the thong of his sandals').

---

[35] So R. Alan Culpepper, *Anatomy of the Fourth Gospel: A Study in Literary Design* (Philadelphia, PA: Fortress, 1983), 103.

John 1.27b: οὗ οὐκ εἰμὶ [ἐγὼ] ἄξιος ἵνα λύσω αὐτοῦ τὸν ἱμάντα τοῦ ὑποδήματος ('I am not worthy to untie the thong of his sandal').[36]

That John's statement on the timing of their respective ministries is followed immediately by John's statement of his unworthiness in both gospels is hardly coincidental; the simplest understanding suggests it is a prime example of the author of John following his source quite closely. The Fourth Gospel includes it since it is the genesis of all the other negations about John in the narrative, as we have already noted.

In light of the Fourth Gospel's prologue and its emphasis on the pre-existence of the Word, however, the narrator's expansion of John's confession, once Jesus approached 'the next day' (1.29), makes perfect sense. What was a straightforward assertion in Mark – Jesus' ministry will follow after John's – now turns into a riddle in the Fourth Gospel, when John says: '*After* me comes a man who ... was *before* me' (1.30; cf. 1.15). The riddle itself may very well explain why Mark's emphasis on the power differential between the two gives way to an emphasis on John's inferior 'rank' in the Fourth Gospel. Simply put, in John's view in the Fourth Gospel, Jesus outranks him because he was before him. Again, given the readers' knowledge of the prologue, this is not surprising. While John 'was a man sent from God' (1.5), Jesus is the Word who was 'in the beginning ... with God' (1.1) and who then 'became flesh' (1.14). In short, the Fourth Gospel's rewriting of this aspect of the scene only follows the trajectory of the story already set by the prologue.

Briefly, it is worth noting that John's 'proclamation' in Mark 1.4 and 7 gives way in the Fourth Gospel to his 'confession' and 'testimony'. Indeed, in the Fourth Gospel, John is a 'witness'. In addition to what we have already said about John's denials about himself, and his testimony on behalf of Jesus, we should observe how these terms play so perfectly into a major storyline in the Fourth Gospel's overarching plot. Thus, his denials are not just simple denials; they are – to dramatize them – *sworn confessions*.[37] His statements about Jesus are not just plain statements; they are *sworn testimony*. John is a 'witness' in a legal proceeding related to Jesus, and he has clearly signed his affidavit. As a basic rewriting of Mark's language of 'proclamation', these changes are therefore easily understood as a thematic departure from Mark's basic story about John because they are the building blocks of the lawsuit motif in the Fourth Gospel.[38]

---

[36] Whatever one makes of the differences between these two statements (e.g., ἱκανός in Mk, ἄξιος in Jn; plural 'sandals' in Mk, singular 'sandal' in Jn, etc.), they are *not* as pronounced as the differences between Matthew 3:11c and Mark 1:7b. And irrespective of that fact, the majority of scholars continue to maintain Matthew's use of Mark.

[37] The word 'confession' (ὁμολογέω) in 1.20 is used only two more times in John, and both are in the context of a trial with stipulated consequences (see 9.22 and 12.42). While the specific legal language related to 'making promises' or 'taking an oath' (cf., e.g., Mt. 5.33–36) does not occur in the Fourth Gospel, the idiomatic expression 'Give glory to God', which functions similarly, does (see 9.24; cf. Josh. 7.19). Note also that while it is John 'confessing' in the Fourth Gospel, people are confessing (ἐξομολογέω) their sins in Mark 1.5.

[38] Lincoln writes, 'The noun μαρτυρία occurs 14 times [in John] in comparison with four times in the three Synoptics together, while the verb μαρτυρέω is found 33 times [in John] in comparison with twice in the three Synoptics. Together with such concepts as judgement, truth, and life, this language forms part of a larger motif, that of a trial or lawsuit, which shapes much of the narrative' (*John*, 100). See further his outstanding treatment of this theme in *Truth on Trial: The Lawsuit Motif in John's Gospel* (Peabody, MA: Hendrickson, 2000).

Another major change in the narrative of the Fourth Gospel, one even more easily linked to the author's rewriting of Mark 1.2–8, relates to Mark's utterly under-developed theme with respect to Jesus as the one who will baptize 'with the Holy Spirit' (1.8). For whatever reason, Mark makes next to nothing out of this important proclamation going forward in the narrative. In the Fourth Gospel, on the other hand, John's testimony about Jesus as the one 'who baptizes with the Holy Spirit' (1.33) announces a motif that becomes absolutely central to the narrative's overall storyline. The Spirit and water, as complementary and linked (cf. 7.38–39) motifs, run like parallel threads throughout the narrative, only reaching their respective resolutions as plot lines when, with respect to water, Jesus' side is pierced in 19.34, and when, with respect to the Spirit, Jesus breathes on his disciples after the resurrection and says, 'Receive the Holy Spirit' in 20.22. In short, John's early proclamation about Jesus and the Spirit in Mark is slightly retooled in the Fourth Gospel (1.33),[39] but the thoroughgoing use to which the motif gets employed going forward in the narrative clearly pursues the author's own theological agenda.[40]

Finally, the most dramatic departure from the account in Mark 1 occurs when, in the Fourth Gospel, John saw Jesus and said: 'Here is the Lamb of God who takes away the sin of the world' (1.29; the statement is shortened but repeated for emphasis in v. 36). While Mark's John is, as we have seen, baptizing throngs of people for the forgiveness of sins, when we look at John's statement here we begin to move to the very essence of the Fourth Gospel's refashioned account. As Bruner puts it memorably, 'This twenty-ninth verse is the Mount Everest of John's witness to Christ'.[41]

Space will not permit a thorough recounting of the various ways John's statement about Jesus has been understood by scholars. Suffice it to say, most are content to speak about polyvalence and intertextual allusions that require an understanding of this passage in light of any number of texts in the Hebrew Bible. Genesis 22, Exodus 12 and 29, Leviticus 16, Isaiah 53 and Jeremiah 11 have all been suggested, as have a few Jewish apocalyptic texts, including the Book of Revelation. C. K. Barrett's sense that the author is involved in the 'amalgamation . . . of ideas' raised by these texts and their interpretation in antiquity is prevalent among scholars as well.[42]

Building on all of that, and then thinking *intratextually*, John's statement in 1.29 most likely anticipates the Passover motif, a motif that surfaces occasionally in the

---

[39] To offer but one example of this slight retooling, in Mark, John proclaims himself that Jesus is the one who will baptize with the Spirit (1.8), whereas in the Fourth Gospel, John confesses that God said to him that Jesus is the one who will baptize with the Spirit (1.33).

[40] On the Holy Spirit in the Fourth Gospel, see especially Gary M. Burge, *The Anointed Community: The Holy Spirit in the Johannine Tradition* (Grand Rapids, MI: Wm. B. Eerdmans, 1987). On the theme of 'water', see Craig R. Koester, *Symbolism in the Fourth Gospel: Meaning, Mystery, Community* (2nd edn; Minneapolis, MN: Augsburg Fortress, 2003), 175–206.

[41] Frederick Dale Bruner, *The Gospel of John: A Commentary* (Grand Rapids, MI: Wm. B. Eerdmans, 2012), 80; Bruner provides an excellent overview of the various ways John's statement in 1.29 has been understood; see pp. 79–84; 90–95.

[42] Barrett, *John*, 177; Richard Hays explains why such an amalgamation of ideas is eminently possible in the Fourth Gospel: 'John's figural hermeneutic allows him to articulate his extraordinary (and polemical) claim that all of Israel's Scripture actually bears witness to Jesus . . . Thus, even more comprehensively than the other Gospels, John understands the Old Testament as a vast matrix of symbols prefiguring Jesus' (*Echoes of Scripture in the Gospels* [Waco, TX: Baylor University Press, 2016], 343).

gospel if for no other reason than to mark the passing of time (cf. 2.13, 23; 6.4) but also to foreshadow the denouement of the story when the Passover becomes critical, especially to the Passion narrative (cf. 11.55–56; 12.1, 12, 20; 13.1; 18.28; 19.14, 31).[43] There, Jesus is handed over for crucifixion around noon, on the day of preparation for Passover (19.14), the very day when the Passover lambs are being sacrificed in the temple.[44] The author draws attention also to a branch of hyssop in 19.29. Of course, hyssop plays an important role at Passover as well (Ex. 12.22). And, finally, after the soldiers break the legs of the two co-crucified men, the narrator notes, rather awkwardly, that they did not break Jesus' legs since he was already dead (19.33).[45] The link between Jesus and the Passover lamb is made explicit when the narrator then refers to Jesus' unbroken legs as a fulfilment of Scripture, almost certainly alluding to the Passover instructions in Ex. 12.46 (cf. Num. 9.12).

Passover, however, as any number of scholars will quickly point out, is not about the expiation or forgiveness of sins.[46] True enough. But Passover was the time to recall what God had done for Israel when he 'struck down the Egyptians' (Ex. 12.27), and their 'house of slavery' (Ex. 13.3, 14).

The Fourth Gospel could very well be drawing all of these ideas together. To make sense of them in one way only requires that we take the narrative quite simply and quite seriously. A preliminary sketch might suggest the following: Jesus is the lamb of God who takes away the sin – indeed, the singular sin – of the world, a sin already identified in the prologue: '... the world came into being through him; yet the world did not know him. He came to what was his own, *and his own people did not accept him*' (1.10–11). Of course, 'accepting' (or 'receiving') him is synonymous with 'believing' in him, as 1.12 states. The singular sin is paralleled therefore by God's singular requirement described in 6.29: 'this is the *work* of God, that you believe in him whom he has sent'. Add to all of this now the (rather Pauline?)[47] notion about slavery to sin that emerges most clearly in John 8, and one perhaps has enough to begin to tie all of this together.

If receiving Jesus is the singular work required of the world, and rejecting Jesus is the world's singular sin, and results in slavery to sin, then God, who loves the world (cf. 3.16), must somehow defeat and destroy sin. This God has done. Just as God defeated and destroyed Egypt, the house of slavery at Passover, so God defeats and destroys (i.e., 'takes away') sin through Jesus, his lamb, at Passover.[48] Given that the verb here, αἴρω, is clearly used to mean 'destroy' in John 11.48, one cannot rule out this

---

[43] Schnackenburg (*John*, 1.158) writes, 'a line goes from here [in 1.29] to the scene at the Cross'.
[44] On the specific timing ('about noon') and its relationship to the sacrifice of Passover lambs, see the discussion in Keener, *John*, 2.1130–31; cf. Michaels, *John*, 942–43.
[45] Awkward in that first the soldiers break the legs of the one co-crucified man and then of the other before coming to find Jesus already dead. But why that order if Jesus was between the two men as indicated in 19.18?
[46] See, e.g., C. H. Dodd, *The Interpretation of the Fourth Gospel* (Cambridge: Cambridge University Press, 1953), 234; Barrett, *John*, 176.
[47] On the relationship of the Fourth Gospel to Paul or Pauline thought, see the judicious discussion in Barrett, *John*, 54–59.
[48] Dodd quite literally equates 'the lamb of God who takes away the sin of the world' with 'God's Messiah who makes an end of sin' (*Interpretation*, 238).

possible inference.⁴⁹ Moreover, a subtle verbal link between Jesus who 'takes away' the sin of the world and the crucifixion as the means by which it gets taken away may well be hinted at when the authorities, if we translate them literally, say to Pilate, 'Take away! Take away! Crucify him!' (19.15). Since the narrator employs the same verb here as in 1.29,⁵⁰ and delights in putting unwitting, profoundly ironic truths in the mouths of Jesus' opponents, this reading is at least suggestive.⁵¹

However one understands the material, this major departure from Mark's narrative about John the Baptist, should certainly be recognized as in keeping with the basic storyline of the Fourth Gospel, and it goes a long way to explaining why Mark's emphasis on confession of sins and forgiveness of sins drops from view. Indeed, forgiveness is only on the periphery in our author's mind (in fact, only in Jn 20.23), since the Fourth Gospel is about the revelation of God as one full of 'grace and truth' (1.14, 17; or, as the Hebrew Bible puts it, 'steadfast love and faithfulness'; cf. Ex. 34.6), a revelation made complete in Jesus' victory over sin on the cross at Passover time.

Conclusion – Similarities as evidence of use; differences as evidence of writing

John 1.19–34 can well be understood as a thoughtful rewriting of Mark's account of John the Baptist in Mark 1.2–8. Mark and the Fourth Gospel share several features: they both begin their basic story about Jesus with a story about John the Baptist. Both texts cite Isaiah 40, and make use of negation as it relates to John. Both offer John's statement of unworthiness and note John's own sense that his ministry simply precedes that of Jesus. Finally, both emphasize John's baptism with water and compare it to Jesus' baptism with the Spirit, although only the Fourth Gospel develops this latter motif in any significant way. Once these similarities are noted for what they are (i.e., as evidence of the Fourth Gospel's use of Mark), if the remaining differences between them can be understood satisfactorily in terms of the theological trajectory of the Fourth Gospel itself (i.e., as evidence of an author 'writing' and not just 'copying'), then the simplest explanation – that is, the preferred explanation – is to understand the Fourth Gospel as, at least in part, a creative rewriting of the Markan account.

---

[49] Note how the verb is also used in reference to the branches 'he removes' (αἴρει) in 15.2 and then consider their eventual fate in 15.6.

[50] Bruner (*John*, 1075–6) draws attention to the use of the verb αἴρω in both passages as well.

[51] As a classic example, note how Pilate unwittingly proclaims Jesus' kingship by insisting on the placard on the cross (19.19–23); see further, Paul D. Duke, *Irony in the Fourth Gospel* (Atlanta, GA: John Knox Press, 1985), 136–37; David W. Mead, *The Literary Devices in John's Gospel* (revised and expanded edn; Eugene, OR: Wipf & Stock, 2018), 75.

11

John the Baptist in Mark and John: An Exercise in Comparison

Troels Engberg-Pedersen

Comparison

Comparison is an art that requires the utmost care about the logic of its exercise, including its scope and purpose. Elsewhere, I have distinguished so-called 'parallel comparison' from 'heuristic comparison'.[1] In parallel comparison, the scholar analyses two (or more) configurations that initially appear similar in certain respects, as individual wholes and each for their own sake. The scholar attempts to situate and understand each individual part of any of the two wholes within that configuration, itself viewed as a whole. In this way, one may ascertain both similarities and differences between the features that initially gave rise to the comparison without distorting the meaning of the individual features, each as part of their own whole. Here the comparison may therefore result in a state of 'deep parallelism', in which the scholar may grasp similarities and differences between the two comparanda in a single view. If we apply this approach to our immediate theme, we should end up with a coherent view of the features of the figure of John the Baptist in Mark and John, respectively. Initially, we would not make any suggestions concerning any 'genealogical' relationship between the two configurations, but consider them only 'analogically'.

'Heuristic comparison', by contrast, presupposes parallel comparison, thus avoiding any distortion of features that initially appear similar, but it aims to take an additional step from merely placing the comparanda in (deep) parallelism. Instead, it focuses specifically on one of the comparanda, using the comparison to throw as much light as possible on *that*. In this way, it brings out particularly sharply any *differences* between the features that initially appeared similar. Heuristic comparison, then, is a particularly helpful tool to make us understand even better the individual features of any configuration that we may want to understand. But here, too, we are in principle only

---

[1] See my 'The Past Is a Foreign Country: On the Shape and Purposes of Comparison in New Testament Scholarship', in *The New Testament in Comparison: Validity, Method, and Purpose in Comparing Traditions*, ed. John M. G. Barclay and Benjamin G. White (LNTS, 600; London: T & T Clark, 2020), 41–61.

comparing 'analogically'. In both parallel and heuristic comparison, the distinctly genealogical perspective is an additional one: *once* we have set out two comparanda as wholes, we may take the additional step of asking whether one has been directly, that is, 'genealogically', influenced by the other.

In this chapter, however, I will proceed in a somewhat different way. I will insist on the need for doing a parallel comparison of Mark and John on John the Baptist. I cannot in fact do that fully here, not least with respect to Mark, but that is the first basic perspective to be applied. However, I will also bring in the genealogical perspective from the start, but only in a hypothetical manner. Since we cannot presumably ever *know* about a genealogical relationship between these two gospels, the basic aim will not be to argue *that* John knew and used Mark (which I take to be the earliest gospel) in what he says about the Baptist, but rather this: *if we take it* that John did know and use Mark not just in general (as I have argued elsewhere), but also in what he says about the Baptist, do we then understand *John's* treatment of the Baptist *better* than we would have done if we had just attempted to analyse that treatment on its own?[2] Thus, I will be using my (rudimentary) *parallel* comparison, *enlarged* with the *genealogical* perspective, for basically *heuristic* purposes, trying to understand John's treatment of the Baptist even better through the comparative exercise. One may well draw the additional conclusion – and I will be happy to do so – that if the heuristic exercise succeeds in a clear and striking manner, then that fact will in itself give added force to the genealogical claim, which I have only posited hypothetically. Such a conclusion will fit in closely with the profile of the present volume. But my main aim in this chapter will be the heuristic one, focusing on John. Why? Because I very strongly feel that all the comparative work that is done by New Testament scholars should in the end be sharply focused on genuinely elucidating the *text* that gave rise to the comparison.[3] In the present case, that text is what John writes about the Baptist.

It so happens that there is available an excellent, recent analysis of John's treatment of the Baptist from a non-comparative, internally narrative perspective: Catrin Williams' 'John (the Baptist): The Witness on the Threshold'.[4] For my question – whether the comparative analysis may heuristically give us *more* for an understanding

---

[2] In *John and Philosophy: A New Reading of the Fourth Gospel* (Oxford: Oxford University Press, 2017), 312–20, I have argued that John knew and exploited in his own way the Messianic secret motif that is fundamental (and specific) to Mark. Earlier, Jörg Frey had made the same case for three specific motifs in Mark and John, one of which is in fact Mark 1.4-11 on the Baptist. See his 'Das vierte Evangelium auf dem Hintergrund der älteren Evangelientradition', in *Johannesevangelium – Mitte oder Rand des Kanons?*, ed. Thomas Söding (Quaestiones Disputatae, 203; Freiburg: Herder, 2003), 60–118. (Also in Frey, *Die Herrlichkeit des Gekreuzigten. Studien zu den johanneischen Texten I* [WUNT, 307; Tübingen: Mohr Siebeck, 2013], 239–94.) I strongly recommend the reader to study this extremely well documented and convincing analysis. For John's use of Mark in general, see now also Frey, *Theology and History in the Fourth Gospel* (Waco, TX: Baylor University Press, 2018), 64–77 and passim.

[3] Of course, the primary comparandum may also very well be some social entity like, for instance, the Pauline ἐκκλησία in Wayne Meeks' comparison of this with the 'household', the 'voluntary association', the 'synagogue', and the 'philosophic or rhetorical school' in *The First Urban Christians: The Social World of the Apostle Paul* (New Haven, CT: Yale University Press, 1983), 75–84.

[4] Catrin H. Williams, 'John (the Baptist): The Witness on the Threshold', in *Character Studies in the Fourth Gospel: Narrative Approaches to Seventy Figures in John*, ed. Steven A. Hunt, D. Francois Tolmie and Ruben Zimmermann (WUNT, 314; Tübingen: Mohr Siebeck, 2013), 46–60.

of John than a merely internal analysis will give – I may therefore use that article by Williams and compare her results with my own.

The Baptist in Mark

The Baptist makes an appearance in Mark in the following places: 1.4, 6, 9, 14 as part of 1.1–14 (the ἀρχή of the gospel about Jesus Christ); 2.18 as part of 2.18–22 (on fasting and wine in new wineskins); 6.14 as part of 6.14–16 (on who Jesus is) and 6.17–29 (the Baptist's death); 8.28 (on who Jesus is); 9.11–13 (implicitly: on Elijah *redivivus*); 11.30, 32 as part of 11.29–33 (was the Baptist's baptism from heaven?).

Were one to make a thorough analysis of the character of the Baptist in Mark, I think one would come out with a characterization of him as (1) a *Vorläufer* (predecessor), (2) a *Vorbild* (model), and (3) a *Zeuge* (witness), or even all three together.[5] *Vorläufer*: Mk 1.1–3 (including 'See, I am sending my messenger ahead of you, who will prepare your way etc.') clearly leads directly into 1.4-6 ('John the baptizer appeared etc.'); note also 1.7–8 ('The one who is more powerful than I is *coming after me* etc.') and 9.11–13 (on the Baptist as Elijah *redivivus*: 'But I tell you that Elijah *has* come, and they did to him whatever they pleased'). *Vorbild*: 6.29 as the conclusion to 6.14–29 (the Baptist's disciples 'came and took his body, and laid it in a tomb' – as Jesus' disciples will eventually do);[6] note also 9:13 (just quoted). *Zeuge*: particularly 1.7–8 (just quoted), plus: '*I* am not worthy to stoop down and untie the thong of *his* sandals. *I* have baptized you with water; but *he* will baptize you with holy πνεῦμα'). We shall see the huge importance for John of this particular feature in Mark's picture of the Baptist.

This must suffice here for Mark. It is presumably correct to say that the picture of the Baptist in Mark has several features (*Vorläufer, Vorbild* and *Zeuge*) that are not intrinsically very closely connected, but also that the Baptist is clearly subordinated to Jesus, both in his own words (1.7–8) and in those of Jesus (2.18–22, 9.11–13). Apart from making the latter point clear, Mark has not wanted, or managed, to fuse the various features he ascribes to the Baptist into a single image. John did.

An exclusively narrative analysis of the Baptist in John

The Baptist (though not explicitly named in that way) figures in John in the following four places: (i) 1.1–37(40–41) – the so-called prologue and its immediate sequel; (ii) 3.23–36/4.1 (on baptism with the πνεῦμα); (iii) 5.33–37 (on the Baptist as witness); (iv) 10.40–42 (the Baptist was right about Jesus).

---

[5] I take these categories from a book by Angelika Ottillinger, *Vorläufer, Vorbild oder Zeuge? Zum Wandel des Taüferbildes im Johannesevangelium* (Dissertationen, Theologische Reihe, 45; St. Ottilien: EOS Verlag, 1991). Ottillinger speaks of the Fourth Gospel. I transfer her title to Mark.
[6] It remains a mystery why, within his overall conception of the gospel, Mark decided to tell the story of the Baptist's death in such striking detail in 6.14–29. Perhaps 6.29 gives the clue to the answer as taken up again in 9.13 (just quoted).

In her fine article on the Baptist in John, Catrin Williams takes it for granted as a general, scholarly insight that the Baptist's main role in John is the single one of being a 'witness'.[7] She therefore focuses not so much on 'character' as on 'characterization', to be understood as John's different ways of bringing out the single character of the Baptist as witness. Following Dodd and others, Williams also presents a threefold *schema* that is found already in 1:6-8 and then 'controls subsequent sections dealing with the Baptist':[8]

1. John was not the light (1.8a; see 1.19-21; 3.28; 10.41).
2. He came to bear witness to the light (1.7a; 8b; see 1.29-34, 36; 3.26; 5.33; 10.41).
3. He bore witness so that all might believe in the light (1.7b; see 1.35-37; 3.26; 5.34; 10.40-42).

To these three points, Williams adds a fourth aspect:

4. John is subordinate to Jesus (1.15; see 1.27, 30; 3.28-30; 5.34-35).

From Williams we may also take these points: a distinction between 'telling' of the Baptist (as, e.g., in 1.6-8) and something verging on 'showing' (as in 1.19-34);[9] a concern with *seeing* (as in 1.29b-34) as part of 'witnessing';[10] the balance between asserting John's significance and his limitations (as particularly relevant to the 'narrative dwindling and departure' of the Baptist in 5.33-36 and 10.40-42, where Williams also speaks nicely of 'character closure').[11] In these ways, a non-comparative analysis focusing on 'characterization' adds some richness to the Baptist's otherwise rather uniform 'character'.[12]

How John has – *ex hypothesi* – transformed Mark on the Baptist

I now take the methodological step announced above. Suppose that John both knew and used Mark in his account of the Baptist: what does this show us about John's writerly practice? And how may such an analysis enrich our understanding of John's

---

[7] Of course, John also has the material that made the Baptist a *Vorläufer* in Mark, but here, as we shall see, it is constantly made a part of the Baptist's own witness.
[8] Williams, 'Witness', 50, quoting C. H. Dodd, *Historical Tradition in the Fourth Gospel* (Cambridge: Cambridge University Press, 1963), 248-49.
[9] Williams, 'Witness', 50, with excellent references on telling and showing to Wayne Booth, Mark Powell, and James Resseguie.
[10] Williams, 'Witness', 54
[11] Williams, 'Witness', 57-58.
[12] Williams, 'Witness', 47 with references in n. 6, also refers to the recent work of Cornelis Bennema on 'character' in John, as also applied to the Baptist. On Bennema's reading, the Baptist's characterization in the Fourth Gospel is 'complex, hovering between "type" and "personality"'. To my mind, a character may very well be quite complex in terms of the features that go into it, but still remain a 'type'. As we shall see, John's account (or 'portrait') of the Baptist entirely focuses on making certain theological points about him and Jesus. He thus very much serves as a 'type'.

picture of the Baptist? We should go through all passages on the Baptist in Mark and ask what – on the stated supposition – they may have '*given*' John.

Mk 1.1–3 ('The beginning of the good news etc.') may (or may not) have given John the idea of himself beginning in 1.1–5 with the *ultimate* ἀρχή – together with the precise way of introducing the Baptist in John 1.6 (ἐγένετο ἄνθρωπος, cf. **Mk 1.4**: ἐγένετο Ἰωάννης).[13] It seems certain, though, that Mk 1.3 on the voice of somebody crying in the wilderness has given John his 1.23, in which the Baptist states that he himself is that voice ('*I* am the voice etc.'). Here we clearly go from 'telling' to 'saying' in the first person singular as part of the Baptist's 'witnessing' (1.19, cf. 1.20). As we shall see, this move – well prepared for in Mark, but *not* so fully developed – is crucial to John's treatment of the Baptist: from third person telling to first person saying.[14]

Mk 1.4–6 (on the Baptist's message and appearance) is completely left out by John. *However*, he transforms Mark's account of the Baptist's baptism as being one of 'repentance for the forgiveness of sins' into something entirely different when he has the Baptist speak of *Jesus* as 'the lamb of God who *removes* the *sin* of the world' (1.29). Here we have two things: first, the Baptist pointing away from himself to Jesus and, second, the idea of Jesus as *removing* sin. Initially, as one reads the Fourth Gospel from the beginning until 1.34, one may wonder what the exact point is of 1.29, which comes in somewhat abruptly. This, however, can be seen more clearly if one reads John in the light of Mark. John aims to make the Baptist say something about *Jesus* (as different from himself) that furthermore brings to the conclusion (by the complete *removal* of sin) something that in the Markan account of the Baptist's own preaching was only preparatorily moving in the same direction (repentance and forgiveness of sins). How, then, will such a complete removal of sin take place? That is what the rest of the material on the Baptist in both John 1 and 3 goes on to show: through baptism with the πνεῦμα. When, in the rest of John's story about Jesus Christ, the πνεῦμα, which to begin with – as we are about to hear – only Jesus had received directly from God, was transmitted further in (Christian) baptism to believers, then their sin would not only be forgiven, but removed.[15] In this way, the comparison with Mark shows something of central importance to the overall conception of the Fourth Gospel itself.

---

[13] No commentary I have consulted (that is, Bultmann, Barrett, Brown, Lincoln, Schnelle, Theobald, Zumstein, and Wilckens) explicitly combines John 1.6 ἐγένετο with Mk 1.4. Hartwig Thyen at least notes that ἐγένετο 'hier wie Mk 1,4 (vgl. Mt 3,1) weniger das *Werden* des Täufers im strengen Sinne [but why not *also* that? Cf. 1.3] als sein geschichtliches Auftreten bezeichnet' (*Das Johannesevangelium* [HNT, 6; 2nd edn; Tübingen: Mohr Siebeck, 2015), 73.

[14] Compare C. H. Dodd, *The Interpretation of the Fourth Gospel* (Cambridge: Cambridge University Press, 1953), 292 (my italics): 'in John as in Mark he [the Baptist] is simply a witness to the coming of the Messiah. In the Fourth Gospel however his testimony is more detailed and definite than in Mark. In fact, the testimony of the Baptist here *absorbs* what Mark has given as from his own pen. In the first place, the Baptist is *made to cite* precisely the scripture that Mark cites in his own pen in the exordium: … (i. 23) etc.' (Please remember also the second sentence in this: that the Baptist's testimony is 'more detailed and definite' in John than in Mark. Here Dodd gives the line for the more explicit proposal that I will eventually make in this essay.)

[15] Let it be noted already here that in what I say in this essay about John 3, in particular, I am drawing quite heavily on my analysis of that chapter in *John and Philosophy*, 123–31 (with references to the scholarly literature).

Mk 1.7-8 has given John three crucial things: (1) the idea of 'the one to come after me', as in the Baptist's own witness in John 1.15, 17, and 30; (2) the idea of his not being worth untying his shoes, as in John 1.27; and (3) the idea that '*I* am baptizing with water, but he will baptize you with holy πνεῦμα', as stated in John 1.33 and hinted at in 1.26. Most importantly, however, (4) Mk 1.7-8 has also given John the idea of the Baptist himself *saying* who he is, in a '*self*-identification' that at the same time points *forward* to Jesus. The crucial move here (from third person telling something about the Baptist to first person having himself say the same thing) is, of course, made already in John 1.15, where the Baptist bears 'witness' to Jesus by saying this: 'It is about this one that I said: "He who comes after me ranks ahead of me because he was before me".' This move of making the Baptist himself state his own role in relation to Jesus constitutes the core of 1.19-34, which, as I have argued elsewhere, is to be understood as the evangelist's *spelling out* what he has already told about the Baptist in the prologue: 1.6-8 and 1.15.[16] What we see here is that John takes something from Mark and *develops* it much further. In John, the Baptist repeatedly himself directly speaks about his own role. That role is not just indirectly stated.

Mk 1.9-11 (on Jesus' baptism by the Baptist) has given John two things: (1) a location 'beyond the Jordan (river)' (1.28) for what happened on the 'first' day (Jn 1.19-28) – and then also for the events on 'the day after' (1.29-34); (2) a topic (of Jesus' baptism) that John would then greatly transform in 1.29-34 in a manner to which we shall come back.

Mk 1.14 (on the Baptist's having been 'arrested') has *possibly* given John his 3.24 (that the Baptist had '*not yet*' been thrown into prison) with two twists: the mention of 'prison' *may* contain a hint at the story in Mk 6.17-29 on the Baptist's imprisonment (cf. 'prison' in Mk 6.17) – so John will be presupposing that part of Mark's account, too; also, John may have wished to emphasize that what happens in 3.22-36 happened precisely *before* the Baptist was imprisoned – whereas in Mark, Jesus' appearance as a preacher took place '*after*' the Baptist had been arrested. If so, why? The answer may well be that only in this way could John make the Baptist himself *say* what he goes on to say in 3.27-36 about his own role in his relationship with Jesus.[17] Once again we see that John has developed a motif (of the Baptist's own saying what his role is) that he had found in Mark, though with much smaller significance there.

Mk 2.18-20 (on the difference between 'the Baptist's disciples' and Jesus' disciples with respect to fasting) has given John two things: (1) the mention of 'John's disciples' in John 3.25-26 and their criticism of Jesus' baptismal practice in an address to their own master, the Baptist; and (2) an answer in Mark by Jesus himself as a 'bridegroom', which John has in 3.29-30 again put into the mouth of the Baptist himself when *he* speaks of Jesus as a 'bridegroom' and of himself as the bridegroom's 'friend', who must

---

[16] See *John and Philosophy*, 65-71. Compare for the point about spelling out (which is crucial for understanding *everything* in 1.1-34) also C. K. Barrett, *The Gospel According to St John* (2nd edn; London: SPCK, 1978), 170 (my italics): 'It [1.19-34] *resumes in narrative form* the more purely theological statements of the Prologue.'

[17] Barrett almost sees this (*Gospel*, 221): 'it seems probable that John's aim [in 3.24] is not to furnish an interesting piece of historical information but to provide a background for v. 30' ('He must increase, but I must decrease').

diminish while the other one grows. This, it seems to me, is an exciting example of John's use of Mark. He has found something in Mark that makes good sense there – and then adopted and transformed it quite drastically to fit his own aims.

There are several purposes with John's changes here, including the fact that Mark is speaking of fasting where the Johannine text is all through (3.22–36) in fact speaking of the proper kind of *baptism*.[18] John makes the Baptist say a number of things that bring the reader directly back to chapter 1. First, he explicitly repeats in 3.28 the point made in chapter 1 that he is not himself the Christ (cf. 1.20), but one who has been 'sent' (ἀπεσταλμένος, also in 1.6) ahead of him' (cf. the earlier idea of Jesus 'coming after' the Baptist, 1.15, 27, 30). Second, in 3.31–36 the Baptist speaks primarily of Jesus, as one who has come 'from above' (3.31, as opposed – one may suppose – to himself, who is 'of the earth'), namely, when he was 'sent' by God *by having the* πνεῦμα *given to him* (3.34). This last point clearly refers to 1.29–34 (on which more later), which is thus kept vividly alive. Third, however, and very importantly, the Baptist also speaks of *believers* (3.35–36), whose faith in the πνεῦμα-receiving Son (again 3.35–36) will mean that they both have (ἔχει) and will see (cf. ὄψεται) eternal life (3.36). How so? Here we must note that 3.35–36 clearly refers to Jesus' statements in the first half of the chapter of how human beings may come to 'see' (3.3) and 'enter' (3.5) the kingdom of God, namely, by being (re)born (3.4, 5, 8) by the πνεῦμα (3.8), or indeed, by '*Christian' baptism* 'with water and πνεῦμα' (3.5). This unmistakably shows that believers will both have and see eternal life when they themselves receive the πνεῦμα in 'Christian' baptism. Thus, in 3.27–36 the Baptist not only speaks of his own relation to Jesus and of Jesus' πνεῦμα-generated identity as having come 'from above', but also of what this all means for believers. The two last points are utterly central to John's overall conception of Jesus. What he has done, therefore, in the present text is to transform a fairly innocent story in Mark 2.18–20 into a comprehensive statement by the Baptist that articulates what lies at the core of his own understanding of the whole meaning of the Christ event. John makes the Baptist *say* that the aim of what God did to Jesus, as described in John 1.29–34, was to make baptism with πνεῦμα available to *believers* in Jesus Christ so that they might be saved. John's Baptist thus saw 'the truth' (compare this with 5.33 and 10.41), not only about Jesus, but also about Jesus' significance for believers.

Mk 6.14–16 and **8.27–29** (on who *Jesus* is: the Baptist or Elijah *redivivus*, or just 'one of the prophets'?) have given John – in an entirely paradoxical, but also in fact quite logical manner – his 1.20–21 and 25 (on who the *Baptist* is *not*). This is again an exciting example of the transformation wrought by John on Mark. Mark had twice told a story about who people took Jesus to be. John transforms this into a story in which the Baptist *himself says* (in response to a question who *he* is, 1.19) that *he* is *neither* the Christ *nor* Elijah *nor* 'the prophet' (1.20–21, 25). John then uses this statement by the Baptist to have his interlocutors ask the question that is the single, basic, underlying question in his whole presentation of the Baptist: if you are neither of the three figures, *then why do you baptize?* (1.24). This crucial question is then answered – and again by the Baptist himself – in 1.29–34, to which we will return in a moment.

---

[18] For arguments for this overall reading of John 3, see my *John and Philosophy*, 128–31.

Mk 9.11-13 (implicitly on the Baptist as Elijah *redivivus* in relation to 'the Son of Man'), which should (I believe) be read together with Mk 12.35-37 (about *Jesus* as the 'lord', not the 'son', of even David), has given John – once again – 1.20-21 and 25 at the same time as it marks one of the strongest differences between Mark and John, duly noted by almost all commentators. While the Baptist in fact was, so Jesus implies in Mark, 'Elijah *redivivus*', John has the Baptist himself explicitly *deny* this. Why? Because in John, the Baptist is *just* a human being (cf. 1.6 and 5.33–34: ἄνθρωπος), though with divine knowledge, as we shall see.

Finally, and similarly, **Mk 11.29-33** (was the Baptist's baptism from heaven?) has given John the *almost* paradoxical claim – made by the Baptist himself in John 3.27–36 – that *his* baptism was *not* 'from heaven', but only in some way preparatory. Again, we have an exciting Johannine use of Mark. John goes against Mark (who surely implies that the Baptist's baptism was in fact 'from heaven') to make the Baptist himself make a *related* point: that *Jesus'* baptism was indeed 'from heaven' (cf. 3.31–34), but his own, human (cf. 3.31) baptism only had a preparatory purpose.

So far, we may summarize the result of these remarks as follows. What we have seen – on our hypothesis that John knew Mark – is that John has done three things with the Markan input on the Baptist. First, he has greatly developed some motifs to be found in Mark, first and foremost the 'witnessing' motif of the Baptist himself stating what his role and relationship is vis-à-vis Jesus. Second, he has rejected some interpretations in Mark of the Baptist's identity: *not*, for instance, Elijah *redivivus*, but just a human being (though with divine knowledge). In this way John in effect sharpens the difference between the Baptist and Jesus, as we will also see in connection with 1.29-34 (Jesus is not at all baptized by the Baptist, but in some way 'baptized' directly by God). Third, John has developed certain motifs from Mark (e.g., repentance for the forgiveness of sins and the Markan Baptist's claim that Jesus will baptize with holy πνεῦμα) into a coherent conception of the character and function of Jesus Christ also in relation to believers, a conception that John's Baptist is then made to articulate (for instance, in 3.27-36) in a manner that turns him into a veritable mouthpiece for the Johannine author himself. In John's Baptist speaks John himself – when he makes his Baptist say all the things that he says.[19]

I believe these results of reading Mark and John together (on our hypothesis) are quite illuminating in relation to John. They thus serve the heuristic purpose of the comparison. They show us something *more* about John than we perhaps knew before, something that is certainly there, but can now also be seen even more clearly.

We are now ready to consider **John 1.29-34**, where John has the Baptist both declare and show *why* he baptized (with water, as we know) when he himself was neither the Christ, nor Elijah, nor 'the prophet'. The text for comparison is of course Mk 1:9-11.

Mk 1:9-11 is simple. Jesus 'came' and was baptized by the Baptist. *Jesus* then *saw* the πνεῦμα descend upon himself from the open heaven and *he heard* a heavenly voice speaking to *him* (alone): 'You are my son etc.' John 1.29-34 is much more complicated. Here everything is focused on the Baptist. *He 'saw'* (NB) Jesus 'coming' towards him

---

[19] Think of John's Baptist, e.g., in Jn 3.27–36, as a puppet in his authorial master's hand.

and then – slightly out of the blue, as we have seen – declared to some unspecified others who Jesus was: 'See the lamb of God who takes away the sin of the world'. This declaration in 1.29 forms an *inclusio* with a similar one at the end of the text (1.34): 'I have seen and have witnessed that this one is the Elect (or Son) of God'.[20] These statements are made by the Baptist at **time(=t)**[4], 'on the second day'. Previously, in fact at **t¹**, the Baptist did not 'know him' (1.31, 33), but, so he says, '*I* came baptizing with water in order that *he* might be revealed to Israel' (1.31). This, then, is the Johannine reason why the Baptist did his baptizing (remember 1.25: 'Why, then, do you baptize ...?') – utterly differently, as we know, from what we find in Mk 1.4–6. The Baptist in John did not baptize (with water) directly for the forgiveness of sins. Instead, he baptized in order that the lamb of God who *takes away* the sin of the world might be *revealed* to Israel. How would he be revealed to Israel in that way? This question is immediately answered: because 'the one (i.e. God) who had sent me to baptize with water, he had told me' – at **t²** – that 'the one (i.e. Jesus) upon whom you will see the πνεῦμα descend and remain upon him, *he* is the one who baptizes with holy πνεῦμα' (1.33). This the Baptist then saw happen at **t³** (1.32). And this is the event to which he now bears witness (at **t⁴**), thereby 'revealing it to Israel'.

So, the Baptist did his baptizing with water for the single purpose that God might then, first (at **t²**), *foretell* him about the descent of the πνεῦμα upon Jesus, which would make *him* baptize with holy πνεῦμα, and next (at **t³**), and second, make that very thing *happen*. In this way, Jesus might be revealed to Israel – namely, when the Baptist bore witness to Israel about it as something he had actually seen, as he is doing right now in the story, at **t⁴**.

In all this the Baptist's own water baptism is in effect denied any significance of its own. Instead, it points exclusively towards the baptism that really matters, the one with holy πνεῦμα with which Jesus will (also) baptize. The Baptist's only function is to bear witness to *that*. Water baptism does not matter, neither as performed for its own sake by the Baptist nor, one must suppose, for those who were only baptized with *that*. The only thing that matters is baptism with holy πνεῦμα.

Was Jesus himself then *not* baptized in John's picture? Certainly not by the Baptist. Since the whole point of the Baptist's baptizing activities was that something *other* (though, as we shall see, somehow 'overlapping') might happen to *Jesus*, his having been baptized with water by the Baptist would be entirely pointless. However, I believe that in John's picture Jesus was in fact baptized (or 'baptized', see in a moment): by *God* when *he* sent his πνεῦμα down upon him. That is what the Baptist saw. That is

---

[20] For the textual crux here ('Elect' or 'Son'?), see, e.g., Barrett, *Gospel*, 178, who (rightly to my mind, but against Nestle Aland) prefers ἐκλεκτός ('elect') and Raymond E. Brown, *The Gospel According to John (I-XII)* (Anchor Bible, 29; Garden City, NY: Doubleday, 1966), 57, who agrees with Barrett. For the opposite view, see Michael Theobald, *Das Evangelium nach Johannes, Kapitel 1-12* (Regensburger Neues Testament; Regensburg: Friedrich Pustet, 2009), 173, who gives noteworthy arguments, as does Thyen, *Johannesevangelium*, 123–24. However, it is not quite clear to me that it matters hugely whether one reads one thing or the other. The reading 'Son' fits well with the special meaning given to Jesus as Son of God in the rest of the gospel. Similarly, the reading 'Elect' will have to be filled in with the content given to Jesus' relationship to God in the rest of the gospel – and indeed in 1.29-34 itself.

what happened. *Instead* of water, Jesus received πνεῦμα upon him to remain there (1.32, 33).[21]

Few scholars will accept the claim that in John's picture Jesus was baptized by God. (1) I think it follows from the *displacement* that takes place from the Baptist's baptism with water (1.26, 33) to something else in 1.29–34. That something takes two forms. One concerns something done by *God*, namely, two things: (i) his announcing to the Baptist at t² that he will make the πνεῦμα descend upon Jesus so that *he* might baptize with πνεῦμα (NB, instead of water, 1.33) and (ii) God's making that thing happen at t³ (1.32). The other concerns something happening to the *Baptist* in consequence, namely, that in his relationship with Jesus he now becomes nothing other than a witness: no longer a baptizer, but a witness (which is, of course, the basic point of the whole passage). In all this, there is a displacement: God is *taking over* from the Baptist's baptizing activity and transforming his role accordingly. The simplest way of understanding together all aspects of this change is to see God as doing to *Jesus* – but in an altogether different way – what the Baptist had up to then been doing: baptizing.

(2) This, I propose, is the best way of reading the Johannine text itself. But one can also see the same displacement if one compares John's account with Mk 1.9–11. Where Mark has two things happening, one concerning the Baptist and Jesus (1.9) and the other concerning Jesus and God (1.10–11), John combines the two within the Baptist's witness and places a strong emphasis on the second one (God's double intervention). The logical conclusion to be drawn from this is that Jesus was *baptized*, not by the Baptist (as in Mk 1.9) *but* by God (in Jn 1.32).

(3) I also think this follows from John chapter 3: there, as we have already seen, the Baptist in a way repeats what he has said of Jesus in chapter 1; but there, what is true of Jesus (that he 'came from above', 3.31, namely, when he received the πνεῦμα) is also said to hold for Christ-believers when *they* are *baptized* – with water *and* πνεῦμα (3.5–8). If this is true of *believers*, it will also hold for Jesus himself. *He* was *baptized* with πνεῦμα by God in order that he might then himself *baptize them* with πνεῦμα. The connection of 3.22–36 (which in 3.28 refers explicitly back to 1.19–34) with 3.1–21 shows that the pneumatic baptism of believers is grounded in the pneumatic *baptism* of Jesus himself.

So far, so good. To the likely astonishment of my readers, I will now take back half (but only half) of what I have just said. If the picture given is the one that John wishes to bring across, then why does he not explicitly *say* that Jesus was baptized by God? I think there is one very good answer to that question. In John (and early Christianity much more broadly) the term βαπτίζειν may very well have been indissolubly connected with water. Some water had to be present for an act to fall under the concept of 'baptism'. That is precisely the case in John 3 where Jesus speaks of believers as 'being born from water and πνεῦμα' (3.5). And that is why the conjecture by Wendt of

---

[21] Note here the 'overlapping' character of the Baptist's baptizing with water and Jesus' receiving the πνεῦμα with which *he* will be baptizing. It is because of this 'overlap' that one can understand why the Baptist did baptize with water (1.26, in answer to the question asked by the Pharisees in 1.25) when this was in itself apparently completely ineffectual – and why he was even sent to do so by God (1.33). The Baptist baptized (with water) *so that* Jesus might receive the πνεῦμα and baptize with *that*. I go immediately on to spell out the logical consequences of this 'overlap'.

excluding 'water and' – listed in the apparatus of Nestle-Aland 27, but rightly dropped in Nestle Aland 28 – is not only unnecessary, but distinctly false. Here, where Jesus is in fact (though the term itself is not used) speaking of baptism, his reference to water (*and*, of course, in this case also πνεῦμα) is exactly right. By contrast, in John 1.32–33 there is *only* πνεῦμα. No water is involved. So, in that sense Jesus was not *baptized* by God. It remains the case, however, that there is a formal analogy between what happened to those who were baptized by the Baptist, to Jesus, and to those who will be baptized in *his* baptism:

John the Baptist	Jesus	Christ-believers
water	πνεῦμα	water and πνεῦμα
baptism	'baptism'	baptism

We should conclude that although Jesus may not have been *baptized* by God (as the ancients understood βαπτίζειν), since he only received πνεῦμα from above, not water, he was in fact 'baptized' by God in the sense that he received what he would henceforth transmit to believers in (Christian) baptism, namely, God's own πνεῦμα, which is of course *the* important element in Christian baptism with water and πνεῦμα.[22]

The Baptist in John

Let us go back to Catrin Williams' four aspects. (1) The Baptist was not the light (or Christ or Elijah or 'the prophet'). (2) Instead, he came to bear witness to the light (etc.). This is all true enough. However, what is most striking about John's picture of the Baptist is a point that Williams does not stress: that John puts special emphasis on *quoting* the Baptist's 'witness'. After the initial 'telling' about the Baptist (1.6–8), what we get are his direct '*sayings*' about Jesus (1.15, 19–34, and again in 3.27–36). And what we later hear about him is that 'All that John [the Baptist] *said* about this one [Jesus] was true' (10.41) and that the Baptist 'has borne witness [in what he was *saying*] to the truth' (5.33). The aim of putting whatever should be said of the relationship between the Baptist and Jesus into the Baptist's own mouth is partly to diminish his own importance (1.19–28) and to aggrandize that of Jesus (1.29–34) – and similarly in 3.27–36 – but

---

[22] The suggestion I have made on the connotations of the term βαπτίζειν in ancient Christian texts should evidently be checked against the occurrences of the term at least in the whole New Testament. The references given by Danker under the lemma 'to use water in a rite etc.' are obviously unproblematic. Those (relatively few) under 'to cause someone to have an extraordinary experience *akin to* an initiatory water-rite, *to plunge, baptize*' (my italics in 'akin to') are more intriguing. Especially noteworthy are Acts 1.5, where ἐν πνεύματι βαπτισθήσεσθε ἁγίῳ ('you will be baptized with holy πνεῦμα') will refer to the immediately following account in 2.1–4 of the coming of the πνεῦμα over the apostles (where no water is involved), and Acts 11.16 ('you will be baptized with holy πνεῦμα'), which has a similar import (the coming of the πνεῦμα over those whom Peter has been addressing in Acts 10). Note, however, that both verses explicitly contrast this being 'baptized' with holy πνεῦμα with the Baptist's baptizing with water – and also that Peter concludes in 10.47 as follows: 'Can anyone withhold the *water* for baptizing these people who have received the holy πνεῦμα just as we have?' It seems likely, therefore, that Luke is here *playing* on the normal set of connotations: that βαπτίζειν was connected with water.

partly also, and through that very means, to bring out what is uniquely special about *Jesus*: that *he* was 'baptized' with πνεῦμα directly by God and that he will similarly baptize human beings (believers) with πνεῦμα. John's Baptist is not just 'a witness to Jesus'. He is himself just a human being (ἄνθρωπος in 1.6 and again, by implication, in 5.33–34) – neither Christ nor Elijah nor 'the prophet'; but he is also a witness to something highly specific connected with Jesus: *the baptism with* πνεῦμα *of both* Jesus (in his 'baptism') *and* Christ-believers (in genuine baptism with water and πνεῦμα). We might certainly also include in the Baptist's witness the two points he makes about Jesus in 1.29 and 1.34: that Jesus is 'the lamb of God etc.' and 'the Elect of God'. But both these identifications are probably meant to be understood in the light of the Baptist's central claim about what he has both directly heard and seen from God: that Jesus was 'baptized' by God with holy πνεῦμα – as described in the text *between* 1.29 and 1.34. Thus, Jesus will be God's Elect *by* having been given the πνεῦμα, and he will be God's lamb by transmitting the πνεῦμα (through his own death and resurrection) to believers, thereby taking away their sin.

Here the point becomes relevant that the Baptist (3) 'bore witness *so that all might believe* in the light' (etc.). That, surely, was the aim. However, I have argued elsewhere that nobody in the Fourth Gospel did come to believe in Jesus in the proper way while he was still alive. For that, they would themselves need to be in possession of the πνεῦμα, and we learn from 7.37–39 that nobody other than Jesus came to possess the πνεῦμα before he had died and been resurrected.[23] How, then, might the Baptist himself (who surely had not received the πνεῦμα, either) know the crucial point about Jesus (his reception of the πνεῦμα) so as to become able to bear witness to him (and that)? The answer must be that although the Baptist was only a human being and in no way to be compared with Jesus, he was able to identify Jesus (and – though initially only ineffectually – reveal him to Israel) for what he in fact was – because, as he himself explains, he had been directly *told* by God (1.33).

Thus understood, John's Baptist is just a human being who bears witness to what he has heard and seen. But he is also special in that *he alone* has *heard* and *seen* (and in both cases as something coming directly from God) what he then bears witness to and reveals to Israel. Moreover, what he bears witness to is the unique character of Jesus *as* having been 'baptized' with πνεῦμα (he is God's Elect) and *as* being meant similarly to baptize believers with πνεῦμα (thereby as God's lamb removing their sin).

Is John's Baptist also (4) 'subordinate to Jesus'? Evidently, yes. But that point is already part of his witness in 1.15, 27, and 30 – and also in 3.28–30. No wonder, then, that once the Baptist has himself made the point wholly clear, John may also make either Jesus (5.33–37) or 'the Jews' (10.40–42) make the same point when he recounts the Baptist's 'narrative dwindling and departure'.

John's Baptist, then, is a quite complex figure: one who *himself* bears witness to his own relative *in*significance, but who is also enabled by God to bear witness to *Jesus's true sig*nificance. This, it seems to me, is both very sharply focused and also quite elegant. Moreover, it certainly gives the Baptist a remarkable stature within John's

---

[23] See *John and Philosophy*, 111, and chapters VI and VIII.

overall conception: not just a *Vorläufer* or an ever so vague *Vorbild*, but in his capacity as witness (*Zeuge*) a figure who, as part of the narration, turns himself into a veritable mouthpiece for the author. He is one who has actually seen 'the truth' – the whole truth and nothing but the truth – about Jesus and 'borne witness' to *that* (5.33). This is the core of my proposal. The Baptist in John is not just a witness to Jesus. *As* a witness to Jesus, John's Baptist becomes the author's mouthpiece for the understanding of the *full* meaning of the story about Jesus. Surely, it is something of a feat to have extracted this specific picture from the much more sprawling account of the Baptist given by Mark. To put it in a slightly drastic image, what John has done is to suck all the Markan material into his own theologizing narrative system and to spit it out again in the transformed shape of *his* Baptist, who acts as nothing but John's own mouthpiece.

From the heuristic to the genealogical point of comparing Mark and John on the Baptist

From *Vorläufer*, *Vorbild*, and *Zeuge* to *Zeuge* alone: the comparison of John with Mark shows how John has narrowed what was available in Mark into something with a much sharper focus on the Baptist's witnessing role alone. But the comparison also shows how John has *developed* (via-à-vis Mark) exactly what it is *to* which the Baptist bears witness, namely, *the idea of the role of baptism with* πνεῦμα – in Jesus and correspondingly in believers – which is John's fundamental idea. In this way, John has made the Baptist much more than a *Zeuge*. He has turned him into a mouthpiece for his own understanding of Jesus' full significance. This is something one might perhaps see from reading John alone, but the comparison with Mark makes the point stand out much more clearly.

Do we then *know* that John had read and used Mark in the ways I have explained? Here the answer I suggested is this: if we can see a *sharp point* in the similarities *and* differences between the two, that is, in what John has supposedly 'taken over' *and* 'left behind' from Mark, then that may be enough for us to conclude that John did read and use Mark's account of the Baptist – in addition to using Mark in any other way that we may find in John. Everything depends, then, on whether I have been able to convince the reader that there *is* such a sharp point.[24]

---

[24] I am most grateful for helpful feedback to the participants and organizers of the delightful conference in Athens in August 2018 that lies behind this chapter. The conference was a model of constructive thinking.

12

How John 'Rewrites' Mark as Seen in John 5.1–18

Gilbert Van Belle

Introduction

In recent research into the relation between the Gospel of John and the Synoptic Gospels and the Gospel of Mark in particular, several scholars have studied the bread miracle (Jn 6.1–16) as a test case. While some exegetes have concluded that John is directly dependent on the Synoptics and especially Mark, others persist in defending the *semeia* hypothesis.[1] With its 'two prongs', namely the defence of John's dependence on the Synoptics and the rejection the signs source,[2] the so-called 'Leuven School' reacts against the hypothesis that John is dependent on a non-Synoptic oral tradition. This hypothesis has been defended by Percival Gardner-Smith,[3] and many exegetes have taken it over in one form or another.[4] In this contribution we wish to examine

---

[1] See Ruben Zimmermann, 'Frühchristliche Wundererzählungen – Eine Hinführung', in *Kompendium der frühchristlichen Wundererzählungen. Band 1: Die Wunder Jesu*, ed. Ruben Zimmermann et al. (Gütersloh: Gütersloher Verlagshaus, 2013), 20–21; Uta Poplutz, 'Die Wundererzählungen im Johannesevangelium: Hinführung', in Ruben Zimmermann et al. (ed.), *Kompendium*, 662: 'Die Diskussion um die Semeiaquelle ist bis heute nicht abgeschlossen'. In the same volume (690–704), Michael Theobald, who defends the *semeia* source, contributed the article on Jn 5.1–18: '"Steh auf!" – Erweckung zum Leben hier und jetzt (Die Heilung eines Gelämten). Joh 5,1–18'; see also his commentary: *Das Evangelium nach Johannes: Kapitel 1–12* (RNT, Regensburg: Pustet, 2009), 367–68. In contrast with Zimmermann and Poplutz, Jörg Frey notes as follows in 'From the *Sēmeia* Narratives to the Gospel as a Significant Narrative: On Genre-Bending in the Johannine Miracle Stories', in *The Gospel of John as Genre Mosaic*, ed. Kasper Bro Larsen (SANt, 3; Göttingen: Vandenhoeck und Ruprecht, 2015), 214: 'At the present, only a minority of Johannine scholars still maintain the assumption of a coherent source of John's signs or a narrative predecessor of the whole Gospel.' Frey refers to the commentary of Theobald and 'the two commentaries that try to renew a very idiosyncratic type of *Literarkritik*' (214 n. 32): Folker Siegert, *Das Evangelium des Johannes in seiner ursprunglichen Gestalt: Wiederherstellung und Kommentar* (Schriften des Institutum Judaicum Delitzschianum, 7; Göttingen: Vandenhoek & Ruprecht, 2007); Urban C. von Wahlde, *The Gospel and Letters of John*, 3 vols (Eerdmans Critical Commentary; Grand Rapids, MI: Wm B. Eerdmans, 2010).
[2] Cf. Andrew T. Lincoln, *The Gospel According to St John* (BNTC, 4; London: Continuum, 2005), 28–29.
[3] Percival Gardner-Smith, *Saint John and the Synoptic Gospels* (Cambridge: Cambridge University Press, 1938). On Gardner-Smith, see Joseph Verheyden, 'P. Gardner-Smith and "The Turn of the Tide"', in *John and the Synoptics*, ed. Adelbert Denaux (BETL, 101; Leuven: Leuven University Press and Peeters, 1992), 423–52.
[4] See C. H. Dodd, *Historical Tradition in the Fourth Gospel* (Cambridge: Cambridge University Press, 1963), 8–9. On Dodd and Gardner-Smith, see Gilbert Van Belle and David R. M. Godecharle, 'C. H. Dodd

the hypothesis that the Fourth Evangelist has made use of the Synoptics and thus also of Mark. We will do this in three steps. First, we will analyse the methods and criteria that are used to defend the hypothesis of dependence. Second, we will consider whether the story of the healing of a lame man (Jn 5.1–18) is clearly indicative of dependence on the Synoptics or not. Third, we will evaluate our approach in light of recent research on oral tradition, media culture and social memory.

Methods and criteria used to determine dependence or independence

Ismo Dunderberg and Jörg Frey have rightly pointed out that methodological questions in former exegesis are not explicitly discussed.[5] In Leuven, neither Frans Neirynck nor Maurits Sabbe described their methods.[6] Two of Neirynck's students, Gabriel Selong and Johan Konings, offered methodological reflections in their doctoral dissertations. I have described their methods in the past.[7] More recently, both Dunderberg and Frey have discussed methodology.[8] Here we follow the excellent exposition of Frey.

1. There is a clear difference between accepting either dependence (and knowledge) of John on the Synoptics or independence. Dependence is established by performing concrete textual comparisons. Certain preconditions are set and the determination of dependence is exegetically acceptable. The manner of arguing independence on the other hand is less clear. Indeed, complete independence cannot be proven when textual comparisons and the use of one of the Synoptics are disputed. Moreover, the arguments in favour of independence are not reliable: the references to oral traditions are too vague and the so-called contacts with a Johannine tradition can hardly be controlled.

---

on John 13:16 (and 15:20): St. John's Knowledge of Matthew Revisited', in *Engaging with C. H. Dodd on the Gospel of John: Sixty Years of Tradition and Interpretation*, ed. Tom Thatcher and Catrin H. Williams (Cambridge: Cambridge University Press, 2013), 86–106.

[5] Ismo Dunderberg, *Johannes und die Synoptiker: Studien zu Joh 1–9* (AASF Dissertationes Humanarum Litterarium, 69; Helsinki: Suomalainen Tiedeakatemia, 1994), 2–24; Jörg Frey, 'Das vierte Evangelium auf dem Hintergrund der älteren Evangelientradition: Zum Problem: Johannes und die Synoptiker', in *Johannesevangelium – Mitte oder Rand des Kanons? Neue Standortbestimmungen*, ed. Thomas Söding (Quaestiones Disputatae, 203; Freiburg: Herder, 2003), 79; reprinted in Jörg Frey, *Die Herrlichkeit des Gekreuzigten: Studien zu den Johanneischen Schriften I*, ed. Juliane Schlegel (WUNT, 307; Tübingen: Mohr Siebeck, 2013), 257.

[6] On Sabbe and Neirynck, see *In Memoriam Maurits Sabbe*, ed. Gilbert Van Belle (Annua Nuntia Lovaniensia, 50; Leuven: Peeters, 2004); Van Belle, 'In Memoriam Frans Neirynck (1927–2012)', *ETL* 89 (2013): 116–57.

[7] Gilbert Van Belle, 'Tradition, Exegetical Formation, and the Leuven Hypothesis', in *What We Have Heard from the Beginning: The Past, Present, and Future of Johannine Studies*, ed. Tom Thatcher (Waco, TX: Baylor University Press, 2007), 333–36.

[8] Dunderberg, *Johannes und die Synoptiker*, 23–30; Frey, 'Das vierte Evangelium', 79–82 (reprinted in Frey, *Die Herrlichkeit*, 237–40).

2. When it is determined that a Johannine text is dependent on an editorial element of one of the Synoptic Gospels, one cannot defend independence. But to establish dependence, what should the scope of a similarity with the Synoptics be? When comparing the texts, it can be said that at least three words must be the same (or two when it concerns unusual words), at least if it is not a general way of speaking or concerns a common source. The use of a Synoptic Gospel can then only be established if it is clear in the given Johannine text that editorial elements of this gospel are involved. In addition, one should accept dependence: (i) in the case of citations that have been modified linguistically to fit in the new context, but where there are still clear references to the original context; (ii) in a text where there are similarities in the story's sequence (*akoloutheia*). In addition, anomalies in the Johannine text might reveal its 'subtext'; they could also indicate intertextual relationships and in this way expose literary processes. According to recent discussions on intertextuality, one can clarify whether a reference to the pretext is intentional or unconscious and also whether the relationship with the (implied) readers is conscious (whereby they draw a textual comparison) or unconscious.

3. In the context of such differences, it also needs to be explained how the Fourth Evangelist could have utilized the older texts. In Matthew and Luke we clearly see how an author has used and processed sources. But in no way does this mean that the Fourth Evangelist took over 'a Synoptic form' of redaction. Nevertheless, many defenders of John's independence think that its author used this model, and this leads them to conclude that John is not dependent on any of the Synoptic Gospels. However, the Fourth Evangelist has clearly not limited himself to such an assembly of sources; rather he is an author who works eclectically and independently and does not exclude the use of written sources. It would certainly remain an unprovable presumption to claim that if he knew the Synoptics in their totality, then he would always have to concede to them as 'standard works'.

4. When knowledge of the Synoptic tradition is considered at the level of the 'redactor' of the Fourth Gospel (i.e., in the case of Jn 21), then the question arises whether it is historically plausible to exclude such knowledge from the Fourth Evangelist. It is currently often argued that the 'Johannine' editors worked very shortly after the Fourth Evangelist. Consequently, regarding their knowledge and use of the Synoptic tradition, one would have to accept that there would not be such large differences between the Evangelist and the 'redactor'. In a similar way one could argue against exegetes who suspect a Synoptic influence at the level of a pre-Johannine source. If it is accepted that the pre-Johannine tradition had knowledge of one of the Synoptic Gospels, then it becomes improbable that the Evangelist himself would not have had knowledge of the specific Synoptic Gospel. If, on the other hand, the peculiarities of the Johannine arrangement can be explained in the context of the Fourth Evangelist's theological tendencies, then assuming an influence at the level of tradition becomes problematic and itself superfluous.

Dependence or independence in John 5.1–18?

The 1984 Jerusalem Symposium

The dialogue between Peder Borgen and Frans Neirynck at the 1984 Jerusalem symposium on the 'Interrelations of the Gospels' is without doubt an important milestone in the study of John and the Synoptics.[9] D. Moody Smith only mentions this discussion in a footnote in the second edition of *John among the Gospels* (2002).[10] But in 2014, Borgen reissued earlier studies on the relations between John and the Synoptics that include this debate.[11] Based on this dialogue, we will endeavour to answer the question of whether John is dependent on Mark regarding the healing miracle at the pool of Bethesda (Jn 5.1–18). It is of course not possible to cover all aspects of the dialogue here, so we will limit ourselves to some striking similarities and differences between John and Mark.

In 1959 Borgen published an article on 'John and the Synoptics in the Passion Narrative' with the following thesis: 'A direct literary relationship between John and the Synoptics cannot be considered, but on the other hand, units of Synoptic material have been added in the Johannine tradition.'[12] In his doctoral thesis, *Bread from Heaven*,

---

[9] The symposium papers have been published six years later in *The Interrelations of the Gospels: A Symposium Led by M.-É. Boismard – W.R. Farmer – F. Neirynck, Jerusalem 1984*, ed. David L. Dungan (BETL, 95; Leuven: University Press and Peeters, 1990). At the conference, on Monday, April 16, 1984, Borgen presented his article ('John and the Synoptics', 408–37), Neirynck responded to Borgen's paper ('John and the Synoptics: Response to P. Borgen', 438–50), then followed a reply by Borgen and finally the morning session ended with an open discussion ('John and the Synoptics: A Reply', 451–58). Both Borgen's and Neirynck's contributions have been published several times, see the Bibliography. In this article I refer only to the 'first publication' edited by Dungan in the following way: Borgen, 'John and the Synoptics'; Neirynck, 'Response', 1990; Borgen, 'Reply'.

[10] D. Moody Smith, *John among the Gospels* (2nd edn; Columbia, S.C.: University of South Carolina Press, 2001), 186 n. 5.

[11] Peder Borgen, *The Gospel of John: More Light from Philo, Paul and Archaeology. The Scriptures, Tradition, Exposition, Settings, Meaning* (NovTSup, 154; Leiden: Brill, 2014). The volume contains eight previously published articles from 1959 through 2010 and seven new chapters and is, after an introduction, divided into five parts. Part C, the central part of the book, deals with the question of the relationship between the Gospel of John to the Synoptic Gospels and is entitled 'From John and the Synoptics to John within Early Gospel Traditions' (101–64). Borgen explains that 'The formulation of the title of Part C reflects that the present author has increasingly moved into also comparing John with the Gospel traditions found in Paul's letters, primarily in his First Letter to the Corinthians, to see how the traditions have been subject to expository use. My journey in this area has step by step led me into reaching the conclusion that John's independence is the most probable understanding. More light from Paul has illuminated this subject area' (XIII). With regard to Borgen's journey, see also his contribution 'The Scriptures and the Words and Works of Jesus', and Michael Labahn's response 'Living Word(s) and the Bread of Life', in Tom Thatcher (ed.), *What We Have Heard*, 39–58 and 59–62; repr. Borgen, *The Gospel of John*, 3–22 and 23–26 (followed by 'Reflections by the Author', 26–27). For an extensive review of Borgen's book, see Harold W. Attridge, *RBL* 12 (2016). He concludes: 'The analysis of the relationship of John to the Synoptics unduly minimalizes the parallels in both form and content, but Borgen's suggestions will no doubt stimulate further fruitful debate on this and other crucial issues.' Compare the review of Jutta Leonhardt-Balzer, *JSNT* 37.5 (2015): 56: 'Whether his overall conclusions on the Synoptics and dating are going to be accepted seems more doubtful.'

[12] Peder Borgen, 'John and the Synoptics in the Passion Narrative', *NTS* 5 (1958–59): 259; repr. in *Peder Borgen, Logos Was the True Light and Other Essays on the Gospel of John* ('Relieff's Publications Edited by the Department to Religious Studies, University of Trondheim, 9; Trondheim: Tapir Academic Publishers, 1983), 80; repr. in Peder Borgen, *The Gospel of John*, 118.

published in 1967, Borgen takes Paul into account regarding his research on the Gospel of John. He compares Jn 6.51b–58 with 1 Cor. 11.23–26, 27–29 and argues that fragments of the Eucharist traditions in Jn 6.51b–58 may have been paraphrased in the same way that Paul paraphrases fragments.[13] Moreover, he concludes: 'The corresponding points between John and the *haggadah* of 1 Cor. 10.1–4 . . . indicate that fragments from a haggadic story of the manna and the well are also used in this section.'[14] In his contribution on the use of tradition in Jn 12.44–50 (1979), he reformulated his hypothesis and applied it to other Johannine discourse material. First, he shows that a traditional Jesus-logion is quoted in Jn 12.44–45 in a way that can be compared with Paul's quotation of the Eucharistic tradition in 1 Cor. 11.23b–25, (26) and 27–34, and, second, he shows that Jn 12.46–50 is an expository elaboration of a Jesus logion corresponding to Paul's paraphrasing of the Eucharistic words in 1 Cor. 11.27–34 and 10.16–17, 21.[15]

In his Jerusalem paper, 'John and the Synoptics', Borgen deals first with 'the agreements between Jn 2.13–22; 5.1–18; 6.51–58 and the Synoptics against the background of the two mutually independent traditions recorded in 1 Cor. 10.3–4, 16, 17, 21; 11.23–29 and Mk 14.22–25'.[16] He is not convinced that the agreements between Jn 2.13–22; 6.51–58 and the Synoptics are significant, and he points out that Jn 5.1–18 has even fewer agreements with the Synoptics. From his analysis he then concludes that John and the Synoptics are mutually independent.[17] Second, in Borgen's endeavour to understand the workings of the Eucharist tradition in the Gospel of John, he finds relevant parallels of transmission, expository and the use of paraphrasing in 1 Cor. 10 and 11.[18] Essentially, he stresses that an oral tradition seems to be the primary source behind the documents. Here too he finds parallels between the Johannine and Pauline passages that support his interpretation, because, as he argues, both sets of passages interpret tradition 'to meet the challenges which existed in the Christian communities'.[19]

Neirynck, who was one of the organizers of the Jerusalem symposium, had at that time already played an important role in research on the gospels. He was mainly known as a determined defender of the two-source theory and the hypothesis of John's dependence on the Synoptics. Although he acknowledges that expository interpretation and paraphrasing commentary can be used to interpret the Fourth Gospel, he remains sceptical of how Borgen applies this interpretation, and insists that 'it has no relevance in a discussion about John's dependence on the Synoptics'. In a similar dismissive line of reasoning, he first says that the application of the 'model' of 1 Cor. 11.23–25, (26) and 27–34 to the Fourth Gospel is limited, because it only shows that John could have used a 'tradition (saying or narrative) as a starting point for further elaboration'. He then

---

[13] Peder Borgen, *Bread from Heaven: An Exegetical Study of the Concept of Manna in the Gospel of John and the Writings of Philo* (NovTSup, 10, Leiden: Brill, 1965; repr. 1981), 91.
[14] Borgen, *Bread from Heaven*, 92.
[15] Borgen, 'The Use of Tradition in John 12:44–50', *NTS* 26 (1979-80): 18–35; repr. Borgen, *Logos*, 49–66 (see his summary in the 'Preface').
[16] Borgen, 'John and the Synoptics', 437.
[17] Borgen, 'John and the Synoptics', 437.
[18] Borgen, 'John and the Synoptics', 437.
[19] Borgen, 'John and the Synoptics', 437.

states that one cannot use the presence of the structure 'text and commentary' to draw a conclusion about either a Pre-Johannine or a Synoptic origin of such a tradition.[20]

In reply to Neirynck, Borgen defended his position. Under the title 'Tradition Received and Handed on: A Paraphrasing Commentary Attached', Borgen treated the following topics in succession: 'The Eucharistic Tradition', 'Jn 6.51b–58', and 'Jn 5.1–18'.[21] He then summarized the points of 'Agreement, Disagreements, Desiderata' reached during the deliberations of the symposium.[22] The first disagreement he notes relates to Jn 5.1–18.[23] The two authors hold different views on dependence and sources, what evaluations are required to prove either dependence or independence. They also disagree on what constitutes a similarity, or a parallel, and cannot agree on 'what kinds of agreements are normal in mutually independent written or oral stories.' For example, Borgen regards the sentence, 'take up your mat and walk' (Jn 5.8, etc. and Mk 2.9 etc.), as a stereotype phrase that could occur in different contexts without them being dependent on each other. Alternatively, 'Neirynck and others think that the phrase comes from Mk 2.9 and cannot be isolated from its context'. Whereas Borgen determines that other similarities between Jn 5.1–18 and Mk 2.1–3.6 are 'too distant and vague to indicate John's dependence on Mark', Neirynck and others in fact think that the verbatim agreement between Jn 5.8 and Mk 2.9, as well as similar sequences between Jn 5.1–18 and Mk 2.1–3.6, indicate that John is dependent on Mark.

These two examples of interpretations are also clearly indicated in the first paragraph of Neirynck's discussion of Jn 5.1–18,[24] in which Borgen's analysis of Jn 5.1–18 is summarized and critically evaluated.[25] Neirynck first notes that Borgen compares Jn 5.1–18 with the Sabbath controversies in Mt. 12.1–8 and Lk. 13.10–17. He then highlights Borgen's conclusion that the three passages follow a traditional structure of a controversial case followed by a judicial dialogue. Hereafter, based on the premise that 'Mt. 12.5–7 is probably Matthew's interpretative expansion of Mk 2.23–28', Neirynck is critical of Borgen for rejecting 'such an interpretative use of Markan material in Jn 5.1–18, because of some distinctive features in Jn 5.10–18'. He mentions two more shortcomings in Borgen's analysis. First, he is critical of Borgen for waving aside the verbatim agreement between Jn 5.8 and Mk 2.9 as a stereotyped phrase.[26] Second, he is critical of Borgen for using the word 'arbitrary' to describe the possible connections between Jn 5.18 and Mk 2.7 (concerning blasphemy) and between Jn 5.16, 18 and Mk 3.6 (concerning the persecution and attempt to kill Jesus). According to Borgen there are no verbal agreements between these texts, a standpoint that contradicts Neirynck's eagle-eyed analysis. Whereas Borgen does not find sufficient reflection of textual structure, because, 'contrary to the expository commentary in Jn 5.10–18, the

---

[20] Borgen, 'John and the Synoptics', 450.
[21] Borgen, 'John and the Synoptics: A Reply', 451–56.
[22] 'John and the Synoptics: A Reply', 457–58.
[23] 'John and the Synoptics: A Reply', 453.
[24] Frans Neirynck, 'John and the Synoptics: Response to P. Borgen', 442–47.
[25] 'John and the Synoptics: Response to P. Borgen', 442. With regard to the Sabbath controversies, see Martin Asiedu-Peprah, *Johannine Sabbath Conflicts as Juridical Controversy* (WUNT, 2/132; Tübingen: Mohr Siebeck, 2001).
[26] Neirynck, 'Response', 442. See below n. 30.

corresponding discussion in Mk 3.1–6 precedes the healing', as we have noted, Neirynck finds Borgen's observations of interpretative forms vague.

We will now investigate the two different interpretations of the verbatim agreements between John 5.8 and Mark 2.9 and the similarity of the sequencing between John 5.1–18 and Mark 2.1–3.6.

John 5.8 and Mark 2.9

According to Borgen, 'The strongest argument in favour of John's dependence' (5.1–18) upon the Synoptics (Mt. 12.1-8, Mk 2.23-28 and Lk. 13.10-17) is 'the verbatim agreement' between Jn 5.8 etc. and Mk 2.9 (see Table 1 and 2, p. 167).[27] He compares Jn 5.8 etc. with a different 'stereotyped phrase'. Borgen uses this term to disengage from the idea that John's language is unique and to dissolve the arguments of John's dependence on the Synoptics that involve verbatim agreements. He thus identifies μηκέτι ἁμάρτανε (Jn 5.14) as a stereotyped phrase that he asserts would have been common to the gospel tradition in general. He notes a second usage of this phrase in Jn 7.53–8.11, which is a different story and which he emphasizes is 'a non-Johannine pericope'.[28] In a second move, Borgen draws an analogy between this stereotyped phrase and 'take up your pallet and walk', which he also calls a stereotyped phrase. He argues that just as μηκέτι ἁμάρτανε can occur in two mutually independent stories, it is possible that the phrase 'take up your pallet and walk' could occur in different stories that are independent of each other. He draws attention away from this phrase, which occurs in both Jn 5.1–9 and Mk 2.1–12, by insinuating that it would constitute the only substantial communality between these two texts, because 'the two stories of healing', in which they occur, 'are very different with hardly any further verbal agreement'.[29]

We have already indicated above that Neirynck is of the opinion that Borgen has 'waved aside ... the verbatim agreement between Jn 5.8 and Mk 2.9 ... as a stereotype phrase'.[30] Neirynck himself describes this agreement as follows (see Table 4, p. 168): 'In the healing stories of John 5 and Mark 2 special emphasis is given to the order of Jesus: "rise, take up your bed and walk" (Jn 5.8; Mk 2.11). In both gospels the phrase is repeated in the description of the healing as an immediate execution of Jesus' order (Jn 5.9; Mk 2.12) and, more significantly, the phrase is also used in the debate, in Jn 5.12 (cf. v.11) in the Sabbath discussion (τίς ἐστιν ... ὁ εἰπών σοι), and in Mk 2.9 in the debate about forgiveness of sin (τί ἐστιν εὐκοπώτερον ... ἢ εἰπεῖν·)'.[31]

Regarding (ἴδε ὑγιὴς γέγονας,) μηκέτι ἁμάρτανε (Jn 5.14), which replicates the other stereotyped sense, Neirynck reasons: 'The healing and the forgiveness of sin are closely connected in the story of Mk 2.1-12. Compare 2.9 and 5b,10b–11. In light of the parallel in Mark, the healed paralytic is a man to whom Jesus has said: your sins are

---

[27] Borgen, 'John and the Synoptics', 429.
[28] Borgen, 'John and the Synoptics', 429.
[29] Borgen, 'John and the Synoptics', 429.
[30] See above, n. 26. Cf. Neirynck, 'Response', 443.
[31] Neirynck, 'Response', 445–46.

forgiven. As far as I see, this distinctive feature, the association of forgiveness and healing, is wholly absent in the case of the *adultera*'.[32]

The similarity of sequence between John 5.1–18 and Mark 2.1–3.6

(1) Borgen pays particular attention to a comparison between Jn 5.1–18 and three Synoptic texts (Mt. 12.1-8; Mk 2.23-28 and Lk. 13.10-17) in his survey, because of their form and agreement of content (see Table 1, p. 167). He argues that if the texts had the same form, then 'the question of John's dependence on (or independence of) the Synoptic Gospels' would become relevant. He defines the form of the texts in Matthew, Luke and John generally as traditional, and then especially as 'a case followed by a judicial exchange' or dialogue. He indeed sees 'interesting' parallels and agreement of form between Mt. 12.1-8 (plucking grain on the Sabbath), Lk. 13.10-17 (the healing of a crippled woman on the Sabbath), and Jn 5.1-18. He includes Mk 2.23-28 in his survey because of its closeness to Mt. 12.1-8.[33] Neirynck regretted that Borgen's comments on this comparison were limited: 'Unfortunately, the presentation of the "text" (with the separation of "the case" and the "expository dialogue": Mt. 12.1, 2-8 and Lk. 13.10-13, 14-17) is not followed by a real "commentary".[34]

(2) Borgen plays down the agreement of Jn 5.16, 18 with Mk 3.6. He indeed asserts that both Jn 5.16, 18 and Mk 3.6 par., connect the motif of the persecution of Jesus and the intent to kill Jesus in the gospel tradition with Jesus' apparent violation of the Sabbath, but then adds 'in different ways', thereby creating a distance between the texts. He says Neirynck's assertion that John is here dependent on Mark 'seems arbitrary', because there are no verbal agreements, or to use his terms, the 'subject matter [is the same, but] not [the] Words'.[35] As a counter-argument to promote the hypothesis of John's independence, Borgen observes that 'the expository commentary in Jn 5.10-18 is attached to the story (the case), [the same] as Mt. 12.1-18 and Lk. 13.10-17, while the corresponding discussion in Mk 3.1-6 precedes the story of healing'.

(a) Borgen refers to Neirynck's reaction to the exegesis of Marie-Émile Boismard.[36] Boismard attributes the oldest layer of the story to John II-A, that is, it was written by the Evangelist: 'After this there was a feast and Jesus went up to Jerusalem. And a certain man was there who had been ill. When Jesus saw him, he said to him: "Rise, and take your pallet and walk." And at once the man (rose) and took up his pallet'. The Evangelist (John II-B) rewrote this story and is responsible for Jn 5.1-18; he made all the additions, with the exception of vv. 17-18, which were written by John III. Verse 18 of John III resumes the theme of John II-B in verse 16. The climax is clear: 'the Jews started persecuting' Jesus in v. 16 and 'the Jews were seeking to kill' him in v. 18. Moreover, John III changed the text of John II-B in verse 16 in order to achieve a climax between

---

[32] Neirynck, 'Response', 446.
[33] Borgen, 'John and the Synoptics', 424–25.
[34] Neirynck, 'Response', 442.
[35] Borgen, 'John and the Synoptics', 430.
[36] Borgen, 'John and the Synoptics', 427–28. Cf. Marie-Émile Boismard and Arnaud Lamouille, in collaboration with Gerard Rochais, *L'Évangile de Jean. Commentaire* (Synopse des quatre évangiles en français; Paris: Éditions du Cerf, 1977), 156–65.

verses 16 and 18. At the level of John II-B, verse 16 thus read: 'Therefore the Jews were seeking to kill him'.

According to Neirynck,[37] however, one should not distinguish between the stages designated as John II-A and John II-B. If Boismard can assume that John II-B had extended and reworked the story of John II-A, why then should it not be assumed that John II-B himself reworked the healing story based on Mk 2.1–12 (the healing story of the lame man) and further clarified it with the Sabbath controversy (Mk 3.1–6)?

(b) With regard to Jn 5.16 and 18, Borgen states that the persecution of Jesus and the intent to kill him are features that belong to the gospel tradition. He also states that these two features are central elements in John, as shown in 5.16, 18; 15.20; 7.19–20, 25; 8.37, 40; 11.53, besides being central to the Johannine community. He bases this assertion on a direct correlation between the persecution of Jesus and attempts to kill him, and the persecution of the disciples/the Christians and attempts to kill them (Jn 15.20; 16.2). Then he reiterates that 'the passion narratives and the killing of Jesus show that these elements have a firm basis in the Gospel tradition and in history'.[38]

Neirynck objects against Borgen by emphasizing the common structural treatment of the intent to kill Jesus.[39] First, he agrees with Borgen that this motif 'is indeed "central in John" (5.18; 7.1, 19, 20, 25; 8.37, 40; 11.53; cf. persecution: 5.16; 15.20)', but then adds directly that in both gospels this is the first time that the motif appears (i.e. Jn 5.18; Mk 3.6). Neirynck adds a second argument, steering deeper into form and structural analysis. (We are reminded that he called Borgen's analysis 'vague'.) He observes that the motif is found at the conclusion of the same pattern in both gospels: 'first the healing, then a controversial Sabbath case'. He does not stop there, but adds further details that are common to the two gospels. He indicates that in both instances, the action involves people who are related to Jesus: the healed man and the disciples. In both instances too, the pattern includes a reminder of Jesus' healing activity as a violation of the Sabbath. Perhaps to intimidate Borgen, Neirynck then remarks, 'No modern interpreter of the Gospel of Mark can blame the Fourth Evangelist for having made the connection between Mark 2.1–12 and Mark (2.23–28) 3.1–6'.[40]

(c) In his analysis, Borgen reiterates that Jn 5.16, 18 and Mk 3.6 differ in how they connect the motif of Jesus' persecution and intent to kill him in the gospel tradition with Jesus' apparent violation of the Sabbath. He finds that the establishment of verbal agreement, required by 'modern interpreters' to prove dependence, is missing between Mk 3.6 and Jn 5.16, 18. He therefore dismisses Neirynck's proof that 'John here is dependent on Mark' and repeats the substantiation of his own position: 'John's independence is supported by the observation that the expository commentary in Jn 5.10–18 is attached to the story (the case) just as Mt. 12.1–18 and Lk. 13.10–17, while the corresponding discussion in Mk 3.1–6 precedes the story of healing'.[41]

---

[37] Frans Neirynck et al., *Jean et les Synoptiques: Examen critique de l'exégèse de M.-É. Boismard* (BETL, 49 ; Leuven: Leuven University Press, 1979), 177–80. See Borgen, 'John and the Synoptics', 428.
[38] Borgen, 'John and the Synoptics', 428–30.
[39] Neirynck, 'Response', 444.
[40] Neirynck, 'Response', 445.
[41] Borgen, 'John and the Synoptics', 430.

Neirynck is very careful in his reply to Borgen.[42] He weaves German citations from two prominent New Testament scholars of the twentieth century, Joachim Gnilka and Rudolf Schnackenburg, as well as the Greek text and several verse references into his response. He wants to show that the verses are connected intimately, and that the readings in Jn 5.18 and Mk 3.6 have more in common than verbal agreement within the scope of the two gospels would show. Furthermore, he does not want to reduce the theme of the verse to a single notion as is typical of some formalists. He thus states: 'The motif for the Jews seeking to kill Jesus is not only a violation of the Sabbath (Jn 5.18)'. He compares this point of view with a reading of Mk 3.6, using the words of the German scholars. First, Gnilka, who reasons that the motif of the intent to kill Jesus does not feel appropriate at the end of the pericope.[43] Hereby Neirynck counters Borgen's observations on the form of the text. Second, Schnackenburg, who connects parts of the texts, Mk 2.7 and 3.6, concerning the accusations of blasphemy.[44] Neirynck then quotes the Greek text of Jn 5.18 (οὐ μόνον ἔλυεν τὸ σάββατον, ἀλλὰ καὶ πατέρα ἴδιον ἔλεγεν τὸν θεὸν ἴσον ἑαυτὸν ποιῶν τῷ θεῷ) in relation to 5.17 ('My Father is working still and I am working'). He references Schnackenburg's commentary to make a christological observation on the meaning of the particular verses in John and compares this directly to the Greek text of Mk 2.7: βλασφημεῖ· τίς δύναται ἀφιέναι ἁμαρτίας εἰ μὴ εἷς ὁ θεός; Neirynck then makes a cross-reference to Jn 10.33 (cf. v. 36) as further substantiation of common material between the two gospels.[45]

(d) On the topic of literary form, Borgen opines that because the motif of blasphemy is used differently in Jn 5.18 and Mk 2.7 par. (also Mk 14.64 par.), these parallels do not prove that John is dependent upon the Synoptics. Instead, he insists that arguments based on form analysis demonstrate that John is not dependent on the Synoptics. He is cautious, though, because there are similarities in form, and therefore he stipulates that '[i]n spite of the similarity of form between, on the one hand Jn 5.1–18 and on the other Mt. 12.1–8 and Lk. 13.10–17, John has a distinctive use of this common form'. Borgen provides two arguments against seeing the form of Jn 5.1–18 being derived from the Synoptics. The first regards function, in which John's presentation of the legal debate in Jn 5.1–18 is different from the Synoptic passages. In John it has 'the function of changing the stage (vv. 10–13: the Jews and the person healed; v. 14: Jesus and the healed person; vv. 15–18: the healed person, the Jews and Jesus)'. The second argument regards John being different from the Synoptics because he alone repeats 'phrases from the story (the case) ... quite mechanically in the subsequent legal debate'. He then determines regarding John's uniqueness, 'Only John has, therefore, an extensive paraphrase of parts of the case-story used as a "text"'.[46]

---

[42] Neirynck, 'Response', 446–47.
[43] Cf. Joachim Gnilka, *Das Evangelium nach Markus*, vol. I (EKKNT, II/1; Zürich: Benziger Verlag; Neukirchen-Vluyn: Neukirchener Verlag, 1978), 126: 'Die Tötungsabsicht der Gegner erscheint am Ende der Perikope nicht besonders angemessen, wohl nach 2,1–3,5'. Cf. page 100: 'Der Vorwurf der Lästerung [2:7] muβ ... mit 3,6 in Verbindung gesehen werden', and cf. page 102.
[44] Cf. Rudolf Schnackenburg, Das *Johannesevangelium*, vol. II (HThKNT, IV/2; Freiburg: Herder, 1971), 123: 'Dem Mann ist mit der Heilung zugleich seine Sünde von Gott vergeben worden; das ist es, was Jesus mit dem Satz meint: "Mein Vater arbeitet bis jetzt."'
[45] Neirynck, 'Response', 446–47.
[46] Borgen, 'John and the Synoptics', 430.

Neirynck's reply takes up Borgen's arguments on how the form is different in John, refines them, and uses them to support the hypothesis of dependence.[47] First, he quotes elements of Borgen's position: 'Another "distinctive feature" and one of the "stronger arguments against John's dependence on the Synoptics" is the elaborate form of changing the stage in Jn 5.10-18.' Second, he corrects Borgen, and, picking up on his use of the dramaturgical term 'stage', Neirynck then uses C. H. Dodd's observations on dramaturgy in John to school him. Neirynck writes: 'In fact, this feature is "distinctively Johannine", and not "distinctively traditional". It has been described by Dodd as "a kind of dramatic technique", "the device of two stages upon which the action is exhibited".'[48] In a third move, Neirynck offers a detailed structural analysis of the pericope in John 5 that reveals the changing locations and personages:

[The healed person interacts with]:
1–9   Jesus (at the Sheep Pool)
10–13   The Jews
14   Jesus (in the temple)
15–18   The Jews and Jesus

Neirynck offers a series of comparisons with Jn 9 and determines, 'There is nothing similar in Mt. 12.1-8'. Hereby he seems to be suggesting that Borgen is avoiding the most crucial evidence. Neirynck continues: 'This is most curious since it is normally not Mt. 12.1-8 but Mk 2.1-3.6, and especially 2.1-12 and 2.23-28; 3.1-6, which is cited as the synoptic parallel.' He then points out differences and similarities between the pericopes in Mark and Matthew. First, the differences: in Mark the two Sabbath pericopes are closely connected. Together they form the conclusion of the section of controversies (2.1–3.6). In Matthew they are separated from Mt. 9.1–17 = Mk 2.1–22 and, as a result of the Matthean expansions in 12.5-7 and 11-12a, and the traditional formula μεταβὰς ἐκεῖθεν in 12.9a, the two pericopes are more clearly distinguished than they are in Mark.

Second, he presents a form-critical connection, demonstrating that he is cautious about determining sources and has a command of both form-critical exegesis and the exegetes: 'I can agree with R. Pesch's form-critical description of the connection of 3.1-6 with 2.23-28, at least with this reservation: the connection is not necessarily pre-Markan.'[49] Neirynck thereby strengthens his hand and insistence that John is dependent on Mark. After viewing the segments of Mark in relation to Matthew, he considers the Markan text as a unit in form: 'When we take Mk 2.23–3.6 as one section in Mark there is no ground for the objection that the discussion precedes the healing since the second pericope is a continuation of the debate following the plucking of grain on the Sabbath.' In the same breath, he retakes Borgen's use of dramaturgical terminology and points to a further connection between Jn 5.1-18 and Mark. He says: 'And the Johannine change of the stage has a synoptic analogy in Mk 3.1'.

[47] Neirynck, 'Response', 443–44.
[48] Cf. Dodd, *Historical Tradition*, 96.
[49] Neirynck, 'Response', 444. Cf. Rudolf Pesch, *Das Markusevangelium*, vol. I (HThKNT, II/1; Freiburg: Herder, 1976), 188.

(e) According to Borgen, 'The agreement between Jn 5.10 ... οὐκ ἔξεστίν ... and Mt. 12.2 is due to the fact that a traditional form corresponding to Paul's use of tradition (Gospel) forms in 1 Cor. 10.21 and 11.27ff. is used in Jn's paraphrase'.[50] Neirynck rejects this 'most typical sentence' as follows: 'Οὐκ ἔξεστίν is treated as an isolated phrase and the striking parallelism between the structure of Jn 5.1–18 and Mk 2.1–12; 2.23–3.6 receives no consideration' (see Table 3, p. 168).[51]

The origin of John 5.1–18: Oral or written?

How does Borgen respond to the question as to whether the passage comes from an oral tradition or whether it is based on a written document? He formulates his answer using the following outline. He makes three points to support his theory that 'Jn 5.1–18 not only draws on oral tradition, but is itself an oral unit which has been written down'.[52]

1. The first point deals with the 'transmitted tradition' within the Johannine community. Borgen wants to say that John and the Synoptics are similar because they all knew and used Paul's writings. Thus, the first part of the passage, Jn 5.1–9, which tells the story of the healing, and has the same form as the parallel stories in the Synoptics, is not dependent on them. Borgen says it seems that John is reproducing 'transmitted tradition corresponding to Paul's rendering of the Eucharistic tradition in 1 Cor. 11.23–25(26)'. He labels the second part of the passage (Jn 5.10–18) 'an expository commentary', and says that this 'corresponds to Paul's commentary in 1 Cor. 11. (26)27ff.'. He thus draws the following conclusion on the whole passage: 'Jn 5.1–18, as a whole, is therefore a unit parallel to 1 Cor. 11.23–34, and results from a corresponding expository activity in the Johannine community.'
2. The second point deals with the *Sitz im Leben* of Jn 5.1–18, which Borgen places contextually within Jn 9.1–41. He draws for support on the studies of J. Louis Martyn and Severino Pancaro about the Johannine community. Borgen's theory of '[t]he life setting of the passage concerns the controversy between the church and the synagogue, in which Christology, the Sabbath and the Law of Moses were central issues'. The importance of these questions for understanding the actual situation of the Johannine community is evident from Jn 9.1–41. Martyn and Pancaro have shown that the history of the Johannine community is reflected in these two passages.
3. The third point is theological. Borgen assesses that '[t]he Evangelist has more interest in the Christological aspect as such than in the Sabbath question'. This explains to him why 'phrases and terms about the Sabbath and the Sabbath controversy are not repeated' in the discourse that follows Jn 5.19, 'whereas the Christological idea in Jn 5.17 ... *is* developed'.

---

[50] Borgen, 'John and the Synoptics', 429.
[51] Neirynck, 'Response', 445.
[52] Borgen, 'John and the Synoptics', 430–31.

Neirynck, who mainly focuses on written texts and believes that oral tradition is difficult to trace, refutes only the third point: 'In a final objection, Borgen opposes to the (traditional) Sabbath question in Jn 5.10–18 the Evangelist's own discourse in 5.19ff. in which "the Christological idea in 5.17 is developed more independently". The Evangelist's interest in the Christological aspect is rightly emphasized, but it is precisely the weakness of Borgen's analysis, it seems to me, that he has not been able to grasp the Christological (!) orientation in the progression from the healing in 5.1–9 to 5.18.'[53]

Neirynck's 1991 reply to Borgen

In his brief overview of research, Borgen notes with regard to the Leuven school: 'In recent years the view that John is dependent upon the Synoptics has gained new impetus. For example, F. Neirynck and M. Sabbe reject theories of "unknown" and "hypothetical" sources behind John, whether they are supposed to be written or oral. Neirynck writes that "... not traditions lying behind the Synoptic Gospels but the Synoptic Gospels themselves are the sources of the Fourth Evangelist"'.[54]

Neirynck responds to this in an 'Additional Note'.[55] He refers to Robert T. Fortna and Johannes Beutler who formulated the same criticism against him.[56] Neirynck answers confidently: 'The truth is that I am skeptical with regard to the classic source theories such as the signs source and a continuous passion narrative, or the combination of both in a *Grundschrift* or signs Gospel. But I am not aware that I ever gave such an exclusiveness to the Synoptic Gospels as to exclude John's use of oral-tradition or source material.'[57] The misunderstanding is refuted: 'In my 1975 reply to A. Dauer, I expressly made the observation that "direct dependence on the Synoptic Gospels does not preclude the possibility of supplementary information". The phrase "not the sources of the Synoptic Gospels but the Synoptic Gospels themselves" was used with reference to Jn 20.1–18, and has been generalized by Borgen far beyond the meaning it had in my paper. It is true, however, that I continue to regard the section Jn 20,1–18 as a pertinent test case for the thesis of John's dependence.'[58] In this note Neirynck also addresses the

---

[53] Neirynck, 'Response', 447.
[54] Borgen, 'John and the Synoptics', 409.
[55] Frans Neirynck, *Evangelica II: 1982-1990: Collected Essays*, ed. Frans Van Segbroeck (BETL, 99; Leuven: Leuven University Press and Peeters, 1991), 711–12.
[56] Robert T. Fortna, *The Fourth Gospel and Its Predecessor: From Narrative Source to Present Gospel* (Philadelphia, PA: Fortress, 1988), 216–18: 'The Source and the Synoptic Gospels' and 46 n. 95: 'Neirynck holds here as everywhere that 4E is dependent not on any pre-Johannine source, but simply on the Synoptics'; Johannes Beutler, 'Méthodes et problèmes de la recherche johannique aujourd'hui', in *La Communauté johannique et son histoire: La trajectoire de l'évangile de Jean aux deux premiers siècles*, ed. Jean-Daniel Kaestli, Jean-Michel Poffet and Jean Zumstein (MoBi, 20; Genève: Labor et Fides, 1990), 19: '[les] travaux de Neirynck ... contribuent à étayer sa propre thèse, selon laquelle les synoptiques constituent la seule source de Jn.' In his recent commentary on John, Beutler writes that through his research he has gradually revised his previous defence of written sources behind the Gospel, and that, under the influence of the Leuven school of Neirynck, he has increasingly come to see the Synoptic Gospels as its sources. In his interpretation of Jn 5.1–18, *to a large extent* he follows Neirynck's answer to Borgen. I paraphrase Beutler's point of view. Cf. Johannes Beutler, *Das Johannesevangelium: Kommentar* (Freiburg: Herder, 2013), 183–84.
[57] Neirynck, *Evangelica II*, 711–12.
[58] Neirynck, *Evangelica II*, 712.

objection of Jürgen Becker, who states that Neirynck turns the Evangelist into 'ein Schreibtisch gelehrte, [der] zwischen den dreien kurzfristig hin- und herpendelnd, sein Evangelium schrieb'.[59] Neirynck answers: 'But the phenomenon of conflation and harmonization of overlapping traditions is already found in the Synoptic Gospels, and it is undeniably one of the characteristics of the early use of the canonical Gospels in the apocryphal literature. If the Fourth Evangelist was a teacher and preacher in his community who knew the earlier Gospels, conflation and harmonization may have been quite natural to him. Such an objection not only concerns the work of the Fourth Evangelist.' Neirynck adds with reference to Eduard Simons,[60] 'Of course, the objection is not new; neither is the answer'.[61]

The Borgen-Neirynck dialogue summarized

Both Borgen and Neirynck have the comparison of written texts as their point of departure. However, since they do not compare the same texts or attach the same value to these texts, it goes without saying that they arrive at different solutions to their research questions regarding John's relationship with the Synoptics. Borgen principally discusses John 5.1–18 and compares this text with Mt. 12.1–8 // Mk 2.23–28 and Lk. 13.10–17. In line with his earlier contributions, he sees a fixed structure of 'the case' and an 'expository dialogue' and attributes this to the oral tradition. Moreover, Borgen provides a fairly complete overview of similarities between the Fourth Gospel and the Synoptics, but according to him they do not indicate literary dependence. Thus, for example, the parallel between Mk 2.9 and Jn 5.8 refers only to a fixed formula in the oral tradition of Early Christianity. Neirynck rejects both conclusions: Jn 5.9–18 is a christological exposition of the Evangelist himself, with the verse in Jn 5.8 playing an important role. This verse, which is parallel with Mk 2.9, points to John's literal dependence on Mark, because of their written similarities. But more than their verbal agreement, the argument of *akolouthia* also plays an important role: the Markan composition in Mk 2.1–3.6 was used by the Fourth Evangelist.

Oral tradition and the Leuven approach

Our point of departure has been a dialogue between Borgen and Neirynck, which is also central to Borgen's latest book. But with which literary theories can Borgen's point of view be compared, and what is our position?

The Borgen-Dauer hypothesis

As we have already noted, akin to Anton Dauer, Borgen 'accepts a mediate contact of John with the Synoptics, some elements of the written Synoptic Gospels being fused

---

[59] Jürgen Becker, 'Das Johannesevangelium im Streit der Methoden (1980–1984)', *ThRu* 51 (1986): 22 and 24.
[60] Eduard Simons, *Hat der dritte Evangelist den kanonischen Matthäus benutzt?* (Bonn, Georgi, 1880), 110.
[61] Neirynck, *Evangelica II*, 712.

together with the pre-Johannine oral tradition.'⁶² But according to Neirynck, one has to take into account that 'some significant variations can be observed in Dauer's defence of the common thesis'.⁶³ Dauer does not avoid calling it a pre-Johannine written source: 'eine zusammenhangende – schriftliche (?) Quelle',⁶⁴ while Borgen places far more emphasis on 'parallel tendency', 'common tradition', and on 'mutually independent tradition'.⁶⁵ However, in the conclusion to his 1959 article, Borgen notes that three sections of the passion story (Jn 18.10–11, 26; 19.31, 38 and 19.40-42) consist of Synoptic material that has been added to the Johannine tradition. In the reprint of his 1983 contribution, his view did not change; in the Preface, he introduces his article as follows: 'John is based essentially on an independent tradition, even though it has been influenced by the synoptic accounts.'⁶⁶

Secondary orality⁶⁷

In the second edition of *John among the Gospels*, D. Moody Smith openly states that 'John's independence, in the sense of ignorance and disuse, of the Synoptics is no longer taken for granted, as much recent investigation moves in the opposite direction. The influence of Frans Neirynck and the Louvain school has been deeply felt on the Continent, as well as in the English-speaking world'.⁶⁸ Smith refers especially to the studies of Manfred Lang, Udo Schnelle and Michael Labahn, who were at that time already colleagues in Halle-Wittenberg:⁶⁹ 'Thus in his intensive redaction-critical study of the Johannine passion narrative, *Johannes und die Synoptiker*, Manfred Lang argues for John's use of Mark particularly, and also for Luke. In this he agrees with his

⁶² Neirynck, 'Response', 439.
⁶³ Neirynck, 'Response', 439.
⁶⁴ Anton Dauer, *Die Passionsgeschichte im Johannesevangelium: Eine traditionsgeschichtliche und theologische Untersuchung zu Joh 18,1–19,30* (SANT, 30; München: Kösel-Verlag, 1972), 335, 227. See also his later study: *Johannes und Lukas: Untersuchungen zu den johanneisch-lukanischen Parallelperikopen Joh 4,46–54/Lk 7,1–10 – Joh 12,1-8/Lk 7,36–50; 10,38–42 – Joh 20,19–29/Lk 24,36–49* (FzB, 50; Würzburg, Echter Verlag, 1984).
⁶⁵ See the critical remarks of Dauer, *Passionsgeschichte*, 131 n. 200, 170 n. 33 and 171 n. 38.
⁶⁶ Borgen, 'John and the Synoptics in the Passion Narrative', 246–59; repr. in Borgen, *Logos*, 67–80; *The Gospel of John*, 103–19. See especially Borgen, *Logos*, 6, where he adds: 'Anton Dauer uses this thesis and builds further on my studies.'
⁶⁷ For the following paragraph, see also Gilbert Van Belle 'Introduction', in Michael Labahn, *Ausgewählte Studien zum Johannesevangelium: Selected Studies in the Gospel of John: 1998–2013*, ed. Antje Labahn (Biblical Tools and Studies, 28; Leuven: Peeters, 2017), XXVII–VIII. See also Labahn's two monographs: *Jesus als Lebensspender: Untersuchungen zu einer Geschichte der johanneischen Tradition anhand ihrer Wundergeschichten* (BZNW, 98; Berlin: de Gruyter, 1999); *Offenbarung in Zeichen und Wort: Untersuchungen zur Vorgeschichte von Joh 6,1–25a und seiner Rezeption in der Brotrede* (WUNT, 2/117; Tübingen: Mohr Siebeck, 2000).
⁶⁸ Smith, *John among the Gospels*, 196.
⁶⁹ Manfred Lang, *Johannes und die Synoptiker: Eine redaktionsgeschichtliche Analyse von Joh 18–19 vor dem markinischen und lukanischen Hintergrund* (FRLANT, 182; Göttingen: Vandenhoeck & Ruprecht, 1999); Udo Schnelle, *The History and Theology of the New Testament Writings*, trans. by M. Eugene Boring (London: SCM Press, 1998), 492–504. See also U. Schnelle, *Das Evangelium nach Johannes* (5th edn; ThKNT, 4; Leipzig: Evangelische Verlagsanstalt, 2006), 17–21. With regard to Jn 5.8, he notes: 'Das Befehlswort zeigt beachtliche Übereinstimmungen mit Mk 2,11; ob eine direkte Abhängigkeit vorliegt oder ein Einzellogion aus der mündlichen Überlieferung verarbeitet wurde, lässt sich nicht mehr mit Sicherheit entscheiden.'

mentor Udo Schnelle, who outlines a similar position in his introduction, which is also reflected in Schnelle's commentary on John. In a massive study of the Johannine miracle tradition, *Jesus as Lebensspender*, Michael Labahn sees Synoptic influence on John, but principally at the level of a secondary orality (a position not dissimilar to that of Anton Dauer ...). That is, the continued telling of Synoptic stories has affected the Johannine accounts.[70]

However, Smith defends the Fourth Gospel as an independent gospel and with regard to 'secondary orality' he remarks: 'The concept of secondary orality is a useful one, underscored as it is by Papias's famous preference for the living voice over the written word. Labahn's conception of its relation to the Johannine tradition is conceivable, and it is hard to imagine how a more thorough case for the position could be made. Yet is there not also the possibility that such secondary orality affected, not the Johannine tradition, but the text of the Gospel of John at the early stage of transmission for which there is no manuscript evidence? If so, elements of Markan redaction could as easily as tradition find their way into manuscripts of the Gospel of John. Such possibility is in the very nature of the case not subject to scholarly controls. But that does not mean it does not exist. Short of new manuscript discoveries, it cannot be established, but neither can it be excluded.'[71] He concludes:

> The work of Lang and Labahn, as well as Schnelle, manifests an ever-growing complexity in the grasp and nuancing of the issues and the evidence. Ironically, in this respect their investigations run counter to the original impetus and thrust of Neirynck's own work. For in contrast to Boismard's solution of the problem of John and the Synoptics, and in particular to his complex diagram of relationships..., Neirynck offers a diagram that is simplicity itself. John draws from each of the Synoptics Gospels: ... Yet, as the problem is now closely studied, the explanation of how John uses, or reflects knowledge of, the Synoptics once again grows, with a seeming inevitability, increasingly complex. The basic problem is again that the evidence points in different directions.[72]

---

[70] Smith, *John among the Gospels*, 196. On 'secondary orality', see now also Michael Labahn, '"Secondary Orality" in the Gospel of John: A "Post-Gutenberg" Paradigm for Understanding the Relationship between Written Gospel Texts', in *The Origins of John's Gospel*, ed. Stanley E. Porter and Hughson T. Ong (Johannine Studies, 2; Leiden, Brill, 2016), 53–80.

[71] Moreover, Smith accepts that 'Labahn's view of the Johannine miracle tradition would seem in principle to stand as an alternative to Lang's contention that John's passion narrative reflects direct knowledge of Mark and Luke, since it would be unlikely that John had direct access to Mark's passion, and Luke's, but not to the miracle stories, or the narrative of Jesus' public ministry generally (or that having direct access to Mark and Luke, John would have used the passion narratives directly, but not the early narratives). To summarize briefly, on the one hand Labahn's thesis could accommodate the implications of my findings in this chapter. On the other, my observations will count against the view that John knew, or at least that John used, any of the synoptic passion narratives' (*John Among the Gospels*, 197). See Labahn's reaction in his review of Smith's monograph: 'S[mith] äußert Sympathie für das Modell der "second orality" (Labahn) und findet eine Koinzidenz mit seine eigenen Beobachtungen. Er bezweifelt, dass ein Nebeneinander der *secondary orality* mit dem Modell der literarischen Abhängigkeit (Lang) denkbar ist – hier mag man erwidern, dass dann, wenn hinter der "secondary orality" synoptischen Texten stehen, auch der Zugriff auf diese Evangelien nicht ausgeschlossen ist' (*TLZ* 129 [2004]: 290).

[72] Smith, *John and the Synoptics*, 198.

In addition to this presentation of Labahn's literary theory, we will note that none other than Borgen, in his critical review of Labahn's *Offenbarung in Zeichen und Wort*, has emphasized the following strong aspects of Labahn's form-critical approach: 'Labahn is to be commended for making an attempt to bring together different approaches and methods of research. He examines the text from the viewpoints of literary criticism, oral tradition and its community setting. The relationship between the miracle stories and the subsequent discourse is defined. The perspective of the history of tradition is combined with the consideration of the communicative appeal of the tradition/text on its hearers/readers. The dual concern in the Johannine community for preservation and innovations is illuminated. Labahn also broadens his study by bringing in comparative material from the surrounding world. In conclusion, the book is a rich and stimulating contribution to the study of John. As such it invites the reader to a dialogue and debate.'[73]

On the basis of a narrative analysis of John 5,[74] Labahn perceives formal and literary anomalies in the narrative structure and the context of the miracle of the paralytic at the pool of Bethesda. He concludes that it is possible to discern three phases of development of the story: a miracle story of the healing of a paralytic (5.2–9c), the traditional story of the Sabbath conflict between the Johannine-Jewish Christian group and the synagogue (5.2–16; 7.21–24), and the incorporation of this conflict story into the Fourth Gospel from the christological viewpoint of the Evangelist. Labahn stresses that if this hypothetical reconstruction of the pre-history of the text is correct, then we have obtained insight into the pre-history of the Johannine community and its controversy with the Jewish environment.

Media culture: Orality, performance and memory

One of the shortcomings of the Leuven hypothesis is that it takes almost no account of 'oral tradition', for which it compensates by speaking instead of the Fourth Evangelist's literary creativity. Like Neirynck, I do not want to exclude 'oral tradition' completely. The studies by Tom Thatcher, Alan Kirk and others of media culture in the first century indeed pose a challenge for me to continue refining my own hypothesis, and rightly one might wonder whether one should not state that:

> ancient Jesus traditions and other early Christian communications were created and recreated in a media culture quite different from that of the modern Western world. Rather than describing the traditioning process in terms of 'transmitting', 'writing', 'revising' and/or 'copying' fixed text, oral-traditional culture is better characterized as a complex matrix of communicative influences upon multiple

---

[73] Peder Borgen, 'Review of M. Labahn, *Offenbarung in Zeichen und Wort*', *JTS* 53 (2002): 218–19.
[74] Michael Labahn, 'Eine Spurensuche anhand von Joh 5,1–18: Bemerkungen zu Wachstum und Wandel der Heilung eines Lahmen', *NTS* 44 (1988): 159–79; repr. Michael Labahn, *Ausgewählte Studien*, 391–411. For this summary, see ibid., XXXV.

trajectories of the past – recollections of both the actual past and of the past discussions/commemorations of those events.[75]

Conclusion

When I was asked to write a contribution about the miracle stories and the Gospel of Mark, I hesitated for a long time. In the end, I chose to orientate my contribution towards a discussion between Borgen and Neirynck, which took place more than thirty years ago and has recently been brought into the spotlight again by Borgen himself. I have drawn attention to two aspects of this discussion in particular that convince me in one way or another that one should not neglect the close contacts between the Gospel of John and the Gospel of Mark: first, the argument of striking word agreements, and, secondly, the argument of the order. Due to this focus, many topics, problems and methods that are mentioned in the history of the exegesis of Jn 5.1–18 have not been discussed. Here I am thinking of the intertextual approach of Jean-Marie Sevrin[76] and the relecture model of Jean Zumstein,[77] the various text-critical problems, the fascinating discussion about the meaning of the archaeological findings related to the Pool of Bethesda,[78] the sequence of chapters 5–7, and the reference to the miracle of chapter 5 in Jn 7.19–24.

I must confess that I myself have always seen the 'Louvain Hypothesis' as an eminent means to understand the theology, Christology and soteriology of the Gospel of John. Thanks to this hypothesis, through the intertextual comparison of written documents, it is easier to understand the redaction of the Fourth Evangelist without having to take an oral tradition *a priori* into account. But as such this cannot be excluded.

---

[75] *The Fourth Gospel in First-Century Media Culture*, ed. Anthony Le Donne and Tom Thatcher (LNTS, 426; London: T&T Clark International, 2011), 2.

[76] Jean-Marie Sevrin, 'Jésus et le sabbat dans le quatrième évangile', in *La Foi dans l'un et l'autre Testament*, ed. Camille Focant (LD, 168; Paris, Éditions du Cerf, 1997), 229–32 : 'Les deux guérisons johanniques et les deux guérisons de la section polémique de Mc 2,1–3,6'; repr. Sevrin, *Le quatrième évangile. Recueil d'études*, ed. Gilbert Van Belle (BETL, 281; Leuven University Press and Peeters, 2016), 186–88.

[77] Jean Zumstein, *L'Évangile selon saint Jean (1–12)* (Commentaire du Nouveau Testament, 4b; Genève : Labor et Fides, 2014), 30-2; Zumstein, *Das Johannesevangelium* (KEK, 2; Göttingen, Vandenhoeck & Ruprecht, 2016), 42–44.

[78] See esp. the commentary of Theobald, *John*, 372–75: 'Exkurs: Zur "Wiederentdeckung" von Bethesda'; see also von Wahlde, 'The Gospel of John and Archaeology', in James H. Charlesworth (ed.), *Jesus and Archaeology* (Grand Rapids, MI: Wm B. Eerdmans, 2006), 523–86; von Wahlde, *The Gospel and the Letters of John*, 216–18.

Appendix

Table 1. Borgen on 'Text' and Commentary in Jn 5.1–18 and Synoptic Parallels

	Jn 5.1–18	Mt. 2.1–8	Mk 2.23–28	Lk. 13.10–17
The case	5.1–9	12.1	2.23	13.10–13
Expository dialogue	5.10–18	12.2–8	2.24–28	13.14–17

Source: Peder Borgen, 'John and the Synoptics', 425–27.

Table 2. Borgen on 'Agreements' between John 5.1–18 and the Synoptics

Sentences (almost verbatim agreement)	
Jn 5.8 ἔγειρε ἆρον τὸν κράβαττόν σου καὶ περιπάτει.	
Jn 5.9 ... εὐθέως ... ἦρεν τὸν κράβαττον αὐτοῦ καὶ περιεπάτει.	Mk 2.9 ἔγειρε καὶ ἆρον τὸν κράβαττόν σου καὶ περιπάτει;
Jn 5.10 ἆραι τὸν κράβαττον	Mk 2.11 ἔγειρε ἆρον τὸν κράβαττόν σου καὶ
Jn 5.11 ἆρον τὸν κράβαττόν σου καὶ περιπάτει	Mk 2.12 ἠγέρθη καὶ εὐθὺς ἄρας τὸν κράβαττον
Jn 5.12 ἆρον καὶ περιπάτει	
Jn 5.14 μηκέτι ἁμάρτανε	(Jn 8.11 μηκέτι ἁμάρτανε)
Part of sentences	
Jn 5.10 σάββατόν ... οὐκ ἔξεστίν σοι (ἆραι)	Mt.12.2 (cf. Mk 2:24) ὃ οὐκ ἔξεστιν ποιεῖν ἐν σαββάτῳ.
Words	
Jn 5.6 ... ἰδὼν ὁ Ἰησοῦς ... λέγει	Mk 2.5 ἰδὼν ὁ Ἰησοῦς ... λέγει
Jn 5.10 ἔλεγον ... οἱ (Ἰουδαῖοι) ...	Mk 2.24 οἱ (Φαρισαῖοι) ἔλεγον
(Jn 5.3d παραλυτικῶν)	Mk 2.3 παραλυτικόν
Subject matter, not words	
Jn 5.18 making himself equal with God	Mk 2.7 It is a blasphemy. Who can forgive sins but God alone?
Jn 5.14 Sin no more	
Jn 5.16 The Jews persecuted Jesus	Mk 3.6 The Pharisees went out, and immediately held council with the Herodians against him, how to destroy him.
Jn 5.18 the Jews sought all the more to kill him.	
Jn 5.17 My Father is working still and I am working	Mt. 12.8 (cf. Mk 2.27; Lk. 6.5) For the Son of Man is lord of the Sabbath

Source: Peder Borgen, 'John and the Synoptics', 427.

Table 3. Neirynck on John 5.1–18 and the Markan Parallels

John	Mark
5.1–9a the healing	2.1–12 the healing
5.8 ... ἆρον τὸν κράβαττόν σου	2.11 ... ἆρον τὸν κράβαττόν σου
5.9 ... ἦρεν τὸν κράβαττον αὐτοῦ	2.12 ... ἄρας τὸν κράβαττον
5.9 ἦν δὲ σάββατον ἐν ...	2.23 ἐν τοῖς σάββασιν
5.10 ἔλεγον οὖν οἱ Ἰουδαῖοι ...· σάββατόν ἐστιν, καὶ οὐκ ἔξεστίν σοι ἆραι τὸν κράβαττόν σου.	2.24 καὶ οἱ Φαρισαῖοι ἔλεγον ...· ... ποιοῦσιν τοῖς σάββασιν ὃ οὐκ ἔξεστιν;
The *man* carrying his bed	the *disciples* plucking grain
5.11–16 *Jesus* ὁ ποιήσας αὐτὸν ὑγιῆ ... ἐν σαββάτῳ (cf. 7.23)	3.1–6 *Jesus* εἰ ... θεραπεύσει αὐτόν 3.2 τοῖς σάββασιν 3.4 ἔξεστιν τοῖς σάββασιν ἀγαθὸν ποιῆσαι ... ἢ *ἀποκτεῖναι;*
5.17 ... ἐργάζομαι.	3.6 συμβούλιον ἐδίδουν κατ' αὐτοῦ
5.18 ἐζήτουν αὐτὸν ... *ἀποκτεῖναι*	ὅπως αὐτὸν ἀπολέσωσιν.

Compare Mk 3.6 (and Jn 5.18) with:

Mk 11.18	ἐζήτουν	πῶς αὐτὸν	ἀπολέσωσιν
Mk 12.12	ἐζήτουν	αὐτὸν	κρατῆσαι
Mk 14.1	ἐζήτουν ...	πῶς αὐτὸν ...	κρατήσαντες ἀποκτείνωσιν.

Source: Frans Neirynck, 'Response', 445.

Table 4. Neirynck on the Parallels between Jn 5.8–12 and Mk 2.9, 11–12

John 5	Mark 2
	2.11 σοὶ λέγω,
5.8 ἔγειρε ἆρον τὸν κράβαττόν σου καὶ περιπάτει	ἔγειρε ἆρον τὸν κράβαττόν σου καὶ ὕπαγε ...
5.9 καὶ εὐθέως ἐγένετο ὑγιὴς ...	2.12 καὶ ἠγέρθη
καὶ ἦρεν τὸν κράβαττον αὐτοῦ καὶ περιεπάτει	καὶ εὐθὺς ἄρας τὸν κράβαττον ἐξῆλθεν ...
(10) ἆραι τὸν κράβαττόν σου (11) ... μοι εἶπεν· ἆρον τὸν κράβαττόν σου καὶ περιπάτει.	
5.12 τίς ἐστιν ὁ ἄνθρωπος ὁ εἰπών σοι·	2.9 τί ἐστιν ... ἢ εἰπεῖν· ἔγειρε
ἆρον καὶ περιπάτει;	καὶ ἆρον τὸν κράβαττόν σου καὶ περιπάτει;

Source: Frans Neirynck, 'Response', 446.

13

From the Expectation of the Imminent Kingdom to the Presence of Eternal Life: Eschatology in Mark and John

Jörg Frey

Eschatology is one of the most central and disputed fields in New Testament scholarship, in particular due to the fact that this subject became especially problematized with the rise of modern interpretation in the late eighteenth century.[1] The expectation of an imminent Parousia, traditionally attributed to Jesus himself and also his apostles, was questioned as an erroneous view that had to be reinterpreted as an 'accommodation' of Jesus and the apostles to the views of their time,[2] in order to protect the whole of Christian doctrine from devastating criticism. With the discovery of differences between the Synoptic and Johannine views, in particular between the plain expectation of the coming of the Son of Man with the heavenly clouds and the more spiritual view of Jesus' coming or internal presence in John, the debate about eschatology and even the eschatology of Jesus became an intra-canonical issue: which tradition is historically closer to Jesus, closer to the theological truth, or philosophically more acceptable? Whereas in the nineteenth century, Jesus' views were usually understood in a spiritualizing (or somewhat Johannized) manner,[3] scholarship around 1900 'discovered' or uncovered the 'thoroughly eschatological' view of the earthly Jesus,[4] while removing

---

[1] On the history of early New Testament scholarship and the criticism of New Testament eschatology by scholars such as Hermann Samuel Reimarus or Johann Salomo Semler as well as by the philosophical schools of the 19th century, see Jörg Frey, *Die johanneische Eschatologie, vol. 1: Ihre Probleme im Spiegel der Forschung seit Reimarus* (WUNT, 96; Tübingen: Mohr Siebeck, 1997), 10–21. See also Jörg Frey, 'New Testament Eschatology – an Introduction: Classical Issues, Disputed Themes, and Current Perspectives', in *Eschatology of the New Testament and Some Related Documents*, ed. Jan G. van der Watt (WUNT, 2/315; Tübingen: Mohr Siebeck, 2011), 6–19.
[2] In particular Johann Salomo Semler; see Gottfried Hornig, *Die Anfänge der historisch-kritischen Theologie: Johann Salomo Semlers Schriftverständnis und seine Stellung zu Luther* (Forschungen zur Systematischen Theologie und Religionsphilosophie, 8; Göttingen: Vandenhoeck & Ruprecht, 1961), 211–31.
[3] Cf. Frey, *Die johanneische Eschatologie 1*, 22–8.
[4] In particular Albert Schweitzer, *Von Reimarus bis Wrede: Eine Geschichte der Leben-Jesu-Forschung* (Tübingen: Mohr Siebeck, 1906), and the second, thoroughly revised, version: Albert Schweitzer, *Geschichte der Leben-Jesu-Forschung* (Tübingen: Mohr Siebeck, 1913). See the English translation: Albert Schweitzer, *The Quest of the Historical Jesus*, ed. John Bowden (Minneapolis, MN: Fortress, 2001).

John from the quest for the Jesus of history.[5] A number of more recent attempts to re-Johannize Jesus and to re-historicize John follow a revisionist agenda,[6] but their approach is methodologically unclear and therefore rather vague.[7] On the other hand, twentieth-century scholarship has also distanced the Synoptics from the views of the Jesus of history in order to validate the gospel authors as theologians in their own right and in their own place. So when comparing Mark and John today, we can do so without the burdensome question about the 'real' teaching of Jesus, but more simply compare two concepts with regard to their literary and theological relationship.

Preliminaries

Comparing the eschatology of Mark and John can simply mean enquiring about their mutual agreements and differences, not only with regard to terms and ideas but also concerning the concept of time and the author's localization within time. It can also mean looking for literary or theological developments or changes between their respective concepts. Such a comparison is based on the presupposition that there is a reception or deliberate modification of the earlier concept in the later one (i.e., of Mark in John). In the context of this chapter, there is not sufficient space to discuss or prove such a reception, but, as I have argued elsewhere,[8] the theory of John's independence from the Synoptics or Mark – which was widely held in the second half of the twentieth century[9] – has rightly been questioned and replaced by the assumption that the Fourth Evangelist actually knew Mark and used it as selectively as he used other sources, in particular the Scriptures. The evangelist even seems to presuppose knowledge of Mark's story or also Mark's text among some of

---

[5] On the 'De-Johannification of Jesus' and the related 'De-Historicization of John', see Paul N. Anderson, *The Fourth Gospel and the Quest for Jesus: Modern Foundations Considered* (LNTS, 321; London: T&T Clark, 2006), 43–99; on the 'critical consensus' established around 1900, see Frey, *Die johanneische Eschatologie 1*, 36–42.

[6] Thus in particular the approach adopted by Paul N. Anderson and the SBL Seminar group 'John, Jesus, and History'. On Anderson's 'Bi-Optic Perspective on John and the Synoptics', see Paul N. Anderson, *Fourth Gospel*, 127–73.

[7] For criticism, see Jörg Frey, *Theology and History in the Fourth Gospel: Tradition and Narration* (Waco, TX: Baylor University Press, 2018), 78–97; on Anderson's approach in particular, see pages 91–93.

[8] Jörg Frey, 'Das vierte Evangelium auf dem Hintergrund der älteren Evangelientradition: Zum Problem: Johannes und die Synoptiker', in Jörg Frey, *Die Herrlichkeit des Gekreuzigten: Studien zu den johanneischen Schriften 1*, ed. by Juliane Schlegel (WUNT, 307; Tübingen: Mohr Siebeck, 2013), 239–94; see also Jörg Frey, *Theology and History*, 64–78.

[9] The breakthrough, as far as this view is concerned, was the booklet by Percival Gardner-Smith, *Saint John and the Synoptic Gospels* (Cambridge: Cambridge University Press, 1938). Gardner-Smith emphasized the differences between Mark and John while only superficially looking at their commonalities, and from those differences he postulated, rather than demonstrated, John's independence. In spite of Gardner-Smith's relatively weak argument, his views were embraced by the leading scholars of that period, C. H. Dodd and Rudolf Bultmann, and so the view of John's independence came to scholarly dominance in the post-Second World War period. See the critical analysis by Joseph Verheyden, 'P. Gardner-Smith and the "Turn of the Tide"', in *John and the Synoptics*, ed. Adelbert Denaux (BETL, 101; Leuven: Leuven University Press and Peeters, 1992), 423–52.

his readers.[10] If such knowledge or even a deliberate reference to Mark can be demonstrated for some instances, it has to be presupposed for the whole (i.e., even for those instances where John apparently ignores or contradicts Mark). The differences call for explanation, but they cannot be counted simply as evidence of ignorance or independence.

I can mention only a few examples for which I consider it certain that John draws on Mark or presupposes knowledge of Mark. First, when John 3.24 presents the simultaneous ministry of John the Baptist and Jesus and then explicitly explains that 'John the Baptist had not yet been imprisoned', this demonstrates that he regards it as necessary to explain his tradition about the simultaneous ministry of Jesus and John in view of a different chronological timeline, as presented in Mark 1.12.[11] Second, when John 12.27–28 depicts Jesus as praying, 'Now my soul has become troubled; and what shall I say, "Father, save me from this hour"? No, for this purpose I came to this hour. "Father, glorify your name"', this prayer appears to amount to a clear rejection of Jesus' prayer for deliverance from the 'hour' of death in Gethsemane according to Mark. When he later rebukes Peter with the words: 'The cup which my Father has given me, shall I not drink it?' (Jn 18.11), the rejection of Mark's Gethsemane narrative is further confirmed.[12] According to John, Jesus – acting in unity with the Father and his will – could not really have asked for deliverance from his passion and death, but only for the fulfilment of God's salvific will and for his glorification, and, accordingly, Jesus' last word on the cross in John characteristically differs from his last words in Mark. In John, reception or dependence on earlier traditions does not mean simple continuity, but implies critical reception, correction or even open rejection. John's relationship with Mark therefore differs from Matthew and Luke's way of reception by expansion and recontextualization. We must reckon with a change in terms and ideas, most probably due to John's distinctive Christology that causes further changes in numerous aspects. Furthermore, John claims to present the christologically true and thus 'definitive' interpretation of Jesus. This does not mean, however, that readers should abandon Mark. Rather, they are challenged to read all available Jesus traditions through the perspective presented here by the Spirit or – as John 21.24–25 claims – through the insight represented by the anonymous Beloved Disciple who is depicted in intimate closeness to Jesus, thus surpassing all the other named disciples.

With regard to the comparison of the two gospels' eschatological concepts, I will briefly outline some aspects of eschatology in Mark before discussing a number of aspects where John departs from Mark. In both cases, I will draw on the entirety of the gospel composition without speculating about pre-redactional sources or layers.

---

[10] Cf. Richard J. Bauckham, 'John for Readers of Mark', in Richard J. Bauckham, *The Gospels for All Christians* (Grand Rapids, MI: Wm B. Eerdmans, 1998), 147–71.

[11] Cf. Jörg Frey, 'Baptism in the Fourth Gospel, and Jesus and John as Baptizers: Historical and Theological Reflections on John 3:22–30', in *Expressions of the Johannine Kerygma in John 2:23–5:18: Historical, Literary, and Theological Readings from the Colloquium Ioanneum 2017 in Jerusalem*, ed. R. Alan Culpepper and Jörg Frey (WUNT, 423; Tübingen: Mohr Siebeck, 2019), 87–115, here 91–92.

[12] See Frey, *Theology and History*, 73–75; more extensively Frey, 'Das vierte Evangelium auf dem Hintergrund', 265–71.

The proclaimed kingdom, appointed times, and the return of the Son of Man: Glimpses at the eschatology of the Gospel of Mark

Since 'eschatology' is a modern term, rooted in orthodox Protestant dogmatics[13] where it was used for the teaching of the 'last things', we must be cautious not to project those anachronistic concepts onto the New Testament, but instead understand the concept of time within this ancient text. Thus we can generally state that in Mark,[14] 'eschatology' is not simply one part of the overall teaching, or a final chapter of Mark's theology, merely focused on some 'last things'. As is widely attested in the early Jesus movement, eschatology frames all of the views about Jesus' sending and ministry, and also about the time of Mark's readers. If eschatology includes the entirety of what was traditionally expected to happen or be bestowed at the end of time or in the period before (the 'messianic' period), it is characteristic for the Jesus movement – with the coming of Jesus as the 'Messiah', with his preaching of 'the kingdom of God', or with the events of his death and resurrection considered the foundation of 'eschatological' salvation – that these end-time events were held to be imminent or even already inaugurated. Consequently, the entirety of the proclamation, including Christology, was 'eschatology' or framed by 'eschatology', rooted in the Scriptures of Israel that were themselves read as referring to the present, 'eschatological' period. Thus, the entirety of Jesus' coming, ministry and death is considered part of the eschatological events or as the inauguration of the 'last' period.

All the views of the early Jesus movement are based on a concept of time and eschatology as developed within Second Temple Judaism, in particular Apocalypticism, with its expectation of a messianic or eschatological restoration or salvation, including the resurrection of the dead, a final judgement of the God of Israel, the destruction of evil powers and the inauguration of God's universal kingdom over humans and the world. Such an eschatological framework was characteristic of all the early views of Jesus' sending and ministry, notwithstanding the differences in their various aspects. Thus even Mark's 'outlook can be termed "apocalyptic" because his narrative is from start to finish set within the context of the approaching end of the world', although Mark 'holds this note of imminent expectation in tension with a sense of present fulfilment', as 'numerous sayings and stories imply the presence of salvation already in Jesus' ministry'.[15]

---

[13] The term was introduced by Philipp Heinrich Friedlieb, *Eschatologia seu Florilegium theologicum exhibens locorum de morte, resurrectione mortuorum, extremo iudicio, consummatio seculi, inferno seu morte aeterna et denique vita aeterna*, the fifth part of his dogmatics, published in 1644, and the title shows that the term was used to summarize the doctrine of the 'last things': death, resurrection, last judgement, end of the world, hell and eternal death, and eternal life. On the early usage, see Sigurd Hjelde, *Das Eschaton und die Eschata: Eine Studie über Sprachgebrauch und Sprachverwirrung in protestantischer Theologie von der Orthodoxie bis zur Gegenwart* (Beiträge zur evangelischen Theologie, 102; München: Kaiser, 1987), 37.

[14] On Mark's eschatology, see Cilliers Breytenbach, *Nachfolge und Zukunftserwartung nach Markus: Eine methodenkritische Studie* (AThANT, 71; Zürich: Theologischer Verlag Zürich, 1984); Klaus Scholtissek, 'Der Sohn Gottes für das Reich Gottes: Zur Verbindung von Christologie und Eschatologie bei Markus', in *Der Evangelist als Theologe: Studien zum Markusevangelium*, ed. Thomas Söding (SBS, 163; Stuttgart: Katholisches Bibelwerk, 1995), 63–90.

[15] All quotations are from Joel Marcus, *Mark 1–8: A New Translation with Introduction and Commentary* (Anchor Bible, 27; New York: Doubleday, 1999), 71.

The beginning of the Gospel (Mk 1.1–4)

From the very beginning, Mark addresses this general concept, when the term εὐαγγέλιον is used with reference to the name Ἰησοῦς Χριστός whose 'messianic' implications can hardly be denied. Mark 12.35 shows 'that the Greek word "Christ" refers to the Jewish concept of an anointed one from the line of David'.[16] In particular, when the opening verses present the scriptural perspective of the eschatological messenger (Mal. 3.1) who is sent to prepare the way of the one following him, the framework of scriptural eschatology (Isa. 40.3; Mal. 3.1) is clearly adopted and introduced as a clue for understanding the subsequent story of the Baptizer and Jesus. Thus, Jesus' coming, his baptism and ministry and ultimately his death are to be understood as the story of God's eschatological messenger and 'Messiah', prefigured in the Scriptures of Israel.

The summary at the beginning of Jesus' ministry (Mk 1.14–15)

If we proceed from here to the beginning of Jesus' ministry and the summary of his proclamation of the εὐαγγέλιον τοῦ θεοῦ (a term which again points to the prophetic or scriptural framework),[17] the proclamation, 'The time has been fulfilled, and the dominion of God has come near!' (1.15), is the first explicit announcement of the eschatological time. The question, however, is in what manner, or what kind of temporality of the idea of the dominion of God and its nearness is here conceptualized. And what does the time-qualification of 'fulfilment' actually mean?

If we read this proclamation not as a summary of the views of the earthly Jesus (which may also be true) but first and foremost as part of the Gospel of Mark, with all its subsequent stories and discourses, and as the 'retrospective' from the author's perspective, several aspects can be elucidated:

- The idea of the fulfilment of time (cf. Gal. 4.4) is a characteristic reference within the scriptural and early Jewish range of thought to a previous divine plan or order of time, in which times are measured and set (by God); the expected 'fulfilment' means that a certain previously announced time has arrived. This is not necessarily the very end but rather a period within an expected sequence of eschatological periods or events. Although the presentation is not supported by eschatological reckoning or by a detailed schedule of eschatological events,[18] it presupposes the general imagination of previously announced and divinely measured times[19] and also the fullness of time. This includes the idea of an expected

---

[16] Marcus, *Mark 1–8*, 141.
[17] Cf. Isa. 61.6 and 52.7; see Rudolf Pesch, *Das Markusevangelium. 1. Teil: Einleitung und Kommentar zu Kap. 1,1–8,26* (HThK, 2.2; 4th edn, Freiburg: Herder, 1984), 101; and, for the background of the term and its earliest usage, see the groundbreaking work by Peter Stuhlmacher, *Das paulinische Evangelium: I. Vorgeschichte* (FRLANT, 95; Göttingen: Vandenhoeck & Ruprecht, 1968); on Mark, see pp. 237–38.
[18] Such a schedule is, however, adopted in Mark 13; on this, see below.
[19] Cf., in particular, the idea in Mark 13.19–20 that God has shortened the period of tribulation. This shows that the duration of periods and also their 'quality' is subject to the power of God the creator and judge.

removal or defeat of evil powers and of the restoration of Israel, creational integrity, or the dominion of God.
- If Jesus is in fact 'the Messiah' (as is confirmed in Mark only at the end,[20] even though it is regarded as true from the beginning), if he is the eschatological messenger of God's good news, then the period inaugurated with this proclamation is the messianic time which, according to most Jewish traditions, is a time *before* the end, before the never-ending final state of salvation and, yet, a time after which further judgements, struggles and tribulations are still to come. Thus, the announcement of fulfilment here does not contradict the fact that, in Mark, a further period of the proclamation of the good news and also further tribulations are still to be expected, as presented in Mark 13. With Jesus' coming and proclamation, that time of fulfilment has come, or rather, has been inaugurated.
- With the Greek phrase βασιλεία τοῦ θεου, Mark adopts the central term of Jesus' own proclamation, a term which in its Jewish background was multi-dimensional, encompassing not only dominion or kingship but also a space or kingdom within which God's rule is effective and in force.[21] It is expressed, for example, in some Psalms, as God's eternal kingdom over the universe. In view of the dominion of foreign kingdoms over Israel and the disobedience of humans, it is also used of an expected and powerful manifestation of God's kingdom over against hostile forces. In Mark, the term is used fourteen times with reference to God's kingdom, not only in Jesus' parables, but also in sayings and comments articulated by the evangelist.
- With the temporal qualification ἤγγικεν, Mark does not claim a present completion of God's dominion but its closeness in both a temporal and existential sense. 'The time is fulfilled, and the kingdom of God has drawn near'. The perfect ἤγγικεν does not necessarily express a completed arrival or 'inauguration' of God's reign, but a closeness that still lacks the final completion and calls for immediate reaction, namely repentance and belief in that 'good news': God's dominion is to be expected in the very near rather than indefinite future, but the nearness is only proclaimed and is not further specified. Thus, in its Markan context, the term (which has been intensely debated with reference to the eschatological views of the earthly Jesus) still leaves space for a further expectation of the manifestation of God's kingdom in the time of Jesus' physical absence.[22]

---

[20] Mark 14.61–62.
[21] God's 'kingdom' or 'kingship' as such (Hebrew: *malkut*) was considered present within some contemporary Jewish texts, from the Psalms through the Temple liturgy and Jewish prayer formulas (where God's eternal kingdom was praised), but apart from that, there was the apocalyptic expectation as developed, e.g., in the Book of Daniel and adopted in several texts from the Qumran library and also in later apocalyptic texts. A particularly dense usage of the *malkut*-terminology is found in the 'angelic liturgy' of the *Songs of the Sabbath Sacrifice* in the Qumran library (4Q400–40X). On the insights gleaned from those texts, see in particular Anna Maria Schwemer, 'Gott als König und seine Königsherrschaft in den Sabbatliedern aus Qumran', in *Königsherrschaft Gottes und himmlischer Kult im Judentum, Urchristentum und in der hellenistischen Welt*, ed. Martin Hengel and Anna Maria Schwemer (WUNT, 55; Tübingen: Mohr Siebeck, 1991), 45–118, whose work highlights a large number of passages that focus on God's *malkut*.

- This is in accordance with the further use of the term βασιλεία τοῦ θεοῦ in Mark: In 4.26 and 4.30 – the parables of the 'automatically' growing seed and the mustard seed – the kingdom of God grows powerfully, hidden from human observation, but it will ultimately become manifest in the eschatological 'harvest'. According to 9.1, the dominion of God is to be expected by the end of the messianic generation, that is, before the death of the contemporaries and testimonies of Jesus. According to the entrance saying in 9.47, it is a space to be entered for final salvation. According to 10.14–15, it is a gift to be received in the way children are able to receive (not as a state to be achieved by one's own activity – as the parable in 4.26–29 has shown). With regard to the rich, Mark 10.23–25 even stresses how hard it is to get into the kingdom although (or rather, because) it is just to be received. The saying in Mark 14.25 links Jesus himself with the kingdom (as a space, or even an eschatological feast), when he expresses his hope of drinking wine again on the *day* – which is also an eschatological term – in the kingdom of God.

The sayings about entering the kingdom thus express the possibility of participation or entry, and the composition in Mark 9.1–10 explains participation in the kingdom as not tasting death and as participation in everlasting life, which is prefigured in Jesus' transfiguration and brought about through his resurrection. The so-called parable theory in Mark 4.11 also stresses that the kingdom is mysterious: it is not understood by everybody but only by those who are with Jesus and, thus, have been given the ability to understand the mystery of the kingdom.[23]

According to Mark 1.15, the way to enter or participate is described as 'repenting' (as prefigured in the ministry of the Baptizer) and 'believing in the good news', that is, responding faithfully to the proclamation presented by Jesus in the gospel or in the post-Easter proclamation of the gospel. Already within the narrative of the Jesus story, Mark directs readers towards the universal proclamation of that εὐαγγέλιον 'in the whole world' (14.9), and it is probable that εὐαγγέλιον is focused on the Jesus story as a whole, including his passion and resurrection. It is only in this way that the unnamed woman who anointed Jesus for his burial can be a part of the εὐαγγέλιον that will be proclaimed throughout the world. The εὐαγγέλιον τοῦ θεοῦ, therefore, is not only the proclamation that the Messiah has come but also that the Messiah Jesus was delivered over to the authorities and crucified 'for the sake of' or 'as a ransom for' 'the many' (Mk 14.25 and 10.45) and that he was raised from the dead and walks ahead of his disciples (16.6–7).

---

[22] On the motif of Jesus' physical absence in the post-Easter period as a formative element of the Gospel of Mark, see David S. du Toit, *Der abwesende Herr: Strategien im Markusevangelium zur Bewältigung der Abwesenheit des Auferstandenen* (WMANT, 111; Neukirchen-Vluyn: Neukirchener Verlag, 2006).

[23] According to 12.34, there are even others who may be 'not distant'.

Christology and eschatology – Looking back and looking forward

Eschatology in Mark, as a result, is inseparably linked to or based upon Christology, the way and fate of Jesus. Thus, the proclamation of Jesus' death and resurrection discloses the mystery of the kingdom (Mk 4.11) that develops and grows also in the presence of the community and will definitely come to its final completion.[24] In Mark 1.17, the first call to discipleship follows the proclamation of 'the good news' about the imminence of the 'kingdom of God'; the post-Easter proclamation of the kingdom implies discipleship, or following Jesus, the crucified and risen one.

The period that is addressed by Mark's Gospel is the post-Easter period of the community, and the Jesus it presents is, quite obviously, the Jesus who is physically absent from his disciples. Thus, Jesus' earthly ministry is actually remembered from a post-Easter perspective, although it is adopted less programmatically than in John. The post-Easter period is addressed as a time in-between, in which the lord of the house is absent for a while until he returns (Mk 13.34–37), and also as a period of danger and distress (10.38–39; 14.38), in which the disciples will again be fasting and mourning (2.18–22). It is one of the primary aims of the gospel to instruct its readers in the post-Easter period to cope with tribulations caused by the absence of Jesus and to see the gospel writing as a kind of substitute for Jesus in the time of his absence.[25]

When the narrative ends with the empty tomb and the proclamation of the angel, this proleptic announcement of the disciples' new encounter with Jesus when they 'will see him' in Galilee (16.7) has the rhetorical effect of prompting the readers to recall their own knowledge about Jesus' resurrection and the ongoing story of the proclamation of the gospel and, possibly, to go back to the beginning of the gospel book and read the story again in order to see him present in his ministry in Galilee.[26] But the christological retrojection to the ministry of Jesus is always complemented by the looking ahead to his expected coming as the Son of Man,[27] as this is presented not only,[28] but most densely, in the eschatological discourse Mark 13.

The eschatological discourse in Mark 13

Only from this perspective can we look, briefly, at the 'eschatological outlook' in Mark 13. This chapter is often only read in order to date the gospel as precisely as possible by locating it during a period of political crisis (e.g., the Caligula crisis or the Jewish war); however, first and foremost it should be read as an expression of eschatological expectation in Mark's Gospel, that is, before we can consider which situation or crisis might have prompted the nuancing and clarifying of earlier expectations in the manner they are depicted here. The chapter uses various earlier materials, but I am sceptical as

---

[24] Cf. Udo Schnelle, *Theologie des Neuen Testaments* (UTB, 2917; Göttingen: Vandenhoeck & Ruprecht, 2007), 396.
[25] Cf., in general, du Toit, *Der abwesende Herr*, 25–37, 113, 116, 237–44, 267–400.
[26] Thus the suggestion by Jan Heilmann, *Lesen in Antike und frühem Christentum: Kulturgeschichtliche, philologische sowie kognitionswissenschaftliche Perspektiven und deren Bedeutung für die neutestamentliche Exegese* (Habilitationsschrift, Ruhr-Universität Bochum, 2019), 326–28.
[27] Thus Breytenbach, *Nachfolge und Zukunftserwartung*, 338.
[28] Cf. also Mark 8.38; 9.1; 14.25.

to whether it is still possible to reconstruct its layers, ingredients or compositional history. A good deal of the predictions, from the Temple logion in Mark 13.2 to the mention of the 'abomination of desolation' in Mark 13.14, could have been developed from earlier prophetic tradition and are not necessarily a reflection of certain historical events.[29]

Be that as it may, the discourse expresses, from Jesus' own perspective, a number of expectations that are still awaited by the addressees during the time of the composition of the gospel. The intention indeed seems to be to warn the community not to follow premature claims of 'the end', because several things 'must' come to pass before the end (13.7). And, as already stated, such a series of expectations aligns with the perspectives offered at the beginning of the gospel.

There is, first, the coming of deceivers or false Messiahs or prophets, claiming 'I am he' (13.6, 21–23). Furthermore, there will be wars, earthquakes, famines (13.7–8), then persecutions and accusations before Gentile and Jewish councils (13.8, 11) and in particular synagogal punishment (13.9), divisions in families and between generations (13.12), and, finally, universal hatred (13.13). All of these elements belong to the category of messianic or apocalyptic woes and lack specificity. They only maintain that the deplorable situation of the world and, in particular, the community are in fact 'birth pangs' of something new, the messianic fulfilment, so that even the experiences of persecution and tribulation are in fact a confirmation of eschatological hope.[30]

The most specific expectation, yet a factor that causes the further delay of the end, is expressed in the announcement that 'the gospel must be proclaimed to all the nations' (13.10). Here, the traditional apocalyptic scenario is modified through a particular reference to the 'good news', the proclamation of the kingdom. Thus, the apocalyptic pattern is changed or expanded in light of the Jesus story, and it becomes necessary to proclaim faith in Jesus universally before the very end, the final completion, can come.

The subsequent passage about the great tribulation also follows an apocalyptic pattern, and it is not plausible to relate it precisely to certain events (e.g., the Jewish war), notwithstanding the question of how an author and readers outside Palestine could have understood those references: fleeing into the mountains, particular hardships for the pregnant and those nursing – this is a very general description of unsurmountable tribulations, and it is not even particularly 'Christian'. There is only

---

[29] Regarding the tendency in recent research to date Mark after 70 CE, it should be noted that Mark 13.14 does not match the events of the destruction of the Temple in 70 CE, so that the dating of the saying after those events is questionable. From the strong encipherment in Mark 13 Martin Hengel concludes in favour of the discourse's origin during the political tensions of 67–70 CE; cf. Martin Hengel, 'The Gospel of Mark: Time of Origin and Situation', in *Studies in the Gospel of Mark*, trans. by John Bowden (Minneapolis, MN: Fortress, 1985), 1–30, here 28. The threat of the Temple's destruction in Mark 13.2 could also be expressed against the background of earlier tradition. Hengel writes, 'The threat of the destruction of the temple had a long prehistory' (*Studies*, 15), and, interestingly, the saying only mentions the destruction of the Temple, not that of the city. For Mark 13.2 we cannot even exclude the possibility that an early form of the prophecy originated with the earthly Jesus and formed the point of departure for the discourse. But these issues can be left aside in the present context.

[30] This is a pattern which has similarly functioned quite often in Christian history up until today.

one phrase of consolation: God has shortened the days of the coming period of tribulation (Mk 13.20). God is still in charge of history, even if the suffering is overwhelming.

The main point, however, is that after the inauguration of the messianic period, but before the end, there 'must' be a time of tribulation, and the end can come only after those woes or birth pangs. But also the following description of the end is full of elements common to an apocalyptic scenario: cosmic changes involving the sun, moon and stars, a shaking of the cosmic order. Only after that will the Son of Man come on the clouds and send his angels for 'harvest' or judgement (13.26–27).

The instruction for readers is, finally, summarized in the parable of the fig tree. They should know that the end is near, at the gates (13.29), they should be alert and awake, but they should not erroneously think that the end is already present, nor be deceived by false prophets or claimants. Furthermore, to guard against any premature enthusiasm, there is still the eschatological reservation that all of the coming tribulations do not yet imply completion, but only signal that the end is imminent.

Remaining tensions in Mark's eschatology

Tensions remain between an expectation that points to a period of one generation (Mk 9.1; 13.30) and a tendency to avoid relating any of the signs directly to the end, as well as tension between knowledge of appointed times and events (13.7, 10) and the impossibility of knowing the exact time (13.32, 35). Here, Mark's eschatology seeks to maintain a balance between the now and the not yet, between the presence of proclamation, persecution and signs of coming tribulation, and the hope for a final deliverance through an encounter with the coming Son of Man. Thus, Mark keeps or even intensifies hope for the Parousia, although there is already the idea of a certain delay, which is explained by the need for the universal proclamation of the gospel, that is, a divine need that the appointed events have yet to be fulfilled.

Judgement and eternal life made available in the presence of Jesus: The reshaping of eschatology in John

When we turn to the Fourth Gospel we seem to enter a different world, and it is no coincidence that the difference, even opposition, between the eschatology of the Synoptics and that of John has stimulated scholarship on Jesus and on the Fourth Gospel from the very beginning of modern New Testament interpretation.[31] For modern readers, John's supposedly more interior and individualistic views appeared much more acceptable than the apocalyptic expectation of the Parousia of the Son of Man, or the 'near' expectation of the end of the world with which Jesus, Paul and also Mark had obviously erred.

---

[31] On those issues, cf. Frey, *Eschatologie 1*, 11–28; Frey, 'New Testament Eschatology', 9–13.

Apocalyptic transformed

It is tempting to state at first what John lacks, avoids or at least thoroughly reinterprets. In John, there is no notion of a universal tribulation as in Mark 13.14–20, no expectations of cosmic 'birth pangs' or signs as in Mark 13.4–8 and 13.24–27, and – most obviously – no colourful description of the coming of the Son of Man with his angels on the clouds as in Mark 13.26. All those apocalyptic scenarios seem to have been removed – or at least reduced and significantly transformed, for example, in the saying about the heavenly mansions and Jesus' return in John 14.2–3, the discussion about the meaning of 'seeing him again' in John 16.16–19, or the metaphorical image of the woman giving birth in John 16.20–22. Thus, the cosmic and future-oriented aspects of eschatology, rooted in the apocalyptic tradition, seem to be transformed from the external to internal dimension, and from the more future to a present reality.[32] Or, as J. Louis Martyn has noted, 'John handles the temporal distinction between the two stages in a way quite different from that which is characteristic of Jewish apocalyptic'[33] – and, we may add, from the eschatology of the Synoptics. In Martyn's words, 'The initial stage is not the scene of "things to come" in heaven. It is the scene of Jesus' life and teaching.... John's two stages are past and present, not future and present'.[34]

In fact, John is the most elaborate canonical testimony to an eschatology focused not on a certain period or sequence of events in the future but in the present: the presence of salvation or judgement in the presence of Jesus or in the proclamation of the gospel. Interpreters are puzzled by the remarkable difference between Synoptic eschatology, orientated towards the imminent kingdom of God and the events related to the 'Parousia' of Jesus, the coming of the Son of Man, and the last judgement (most prominently presented in Mt. 24–25), and the Johannine view that judgement and the gift of eternal life do not happen in a distant future but happen *now* (Jn 3.18) so that believers already '*have* eternal life' in the present (3.36; 5.24)

'The hour is coming, and now it is' (Jn 4.23 and 5.25)

The tension within Johannine eschatology is concisely captured in John 4.23 and 5.25 in the short phrase ἔρχεται ὥρα καὶ νῦν ἐστιν ('the hour is coming, and now is'). In this double expression, the traditional expectation of a 'coming' hour (as in Jn 4.21 and 5.28) is linked with the idea that this very hour is already present. This is clearly related to a traditional usage of the term ὥρα or 'the last hour' probably known from the Johannine community, although the more prominent Johannine usage of the term ὥρα for the 'hour of Jesus' (2.4; 7.30; 8.20; 12.23) as the hour or time of his death seems to draw more strongly on Mark's Gethsemane scene where this term is used. John, who creatively draws on the Markan Gethsemane scene in John 12.27–28 and

---

[32] Cf. John Ashton's well-known description of John's concept as 'an apocalypse – in reverse, upside down, inside out', in John Ashton, *Understanding the Fourth Gospel* (2nd edn; Oxford: Oxford University Press, 2007), 328–9. See also the volume *John's Gospel and Intimations of Apocalyptic*, ed. Catrin H. Williams and Christopher Rowland (London: Bloomsbury, 2013).
[33] J. Louis Martyn, *History and Theology in the Fourth Gospel* (New York: Harper & Row, 1968), 136.
[34] Martyn, *History and Theology*, 137.

18.1 (cf. 14.31), can expand this term into a wider concept so that the focus on Jesus' death is prepared and developed in advance. Thus, while the predominant usage of ὥρα in John, probably adopted from Mark 14.35, refers to the 'eschatological' hour of Jesus' death and resurrection, John is also aware of the traditional use of the term 'last hour' or end of time, linked to judgement and resurrection and the true veneration of God. Despite this awareness, he deliberately relates the expected last hour to the presence of Jesus and his word: the hour that comes, the eschatological event, is already now, in the present. This is what Mark had explicitly denied in view of the tribulations or claims of false Messiahs (13.6–7, 22–23).

Eschatological traditions in the Johannine circle and in the Fourth Gospel

There are more eschatological traditions in John (and also in the Johannine epistles), some of which are conceptually parallel, though without explicit reference, to what we know from Mark:[35]

> The Johannine epistles attest to a tradition about an eschatological opponent figure called 'antichrist' (ἀντίχριστος: 1 Jn 2.18; 4.3; 2 Jn 7). The term points to an individual figure who is eschatologically opposed to Christ or put in the place of Christ, a figure whose coming was expected in the final period, shortly before the end. Such an eschatological teaching within the Johannine school closely parallels the teaching about coming deceivers and pseudo-Messiahs in Mark 13. But in John, there is no direct reference to the sequence of events from Mark, not even to the coming of the Son of Man. John seems to ignore those traditions of which he was probably aware. Conceptually, the eschatological discourse in the Synoptics is replaced by another discourse, the Farewell Discourse.[36]

In the Johannine epistles, however, there is a more intense adoption of eschatological traditions similar to those found in Mark. There is awareness that the community is living in the 'last hour' (1 Jn 2.18), that time is heading towards the end (1 Jn 2.8, 17), that the present conflicts with false teachers are a sign of the arrival of the period of eschatological tribulations and that final salvation is near, so that the community of disciples has to be particularly alert in order not to be led astray. In the context of a particular crisis within the community (1 Jn 2.18–22; 4.1–3; 2 Jn 7–8), the author also

---

[35] Cf. extensively Jörg Frey, *Die johanneische Eschatologie, vol. 3: Die eschatologische Verkündigung in den johanneischen Texten* (WUNT, 117; Tübingen: Mohr Siebeck, 2000), 13–97; Jörg Frey, 'Eschatology in the Johannine Circle', in *Die Herrlichkeit des Gekreuzigten*, 663–98, here 671–81.

[36] This is true, although the point in the narrative where the Farewell Discourse is inserted, after the last meal of Jesus and his disciples, differs from the place where the eschatological discourses are placed in the Synoptics. In Mark, there is only a brief hint that Jesus was still talking when Judas and the soldiers appeared (14.43). Before the garden scene, Luke inserted some brief dialogue scenes between Jesus and the disciples (22.24–38), and John actually expands those dialogues to his extended Farewell Discourses.

expresses the expectation of a last 'day of judgement' (1 Jn 4.17), the Parousia of Christ (2.28), and – specifically Johannine – the transfiguration of believers into the likeness of the glorified Christ (3.2–3; cf. Jn 17.24).[37]

From the very concise and abbreviated introduction to eschatological material in the Epistles we can assume that the Fourth Gospel also draws on a set of 'apocalyptic' views or teachings that are well-known in the Johannine communities. Among the sayings adopted in the gospel, there is the remarkable promise of Christ's 'coming again' and the unification with the disciples in the Father's House (Jn 14.2–3), which most closely parallels the tradition presented in 1 Thess. 4.16–17.[38] Additional sayings about Jesus' 'coming' (Jn 14.18; cf. 21.22) or about 'seeing him again' (16.16–19; cf. 14.19) probably also draw on community traditions, even if their traditional shape can no longer be ascertained.[39] The Fourth Gospel, therefore, is obviously aware of the expectation of the Parousia. In 16.16–19 it seems to draw on some discussions about the real meaning of Jesus' promise of return, and in the final and perhaps redactional chapter, Jesus' return is mentioned without any further attention, as if it were a commonplace in the community teaching. However, the gospel not only avoids describing the Parousia in its full apocalyptic picture – as in Mark 13, followed by the other Synoptics – but presents it in John 14.2–3 without the picturesque scenario, focusing instead only on the reunification of the disciples with Jesus. Here, John is closer to Paul in 1 Thess. 4.13–18 than to Mark.

The saying about the 'coming hour' of the resurrection (cf. Jn 5.25, 28–29) was most likely one of these traditional sayings, which is adopted twice in the Gospel of John in two different versions: John 5.28–29 lacks the καὶ νῦν ἐστιν, thus the verses refer to a future point of time, an eschatological resurrection of the dead in which the saved and the sinners hear the voice of Jesus (or the 'Son of Man'; cf. 5.27) and come out of their tombs for life or destruction, apparently based on a decision already made during their lifetime. Accordingly, this saying has a certain 'Johannine' colouring, but not as strong as the one in John 5.25, where the addition of καὶ νῦν ἐστιν reshapes the traditional saying into an announcement of present 'spiritual' resurrection.[40] Furthermore, the insertion of John 5.28–29 and 5.25 is not simply parallel: while 5.25 is a revelatory saying, introduced by the double 'Amen' formula, 5.28 seems to be an argument from tradition, inserted to make plausible for the Jerusalem Jews, the fictive addressees of the discourse, the provoking statements about Jesus' present eschatological authority.

---

[37] On these traditions, see Frey, *Die johanneische Eschatologie 3*, 71–97.
[38] Cf. Frey, *Die johanneische Eschatologie 3*, 134–48.
[39] On Jn 14.18, see Frey *Die johanneische Eschatologie 3*, 164–66, but cf. the criticism by Michael Theobald, *Herrenworte im Johannesevangelium* (HBS, 34; Freiburg im Breisgau: Herder, 2002), 20, who thinks that only the motif of the ὀρφανοί has a traditional background, while it is not possible to reconstruct a coherent unity that could have been transmitted within the community. However, if the sayings in Jn 14.2–3 and 21.22 are part of the tradition, it is quite probable that the evangelist draws on traditions in the present case, even if we cannot determine the extent to which the form of the saying in Jn 14.18 is his own. On Jn 16.16–19, see Frey, *Die johanneische Eschatologie 3*, 205–9.
[40] Cf. the similar phenomenon in Jn 4.23 and 4.21.

Christology and eschatology: Judgement and life made present

In both Mark and John, eschatology is linked to Christology, but in John, unlike Mark, eschatology is most strongly based on and reshaped from Christology.[41] Whereas in Mark, Jesus' true identity and dignity is only revealed at the end of the story (14.62), in John Jesus is the Messiah (1.41, 45) but he is also more than this. He is the Son of God (1.49), the Son of Man (1.51), even God (1.1–2, 18), so that John can present the whole earthly ministry of Jesus as characterized by and imbued with his glory. This presentation is made possible in the light of the insights gained in the post-Easter period alone. In all his deeds and words, the earthly Jesus already reveals the divine glory and is presented with an identity that the disciples could only later understand through the Spirit. For this reason, the Johannine image of Jesus and also his preaching differ markedly from the images found in the Synoptics. This decisively shaped Christology is also the reason for the fact that, in his person, Jesus already incorporates the divine acts of judgement and resurrection (cf. 11.25–26) and that those divine eschatological acts are made present in his presence.

This is made prominently evident in John 5.19–30:[42] Jesus claims to have divine authority, which is not blasphemous because this authority to enact the (eschatological) judgement and to offer eschatological or 'eternal' life is given to him by the Father. In two different sequences, the authorization of 'the Son' (5.21–23) or 'the Son of Man' (5.26–27) is presented. Interestingly, the term 'Son of Man' is adopted here without the definite article, which creates a striking allusion to Dan. 7.14 and the authorization discourse in Dan. 7. Unlike in Mark, the Johannine 'Son of Man' seems to be clearly shaped from apocalyptic tradition, referring to Jesus as a 'heavenly' being, who has come from the realm of God (3.13; 6.62; cf. also 1.51) and who is authorized to reveal the 'heavenly things' (cf. 3.12) or to act as God's authorized eschatological agent. The titles 'Son of God' and 'the Son', albeit from a different background, express the same divine authority, which is also the reason for his eschatological authority to give life and to enact judgement.

Since Jesus, the incarnate one, is entrusted with eschatological judgement, it is made present in his presence. The decision about the eschatological fate of humans take place in the encounter with him (Jn 3.18). Here, John only continues the idea expressed in earlier Jesus tradition (cf. Lk. 12.8–9) that the acceptance or denial of Jesus is the criterion for the final acceptance or rejection in the judgement enacted by the Son of Man.[43] But since the eschatological judge is now present, belief in Jesus presently brings about eschatological salvation and 'eternal life', so that believers have already passed judgement and there is no future expectation of judgement (5.24). The opposite is also

---

[41] The influential interpretation by Rudolf Bultmann reversed the sequence and considered eschatology or the understanding of time as the basic element from which the expression of Christology was shaped (as soteriology, in a non-ontological, existential manner); on Bultmann's interpretation of John's Christology and eschatology, see Jörg Frey, 'Johannine Christology and Eschatology', in *Beyond Bultmann: Reckoning a New Testament Theology*, ed. Bruce W. Longenecker and Mikeal C. Parsons (Waco, TX: Baylor University Press, 2014), 101–32.

[42] On the interpretation of this passage, see Frey, *Die johanneische Eschatology 3*, 322–402.

[43] Cf. Jörg Frey, 'Continuity and Discontinuity between "Jesus" and "Christ": The Possibilities of an Implicit Christology', *RCatT* 36 (2011): 69–98. There is no need to discuss here whether Jesus and the Son of Man are distinguished or identical – the eschatological relevance of confessing Jesus is clear enough.

true: The one who does not believe 'has already been condemned' (3.18), and he or she is under the negative verdict or wrath (3.36).[44]

As in the case of eschatological judgement, salvation and the gift of eschatological life are also made available in the presence of Jesus and his word. He has life in himself (Jn 5.26) and is 'the resurrection and the life' in person (11.25), although such a view actually presupposes his resurrection and is only expressed through the post-Easter insight into Jesus' true identity and dignity.[45] Those who believe '*have* eternal life' (6.47; cf. 3.36; 5.24; 20.31; 1 Jn 5.12–13); they will not face further judgement or condemnation (Jn 3.18), they will not see or taste death (8.51-52) for they have definitively passed from death unto life (5.24; 1 Jn 3.14). Thus, readers are assured that those who believe have their share in everlasting life, not only as a final reward at a last judgement but as a present possession in and through their encounter with Jesus.

Life (ζωή) or 'eternal life' (ζωὴ αἰώνιος) is the most prominent term for 'salvation' in John, replacing the central term of the earlier Jesus tradition: βασιλεία τοῦ θεοῦ ('kingdom of God'). Here we may possibly encounter the most important direct connection between the eschatologies of Mark and John. Just as the term βασιλεία τοῦ θεοῦ is presented as the central term of salvation at the beginning of Mark (1.15), it is also adopted in Jesus' first dialogue in John 3. Here, the term is introduced in Jesus' answer to Nicodemus in two parallel sayings (3.3, 5), which are most probably different variants of a community tradition. That tradition was likely shaped as an entrance saying about 'entering the kingdom of God', and was already related to baptism in the Johannine community (cf. Jn 3.5), while John 3.3 is a 'riddling' variant created by the evangelist himself.[46] Most strikingly, however, the term is then abandoned in the Fourth Gospel. After the two references in question, βασιλεία and also βασιλεύς are only applied to Jesus who is then presented as the true 'king', for example, in the encounter with Pilate (18.36–37),[47] whereas in John 3, the term is replaced by a new and, what is

---

[44] Despite the definitive use of the perfect tense, there is no reason to think that it precludes a later, positive reaction to Jesus resulting in salvation from death unto life. The expressions of Johannine 'dualism' should not be systematized. In the Johannine views of salvation and judgement, there is no clear-cut system, no equilibration between the positive and negative side, but rather a remarkable 'asymmetry' which always leaves space for movement 'from darkness toward the light'. Cf. Hans Weder, 'Die Asymmetrie des Rettenden: Überlegungen zu Joh 3,14–21 im Rahmen johanneischer Theologie', in *Einblicke ins Evangelium*, ed. Hans Weder (Göttingen: Vandenhoeck & Ruprecht, 1992), 435–65. On the meaning and function of dualistic language and dualistic oppositions in John, see Jörg Frey, 'Johannine Dualism: Reflections on its Background and Function', in *The Glory of the Crucified One: Christology and Theology in the Gospel of John*, trans. by Wayne Coppins and Christoph Heilig (BMSEC, 6; Waco, TX: Baylor University Press, 2018), 101–67.

[45] On the retrospective view in John, see Jörg Frey, 'The Glory of the Crucified One', in *The Glory of the Crucified One*, 237–58, cf. also Jörg Frey, 'The Gospel of John as a Narrative Memory of Jesus', in *Memory and Memories in Early Christianity*, ed. Simon Butticaz and Enrico Norelli (WUNT, 398; Tübingen: Mohr Siebeck, 2018), 261–84.

[46] See Frey, *Die johanneische Eschatologie 3*, 252–54; see also Jörg Frey, 'From the "Kingdom of God" to "Eternal Life": The Transformation of Theological Language in the Fourth Gospel', in *John, Jesus, and History*, Vol. 3: *Glimpses of Jesus through the Johannine Lens*, ed. Paul N. Anderson, Felix Just, S.J., and Tom Thatcher (ECL, 18; Atlanta, GA: Society of Biblical Literature, 2016), 439–58.

[47] On the Johannine passion narrative as the enthronement of the true king, see Jörg Frey, 'Jesus und Pilatus: Der wahre König und der Repräsentant des Kaisers im Johannesevangelium', in *Christ and the Emperor: The Gospel Evidence*, ed. Gilbert Van Belle and Joseph Verheyden (BTS, 20; Leuven: Peeters, 2014), 337–93; Frey, *Theology and History*, 186–96.

for John, central term of salvation, ζωὴ αἰώνιος (3.15, 16, 36).[48] This transformation or replacement is already prefigured in some sayings in Mark 9.43, 45, 47 where the two terms are connected and maybe interchangeable.

John's preference for ζωή terminology may be due to the transfer of early Jesus tradition from the Palestinian Jewish milieu to a Graeco-Roman context, but there are also theological reasons for the prominence of 'life' as the gift of the Risen One. The semantic development can be perceived earlier in Paul's letters. Whereas in some Pauline passages 'life' is still understood as a gift to be granted in future salvation (Rom. 2.7; 5.21; 6.22–23; Gal. 6.8), other passages (Gal. 2.20; 5.25; Rom. 6.8; 8.2, 6, 10; 2 Cor. 4.10–12) conceptualize 'life' as a present gift mediated through participation in the life-giving Spirit (1 Cor. 15.45).[49] As Nadine Ueberschaer has recently demonstrated, the insertion of life terminology into traditional formulaic material about Jesus' death and resurrection (1 Thess. 4.14; 2 Cor. 5.14–15; Rom. 6.3–8; 14.7–9) is an innovative step in Pauline thought; it is also adopted in John when faith and life terminology are linked in programmatic sayings, such as in John 3.15, 16; 5.24–25; and 11.25–26.[50] For those who believe, 'life' is a present gift that continues even in case of physical death.

In John this expectation of eschatological life, now made available for the disciples, undergoes a particular transformation in the Farewell Discourses, which – as mentioned above – replace, to a certain degree, the eschatological discourse of the Synoptics. Here, Jesus addresses the post-Easter community represented by the group of disciples. Apparently, the community members struggled with Jesus' absence or his invisibility (Jn 16.10), or felt abandoned like orphans (cf. 14.18), and the Farewell Discourses answer their concern with a double strategy. The author emphasizes that the disciples already participate in all the benefits of salvation, such as peace (14.27; 16.33), joy (16.22, 24) and, in particular, the Spirit (14.16–7), although this is supplemented by several promises of a new encounter between the disciples and Jesus: they will see him again (cf. 14.19; 16.16–19), and – for the community of readers – this is not only related to Easter but points further into the future. Thus, there is a blurring of traditional hope for the Parousia with a reference to the reunion mediated through the Spirit within the community. The disciples are promised that they will be 'where he is' (cf. 12.26; 14.3; 17.24). The hope for the Parousia so colourfully expressed in Mark is transposed into a less 'mythological' expression of closeness at an unspecified location.[51] The eschatological promise is not abandoned but rather confirmed by the idea that the risen Jesus is already with the Father, and that his followers can hope for a reunion that will no longer be endangered by the hostility of the world or by the uncertainties of their own faith. Instead, they will be brought to fulfilment by Jesus himself.

[48] Cf. also Frey, *Die johanneische Eschatologie 3*, 260–61
[49] Already in Paul, ζωὴ (αἰώνιος) is not only understood as a future gift, but in some passages is also depicted as a present gift of salvation mediated through participation in the life-giving Spirit (1 Cor. 15.45); this is the case in Gal. 2.20; 5.25; Rom. 6.8; 8.2, 6, 10; 2 Cor. 4.10–12. This tendency is then continued in Col. 3.3–4 (cf. 1 Jn 3.2–3). See Frey, *Die johanneische Eschatologie 3*, 267–68.
[50] Nadine Ueberschaer, *Theologie des Lebens: Glaube und Leben bei Paulus und Johannes – ein theologisch-konzeptioneller Vergleich* (WUNT, 389; Tübingen: Mohr Siebeck, 2017).
[51] On the eschatological proclamation of the Farewell Discourses, see Frey, *Die johanneische Eschatologie 3*, 232–39.

Some points of comparison and concluding reflections

Comparing the eschatologies of Mark and John is fraught with difficulties because there are so few terminological links that enable one to make clear comparisons between them or even to pinpoint transformations or developments. The differences exist instead in the wider context, and they have to be assessed in light of basic agreements between them as well:

1. Eschatology in Mark and John is based on Christology: all the traditional hopes for the future and the qualification of the present time are determined by the fact that the Messiah Jesus has come and that with him the eschatological salvation has come near. Both writings agree that the Christ event and its implications accord with the Scriptures (i.e., with the salvific will of God). Only on that common ground can the differences between their eschatological concepts be established.
2. Whereas the Jesus story is narrated in both gospels from a post-Easter perspective and that they have to cope with the situation of Jesus' physical absence, their temporal orientation is quite different. When Mark narrates the Jesus story as a sequence of past events, the basic orientation is primarily towards the future, so that the community of addressees is closely linked to the expected Parousia of the Son of Man. John, however, programmatically narrates the past story of Jesus in relation to the present situation of his time and to the insights and problems of his addressees, so that readers can understand the foundational relevance of the Jesus story for their own existence in faith. Compared with Mark, the basic temporal axis in John is not between the present and the future, but between the past and the present.
3. In Mark, the struggles and tribulations of the community as well as external events and cosmic signs are regarded as signs or birth pangs of the end times. The view that tribulations within the community, not just in the external world or cosmos, is a sign of the eschatological period was also expressed in the Johannine context, albeit only in the epistles (1 Jn 2.18-19). The eschatological tradition is utilized here to stress the decisive quality of the decision that must presently be made. In John's Gospel, in contrast, the community's hardships are addressed through a different strategy. The community is not only to anticipate future salvation, their expected encounter with Christ (14.2; 17.24), but also, predominantly, to look upon the fruits of the work of Jesus and the gifts of the Spirit that can be experienced in the present.
4. However, whereas the community's expectation is still oriented in Mark towards Jesus' Parousia, John hints at a discussion about the true meaning of that promise (16.16-19: 'what does this mean'), and while the expectation of Jesus' coming is expressed without any further comment in John 21.22-23, it is focused on the disciples in 14.2-3 and even transformed into an individual promise that Jesus will dwell within his followers. The traditional hope is not denied, but is partly reinterpreted in a matter that strips it of its cosmic and apocalyptic imagery.
5. Obviously, John adopts the earlier (though not exclusively Markan) tradition of eschatology focused on the term βασιλεία τοῦ θεοῦ. It is striking, however, that the evangelist deliberately replaces this traditional term with the central new salvific term 'eternal life'. Kingship is now centred on Jesus, in whom God's kingdom is

realized, and salvation is now expressed by the term '(eternal) life'. Here we can even see that the evangelist develops a new theological language, which is arguably more accessible to his audience, but he is also eager to let his readers perceive that his gospel's different language is not entirely new: it has been taken from and is equivalent to the terms encountered in the earlier Jesus tradition.

Apart from general conceptual transformations derived from Johannine Christology, immediate connections between John and Mark in the field of eschatology are rare. Conceptual and terminological developments in John's eschatological views are not drawn primarily from Mark, but, more strongly, from developments within the Johannine community tradition and, in part, insights from the Pauline tradition. Notwithstanding John's knowledge of Mark, the Fourth Evangelist ignores specific passages, such as the eschatological discourse, and replaces them with discourses having a different focus. And while the core of the earlier Jesus tradition – the 'kingdom of God' theme – is adopted in the opening part of John's Gospel, theological interests and themes are developed differently. Judgement and Life are set in the present, and the expectation of the Parousia, which apparently was already questioned in the Johannine community, is thoroughly transformed.

14

Ethical Concepts in Mark and John: A Comparative Approach

Oda Wischmeyer

Introductory remarks

When I first began to think about the topic in question, I was puzzled by my limited knowledge of related ethical concepts in the Gospels of Mark and John. Do both gospels share certain concepts beyond the well-known *agapān*-theme?[1] I wondered whether both gospels could have more in common than love ethics. I also pondered how it might be possible, especially in the Gospel of John, to identify a *range* of ethical topics, and, finally, whether I would be able to offer an appropriate definition of *ethics* and *comparison* as well as *connections* and *relations*. What I present in this chapter are the results of a comparative investigation that have in fact altered my appreciation particularly of John's ethical passages, and this has paved the way for me to read the Gospel of John against the backdrop of the Gospel of Mark.

What is an 'ethical text'?

I want to begin with as clear a definition as possible of what we mean by *ethics* with reference to New Testament texts. Michael Labahn has, in this respect, formulated a well-conceived and carefully nuanced definition for investigating *'ethics' in the world of texts*. He states:

> [A]n 'ethical text' [is] a text that
>
> (a) *provides a reflective orientation toward the reader's actual 'way of life'*[2]
> (b) *by* defining *how to behave and act*
> (c) *according to* a *value system* that is developed or supported by the text, its characters, and/or its setting,

---

[1] Oda Wischmeyer, *Liebe als Agape: Das frühchristliche Konzept und der moderne Diskurs* (Tübingen: Mohr Siebeck, 2015).
[2] Italics mine.

(d) *in relation to* a *specific social group* and/or in relation to the surrounding society at large.[3] And I would like to add here: or *against* a group or society at large.[4]

I shall take his clear-cut definition of 'ethical texts and concepts' as my point of departure. It is only in the last part of this essay that I will broaden this definition in line with new trends in Johannine scholarship. On the basis of Labahn's definition I shall formulate five preliminary questions of my own – questions that may shed light on the character and meaning of ethical texts. It is necessary to emphasize from the outset that it is *texts*, not individual and social behaviour, or the actual way of life of early Christians, which are being interpreted when we read Mark and John comparatively. I do not aim to reconstruct either the social milieu of the individual communities that presumably existed behind both gospels or to discuss their personal ethical standards and daily conduct. The questions, rather, that I intend to ask in relation to these texts are as follows:

1. Who is the *author* and/or who authorizes the text in question?
2. Who is the intended *audience*/community of the text?
3. Which *norms* and values/authorities underlie the text or are alluded to or contested or disputed by the text?

Two further questions will also necessarily play a role in my investigation, although I cannot discuss them in detail here:

4. What is the literary *form* of the text?
5. In which broader literary *context*/genre/form is the text embedded?

The superordinate role of Christology

In what follows I will present the most important ethical passages in both gospels. I will comment on their main topics in line with my questions, discuss possible ways of comparing Mark's and John's ethical concepts, and eventually propose how ethics – in both gospels – relate to their *Christology*. I will argue that both authors shape their ethical concepts primarily in relation to their respective Jesus narratives. For clarification purposes, I shall first provide a short introduction to my comparative reading of ethical aspects in both narratives in light of their christological views.

---

[3] Michael Labahn, '"It's Only Love" – Is That All? Limits and Potentials of Johannine "Ethic". A Critical Evaluation of Research', in *Rethinking the Ethics of John: "Implicit Ethics" in the Johannine Writings*, ed. Jan G. van der Watt and Ruben Zimmermann (WUNT, 291; Tübingen: Mohr Siebeck, 2012), 3–43, especially 6–7. See also the brief definition offered by Wayne E. Meeks, *The Origins of Christian Morality: The First Two Centuries* (New Haven, CT: Yale University Press, 1993). Meeks characterizes '"ethics" in the sense of a reflective, second-order activity: it is morality rendered self-conscious ...' (p. 4). Meeks differentiates between ethics/ethos and morality: '"Morality", on the other hand, names a dimension of life, a pervasive and, often, only partly conscious set of value-laden dispositions, inclinations, attitudes, and habits' (p. 4).

[4] I am thinking here of the Markan controversy stories.

The author of *Mark's Gospel* pursues a twofold objective in his narration of the Jesus story: on the one hand, he presents Jesus as an authoritative teacher of the Torah (12.28–34); by doing so, Mark is able to transmit historical traditions about Jesus of Nazareth and, at the same time, shape those traditions in accordance with his own christological emphases. To illustrate Jesus' role as authoritative teacher, Mark opts for the literary device of controversy stories.[5] On the other hand, Mark presents Jesus as the Messiah who announces the Kingdom of God and who preaches a new ethos of diakonia and discipleship. Lev. 19.18, the commandment of love, remains part of the Torah and connects Jesus' ethos to that of the scribes in Mark's narrative (12.31, 33). The new ethos of diakonia and discipleship, however, *exceeds* obedience to the Torah (10.17–22). This discipleship includes some specific rules pertaining to the disciples' individual lifestyle, which separate them from the 'ordinary Jewish' way of life. It is noteworthy that, according to Mark, ἀγάπη/ἀγαπᾶν is not a part of the new ethos of discipleship but the cornerstone of both the Jewish ethos and Jesus' interpretation of the ethos of the Law.

The author of *John's Gospel* attributes the title 'son of God' to Jesus from the beginning of his Jesus narrative (1.14, 34). According to the prologue, Jesus is the beloved one (μονογενής). During his mission, therefore, Jesus proclaims a comprehensive love concept that includes the 'new commandment' of mutual love among the disciples (chs 13–17). The Gospel of John thus reformulates and develops Mark's ethical concept of discipleship on the basis of his Christology. In contrast, Matthew and Luke follow a different track by inserting and arranging material from the Sayings source into their Jesus narratives and by conceptualizing the speeches of Jesus as those belonging to the authoritative teacher of Law.

What, then, do Mark and John have in common? In general terms, both gospels focus on a *christologically-based ethics* that does not stand apart from or against the ethics of Torah, but works from a newly formulated basis. In both gospels ethics is connected to the person of Jesus, to his mission, his life and death. Thus, the ethical concepts of both gospels are part of their specific Jesus narrative, not only with regard to the gospel genre but also in relation to the content of the Jesus story. Both evangelists agree that Jesus' ethics cannot be reduced to instructions of moral conduct in the sense of a fresh interpretation of Torah; rather, Jesus' ethics are related to a *personal* connection between himself and his disciples. Ethics are part of the disciples' new way of life with Jesus, both during and after his earthly life. During Jesus' mission the disciples accompany him as μαθηταί, and after his death they live in a state of constant 'discipleship'. According to Mark, Jesus formulates an ethics of *discipleship*, while, according to John, he focuses exclusively on the concept of *love between 'friends'*. Within the Johannine narrative these friends are the apostles, but for the readers of the Gospel of John, who are members of the Christ-believing communities, they are also to become friends of Jesus and to understand the sayings and stories about the apostles in a paradigmatic fashion.

---

[5] Lorenzo Scornaienchi, *Der umstrittene Jesus und seine Apologie: Die Streitgespräche im Markusevangelium* (NTOA/StUNT, 110; Göttingen: Vandenhoeck & Ruprecht, 2016).

Ethical texts in Mark

According to the definition of ethics provided by Labahn, we might first and foremost identify the following Markan passages as ethical texts:[6]

- Mk 6.7–9: mission instructions[7] (internal audience: 'the Twelve').
- Mk 7.1–13: on purity and on the commandment to honour one's parents (hostile audience: Pharisees and scribes).[8]
- Mk 7.14–16: once more on purity (general audience: crowds).
- Mk 7.17–23: third discourse on purity, concluding with a comprehensive catalogue of vices[9] (internal audience: disciples).
- Mk 8.34–37: teaching about the way of life that accords with discipleship[10] (general audience: crowds and disciples).
- Mk 9.33–37: *apophthegma* on 'the style of leadership in the early church'[11] (internal audience: the 'Twelve').
- Mk 10.1–12: instruction on divorce[12] (v. 1: general audience: crowds; vv. 2–9: hostile audience: Pharisees; vv. 10–12: internal audience: disciples).
- Mk 10.13–15: saying about children and the kingdom of God (general and internal audiences: crowds and disciples).
- Mk 10.17–31: 'property and the kingdom of God'[13] (internal and individual audiences: vv. 17–22: young man; vv. 23–27: disciples; vv. 28–31: Peter).
- Mk 10.35–45: 'instruction on leadership'[14] (individual and internal audiences: vv. 35–40: James and John; vv. 41–45: 'the Ten').
- Mk 12.13–17: on taxes[15] (hostile audience: Pharisees and Herodians).

---

[6] I cannot here discuss my selection in detail. Other texts that fluctuate between the topic of obedience to the Torah and ethos could be added to the list.

[7] Adela Yarbro Collins, *Mark: A Commentary* (Hermeneia; Minneapolis, MN: Fortress, 2007), 299, remarks that the ethical impact of the text is the invitation to Christian communities to provide *hospitality* to missionaries. Mark develops an ascetic *Wanderethos* (Gerd Theißen) for the missionaries and, at the same time, places demands on the communities to show hospitality; these are two sides of the same coin.

[8] The text is primarily concerned with the right application of Torah commandments (see also Mk 12.28–34).

[9] Mk 7 is a core text of common early Christian ethics. Mark shifts the theme of purity from ritual obedience to ethics, thus secretly devaluing ritual purity. Yarbro Collins, *Mark,* 359, traces this back to Gen. 6.5. We also find parallels in Rom. 7.7 and Jas 1.13–15. For catalogues of vices and virtues, see Yarbro Collins, *Mark,* 357–58. Basically, Mk 7 demonstrates that Mark shares the ethical values of early Judaism and early Christianity, although he does not make them a subject of longer discussion. They are not the focus of his ethical concerns.

[10] Yarbro Collins, *Mark,* 409: in the Markan context 'verse 35 advocates not wishing to save one's (physical) self'.

[11] Yarbro Collins, *Mark,* 444.

[12] The pericope is about the interpretation of the Law: Jesus argues against the wording of Deut. 24.1, 3 and in favour of Gen. 1.27.

[13] Yarbro Collins, *Mark,* 473. This is a core ethical text. In this lengthy passage, Mark shifts the ethical emphasis several times: from the topic of Torah observance to the renunciation of wealth to discipleship in the sense of 'leaving everything'.

[14] The clue to the instruction is the Christological logic of v. 45: the disciples ought to serve as the Son of Man serves.

[15] Obviously, Mark is primarily interested in Jesus rebuking the Pharisees and in demonstrating his superiority in the debate. These are the patterns for the whole of chapter 12.

- Mk 12.28–34: the question about the greatest commandment[16] (individual audience: one scribe).
- Mk 12.38–40: moral critique of the scribes[17] (general audience: πολὺς ὄχλος).
- Mk 12.41–44: the paradigm of the poor widow[18] (internal audience: disciples).
- Mk 14.7: allusion to the social circumstances, duties and challenges of the early Christian communities: poverty and charity (*ad lectores*: Christian communities).
- Mk 14.66–72: Peter as an example of the personal vices of cowardice and denial (*ad lectores*).

The listed texts demonstrate a variety of themes, making it difficult at first glance to label one or two ethical norms or values as key concepts. More promising, as a first step, is to read the texts through the lens of the different questions I listed earlier (1–5) and only then to discuss the themes they may have in common.

My first question (1), concerning the *author(s)*, leads to some different insights. From a historical-critical perspective, the ethical text-units often point back to different layers of traditions: a historical Jesus tradition and later traditions as well as traces of reinterpretation by members of the Jesus movement. All text-units are the result of a rather complex process of formation that can be traced back to specific historical contexts, situations and audiences, so that the idea of one particular ethical value system or the search only for the original meaning of an individual saying or story would not be sufficient. Each text results from a different ethical perspective attributed to an original story or saying during the process of textualization. As *redactor* each evangelist intertwines different traditions and topics. As *author* each one works with the aim of creating his own ethical texts and of integrating those texts into his overall narrative (εὐαγγέλιον) about Jesus as the Christ, the Son of God. By framing diverse types of traditions in and through narrative, Mark furnishes traditions with a new significance so that exegesis always has to look for both: different levels or layers of tradition and the evangelist's new narrative framing and fresh interpretation. While the literary work of the author – i.e., the evangelist – is important as far as the authority of the text of the gospel as a whole is concerned, from Mark's narrative perspective the author is always Jesus himself.

Second, in order to classify the texts from different perspectives, I have grouped them according to intended *addressees* (question 2). In Mark, ethical themes are discussed in five different settings: first, among the narrow circle of Jesus' *disciples* (internal audience) and, second, in what we may label the *public sphere* (general audience). Repeatedly Jesus addresses both groupings successively (chs 7 and 10).[19] There are two other settings: on one hand, Jesus' discussion with opponents, the unyielding or even hostile Pharisees,

---

[16] In this pericope the stress is not on Lev. 19.18 but on the *double* love command. To love God is the first priority. The text is not primarily an ethical text but a hermeneutical interpretation of Torah, responding to the question regarding the highest commandment (see also Mk 7.9–13).
[17] This is an ethical text that draws attention to the thirst for social recognition combined with greed and pretended piety.
[18] The anecdote has a strong social-ethical intention ('Armentheologie'), but it also belongs to the ethics of discipleship. See Eve-Marie Becker, 'Was die "arme Witwe" lehrt: Sozial- und motivgeschichtliche Beobachtungen zu Mk 12, 41–44par', *NTS* 65 (2019), 148–65.
[19] John's narrative reflects this division in chapters 13–17 (Jesus and his friends).

scribes and Herodians, and, on the other hand, his instructions to individuals. Eventually, in Mark 14.7 and 14.66–72, the gospel's potential readers are addressed: here it becomes clear that the evangelist has a Christ-confessing readership in mind.

Third, on the basis of observations about the author or authorization and addressees of the ethical passages, the issue of underlying norms and values (question 3) can also be resolved. Those passages that are exclusively or predominantly addressed to the disciples proclaim and enhance the following values:

- ascetic ethos and lifestyle adopted by the missionaries ('Wanderradikale'), especially poverty combined with the ethos of hospitality on the part of the communities;
- inward purity;
- leadership as service and, at the same time, renunciation of status and power;
- children and a poor widow as examples for the Jesus-followers.

The concept that binds together these ethical topics in Mark is *discipleship*. Accordingly, Richard B. Hays defines discipleship as Mark's primary ethical concept.[20] His statement, 'Strikingly, the concept of love, a common theme of early Christian teaching, receives very little attention in Mark',[21] warrants our approval. Richard Hays is certainly correct regarding those passages addressed to the disciples as the primary target of Jesus' teaching. What Mark conceptualizes in these pericopes is the distinct new ethos of Jesus followers that commences with the first generation of his disciples,[22] and, beyond that, an ethos adjusted to the living conditions and challenges of the Christ-believing communities in Mark's own time. Discipleship means following Jesus in terms of lifestyle and ethical values.

However, the passages addressed to a more general audience – the crowds and/or the Jewish authorities – deal with topics belonging to the wider ancient Jewish and early Christian discourse on Torah: the text-units are concerned with virtues and vices, with purity, divorce, taxes, with obligations towards parents, and with the greatest commandment.[23] Three of these ethical topics pertain to the interpretation of the Decalogue, 'the law of Moses'. In these text-units Mark has one main objective: to demonstrate that Jesus' supreme authority exceeds that of the scribes.[24] The author of Mark's Gospel is not interested in establishing internal coherence between the single commandments to enable a concept of ethical teaching, whether old or new, to emerge. Instead, Mark molds *Jesus as the perfect teacher of the Torah*, in discussion in each individual case with the Jerusalem authorities, particularly in 12.28–34. In this anecdote or 'quest story' (Robert C. Tannehill),[25] the author's intention is 'the praise of Jesus' as

---

[20] Richard B. Hays, *The Moral Vision of the New Testament: A Contemporary Introduction to New Testament Ethics* (San Francisco, CA: Harper Collins, 1996), 75–85.
[21] Hays, *The Moral Vision*, 84.
[22] To which degree it can be traced back to the way of life and sayings of Jesus himself cannot be pursued in this essay.
[23] The degree to which these themes have already been part of the instruction of the 'historical Jesus' cannot be discussed in this essay. See Cilliers Breytenbach, 'Die Vorschriften des Mose im Markusevangelium: Erwägungen zur Komposition von Mk 7,9–13; 10,2–9 und 12,18–27', *ZNW* 97 (2006): 22–43.
[24] Scornaienchi, *Der umstrittene Jesus, pass.*
[25] Yarbro Collins, *Mark*, 565.

Adela Yarbro Collins puts it.[26] It is *not* so much about creating an ethical concept of love (of one's neighbour),[27] since both Jesus *and* the scribe cite Lev. 19.18. Instead, Mark portrays Jesus as prevailing against an excellent scribe, so that, in the hierarchy that exists between both teachers, Jesus is given the pre-eminent position. In 12.28–34, therefore, Mark does not draft an ethical concept of love, but emphasizes Jesus' superior ability to interpret Scripture in direct competition with the Jerusalem scribes. Mark's distinct idea when highlighting Jesus' ethical message is to bring the concept of *discipleship* (Hays)[28] into focus.

Observations concerning the *fourth* issue, the literary genres of the ethical texts (question 4) match the results of the third question. As mentioned above, Mark uses the controversy stories for his portrait of Jesus as teacher of the Law. Sayings units are used for instructing the disciples. Biographical scenes like Mk 12.41–44 and 14.16–72 serve paradigmatic purposes. Finally, the overall literary context (question 5), as already noted, is the Jesus narrative of the gospel.

Ethical texts in John

While scholars do not deny that there are important ethical topics and texts in Mark, the situation regarding *John* is different. Many scholars of my generation and of the generation with whom I studied generally denied that there is anything resembling ethics in John. Rudolf Bultmann does not write a single line about ethics in his chapters on John's theology nor does Jean Zumstein in his most recent seminal commentary.[29] We have Ernst Käsemann's *dictum* in our ears: 'Objekt christlicher Liebe ist für Johannes allein . . . die Bruderschaft Jesu'.[30]

In the wake of these verdicts, heated debates on the rather clumsy term *Konventikelethik* have filled the pages of the most comprehensive volumes on New Testament ethics in earlier decades, and Jörg Frey has revisited these debates in a recent contribution.[31] Up to now, several questions remain under dispute. Scholars discuss whether, or to what degree, John 13.34–35 is to be read as a general ethical text; whether the commandment of love points back to Lev. 19.18; and to whom the καινὴ ἐντολὴ applies.

---

[26] Yarbro Collins, *Mark*, 566.
[27] Thomas Söding argues in favour of this interpretation in 'Das Liebesgebot bei Paulus und Markus: Ein literarischer und theologischer Vergleich', in *Paul and Mark. Comparative Essays Part I: Two Authors at the Beginnings of Christianity*, ed. Oda Wischmeyer, David C. Sim, Ian J. Elmer (BZNW, 198; Berlin/Boston: de Gruyter 2014), 465–503.
[28] Mark also draws on tradition here, but he emphasizes the ethical pre-eminence of the topic.
[29] Jean Zumstein, *Das Johannesevangelium* (KEK, 2; Göttingen: Vandenhoeck & Ruprecht, 2016).
[30] Ernst Käsemann, *Jesu letzter Wille* (Tübingen: Mohr Siebeck, 1966), 136.
[31] E.g., Siegfried Schulz, *Neutestamentliche Ethik* (Zürich: Theologischer Verlag, 1987), 486–511. See the articles of Friedrich Wilhelm Horn, 'Ethik des Neuen Testaments 1982–1992', in *ThR* 60 (1995): 32–86; 'Ethik des Neuen Testaments 1993–2009. Teil I', in *ThR* 76 (2011): 1–36; 'Teil II', in *ThR* 76 (2011): 180–221. More recently, see Jörg Frey, 'Glauben und Lieben im Johannesevangelium', in *Glaube, Liebe, Gespräch: Neue Perspektiven johanneischer Ethik*, ed. Christina Hoegen-Rohls and Uta Poplutz (BThS, 178; Göttingen: Vandenhoeck & Ruprecht, 2018), 33–35 (especially nn. 55 and 59, *pace* Wayne A. Meeks). Jörg Frey also refers to the concept of 'Konventikelethik'.

During the last few decades, however, the overall exegetical perspective on John has undergone a significant change, and new questions warrant new answers.[32] Udo Schnelle has recently recapitulated and summarized scholarly developments on Johannine ethics under three important headings: the ethical relevance of (1) the gospel genre, (2) metaphorical language and (3) narrative ethics.[33] Here we meet a *language- and literary*-based approach that is having a stimulating impact on the study of Johannine ethics. In addition, Jörg Frey points to the fact that, not only in recent Johannine studies, but also in the whole area of New Testament exegesis, the study of ethics is nowadays a field of crucial interest.[34] Fresh interpretative models have been developed, such as the model of 'implicit ethics' proposed by Jan G. van der Watt and Ruben Zimmermann.[35] These models move beyond the genre-based *parenesis*-discourse initiated by Martin Dibelius and developed by the previous generation of exegetes.[36] Sookgoo Shin has recently provided a short 'overview of recent scholarship on John's ethics'.[37] Like Schnelle, he draws attention to 'hidden ethical meanings'[38] and to the gospel narrative as the vehicle for ethics,[39] thus opening up new scholarly perspectives on ethics in the Gospel of John. It goes without saying that the contributions of van der Watt, Zimmermann and Shin modify the precise profile of ethics formulated by Michael Labahn. Ethics is no longer primarily understood as a system of rules concerning the behaviour and *actions* of individuals, but also pertains to the fields of emotions and of psychological-cultural modes of communal life and social standards.

Before I proceed with a discussion of Schnelle's criteria, I shall present a very short list of passages in the first part of John's Gospel that can be labelled ethical texts, again following Michael Labahn's definition:

- Jn 5.29: sentence on good and evil from an eschatological perspective.
- Jn 7.19: on Moses-Torah.
- Jn 8.1–11: on divorce.
- Jn 12.1–8: anointing by Mary in Bethany.

A different picture emerges in the second part of the gospel:

- Jn 13.1–20: washing of feet.
- Jn 13.34: the new commandment.
- Jn 14.15–21: keeping the new commandment.
- Jn 15.9–17: keeping the commandments of Christ.

---

[32] See Hoegen-Rohls and Poplutz (eds), *Glaube, Liebe, Gespräch, pass.*
[33] Udo Schnelle, *Theologie des Neuen Testaments* (3rd edn; Göttingen: Vandenhoeck & Ruprecht, 2016), 708–15. See especially the contributions on the history of the interpretation of Johannine ethics in Hoegen-Rohls and Poplutz (eds), *Glaube, Liebe, Gespräch*.
[34] Frey, 'Glauben und Lieben im Johannesevangelium', 37–38.
[35] See van der Watt and Zimmermann, *Rethinking the Ethics of John*.
[36] An outstanding contribution to this discussion is James M. Starr and Troels Engberg-Pedersen (eds), *Early Christian Paraenesis in Context* (BZNW, 125; Berlin/New York: de Gruyter, 2004).
[37] Sookgoo Shin, *Ethics in the Gospel of John: Discipleship as Moral Progress* (BIS, 168; Leiden: Brill, 2019), 5–25. Shin deals with several contributions adopting the approach of Jan G. van der Watt.
[38] Shin, *Ethics in the Gospel of John*, 13–21.
[39] Shin, *Ethics in the Gospel of John*, 21–25.

- Jn 16.8–11: new definition of sin, justice and last judgement.
- Jn 18.25–27:[40] on Peter (see Mk 14.66–72).

In his speeches in the first part of the gospel, Jesus rarely addresses the question of ethics. It is only in the second part of the book, in the context of the Farewell Discourses where his 'friends' or 'his own' are addressed, that the evangelist allows Jesus to elaborate on the ethical theme of ἀγάπη/ἀγαπᾶν. In the first part of the gospel, the evangelist only touches briefly upon some of the ethical topics belonging to the traditional inventory of ethical issues found in the Torah and the Synoptic Gospels. Although the number of passages belonging to this category is limited, it is still crucial to analyse the pre-history and ideological contexts of their ethical themes. John 5.29, 7.19 and the very distinctive 8.1–11,[41] are fragments drawn from discourses on Torah that already feature in Markan ethics: the relationship between good and evil deeds (ἔργα) and the last judgement, acting according to the Torah, and adultery. None of these three passages is particularly characteristic of Johannine ethics; they rather demonstrate the author's knowledge of Torah-discourse and his awareness of Jesus' traditional status as a teacher of Torah. Quite the opposite is true of 16.8–11, where the author redefines key terms found in Jewish and early Christian ethical-eschatological discourses: ἁμαρτία, δικαιοσύνη und κρίσις. In 16.8–11 John clearly limits these discourses to the core issues of 'faith' and Christology. Here we find the *new* ethical ideas that the author attributes to 'his' Jesus figure. Sin (ἁμαρτία), justice (δικαιοσύνη) and last judgement (κρίσις) – the key components of Israel's ethics – are reinterpreted along christological lines. Sin is defined as faithlessness (towards Jesus), justice as Jesus' return to God, i.e. his being righteous, and judgement as already fulfilled (through the coming of Jesus). Jean Zumstein illuminates the literary and religio-historical form of the text-unit by observing that John uses the form of an accusation saying originating in Old Testament accusations by the God of Israel against his people or the nations.[42] To express the point sharply, in 16.8–11 the evangelist changes ethics into Christology. In contrast, John 12.1–11 offers a glimpse into a certain practical issue within the Johannine communities, namely the proper handling of community finances. John is the only evangelist to introduce Judas as a thief.[43] Different from Mark, the Johannine version of the anointing concentrates on the issue of money and the use of funds – a matter already of importance within communities during Paul's missionary activity. The virtue of supporting the poor stands against the vice of the unlawful use of money.

Sookgoo Shin examines three more text-units in the first part of the gospel: the conversation between Jesus and Nicodemus (3.1–21), the encounter with the Samaritan woman (4.1–42), and the healing of the man born blind (9.1–41). In 3.17–21 the evangelist anticipates the statement in 16.8–11 about final judgement and the connection between faith and judgement. Moreover, Shin describes the narrative as 'a story that is aimed at persuading its readers to adopt a Johannine worldview ... and

---

[40] For other ethical texts in the Gospel of John, see the contributions on Jn 4.43–53, 9.1–41 and 14.6 in Hoegen-Rohls and Poplutz (eds), *Glaube, Liebe, Gespräch*.
[41] While 8.1–11 is a later addition, its moral message meets the overall Johannine ethical concept.
[42] Zumstein, *Das Johannesevangelium*, 596–601.
[43] For the synoptic analysis, see Zumstein, *Das Johannesevangelium*, 439–44.

thus to walk in the way of Johannine discipleship'.⁴⁴ In chapter 4 also, faith is the focus of the conversation between Jesus and the Samaritan woman, with Jesus serving as the central figure of the narrative. The moral issue surrounding the woman's life, in the company of an unmarried man, serves only as a starting point for Jesus' self-presentation. Shin is correct in stating that John does not offer 'any explicit guidance on moral behavior', but rather that the 'narrative has the intrinsic power to change the reader's moral vision'.⁴⁵ The christological intention of the story of the man born blind can be seen most clearly in 9.2–3:

> 2 His disciples asked him, 'Rabbi, who sinned, this man or his parents, that he was born blind?' 3 'Neither this man nor his parents sinned', said Jesus, 'but this happened so that the works of God might be displayed in him.'

Jesus rejects his disciples' question regarding the origin of the blind man's *sin* – a key ethical term (cf. 16.8–11). Instead Jesus explains that God's works shall be revealed and that he himself is the one who performs these works. The narrative leads to the man's confession: πιστεύω, κύριε (v. 38). In vv. 39–41 John deals once more with judgement and sin. Shin thus offers the following ethical summary: 'The man who seemed most inadequate and unqualified to do the works of God has become the role model *par excellence* of discipleship for both witnesses and readers'.⁴⁶

In the second part of the gospel, the tendency to move from ethics to Christology is evident. The evangelist begins his narration of the passion with the footwashing (13.12–20), in which Jesus gives his disciples a final *example* of mutual love and service. After this Jesus establishes a general rule for his disciples under the heading of a 'new commandment' (καινὴ ἐντολή, 13.34). By using ἐντολή, the evangelist points back to Lev. 19.18 but also to Jesus' earlier speech in chapter 12, where ἐντολή is used in the comprehensive sense of God's advice to Jesus:

> For I did not speak on my own, but the Father who sent me commanded (ἐντολὴν δέδωκεν) me to say all that I have spoken. I know that his command (ἐντολὴ αὐτοῦ) leads to eternal life. So whatever I say is just what the Father has told me to say.
>
> 12.49, 50

So, John builds a bridge to Lev. 19.18, but at the same time he underlines the new dimension of Jesus' ethical rule. The 'new commandment' differs from Lev. 19.18 in significant ways: it is not the Israelites but the Twelve who are addressed by Jesus. The intensity or strength of love is measured not through comparison with the self-love of a person but by imitation of *Jesus'* love to 'his own'. This new kind of mutual love will be a sign of the lasting discipleship of the Twelve. In sum, the καινὴ ἐντολή is different

---

⁴⁴ Shin, *Ethics in the Gospel of John*, 78.
⁴⁵ Shin, *Ethics in the Gospel of John*, 99.
⁴⁶ Shin, *Ethics in the Gospel of John*, 120.

from the love of neighbour in ancient Judaism,⁴⁷ though it builds on Lev. 19.18 and on the Synoptic tradition (Mk 12.31, 33 par.). As already noted, John follows Mark in the sense that Lev. 19.18 is not at the core of Jesus' ethical teaching. Mark spells out Jesus' own ethical message in terms of discipleship. John adheres to the value of Love, but alters the object from neighbour to 'friends'. The Gospel of John thus limits Jesus' ethical message to love among the disciples. Whether or not we want to label this kind of ethics as *Konventikelethik*, in John we find the concept of mutual love among those community members who are Christ's 'friends' and who live according to his commandments (Jn 15.14).

But what are Jesus' commandments? The evangelist appears to refuse to answer this question and insists instead on the mere repetition of the 'new commandment'. Shin states regarding John 3: 'through the Nicodemus narrative, John leads his readers to challenge and reconsider their moral assumptions and to accept the Johannine understanding of "what is ethical". To do so, John does not give readers a list of "do's or don'ts" but he rather presents them with a story that is aimed at persuading its readers to adopt a Johannine worldview'.⁴⁸ In 14.15–21 John intensifies this veiled kind of ethical message. He enhances the significance of the new commandment by highlighting the relationship between keeping the commandment and loving Jesus. In John 15.9–17 a further deepening of the theological motif of love is developed:

> *9* As the Father has loved me, so I have loved you. Now remain in my love. *10* If you keep my commands (ἐντολάς), you will remain in my love, just as I have kept my Father's commands (ἐντολάς) and remain in his love. *11* I have told you this so that my joy may be in you and that your joy may be complete. *12* My command (ἐντολή) is this: Love each other as I have loved you. *13* Greater love has no one than this: to lay down one's life for one's friends (ἵνα τις τὴν ψυχὴν αὐτοῦ θῇ ὑπὲρ τῶν φίλων αὐτοῦ). *14* You are my friends if you do what I command (ἐντέλλομαι). *15* I no longer call you servants, because a servant does not know his master's business. Instead, I have called you friends, for everything that I learned from my Father I have made known to you. *16* You did not choose me, but I chose you and appointed you so that you might go and bear fruit – fruit that will last – and so that whatever you ask in my name the Father will give you. *17* This is my command (ἐντέλλομαι): Love each other.

This text gives expression to the ultimate Johannine notion of the circular flow of love:⁴⁹ God loves his son, the son loves his friends and lays down his life for them. The friends love each other in the same way as the son has loved them. For this purpose, the evangelist uses the phrase μένειν ἐν τῇ ἀγάπῃ τῇ ἐμῇ.⁵⁰ It is the stream of love between

---

⁴⁷ See recently Kengo Akiyama, *The Love of Neighbour in Ancient Judaism: The Reception of Leviticus 19:18 in the Hebrew Bible, the Septuagint, the Book of Jubilees, the Dead Sea Scrolls, and the New Testament* (AJEC, 105; Leiden: Brill, 2018).
⁴⁸ Shin, *Ethics in the Gospel of John*, 78.
⁴⁹ See Wischmeyer, *Liebe*, 109–15.
⁵⁰ This phrase occurs frequently in John.

God, Jesus and the disciples that is imagined by the evangelist. Mutual love is the new definition of ethics within the Johannine communities.

On the comparison of texts

Before offering a final comparison of the ethical concepts expressed by both evangelists, I wish to include some methodological reflections on the study of *comparison* or on the reconstruction of putative *connections*. What do we mean when we speak of connections between John and Mark? What does it mean to compare their ethical concepts, and what is the possible outcome of a comparison of this kind? Our investigation can be narrowed to the following question: How can we identify appropriate comparative tools that lead us *beyond* the three well-established tools of *Motivgeschichte* (motif criticism), *Traditionsgeschichte* (tradition criticism) and *intertextuality*?

I shall begin my methodological reflections by revisiting the ways in which *Motivgeschichte*, *Traditionsgeschichte* and intertextuality can contribute to a comparison of ethical texts. First, *motifs*: the philological analysis of literary or philosophical-ethical motifs in narrative or discursive texts has always been an effective instrument in comparative literary studies. *Motivgeschichte* works as a storehouse of specific terms, metaphors, topics, sayings, aphorisms and figures.[51] This storehouse preserves fundamental human convictions, experiences, values and attitudes. Literary motifs have a time-transcending character and serve as helpful hermeneutical tools with the capacity to bridge different temporal epochs and cultures. By motifs, readers are enabled to understand narratives and arguments that transcend their own personal experience as well as the boundaries of their particular historical and cultural worlds. *Motivgeschichte* thereby helps to avoid the determinacy of personal and historical conditions – with their specific and limited possibilities of experience, contexts and interchanges – and, in its place, negotiates the obstacles of cultural otherness and strangeness. *Motivgeschichte* is thus a *lingua franca* for the study of both narrative literature and popular philosophical or ethical texts. The study of *Motivgeschichte*, for instance, helps to illuminate the concept of *parenesis* within the context of Hellenistic-Roman and ancient Jewish culture. To interpret ethical texts by means of *Motivgeschichte* reveals *similar* or identical cultural patterns, experiences and values in *different* texts and cultures containing topical or stereotyped literary terms, phrases or figures. In short, *Motivgeschichte* casts a wide hermeneutical net over the literary, religious and philosophical heritage of the ancient world. Motifs, however, are not *concepts* as such, but rather important *tessera* in the broader mosaic of multifarious textual worlds.

Thus, when applied to the topic of this investigation, we encounter the widespread motif of doing good or evil (Mk 3.4; Jn 5.29)[52] or the catalogue of vices in Mk

---

[51] Udo Schnelle, *Einführung in die neutestamentliche Exegese* (6th edn; Göttingen: Vandenhoeck & Ruprecht, 2005), 134.
[52] Oda Wischmeyer, 'Gut und Böse: Antithetisches Denken im Neuen Testament und bei Jesus Sirach', in *Treasures of Wisdom: Studies in Ben Sira and the Book of Wisdom. FS M. Gilbert S.J.*, ed. Núria Calduch-Benages and Jacques Vermeylen (BETL, 143; Leuven: Peeters, 1999), 129–36; Oda Wischmeyer,

7.22;[53] indeed, four of the twelve vices mentioned in Mk 7 also occur in John.[54] A list of cross-references demonstrates that vices belong to the common ethical *lingua franca* shared by John and Mark. Nevertheless, it is striking how little interest both authors show in building a moral concept on the mere basis of, for example, 'Good and Evil' or vices and virtues. In fact, John is even less interested than Mark in referring to common moral values. At the same time, neither of these authors completely removes those motifs belonging to the huge reservoir of ancient moral convictions. We must not underestimate the layer of ethical stereotypes that continued to serve as a common resource for both gospel writers and also acted as a hermeneutical bridge for readers from outside the early Christian communities. In this bridging function, ancient ethical stereotypes or motifs constantly reappear in Christian literature during the 2nd century CE and onwards.

Second, through *Traditionsgeschichte* we study the development and mutual interdependence of traditions that are embedded in foundational narratives about the origin or end of institutions, persons, eminent places, sayings, customs and rites. The concept of *Traditionsgeschichte* is multifaceted. *Traditionsgeschichte*, in the way it is applied here, is closely connected to oral history and oral traditions and to the processes of transmitting traditions, either in unwritten or written form. In any case, traditions exist before the written texts or records. *Traditionsgeschichte* goes back to the past and opens up the historical dimension of ethical texts. Traditions, like motifs, are not concepts; nevertheless, different from motifs, traditions can be the point of departure for a concept that will later develop ('invented traditions').

The fact that 'tradition' is not a 'concept' is fundamental to the interpretation of the commandment of love in both Mark and John. In Mark 12, Jesus and the scribe successively quote Lev. 19.18, thereby ascribing utmost importance to the commandment of love. Scholars like Thomas Söding tend to detect an ethical *concept* in this text-unit.[55] I have earlier indicated why I disagree with this position. Certainly Mark 12 is an important text within the *Traditionsgeschichte* of Lev. 19.18, especially because of the way in which Mark combines Lev. 19 with Deut. 6.5. But Mark 12 has no *concept* of love. It is this double citation of ἀγαπᾶν in Mark 12 that, nevertheless, stimulated John to develop his particular, and comprehensive, concept of love.[56] The connections between the Markan and Johannine statements on love are not sufficiently explained by *Traditionsgeschichte* alone. Instead, we need to take another step and proceed from *Traditionsgeschichte* to intertextuality.

Intertextuality, as Jean Zumstein has argued, offers a rationale for comparing Mark and John. He analyses the interconnections between Mark and John with reference to Gérard Genette's concept of hypertextuality.[57] Different from Luke and Matthew, John

---

'Zwischen Gut und Böse: Teufel, Dämonen, das Böse und der Kosmos im Jakobusbrief', in *Das Böse, der Teufel und Dämonen – Evil, the Devil, and Demons*, ed. Jan Dochhorn, Susanne Rudnig-Zelt, Benjamin Wold (WUNT, 2/412; Tübingen: Mohr Siebeck, 2016), 153–68.

[53] Also the motif of evil: πονηρός (Mk 7.23; Jn 3.19; 7.7).
[54] πορνεία (Jn 8.41); μοιχεία (8.3); δόλος (1.47); βλασφημία (10.33).
[55] Söding, 'Das Liebesgebot bei Paulus und Markus', 465–503.
[56] See Wischmeyer, *Liebe*, pass.
[57] Gérard Genette, *Palimpseste: Die Literatur auf zweiter Stufe*, tr. Wolfram Bayer and Dieter Hornig (Edition Suhrkamp: Aesthetica, 1683; Frankfurt am Main: Suhrkamp, 1993); see Zumstein, *Das Johannesevangelium*, 46.

'reconfigures all Jesus materials and integrates them into his own narrative and theological concept'.[58] Zumstein's loose definition enables us to gain a better understanding of the place of ethics in both gospels. The perspective offered by *Traditionsgeschichte* is of limited significance for interpreting the commandment of love in Mark and John: John does not use the Jewish tradition of love of one's neighbour when construing the 'new' commandment of mutual love. He neither refers to the important Torah commandment of Lev. 19.18 nor to Mk 12.31 as the primary commandment in Jesus' ethical advice; rather, John 'reconfigures' both sources of tradition without citing or even mentioning them. Moreover, John boldly changes the addressees of the commandment: it is no longer 'neighbours', i.e. the Israelites, who are to be loved, but Jesus' 'friends'. In that sense the commandment given by the Johannine Jesus in 13.34 is 'new', and it is through the lens of intertextuality that this interpretative result is achieved.

In brief, only a combination of *Motivgeschichte*, *Traditionsgeschichte* and intertextuality offers indispensable insights into the foundations of ethics in both Mark and John. Jean Zumstein gets to the heart of the matter when he argues: 'We are no longer engaged in a quest for origins, nor does documentary authenticity stand at the centre of the investigation, but rather the type of relationship between two complete literary works that succeed each other in time'.[59] Nevertheless, it is the *fourth* approach, *Literaturgeschichte*, as highlighted by Udo Schnelle, that will take us one step further. Literary criticism leads us to a perception of the *individual* literary text in which ethical topics are embedded, or, in other words, the text's 'structural design'. The study of *Literaturgeschichte* provides appropriate questions and answers in the quest for the literary profile and genre of ethical discourse, and, according to Schnelle, this is where we meet one of the most important aspects of the study of early Christian ethics: *genre* as a tool of literary criticism.[60]

Mark is the first gospel to compose a *Jesus narrative* for a Christ-believing audience. From the outset he offers his own interpretation of the narrative through the introductory phrase εὐαγγελίον Ἰησοῦ Χριστοῦ υἱοῦ θεοῦ. To put it simply: what *Mark* records is not an ethical compendium but a book about the message of Jesus, the Christ. Accordingly, the kind of ethical vision and advice that Mark as author wishes to convey is the concept of *discipleship* that connects the readers to Jesus and enables other readers to align themselves with this kind of discipleship. Those parts of Mark's Jesus book that centre on ethical topics, particularly chapter 12, work primarily as demonstrations of Jesus' superiority and insightful wisdom as teacher. In *John's* Christ narrative, by contrast, almost every ethical topic is subsumed under Jesus and his new commandment of *love*. John's christological message speaks of the stream of love that creates unity between God, his son and the disciples. Only through love are the Christ-confessing communities for whom John writes his gospel to conduct their lives.

---

[58] Translation of Zumstein, *Das Johannesevangelium*, 47.
[59] Zumstein, *Das Johannesevangelium*, 7.
[60] See questions (4) and (5) above.

From *Jesus, the Christ*, who framed a new ethics of discipleship to *Jesus, Son of God*, who loved his own to the end: The development of Christological ethics in the Jesus narratives of Mark and John

The summary of this investigation will be brief. The author of Mark's Gospel shapes a narrative about Jesus, the Christ, as the most authoritative teacher of Torah. At the same time, Jesus appears as the one who initiates an eschatological way of life and as the one who calls for a discipleship characterized by service and the renunciation of power and status. Discipleship, for Mark, is tantamount to following Jesus' way to the cross.

It is reasonable to assume that the author of John's Gospel had read the Gospel of Mark. John does not seem to be as bound as Mark to the ethical teaching of the 'historical Jesus'; instead, his aim is to work out the inner connection between Jesus' life and mission and the disciples' way of life. Thus ἀγάπη/ἀγαπᾶν emerges as a concept associated with emotional and practical behaviour. ἀγάπη/ἀγαπᾶν encompasses God's relationship to his son and vice versa, and also Jesus' relation to humankind and the relationship between his friends. By combining these different aspects of love, John configures the Jesus story as a network of love, even as the great and ultimate love story.[61] He thereby draws on Mark's concept of discipleship and develops the emotional and personal dimension of that concept. The μαθηταί in John 13.35 are identical to the μαθηταί in Mark 8.34–38. A similar close link exists between the footwashing scene in John 13 and Jesus' sayings about the renunciation of status in Mark 10.41–45.

It seems to me that the author of the Johannine Gospel has drafted his ethical concept of love among Jesus' friends on the basis of two pillars already established by Mark: the double love commandment in Mark 12 (see Lev. 19.18; Deut. 6.4) and Mark's concept of discipleship. John's ethical concept of love discloses its actual power when read against Mark's gospel narrative. Mark provided John with basic ethical traditions and motives that were developed into elements of his own narration of Jesus who, 'having loved his own who were in the world, he loved them to the end' (Jn 13.1).

---

[61] Wischmeyer, *Liebe, pass.*

15

The 'Speeches' in Mark and John: Comparative Readings

Susanne Luther

'Speeches', discourses, and dialogues

Martin Luther drew attention to the significance of Jesus' speeches in John's Gospel by stating: 'Now John writes very little about the works of Christ, but very much about his preaching, while the other evangelists write much about his works and little about his preaching. Therefore John's Gospel is the one, fine, true, and chief gospel, and is far, far to be preferred over the other three and placed high above them'.[1] However, an analysis of direct speech in the four canonical gospels shows that the quantity of speech material over against narrative passages takes up 58% of the text in John's Gospel, but only 46% of Mark's, while it is 60% and 66% in Luke and Matthew respectively.[2] In all four canonical gospels, most of the direct speech is attributed to Jesus,[3] although it seems to be of greater importance in the Gospel of John in comparison with the Synoptics. This has led scholars to observe that 'if narrative is typical of Mark, discourse is typical of John',[4] and '[i]n contrast to the Synoptics, the Johannine Jesus is all talk and (almost) no action'.[5] When comparing John and Mark, it becomes evident that not only is the amount of direct speech lower in Mark than in John, but also the number of longer speech-compositions in both gospels is strikingly at variance. Mark has only two

---

[1] Martin Luther, 'Word and Sacrament', in *Luther's Works*, ed. E. Theodore Bachmann (vol. 35; Philadelphia, PA: Muhlenberg Press, 1960), 362.
[2] Cf. Lars Kierspel, *The Jews and the World in the Fourth Gospel: Parallelism, Function, and Context* (WUNT, 2/220; Tübingen: Mohr Siebeck, 2006), 133–34.
[3] Kierspel, *The Jews and the World*, 134: In Matthew 56% of the text is Jesus' speech, in Mark 35%, in Luke 47% and in John 42%.
[4] Morna D. Hooker, 'The Johannine Prologue and the Messianic Secret', *NTS* 21 (1974): 41.
[5] Adele Reinhartz, '"And The Word Was God": John's Christology and Jesus's Discourses in Jewish Context', in *Reading the Gospel of John's Christology as Jewish Messianism: Royal, Prophetic, and Divine Messiahs*, ed. Benjamin Reynolds and Gabriele Boccaccini (Leiden: Brill, 2018), 69. However, Jo-Ann A. Brant, *Dialogue and Drama: Elements of Greek Tragedy in the Fourth Gospel* (Peabody, MA: Hendrickson, 2004), 35, considers the discourses as the 'true action of the gospel, just as dialogue is the action of a drama'. Cf. Jo-Ann A. Brant, *John* (Paideia Commentaries on the New Testament; Grand Rapids, MI: Baker, 2011), 10 and 13.

speech-compositions,[6] the parable discourse in Mark 4.1–34 and the eschatological or Olivet discourse in 13.5–37,[7] while in the Gospel of John about one third of the direct speech attributed to Jesus occurs in the context of longer speech-compositions,[8] which are traditionally described as the Johannine 'discourses':[9]

1. the Discourse on New Birth (Jn 3.1–21)
2. the Water of Life Discourse (4.1–42)
3. the Discourse on the Divine Son (5.19–47)
4. the Bread of Life Discourse (6.22–59)
5. the Discourse on the Life-Giving Spirit (7.1–52)
6. the Light of the World Discourse (8.12–59)
7. the Good Shepherd Discourse (10.1–21)
8. the Words on the Glorification of the Son (12.23–50)
9. the Farewell Discourses and the Prayer of Jesus (13.31–16.33; 17.1–26).[10]

By comparing the speech material in the Gospel of John with that contained in the Synoptics, especially Mark, the unmissable differences between both texts become evident: 'That the speech of Jesus in the Fourth Gospel is usually quite different from that of Jesus in the Synoptics goes without saying. John certainly made no attempt to conceal his own pervasive idiom in this discourse material. In fact, if we omit Jesus' discourses, John's basic accounts about Jesus often resemble the traditions behind the Synoptics'.[11] Despite this slightly discouraging statement, this chapter will venture to

---

[6] Cf., however, also David M. Young and Michael Strickland, *The Rhetoric of Jesus in the Gospel of Mark* (Minneapolis, MN: Fortress, 2017), who discuss four 'discourses' in the Gospel of Mark (3.20–35; 4.1–34; 6.53–7.23; 11.27–13.37), including controversy stories and speech-compositions that are linked together in longer narrative sections.

[7] Ben Witherington III, *The Gospel of Mark. A Socio-Rhetorical Commentary* (Grand Rapids, MN: Wm B. Eerdmans, 2001), 162, speaks of a 'rhetorical unit or speech proper' in the case of Mark 4, and of a 'single discourse or block of continuous teaching' (p. 336) as well as a 'speech' (p. 338) with regard to Mark 13. Richard T. France, *The Gospel of Mark: A Commentary on the Greek Text* (NIGTC; Grand Rapids, MN: Wm B. Eerdmans, 2002), 13–15, refers to both Mark 4 and 13 as 'explanatory discourses'. Cf. also Willem S. Voerster, 'Literary Reflections on Mark 13.5–37: A Narrated Speech of Jesus', in *The Interpretation of Mark*, ed. William R. Telford (Edinburgh: T&T Clark, 1995), 269–88.

[8] Cf. Philipp F. Bartholomä, *The Johannine Discourses and the Teaching of Jesus in the Synoptics* (TANZ, 57; Tübingen: Francke, 2012), 1–2, who counts speeches that exceed 200 words as longer speech-compositions.

[9] The first seven discourses are widely linked with the seven signs narrated in John; see, e.g., Leon Morris, *Jesus is the Christ: Studies in the Theology of John* (Grand Rapids, MN: Wm B. Eerdmans, 1989), 23. Because of the greater volume of dialogic material in John, the gospel has been characterized as a drama; see, e.g., Ludger Schenke, *Johannes: Kommentar* (Düsseldorf: Patmos, 1998), 398; further, Brant, *Dialogue and Drama*, passim; and also George L. Parsenios, 'The Silent Spaces between Narrative and Drama: Mimesis and Diegesis in the Fourth Gospel', in *The Gospel of John as Genre Mosaic*, ed. Kasper Bro Larsen (SANt, 3; Göttingen: Vandenhoeck & Ruprecht, 2015), 85–97.

[10] Cf. here Gail R. O'Day, '"I have said these things to you . . .": The Unsettled Place of Jesus' Discourses in Literary Approaches to the Fourth Gospel', in *Word, Theology and Community in John*, ed. John Painter, R. Alan Culpepper and Fernando F. Segovia (St. Louis, MO: Chalice Press, 2002), 143–54.

[11] Craig S. Keener, *The Gospel of John: A Commentary* (2 vols, Grand Rapids, MN: Baker, 2003), 1:53. Cf also Bartholomä, *Johannine Discourses*, 3–4: 'Already the literary form of the elaborate discourses used by the author of the Fourth Gospel stands in general contrast with the Synoptists' portrait of

offer a comparison of the 'speech-compositions', 'speeches' or 'discourses' – not Jesus' 'speech' as a narrative character as such – in Mark and John. The focus will be on the following questions:

- To what extent is an analysis of the speech-compositions in Mark and John able to clarify the relationship between the two gospels?
- Which perspectives on the speech-compositions can shed new light on the question of whether John knew (and used) Mark?

In this paper I will read the extended speech-compositions in both gospels against the background of ancient historiography. I will *first* examine the specific form, narrative structure and audience of the speeches in both gospels; *second*, I will discuss the use of sources and traditions for the composition of the speeches; and, *third*, I will assess the function of the speeches in relation to the historiographical claim of both texts.

Taking stock: Form, narrative structure and the audience of the speeches in Mark and John

An analysis of form, narrative structure and audience brings to the fore the distinctive characteristics of the extended speech-compositions in the Gospels of Mark and John. The two Markan speeches differ significantly from each other: Mark 4.1–34 opens with a scene of public teaching (v. 1), which, from v. 10 onwards, turns into an interpretation of the parables for a limited, and yet extended, circle of disciples (v. 10). Jesus' direct speech is repeatedly interrupted by narrative elements (4.1–2, 10, 33–34) and transitional formulations (4.9, 11, 13, 21, 24, 26, 30);[12] these are superfluous in narrative terms since they interrupt Jesus' speech. From a narratological perspective, this disruption to the parable speech divides the text into individual units (4.3–8, 9, 10–12, 13–20, 21–23, 24–25, 26–29, 30–32, 33–34) and reduces the immediacy of Jesus' speech.[13] In Mark 13.1–37 Jesus offers his teaching to a circle of four selected disciples – Peter, James, John and Andrew – and is therefore presented as a teacher to a small group of insiders.[14] After the setting of the scene through a short dialogue between

---

Jesus' teaching that predominantly features short, pithy sayings and parables. [...]. Several of the singular sayings, parables, and metaphorical words in John cannot obscure the fact that the Johannine pattern of extensive speeches is unique among our canonical accounts of the life of Jesus. [...] Differences in vocabulary are obvious as well: distinctive Johannine terms commonly used by Jesus in the Fourth Gospel (e.g., light, darkness, eternal life, truth, or witness) do not occur frequently, if at all, in the Synoptics. [...] The distinctive nature of Jesus' words in John's Gospel may also be seen in their theological emphases [...]'.

[12] The transitional formulations may be due to isolated units of literary tradition which the evangelist compiled into one extended speech in Mark 4; cf. below note 23.

[13] See here Eve-Marie Becker, 'Markus 13 Re-visited', in *Apokalyptik als Herausforderung neutestamentlicher Theologie*, ed. Michael Becker and Markus Öhler (WUNT, 2/214; Tübingen: Mohr Siebeck, 2006), 103.

[14] For a discussion of the genre of Mark 13 and its eschatological and apocalyptic elements, see Gertraud Harb, *Die eschatologische Rede des Spruchevangeliums Q: Redaktions- und traditionsgeschichtliche Studien zu Q 17,23–37* (BTS, 19; Leuven: Peeters, 2014), 128–38.

Jesus and one of his disciples (vv. 1–2) and then a change of setting (v. 3) combined with a question from the four disciples to initiate the speech that follows (v. 4), Mark 13.5b–37 provides a monological speech by Jesus introduced in v. 5a by a *verbum dicendi*.[15] The reader is directly confronted with the character's speech, which contains no narrative transitions or interruptions, thus bringing about an immediacy of speech.[16] In contrast to John's Gospel, 'Mark himself does not act as the actual composer of these speeches – he rather appears as collector and compiler of sayings material, since he does not give rhetorical shape to an elaborated speech: there is no single argumentum which runs through the entirety of the speech'.[17]

The Johannine discourses are often initiated with a dialogue, in which Jesus answers the questions posed by his interlocutors.[18] In the Discourse on New Birth (3.1–21), for example, Jesus' responses to Nicodemus are what constitute the discourse, the latter's continuous interlocutions serve to advance the dialogue (cf. also 7.1–52; 8.12–59; 12.23–50; 13.31–16.33). In the Discourse on the Water of Life (4.1–42), it is Jesus' dialogical exchange with the Samaritan woman that accelerates the progress of his speech, even though the verbal contributions of both parties are almost equal in length.[19] To speak of Johannine 'discourses' rather than 'speeches' therefore seems appropriate. In addition to the interlocutions of Jesus' dialogue partners, the Johannine discourses also contain narrative transitions, such as in John 10.6–7 where an explanation of the disciples' incomprehension interrupts the flow of Jesus' speech on the level of narration. In the Bread of Life discourse (6.22–59), the text opens with an introductory section (vv. 22–26a) and a dialogue between Jesus and the people (vv. 26b–34), which is then followed by Jesus' monologue (vv. 35–59). This speech is interrupted by the narrator's explanatory comment about the disbelieving murmuring of the Jews, although this forms an aside rather than contributing to the dialogue; the

---

[15] Cf. Joachim Gnilka, *Das Evangelium nach Markus* (EKK, II/2; 5th edn; Zürich: Benziger, 1999), 179–216, who emphasizes the 'kompositorische Geschlossenheit' of the chapter (p. 179).

[16] See Becker, 'Markus 13 Re-visited', 103; for the narrative structure of this speech, see pp. 102–104; for the reconstruction of possible traditions in Mark 13, cf. Eve-Marie Becker, *Das Markus-Evangelium im Rahme antiker Historiographie* (WUNT, 194; Tübingen: Mohr Siebeck, 2006), 89–98.

[17] Eve-Marie Becker, *The Birth of History: Memory and Time from Mark to Luke-Acts* (New Haven, CT: Yale University Press, 2017), 97; see also, however, the analysis of rhetorical elements in the Markan speeches according to the principles of ancient rhetoric provided in Young and Strickland, *Rhetoric of Jesus*, 119–83 and 213–87.

[18] Cf. Keener, *Gospel of John*, 68, who describes the structure of the Johannine discourse as (a) Jesus' statement, (b) the interlocution of a person who misunderstands, (c) the discourse, which can be monologic or contain several more interlocutions. See also Douglas Estes, *The Questions of Jesus in John: Logic, Rhetoric and Persuasive Discourse* (BIS, 115; Leiden: Brill, 2013), 57–67, esp. 59–61. Estes speaks of John as a 'dialectical gospel', for the question-answer-scheme in the narrative evokes an active response from the reader. '[T]he Fourth Gospel is dialectical as it purposely uses a repetitious question scheme between the narrator and the reader in order to narrow the reader down to the reasonable position that Jesus is the Christ' (p. 166).

[19] Cf. R. Alan Culpepper, 'The Weave of the Tapestry: Character and Theme in John', in *Characters and Characterization in the Gospel of John*, ed. Christopher W. Skinner (LNTS, 461; London: T&T Clark, 2013), 35, who emphasizes the role of these Johannine characters as 'plot functionaries' in the thematic development of the gospel, that is, beyond their function of illustrating different responses to Jesus. See also Marion Moser, *Schriftdiskurse im Johannesevangelium: Eine narrative-intertextuelle Analyse am Paradigma von Joh 4 und Joh 7* (WUNT, 2/380; Tübingen: Mohr Siebeck, 2014), on the dialogic interaction between Jesus and his counterparts.

continuation of Jesus' speech is then interpreted as his knowledge of and response to the reaction of the Jews. Here again the narrator deliberately interrupts Jesus' speech, but does so for the sake of explaining Jesus' subsequent words (cf. also Jn 7.25–27). The Johannine discourses – as in historical narrative – often serve to interpret or explain the preceding narrative.[20] John presents only two speeches in the form of longer monologues by Jesus that contain no narrative transitions or interlocutions by other parties: both John 5.19–47 and 17.1–26 are introduced by short preludes that provide the framework for and open Jesus' monologue through a *verbum dicendi* (5.19; 17.1). The Johannine discourses address different individual or group characters:[21] in the public discourses, individuals like Nicodemus (3.1–21) or the Samaritan woman (4.1–42), or groups like 'the Jews', 'the Pharisees' or 'the crowd' (5.19–47; 6.22–59; 7.1–52; 8.12–59; 10.1–21; 12.23–50) are presented as Jesus' conversation partners. In the Words on the Glorification (12.23–50) and in the Farewell Discourses (13.31–16.33), the disciples are the ones addressed by Jesus. In several Johannine discourses the addressees also change (e.g., 6.22–59).

This brief overview confirms that the Johannine discourses and Markan speeches deal with different topics and present their material in different ways: John presents his speech material in the form of extended dialogues or discourses rather than, as in the Synoptics, in short 'proverbial' sayings, parables and controversy dialogues.[22] A comparison of speeches or discourses in Mark and John also suggests, nevertheless, that both evangelists exhibit certain similarities in their aim of presenting Jesus' teaching in the form of longer monologues that mirror his character and actions. This also highlights the possibility that the form and purpose of John's longer speeches, like those in Mark, might be influenced by the ancient rhetorical practice of *prosopopoiia*, as attested in the speeches of ancient historiographical works.

The use of sources and traditions in Mark and John

When reading Mark and John from the perspective of ancient historiographical works, it is necessary to focus on the sources and traditions upon which the two evangelists base their speech-compositions. This is required in order to consider the possible origins and application of the material, but also to discern how the Johannine discourses relate to Synoptic material, especially whether and to what extent the speeches in Mark's Gospel can be plausibly viewed as a textual template for the Johannine compositions.

---

[20] Cf. Keener, *Gospel of John*, 69; C. K. Barrett, *The Gospel according to St. John* (2nd edn; London: SPCK, 1978), 20; Christoph Demke, 'Das Evangelium der Dialoge: Hermeneutische und methodologische Beobachtungen zur Interpretation des Johannesevangeliums', *ZThK* 97 (2000), 164–82, who also stresses the broad hermeneutical spectrum of possible interpretations of the Johannine dialogues.

[21] Cf. Brant, *Dialogue and Drama*, 27–29.

[22] See Keener, *Gospel of John*, 53: 'That even the content and structure of the discourses diverge significantly from the Synoptics could indicate that John received his tradition through a different means of transmission. In this case, the Synoptics would reflect the more common forms used in transmission of teacher's deeds and sayings (shorter anecdotes rather than long discourses, except in whole epics), and John transmitted longer units of speech'.

Mark 4 repeatedly contains transitional formulations (e.g., 4.9, 11, 13, 21, 24, 26, 30), which may indicate that this chapter constitutes a 'grown tradition complex' edited by the evangelist.[23] Mark 13 appears as a compositional unit that does not lend itself for close literary-critical analysis. Either Mark composed the speech independently on the basis of individual traditions – similar to how Matthew composed the Sermon on the Mount or John composed his discourses – or Mark used and, at best, edited an existing source which contained Jesus' speech as an established complex of traditions.[24]

In the case of the Johannine discourses, it has been shown that John takes up a multitude of Synoptic Jesus traditions and also composes the speeches he attributes to Jesus by using various strands of Jesus tradition.[25] In scholarly debates about the relationship between the Gospel of John and the Gospel of Mark,[26] three main theories have been proposed:

1. the theory of literary dependence, which assumes that John knew one or more of the Synoptic Gospels and used them as a source[27]
2. the theory of literary independence of John from the Synoptics, which proposes that John and the Synoptics used common early Christian tradition[28]
3. the theory that John knew one or more of the Synoptics, but used them in a distanced and free way that can best be described with the aid of intertextuality theory.[29]

---

[23] Cf., e.g., Dieter Lührmann, *Das Markusevangelium* (HNT, 3; Tübingen: Mohr Siebeck, 1987), 80–81, who considers the 'Überleitungsformeln' in vv. 2, 11, 21, and 24 as redactional, while those in vv. 9, 26, and 30 are attributed to tradition. See further Joachim Gnilka, *Das Evangelium nach Markus* (EKK, II/1; 5th edn; Zürich: Benziger, 1998), 155–67 and 173–92, esp. 191–92; cf. also Ludger Schenke, *Das Markusevangelium. Literarische Eigenart – Text und Kommentierung* (Stuttgart: Kohlhammer, 2005), 125.

[24] See Becker, 'Markus 13 Re-visited', 101–2 and 104; cf. also Becker, *Das Markus-Evangelium*, 82–89.

[25] Cf. Bartholomä, *Johannine Discourses*, passim.

[26] See Jörg Frey, 'Das vierte Evangelium auf dem Hintergrund der älteren Evangelientradition: Zum Problem: Johannes und die Synoptiker', in *Die Herrlichkeit des Gekreuzigten. Studien zu den johanneischen Schriften I*, ed. Juliane Schlegel (WUNT, 307; Tübingen: Mohr Siebeck, 2013), esp. 240–55; Michael Labahn and Manfred Lang, 'Johannes und die Synoptiker: Positionen und Impulse seit 1990', in Michael Labahn, *Ausgewählte Studien zum Johannesevangelium. Selected Studies in the Gospel of John: 1998–2013*, ed. Antje Labahn (BTS, 28; Leuven: Peeters, 2017), 3–78; D. Moody Smith, *Johannine Christianity. Essays on its Setting, Sources, and Theology* (Columbia: University of South Carolina Press, 1984), 39–61.

[27] Cf. Barrett, *Gospel according to St. John*; and Frans Neirynck, 'John and the Synoptics 1975–1990', in *John and the Synoptics*, ed. Adelbert Denaux (BETL, 101; Leuven: Peeters, 1992), 3–62.

[28] See Percival Gardner-Smith, *Saint John and the Synoptic Gospels* (Cambridge: Cambridge University Press, 1938); Rudolf Bultmann, *Das Evangelium des Johannes* (KEK, 2; 21st edn; Göttingen: Vandenhoeck & Ruprecht, 1986); C. H. Dodd, *Historical Tradition in the Fourth Gospel* (Cambridge: Cambridge University Press, 1963); Jürgen Becker, *Das Evangelium nach Johannes: Kapitel 1–10* (ÖTBK, 4/1; 3rd edn; Würzburg: Echter, 1991), 41–45; Michael Theobald, *Das Evangelium nach Johannes. Kapitel 1–12* (RNT; Regensburg: Pustet, 2009), 81.

[29] Cf. Jean Zumstein, *Das Johannesevangelium* (KEK, 3; Göttingen: Vandenhoeck & Ruprecht, 2016), 46; Hartwig Thyen, *Das Johannesevangelium* (HNT, 6; Tübingen: Mohr Siebeck, 2005), 4; Hartwig Thyen, 'Johannes und die Synoptiker: Auf der Suche nach einem neuen Paradigma zur Beschreibung ihrer Beziehungen anhand von Beobachtungen an Passions- und Ostererzählungen', in *John and the Synoptics*, ed. Adelbert Denaux (BETL, 101; Leuven: Leuven University Press and Peeters, 1992), 81–107.

With a view to the focus of this particular collection of essays, it needs to be reinforced that an analysis of the Johannine speeches actually confirms what has also been claimed for the Gospel of John as a whole: the evangelist draws on material from the Old Testament, the Synoptic tradition and special material,[30] but these written and/or oral pretexts are reconfigured and integrated into the evangelist's own narrative structure and theological aims.[31] This means that clues about the scope, origin and handling of the material, as well as an answer to the question as to whether John knew and used the Synoptics, are difficult or impossible to discern, even if common early Christian tradition can be detected.[32] Thus, although we find no literary dependence of the 'Synoptic type', it can be assumed that John knew and used the Synoptic tradition.[33] The exact scope and origin of John's pretexts can, however, no longer be reconstructed.[34]

Moreover, it is noteworthy that neither John nor Mark explicitly addresses the issue of their use of tradition and sources – as Luke does in his proemium. They do not indicate that the use and identification of sources or traditions is even relevant to their presentation of past events, and they are not used with a view to creating an authentic account of what is depicted in their narratives. An authoritative and thus authenticating use of Synoptic or non-Synoptic early Christian sources or traditions does not seem to be of significance for either of the two gospels; neither text refers to its pretexts for the authentication of its own presentation of historical events. Nevertheless, both texts claim to narrate past events and thus to align themselves with the tradition of ancient historiographical works that engage with and interpret received tradition in order to present an authoritative account of the past.

---

[30] Michael Theobald, '"Johannes" im Gespräch – mit wem und worüber?', in *Studien zum Corpus Iohanneum*, ed. Michael Theobald (WUNT, 267; Tübingen: Mohr Siebeck, 2010), 193–203, for an enquiry into the source texts with which the Gospel of John is 'in dialogue'. For an extensive analysis of the Synoptic material used in the Johannine discourses, see Bartholomä, *Johannine Discourses*, passim.

[31] Zumstein, *Johannesevangelium*, 46–47, rightly states that the evangelist displays considerable freedom by reconfiguring the material at his disposal and integrating it into his own narrative structure and theological purpose; cf. also Frey, 'Das vierte Evangelium auf dem Hintergrund', 115.

[32] See Theobald, *Evangelium nach Johannes*, 77: 'Was die Frage der Synoptiker*kenntnis* durch den vierten Evangelisten angeht, ist einzuräumen, dass sie weder positiv noch negativ entscheidbar ist, ja dass Verifikationsmöglichkeiten in der einen oder anderen Richtung fehlen'.

[33] Frey, 'Das vierte Evangelium auf dem Hintergrund', 113–14: 'Die literarische Kenntnis (und punktuelle Benutzung) des Markus- und vielleicht auch des Lukasevangeliums durch den Vierten Evangelisten schließt die zusätzliche Rezeption von weiteren (mündlichen oder auch schriftlichen) *Traditionen aus dem eigenen Gemeindekontext* nicht aus, sondern ein. Doch ist auch für diese eine ebenso selektive und partiell kritische Aufnahme anzunehmen, wie dies im Blick auf die Elemente der synoptischen Tradition festgestellt werden muss. Der Vierte Evangelist ist alles andere als ein bloßer Kompilator'.

[34] It seems likely that John used sources and traditions in his gospel; see Zumstein, *Johannesevangelium*, 43–44, who works with a 'Minimal-Hypothese', which assumes that the Johannine school had access to a range of miracle stories, Jesus sayings and a Passion story, but that it is not possible to reconstruct these sources in detail, 'und zwar nicht aufgrund inkompetenter Forschung, sondern aufgrund des Charakters des zu interpretierenden Textes selbst' (p. 43).

The function of speeches in relation to the historiographical claim of Mark and John

Both the Gospels of Mark and John narrate past events centred on a historical person, Jesus of Nazareth. Both reveal a claim to historical referentiality in their factual narratives[35] and can thus be read in relation to ancient historiographical texts. Both Mark and John also ascribe long speeches to their main character, as is also attested in ancient historiography.[36] At the same time, both use the 'gospel' genre – and in this regard the controversial debate as to whether they both invented this genre independently of each other, or whether John knew Mark's Gospel, becomes a relevant issue.[37] Before considering whether the use of speeches in Mark and John testifies to the relation between the two gospels when read in the light of ancient historiography, the historiographical character of both works needs to be considered.

Mark and John as factual texts with a historiographical claim

The historiographical characteristics of the Synoptic Gospels have long been the focus of research. Eve-Marie Becker has shown that Mark created a new genre with his gospel text – an early Christian factual narrative with historiographical characteristics and a claim to historical referentiality. She describes Mark as a pre-historiographical author[38] who created not an auto-referential and autonomous literary work, but a hetero-referential text based on eyewitnesses or sources, in which he

---

[35] Both texts are presented in a factual mode of speech and display a claim to historical referentiality, i.e. the texts convey the 'claim to represent historical facts'; see further Christian Klein/Matías Martínez (ed.), *Wirklichkeitserzählungen: Felder, Formen und Funktionen nicht-literarischen Erzählens* (Stuttgart/Weimar: Metzler, 2009), 2.

[36] The frequently discussed question as to whether the Gospel of John can contribute to historical Jesus research becomes even more controversial in relation to Jesus' speeches, when the authenticity of Jesus' words (authenticity of wording) or teachings (authenticity of content) is addressed. Cf. here Keener, *Gospel of John*, 53: 'Could these distinctive parts of John's Gospel [i.e., the discourses, S.L.] function as theological commentary, analogous to the function of speeches in many ancient histories [...]? If so, to what extent do they reflect John's sources about Jesus, and to what extent do they simply reflect his interpretation of Jesus? To the extent that they reflect John's interpretation, to what degree would it have been consistent with the historical Jesus' perspectives, perhaps not emphasized or developed in the Markan stream of tradition?'.

[37] See Rudolf Bultmann, *Gospel of John: A Commentary* (Eugene: Wipf & Stock, 2014), 6: 'Since Mark created the literary type of Gospel, to which John's writing also belongs, a direct or indirect acquaintance with the Gospel of Mark must surely be accepted'. Cf. also Udo Schnelle, 'Johannes und die Synoptiker', in *The Four Gospels 1992: FS F. Neirynck*, ed. Frans Van Segbroeck *et al.* (BETL, 100; Leuven: Peeters, 1992), 1799–814; Jürgen Becker, 'Das vierte Evangelium und die Frage nach seinen externen und internen Quellen', in *Fair Play: Diversity and Conflicts in Early Christianity: FS H. Räisänen*, ed. Ismo Dunderberg, Christopher Tuckett, and Kari Syreeni (NT.S, 103; Leiden: Brill, 2002), 203–41.

[38] Eve-Marie Becker, 'Die Konstruktion von "Geschichte": Paulus und Markus im Vergleich', in *Paul and Mark. Comparative Essays Part I: Two Authors at the Beginnings of Christianity*, ed. Oda Wischmeyer, David C. Sim, and Ian J. Elmer (BZNW, 198; Berlin: de Gruyter, 2014), 393 and 412. Cf. also Eve-Marie Becker, *The Beginnings of History*, 18, 111, 119.

arranges temporal sequences, and constructs and interprets them in literary and theological terms.³⁹

With regard to the Gospel of John, I have elsewhere shown that this text also presents itself as a factual text with a claim to historical referentiality.⁴⁰ It makes use of the literary strategies of authentication to create the perception that it is an authentic representation of the past and to construct the authenticity of the narrated events.⁴¹ The Johannine representation of the past does, however, go beyond mere earthly historiography, in that the narrative of the historical events surrounding the earthly Jesus also takes into account the time before the incarnation, i.e. the time of the pre-existence of the Logos, as well as the time after Jesus' earthly life, death and resurrection, i.e. the time of his return to the Father. The Jesus story is thus inscribed into contemporary history, but it is also aligned with the all-encompassing and 'historiography-surpassing' history of God with his creation.⁴²

It can therefore be stated that both Mark and John present themselves as factual narratives, which describe events of the past as well as claiming historical referentiality and constructing authenticity through various literary strategies, such as the speeches of their main characters, in order to communicate to the reader that 'truth' is being reported about historical events and persons.⁴³ Both gospels can thus be read in the context of ancient historiography.⁴⁴

---

³⁹ Cf. also Becker, 'Konstruktion von "Geschichte"', 414, who states that Mark is more than a collector and tradent of traditions. Rather, he proves to be a pre-historiographical author in that he creates a coherent narrative context and contributes to the interpretation of an 'overall history' that goes beyond the narration of scenic individual events in Galilee or Jerusalem. The historiographical achievement of Mark as writer consists in him linking the heterogeneous areas of available tradition and constructing a coherent history of events as well as creating a chronological and causal connection and interpretation between the event sequences.

⁴⁰ Susanne Luther, *Die Authentifizierung der Vergangenheit: Literarische Geschichtsdarstellung im Johannesevangelium* (WUNT; Tübingen: Mohr Siebeck, 2021); Susanne Luther, 'The Authentication of the Past: Narrative Representations of History in the Gospel of John', JSNT (2020), forthcoming.

⁴¹ The literary construction, however, is not to be equated with fictitiousness; cf. Zumstein, *Johannesevangelium*, 37: '"Fiktion" bedeutet nicht, dass Joh Elemente aus dem Leben und der Botschaft Jesu völlig frei erfunden hätte. Die joh Schule arbeitete mit diversem traditionellem Material, das ihr vorlag. Unter Fiktion ist vielmehr die Art und Weise zu verstehen, in der der Erzähler sein Material auswählt und es in Erzählform bringt, indem er es an einen bestimmten Platz in der erzählten Geschichte bringt, indem er es hervorhebt, entfaltet, umformuliert oder interpretiert. Eine historische Darstellung, die immer ein Konstrukt ist, kommt nicht umhin, Geschichte und Fiktion miteinander zu verflechten. Im Gebiet der Geschichtsschreibung entstammt die Fiktion also nicht primär der Phantasie, sondern gehört in den Bereich der Interpretation'.

⁴² See Richard Bauckham, 'Historiographical Characteristics of the Gospel of John', in *The Testimony of the Beloved Disciple: Narrative, History, and Theology in the Gospel of John* (Grand Rapids, MN: Baker, 2007), 103: 'Ordinary history is transcended in metahistory, but this can happen only through Jesus' real presence in ordinary history. Thus the story bears emphatically the marks of historiography at the same time as it bursts the boundaries of space and time'.

⁴³ Though not necessarily historical truth; see Luther, *Die Authentifizierung der Vergangenheit*.

⁴⁴ Cf. here Carlo Scardino, *Gestaltung und Funktion der Reden bei Herodot und Thukydides* (Beiträge zur Altertumskunde, 250; Berlin: de Gruyter, 2007), 717–18, who claims that both gospels are oriented towards ancient historiography: Mark models Herodotus' historiography with regard to formal composition though not in its subject matter and function of speeches, while John's longer reflexive speeches – also with regard to composition but not subject matter and function – may exhibit parallels to Thucydides' historiography.

Speeches in ancient historiography

According to the ancient progymnasmata and rhetorical handbooks, enriching historical accounts with speeches makes the presentation believable and persuasive to audiences.[45] The speeches attributed to historical persons in ancient historiography are composed by the author of the historiographical work in question; the speeches may be fictitious in terms of their wording, but they aim to reproduce a speech that is appropriate to the situation and to the character of the speaker, adhering as closely as possible to the general sense of what was or could actually have been said.[46] In his *History of the Peloponnesian War* Thucydides identifies three literary functions for the use of speeches in ancient historiography: they serve (a) to diversify the narrative, (b) to increase the immediacy of a character's presentation, and (c) as a means of emphasis.[47] Beyond this, speeches fulfil a number of different functions in the various attested forms of ancient historiography:

> speeches prepare an action, lead over to it, interrupt it and dramatically emphasize the tension. While some are causative, mark the change from calm to action, are usually at the beginning of the chain of action and prepare and motivate it mentally, others are explicative, [...] illuminate, explain and comment indirectly on a situation described in the narrative of the narrator. Above all, longer speeches, antilogies and conversations, [...] serve to give patterns of interpretation and indirectly control reception [...]'.[48]

They also mediate between the past and the present.[49]

It has been repeatedly stated that the Johannine discourses are closely linked to the narrative sections of the gospel; the significance of the narrated incidents is drawn out and interpreted in the discourses, or the truths enunciated in the discourses are given dramatic expression in the actions described in the narrative sections.[50]

---

[45] See Alicia D. Myers, 'Prosopopoetics and Conflict: Speech and Expectations in John 8', *Biblica* 92 (2011), esp. 581–83, with references to ancient sources; cf. also John Marincola, 'Speeches in Classical Historiography', in *A Companion to Greek and Roman Historiography*, ed. John Marincola (Oxford: Blackwell, 2007), 118–32.

[46] See Keener, *Gospel of John*, 54: 'Sayings of famous teachers were memorized and circulated, and often gathered into collections. Whole speeches, however, were usually preserved only in their general sense, hence redeveloped by historical writers according to basic rules of rhetorical and historical verisimilitude. Speeches could have a historical kernel, and John could have developed such a kernel, based on sayings, controversy-dialogues, or eyewitness notes or memories, without violating its basic sense'. Cf. also Dennis Pausch, *Stimmen der Geschichte: Funktionen von Reden in der antiken Historiographie* (Berlin: de Gruyter, 2010), 1; and Armin D. Baum, 'Zu Funktion und Authentizitätsanspruch der *oratio recta* Hebräische und griechische Geschichtsschreibung im Vergleich', *ZAW* 115 (2003), esp. 598–606; cf. also Becker, *Birth of History*, 98–101.

[47] I:22; cf. Christoph G. Müller, 'Διήγησις nach Lukas: Zwischen historiographischem Anspruch und biographischem Erzählen', in *Historiographie und Biographie im Neuen Testament und seiner* Umwelt, ed. Thomas Schmeller (NTOA/StUNT, 69; Göttingen: Vandenhoeck & Ruprecht, 2009), 114.

[48] Scardino, *Gestaltung und Funktion der Reden*, esp. 717–42 (quotation from p. 718).

[49] Cf. Marincola, 'Speeches in Classical Historiography', 130–32.

[50] C. H. Dodd, *The Interpretation of the Fourth Gospel* (Cambridge: Cambridge University Press, 1953), 384.

The Johannine discourses function as a theological explanation of the narrated events and actions, especially at key points of the narrative. This means that 'Jesus' words are foundational for the literary and theological purposes of the Gospel of John',[51] in that 'the spoken words function as the main vehicle for communicating the author's point of view'.[52] The same applies to the Gospel of Mark, in that, for example, the apocalyptic speech in Mark 13 is situated at a central turning point in the narrative and serves to explain and justify Jesus' preceding teaching and actions. Thus, the two speeches in Mark 4 and 13 'allow the reader a pause in the otherwise rapid pace of the narrative to think through the implications of the story so far, and provide a theological framework for understanding the new thing that is happening with the coming of Jesus of Nazareth'.[53] But the speeches in Mark and John do not explain and interpret historical situations and developments in the same way as the speeches of great statesmen in ancient historiography. Rather they provide the main character, Jesus, with a platform to address directly the recipients of the gospels through speeches that convey the content of his teaching and disclose his role and mission.[54] In this way, the speeches serve to dramatize the narration of Jesus' life; they contribute to the characterization of the main character, Jesus, and bring the narrative to life. The speeches also create immediacy, because they reach over metaleptically into the world of the recipients of the text: the direct speech of the discourses is not only directed text-internally but also at the text-external addressees. Thus, for example, the dialogical discourse in John 3 explicitly turns to the reader. Nicodemus is presented as Jesus' interlocutor and as διδάσκαλος τοῦ Ἰσραὴλ (v. 10) who is addressed in the second person singular. In v. 11 however, Jesus' response switches to the second person plural. If this tension is to be resolved on the intradiegetic level, it might indicate the contrast between the implied group of Israel's teachers and the Jesus group. If one interprets this passage as a narrative metalepsis, the reader becomes directly involved in the conversation between Jesus and Nicodemus through its grammatical form of address. Thus, the speeches in Mark and John are oriented towards the use and function of speeches in ancient historiographical writings; within the gospel narrative they serve to enrich the historical account and to make the presentation believable and persuasive to the audience.

Mark and John – Is there a relation?

The speech-compositions in John's Gospel exhibit substantial differences in terms of their language, style and narrative mode when compared with the speeches found in Mark's Gospel. This may be due to John's individual literary skill and intention, the differences in the ways both authors worked with their pretexts and traditions, the

---

[51] Bartholomä, *Johannine Discourses*, 3.
[52] Kierspel, *The Jews and the World*, 138.
[53] France, *Gospel of Mark*, 15.
[54] Cf., e.g., George L. Parsenios, *Departure and Consolation: The Johannine Farewell Discourses in Light of Greco-Roman Literature* (NT.S, 117; Leiden: Brill, 2005), esp. 142–49 and 153–54.

further development of the gospel genre, or even because of the characteristic presentation of the main characters' speeches in each gospel narrative.

Literary dependence cannot be corroborated for the speeches in Mark and John, and, as a result, the Markan speeches cannot be considered as sources used by John. From a historical perspective, however, it seems unlikely that John's Gospel can be read as wholly independent from Mark's Gospel. John knew and used Synoptic tradition, and it is unlikely that two authors invented the same 'gospel' genre independently of each other; it is therefore just as unlikely that both invented similar speech forms, together with their application and function, from within that genre. If we assume that Mark, as the earlier text, invented the 'gospel' genre and that John chose a similar literary form for his depiction of the Jesus story, then we can also posit that John knew or was influenced by Mark's Gospel and its use of speeches, or even regarded Mark's genre as a basic template – either through direct knowledge or through knowledge of Mark's reception in other early Christian gospels.

By reading Mark and John in the context of ancient historiographical works, it is noteworthy that John does not (explicitly or implicitly) indicate that his presentation is designed to replace previous works or that it offers a version of events surpassing its predecessors, at least not with a view to previous gospels.[55] John does not replace earlier Markan or Synoptic tradition; he does not even directly refer to it. John rather presupposes early Christian gospel tradition, in whatever form it was transmitted and received by him.

---

[55] That John's Gospel claims to substitute the Scriptures – in that it considers itself to be the fulfillment of Scripture or even presents itself as the new Scripture – will have to be considered in a different context; see Luther, *Authentifizierung der Vergangenheit,* chapter 6; cf. also Reinhartz, 'And The Word Was God', 89, who, on the basis of passages like Jn 17.17 and 14.6, interprets Jesus as 'God's Word, and God's Truth', and that, as such, 'Jesus embodies the divine essence and is empowered to act in the world not merely as God's spokesman or representative, but, fundamentally, as God himself'; thus 'the Gospel itself [...] is the means through which the Gospel's audience – its hearers – hear the voice of the Son of God, and in so doing, attain eternal life' (p. 90).

16

The Lost Temptation of Christ?
John's Philosophical Rewriting of
Markan Temptation Scenes

Kasper Bro Larsen

Introduction[1]

One of the never-ending subjects of debate in Johannine scholarship is still an open question: was the author behind the Gospel of John an originator and exponent of independent traditions about Jesus, or rather a creative and critical re-writer of the Synoptic Gospels, in particular Mark's Gospel and Markan traditions? Is the Fourth Gospel, in other words, the fourth Synoptic Gospel?[2] One of the stronger indications in favour of John's dependence on Mark is John's creative use of Synoptic and specifically Markan material from Jesus' temptation prayer at Gethsemane (Mk 4.32–42; cf. Mt. 26.36–46; Lk. 22.39–46). However, whereas Mark presents Jesus in doubt and temptation, asking the Father to take the cup of suffering away from him, the Johannine Jesus reaches out for the cup: '... it is for this reason that I have come to this hour. Father, glorify your name' (Jn 12.28, NRSV; see also v. 27). The Johannine emphasis on Jesus' dismissal of temptation is one of many unique features in John that transform the Markan passion narrative into something that we might call an 'action narrative': that is, a passion narrative in which Jesus is emphatically active and takes the initiative.[3]

---

[1] This chapter was presented to the 'Gospel of John and the Synoptics' session co-organized by the Synoptic Gospels Section and the Johannine Literature Section at the Society of Biblical Literature Annual Meeting, San Diego, 24 November 2019. The author wishes to thank the two respondents, Professors Jennifer Knust and Sherri Brown, for constructive comments and discussion.

[2] For reviews of research, see, for example, D. Moody Smith, *John Among the Gospels: The Relationship in Twentieth-Century Research* (Minneapolis, MN: Fortress, 1992); Ismo Dunderberg, *Johannes und die Synoptiker: Studien zu Joh 1–9* (AASF. Dissertationes Humanarum Litterarum, 69; Helsinki: Suomalainen Tiedeakatemia, 1994); and Harold W. Attridge, 'John and Other Gospels', in *The Oxford Handbook of Johannine Studies*, ed. Judith M. Lieu and Martinus C. de Boer (Oxford: Oxford University Press, 2018), 44–62.

[3] To mention some well-known examples, the Johannine Jesus directly prompts Judas to action (13.27) and surrenders himself to the soldiers, thus pre-empting the kiss of Judas (18.4–8). In custody, Jesus' attitude is generally not one of silence, but he addresses authorities like Annas and Pilate with still greater authority than before (18.13–19.25a). He carries the cross by himself, without the assistance of Simon of Cyrene (19.17), and when the soldiers give him sour wine to drink, they

John's transformation of the passion narrative into an action narrative has been explained in various ways in scholarship, for example as an expression of John's 'high' Christology,[4] as docetic Christology in embryonic form,[5] as a consequence of Jesus' omniscience in the gospel narrative,[6] as a generic break from Synoptic narrative gospel writing in the direction of didactic and discursive gospel writing,[7] as an expression of Jesus' messianic royal determination and sovereignty,[8] and as a masculinized image of Jesus according to ancient gender stereotypes.[9]

It is the purpose of the present chapter to contribute to this discussion of John's action narrative by analysing how John rewrites the Markan temptation scenes. As already mentioned, John is highly critical of the idea that Jesus is subject to serious temptation, and his criticism appears in the form of revisions of previous Jesus tradition. It is my assertion that these revisions were something that ancient readerships would have recognized as philosophical revisions. In Greco-Roman philosophical tradition from Socrates onward, not least in the Stoic tradition, which was highly influential in the first century CE, there was wide agreement that the philosophical sage should act with initiative and steadfastness in times of trial when adversity was to challenge the ideal and virtuous way of life. Unlike the fool, who carries different masks and changes his mind, the philosophical sage has one determined persona. As Seneca phrased it:

> Everyone changes his plans and prayers day by day ... That is how a foolish mind is most clearly demonstrated: it shows first in this shape and then in that, and is never like itself – which is, in my opinion, the most shameful of qualities. Believe me, it is a great role – to play the role of one man. But nobody can be one person except the wise man; the rest of us often shift our masks.
>
> Seneca, *Ep.* 120.21–22 [Gummere, LCL]

---

do so at Jesus' own request, thereby staging the fulfillment of scripture (19.28). Finally, Jesus dies in triumph and without despair: 'It is finished' (19.30).

[4] Jörg Frey, *Theology and History in the Fourth Gospel: Tradition and Narration* (Waco, TX: Baylor University Press, 2018), 56–58.

[5] Ernst Käsemann, *Jesu letzter Wille nach Johannes 17* (2nd unrevised edn; Tübingen: Mohr Siebeck, 1967), 51–52.

[6] R. Alan Culpepper, *Anatomy of the Fourth Gospel: A Study in Literary Design* (Philadelphia, PA: Fortress, 1983), 106–12; Kasper Bro Larsen, 'Narrative Docetism: Christology and Storytelling in the Gospel of John', in *The Gospel of John and Christian Theology*, ed. Richard Bauckham and Carl Mosser (Grand Rapids, MI: Wm B. Eerdmans, 2007), 346–55.

[7] William Wrede, *Charakter und Tendenz des Johannesevangeliums* (Tübingen: Mohr, 1903), 5; Anders Klostergaard Petersen, 'Generic Docetism: From the Synoptic Narrative Gospels to the Johannine Discursive Gospel', in *The Gospel of John as Genre Mosaic*, ed. Kasper Bro Larsen (SANt, 3; Göttingen: Vandenhoeck & Ruprecht, 2015), 99–124.

[8] Manfred Lang, *Johannes und die Synoptiker: Eine redaktionsgeschichtliche Analyse von Joh 18–20 vor dem markinischen und lukanischen Hintergrund* (FRLANT, 182; Göttingen: Vandenhoeck & Ruprecht, 1999), 318–21; Frey, *Theology and History*, 195.

[9] Colleen M. Conway, '"Behold the Man!" Masculine Christology and the Fourth Gospel', in *New Testament Masculinities*, ed. Stephen D. Moore and Janice Capel Anderson (Atlanta, GA: Society of Biblical Literature, 2003), 163–80; Colleen M. Conway, *Behold the Man: Jesus and Greco-Roman Masculinity* (Oxford: Oxford University Press, 2008), 143–57; Karl Olav Sandnes, *Early Christian Discourses on Jesus' Prayer at Gethsemane: Courageous, Committed, Cowardly?* (NovTSup, 166; Brill: Leiden, 2016), 173–96.

In this intellectual context, Jesus' tribulations in Mark might appear quite unphilosophical. As a matter of fact, Celsus, the second-century philosopher and critic of early Christianity, gave voice to philosophical criticism of the Markan Jesus in temptation: 'Why does he mourn, and lament, and pray to escape the fear of death, expressing himself in terms like these: "O Father, if it be possible, let this cup pass from me?"' (Origen, *Cels.* 2.24 [*ANF* 4.441]; see also 2.9, 38, 47; cf. 10.3, 10).[10] The Letter to the Hebrews, one of the most philosophical texts in the New Testament, stresses that Jesus, even though he was tested by God, did not fail: 'For we do not have a high priest who is unable to sympathize with our weaknesses, but we have one who in every respect has been tested (πεπειρασμένον) as we are, yet without sin' (Heb. 4.15; see 2.18; 5.7). Similar philosophical considerations regarding Jesus in temptation may lie behind John's rewriting of the Markan temptation scenes, as I rather loosely term the narratival episodes in which Jesus' true will is put to the test. After all, the Gospel of John invites a philosophical reading from the very beginning in introducing Jesus as the eternal λόγος (1.1, 14) and quickly establishing philosophical concepts like πίστις (1.7, 12) and ἀλήθεια (1.14, 17) as main subjects. Though I neither find evidence that John had read the ancient philosophical canon nor detect use of a very specific, technical philosophical vocabulary in John, his portrayal of Jesus depicts him in the likeness of the philosophical sage of the Greco-Roman world – just as, for example, Philo and Josephus' rewritten portrayals of Moses.[11]

Temptation scenes in the Gospel of Mark

In order to ascertain John's rewriting of Markan temptation stories, it is necessary first to recall how Jesus' temptations are framed in Mark. Mark portrays Jesus as God's chosen but elusive Son who is walking and teaching the 'way of the Lord', i.e., a way of life that is according to the will of God even if it is to lead to opposition and suffering (1.3; see 8.27; 9.33–34; 10.52; 12.14; Mal. 3.1; Isa. 40.3). An important plot catalyst in Mark is the question whether or not Jesus really wishes to succumb to the will of God. Does he accept his task of walking in the way of the Lord? Jesus, in other words, is subject to so-called 'tests of volition': does he want to do what he has to do?[12] Such temptations, testings and trials of the main character's true will and sentiment – the ancient Greek πειρασμός covers all three meanings – are common in ancient narrative. One type of narrative situates the test of volition at the beginning of the story. That is the case, for example, in the call narratives of the Hebrew Bible (e.g., Gen. 12.1–5; Exod.

---

[10] For later examples of philosophical criticism of Jesus in temptation, see Sandnes, *Early Christian Discourses*, 63–97.
[11] George van Kooten has argued that John was acquainted especially with the Platonic dialogues. See, for example, George van Kooten, 'The Last Days of Socrates and Christ: *Euthyphro, Apology, Crito,* and *Phaedo* Read in Counterpoint with John's Gospel', in *Religio-Philosophical Discourses in the Mediterranean World: From Plato, through Jesus, to Late Antiquity,* ed. Anders Klostergaard Petersen and George van Kooten (Ancient Philosophy & Religion, 1; Leiden: Brill, 2017), 219–43.
[12] Regarding 'tests of volition' in narratology, see Claude Bremond, *Logique du récit* (Poétique; Paris: Seuil, 1973), 176–206; Ole Davidsen, *The Narrative Jesus: A Semiotic Reading of Mark's Gospel* (Aarhus: Aarhus University Press, 1993), 280–82, 286–87.

3.4; 1 Sam. 3; Isa. 6), where the main characters rather quickly accept the task (once the conventional hindrance motif is overcome) so that they can move into action. In other types of narrative, the main character's motivation is under negotiation during large parts of the story, with the consequence that the reader does not know whether or not the hero will actually accept and perform his task. In Homer's *Iliad*, for example, suspense builds on the question whether or not Achilles will take action and join in the fight against the Trojans.

Mark's Gospel takes the latter approach. As in the *Iliad*, the story contains a whole series of tests of volition or scenes of temptation.[13] Six scenes seem to stand out as tests of volition. The first of these, often simply described as 'The Temptation of Jesus' (see NRSV), is Satan's test of Jesus in the wilderness in 1.12-13 (see 1.13: πειραζόμενος ὑπὸ τοῦ σατανᾶ). The text does not directly say so, but since Jesus in the preceding baptism has just received his calling as the Son of God (1.9-11), the trial concerns Jesus' adherence to that calling. In passing that test, he confirms his willingness to act according to God's will as the Son of God. The second test appears already in 1.35-45 where Jesus' popularity as a healer and exorcist among the crowds becomes a temptation that challenges his mission. But Jesus once again resists temptation: 'Let us go on to the neighbouring towns, so that I may proclaim the message there also; for that is what I came out to do' (1.38). The third test of volition is staged by Jesus' family. In 3.20-35, right after Jesus' declaration of the twelve disciples as his new spiritual family (3.13-19), his natural family arrives at his home. They believe him to have gone mad and want to restrain him (3.20-21, 31-32). But Jesus answers, 'Who are my mother and my brothers? ... Whoever does the will of God (τὸ θέλημα τοῦ θεοῦ) is my brother and sister and mother' (3.33-35). The fourth test is an important turning point in the story, where Jesus begins to teach that the way of the Lord leads past suffering and rejection in Jerusalem (8.27-10.45). Peter rebukes Jesus and counters his understanding of God's will (see 8.31: δεῖ), but once again Jesus resists the temptation and rebukes Peter in return: 'Get behind me, Satan! For you are setting your mind not on divine things but on human things' (8.33). Mark's fifth temptation scene, in which Jesus is portrayed as seriously in doubt, takes place in Gethsemane (14.32-42) – I shall return to that below – and the final temptation is on the cross. The passers-by, along with the Jewish authorities, mock Jesus by saying: 'He saved others; he cannot save himself. Let the Messiah, the King of Israel, come down from the cross now, so that we may see and believe' (15.31-32). But Jesus does not divert from the way of the Lord and gives his life 'as a ransom for many' (10.45).[14]

It could be argued that the above tests of Jesus' will represent no more than a conventional hindrance motif in Mark and that they fall short of seriously challenging

---

[13] Susan R. Garrett, *The Temptations of Jesus in Mark's Gospel* (Grand Rapids, MI: Wm B. Eerdmans, 1998).

[14] Beyond these six tests of volition or temptation scenes, temptation and trial also appears as a recurrent motif in Mark, for example when the Pharisees put Jesus' knowledge of God's will to the test by challenging his understanding of the Torah. Mark explicitly speaks of πειρασμός in some of these disputes. They ask him for a sign from heaven in order to test him (πειράζοντες αὐτόν; 8.11), but Jesus refuses. They test him regarding his view on the divorce regulations of the Torah (10.2: πειράζοντες αὐτόν) and on paying taxes to the emperor (12.15: τί με πειράζετε).

the will of Jesus. However, Jesus' petition in the Gethsemane scene (14.36: 'remove this cup from me') implies that in Mark the will of Jesus, the suffering Messiah, is an agonistic battle zone. True, the Markan temptation scenes emphasize that Jesus wins his inner battles, but the *ultima verba* of Jesus on the cross are famously ambiguous (15.34: 'My God, my God, why have you forsaken me?'). The words hardly indicate that Jesus has given in to temptation and is tragically denouncing the way of the Lord. Rather, it is the prayer of the righteous sufferer (Ps. 22). But the ambiguity evidently gave rise to discomfort in later tradition, because the evangelist Luke significantly redacted Mark's Gethsemane scene and *ultima verba*, rendering the passion narrative less open to philosophical criticism.[15] After all, as Socrates famously said, true philosophers lead a life in training for dying: 'Would it not be very foolish if they should be frightened and troubled when this very thing happens ... ?' (Plato, *Phaed*. 67e [Fowler, LCL]; see also, for example, Cicero, *Tusc*. 1.74; Epictetus, *Diatr*. 3.26; 4.7.3–4; Philo, *Prob*. 111).[16]

The Socratic philosopher in temptation

How should the wise act in times of temptation? The question had been a frequently occurring *topos* in ancient philosophy ever since the noble death of Socrates as described by Plato and Xenophon (Plato, *Euthyphro*; *Apology*; *Crito*; *Phaedo*; Xenophon, *Apology*; *Memorabilia* 1.1.1–1.2.64). For his unwavering steadfastness, Socrates became a symbol of the ideal philosopher, one who practiced his own teaching unto death. Socrates was depicted as an example and role model for the truly wise man to emulate; and this image of Socrates was carried into the first century CE by authors like Seneca, Epictetus and Dio Chrysostom: 'If, however, you desire a pattern (*exemplum*), take Socrates' (Seneca, *Ep*. 104.27 [Gummere, LCL]).[17] Socrates' ability to resist temptation in the midst of turmoil was, even in the Platonic dialogues, an important aspect of his virtue. In the *Apology*, Socrates refuses to give up philosophizing (*Apol*. 29d) or to be

---

[15] Greg Sterling, '*Mors philosophi*: The Death of Jesus in Luke', *HTR* 94 (2001): 383–402. For Matthew's redaction of Mark's Gethsemane scene in light of the *aqedah*, see Leroy A. Huizenga, 'Obedience unto Death: The Matthean Gethsemane and Arrest Sequence and the Aqedah', *CBQ* 71 (2009): 507–26; Leroy A. Huizenga, *The New Isaac: Tradition and Intertextuality in the Gospel of Matthew* (NovTSup, 131; Brill: Leiden, 2009), 237–62. See also Sandnes, *Early Christian Discourses*, on the Gethsemane scene and its reception in early Christianity.

[16] For discussions of possible philosophical or anti-philosophical traits in Mark's depiction of the death of Jesus, see Adela Yarbro Collins, 'From Noble Death to Crucified Messiah', *NTS* 40 (1994): 481–503; and Runar M. Thorsteinsson, *Jesus as Philosopher: The Moral Sage in the Synoptic Gospels* (Oxford: Oxford University Press, 2018), 33–71; on the same topic in the Gospel of John, see Jerome H. Neyrey, 'The "Noble Shepherd" in John 10: Cultural and Rhetorical Background', *JBL* 120 (2001): 267–91; and Jörg Frey, 'Edler Tod – wirksamer Tod – stellvertretender Tod – heilvoller Tod: Zur narrativen und theologischen Deutung des Todes Jesu im Johannesevangelium', in Jörg Frey, *Die Herrlichkeit des Gekreuzigten: Studien zu den Johanneischen Schriften I*, ed. Juliane Schlegel (WUNT, 307; Tübingen: Mohr Siebeck, 2013), 561–66.

[17] Klaus Döring, *Exemplum Socratis: Studien zur Sokratesnachwirkung in der kynisch-stoischen Popularphilosophie der frühen Kaiserzeit und im frühen Christentum* (Hermes Einzelschriften, 42; Wiesbaden: Steiner, 1979); Paul A. Vander Waerdt (ed.), *The Socratic Movement* (Ithaca: Cornell University Press, 1994).

enticed by other people's pity (34b-d), his family (34d), or his own rhetorical skills (35d; 38d). In the end, Socrates is convinced that nothing can harm the morally good man, whether alive or dead (41d). The *Crito*, which takes place in Socrates' cell as he awaits his execution, is virtually one long temptation scene. Crito, Socrates' wealthy friend, tries to convince him to escape by appeal to their friendship, to Crito's reputation, to public opinion, and to the future fate of Socrates' sons. Once again, however, Socrates is immune to temptation, seeing escape as betrayal of his message (Plato, *Crito* 44b-46a). Socrates concludes by confirming his divine mission: 'In that case, Crito, let it be, and let's do it this way since this is the way the god is guiding me' (54e [Emlyn-Jones, LCL]). In first-century receptions of Socrates, this determined attitude in the hour of temptation is equally emphasized:

> But all these measures [i.e., for example, the charges, the imprisonment, and the cup of poison] changed the soul of Socrates so little that they did not even change his features. What wonderful and rare distinction! He maintained this attitude up to the very end, and no man ever saw Socrates too much elated or too much depressed. Amid all the disturbance of Fortune, he was undisturbed (*aequalis*).
>
> Seneca, *Ep.* 104.28 [Gummere]; see also, for example, 24.4; 70.8-9; Epictetus, *Diatr.* 4.1.160-66; 4.7.30-32

In Jewish tradition also, the example of Socrates came to play a role. Temptation and testing had of course already been an important theme in the Jewish Scriptures, for example in the Garden of Eden myth (Gen. 3), in the story of Abraham's binding of Isaac (Gen. 22), and in the narrative of Israel's journey through the wilderness (for example, Num. 11.1-9, 31-35). But in Jewish literature from the Greco-Roman period, Socrates surfaces, in the sense that Jewish heroes were portrayed with philosophical traits: steadfast in temptation, masters of their passions and true to their 'philosophical' way of life. Maccabean martyrs like Eleazar (2 Macc. 6.18-31) and the seven brothers with their mother (2 Macc. 7) were cast in this role.[18] Like Socrates, Eleazar is tempted by his friends to save himself (2 Macc. 6.21-23; see also the temptation in 7.24); and like Socrates, Eleazar refuses, and becomes an example to others by actively pursuing martyrdom: '"Therefore, by bravely giving up my life now, I will show myself worthy of my old age and leave to the young a noble example (ὑπόδειγμα) of how to die a good death willingly (προθύμως) and nobly for the revered and holy laws". When he had said this, he went at once (εὐθέως) to the rack' (2 Macc. 6.27-28; see ὑπόδειγμα in Jn 13.15). Philo and Josephus depict Moses, as well as other characters from scripture, in similar fashion (see below). And later, in the first or second century CE, the author of *4 Maccabees* rewrites the story of the Maccabean martyrs in order to further demonstrate how reason taught by Torah conquers the passions (*4 Macc.* 1.1-19). According to these philosophically inspired accounts, the hero fights temptation actively, acts independently, speaks the

---

[18] Tessa Rajak, 'Dying for the Law: The Martyr's Portrait in Jewish-Greek Literature', in *Portraits: Biographical Representation in the Greek and Latin Literature of the Roman Empire*, ed. M. J. Edwards and Simon Swain (Oxford: Clarendon Press, 1997), 39-67; Jan Willem van Henten, *The Maccabean Martyrs as Saviours of the Jewish People: A Study of 2 and 4 Maccabees* (JSJSupp, 57; Leiden: Brill, 1997), 270-94.

truth openly, lives according to his teachings, consoles his followers, becomes an example to others, and curbs his passions – much like the Johannine Jesus in temptation.

Johannine rewriting of Markan temptation scenes: Omission, reuse, invention

It is striking as we turn to the Gospel of John – not least if John knew Mark's Gospel – how John has toned down Mark's emphasis on temptation scenes as a narratival dynamo. John, for example, omits the significant temptations in the wilderness, at Caesarea Philippi, in Gethsemane and on the cross. Mark's language of πειρασμός has almost disappeared in John, who refrains from describing the Jewish authorities' challenge of Jesus as 'testing'.[19] Whereas the temptations staged in Mark become increasingly dramatic, they are undramatic in John. Real temptation implies that the will of the one tempted is fractured, as with Mark's Jesus in Gethsemane, but in John, Jesus' will is in sync with God's. This is repeatedly expressed by Jesus: 'I can do nothing on my own … because I seek to do not my own will (τὸ θέλημα τὸ ἐμὸν) but the will of him who sent me (τὸ θέλημα τοῦ πέμψαντός με)' (5.30) and '… for I have come down from heaven, not to do my own will (τὸ θέλημα τὸ ἐμὸν), but the will of him who sent me (τὸ θέλημα τοῦ πέμψαντός με)' (6.38; see also 4.34; 9.31; 17.4). In his diatribe *Of Freedom from Fear*, Epictetus' persona describes his philosophical self in a similar manner:

> Who is there, then, that I can any longer be afraid of? … For I regard God's will as better than my will (κρεῖττον γὰρ ἡγοῦμαι ὃ ὁ θεὸς θέλει ἢ ὃ ἐγώ). I shall attach myself to Him as a servant and follower, my choice is one with His (συνορμῶ), my desire one with His (συνορέγομαι), in a word, my will is one with His will (ἁπλῶς συνθέλω).
> Epictetus, *Diatr.* 4.7.19–20 [Oldfather, LCL]; see Plato, *Crito* 54e

The uniformity of the will of the philosopher and of God renders the true philosopher immune to temptation in a manner comparable to the Johannine Jesus. However, John does not simply omit all Markan temptation scenes. He reuses some of them and also presents new ones in order to demonstrate Jesus' fixity of purpose. In John 6–7, we may find echoes of Markan and Synoptic scenes with a temptation motif. The crowd attempts to make Jesus a worldly king (6.14–15; see also 11.12–19; Mk 11.10; Mt. 4.8–9/Lk. 4.5–7), and Jesus' family seeks to control his will, this time by trying to persuade him to go to Jerusalem (7.1–10; Mk 3.20–35).[20] The crowd and Jesus' brothers, however, have no power

---

[19] John employs πειρασμός language only in the context of the feeding of the five thousand in ch. 6, but there Jesus characteristically acts as the active tester and not as the one tested. Jesus asks Philip how to buy food for the people, but the narrator explains: 'He said this to test him (πειράζων αὐτόν), for he himself knew what he was going to do' (6.6).

[20] Raymond Brown has suggested that there are three Johannine temptation scenes in John 6–7, corresponding to Satan's three temptations of Jesus in the wilderness in Matthew's and Luke's double tradition (Mt. 4.11/Lk. 4.1–13). However, in my view the parallels are more or less indistinct; see Raymond E. Brown, 'John and the Synoptic Gospels: A Comparison', in *New Testament Essays* (Garden City, NY: Doubleday, 1965), 259–64.

over Jesus' will, and Pilate too is powerless. He tempts Jesus: 'Do you not know that I have power (ἐξουσίαν) to release you, and power (ἐξουσίαν) to crucify you?' (19.10) – a Johannine equivalent to the temptation at the cross in Mark – but Jesus answers that Pilate has no power over him except the power given him from above (19.11). Jesus sounds like a Stoic such as Epictetus: '... no one has authority over me (εἰς ἐμὲ οὐδεὶς ἐξουσίαν ἔχει). I have been set free by God, I know His commands, no one has power any longer to make a slave of me, I have the right kind of emancipator, and the right kind of judges' (*Diatr.* 4.7.17–18 [Oldfather, LCL]). Pilate tries to tempt Jesus to escape, and Mary Magdalene may perhaps do the same when she apparently seeks to hold on to Jesus' physical presence after his resurrection. But the Johannine Jesus is once again steadfast in the face of temptation (20.17). Jesus encounters some of the same challenges as Socrates – public authorities, the crowd, family, personal ties – but, in common with Socrates and the Stoics, the honour he seeks is not from humans, but from God (Jn 5.41; 6.13; 8.50, 54; 12.43; Plato, *Apol.* 35d; 39b; 40a–b; 41d; *Crito* 54e; Diogenes Laertius, *Vit. Phil.* 7.120).

Dramatizing the philosophical autonomy of the Logos

Jesus' strong adherence to God's will disengages him from human agendas just as, in an ancient philosophical context, the truly autonomous person is guided by divine reason (λόγος). Socrates follows the will of the gods (*Apol.* 30a; 33c; *Crito* 54e); and according to Stoic doctrine, true freedom can only be obtained by the sage who is guided by divine reason and thus lives according to nature (Epictetus, *Diatr.* 3.26.39; Diogenes Laertius, *Vit. Phil.* 7.121–22). Philo, in his Jewish appropriation of Stoic and Platonic notions, devotes a whole treatise to the subject (*Every Good Man is Free* [*Prob.*]) in which he defends the Stoic idea that moral excellence (and not external goods) is the only true good. The true philosopher retains independence even though other people seek to become his masters (*Prob.* 18–19): 'For in very truth he who has God alone for his leader, he alone is free' (20). And this freedom leads to independence of action (21: αὐτοπραγία; see also 109; Diogenes Laertius, *Vit. Phil.* 7.122). In 2 Maccabees, Eleazar embodies such an independence as he welcomes death by walking to the rack 'of his own accord' (6.19–20: αὐθαιρέτως; see 6.27–28). In John, Jesus acts with autonomy that is comparable to the ideal philosopher's. He gives his life freely: 'No one takes it from me, but I lay it down of my own accord. I have power to lay it down, and I have power to take it up again' (10.18: οὐδεὶς αἴρει αὐτὴν ἀπ' ἐμοῦ, ἀλλ' ἐγὼ τίθημι αὐτὴν ἀπ' ἐμαυτοῦ. ἐξουσίαν ἔχω θεῖναι αὐτήν, καὶ ἐξουσίαν ἔχω πάλιν λαβεῖν αὐτήν). Jesus, in other words, is in ἐξουσία (power) over his life/soul (10.17: ψυχή) – something that the philosophical tradition since Socrates and Plato had called ἐγκράτεια (self-control, literally: empowerment or mastery [of the soul]).

This divine autonomy of Jesus is illustratively dramatized in three scenes that can be regarded as temptation scenes in the sense previously described. In all three scenes, John once again puts Jesus' steadfastness on display. First, at the wedding in Cana, Jesus' first public and programmatic act, Jesus' mother discloses that the wine has run out, presumably wishing him to take action. But Jesus answers: 'Woman, what concern is that to you and to me? My hour has not yet come' (2.4: τί ἐμοὶ καὶ σοί, γύναι; οὔπω ἥκει ἡ ὥρα μου). The peculiar Semitism, τί ἐμοὶ καὶ σοί, γύναι, is perhaps better translated as, 'Woman, what do we have in common?'.[21] If so, Jesus is distancing himself from the mother's attempt to nudge him into taking action and thus obeying mundane agendas. However, his imperative is to follow divine timing ('my hour'). The fact that Jesus in the following verses does supply new wine, on the face of it obeying his mother's wish, may seem a self-contradiction, but the delay of Jesus' action shows that he acts on his own divine initiative (see 10.18: 'on my own accord') without following a human schedule. The second temptation scene is the already mentioned occasion in 7.1–10, when Jesus' brothers encourage him to leave Galilee and go to Judea to reveal himself to the world. Jesus once again declines, stating that his hour has not yet come (7.6–8); nevertheless, he goes to Jerusalem secretly when the brothers have left (7.10). The third scene leads to the raising of Lazarus. Jesus receives an ominous message from the sisters: 'Lord, he whom you love is ill' (11.3). The message implies that Jesus should react (see 11.21), but he hesitates. Two days later, however, he does embark on a journey to Bethany: 'Let us go to Judea again' (11.7). The same pattern is dramatized in these three temptation scenes: (1) human characters attempt to take the initiative, (2) Jesus rejects it but (3) takes action on his own initiative.[22] Like the philosophical sage, Jesus does not react, but acts autonomously – just as his passion narrative is an action narrative. The sage does not fear human requests or orders. As Philo says: 'Naturally too in matters indifferent he does not act under compulsion.... Whence it is clear that he does nothing unwillingly and is never compelled, whereas if he were a slave he would be compelled, and therefore the good man will be a free man' (*Prob.* 61; see 154). The sage follows the will of God, and is thus free from and superior to external temptation. His autonomy is determined by λόγος (Plato, *Crito* 46b; Philo, *Prob.* 25, 46), just as the Johannine Jesus is himself the λόγος.

John's dispersion and inversion of the temptation scene in Gethsemane

Let us now turn to the Markan temptation scene that was briefly mentioned in the introduction. The Johannine allusions to the temptation scene in Gethsemane constitute some of the best arguments in favour of Johannine dependence on Mark, and they illustrate Jesus' philosophical determination of will. Whereas Matthew and Luke both rewrite this scene so as to modify it, John's mode of rewriting is more complex. He omits the actual temptation prayer but alludes to it in two sayings by Jesus that are dispersed in John's narrative. As has often been noticed by scholars, these allusions to Mark seem highly critical of Mark's portrayal of Jesus as a character subject to temptation, doubt, and irresolution vis-à-vis his divine mission.[23] In

---

[21] Athur H. Maynard, 'ΤΙ ΕΜΟΙ ΚΑΙ ΣΟΙ', *NTS* 31 (1985): 582–86.
[22] The pattern may also be implied in 4.47–53 and 11.53–54; see Charles H. Giblin, 'Suggestion, Negative Response, and Positive Action in St John's Portrayal of Jesus (John 2.1–11; 4.46–50; 7.2–14; 11.1–44)', *NTS* 26 (1980): 197–211.
[23] See, for example, Brown, 'John and the Synoptic Gospels'; and Jörg Frey, *Theology and History*, 64–77.

Mark, Jesus theatrically throws himself on the ground in deep grief and prays that '...if it were possible, the hour might pass from him (ἵνα εἰ δυνατόν ἐστιν παρέλθῃ ἀπ' αὐτοῦ ἡ ὥρα)' (14.35). He wishes that his suffering may pass him by: 'Abba, Father, for you all things are possible; remove this cup from me (παρένεγκε τὸ ποτήριον τοῦτο ἀπ' ἐμοῦ); yet, not what I want, but what you want' (Mk 14.36; see also Matt. 26.39; Lk. 22.42). The Markan Jesus is obviously in unphilosophical despair and anguish. In the *Apology*, Socrates frowns upon such a beseeching attitude in the face of temptation:

> But perhaps one or other of you may be annoyed on calling to mind his own situation, if, in defending a less important case than this one, he begged and implored the jurors with many tears (τοῦ ἀγῶνος ἀγῶνα ἀγωνιζόμενος ἐδεήθη τε καὶ ἱκέτευσε τοὺς δικαστὰς μετὰ πολλῶν δακρύων), and brought forward his children to arouse the maximum sympathy as well as many other members of his family and friends. But I shall do none of these things even though, as it might seem, I'm running the ultimate risk (ἐγὼ δὲ οὐδὲν ἄρα τούτων ποιήσω, καὶ ταῦτα κινδυνεύων, ὡς ἂν δόξαιμι, τὸν ἔσχατον κίνδυνον).
>
> *Apol.* 34c [Emlyn-Jones]; see 35c; 38e

The Johannine Jesus certainly approaches his death with more Socratic confidence than Mark. Accordingly, John's first allusion to the Gethsemane prayer contains a retraction of the above-mentioned Markan 'hour' petition. The allusion appears in the dialogue that follows Jesus' triumphal entry to Jerusalem, when the Greeks seek him: 'Now my soul is troubled. And what should I say – "Father, save me from this hour (πάτερ, σῶσόν με ἐκ τῆς ὥρας ταύτης)?" No, it is for this reason that I have come to this hour (ἀλλὰ διὰ τοῦτο ἦλθον εἰς τὴν ὥραν ταύτην). Father, glorify your name' (Jn 12.27-28; see also 12.23; 13.1; 17.1; 18.11). John's Jesus reuses and rejects the 'hour' petition, which is specifically Markan, since neither Matthew nor Luke present it in their versions of the temptation prayer (Mk 14.35; yet, in a different context, see ὥρα in Mt. 26.45; Lk. 22.53). John here seems to be critically rewriting Mark. In John, Jesus refuses to pray a temptation prayer and replaces it with a glorification prayer, thus announcing the hour of his passion with a call for action: 'Father, glorify your name'.

John's second allusion to Mark's Gethsemane prayer once again alludes to and rejects it. This time the inversion concerns the 'cup' petition in Mark (14.36: 'remove this cup from me'). When the Johannine Jesus surrenders himself to the soldiers and Peter cuts off the ear of the High Priest's slave, he reproaches Peter and explains why he needs to drink the 'cup': 'Put your sword back into its sheath. Am I not to drink the cup that the Father has given me (τὸ ποτήριον ὃ δέδωκέν μοι ὁ πατήρ)?' (Jn 18.11). The Johannine Jesus does not call the 'cup' of his suffering into question. In both of these Johannine allusions to Mark's Gethsemane prayer, Jesus' determinacy conforms with philosophical ideals: 'Thus no fortune, no external circumstance, can shut off the wise man from action. For the very thing which engages his attention prevents him from attending to other things.... Hence neither poverty, nor pain, nor anything else that deflects the inexperienced and drives them headlong, restrains him from his course' (Seneca, *Ep.* 85.38-39 [Gummere, LCL]).[24]

'My soul is troubled': Cracks in the philosophical picture?

In broad strands of Greco-Roman philosophical tradition, not least among the Stoics, mastery over the passions was seen as one of the hallmarks of the wise sage. As already mentioned, in this intellectual context the Markan Jesus in Gethsemane may appear unphilosophical. John clearly takes Jesus in a more philosophical direction, but there are limits to the tendency. On the one hand, as we have seen, the Johannine Jesus is indeed not seriously affected by temptation. And John has deleted Synoptic (and Pauline) passion language regarding Jesus' suffering. So when Jesus predicts his death, it is not as suffering (verb., πάσχω; Mk 8.31; 9.12; Mt. 16.21; 17.12; Lk. 9.22; 17.25; 22.15; 24.26, 46), but as uplifting (verb., ὑψόω) and glorification (verb., δοξάζω). So far, Jesus may be said to embody the Stoic ideal of ἀπάθεια. But on the other hand, the Johannine Jesus is a man of emotions. The disciples interpret his action in the temple with a citation from scripture: 'Zeal (ὁ ζῆλος) for your house will consume me' (2.17; see Ps. 69.10). Jesus loves Lazarus and his sisters (11.3, 5, 36), the beloved disciple (13.23; 19.26; 20.2; 21.7, 20), and 'his own' (13.1; 15.9, 13), just as God loves the world, his Son, and 'his own' (3.16; 14.23; 17.23) and shows wrath to the disobedient (3.36). Jesus becomes deeply indignant and weeps at Lazarus' death: 'When Jesus saw her weeping, and the Jews who came with her also weeping, he was greatly disturbed in spirit and deeply moved (ἐνεβριμήσατο τῷ πνεύματι καὶ ἐτάραξεν ἑαυτὸν) ... Jesus began to weep (ἐδάκρυσεν)' (11.33-35; see 11.38).

Regarding temptation in John, it is also important that Jesus, in spite of his clear rejection of the Markan temptation prayer in Gethsemane, is in fact moved: 'Now my soul is troubled (ἡ ψυχή μου τετάρακται)' (Jn 12.27; see 11.33; 13.21; 14.1, 27). This description of Jesus stands in contrast to the tranquil image of the ideal philosopher whose soul remains undisturbed (e.g., Seneca, *Ep.* 104.28; Diogenes Laertius, *Vit. Phil.* 7.117).[25] In spite of their scepticism toward the irrational passions, however, the Stoics granted that the wise person may entertain positive emotions (εὐπάθειαι) attached to reason. Such rational emotions were joy (χαρά, the counterpart of negative pleasure, ἡδονή), caution (εὐλάβεια; the counterpart of negative fear, φόβος) and wishing (βούλησις; the counterpart of negative ἐπιθυμία, desire; see Plutarch, *Virt. mor.* 449b;

---

[24] There is a third Johannine allusion, not to the Gethsemane prayer as such but to the Gethsemane scene in a broader sense. It appears at the end of the first Farewell Discourse, when Jesus states that 'the ruler of this world is coming' (Jn 14.30: ἔρχεται γὰρ ὁ τοῦ κόσμου ἄρχων) and instructs his disciples: 'Rise, let us be on our way' (14.31: ἐγείρεσθε, ἄγωμεν ἐντεῦθεν). The saying echoes Jesus' words in Mark and Matthew right before Judas' arrival in Gethsemane: 'Get up, let us be going. See, my betrayer is at hand (ἐγείρεσθε ἄγωμεν· ἰδοὺ ὁ παραδιδούς με ἤγγικεν)' (Mk 14.42; Mt. 26.46). John's allusion contains not a retraction of a Markan Jesus saying, as in the two examples above, but a reinterpretation. Instead of speaking about the approaching Judas as 'betrayer', the Johannine Jesus addresses the arrival of 'the ruler of this world', i.e., Satan, who stands behind Judas (6.70; 13.20).

[25] Notice the same vocabulary in Plato when Socrates describes how the body disturbs the soul (verb., ταράττω, Attic for ταράσσω; *Phaed.* 66a; see also 103c).

Diogenes Laertius, *Vit. phil.* 7.116). But the Stoics did not formulate a fourth positive emotion to be a counterpart of the fourth cardinal vice, λύπη (grief). Gitte Buch-Hansen has argued that Philo developed 'virtuous lament' as a fourth εὐπάθεια (the counterpart of λύπη) in order to assimilate emotional biblical figures into the Stoic theory of the passions.[26] Philo thus interprets the phrase 'and the Israelites also wept again' from Numbers 11.4 in the following manner: 'And yet indeed it is not unusual for the devotees of virtue themselves to be much moved and to shed tears (σφαδᾴζειν καὶ δακρύειν), either when bemoaning the misfortunes of the unwise owing to their innate fellow-feeling and humaneness (τὸ φύσει κοινωνικὸν καὶ φιλάνθρωπον), or by reason of being overjoyed' (*Migr.* 156 [Colson & Whitaker, LCL]). According to Buch-Hansen, in other words, John's image of an emotional Jesus can be integrated into the Stoic philosophical system by means of Philo's idea of unselfish and philanthropic emotions.[27]

Buch-Hansen's argumentation is maybe too technical by focusing on very specific philosophical vocabulary, but it is remarkable, if I should add an observation along these lines, that the Johannine emotional Jesus is never portrayed in a state of highly unphilosophical grief (λύπη; see Diogenes Laertius, *Vit. Phil.* 7.118; but see the disciples in Jn 16.6, 20–21; 21.17). Whereas the Markan Jesus in temptation is described as deeply grieved (περίλυπος), the Johannine Jesus' soul is troubled (τετάρακται). Whether or not this change reflects a Stoic theory of emotions in John, it is certainly biblical idiom. Just as Mark's language echoes the first parallelism in Ps. 41.6 LXX, John's language reflects the last part: 'Why are you deeply grieved, my soul, and why do you trouble me (ἵνα τί περίλυπος εἶ, ψυχή, καὶ ἵνα τί συνταράσσεις με)' (Ps. 41.6, 12 LXX; 42.5; see also 41.7). John's rewriting of Mark is not solely philosophical, but also contains reinterpretation of biblical tradition.[28]

This kind of rewriting looking to a double horizon – both philosophy and tradition – is also typical in Philo and Josephus. Rewriting the life of Moses, these two authors, on the one hand, emphasize his philosophical temperance, toning down his emotional outbursts, and on the other hand retain some emotional elements from tradition. According to Philo, whereas Aaron had to struggle not to be overcome by passions (almost like a Markan Jesus), Moses completely mastered them without toil (*Leg.* 3.129, 134–35). He exercises temperance and self-control (σωφροσύνη; *Mos.* 1.25), tames the passions (πάθος; *Mos.* 1.25), and lives according to his own teaching of reason (1.26, 29, 48, 162). Yet, on the other hand, Moses was zealous (ἐζήλωσε) for the traditions of his people (1.32; see also 1.153), lost courage, and was disgusted by his people's captivity in Egypt (1.40), to the extent that he finally – but righteously – killed the cruelest of all Egyptians (1.44). Like Philo, Josephus opts for a more philosophical image of Moses. For apologetic reasons, he practices rewriting by omission as he elides philosophically

---

[26] Gitte Buch-Hansen, 'The Emotional Jesus: Anti-Stoicism in the Fourth Gospel?', in *Stoicism in Early Christianity*, ed. Tuomas Rasimus, Troels Engberg-Pedersen, and Ismo Dunderberg (Grand Rapids, MI: Baker Academic, 2010), 93–114.

[27] See also Seneca's view on the philosopher's emotions in *Polyb.* 18.5–7.

[28] Johannes Beutler, 'Psalm 42/43 im Johannesevangelium', *NTS* 25 (1987): 33–57. See also Harold W. Attridge, 'An "Emotional" Jesus and Stoic Tradition', in *Stoicism in Early Christianity*, ed. Tuomas Rasimus, Troels Engberg-Pedersen and Ismo Dunderberg (Grand Rapids, MI: Baker Academic, 2010), 77–114; and Stephen Voorwinde, *Jesus' Emotions in the Fourth Gospel: Human or Divine?* (LNTS, 284; London: T&T Clark, 2005).

embarrassing episodes about Moses' wrath (Exod. 32.15-20; *Ant.* 3.95-102) and his murder of the Egyptian (Exod. 2.11-15; *Ant.* 2.254).²⁹ And Josephus presents Moses' farewell discourse from Deut. 31-34 as a call to philosophical moderation. Moses warns his people against rebellion against the authorities, presenting himself as an example of one who refrains from wrath (ὀργή), controls the passions and lives in temperance (σωφρονήσειν; *Ant.* 4.189; see 4.49; 4.328-29). Yet, on the other hand, Josephus describes Moses as 'terrified' (κατεπλάγη; 2.267) when he encounters the Lord in the burning bush, and highly sympathetic to his people at his impending death: 'For he, who had ever been persuaded that men should not despond as the end approached, because this fate befell them in accordance with the will of God and by a law of nature, was yet by this conduct of the people reduced to tears (ἐνικήθη δακρῦσαι)' (4.322). In other words, Philo's and Josephus's rewritten portrayals of Moses as philosophical sage do not imply a total extinguishing of his emotions. Instead, they seek to negotiate between traditional biblical material and contemporary philosophical ideals. The same can be said of John's depiction of Jesus in temptation. The portrait is painted in traditional (Ps. 41 LXX; Mark's Gospel) and philosophical colours.

Conclusion

Does it make sense to speak of the lost temptation of Christ in the Gospel of John? If John knew Mark's Gospel – and as we have seen, there are some indications of that in John's use and rejection of the temptation prayer in Gethsemane – then he rewrites the Markan temptation scenes through omission, reuse and dispersion. He also presents new temptation scenes, like the dialogue between Jesus and his mother at the wedding in Cana, but the Johannine temptations are different from Mark's. Whereas in Mark the will of Jesus wavers and becomes an element of narrative suspense, the Johannine Jesus is more steadfast, active and in control. John, in other words, moves Jesus closer to Socratic and Stoic philosophical ideals of the wise sage's independent and active attitude in the face of temptation. While it could be argued (and was in fact argued by Origen, *Cels.* 2.24) that even Mark's Jesus appears philosophical in so far as he overcomes temptations, the Gethsemane scene and Jesus' cry on the cross are open to ambiguity. Anti-Christian authors like Celsus found this ambiguity philosophically embarrassing, and the Johannine, still more than the Lukan, redaction of Mark reflects attempts to overcome such embarrassment. Like the ideal philosopher, the Johannine Jesus fights temptation actively and acts independently; but does he control his passions? Regarding the latter, John retains some ambiguity by presenting Jesus as emotional.

John's practice of rewriting in a philosophical mode apparently had its limits – limits that can also be detected in Jewish-Hellenistic practices of rewriting Moses in a philosophical mode. Philo and Josephus navigate between traditional narrative and

---

[29] Louis H. Feldman, 'Josephus' Portrait of Moses', *JQR* 82 (1992): 285-328 and *JQR* 83 (1993): 7-50, 301-30.

philosophical ideas, Josephus even omitting the most philosophically disturbing episodes from tradition; and both create an image of Moses as philosophical *and* emotional. John also navigates between traditional narrative and philosophical ideas, possibly with a similar purpose, namely that of presenting Christ-centered Judaism to the Greco-Roman world. After all, it is when the Greeks seek Jesus (12.20) that Jesus proclaims his inverted Gethsemane prayer and thus reveals his philosophy-compatible steadfastness in temptation. John does not portray Jesus as the ideal Stoic sage embodying ἀπάθεια, but John's rewriting of Markan temptation scenes is best described as philosophical. However, Jesus is not only portrayed with the god-like traits of the philosopher (Diogenes Laertius, *Vit. Phil.* 7.119); he is the divine λόγος himself. What Johannine scholars traditionally call 'high' Christology may better be described as philosophical Christology.

17

The Plot to Kill Jesus in Mark and John: Reflections on the Literary Relationship between Two Early Christian Theological Biographies of Jesus on the Basis of a Detail in Their Storytelling

Michael Labahn

Introduction

The nature of the literary relationship between John and the Synoptic Gospels is an important issue in the history of the study of the Fourth Gospel.[1] As part of this debate, the question of the significance of the use of the same genre, 'gospel', in the Gospels of Mark and John plays a key role. For some scholars, acquaintance with the 'gospel' genre is a central argument in support of John's knowledge of Mark (e.g., Udo Schnelle[2]). Others assume a kind of double invention of the 'gospel' genre by both Mark and John (e.g., Jürgen Becker[3]). It is necessary in this respect to ask whether these alternatives are

---

[1] For an introduction and overview, see, e.g., Michael Labahn and Manfred Lang, 'Johannes und die Synoptiker: Positionen und Impulse seit 1990', in Michael Labahn, *Ausgewählte Studien zum Johannesevangelium: Selected Studies in the Gospel of John. 1998-2013*, ed. Antje Labahn, with an Introduction by Gilbert Van Belle (BTS, 28; Leuven: Peeters, 2017), 3–78.

[2] Udo Schnelle, 'Johannes und die Synoptiker', in *The Four Gospels 1992: FS F. Neirynck*, ed. Frans Van Segbroeck, Christopher M. Tuckett, Gilbert Van Belle and Joseph Verheyden (BETL, 100; Leuven: Leuven University Press and Peeters, 1992), 1799–814; see also Udo Schnelle, *Theologie des Neuen Testaments* (3rd edn; UTB, 2917; Göttingen: Vandenhoeck & Ruprecht, 2016), 415.

[3] See Jürgen Becker, 'Das vierte Evangelium und die Frage nach seinen externen und internen Quellen', in *Fair Play: Diversity and Conflicts in Early Christianity. FS Heikki Räisänen*, ed. Ismo Dunderberg, Christopher Tuckett and Kari Syreeni (NovTSup, 103; Leiden: Brill, 2002), 203–41, 223–25, in discussion with Schnelle; idem, *Mündliche und schriftliche Autorität im frühen Christentum* (Tübingen: Mohr Siebeck, 2012), 145: 'Das Johannesevangelium bezeugt eine selbständige Literalisierung der Jesus-Tradition, wie sie im johanneischen Kreis in einer besonderen Gestalt vorlag'. Of particular interest for our topic is James D. G. Dunn, 'John and the Synoptics as a Theological Question', in *Exploring the Gospel of John: In Honor of D. Moody Smith*, ed. R. Alan Culpepper and C. Clifton Black (Louisville, KY: Westminster John Knox, 1996), 301–13, 306, who emphasizes the climactic character of the passion narrative in the earliest gospels. One could easily include the plot to kill Jesus among the range of consequences to the genre analogy; in the judgment

methodologically justified. First, one must ask whether it is permissible to speak of a new, independent 'gospel' genre in early Christian literature.[4] Parallels to the ancient biographical genre[5] relativize the force of this argument. If we understand the gospels as biographical,[6] or even as belonging to a historical genre,[7] it is hardly surprising that the portrayal of Jesus starts with the earliest stages of his public ministry, which – as is well known – is extended further by Matthew, Luke and John to before Jesus' baptism. The story ends with the cross and resurrection of Jesus, which offers a different openness and orientation towards the respective addressees. Both ends of Jesus' biography, the *beginning* of his public activity and his *end* in death and resurrection, need to be linked together by the argumentation or narrative plot. This belongs to the literary but also theological tasks of a successful biographical narrative of Jesus' life.

In line with this research-historical framework, the aim of my contribution is not so much to pursue the question of genre and consider its significance for John's relationship with Mark. Rather, I will focus on one element in the presentation of Jesus' life: a conflict scene during the public ministry of the story's hero, one that prepares for the subject of his passion, death and resurrection. My article centres on the striking parallel between the Markan and Johannine accounts of the decision of Jesus' opponents to kill him because of a healing he performed on a Sabbath (Mk 3.1–6; 11.18 and Jn 5.1–18; 11.47–53).[8] This plot presents a remarkable analogy between the two accounts. It is all

---

of Dunn this does not prove dependence. On the relevant debate, see Labahn and Lang, 'Johannes und die Synoptiker', 57–61.

[4] Thus, e.g., Schnelle, *Theologie*, 386, notes the following elements that belong to the 'gospel' genre: Mark 'schuf mit der neuen Literaturgattung Evangelium die erste ausführliche Jesus-Christus-Geschichte und bestimmte durch die Präsentation der Ereignisse/Charaktere, durch den geographisch/ chronologischen Rahmen, den Geschehensverlauf, die Erzählperspektive und seine theologischen Einsichten wesentlich das Jesus-Christus-Bild des frühen Christentums'; see also pp. 402–3. For Schnelle, the 'gospel' genre is to be defined in terms of content rather than form: 'Die Literaturgattung Evangelium ist somit eine Form sui generis, die sich der theologischen Einsicht verdankt, dass in der einmaligen und unverwechselbaren Geschichte des Jesus von Nazareth Gott selbst handelte. Eine Spannung zwischen vor- und nachösterlich, Geschichte und Kerygma oder textinterner und textexterner Ebene besteht dabei für Markus nicht, sondern seine theologische Leistung besteht gerade darin, beides jeweils entschieden als Einheit verstanden und dargestellt zu haben'.

[5] Cf. e.g., Holger Sonnabend, *Geschichte der antiken Biographie: Von Isokrates bis zur Historia Augusta* (Stuttgart, Weimar: J.B. Metzler, 2002); Richard A. Burridge, *What are the Gospels? A Comparison with Graeco-Roman Biography* (SNTSMS, 70; Cambridge: Cambridge University Press, 1992); see also Widu Wolfgang Ehlers (ed.), *La Biographie antique* (Fondation Hardt, Entretiens, 44; Genève: Librairie Droz, 1998); Dirk Wördemann, *Das Charakterbild im bíos nach Plutarch und das Christusbild im Evangelium nach Markus* (Studien zur Geschichte und Kultur des Altertums, 1/19; Paderborn: Schöningh, 2002).

[6] Cf., e.g., Gerd Theißen, *Die Entstehung des Neuen Testaments als literaturgeschichtliches Problem* (Schriften der Philosophisch-historischen Klasse der Heidelberger Akademie der Wissenschaften, 40; Heidelberg: Winter, 2007), 84–92; Detlev Dormeyer, *Das Markusevangelium als Idealbiographie von Jesus Christus, dem Nazarener*, 2nd edn (SBB, 43; Stuttgart: Katholisches Bibelwerk, 2002), especially 4–11.

[7] Cf., e.g., Eve-Marie Becker, *Das Markus-Evangelium im Rahmen antiker Historiographie* (WUNT, 194; Tübingen: Mohr Siebeck, 2006).

[8] The intention and decision to kill Jesus are continued in the passion narratives of Mark and John, where they are also connected to the motive of blasphemy (Mk 14.64; Jn 19.7). One can read the intention to kill Jesus in each presentation of his public life as an anticipation of the condemnation that follows in the passion narratives; nevertheless, the parallels described in this chapter cannot be ignored and, in my opinion, require further explanation.

the more noteworthy since, in both cases, the decision is made much earlier than what is required by the narrative frame of the biographical structure, long before the very different presentations of Jesus' passion offered in both narratives.[9] Does this plot to kill Jesus belong to the gospel genre or to the basic building-blocks of the historical memory of Jesus' life? Or does it point to a direct or indirect connection between two gospels that are undoubtedly characterized by their considerable focus on the cross and resurrection of Jesus, albeit with different emphases on the divine necessity of Jesus' death? In the Gospel of Mark it is the divine plan (δεῖ: 8.31) that leads to Jesus' vicarious suffering and death for the many (δοῦναι τὴν ψυχὴν αὐτοῦ λύτρον ἀντὶ πολλῶν; 10.45). True knowledge of the revelation of God in Jesus can, according to Mark, only be gained in and through the cross, which is why the narrator never tires of shaping Jesus' public activity through the theological lens of the cross and the motif of misunderstanding. Even in John the sovereign way of the Son of God is linked to the cross at the precise hour when the Passover lambs are slaughtered (Jn 19.14); this is when Jesus gives up his life in the service of friendship for his own (10.11; 15.13) and does so in accordance with the divine will. The fact that both evangelists are credited with a *theology of the cross*[10] certainly enhances the role of *death* in the overall plot. But do these general remarks on the significance of Jesus' death in their respective accounts adequately substantiate the parallels (described in more detail below) of his opponents' decision to kill him during his public ministry?

In the analysis that follows, the two announcements to kill Jesus (Mk 3.6 and Jn 5.18) and their literary function in the macrostructure of the gospels will be analysed in some detail. As a second step, the results of this analysis of the two accounts will be compared, so that parallels and differences in the content and structure of both plots can be identified. Ultimately, this analysis will show that, despite differences in detail, the plot to kill Jesus is important for understanding the relationship between John and Mark (or the Synoptics in general), because crucial linguistic and structural-narrative similarities between them prove that the Johannine story is based on the Markan representation of the event. The evidence presented here is not, however, evaluated in terms of direct literary reception but rather of an oral culture of remembrance

---

[9] On research into the widely debated relationship between the passion story in John and Mark/the Synoptics, see, e.g., Manfred Lang, *Johannes und die Synoptiker: Eine redaktionsgeschichtliche Analyse von Joh 18–20 vor dem markinischen und lukanischen Hintergrund* (FRLANT, 182; Göttingen: Vandenhoeck & Ruprecht, 1999), 14–56.

[10] On the debate about describing the Johannine account of Jesus' death as a *theologia crucis*, see, e.g., Jörg Frey, 'Die "theologia crucifixi" des Johannesevangeliums', in Jörg Frey, *Die Herrlichkeit des Gekreuzigten: Studien zu den johanneischen Schriften I*, ed. Juliane Schlegel (WUNT, 307; Tübingen: Mohr Siebeck, 2013), 485–554; Thomas Knöppler, *Die theologia crucis des Johannesevangeliums: Das Verständnis des Todes Jesu im Rahmen der johanneischen Inkarnations- und Erhöhungschristologie* (WMANT, 69; Neukirchen-Vluyn, Neukirchener Verlag, 1994), 6–18; Udo Schnelle, 'Markinische und johanneische Kreuzestheologie', in *The Death of Jesus in the Fourth Gospel*, ed. Gilbert Van Belle (BETL, 200; Leuven: Leuven University Press and Peeters, 2007), 233–58; Esther Straub, 'Der Irdische als der Auferstandene: Kritische Theologie bei Johannes ohne ein Wort vom Kreuz', in *Kreuzestheologie im Neuen Testament*, ed. Andreas Dettwiler and Jean Zumstein (WUNT, 151; Tübingen: Mohr Siebeck, 2002), 239–64; see also Michael Labahn, 'Bedeutung und Frucht des Todes Jesu im Spiegel des johanneischen Erzähllaufbaus', in Michael Labahn, *Ausgewählte Studien*, 361–87, especially 361–62.

understood as the use of re-oralized tradition – a technique often described (or named) as 'secondary orality'.

The plot to kill Jesus according to Mark and John

Mark's account of the decision to kill Jesus (Mk 3.6; 11.18)

In the Gospel of Mark the passion and crucifixion of Jesus belong to Jesus' way in accordance with God's will and plan. This is evident in the passion predictions (Mk 8.31; 9.31; 10.32–34) and in the emphasis on the divine 'necessity' of Jesus' passion (8.31), which connect his public ministry to the passion story (chapters 15–16). It must also be borne in mind that the Markan Jesus is already in Jerusalem where he refers to his forthcoming violent death (11.18). In a pointed fashion, though overly marginalizing Jesus' ministry and teaching, Martin Kähler describes the Gospel of Mark as a 'Passion story with a detailed introduction'.[11] Nevertheless, given the orientation of the narrative plot, a reference to the cross can already be detected in the use of the 'Son of God' title in the account of Jesus' baptism (1.11: God calls Jesus ὁ υἱός μου ὁ ἀγαπητός; see further references in 9.7; 15.39); a Markan theology of the cross can therefore be assumed.[12] Jesus' suffering and death are theologically interpreted by Mark and are of decisive significance not only for the gospel's Christology but also for its ecclesiology and ethics.

At the same time, Jesus' proclamation is shaped by dispute and controversy.[13] Such conflicts, which are likely to evoke the memory of discourses drawn from the life of Jesus, may be taken by a narrator as an occasion to develop a tense account of deadly conflict, although this is not necessarily required. Since the New Testament gospels end with Jesus' passion, cross and resurrection, the preparation for this crisis is plausible within each narrative, but questions remain about the extent of linguistic and structural parallels and their interpretation, especially as these conflicts unfold in a different

---

[11] Martin Kähler, *Der sogenannte historische Jesus und der geschichtliche, biblische Christus*, ed. Ernst Wolf (2nd edn, Theologische Bücherei, 2; München: Chr. Kaiser Verlag, 1956), 59–60 n. 1: 'Passionsgeschichte mit ausführlicher Einleitung' (quotation on p. 60).

[12] For a Markan theology of the cross, see, e.g., Élian Cuvillier, 'Die "Kreuzestheologie" als Leseschlüssel zum Markusevangelium', in Dettwiler and Zumstein (eds), *Kreuzestheologie im Neuen Testament*, 107–50; see also Martin Ebner, 'Kreuzestheologie im Markusevangelium', in Dettwiler and Zumstein (eds), *Kreuzestheologie im Neuen Testament*, 151–68, who describes the ecclesiological dimension of Mark's theology of the cross as an alternative to the sociological and religious expectations of the Roman Empire; see further Schnelle, 'Kreuzestheologie', 236–42. Cuvillier, 'Kreuzestheologie', 107–8, locates the identification of Mark's theology of the cross in the emergence of redaction-historical research in the 1960s under the influence of dialectical theology; for examples, see Cuvillier, 'Kreuzestheologie', 107 n. 1.

[13] See, for example, Lorenzo Scornaienchi, *Der umstrittene Jesus und seine Apologie: Die Streitgespräche im Markusevangelium* (NTOA/StUNT, 110; Göttingen: Vandenhoeck & Ruprecht, 2016), who conceives the Markan Jesus as a figure constantly attacked in relation to religious laws and his behaviour towards the Roman state, but who vindicates himself against these attacks, so that the gospel is – rhetorically – understood as an apology. See also, Joanna Dewey, *Markan Public Debate. Literary Technique, Concentric Structure and Theology in Mark 2:1–3:6* (SBLDS, 48; Chico, CA: Scholars Press, 1980); Jarmo Kiilunen, *Die Vollmacht im Widerstreit: Untersuchungen zum Werdegang von Mk 2,1–3,6* (AASF.DHL, 40; Helsinki: Suomalainen Tiedeakatemi, 1985).

'discourse universe' in each gospel narrative.[14] In this respect, the subject of this article can shed new light on the issue of the potential dependence of Mark and John and, possibly, of the parallel narrative genre and its basic structure.

Returning to the Gospel of Mark: the narrator in fact begins his account of Jesus' ministry with a polemical emphasis on Jesus' authority as opposed to that of his opponents, the scribes (1.22; cf. 1.27).[15] It is this group, or at least some of them, who accuse Jesus of blasphemy – shortly after his healing of a paralytic whose sins are forgiven by Jesus (2.7: βλασφημεῖ) – and take action against Jesus until his death.[16] A series of controversies (2.1–3.6) begins with this formally peculiar miracle story about the paralytic,[17] and it ends with a formal decision by Jesus' opponents to kill him. In addition to blasphemy, questions of purity (2.16) and fasting (2.18), as well as the theme of Sabbath-violation (2.24; 3.2–4), are touched upon within the controversy series.

Mk 2.1–12	Healing of a paralytic and the authority to forgive sins	Allegation of blasphemy (βλασφημεῖ) by some of the scribes as opponents (2.6. τινες τῶν γραμματέων)
Mk 2.13–17	Table fellowship with tax collectors and sinners	οἱ γραμματεῖς τῶν Φαρισαίων critically ask how Jesus can share table fellowship with tax collectors and sinners as religiously unclean people (2.16: μετὰ τῶν τελωνῶν καὶ ἁμαρτωλῶν ἐσθίει)
Mk 2.18–22	Fasting	Anonymous request as to why the disciples of Jesus are not fasting
Mk 2.23–28	Sabbath	On the Sabbath, the disciples gather ears of corn (2.23), which is considered by the Pharisees to be Sabbath transgression. ἴδε τί ποιοῦσιν τοῖς σάββασιν ὃ οὐκ ἔξεστιν
Mk 3.1–6	Healing of a man with a paralysed hand on the Sabbath	Order of the Pharisees with the Herodians (οἱ Φαρισαῖοι εὐθὺς μετὰ τῶν Ἡρῳδιανῶν) for the ruin of Jesus (3.2b, 6: 2 καὶ παρετήρουν αὐτὸν . . ., ἵνα κατηγορήσωσιν αὐτοῦ . . . 6 . . . συμβούλιον ἐδίδουν κατ' αὐτοῦ ὅπως αὐτὸν ἀπολέσωσιν)

---

[14] With the term 'discourse universe' I refer – here in relation to a text – to the knowledge required in order to be able to successfully read and understand a text, its action, its reasoning, and/or its pragmatics, i.e. the world and its order as it is linguistically designed. See also Kristina Dronsch, *Bedeutung als Grundbegriff neutestamentlicher Wissenschaft: Texttheoretische und semiotische Entwürfe zur Kritik der Semantik dargelegt anhand einer Analyse zu akouein in Mk 4* (NET, 15; Tübingen: Francke, 2010), 94: 'Das "Diskursuniversum" eines Textes ist dann die Welt, die ein gegebener Text setzt und voraussetzt, damit das vom Text Erzählte oder Behauptete plausibel funktionieren kann'.

[15] On the attribution of the polemic against the scribes to the Markan narrator, see, e.g., Dieter Lührmann, *Das Markusevangelium* (HNT, 3; Tübingen: Mohr Siebeck, 1987), 50.

[16] Cf., e.g., Dieter Lührmann, 'Die Pharisäer und die Schriftgelehrten im Markusevangelium', *ZNW* 78 (1987): 169–85.

[17] On form and tradition/source behind Mark 2.1–12, see (among others) Karl Kertelge, *Die Wunder Jesu im Markusevangelium: Eine redaktionsgeschichtliche Untersuchung* (StANT, 23; München: Kösel, 1970), 75–82; Dietrich-Alex Koch, *Die Bedeutung der Wundererzählungen für die Christologie des Markusevangeliums* (BZNW, 42; Berlin: de Gruyter: 1985), 46–50; Heinz-Wolfgang Kuhn, *Ältere Sammlungen im Markusevangelium* (StUNT, 8; Göttingen: Vandenhoeck & Ruprecht, 1971), 53–58; Ludger Schenke, *Die Wundererzählungen des Markusevangeliums* (SBB, 5; Stuttgart: Katholisches Bibelwerk, 1974), 146–60. Intense discussion has led to different hypotheses about the pre-literary evolution of the story, including the priority of miracle forms over word proclamation, or of the cure over the forgiveness of sins. What is decisive for this essay is that, in Mark, the healing and remission of sins form a unity which, as in the following episodes, leads to contradictions based on religious rules that are the cause of Jesus' actions on behalf of human beings.

In Mark 2.1–3.6, Jesus as teacher and interpreter of the Jewish law makes an extraordinary claim to be able to offer forgiveness of sins, but also by engaging in table fellowship with tax collectors and sinners as a realization of that forgiveness as well as through his interpretation of Jewish fasting and Sabbath regulations. This is, at the same time, a high christological claim with reference to Jesus' authority (2.10: ἐξουσίαν ἔχει ὁ υἱὸς τοῦ ἀνθρώπου), to the eschatological time of joy linked to his work (2.19–20), and to the claim that the Son of Man's interpretation of the law rules over the Sabbath (2.28), which – according to the text's rhetoric of text – accords with God's will.

As a conclusion to the conflict scenes in Mark 2.1–3.6, Jesus heals the hand of the paralytic on the Sabbath (3.5: . . . λέγει τῷ ἀνθρώπῳ· ἔκτεινον τὴν χεῖρα. καὶ ἐξέτεινεν καὶ ἀπεκατεστάθη ἡ χεὶρ αὐτοῦ.). This action corresponds to the Sabbath interpretation offered by the Markan Jesus, in as much as the Sabbath was made for man (2.27: τὸ σάββατον διὰ τὸν ἄνθρωπον ἐγένετο καὶ οὐχ ὁ ἄνθρωπος διὰ τὸ σάββατον·) and that one should do good and save souls on the Sabbath (3.4: ἔξεστιν τοῖς σάββασιν ἀγαθὸν ποιῆσαι ἢ κακοποιῆσαι, ψυχὴν σῶσαι ἢ ἀποκτεῖναι). The claim and action of Jesus (as in the case of his disciples: 2.18, 23) act like a provocation to the opponents,[18] especially since they are expecting Jesus to act: καὶ παρετήρουν αὐτόν . . ., ἵνα κατηγορήσωσιν αὐτοῦ (3.2). This depiction of the situation turns the sequence of disputes into a sequence ending with the decision to kill Jesus, whereby at the beginning and at the end of this unit a miracle story is narrated which is more reminiscent of a pronouncement story/apophthegma.[19] On each occasion Jesus demonstrates his power (2.10: the authority of the Son of Man to forgive sins; lordship of the Son of Man over the Sabbath).

When the individual episodes are brought together, the opposition of the narrated opponents to Jesus' claim to authority leads, within the text's value system, to his fundamental rejection, which only takes place at the end of the narrative. Thus, the plot to kill Jesus not only concludes the Sabbath healings (3.5)[20] but also the entire conflict sequence,[21] beginning with the accusation of blasphemy (2.7). The final sentence of this episode is as follows:

---

[18] The different groups of opponents are brought together by the narrator through reference to the Pharisees; the initial reference to the scribes is replaced by the γραμματεῖς τῶν Φαρισαίων (Mk 2.16), and this is eventually followed by the Pharisees (latterly the Herodians) as spokesmen against Jesus.

[19] Even as an apophthegma Mark 2.1–12 preserves the basic structure of a miracle story, while the account of the miracle in 3.1–6 is formally, and more strongly, transformed into a conflict scene by 3.2,6.

[20] E.g., Lührmann, *Markusevangelium*, 66.

[21] See also Gudrun Guttenberger, *Die Gottesvorstellung im Markusevangelium* (BZNW, 123; Berlin: de Gruyter, 2004), 289. For Kari Syreeni, *Becoming John: The Making of a Passion Gospel* (LNTS, 590; London: T&T Clark, 2018), 17, in his comparison with the Gospel of John, the decision to kill Jesus is reached too early in the Markan narrative, so that, unlike John, no 'linear degration in describing the opponents' hostility' can arise. Whether the Markan decision to kill Jesus is so static has to be seen in a much more differentiated and dynamic way. Unfortunately, Syreeni does not offer a comparable position in relation to Mk 3.6 and Jn 5.16, 18.

Mark 3.6
καὶ ἐξελθόντες οἱ Φαρισαῖοι
εὐθὺς μετὰ τῶν Ἡρῳδιανῶν συμβούλιον ἐδίδουν κατ᾽ αὐτοῦ
ὅπως αὐτὸν ἀπολέσωσιν.

Then the Pharisees went out
and immediately plotted with the Herodians against him,
how they might destroy him.[22]

The Pharisees represent a narrative character whose criticism of Jesus' healings is summarized by Mark. They leave the stage after their expectation is fulfilled that Jesus will break the Sabbath. They immediately join the group of Herodians, whose introduction into the text is surprising. The Herodians are to be understood as supporters of Herod Antipas, the ruler of Galilee, who briefly united power over the whole land, including Jerusalem.[23] They bring a political dimension to the decision to kill Jesus and open up a perspective in Jerusalem that will later be adopted by the chief priests (11.18). Later, within the Markan narrative world, this duo reunites against Jesus by seeking to entrap him through their question about paying taxes (12.13: Καὶ ἀποστέλλουσιν πρὸς αὐτόν τινας τῶν Φαρισαίων καὶ τῶν Ἡρῳδιανῶν ἵνα αὐτὸν ἀγρεύσωσιν λόγῳ). Because they belong to the set of controversies located in Jerusalem (11.1–12.44) and are placed immediately after the parable of the vineyard and the cornerstone, which in Mark anticipates Jesus' death (12.1–9, 10–12),[24] such a constellation of narrative characters forms a connecting line to the passion narrative. The decision (συμβούλιον ἐδίδουν[25]) to destroy Jesus (αὐτὸν ἀπολέσωσιν) is made by two groups representing religious and political power.[26]

It is disputed whether this decision stems from tradition or from the Markan hand.[27] That 2.1–3.6 consists of traditional material used by the narrator is difficult to dispute. It is indeed possible that a collection of conflict stories is being re-told in 2.1–3.6.[28] However, it seems unlikely, for a number of reasons, that Mark 3.6 should be understood as part of such a collection or even of a single tradition. The decision to kill Jesus already looks forward to its completion and therefore only makes sense at the level of the entire Markan story. Formally and linguistically, Mark 3.6, together with its preparation in 3.2, belongs to the hand of the narrator,[29] who defines his conflict tradition(s) as a link between the public ministry of Jesus, whose authority triggers conflict, and his passion, cross and empty grave.

---

[22] All English New Testament translations are taken from NKJV.
[23] Cf. Joachim Gnilka, *Das Evangelium nach Markus: Mk 1–8,26* (EKK, II/1; Zürich: Benziger/Neukirchen-Vluyn: Neukirchener Verlag, 1978), 129.
[24] Cf., e.g., Bas van Iersel, *Markus: Kommentar* (Düsseldorf: Patmos, 1993), 191–93.
[25] A Latinism; cf. Gnilka, *Evangelium*, 126 n. 9.
[26] Cf. Morna D. Hooker, *According to Saint Mark* (Black's New Testament Commentaries; London: A&C Black, 1991), 108.
[27] In favour of tradition, see, e.g., Kertelge, *Die Wunder Jesu*, 83–84; in favour of the evangelist, see, e.g., Koch, *Bedeutung*, 51–2; Kuhn, *Sammlungen*, 222–23.
[28] E.g., Udo Schnelle, *Einleitung in das Neue Testament* (9th edn; UTB, 1830; Göttingen: Vandenhoeck & Ruprecht, 2017), 276–77.
[29] See the evidence gathered in Gnilka, *Evangelium*, 126.

The decision to kill Jesus, which takes place in Galilee, is not carried out until the passion events in Jerusalem, although it already brings the cross into his public life.[30] In fact, the decision is later confirmed by the intention to kill him.[31] In Mark 11–15, the report of Jesus' cleansing of the temple is intended to lead to the plot to kill him (11.18: Καὶ ἤκουσαν οἱ ἀρχιερεῖς καὶ οἱ γραμματεῖς καὶ *ἐζήτουν πῶς αὐτὸν ἀπολέσωσιν· ἐφοβοῦντο γὰρ αὐτόν, πᾶς γὰρ ὁ ὄχλος ἐξεπλήσσετο ἐπὶ τῇ διδαχῇ αὐτοῦ*[32]). Granted, it is not the group of Herodians, but rather the chief priests as representatives of the Jerusalem aristocracy who, together with the scribes, seek to kill Jesus. This would be quite appropriate in the narrative context but, in contrast to 3.6, no direct decision is made. It is simply an intention (ἐζήτουν) prompted by fear (ἐφοβοῦντο). However, as in Mark 2.1–3.6, the statement is justified by Jesus' authority (11.8: πᾶς γὰρ ὁ ὄχλος ἐξεπλήσσετο ἐπὶ τῇ διδαχῇ αὐτοῦ) and is therefore christologically motivated.[33] It refers back to the decision to kill him, although the temple action is the external cause and a politically plausible reason for killing Jesus. As the Jerusalem narrative section progresses, Jesus' path to his crucifixion continues to gain momentum.[34]

Throughout the story, the rejection of and resistance to Jesus are also expressed in different ways. Jesus is declared by the Jerusalem Pharisees to be possessed (3.22: Βεελζεβοὺλ ἔχει καὶ ὅτι ἐν τῷ ἄρχοντι τῶν δαιμονίων ἐκβάλλει τὰ δαιμόνια), which, from a social perspective, amounts to a devastating indictment, though not a συμβούλιον (as in 3.6). There are countless such discourses, as well as expressions of annoyance at Jesus' teaching and success (such as 6.3). Crucial for Mark's theological interpretation of the passion, cross and empty tomb is the middle section (Mk 8.27–10.52), which places Jesus' suffering under the interpretative lens of the divine will and explores the christological, soteriological, ecclesiological and also the ethical consequences of Jesus' death. Against this background, Mark 2.1–3.6 fulfils a specific function by making Jewish leaders responsible for the trial and sentencing of Jesus on the public-political level of the text and thus contributing to the validation of the two poles in Jesus' life: his mighty public ministry and his condemnation to death on the cross.

John's account of the plot to kill Jesus (5.18; 11.47–53)

A significant and fundamental aspect of Johannine Christology is the notion of Jesus coming into the world to offer salvation (3.16; see also, e.g., 4.42; 12.47). Even the

---

[30] Cf. Schnelle, 'Kreuzestheologie', 237: 'Erzählerisch hat Mk 3,6 die Funktion einer Prolepse ...' 'Damit ist der Tod Jesu am Kreuz in der Erzählung präsent'.

[31] Cf. Frans Neirynck, 'John 5,1–18 and the Gospel of Mark', in Frans Neirynck, *Evangelica II*, ed. Frans Van Segbroeck (BETL, 99; Leuven: Leuven University Press and Peeters, 1991), 699–712, especially 707.

[32] See also the repetition and variation of the intention to kill Jesus in 12.12; 14.1: καὶ ἐζήτουν οἱ ἀρχιερεῖς καὶ οἱ γραμματεῖς πῶς αὐτὸν ἐν δόλῳ κρατήσαντες ἀποκτείνωσιν.

[33] Differently Martin Meiser, *Die Reaktion des Volkes auf Jesus: Eine redaktionskritische Untersuchung zu den synoptischen Evangelien* (BZNW, 96; Berlin/New York: de Gruyter, 1998), 188, seeks to interpret 11.18b as 'epiphanietheologisch'. With regard to the interpretation of the cleansing of the temple (through Jesus' teaching), however, Mark's perspective on the authority and success of Jesus as teacher is inserted into 11.17–18.

[34] According to Dormeyer, *Markusevangelium* 244, Mark's narrative code is dominant 'seit dem Auftreten der Gegner (Mk 2,1) bis zum Schluß von dem Kampf um Leben und Tod ... und der Möglichkeit der Versöhnung ...'.

prologue, an essential introduction to the Johannine 'discourse universe',[35] conveys this coming into the world as an event aimed at acceptance and life (1.12; see also 1.9), but which also leads to rejection of God's offer of salvation (1.11: εἰς τὰ ἴδια ἦλθεν, καὶ οἱ ἴδιοι αὐτὸν οὐ παρέλαβον; see also 1.10). Despite the lack of direct references to Jesus' death in the prologue, readers are already prepared for violent conflict.[36] As in the Gospel of Mark, the Johannine Jesus comes into conflict with opponents within the world of the text; the narrator portrays the negative character of this conflict in dualistic terms, as a conflict between light and darkness, between good and evil.[37] The fact that the cross is the target or goal of the Johannine plot is signaled by the account of Jesus' temple cleansing (2.13–22).[38] Here Jesus predicts the destruction and rebuilding of his own body: λύσατε τὸν ναὸν τοῦτον καὶ ἐν τρισὶν ἡμέραις ἐγερῶ αὐτόν (2.19). Against the misunderstanding of his opponents, the narrator signposts Jesus' words as the announcement of his death and resurrection (2.21: ἐκεῖνος δὲ ἔλεγεν περὶ τοῦ ναοῦ τοῦ σώματος αὐτοῦ). However, neither the provision of basic information in the prologue – designed for a successful reading of the gospel – nor the narrative preparation for Jesus' death and resurrection[39] include the need to supply a plot or formal death sentence before Jesus' passion.

In striking analogy to Mark 3.6, which will be considered in more detail in the following section of this essay, John 5.18 provides the first reference to the plan to kill Jesus, which, in contrast to the Markan account, is repeatedly mentioned in the lead-up to the formal decision in John 11.53:

John 5.18

διὰ τοῦτο οὖν μᾶλλον ἐζήτουν αὐτὸν οἱ Ἰουδαῖοι ἀποκτεῖναι,
ὅτι οὐ μόνον ἔλυεν τὸ σάββατον,
ἀλλὰ καὶ πατέρα ἴδιον ἔλεγεν τὸν θεὸν
ἴσον ἑαυτὸν ποιῶν τῷ θεῷ.

Therefore the Jews sought all the more to kill him,
because he not only broke the Sabbath,
but also said that God was his Father,
making himself equal with God.

This explanatory comment presupposes a similar statement in John 5.16:

---

[35] Cf., e.g., Michael Labahn, 'A Narrow Gate to the Johannine Gospel? Re-Thinking the Relationship Between the Johannine Prologue (John 1:1-18) and the Gospel of John in Terms of the Theories of Paratext and of "Discourse Universe"', in *Johannine Christology*, ed. Stanley E. Porter and Andrew W. Pitts (Johannine Studies, 3; Leiden: Brill, forthcoming).
[36] See also Schnelle, 'Kreuzestheologie', 245.
[37] On the so-called Johannine dualism, see Jörg Frey, 'Zu Hintergrund und Funktion des johanneischen Dualismus', in Jörg Frey, *Die Herrlichkeit des Gekreuzigten*, 409–82.
[38] Cf. Udo Schnelle, 'Die Tempelreinigung und die Christologie des Johannesevangeliums', NTS 42 (1996), 359–73.
[39] Cf. Labahn 'Bedeutung', 366–71.

καὶ διὰ τοῦτο ἐδίωκον οἱ Ἰουδαῖοι τὸν Ἰησοῦν,[40]
ὅτι ταῦτα ἐποίει ἐν σαββάτῳ.

For this reason the Jews persecuted Jesus,
because he had done these things on the Sabbath.

As in Mark's story, the starting-point of the plot against Jesus in John's Gospel is the healing of a paralytic. The problematic nature of Jesus' deed, which is only noted after the healing, lies in its timing: it was the Sabbath (5.9: Ἦν δὲ σάββατον ἐν ἐκείνῃ τῇ ἡμέρᾳ). It remains unclear as to whether the ostentatious carrying of the mat on the Sabbath in accordance with Jesus' instruction (this offence is at the centre of 5.10–11) or the healing itself (this is the focus of Jesus' actions in 5.17 and 7.23: ὅλον ἄνθρωπον ὑγιῆ ἐποίησα ἐν σαββάτῳ) gives rise to the controversy. In any case, because the events take place on the Sabbath, Jesus comes under the watchful eye of his opponents, who learn about his identity from the healed man and, finally, question Jesus himself (5.10–15). The information provided by the healed man leads to an ongoing[41] persecution of Jesus (5.16), which he counters in 5.17 in the form of a direct reply. Jesus justifies his Sabbath healing by claiming to uphold human life, as his Father does, even on the Sabbath: ὁ πατήρ μου ἕως ἄρτι ἐργάζεται κἀγὼ ἐργάζομαι (see also 7.23: ὅλον ἄνθρωπον ὑγιῆ ἐποίησα ἐν σαββάτῳ).[42] This reply provokes his opponents, whose intentions have already been made explicit in 5.16, to seek to harm Jesus (ἐδίωκον), and this is intensified in v.18a in that they now intend to kill him (ἀποκτεῖναι):

διὰ τοῦτο οὖν μᾶλλον ἐζήτουν αὐτὸν οἱ Ἰουδαῖοι ἀποκτεῖναι, ...

Therefore the Jews sought all the more to kill him ...

The reasoning that follows refers to the accusation of breaking the Sabbath law (ἔλυεν τὸ σάββατον) and also complements the accusation of blasphemy:[43] Jesus makes himself equal to God (ἴσον ἑαυτὸν ποιῶν τῷ θεῷ). Thus Jesus' justification for his act of healing – though identified as blasphemy – becomes the essential occasion for the intention to kill him, although the reference to the unity of Father and Son within the accusation is an essential feature of the Johannine 'discourse universe' (cf. 5.17–30;

---

[40] Some old Greek manuscripts (A K N Γ Δ Θ and others) add καὶ ἐζήτουν αὐτὸν ἀποκτεῖναι. The oldest and best evidence (𝔓⁶⁶·⁷⁵ ℵ B C D L W and others) reads the longer text which, plausibly, adds the sentence from John 5.18. NKJV reads the longer version and therefore adds 'and sought to kill Him'.

[41] On the imperfect tense of ἐδίωκον, see Johannes Beutler, *Das Johannesevangelium: Kommentar* (Freiburg: Herder, 2013), 191.

[42] For Jewish discussion on Sabbath rest and God's ongoing work of preserving creation, see, e.g., Martin Asiedu-Peprah, *Johannine Sabbath Conflicts as Juridical Controversy* (WUNT, 2/132; Tübingen: Mohr Siebeck, 2001), 77; Peder Borgen, 'The Sabbath Controversy in John 5:1–18 and Analogous Controversy Reflected in Philo's Writings', in Peder Borgen, *Early Christianity and Hellenistic Judaism* (Edinburgh: T&T Clark, 1996), 105–20, 110–13.

[43] Even if, unlike Mark 2.7, the charge of blasphemy is not explicitly pronounced, even though it certainly belongs to the polemic of opposition in the Johannine world (10.33, 36), the accusation that Jesus makes himself equal to God refers to the offence of blasphemy; cf. for example, Rainer Metzner, *Das Verständnis von Sünde im Johannesevangelium* (WUNT, 122; Tübingen: Mohr Siebeck, 2000), 190.

10.30; see also the statements about the mutual indwelling of God and his Son in, e.g., 10.38; 14.10). In this sense, accurate information about Jesus leads to wrong conclusions, because the opponents do not share the Johannine viewpoint.

John 5.18 does not express a formal decision to kill Jesus. It is an intention (ἐζήτουν) whose enactment is attempted several times (see 7.30, 32, 44; 8.59; 10.31–39; cf. 7.19–20, 25; 8.37, 40; 11.8). In fact, the plot to kill Jesus can also prompt a different course of action (as in 7.1 and 8.59). Jesus escapes persecution until the arrival of his hour of glorification (12.20–36).

Within the Johannine narrative world, a formal decision to sentence Jesus to death only comes in a political context after Jesus raises Lazarus in a kind of template for his own resurrection (11.47–53).[44] Thus, the raising of Lazarus as an event that prefigures Jesus' own resurrection forms the basis of the final decision to kill Jesus. Having been informed of Jesus' miraculous deed, the Pharisees (!) gather the Sanhedrin with the chief priests and discuss their course of action, given the potential political consequences of Jesus' growing number of followers. Caiaphas, the ἀρχιερεὺς τοῦ ἐνιαυτοῦ ἐκείνου, prepares for the selection of the one who must die for his people (v. 51: ... ἵνα εἷς ἄνθρωπος ἀποθάνῃ ὑπὲρ τοῦ λαοῦ καὶ μὴ ὅλον τὸ ἔθνος ἀπόληται ...); this is the council's final decision regarding Jesus' fate (v. 53):

ἀπ' ἐκείνης οὖν τῆς ἡμέρας ἐβουλεύσαντο
ἵνα ἀποκτείνωσιν αὐτόν

Then, from that day on, they plotted
to put him to death.

After referring to the arrival of Jesus' hour of glory (12.27–35), and after reporting how Jesus prepares his disciples for the period after his return to the Father (Jn 13–17), there follows John's unique portrayal of Jesus' passion, cross and resurrection.

I interpret the death sentence in 11.53, nevertheless, as a 'repetition and variation'[45] of John 5.18, in that 11.53 represents the formal confirmation and enforcement of 5.18, at a time when Jesus proclaims his passion to be his glorification and the last stage of his earthly journey has begun (cf. ch. 12). Therefore, John 11.47–53 also needs to be examined with John 5.18 in a comparative analysis of the Markan and the Johannine presentation of the plot to kill Jesus.

Comparative analysis

As mentioned earlier in this study, the description of Jesus' public ministry, death and resurrection are essentially components of the narrative genre of the gospels. It also seems to be part of the narrative plot of these gospels, as encountered in Mark and

---

[44] On John 11.47–53 within the overall context of John's Gospel, see Camilus Umoh, *The Plot to Kill Jesus: A Contextual Study of John 11.47–53* (EHS, 23/696; Frankfurt: Lang, 2000).
[45] On the literary concept of 'repetition and variation' in John, see Gilbert Van Belle, 'Style Criticism and the Fourth Gospel', in *One Text, a Thousand Methods: Studies in Memory of Sjef van Tilborg*, ed. P. Chatelion Counet and Ulrich Berges (BIS, 71; Boston: Brill, 2005), 291–316.

John, that Jesus' death has already been predicted as a necessity. Mark 3.6 incorporates an early plot to kill Jesus into his narrative, which, in addition to offering theological interpretations of Jesus' death as integral to his service for the many, focuses on the public-political context, even if Mark largely neglects this motif in the narrative that follows. In John's distinctive presentation of Jesus, there are similar anticipatory markers of Jesus' death and resurrection that seemingly belong to a gospel's narrative strategy. Somewhat more surprising is the reporting of a formal agreement to kill Jesus; it is reported in roughly similar narrative time and, particularly, on a similar occasion. Formulated and motivated differently and, unlike Mark, resumed several times, this decision is not due to genre and narrative plot as such but demonstrates an active reception of the Markan-editorial narrative arrangement.

It is noteworthy that in both gospels the decision to kill Jesus is tied to the healing of a paralytic: hand paralysis in Mark, musculoskeletal paralysis in John. Both stories contain certain parallels. Mark 2.1–12 and John 5.1–9 have already been identified as passages that could establish a direct or indirect relationship between John's Gospel and Mark's Gospel.[46] In addition to verbal and thematic links between the two miracle stories, reference has been made to structural parallels in their literary context (to which the plot to kill Jesus belongs). The following comparison focuses only on the opponents' decision to kill Jesus at the editorial level of both texts.[47] We will start with a linguistic comparison of the two decisions in Mark 3.6 and John 5.18:

Mark 3.6	John 5.18
καὶ ἐξελθόντες οἱ Φαρισαῖοι εὐθὺς μετὰ τῶν Ἡρῳδιανῶν συμβούλιον ἐδίδουν κατ' αὐτοῦ ὅπως αὐτὸν ἀπολέσωσιν.	διὰ τοῦτο οὖν μᾶλλον ἐζήτουν αὐτὸν οἱ Ἰουδαῖοι ἀποκτεῖναι,
cf. 3.2: καὶ παρετήρουν αὐτὸν εἰ τοῖς σάββασιν θεραπεύσει αὐτόν, ἵνα κατηγορήσωσιν αὐτοῦ.	ὅτι οὐ μόνον ἔλυεν τὸ σάββατον,
cf. 2.7: τί οὗτος οὕτως λαλεῖ; βλασφημεῖ· τίς δύναται ἀφιέναι ἁμαρτίας εἰ μὴ εἷς ὁ θεός;	ἀλλὰ καὶ πατέρα ἴδιον ἔλεγεν τὸν θεὸν ἴσον ἑαυτὸν ποιῶν τῷ θεῷ.

The terminology used to convey the intention to kill Jesus in Mark 3.6 and John 5.18 differs almost completely in terms of linguistic details.[48] Both texts follow the previous plot, a miracle sequence (Mk 2.1–3.6 and Jn 4.46–5.9) that stirs up the conflict. διὰ τοῦτο οὖν μᾶλλον takes up the brief controversy in John 5.17–18. At the same time, it presupposes the function of the previous Sabbath healing of the paralytic (5.1–9) as an act in which conflict seems to have been inflamed. As the opposing actors οἱ Ἰουδαῖοι

---

[46] On the debate, see Gilbert Van Belle, 'How John "Rewrites" Mark as Seen in John 5.1–18' (in this volume).

[47] I assume the use of tradition not only in Mark 2.1–3.6, but also in John 5.1–16, as I have shown elsewhere; see Michael Labahn, *Jesus als Lebensspender. Untersuchungen zu einer Geschichte der johanneischen Tradition anhand ihrer Wundergeschichten* (BZNW, 98; Berlin: de Gruyter, 1999), 213–64; Michael Labahn, 'Eine Spurensuche anhand von Joh 5.1–18: Bemerkungen zu Wachstum und Wandel der Heilung eines Lahmen', in Michael Labahn, *Ausgewählte Studien*, 391–411.

[48] An image that will change when the full motive is compared.

are mentioned rather than the Pharisees; the *Ioudaioi* are the classic representation of opposition within the Johannine narrative and are a typical feature of the presentation of conflict.[49]

In the Gospel of Mark, the decision to kill Jesus is called συμβούλιον ἐδίδουν[50] and it carries the formal character of a decision. In the Fourth Gospel, however, it is simply noted that the opponents intend to kill Jesus (ἐζήτουν ... ἀποκτεῖναι), and this is to be understood as an intensification of the persecution noted in 5.16; it is unsuccessfully tried out through individual attempts until the final decision is taken in John 11.47–53. However, in view of certain linguistic signals, it is necessary to enquire about the extent to which the influence of Mark 11.18, for example, may be plausibly proposed.[51] As in Mark 11.18 (see also Mk 14.1, although 11.18 uses the verb ἀπόλλυμι, as in 3.6) John 5.18 refers to the intention (ζητέω) to kill Jesus.

The decision already made to persecute Jesus (διὰ τοῦτο ἐδίωκον οἱ Ἰουδαῖοι τὸν Ἰησοῦν) in John 5.16 is tightened and concretized through the use of ἀποκτεῖναι. In Johannine diction Jesus can be killed, but the concept of annihilation (as in Mk 3.6) is inappropriate for the Johannine account since Jesus' death is not annihilation but the sovereign act of Jesus the Son of God; it represents his exaltation to the father, his victory over the ruler of the world, and it is an act of salvation for his followers.[52] In terms of Christology or theology, the Johannine reformulation is completely justified. Moreover, in John 3.16; 6.39; 10.28; 17.12 and 18.9, the verb ἀπόλλυμι is used to offer assurance that Jesus is the guarantor that none of his followers shall be lost; the Johannine focus is therefore on a different semantic code.

As in Mark 3.2 and 6, healing on the Sabbath is, in John 5, the central factor in the plan to kill Jesus. In addition to the Sabbath transgression, John 5.18 explicitly mentions Jesus' claim to act like God. This does not bring about an accusation of blasphemy, although the verdict does seem to be implied[53] (cf. Jn 10.33, 36, referring to Jesus' self-claim: ἐγὼ καὶ ὁ πατὴρ ἕν ἐσμεν [10.30]). This, in turn, is reminiscent of Mark 2.7, where Jesus is accused of blasphemy because he makes a claim (forgiveness of sin) that his opponents attribute exclusively to God. The key elements leading to the plot to kill Jesus in Mark 2.1–3.6 can also be found in John. However, in John 5.16–18 they are fused into the Johannine discourse universe and current narrative context.

A linguistic comparison of the first two plots to kill Jesus (Mk 3.6 and Jn 5.16, 18) seemingly supports the independent development of a similar preparation for Jesus' passion narrative in the presentation of his public activity; this could quite possibly

---

[49] For the various features of οἱ Ἰουδαῖοι as characters in the Johannine narrative, see the brief assessment by Udo Schnelle, 'Die Juden im Johannesevangelium', in *Gedenkt an das Wort: Festschrift für Werner Vogler zum 65. Geburtstag*, ed. Christoph Kähler and Martina Böhm (Leipzig: Evangelische Verlagsanstalt, 1999), 217–30. Cf. the different assessment offered by Adele Reinhartz, 'The Jews of the Fourth Gospel', in *The Oxford Handbook of Johannine Studies*, ed. Judith M. Lieu and Martinus C. de Boer (Oxford: Oxford University Press, 2018), 123–37.
[50] Cf. Gnilka, *Evangelium*, 126.
[51] Cf. Neirynck, 'John 5,1–18', 706.
[52] Cf., e.g., Jörg Frey, 'Edler Tod – wirksamer Tod – stellvertretender Tod – heilschaffender Tod: Zur narrativen und theologischen Deutung des Todes Jesu im Johannesevangeliums', in Jörg Frey, *Die Herrlichkeit des Gekreuzigten*, 555–84.
[53] Cf., e.g. Asiedu-Peprah, *Johannine Sabbath Conflicts*, 77.

have been derived from a comparable narrative plot within the gospel genre. But one should not draw premature conclusions, given that the Johannine narrator adapts his memories, traditions or sources in a creative manner to serve his own narrative of Jesus and according to his own discourse universe.[54] In the Fourth Gospel, therefore, the intention to kill Jesus presupposes the Johannine narrative context and theological interpretation of the Sabbath healing. The opponents also stem from the Johannine narrative universe. Likewise, the death of Jesus cannot destroy him, since the cross is not so much the locus of death but of the triumph of the sovereign Son of God and of his return to the Father. However, as far as terms belonging to βουλ- and συμβουλ- are used in John 11.53 and 18.14,[55] this is again a signal for one to compare in more detail the overall context of the intention to kill Jesus in John and Mark. This applies even if the verbs used in the Fourth Gospel show different semantic shades of meaning and without the Latinism συμβούλιον ἐδίδουν, since the formulations under question closely reflect the decision to kill Jesus (more on which below).

As we have already seen, John 11.47–53 must be regarded as the explicit Johannine expression of the decision to kill Jesus. The formal terminology encountered in Mark 3.6 would, for theological reasons, have been too premature if it had been included in John 5.18. There is no place either for a death penalty in John 5, because the 'hour' – as the time of the cross and glorification (7.30; 8.20; 12.23, 27; 13.1; 17.1; see also 7.6, 8) – has not yet arrived; and from a Johannine theological perspective, the killing of Jesus cannot take place without the agreement of Father and Son (cf. 12.27–28). In light of these basic insights, the various markers linking the decision to kill Jesus in John 11.47–53 with Mark 3.6 are of particular importance.

Unlike John 5.18, and yet similar to Mark, the Pharisees initiate the deliberations leading to the decision to kill Jesus (11.47). The Pharisees are not joined by the Herodians according to John, but 11.57 does include a second group from among the Jerusalem aristocracy, namely the enigmatic group of chief priests who are well known from the Markan narrative context (see Mk 11.18). In the Gospel of Mark, two miracle stories trigger the decision to kill Jesus. Similarly, according to John 11.47, there are signs – a well-established Johannine term, but here in the plural ('many signs') and thus not restricted to the raising of Lazarus – that force the Sanhedrin to take action (... οὗτος ὁ ἄνθρωπος πολλὰ ποιεῖ σημεῖα; v. 47). The High Priest Caiaphas prophesied, as the additional explanatory comment claims (v. 51), that it is better that one man should die (εἷς ἄνθρωπος ἀποθάνῃ; taking up the intention to kill Jesus from Jn 5.18) for the people (ὑπὲρ τοῦ λαοῦ) than for the whole people to perish (ὅλον τὸ ἔθνος ἀπόληται;

---

[54] See the apposite remarks of Schnelle, *Einleitung*, 581: the Fourth Evangelist 'integrierte jene Traditionen in sein Evangelium, die nach seiner Meinung geeignet waren, ein Verstehen des Christusgeschehens und den Glauben an Jesus Christus als den fleischgewordenen Gottessohn zu fördern. Dieser Rezeptionsvorgang lässt die theologische und schriftstellerische Kompetenz des 4. Evangelisten erkennen. Johannes gestaltet Tradition und Redaktion zu einem erzählerisch und theologisch neuen Ganzen aus'.
[55] However, at the time of the Jewish trial before Annas, the verb συμβουλεύω is used in the sense of 'giving advice': ἦν δὲ Καϊάφας ὁ συμβουλεύσας τοῖς Ἰουδαίοις ὅτι συμφέρει ἕνα ἄνθρωπον ἀποθανεῖν ὑπὲρ τοῦ λαοῦ.

cf. Mark 3.6: αὐτὸν ἀπολέσωσιν [v. 50]). The use of the verb ἀπόλλυμι in Mark 3.6 and 11.50 may, of course, form a coincidental parallel, especially since the verb is used frequently in different narrative contexts in both Mark and John.[56] The parallel does, nevertheless, represent a noteworthy detail. The actual decision is expressed with the aid of the phrase ἐβουλεύσαντο ἵνα ἀποκτείνωσιν αὐτόν, which is reminiscent of the wording of the decision in Mark 3.6: συμβούλιον ἐδίδουν. Thus, when John 5.16, 18 and 11.47–53 are compared to the Markan evidence as a whole, a shift takes place from the initial impression of how to interpret the different linguistic evidence and content in the Markan and Johannine accounts of the intention to kill Jesus. If one rules out a model of literary dependence, which is oriented more towards modern desk activity or the postmodern phenomenon of a digital text workshop,[57] then the observations noted above are important: some form of indirect oral rather than direct literary relationship can be considered.

A series of 'soft' criteria for placing John's account in 5.18 within the same horizon as Mark 2.1–3.6 and 11.18 must, then, be duly noted. The immediate starting point for the Johannine presentation of the persecution and plot to kill Jesus is, as in Mark 2.1–3.6, the healing of a paralytic. Although the immediate Markan context of the healing of the paralysed hand bears little resemblance to the healing of the paralysed man at the Jerusalem pool, both healing stories adhere to the theme of deliverance from sin. Forgiveness of sins in Mark 2.1–12 derives from the authority of the Markan Jesus. It is integrated into the miracle story itself, where Jesus' forgiveness of sins precedes the act of healing as confirmation or proof of that authority. In John 5, the healing miracle precedes the call for the healed man to sin no more: ἴδε ὑγιὴς γέγονας, μηκέτι ἁμάρτανε, ἵνα μὴ χεῖρόν σοί τι γένηται (5.14).[58] Healing and the forgiveness of sins are not directly related, as they are in Mark 2.1–12. In John, the paralytic is healed in a holistic way, so that 5.14 concerns the possibility of living a healthy life, including a life without sin. Verse 15, however, exposes the failure of the healed man: in the face of the self-revelation of the Son of God, the man does not recognize God's glory visible in Jesus' performance of miracles (Jn 2.11) and he fails again in and through his report to the

---

[56] Ten times in Mark (1.24; 2.22; 3.6; 4.38; 8.35[twice]; 9.22, 41; 11.18; 12.9) and ten times in John (3.16; 6.12, 27, 39; 10.10, 28; 11.50; 12.25; 17.12; 18.9).

[57] For Jürgen Becker, 'Das Johannesevangelium im Streit der Methoden (1980–1984)', in Jürgen Becker, *Annäherungen: Zur urchristlichen Theologiegeschichte und zum Umgang mit ihren Quellen. Ausgewählte Aufsätze zum 60. Geburtstag mit einer Bibliographie des Verfassers*, ed. Ulrich Mell (BZNW, 76; Berlin: de Gruyter, 1995), 204–81, 228–29, the model of literary dependence between John and the Synoptics is unconvincing because it is depicted as the work of a modern scholar simultaneously working on different texts. This criticism may be based on the individual excesses of the idea of literary dependence. However, even in the context of the Synoptic problem, which has to do with literary dependence, freedom and reliance on an antecedent text, we are dealing with different, even low degrees of verbatim correspondence. Within the field of oral tradition, low degrees of verbatim correspondence together with structural parallels become highly valuable signals of relationships between textual entities (see further below).

[58] In this respect, the themes of Mark 2.7 and John 5.14 are quite closely related, but unlike Rudolf Schnackenburg, *Das Johannesevangelium II. Teil: Kommentar zu Kap. 5–12* (HThK, IV/2; Freiburg: Herder, 1971), 123, I do not think that in John 5 the paralytic's sin has been forgiven by God ('seine Sünde von Gott vergeben worden ist', referring to 5.17). Rather, his life has been restored by Jesus' healing, which should lead to faith because of the revelation of Jesus as God's gift of life (see also 2.11).

Jews.[59] Structural similarities here are impressive, but at the same time there are a number of linguistic variations and differences in factual detail, which again points to the Johannine narrator as an indirect rather than direct literary recipient of Mark.

There is a different motivation in each gospel for the accusation of blasphemy. In Mark 2.6–7 the scribes accuse Jesus of having claimed for himself God's authority to forgive sins. This is not exactly what Jesus says in John 5.17: ὁ πατήρ μου ἕως ἄρτι ἐργάζεται κἀγὼ ἐργάζομαι (compare this with the opponents' representation of Jesus' statement, v. 18: καὶ πατέρα ἴδιον ἔλεγεν τὸν θεὸν ἴσον ἑαυτὸν ποιῶν τῷ θεῷ). However, both texts are extremely close in terms of the basis for the accusation; forgiveness of sins is an act reserved for God,[60] and this causes his opponents to accuse Jesus of blasphemy. In the Fourth Gospel, as already noted, there is no explicit charge of blasphemy in 5.18, but the problem underpinning the reason for killing Jesus is related to the accusation of blasphemy, which is later explicitly stated (cf. John 10.33, 36; 19.7). It remains true that in both cases the intention to kill Jesus implies that he has violated the Sabbath rest and is guilty of blasphemy.

Another analogous feature is the high christological claim in Mark 2.1–3 and 6, which is an essential basis for Jesus' discourse in the Johannine narrative and is reflected in particular in the claim: ὁ πατήρ μου ἕως ἄρτι ἐργάζεται κἀγὼ ἐργάζομαι. In both scenes, opponents are confronted with Jesus' unique authority and special claim before they express their intention to kill him.

The combination of the intention to kill Jesus with the Sabbath transgression creates a comparable matrix of justification in both gospels, reminiscent of Jesus' well-known controversy in relation to Sabbath regulations. Nevertheless, the topic is of structural importance for each narrative and should not be neglected when it comes to determining the nature of a possible relationship between the two gospels.

Despite differences in language, Mark 3.6 and John 5.18 are closely linked in their presentation of the opponents' intention to kill Jesus. As shown, the connection between them becomes linguistically more impressive if John 11.53 (or 11.47–53) is joined to 5.18 as an intra-Johannine co-text. It is likely that John 5.18 (and 11.53) betrays awareness of Mark 2.1–3.6 in view of their shared basic structure of healing miracles (paralysed man/paralysed hand – long-term paralysed man) linked to deliverance from sin (forgiveness of sins – revelation of Jesus as God's messenger leading to salvation), Sabbath transgression with a claim to authority (lord of the Sabbath – continuation of the activity of heavenly Father) and an accusation of blasphemy (Mk 2.7, but only indirectly in Jn 5.18) and the subsequent decision to kill Jesus (Mk 3.6 – Jn 5.18; 11.53).

---

[59] Labahn, *Jesus als Lebensspender*, 377; Michael Labahn, 'Die Gabe des Lebens und kaiserliche Wohltaten – ein unvermeidlicher Gegensatz: Der Jesus des vierten Evangeliums als Wundertäter und der römische Kaiser', in *Christ and the Emperor: The Gospel Evidence*, ed. Gilbert Van Belle and Joseph Verheyden (BiTS, 20; Leuven: Peeters, 2014), 249–77, here 260–1; for a different position, see, e.g. Klaus Scholtissek, 'Mündiger Glaube: Zur Architektur und Pragmatik johanneischer Begegnungsgeschichten: Joh 5 und Joh 9', in *Paulus und Johannes. Exegetische Studien zur paulinischen und johanneischen Theologie und Literatur*, ed. Dieter Sänger and Ulrich Mell (WUNT, 198; Tübingen: Mohr Siebeck, 2006), 75–105.

[60] Cf., e.g., Rudolf Pesch, *Das Markusevangelium. I. Teil: Einleitung und Kommentar zu Kap. 1, 18, 26*, (5th edn; HThK, II/1; Freiburg: Herder, 1989), 158–59.

Finally, particularly impressive is the idiosyncratic chiastic structure, whereby elements linked to Jesus' public activity in Mark are placed at the point where the passion begins in John. In the schema below we see the Pharisees and members of the Jerusalem aristocracy (here as part of the Sanhedrin: Jn 11.47) deciding to kill Jesus, thus transferring the key idiom from Mark 3.6 (συμβούλιον ἐδίδουν ... αὐτὸν ἀπολέσωσιν) to John 11.53 (ἐβουλεύσαντο ἵνα ἀποκτείνωσιν αὐτόν), whereas John 5.18 first mentions the intention to kill Jesus, which we find in Mark after the cleansing of the temple (Mark 11.18; in 12.12 and 14.1 people search to arrest Jesus):

After a healing of a paralytic on Sabbath Mk 3.6:	→	Shortly before the passion narrative starts Mark 11.18:
... οἱ Φαρισαῖοι εὐθὺς μετὰ τῶν Ἡρῳδιανῶν συμβούλιον ἐδίδουν κατ' αὐτοῦ ὅπως αὐτὸν ἀπολέσωσιν		οἱ ἀρχιερεῖς καὶ οἱ γραμματεῖς καὶ ἐζήτουν πῶς αὐτὸν ἀπολέσωσιν
John 5.18:	✕	John 11.53: (Jn 11.47: Συνήγαγον οὖν οἱ ἀρχιερεῖς καὶ οἱ Φαρισαῖοι)
ἐζήτουν αὐτὸν οἱ Ἰουδαῖοι ἀποκτεῖναι		ἐβουλεύσαντο ἵνα ἀποκτείνωσιν αὐτόν

In my view the plot to kill Jesus from Mark's narrative turns into a memory[61] of that incident, with its key features of intention and final decision to kill Jesus, due to the healing of a paralytic on Sabbath combined with the issue of forgiving sin. These memory elements are unfolded anew in the story of the Johannine Jesus. The intention and decision to kill him are placed in a different position, which aligns better with Johannine theology (see above) and possibly offers a more logical chronology placing the intention first and then finally noting the legal decision. Also, the Pharisees as characters are replaced in the context of the passion narrative though still associated with the decision to kill Jesus.

Therefore, the overall picture points to the likely reception of Mark's Gospel by the Johannine narrator, suggesting that the Johannine plot to kill Jesus is a retelling of its Markan counterpart. This need not be understood as a case of direct literary relationship; it is better explained with reference to a culture of orality, as already intimated in this chapter and as will be explained in more detail in the following section.

---

[61] On the psychological theory of memory used here, see below pp. 247–48.

'The plot to kill Jesus' in Mark and John as an example of re-oralization

As shown above, a number of structural, thematic and linguistic factors, mostly in the form of 'soft' criteria, can be adduced in support of John's acquaintance with Mark 2.1–3.6 and 11.18 in his presentation of the decision to kill Jesus (Jn 5.18; 11.47–53). Those who already interpret John 5.1–9 as engaging with Mark 2.1–12 will regard this scenario as persuasive and will interpret these criteria on the level of direct literary dependence.[62] For those who rule out a literary relationship, the factors noted above are unlikely to be regarded as convincing. A third option, which helps to account for some of the obvious parallels as well as the differences and autonomous reception, is John's acquaintance with passages and entire episodes from Mark's Gospel via oral tradition, as suggested by the model of 'secondary orality'. With the term 'secondary orality',[63] I refer to proposals made by Walter Ong for describing the use and reuse of material from written texts in an oral context.[64] The term has subsequently been taken up by Werner Kelber with reference to early Christian use of Old Testament texts. Kelber notes that if a written text:

> ...enters the world of hearers by being read aloud [as was typically the case in antiquity], it functions as secondary orality. But now the story narrated is one that was never heard in primary orality, for it comprises textually filtered and contrived language.[65]

This concept is also used to explain the relationship *between* early Christian writings if the nature of the similarities and differences between them points to some kind of reception, but for which written or literary dependence does not seem a plausible scenario. As far as Ong's original concept is concerned, the term 'secondary' refers to orality in relation to a written communication culture in which the orality *derives* from written texts and their contexts. Therefore, since the original formulation of the term 'secondary orality' assumes a culture of extensive writing, I refer in this connection to the concept as a 'post-Guttenberg paradigm'. The term 'secondary' is not intended to devalue such orality but it does describe an orality derived from written texts. This aspect is the decisive reason for the application of the term 'secondary orality' to describe ancient, especially early Christian, phenomena. The term acknowledges the significant presence of written texts, while allowing at the same time for an oral culture,

---

[62] E.g., Neirynck, 'John 5,1–18', 703–8; Neirynck, 'John and the Synoptics 1975–1990', in *John and the Synoptics*, ed. Adelbert Denaux (BETL, 101; Leuven: Leuven University Press and Peeters, 1992), 3–62, especially 53–55.

[63] Cf. Michael Labahn, '"Secondary Orality" in the Gospel of John: A "Post-Gutenberg" Paradigm for Understanding the Relationship between Written Gospel Texts', in *The Origins of John's Gospel*, ed. Stanley E. Porter and Hughson T. Ong (Johannine Studies, 2; Leiden: Brill, 2016), 53–80; Michael Labahn, 'Secondary Orality', in *The Dictionary of the Bible in Ancient Media*, ed. Tom Thatcher, Chris Keith, Raymond F. Person and Elsie Stern (London: T&T Clark, 2017), 362–64.

[64] Cf., e.g., Walter J. Ong, *Orality and Literacy: The Technologizing of the World* (New Accents, Reprint; London/New York: Routledge, 2007).

[65] Werner Kelber, *The Oral and the Written Gospel: The Hermeneutics of Speaking and Writing in the Synoptic Tradition, Mark, Paul, and Q* (Philadelphia, PA: Fortress, 1983), 217–18.

that is, a culture in which the availability of written texts is not widespread.[66] Above all, the term specifies the scope for possible 'oral' dependence, in contrast to the phenomenon of direct literary dependence. 'Secondary orality' presupposes the *renewed verbalization of a text* that has already been fixed in writing – for example, through the process of reading but also its subsequent retelling or further re-transmission. After a short or longer (itself oral) reception process in the memory of hearers, the material is written down again. It is this phase that is expressed with the aid of the term 'secondary'. While written texts were not as widespread or as accessible in antiquity as they are in the post-Guttenberg period, the concept of secondary orality does help us understand the relationship between passages in ancient texts that exhibit similarities and differences in content, structure and formulation, but, at the same time, are not the result of a purely literary relationship or creative copying. Since, however, the now well-established term 'secondary orality' was perceived to be misleading and anachronistic among participants in the Athens conference on 'Mark and John', the term 're-oralization' is arguably more appropriate for future descriptions of this phenomenon.

It is important, in my view, that the phenomenon described as 'secondary orality' or 're-oralization' can appropriately account for similarities and differences in John as a reception of Mark's Gospel. On the basis of mnemo-psychological factors, structural parallels that are often associated with several core terms can be regarded as characteristic of oral tradition.[67] Against this background, Breytenbach describes how human memory can reorganize stories. His description helps us understand how an author processes or handles sources, especially through oral retelling:

> Wenn der Hörer nun aber zum Erzähler wird, greift er nicht auf die von ihm damals gehörte Phonemkette zurück. Diese hat er nicht mehr im Ohr. Er hat sie aber beim Hören in eine semantische Textbasis, die situationell organisiert ist, umgesetzt. Er greift auf diese kognitive Repräsentation in seinem eigenen Gedächtnis zurück und formuliert mit Hilfe seiner gedanklichen Vorstellung der Situation, von der die Erzählung handelte, eine neue Erzählung, die seinem neuen kommunikativen Kontext entspricht.[68]

In this context, memories do not selectively store texts or even single words, but rather, through meaningful and hierarchical networks, retain 'contents and meanings'

---

[66] In our image of ancient oral culture, we should not forget that, in the world of early Christianity, literary phenomena had a comparatively high presence, for example through numerous inscriptions, even though the question of literacy among ancient people requires a nuanced view that accepts the presence of literary sources (from books to small graffiti); different degrees of literacy, with a relatively small group of people able to read longer texts; and oral culture.

[67] Vgl. Cilliers Breytenbach, 'MNHMONEUEIN: Das "Sich-erinnern" in der urchristlichen Überlieferung – Die Bethanienepisode (Mk 14,3–9/Jn 12,1–8) als Beispiel', in Adelbert Denaux (ed.), *John and the Synoptics*, 548–57. See also Michael Labahn, 'Die Macht des Gedächtnisses: Überlegungen zu Möglichkeit und Grenzen des Einflusses hebräischer Texttradition auf die Johannesapokalypse', in *Von der Septuaginta zum Neuen Testament: Textgeschichtliche Erörterungen*, ed. Martin Karrer, Siegfried Kreuzer and Marcus Sigismund (ANTF, 43; Berlin/New York: de Gruyter, 2010), 385–416, especially 390–92.

[68] Breytenbach, 'MNHMONEUEIN', 554–55.

in long-term memory,[69] so that traditions are preserved in memory through selected key thematic terms and basic structures.[70] While the parallels between John 5.16, 18; 11.47-53 and the Markan representation of the plot to kill Jesus do not amount to quotations or even allusions, in line with mnemo-psychological insights these coincidences are best understood as 'secondary orality'/'re-oralization'. We note that key terms used by Mark to express the decision to kill Jesus (συμβούλιον ἐδίδουν / ἐβουλεύσαντο ... αὐτὸν ἀπολέσωσιν / ἀποκτείνωσιν αὐτόν) or the intention to kill him (ἐζήτουν ... ἀπολέσωσιν / ἀποκτεῖναι) reappear in John. This corresponds to the technique of storing analogous motifs so that recipients can rearrange them in any future re-narration of the incident(s), especially as this exchange fits into their narrative world. Basic components or triggers remain stored in memory; thus John's presentation of the intention to kill Jesus is triggered by an act of healing on the Sabbath and an accusation of blasphemy that – in entirely Johannine diction – lead to opposition. It is noteworthy that the timing and content of the plot to kill Jesus is reported in an analogous position in both texts.[71] Each narrative builds its own narrative inventory of opponents to Jesus; the similarities in the identification of those responsible for the Johannine decision to kill Jesus are therefore striking, since in both texts the Pharisees cooperate with members of the Jerusalem-oriented aristocracy. Modifications to key terms or common basic structures can be easily understood as an adaptation to the discourse universe of the Johannine narrator. The role of oral memory as a 'storehouse' of information plays an important role in the production of a new text drawn from different sources. Emerging from this memory is the motif of the intention to kill Jesus, which has possibly been stored after hearing the Gospel of Mark or from an oral recounting of the Markan account of the life of Jesus.

Conclusion

We return to the starting point of this chapter. The motif of an early plot or decision to kill Jesus on the basis of a Sabbath healing fits well in a narrative whose orientation is towards the cross, but it is not a general characteristic of the genre of biographical or historical gospel. This is a distinctive, though not necessarily unique, motif in the Markan and Johannine narratives; it is a motif that, despite low verbatim correspondence, connects the narrative plot of John's Gospel to that of Mark's Gospel.

It is not possible, however, to establish direct literary dependence between Mark and John on the basis of their accounts of the decision to kill Jesus. The two gospels

---

[69] Labahn, 'Die Macht des Gedächtnisses', 391, with reference to Viktor Hobi, 'Kurze Einführung in die Grundlagen der Gedächtnispsychologie', in *Vergangenheit in mündlicher Überlieferung*, ed. Jürgen von Ungern-Sternberg and Hansjörg Reinau (Colloquium Rauricum, 1; Stuttgart: B.G. Teubner, 1988), 20-24.
[70] Cf., e.g., Gordon H. Bower/Randolph K. Cirilo, 'Cognitive Psychology and Text Processing', in *Handbook of Discourse Analysis Vol. 1: Disciplines of Discourse*, ed. Teun A. Van Dijk (London: Academic Press, 1985), 71-105.
[71] See above pp. 232-39.

formulate distinctive accounts, both linguistically and theologically. Nevertheless, it is also doubtful – and contradictory to form-historical research – that the narrative frame of the decision to kill Jesus stems from an independent oral tradition earlier than Mark and John. As a third alternative, the model of John's knowledge of Mark through oral memory appears to be a good option, particularly the concept of 'secondary orality'/'re-oralization'. It also presupposes some form of contact between Johannine Christians and/or the Johannine narrator with Mark, either as a result of the oral reception of the narrative and its individual episodes, due to some form of contact in oral tradition, or through preservation of the stories in oral memory.

18

The Triumph of the King: John's Transformation of Mark's Account of the Passion

Helen K. Bond

Advocates of the view that John knew one or more of the Synoptic Gospels always have to wrestle with a difficult problem: why did John alter the earlier texts so much? In the case of Mark, how do we explain John's omission of such iconic scenes as the baptism, the transfiguration or the Sanhedrin trial? And how do we account for significant chronological differences, not to mention Jesus' distinctive teaching in this gospel? When the Fourth Evangelist was thought to have been an eyewitness of events, the problem was less pressing: John could appeal to his own authority, perhaps even as a disciple, to tell the story in his own way. Clement of Alexandria famously declared that John, seeing that the bodily facts had already been set down, composed a 'spiritual' gospel (Eusebius, *Hist. eccl.* 6.14.7). As the traditional view receded, however, scholars were forced to come up with other explanations for John's alterations. Did the evangelist hope to supplement the earlier texts, or to interpret them? To correct, or even to replace them?[1]

It was, of course, the numerous *differences* between John and the Synoptics that convinced Percival Gardner-Smith, C. H. Dodd and the majority of mid-twentieth century commentators that John had no knowledge of the earlier gospels.[2] From this perspective, John's many omissions and 'pointless contradictions' were no longer a problem: John could hardly have reproduced what he did not know.[3] What needed

---

[1] Variants on all of these can be found in the works of Brook Foss Westcott, *The Gospel According to St John* (London: John Murray, 1902), lxxvii–lxxxiv; B. H. Streeter, *The Four Gospels: A Study of Origins* (London: MacMillan, 1964 [first published 1924]), 427–61; J. H. Bernard, *A Critical and Exegetical Commentary on the Gospel According to Saint John* (ICC, 2 vols; Edinburgh: T&T Clark, 1928), 1: xciv–cxxii; George H. C. MacGregor, *The Gospel of John* (London: Hodder and Stoughton, 1928). For more recent discussion, see Richard Bauckham, 'John for Readers of Mark', in Richard Bauckham (ed.), *The Gospels for All Christians: Rethinking Gospel Audiences* (Edinburgh: T&T Clark, 1998), 147–71 (who favours a complementary relationship), and Chris Keith, 'The Competitive Textualization of the Jesus Tradition in John 20:30–31 and 21:24–25', *CBQ* 78 (2016): 321–37 (who favours a competitive replacement).
[2] Percival Gardner-Smith, *Saint John and the Synoptic Gospels* (Cambridge: Cambridge University Press, 1938). For full discussion, see D. Moody Smith, *John Among the Gospels* (Columbia: University of South Carolina Press, 2nd edn, 2001).
[3] The quotation is from Gardner-Smith, *Saint John*, 92.

explaining were rather the many *similarities* between John and the Synoptics, similarities that were largely put down to the use of common oral traditions and an emerging early *kerygma* that gave a unified shape to those traditions. The accounts of Jesus' *passion* in the Gospels of Mark and John, however, were treated as a special case. Mark 14–15 and John 18–19 share a significant number of features – from the sequence of events, to shared details, themes and even common vocabulary. Such a high degree of similar material, it was argued, must go back to a shared (probably written) source, most likely an early continuous passion narrative that formed the basis for both Mark and, later, John.[4]

Despite many valiant attempts to reconstruct it, however, recent decades have seen a waning of scholarly confidence in the existence of any kind of primitive, pre-Markan passion narrative.[5] The hypothetical source was first posited by the form critics, for whom the chronological structure, greater coherence and more specific details regarding place and time that characterized Mark 14–16 were hard to reconcile with the more isolated *pericopae* that comprised the earlier portions of the gospel.[6] What the form critics failed to realise, however, is that this is a common structure in an ancient biography (particularly one relating to a philosopher or teacher), whereby a topical arrangement of *chreiai* (or anecdotes) tends to give way to a more chronological account of the hero's death.[7] In the 1970s a number of redaction critics were already questioning the likelihood of any kind of pre-Markan passion account,[8] and this has only increased in the wake of more recent narrative studies, which have detected the same use of *inclusios*, juxtapositions and dramatic irony in the passion narrative as elsewhere. Mark's style may be simple and colloquial, but his work as a whole exhibits

---

[4] On the relationship between the passion narratives in John and Mark, see Smith, *John Among the Gospels*, 111–37.

[5] Some (like Martin Dibelius) imagined an almost complete passion narrative which Mark simply incorporated into his account with only minimal changes – a model which lies behind the influential studies of Rudolf Pesch, Gerd Theissen and Joel Green. Rudolf Bultmann, however, thought in terms of an original kernel (perhaps along the lines of 1 Cor. 15.3–5, or one of the Markan passion predictions) which acquired more material as it was passed along – a model which inspired the 'composite' theories of Vincent Taylor, Johannes Schreiber, and Detlev Dormeyer. Even in their heyday in the 1960s and 70s, attempts to uncover a pre-Markan passion narrative were far from achieving any kind of a consensus; see Marion L. Soards, 'Appendix IX: The Question of a Pre-Markan Passion Narrative', in Raymond E. Brown, *The Death of the Messiah* (New York: Doubleday, 1994), 1492–524.

[6] Curiously, this putative source does not seem to have emerged at the time when Markan source-criticism was at its height. In the late nineteenth and early twentieth centuries, scholars detected various sources behind Mark's Gospel – a miracle source, a Twelve source, a parables source, an *Ur-Markus*, even a boat source! Some of these (such as the Twelve source) may have extended into the final chapters of the gospel, but no scholar seems to have thought to assign Mark 14–15 as a whole to a separate source. Pre-20th century commentaries move straight from 13.37 to 14.1 without mention of a new source; see, for example, Ezra P. Gould, *A Critical and Exegetical Commentary on the Gospel According to St Mark* (Edinburgh: T&T Clark, 1896).

[7] This is a pattern adopted by Suetonius in his *Lives of the Caesars*, and also by Lucian in his *Life of Demonax*, and to some extent in Diogenes Laertius' *Lives of Philosophers* (though the *chreiai* are often very jumbled in the latter). For fuller discussion, see Helen K. Bond, *The First Biography of Jesus: Genre and Meaning in Mark's Gospel* (Grand Rapids, MI: Wm B. Eerdmans, 2020), 98–106.

[8] See, for example, the essays in Werner H. Kelber, *The Passion in Mark: Studies on Mark 14–16* (Philadelphia, PA: Fortress, 1976), and Frank J. Matera, *The Kingship of Jesus: Composition and Theology in Mark 15* (Chico, CA: Scholars Press, 1982).

a unity of outlook and literary expression that suggests that we are dealing with a creative author and sophisticated theologian. Giving the hero an appropriate and fitting end was an important component of any ancient biography, and biographers were allowed a wide range of latitude when it came to describing the hero's death. Whatever sources Mark inherited, he was by no means compelled to use them in the form in which they came down to him, and the needs of his own particular work would doubtless have necessitated a considerable degree of rewriting of whatever already existed.[9]

The more we question Mark's incorporation of a relatively full, early passion account, of course, the less likely it seems that we can explain the significant similarities between Mark and John by appeal to this shared source. In the remainder of this chapter, I wish to join the ranks of B. H. Streeter, C. K. Barrett, Frans Neirynck and the Leuven School, Udo Schnelle, Andrew Lincoln – and, of course, other contributors to this volume – in the working assumption that John knew and used Mark's Gospel.[10] As Dwight Moody Smith has observed, the persuasiveness of this position depends largely on how well it works in exegesis, and how well John's departures from Mark make sense in the light of the evangelist's wider interests.[11] Towards that end, I propose to compare the trial scenes in Mark and John, noting the way in which John has transformed the earlier gospel in accordance with his wider literary and theological aims.[12] First, though, it will be useful to have a clear understanding of the way in which each evangelist presents the death of Jesus more generally.

Jesus' death in Mark

As noted above, recent work on Mark's Gospel has revealed a careful and creative author who composed a compelling biography of the founder of the religious movement to which he belonged. We should not assume that Mark's passion narrative is a 'neutral' account that has then been subjected to John's much more theological retelling. Mark offers a highly theological account of his hero's death, with its own inner coherence and rhetorical force.

Early on, Mark's *bios* presents his readers with an attractive Jesus. Adopted by God as his son (1.9–11), our hero quickly shows himself to be a force to be reckoned with. He travels throughout Galilee with his male companions, attracting crowds, healing

---

[9] For fuller discussion, see Bond, *First Biography*, 106–13.
[10] Two further works worth noting here are: Anton Dauer, *Die Passionsgeschichte im Johannesevangelium: Eine traditionsgeschichtliche und theologische Untersuchung zu Joh 18,1–19.30* (Munich: Kösel-Verlag, 1972) – who, after carefully comparing John with Synoptic parallels, concluded that the Fourth Gospel used a source which was familiar with the final form of the Synoptics; also Manfred Lang, *Johannes und die Synoptiker: Eine redaktionsgeschichtliche Analyse von Joh 18–20 vor dem markinischen und lukanischen Hintergrund* (FRLANT, 182; Göttingen: Vandenhoeck & Ruprecht, 1998) – who offers a redactional overview of John's use of both Mark and Luke.
[11] Smith, *John Among the Gospels*, 183–84.
[12] For a similar analysis of John 20 and its links particularly with Luke, see Helen K. Bond, 'Recognition and "Those who have not Seen": John's Reception of Synoptic Resurrection Narratives', in *Come and Read: Interpretive Approaches to the Gospel of John*, ed. Alicia D. Myers and Lindsey S. Jodrey (Lanham: Fortress Academic, 2020), 171–84.

the sick and besting opponents wherever he goes. He provides food for the hungry, controls the forces of nature and is even able to raise the dead. It is only in the middle section of the work, however, as Jesus journeys to Jerusalem, that we begin to understand his message (8.22–10.52). Here the Markan Jesus turns all contemporary ideas of honour upside down in favour of a deeply counter-cultural and distasteful focus on what society at large would consider shameful. Disciples are called on to deny themselves, to act as slaves to one another, and to shun all markers of prestige. They are asked to give up everything; not only riches (10.17–22), but homes and families too (10.23–30), and possibly even their lives (8.34–38). True honour and greatness in the community that Jesus forms around himself lies not in courting the esteem of others, but in embracing a new understanding of honour based on ignominious service, suffering and disgrace – a path Jesus himself will follow, even to death (as 10.42–45 makes clear).[13]

Nowhere is Mark's literary artifice more apparent than in the careful links between Jesus' central body of teaching and his death. The Markan Jesus goes willingly to his fate, in full appreciation of what he will be asked to endure. Rejected by envious Jewish authorities (15.10), he will submit himself to the will of the Father and die on a Roman cross – the ultimate expression of what it means to be a 'slave of all'. Jesus becomes increasingly passive as the narrative marches inexorably onwards; others assert authority over his body – arresting, beating, binding, scourging and finally crucifying him. Like a slave, Jesus endures it all, disempowered, humiliated, shamed and violated. Throughout, he is subjected to relentless mockery – from the Jewish leaders, Pilate, Roman soldiers, fellow prisoners and even bystanders – until finally he gives up his life with a scream of anguish and abandonment. For Mark's readers, who may themselves have experienced (or fear) persecution, Jesus provides an example of steadfast endurance: openly declaring his identity before the High Priest (14.62), he metaphorically drinks the cup that has been prepared for him and gives up his spirit (ἐκπνέω, 15.37).

Yet this is not the full picture for Mark. As Jesus hangs on the cross, the earth is plunged into the darkness of a solar eclipse, the veil of the Temple is ripped in two (signifying its impending destruction, 15.33), and a hostile executioner acclaims him 'Son of God' (υἱὸς θεοῦ; 15.38–39). Woven into these scenes at a deeper level are hints of the Roman triumph – the gathering of the whole cohort in the *praetorium*, the procession to the place of the skull (evoking the Capitoline Hill in Rome), the refusal of wine mingled with myrrh (aping the triumphator's refusal of wine), Jesus' 'enthronement' between two others (15.27), and the mingling throughout of the twin ideas of kingship and sacrifice.[14] It is surely significant that themes of kingship dominate two Markan passages – the account of the activities of the anti-'King' Herod (6.14–29) and the crucifixion. In the world of radically new values that the work creates, Jesus' shameful death is indeed the triumph of the king – for those with eyes to see.

---

[13] For the ideas in this paragraph, see Bond, *First Biography*, 224–37.
[14] See Thomas E. Schmidt, 'Mark 15.6–32: The Crucifixion Narrative and the Roman Triumphal Procession', *NTS* 41 (1995): 1–18; and Allan T. Georgia, 'Translating the Triumph: Reading Mark's Crucifixion Narrative against a Roman Ritual of Power', *JSNT* 36 (2013): 17–38.

Jesus' death in John

In terms of the sequence of events, John's Gospel is at its closest to Mark's in the passion narrative, though a number of significant changes give his account a very different character. There is little sense of shame, or of the ignominious, 'bad' death so obviously associated with the cross that we find in Mark. And although not entirely lacking, there is far less sense of Jesus' death as an example to others here (at least some of that role has been transferred to the mysterious and idealised 'Beloved Disciple'). Instead, the note of triumph – muted, yet undeniably present in Mark – is now dominant. Jesus' death for John is the hour of his glorification, the completion of his earthly mission and the judgement of this world.[15]

John prepares for Jesus' death as early as the prologue. As the pre-existent Word of God, Jesus takes on flesh and comes to his own, only to be rejected by those who love darkness rather than light. We quickly learn that he will be the new paschal lamb who takes away the sins of the world (1.29, 36), and as the narrative proceeds, it becomes clear that the long-awaited 'hour' of Jesus' death (2.4; 7.30; 8.20; 12.23, 27; 13.1) will paradoxically be his moment of exaltation. Many features associated with the end of Jesus' ministry in Mark, such as the cleansing of the Temple, the words of the Eucharist, and a gathering of the Sanhedrin, are located much earlier in John (2.13–22; 6.52–58; 11.47–53), ensuring that the theme of Jesus' death is constantly in view (at least for those with some knowledge of Mark).[16] Similarly, the lack of exorcisms in John, along with the widespread motifs of trial and judgement, prepare the way for seeing Jesus' cross as the final confrontation with the powers of Satan. For John, Jesus is engaged in a cosmic struggle between good and evil, life and death. The cross represents the ultimate judgement of 'this world', God's victory over Satan and the condemnation of those who do not believe (14.30; 16.33).

Like the good shepherd, Jesus will lay down his life for his friends, willingly following the path laid out for him by the Father (10.17–18), a theme that is reiterated as Jesus explains his coming death to his disciples in the Farewell Discourses (15.13). Jesus' divine knowledge of his status and destiny comes out clearly in the distinctively Johannine account of his arrest. Confronted by not only Jewish temple police but a large detachment of Roman soldiers,[17] Jesus boldly steps forward, identifying himself as the divine 'I am'. Like the prophets Ezekiel (Ezek. 1.28) or Daniel (Dan. 10.9), the arresting party fall to the ground in the face of this theophany, powerless to do anything against him. Clearly no earthly force could have apprehended Jesus if he had not

---

[15] For good overviews of John's account of Jesus' passion, see Donald Senior, *The Passion of Jesus in the Gospel of John* (Collegeville, MN: Liturgical Press, 1991); Jörg Frey, *The Glory of the Crucified One: Christology and Theology in the Gospel of John* (trans. Wayne Coppins and Christoph Heilig; Waco, TX: Baylor University Press, 2018), 171–97, and Jörg Frey, *Theology and History in the Fourth Gospel: Tradition and Narration* (Waco, TX: Baylor University Press, 2018), 186–96.

[16] There are good reasons to assume that John knew Luke, and perhaps also Matthew, though the limitations of the present study mean that these will only occasionally be mentioned in the footnotes. For discussion, see Smith, *John Among the Gospels*, 85–110.

[17] On the Roman cohort here (σπεῖρα, meaning one tenth of a legion, or 600 men), see Raymond E. Brown, *The Gospel According to John* (Anchor Bible, 29; London: Geoffrey Chapman, 1966), 2:807–8; Mark mentions 'the whole cohort (σπεῖρα)' in 15.16.

allowed himself to be taken. John's dramatic narrative shows that all their 'lanterns' and 'torches' are no match for the one who is truly the 'light of the world' (14.30; 16.33).

Jesus maintains his majestic, serene composure throughout the trial narratives and into the crucifixion account. No longer is he too weak to carry his cross (see Mk 15.21); instead, he carries it himself to the place of crucifixion where, with great irony, Pilate's charge on the cross proclaims his universal kingship (19.19–22). Jesus shares his last moments with his mother and the Beloved Disciple (19.26–27) before declaring his mission 'finished' (τετέλεσται, 19.30); these final scenes echo the opening of Genesis, suggesting that John sees the completion of Jesus' ministry and the birth of the Christ-following community as a new creation.[18] The cross for John represents the 'lifting up' of the Son (3.14; 8.28; 12.31–32, 33), in a sense, a royal enthronement that gathers all people to himself. Despite appearances, Jesus' death is the ultimate revelation of God's love for the world and the beginning of his glorious ascent once more to the Father.

With the broader interests and strategies of these two distinctive passion narratives in view, I shall now turn to a more detailed consideration of their trial narratives, looking first at Jesus' Jewish and Roman trials in Mark, and then at the way in which John has transformed the earlier gospel in harmony with his own particular interests.

Jesus' trials in Mark (14.53–15.20)

Mark's two trial scenes form a carefully structured unit, with a number of parallels between the Jewish and the Roman proceedings.[19] In both, the questions revolve around two themes: one general, the other concerned with Jesus' identity. In the Jewish trial, Jesus is first accused by many false witnesses who are unable to agree with one another in their testimony against him. In the end, some stand up and accuse him of threatening not only to destroy the temple but also to build another in three days 'not made with hands' (ἀχειροποίητον). Yet even this is inconclusive, and Jesus resolutely remains silent (14.60–61a). In response, the High Priest introduces a new theme, now questioning Jesus specifically regarding his identity: 'Are you the Christ, the Son of the Blessed?' Jesus' answer is clear and forthright: 'I am; and you will see the Son of Man seated at the right hand of Power, and coming with the clouds of heaven' (14.62). This is blasphemy, the High Priest declares, and all the council condemns him to death (14.64).

The trial before Pilate similarly revolves around two sets of charges, though they are now reversed. Pilate begins with the question of Jesus' identity: 'Are you the King of the

---

[18] See Ruben Zimmerman, 'Symbolic Communication between John and His Reader: The Garden Symbolism in John 19–20', in *Anatomies of Narrative Criticism: The Past, Present and Future of the Fourth Gospel as Literature*, ed. Tom Thatcher and Stephen D. Moore (Atlanta, GA: Society of Biblical Literature, 2008), 221–35; also Frey, *Glory of the Crucified One*, 192.

[19] For fuller discussion of these passages, including the many historical questions they raise, see my earlier studies in *Pontius Pilate in History and Interpretation* (SNTSMS, 100; Cambridge: Cambridge University Press, 1998), 94–119, 194–202, and *Caiaphas: Friend of Rome and Judge of Jesus?* (Louisville, KY: Westminster John Knox, 2004), 98–108. On the deliberate Markan parallelism between the trials, see also Matera, *The Kingship of Jesus*, 7–8, 99.

Jews?' Again, Jesus chooses to answer this, though his response is far more guarded than before the High Priest: σὺ λέγεις, he says, perhaps implying, 'The words are yours, not mine' (15.2). Jesus is a 'king', but not in any sense that the Roman prefect would understand. The chief priests now accuse him of 'many things' (πολλά), but Jesus, as earlier, refuses to engage with their charges and remains silent (15.5a).

Both Markan trials end with mockery and abuse of the prisoner, each appropriate to the charge brought against him. Following the Jewish trial, it is apparently members of the council who spit on Jesus, cover his face, strike him, and call on him to 'prophesy', while unspecified guards (ὑπηρέται) beat him (14.65). In the fuller account that follows the Roman proceedings, Jesus is taken inside the *praetorium* by Roman soldiers who, after scourging him (15.15), subject him to an undignified mockery of what they see as his kingly pretensions, dressing him in imperial purple, crowning him, and paying him mock-homage (15.16–20).

Finally, in both scenes Jesus is contrasted with another character.[20] In the Jewish trial, it is Peter who, alone of the disciples, has followed Jesus to the High Priest's house and now stands warming himself by the fire (14.54). As Jesus is tried before the High Priest, a maid (παιδίσκη) notices Peter and accuses him of having been with the Nazarene. Peter denies it and moves away from the light of the fire, only to be challenged twice more by the maid and other bystanders. Now Peter's denials become more intense: he calls down a curse on himself and swears, 'I do not know this man of whom you speak' (14.71). Mark's hearers are presented with two ways to behave if called upon to answer for their faith: that of Jesus, who calmly declares his identity even before the most powerful religious leader, and that of Peter, who desperately attempts to distance himself from the charge of being a follower of Jesus, even before a lowly serving maid. Should they find themselves called upon to face trial and persecution, to stand before governors and kings (as 13.9–11 predicts), it is clear which model they are to follow.

In the course of the Roman tribunal, the contrast is with Barabbas. Suddenly we are told that a crowd appears, asking Pilate to honour his usual custom of releasing a prisoner of their choosing (15.6, 8). Mark sets up the element of choice from the beginning, noting that there was a man named Barabbas among those in prison who had committed murder in the insurrection (15.7).[21] In response to Pilate's offer to release the 'King of the Jews', the once-friendly crowd, stirred up by the chief priests, shout instead for Barabbas, a choice they maintain until their wish is granted (15.9–15). The persistent use of the title 'king' in this scene heightens what is at stake in the choice between the two men: will the Jewish crowd choose Jesus as their king and leader, or an insurrectionary, tainted with rebellion and murder? Read in the aftermath of the disastrous war of 66–70 CE, when Jews really did put their trust in political aspirants and armed rebellion, the drama of Mark's scene is not hard to appreciate. The true 'king', all along, was none other than Jesus.

---

[20] See Agusti Borrell, *The Good News of Peter's Denial: A Narrative and Rhetorical Reading of Mark 14:54, 66–72* (Atlanta, GA: Scholars Press, 1998), esp. 61, who notes the 'common basic design' between Peter's denial and the Barabbas scene in the Roman trial, including the threefold questioning, and even linguistic links.

[21] The Greek here is ambiguous: Is Barabbas also a murderer, or simply in prison with murderers?

Above and beyond these contrasts is yet another, that between the High Priest and Pilate. As so often in his strongly episodic narrative, Mark provides no connecting link between the two trials. The Jewish court condemns Jesus to death in 14.64 with no suggestion that their verdict is anything but final. In 15.1, however, the whole council hold another consultation before binding Jesus and handing him over to Pilate, at which point the proceedings against Jesus start all over again. Whatever historical reasons necessitated a double hearing,[22] Mark's presentation gives each trial equal weight and invites comparisons not only between the two courts, but more specifically between the two judges.

Of all Markan characters, the High Priest is perhaps the most shadowy. He is presumably part of the high/chief priestly group (οἱ ἀρχιερεῖς) who plot against Jesus in 11.18 and 14.1–2, and who later accuse Jesus before Pilate (15.3), stir up the crowd (15.11), and mock Jesus on the cross (15.31). It is only in the Jewish trial, however, that an independent 'high priest' emerges (now referred to by the singular ὁ ἀρχιερεὺς), who challenges Jesus, secures the death penalty, and once again disappears into the chief priestly group. Not only is the High Priest not named, but he also exhibits no independent character traits whatsoever. We might well suspect that Mark has drawn attention to this figure solely to provide a focal point for the contrast with Pilate. And the depiction of the High Priest, however roughly sketched, is not a flattering one. He, along with his associates, convenes the council with the specific purpose of putting Jesus to death (14.55), but even so, the resulting kangaroo court has difficulty in making charges stick (14.56–59). Later, we find out that the Jewish authorities are motivated by envy (15.10, a charge already implicit in 12.12 and 14.1–2). Only when he takes matters into his own hands and secures Jesus' 'confession' from his own lips does the High Priest finally succeed in his ungodly design.

In many respects, Pilate is the mirror opposite of the High Priest. While the chief pontiff is referred to not by name but only by office, Pilate is referred to by name but not by office. No mention is made of his position as *praefectus* of Judea or to his imperial duties; his official status is as lightly sketched as possible. Similarly, while the High Priest's one concern is to have Jesus put to death, Pilate seems in no hurry to condemn him; and while the High Priest directs others toward a verdict (14.64), in Pilate's court it is the fickle Jewish crowd that, like the mob at a gladiatorial contest, pronounces in favour of crucifixion (15.13–15). I have argued elsewhere that Pilate is not to be read as a friendly, or even weak, character here.[23] He is quite aware of what is going on (15.10), and his repeated use of the title 'king' seems more calculated to rile the people than genuinely to secure Jesus' release. Yet Mark's characterization of the prefect shows that, despite Jesus' *crucifixion*, the prime movers in his death were not the Roman authorities, but hostile Jewish priestly leaders.

---

[22] On the right of Jewish courts to execute, see James S. McLaren, *Power and Politics in Palestine: The Jews and the Governing of Their Land, 100 BC–70 AD* (Sheffield: JSOT Press, 1991).
[23] See Bond, *Pontius Pilate*, 103–16.

Jesus' trials in John

John departs quite considerably from Mark in his trial scenes. Instead of two parallel hearings, he reduces the Jewish interrogation to the briefest of exchanges and expands the Roman trial to five times its Markan length, now establishing it as the centrepiece of his passion narrative. Building on the earlier trial motifs that echo throughout the gospel, John will use Jesus' appearance in a Roman court to explore themes of power, kingship and judgement. Despite the differences between the two accounts at this point, however, we shall see that several themes that we found to be implicit in Mark become much more developed as a result of John's careful rewriting. We shall start with an examination of John's much reduced Jewish hearing.

The Jewish hearing (18.12–27)

After his arrest, Jesus is bound and taken to Annas, the father-in-law of Caiaphas who, we are reminded, had 'advised the Jews that it was better to have one person die for the people' (18.14).[24] The note recalls the earlier gathering of the Sanhedrin, which had already tried and condemned Jesus in his absence (11.47–53). The outcome of this brief hearing, then, like its Markan counterpart, seems assured.

Strikingly, John retains Mark's distinctive intercalation, now turning to the story of Peter's denial. By placing the first denial before the account of the Jewish trial, John heightens the dramatic impact of the technique. Exactly how Peter managed to get into the High Priest's courtyard was left unexplained by Mark (who rarely furnishes us with such details). John's less 'episodic', more flowing narrative requires rather more elucidation. Assuming that the High Priest lives in an *insula*-type house with a doorkeeper, John creates a scene in which another disciple, who was known to the High Priest, arranges Peter's entry.[25] The doorkeeper is presumably cast as a female (ἡ παιδίσκη ἡ θυρωρὸς) because of Mark's 'maid' (παιδίσκη); her question to Peter is now quite natural. After his first denial, Peter takes his place with the slaves and the police, warming themselves in the darkness.

Inside the palace, Jesus is confronted by the High Priest. Much of the material found in the Markan trial narrative has been used earlier by John: 1.51; 2.19; 10.24; and 11.47–53;[26] the effect of this strategy is to give the impression that all of Jesus' public ministry has been a 'trial' before the unbelieving Jews.[27] Nor does John have any need

---

[24] The name 'Caiaphas' may have been supplied from Mt. 26.57; we hear of Annas in Lk. 3.2 (and Acts 4.5–6, though there is no evidence that John knew this second work). For a fuller analysis of Synoptic parallels here, see Lang, *Johannes und die Synoptiker*, 86–115.

[25] John's explanation, of course, raises more questions of its own, particularly surrounding the identity of the 'disciple known to the High Priest'.

[26] Raymond Brown's explanation of this phenomenon was that John, dependent on eyewitness tradition, had retained these elements in their correct historical places, while the disciples (who were not present at the Jewish trial) composed the Sanhedrin scene themselves, based on a scattering of motifs from Jesus' ministry, to create a tradition which made its way into Mark, 'Incidents that are Units in the Synoptic Gospels but Dispersed in St John', *CBQ* 23 (1961): 151–52.

[27] On the trial motif in John, see Anthony E. Harvey, *Jesus on Trial: a Study on the Fourth Gospel* (London: SPCK, 1976), and Andrew T. Lincoln, *Truth on Trial: the Lawsuit Motif in the Fourth Gospel* (Peabody, MA: Hendrickson, 2000).

to present Jesus' Jewish trial as a christological climax – once again, Jesus' exalted identity has been apparent throughout the whole of the work. In place of the Jewish trial in the earlier gospel, John records only a brief exchange that is reminiscent of Jesus' words in Gethsemane in Mark 14.49. The High Priest asks Jesus about his disciples and his teaching, to which he states that he has spoken openly (παρρησία) to the world, that he has always taught in synagogues and in the temple, where all Jews come together. Jesus' answer earns him a slap from an attendant – a detail which seems to have been retained from Mark's Jewish hearing, which also uses the words ὑπηρέται and ῥάπισμα (14.65). The reduction of the multiple to the single is a frequent Johannine technique (as we shall see in a moment); here, the single slap lends the narrative a greater drama than its Markan counterpart.

Despite its brevity, John's Jewish hearing contains three noteworthy elements. First is Jesus' clear declaration that he has said nothing in secret (ἐν κρυπτῷ, 18.20), a claim backed up by his earlier preaching in synagogues (6.59) and the Temple (2.13–22; 7.14; 10.22–30; and 18.2). This may be an attempt to settle a certain ambiguity in Mark. Although the Markan Jesus does speak with boldness, particularly in his controversies with opponents, and most clearly of all in his response to the High Priest (14.62), it is also the case that he frequently gives his disciples instruction in 'secret' (at least inside a house, or in a quiet place) and often enjoins people to secrecy (1.44; 5.43; 8.30; 9.9). This secrecy could easily be misinterpreted. Celsus, for example, claimed that Jesus had preached only in an obscure corner of Galilee to a few countryfolk (Origen, *Contra Celsum* 2.70). And Socrates, in a manner similar to Jesus, is said to have declared to his judges: '[I]f anyone claims he has ever learned anything from me or heard anything in private that none of the others have heard, be well assured that he's not telling the truth' (Plato, *Apology* 33b).[28] Boldness (παρρησία) was considered a particularly good quality in a philosopher, and John attributes this to Jesus on several occasions (7.4, 26; 10.24; 11.54).[29] The Johannine Jesus may be 'congenitally incapable of giving a straight answer', but he is not secretive.[30]

Second, the identity of Jesus' questioner is important here. Although we are reminded in 18.24 that Jesus stands before Annas, the scene opens with a reference to Jesus' accuser as 'the High Priest'. A common motif throughout John's Gospel has been the theme of Jesus as the fulfilment (and therefore replacement) of Jewish feasts and institutions: the Temple, water of purification, the manna in the wilderness, the paschal lamb and so on. As noted earlier, John likes to concentrate on single characters, often where Mark has several, focusing attention on each character's personal encounter with Jesus. In this scene, he brings Jesus face to face with the High Priest. Jesus' boldness and supreme majesty contrasts with the High Priest, whose servant responds to Jesus

---

[28] Plato, *Euthyphro, Apology, Crito, Phaedo*. Edited and translated by Chris Emlyn-Jones and William Preddy (Loeb Classical Library 36; Cambridge, Ma.: Harvard University Press, 2017).

[29] Alicia D. Myers defines it as 'virtuous speech in the Mediterranean world, which friends and good citizens employed to guide others toward truth'; see 'Discerning Characters: *Parresia, Paroimia*, and Jesus's Rhetoric in John 10:1–21', in Alicia D. Myers and Lindsey S. Jodrey (eds), *Come and Read*, 125, see further, pp. 127–28, 130–34.

[30] The phrase is from R. Alan Culpepper, *Anatomy of the Fourth Gospel: A Study in Literary Design* (Philadephia: Fortress, 1983), 112.

with violence and who is himself silenced (and therefore shamed?) by Jesus' reply. For John's audience, all that the Jewish High Priest once provided as God's mediator and revealer is now subsumed by Jesus.[31]

Third, in common with the Markan narrative, John's retelling retains the contrast between Jesus and Peter. Immediately after the brief scene with the High Priest, John notes that Annas has Jesus bound and sent to Caiaphas (18.24), though no details of any second hearing are given, and in 18.28a the prisoner is now taken to Pilate.[32] In place of the proceedings before Caiaphas, John reverts to the story of Peter's denials, which occupies the entire space. Perhaps here, as with the reference to events 'before John the Baptist was arrested' (3.24; see Mk 1.14–15), John gives a nod to readers familiar with Mark, indicating where the trial before Caiaphas should fit. Those of his audience who do not know Mark, however, are hardly likely to note the omission, and the reminder that Caiaphas advocated doing away with Jesus in 18.14 would not lead them to expect any leniency from him now.[33]

John picks up Peter's story with his last two denials, repeating Mark's detail that the disciple was warming himself (θερμαινόμενος, Jn 18.25; Mk 14.66). Now the female doorkeeper has given way to an indeterminate group who ask him again if he is one of Jesus' followers. Peter's replies are pared down considerably by John. Rather than Mark's increasingly desperate denials, the Johannine Peter simply says, 'I am not' (οὐκ εἰμί, 18.17, 25).[34] The tension is raised by the third questioner, 'a relative of the man whose ear Peter had cut off', but again the scene is much sparser than its Markan counterpart: no longer is there a reminder of Jesus' prophecy of Peter's betrayal (Jn 13.38), or a note that Peter broke down in tears.[35] The theme of light and darkness was there to some extent already in Mark, who twice tells us that Peter was warming himself by the fire (φῶς in Mk 14.54, 67). After the first denial, the Markan Peter withdraws to the forecourt, distancing himself not only from the warmth of the fire but also from the light that it casts on his features, thus symbolically moving into the darkness as he denies his master. Shades of this are also present in John, developing the darkness/light imagery so prevalent in this gospel. John's Peter warms himself by a charcoal fire (ἀνθρακιά), although he does not move away from it, and there is surely some significance to his denying the one who is truly the 'light of the world' as he stands bathed in its smoky glow.

---

[31] For fuller discussion, see Helen K. Bond, 'At the Court of the High Priest: History and Theology in John 18:13–24', in *John, Jesus and History*, Vol 2. *Aspects of Historicity in the Fourth Gospel*, ed. Paul N. Anderson, Felix Just, S.J., and Tom Thatcher (ECL, 2; Atlanta, GA: Society of Biblical Literature, 2007), 313–24.

[32] The reference to Jesus taken 'first' (πρῶτον) to Annas in 18.13 might lead us to expect a second trial here, but John does not recount one. See Bauckham, 'John for Readers of Mark', 157–58.

[33] Jean Zumstein refers to John as a 'networked text' which allows, even invites, multiple interpretations depending on the audience's knowledge. See Jean Zumstein, 'Intratextuality and Intertextuality in the Gospel of John', in Tom Thatcher and Stephen D. Moore (eds), *Anatomies of Narrative Criticism*, 121–35.

[34] There are similarities here with Peter's second denial in Lk. 22.58.

[35] Peter disappears from the narrative here, though Mary will find him along with the rest of the disciples in chapter 20. The scene will be recalled in 21.15–19, when Peter has the opportunity to counteract his three denials with three declarations of his love for Jesus.

As in Mark, John's intercalation adds further layers to the meaning of Jesus' Jewish hearing. On a fairly straightforward level, Jesus' openness before the High Priest contrasts with Peter's denials; the two scenes are even closer in John in that Jesus' Jewish accuser asks him about his disciples just as one of them is denying his discipleship. It will be clear to readers which example to follow here. John's narrative, however, brings a third scene into the comparison: the arrest in the garden, where Jesus' threefold acceptance of his identity (twice using the 'I am' formula) provides an almost exact opposite to Peter's threefold 'I am not'. The reference to the High Priest's slave's ear and the garden in conjunction with Peter's third accuser leads the reader back to Jesus' arrest, allowing connections to be made across the two scenes. Both at his arrest and before the High Priest, Jesus spoke openly and proclaimed his identity to those around him; Peter, in contrast, is overwhelmed by the darkness and betrays his identity as one of Jesus' disciples.

Jesus' Roman trial in John (18.28–19.16)

As already noted, John develops Mark's Roman trial quite considerably so that it is now the central episode in his passion narrative. Mark's account extended to three scenes: one inside with Pilate, one outside with a crowd and Barabbas, and one inside the *praetorium* with the mocking soldiers. These are now expanded with great dramatic artistry into seven scenes, arranged in two groups of three with the soldiers' mockery in the middle, and the central scene in each group featuring a dialogue between Jesus and Pilate inside the *praetorium*. Like Mark, John is particularly concerned to highlight Jesus' kingship in the Roman proceedings, showing in what way he could truly be said to be the 'King of the Jews'. While Mark used his parallel trials to explore themes of responsibility, however, John's single trial focuses attention on cosmic themes of power and judgement. In this final, grand denouement, Jesus comes face to face with all the forces of the world – Jewish and Roman – and all are tried and found wanting.[36]

In a similar manner to the start of the Jewish trial, John's first scene sets up the locations of the principal characters (18.28b–32). The chief priests refuse to enter the gentile headquarters on the grounds that they need to preserve their purity for the approaching feast, a stance that necessitates Pilate (who, as in Mark, is introduced simply by his *cognomen*) coming out to them. Throughout the seven scenes, Pilate must move between Jesus (who is at least initially taken inside the *praetorium*) and the chief priests (who resolutely remain outside). Of course, John's readers appreciate a huge irony here: it is clear from the ensuing dialogue that the Jewish authorities are intent on having Jesus executed (18.19–31); they fuss about purity while handing over God's messiah. The opening dialogue also explains the need for two trials: Jesus is now handed over to Rome because Jews do not have the power of capital jurisdiction. The evangelist sees a greater level of fulfilment in all of this: events are unfolding just as Jesus predicted (18.32). Although hostility has so far come almost entirely from 'the

---

[36] For a closer analysis of Synoptic parallels in this passage, see Lang, *Johannes und die Synoptiker*, 115–207.

Jews', his transfer to Roman authority means that Jesus will be crucified, in other words, 'lifted up' for all to see.

The second scene develops Mark's first exchange between Pilate and Jesus (Mk 15.1–5). Like his Markan counterpart, the Johannine Pilate goes straight to the central charge: Are you the King of the Jews? (Jn 18.33; Mk 15.2). As in Mark, this is the first time that kingship has been mentioned since Jesus' arrest and comes as something of a surprise. The Johannine Jesus is rather more loquacious than his Markan counterpart, but his rejoinder to Pilate, 'Do you ask this on your own, or did others tell you about me?', captures something of the Markan Jesus' distance and ambiguity. (The similarities would be even closer if Jonathan Schwiebert is correct to read Jesus' reply in Mark as a counter-question, throwing the charge back at Pilate, along the lines of his response to opponents in 11.27–33 and 12.13–17.[37]) Pilate's answer, 'Am I a Jew?', can be read on several different levels. Ethnically, of course, Pilate is not a Jew. But being a 'Jew' for John is fundamentally connected to a negative response to Jesus, acting as a representative of the hostile and unbelieving 'world'. Pilate – like every other character – will be required to make some kind of response, and as the trial narrative continues, and Pilate fails to respond, it becomes clear that he is indeed a 'Jew'.

But what kind of a king is Jesus? While Mark used the contrast with Barabbas to highlight the differences between Jesus and the violent activities of would-be kings and insurrectionaries, John puts words in the mouth of Jesus so that the prisoner will now control the discourse between him and Pilate. Drawing on the typically Johannine contrasts between what is above/below and of the world/not of the world (8.23; 15.19; 17.14, 16), Jesus declares his kingdom is 'not from this world'. Our author imagines two ultimately conflicting worlds of values and meanings, one ruled by God, the other by the forces of darkness and untruth. Jesus' kingdom clearly belongs to the former. Pilate, however, is not interested in a theological discussion; 'So you are a king?', he demands. For John, Jesus *is* a king (as Nathanael declared in 1.49), but his kingship is subordinated to his witness to the truth (18.37), a witness he has brought to the very heart of Roman power in the governor's court. 'Everyone who belongs to the truth listens to my voice', he continues, to which Pilate famously responds, 'What is truth?' (18.37–38a). For John, of course, Jesus is himself the truth (14.6); Pilate's contempt and refusal to stay for an answer marks him out as one already condemned.

Scene three is a truncated version of Mark's Barabbas scene (Jn 18.38b–40); the presence of 'again' (πάλιν) in v. 40, despite it being the first and only cry of the bystanders, shows that John is trimming a longer account (see Mk 15.13 where 'again' is used of the crowd's second response). Now the custom is a Jewish one, linked specifically to the Passover, but raised by Pilate who claims to 'find no case against him'. Barabbas himself, no longer an insurrectionary foil to Jesus, is simply a robber (λῃστής). Perhaps the greatest change to Mark, however, is that there is no ostensibly neutral crowd in John; Pilate makes his declaration to the same group of Jewish chief priests who have handed Jesus over for execution. The governor can hardly be surprised when they shout for Barabbas instead. The scene has echoes of the Good Shepherd discourse of chapter 10,

---

[37] Jonathan Schweibert, 'Jesus's Question to Pilate in Mark 15:2', *JBL* 136 (2017): 937–47.

where 'thieves and robbers' lead the sheep astray (κλέπτης καὶ λῃστής; 10.1, 10). The Jewish leaders are so blind that they prefer one who comes 'to steal and kill and destroy' rather than the one who brings life. Overall, however, the scene plays a far less central role in John than it did in Mark.[38] Perhaps the evangelist included it simply to maintain his threefold chiastic structure; at all events, the exchange leads on, as in Mark, to Jesus being flogged and mocked by the soldiers (19.1–3).

The soldiers' mockery has much in common with its Markan predecessor, even down to verbal links. Both are, in effect, mock coronations: in both, the soldiers weave a crown of thorns (πλέξαντες στέφανον ἐξ ἀκανθῶν, Jn 19.2; πλέξαντες ἀκάνθινον στέφανον, Mk 15.17), dress him in purple (ἱμάτιον πορφυροῦν; πορφύραν[39]), and cry 'Hail, King of the Jews' (χαῖρε ὁ βασιλεὺς τῶν Ἰουδαίων, Jn 19.3; Mk 15.18). John's account is briefer, but still encourages his audience to see beyond the surface mockery to the reality that Jesus truly is King of the Jews. John's major alteration, of course, is the placement of this scene, which now stands at the central point in the trial narrative, lending an overriding air of mockery and double meaning to the scenes that surround it.[40] Relocating the mockery also allows John to heighten the dramatic potential of the following scenes. Pilate can now take Jesus outside to the waiting authorities and present him to them, still dressed in kingly regalia, with the words 'Here is the man'. Not surprisingly, the chief priests and their officers still want to eliminate Jesus. As in Mark, the cry to 'crucify' comes not from Pilate but from the Jewish authorities. 'Take him yourselves and crucify him', Pilate says, 'I find no case against him'. It is difficult to imagine that this is a serious suggestion; the Johannine Pilate has already been told that the Jewish authorities do not have the right of capital punishment (18.31), and Pilate's comment is surely best understood as an attempt to mock Jewish impotence. Certainly, this is the way that 'the Jews' understand the governor's words, now changing tack and accusing Jesus of claiming to be the Son of God.

At this, Pilate becomes afraid. While the word used here (μᾶλλον) might naturally mean 'more afraid', the fact that Pilate has showed little fear so far might justify a translation such as 'afraid instead'. Perhaps what John intends is a superstitious dread on the part of the pagan governor.[41] Entering the *praetorium* again, he asks Jesus where he is from. Recognizing Jesus' origin as the 'one from above' is an important Johannine motif and a key method of distinguishing between those who have faith and those who do not (see 7.28–29; 8.14; 9.29; 17.8). The very fact that Pilate needs to pose this question shows how far he is from the truth. Picking up on the silence of Mark 15.5, the Johannine Jesus has nothing to say, though as Donald Senior notes, the silence here condemns *Pilate* rather than Jesus.[42] In response, Pilate proclaims his own power over life and death, to which Jesus tells him that all the power he thinks is his has been given

---

[38] Frey, *Glory of the Crucified One*, 192, suggests that the Barabbas scene is part of a larger theme in which Jesus takes the place of others (for example the disciples in the garden).
[39] John uses the same verb here – περιβάλλω – as that used in Lk. 23.12 (of Herod's soldiers, a mockery also situated in the midst of the trial).
[40] John's placement could have been inspired by Lk. 23.22, where Pilate declares his intention to have him 'chastised' (παιδεύω) and released – an intention which in Luke is never carried out.
[41] For fuller discussion, see Bond, *Pontius Pilate*, 187.
[42] Senior, *Passion*, 91–92.

to him from God (who is also the source of Jesus' own ἐξουσία, 17.1–2). At this, Pilate does try to release Jesus, though it is short-lived. Outside again, the Jews shout 'If you release this man, you are no friend of the emperor. Everyone who claims to be a king sets himself against the emperor' (19.12). It is, of course, hugely ironic that it is the Jewish authorities who introduce Pilate's loyalty to Caesar into the discussion, though it has the desired effect on Pilate who brings Jesus out to the tribunal. What happens next is perhaps intentionally unclear – either Pilate sits on the judgement seat himself (as would be natural), or we are to understand that he sits Jesus on the βῆμα.[43] In favour of the latter (transitive) reading are both Justin Martyr (*Apology* 35) and the *Gospel of Peter* (5.7), where Pilate sits Jesus on the seat. Such a reading would also fit well with John's theological outlook in that Jesus, who has maintained his kingly majesty throughout, now takes his seat to judge the world.[44] For this author, it is not Jesus on trial, but the representatives of all those who fail to respond to him.

Before launching into his final scene, John pauses to give details of the location of the trial (on the Λιθόστρωτος, or stone pavement) and the time at which all of this occurred (the day of preparation of the Passover, about noon). This is a deliberate departure from Mark, who carefully situates Jesus' death the following day, that is, on the Passover itself (a setting which equates the last supper with the Passover *seder*). Rather than assume that John changed Mark for 'theological reasons' here, I have argued elsewhere that it is more likely that the evangelist drew on traditions already popular within his own Christ-following circles, traditions that had already begun to equate Jesus' death with the Passover lamb (see also 1 Cor. 5.7–8, 1 Pet. 1.19).[45] Such a view of Jesus' crucified body not only fits John's insistence on Jesus as the replacement of Jewish feasts and institutions, but may have even been the original impetus for this widespread Johannine motif. At all events, John may well be correcting his Markan source here to underscore a more profound theological truth (the Eucharist of course plays no part in John's passion narrative, though Eucharistic-type language appeared at an earlier Passover in 6.52–58). Whether or not noon was the time at which the Passover lambs were slain,[46] high noon was clearly the most appropriate time for the kind of theophanic revelation of glory that John links with the cross.[47]

As John moves towards his dramatic conclusion, Pilate continues to taunt Jesus' Jewish accusers in language highly reminiscent of Mark 15.9–15. 'Here is your King', he says, to which they shout again for crucifixion. 'Shall I crucify your King?', he asks, which prompts the Jewish authorities to reject their ancestral loyalty to the God of Israel with the terrible words, 'We have no King but Caesar'. At this, Pilate hands Jesus over 'to them' for crucifixion. The charge of blasphemy, which was so prominent in

---

[43] The verb may be understood intransitively, in which case Pilate sits on the seat himself, or transitively, in which case he sits Jesus down.
[44] For a similar reading, see Lincoln, *Truth on Trial*, 133–35.
[45] Helen K. Bond. 'Dating the Death of Jesus: Memory and the Religious Imagination', *NTS* 59 (2013): 461–75.
[46] So Brown, *Gospel*, 2:883.
[47] See Georgia Petridou, *Divine Epiphany in Greek Literature and Culture* (Oxford: Oxford University Press, 2015), 210–14. She notes: 'Midday is a critical, ambiguous, and somewhat frightening period of the day; it is the time that the sun is at its highest point in the sky and physical objects cast a small shadow or no shadow on the ground' (p. 210).

Mark's Jewish trial scene, has been turned around and used against Jesus' Jewish accusers. It is they who blaspheme against God, while Jesus is sent to the cross on the basis of false charges that are, of course, ironically true. Pilate's court represents the judgement of this world – both the Roman governor who has refused to respond to the truth and the Jewish authorities who stand condemned by their own blasphemy.

Concluding reflections

Although we have been able to analyse only a short section of John's passion narrative, already certain traits in our author's handling of Mark have emerged. At times, he is happy to change or correct the earlier account. Sometimes this might be for apologetic reasons, for example in the Jewish hearing where the Johannine Jesus is clear that he has said nothing in secret (unlike the Markan Jesus), or we might add Jesus' intervention at his arrest on behalf of his disciples (where their Markan desertion might have cast them in a poor light), or the insistence that Jesus carried his own cross (lending a more majestic feel to John's account). At other times, John's changes might be for theological reasons or to align the narrative with traditions current in his own Christ-following group, such as the date of the crucifixion. John prefers to give fuller explanations than Mark, so he adds material to show how Peter gained access to the High Priest's courtyard and why it was that Jesus needed a Roman trial; he is also happy to move stories to other locations, such as his relocation of the soldiers' mockery so that Jesus' acclamation as king takes place while wearing his mock-regalia, or to tear apart Markan unities and scatter the fragments in other places, as we have with the Jewish trial. And throughout the whole of the section analysed here, we see John drawing out themes already present in Mark and heightening their dramatic quality – both the motifs of kingship and triumph, for example, can be found in Mark, but it is in John's masterly treatment that they reach their full artistic potential.

What we have here is not a cautious scribal editing such as we find in Matthew and Luke; rather, John's is a much freer and more confident appropriation and reworking of Markan motifs.[48] This is an author who values Mark's biography highly, who appreciates the effort to cast theology in narrative form and to make the life and death of Jesus central both to Christian proclamation and to ethics, and yet he is quite happy to alter his Markan source. John's handling of the earlier gospel may strike the modern reader as cavalier. Clearly he had little interest in establishing historical facts, and his work has certain similarities with the apocryphal gospels whose writers are often happy to diverge quite substantially from their canonical predecessors.[49] John's purpose is to

---

[48] See also Richard Bauckham, 'The Gospel of John and the Synoptic Problem', in *New Studies in the Synoptic Problem: Oxford Conference, April 2008: Essays in Honour of Christopher M. Tuckett*, ed. Paul Foster, Andrew Gregory, John S. Kloppenborg and Joseph Verheyden (BETL, 239; Leuven: Leuven University Press and Peeters, 2011), 657–88.

[49] See D. Moody Smith, 'The Problem of John and the Synoptics in Light of the Relation between Apocryphal and Canonical Gospels' in *John and the Synoptics*, ed. Adelbert Denaux (BETL, 101; Leuven: Leuven University Press and Peeters, 1992), 147–62.

draw out the significance of Jesus' life and death for his readers, to present a deeper, more spiritual 'truth', openly collapsing any distinction between the Jesus who was known throughout his ministry and the resurrected, exalted Lord as he has been revealed through the Paraclete (2.17, 22; 12.16; 13.7).[50] But none of this should surprise us. The purpose of ancient biographies was to expose the subject's character – in Plutarch's terms, his soul (ψυχή, *Alexander* 1.3) – and biographers were allowed a great deal of latitude in the manner in which they went about their craft. A degree of artistic license and even fictionalization is always necessary, even in a modern research biography, in order to bring a character to life.[51] The Johannine passion narrative offers a particularly rich example of the way in which an early Christian biographer has creatively refashioned an older source and infused it with new life.

---

[50] See Robert H. Lightfoot, *St John's Gospel: A Commentary* (Oxford: Oxford University Press, 1957), 30–1, who notes that 'truth' to the ancients was not the same as historical facticity; see also Frey, *Theology and History*, 143–203. Frances M. Young argues that postmodern scholars can learn much here from the early Church Fathers, who were more attuned to spiritual meaning; see Frances M. Young, 'John and the Synoptics: An Historical Problem or a Theological Opportunity?', *Louvain Studies* 33 (2008): 208–20.

[51] See the helpful discussion on 'Historicity and Truth', in Lincoln, *Gospel*, 39–50; also Bond, *First Biographer*, 66–71. On fiction in biography more broadly, see the collection of essays in Koen de Temmerman and Kristoffel Deoen (eds), *Writing Biography in Greece and Rome: Narrative Technique and Fictionalization* (Cambridge: Cambridge University Press, 2016).

Bibliography

Akiyama, Kengo. *The Love of Neighbour in Ancient Judaism: The Reception of Leviticus 19:18 in the Hebrew Bible, the Septuagint, the Book of Jubilees, the Dead Sea Scrolls, and the New Testament*. AJEC, 105. Leiden: Brill, 2018.
Alexander, Philip S. 'Retelling the Old Testament'. In *It is Written: Scripture Citing Scripture. Essays in Honour of Barnabas Lindars*, edited by D. A. Carson and H. G. M. Williamson, 99–121. Cambridge: Cambridge University Press, 1988.
Allen, Garrick V. 'Rewriting and the Gospels'. *JSNT* 41 (2018): 58–69.
Anderson, Paul N. *The Christology of the Fourth Gospel: Its Unity and Disunity in the Light of John 6*. WUNT, 2/78. Tübingen: Mohr Siebeck, 1996; 2nd edn, Valley Forge: Trinity Press International, 1997; 3rd edn, Eugene, OR: Cascade, 2010.
Anderson, Paul N. *The Fourth Gospel and the Quest for Jesus: Modern Foundations Considered*. LNTS, 321. London: T&T Clark, 2006.
Anderson, Paul N. 'John and Mark – the Bi-Optic Gospels'. In *Jesus in Johannine Tradition*, edited by Robert T. Fortna and Tom Thatcher, 175–88. Louisville, KY: Westminster John Knox, 2001.
Anderson, Paul N. 'Interfluential, Formative, and Dialectical – A Theory of John's Relation to the Synoptics'. In *Für und Wider die Priorität des Johannesevangeliums*, edited by Peter Hofrichter, 19–58. TTS, 9. Hildesheim: Olms, 2002.
Anderson, Paul N. 'Aspects of Interfluentiality between John and the Synoptics: John 18–19 as a Case Study'. In *The Death of Jesus in the Fourth Gospel*, edited by Gilbert Van Belle, 711–28. BETL, 200. Leuven: Leuven University Press and Peeters, 2007.
Anderson, Paul N. 'Mark, John, and Answerability: Interfluentiality and Dialectic between the Second and Fourth Gospels'. *Liber Annuus* 63 (2013): 197–245.
Anderson, Paul N., Felix Just, S.J. and Tom Thatcher (eds). *John, Jesus and History*, Vol. 1: *Critical Appraisals of Critical Views*. SBLSymS, 44. Atlanta, GA: Society of Biblical Literature, 2007.
Anderson, Paul N., Felix Just, S.J. and Tom Thatcher (eds). *John, Jesus and History*, Vol. 2: *Aspects of Historicity in the Fourth Gospel*. ECL, 2. Atlanta, GA: Society of Biblical Literature, 2009.
Anderson, Paul N., Felix Just, S.J. and Tom Thatcher (eds). *John, Jesus and History*, Vol. 3: *Glimpses of Jesus Through the Johannine Lens*. ECL, 18. Atlanta, GA: Society of Biblical Literature, 2016.
Appold, Mark. '"A Jew": A Search for the Identity and Role of an Anonymous Judean'. In *Character Studies in the Fourth Gospel: Narrative Approaches to Seventy Figures in John*, edited by Steven A. Hunt, D. Francois Tolmie and Ruben Zimmermann, 260–67. Grand Rapids, MI: Wm. B. Eerdmans, 2016.
Asiedu-Peprah, Martin. *Johannine Sabbath Conflicts as Juridical Controversy*. WUNT, 2/132. Tübingen: Mohr Siebeck, 2001.
Ashton, John. *Understanding the Fourth Gospel*. Oxford: Clarendon Press, 1993; 2nd edn, 2007.
Ashton, John. 'Really a Prologue?'. In *The Prologue of the Gospel of John: Its Literary, Theological, and Philosophical Contexts: Papers Read at the Colloquium Ioanneum 2013*,

edited by Jan G. van der Watt, R. Alan Culpepper and Udo Schnelle, 27–44. WUNT, 359. Tübingen: Mohr Siebeck, 2016.
Attridge, Harold W. 'Genre Bending in the Fourth Gospel'. In Harold W. Attridge *Essays on John and Hebrews*, 61–78. WUNT, 264. Tübingen: Mohr Siebeck, 2010.
Attridge, Harold W. 'An "Emotional" Jesus and Stoic Tradition'. In *Stoicism in Early Christianity*, edited by Tuomas Rasimus, Troels Engberg-Pedersen and Ismo Dunderberg, 77–114. Grand Rapids, MI: Baker Academic, 2010.
Attridge, Harold W. 'Genre'. In *How John Works: Storytelling in the Fourth Gospel*, edited by Douglas Estes and Ruth Sheridan, 9–22. Atlanta, GA: Scholars Press, 2016.
Attridge, Harold W. 'Review of Peder Borgen, *The Gospel of John*'. *RBL* 12 (2016).
Attridge, Harold W. 'John and Other Gospels'. In *The Oxford Handbook of Johannine Studies*, edited by Judith M. Lieu and Martinus C. de Boer, 44–62. Oxford: Oxford University Press, 2018.
Attridge, Harold W, Jörg Frey, Judith M. Lieu and Margaret M. Mitchell. Review: 'Troels Engberg-Pedersen, John and Philosophy: A New Reading of the Fourth Gospel', *Early Christianity* 10, no. 2 (2019): 219–60.
Azuma, Yoshimi. 'Reading John 11:1–12:11 through the Lens of the Resurrection in 1 Enoch'. PhD dissertation, Emory University, Atlanta, GA, 2015.
Bachmann, E. Theodore. *Luther's Works, Word and Sacrament*. Vol. 35. Philadelphia, PA: Muhlenberg Press, 1960.
Baldensperger, W. *Der Prolog des vierten Evangeliums, sein polemisch-apologetischer Zweck*. Tübingen: J. C. B. Mohr, 1898.
Barker, James W. 'Ancient Compositional Practices and the Gospels: A Reassessment'. *JBL* 135 (2016): 109–21.
Barrett, C. K. *The Gospel According to St John: An Introduction with Commentary and Notes on the Greek Text*. 2nd edn. London: SPCK; Philadelphia, PA: Westminster, 1978.
Barrett, C. K. 'John and the Synoptic Gospels'. *ExpT* 85 (1974): 228–33.
Barrett, C. K. 'Christocentric or Theocentric: Observations on the Theological Method of the Fourth Gospel'. In C.K. Barrett, *Essays on John*, 1–18. London: SPCK, 1982.
Bartholomä, Philipp F. *The Johannine Discourses and the Teaching of Jesus in the Synoptics*. TANZ, 57. Tübingen: Francke, 2012.
Bauckham, Richard. *Jesus and the God of Israel: God Crucified and Other Studies on the New Testament's Christology of Divine Identity*. Grand Rapids, MI: Wm. B. Eerdmans, 2009.
Bauckham, Richard. 'John for Readers of Mark'. In Richard Bauckham, *The Gospels for All Christians: Rethinking the Gospel Audiences*. Edinburgh: T&T Clark, 1998, 147–71.
Bauckham, Richard. 'Historiographical Characteristics of the Gospel of John'. *NTS* 53 (2007): 17–36. Reprinted in *The Testimony of the Beloved Disciple: Narrative, History, and Theology in the Gospel of John*, edited by Richard Bauckham, 93–112. Grand Rapids, MI: Baker, 2007.
Bauckham, Richard. 'Monotheism and Christology in the Gospel of John'. In Richard Bauckham, *Testimony of the Beloved Disciple*, 239–52. Grand Rapids, MI: Baker Academic, 2007.
Bauckham, Richard. 'The Gospel of John and the Synoptic Problem'. In *New Studies in the Synoptic Problem: Oxford Conference, April 2008: Essays in Honour of Christopher M. Tuckett*, edited by Paul Foster, Andrew Gregory, John S. Kloppenborg and Joseph Verheyden, 657–88. BETL, 239. Leuven: Leuven University Press and Peeters, 2011.
Baum, Armin D. 'Zu Funktion und Authentizitätsanspruch der *oratio recta* Hebräische und griechische Geschichtsschreibung im Vergleich', *ZAW* 115 (2003): 586–607.

Beasley-Murray, G. R. 'The Mission of the Son of God'. In *Gospel of Life: Theology in the Fourth Gospel*, 15–33. Peabody, MA: Hendrickson, 1991.
Becker, Eve-Marie. *Das Markus-Evangelium im Rahmen antiker Historiographie*. WUNT, 194. Tübingen: Mohr Siebeck, 2006.
Becker, Eve-Marie. *Der früheste Evangelist: Studien zum Markusevangelium*. WUNT, 380; Tübingen: Mohr Siebeck, 2017.
Becker, Eve-Marie. *The Birth of Christian History: Memory and Time from Mark to Luke–Acts*. New Haven, CT: Yale University Press, 2017.
Becker, Eve-Marie. 'Markus 13 Re-visited'. In *Apokalyptik als Herausforderung neutestamentlicher Theologie*, edited by Michael Becker and Markus Öhler, 95–124. WUNT, 2/214. Tübingen: Mohr Siebeck, 2006.
Becker, Eve-Marie. 'Die Konstruktion von "Geschichte": Paulus und Markus im Vergleich'. In *Paul and Mark: Comparative Essays Part I: Two Authors at the Beginnings of Christianity*, edited by Oda Wischmeyer, David C. Sim and Ian J. Elmer, 393–422. BZNW, 198. Berlin: de Gruyter, 2014.
Becker, Eve-Marie. 'John 13 as Counter-Memory: How the Fourth Gospel Revises Early Christian Historiography'. In *The Gospel of John as Genre Mosaic*, edited by Kasper Bro Larsen, 269–81. SANt, 3. Göttingen: Vandenhoeck & Ruprecht, 2015.
Becker, Eve-Marie. 'Was die "arme Witwe" lehrt: Sozial- und motivgeschichtliche Beobachtungen zu Mk 12, 41–44par'. *NTS* 65 (2019): 148–65.
Becker, Eve-Marie. *Der verspätete Jesus: Joh 11 als Parusieerzählung?* (in preparation).
Becker, Eve-Marie and Anders Runesson (eds). *Mark and Matthew I: Comparative Readings: Understanding the Earliest Gospels in their First-Century Settings*. WUNT, 271. Tübingen: Mohr Siebeck, 2011.
Becker, Jürgen. *Das Evangelium nach Johannes: Kapitel 1–10*. 3rd edn. ÖTBK, 4/1. Gütersloh, Würzburg: Gütersloher Verlagshaus Gerd Mohn, Echter Verlag, 1991.
Becker, Jürgen. *Das Evangelium nach Johannes: Kapitel 11–21*. 2nd edn. ÖTBK, 4/2. Gütersloh, Würzburg: Gütersloher Verlagshaus Gerd Mohn, Echter Verlag, 1984.
Becker, Jürgen. *Mündliche und schriftliche Autorität im frühen Christentum*. Tübingen: Mohr Siebeck, 2012.
Becker, Jürgen. 'Das Johannesevangelium im Streit der Methoden (1980–1984)'. *ThRu* 51 (1986): 1–78. Reprinted in Jürgen Becker, *Annäherungen: Zur urchristlichen Theologiegeschichte und zum Umgang mit ihren Quellen: Ausgewählte Aufsätze zum 60. Geburtstag mit einer Bibliographie des Verfassers*, edited by Ulrich Mell, 204–81. BZNW, 76. Berlin: de Gruyter, 1995.
Becker, Jürgen. 'Das vierte Evangelium und die Frage nach seinen externen und internen Quellen'. In *Fair Play: Diversity and Conflicts in Early Christianity: FS H. Räisänen*, edited by Ismo Dunderberg, Christopher Tuckett and Kari Syreeni, 203–41. NT.S, 103. Leiden: Brill, 2002.
Bennema, Cornelis. *Encountering Jesus: Character Studies in the Gospel of John*. 2nd edn. Minneapolis, MN: Fortress, 2014.
Berger, Klaus. *Im Anfang war Johannes: Datierung und Theologie des vierten Evangeliums*. Stuttgart: Quell, 1997.
Berger, Klaus. 'Das Evangelium nach Johannes und die Jesustradition'. In *Johannesevangelium – Mitte oder Rand des Kanons? Neue Standortbestimmungen*, edited by Thomas Söding, 38–59. Quaestiones Disputatae, 203. Freiburg: Herder, 2003.
Bergmeier, Roland. 'Die Bedeutung der Synoptiker für das johanneische Zeugnisthema: Mit einem Anhang zum Perfekt-Gebrauch im vierten Evangelium'. *NTS* 52 (2006): 458–83.

Bernard, J. H. *A Critical and Exegetical Commentary on the Gospel According to Saint John.* ICC; 2 vols. Edinburgh: T&T Clark, 1928.

Beutler, Johannes. *Das Johannesevangelium: Kommentar.* Freiburg: Herder, 2013.

Beutler, Johannes. 'Psalm 42/43 im Johannesevangelium', *NTS* 25 (1987): 33–57.

Beutler, Johannes. 'Méthodes et problèmes de la recherche johannique aujourd'hui'. In *La Communauté johannique et son histoire: La trajectoire de l'évangile de Jean aux deux premiers siècles*, edited by Jean-Daniel Kaestli, Jean-Michel Poffet and Jean Zumstein, 15–38. Le Monde de la Bible, 20. Genève: Labor et Fides, 1990.

Blumenthal, Christian. *Allweiser Schöpfer und durchsetzungsstarker Gesetzgeber: Eine Studie zur erzählerischen Entfaltung des Gottesbildes im 4. Makkabäerbuch.* Deuterocanonical and Cognate Literature Studies, 35. Berlin: de Gruyter, 2016.

Boismard, Marie Émile and Arnaud Lamouille, in collaboration with Gerard Rochais. *L'Évangile de Jean: Commentaire.* Synopse des quatre évangiles en français, 3. Paris: Éditions du Cerf, 1977.

Bond, Helen K. *Pontius Pilate in History and Interpretation.* SNTSMS, 100. Cambridge: Cambridge University Press, 1998.

Bond, Helen K. *Caiaphas: Friend of Rome and Judge of Jesus?* Louisville, KY: Westminster John Knox, 2004.

Bond, Helen K. *The First Biography of Jesus: Genre and Meaning in Mark's Gospel.* Grand Rapids, MI: Wm. B. Eerdmans, 2020.

Bond, Helen K. 'At the Court of the High Priest: History and Theology in John 18:13–24'. In *John, Jesus and History*: Vol. 2: *Aspects of Historicity in the Fourth Gospel*, edited by Paul N. Anderson, Felix Just, S.J. and Tom Thatcher, 313–24. ECL, 2. Atlanta, GA: Society of Biblical Literature, 2007.

Bond, Helen K. 'Dating the Death of Jesus: Memory and the Religious Imagination'. *NTS* 59 (2013): 461–75.

Bond, Helen K. 'Recognition and "Those who have not Seen": John's Reception of Synoptic Resurrection Narratives'. In *Come and Read: Interpretive Approaches to the Gospel of John*, edited by Alicia D. Myers and Lindsey S. Jodrey, 171–84. Lanham, MD: Fortress Academic, 2020.

Borgen, Peder. *Bread from Heaven: An Exegetical Study of the Concept of Manna in the Gospel of John and the Writings of Philo.* NovTSup, 10. Leiden: Brill, 1965.

Borgen, Peder. *Logos Was the True Light and Other Essays on the Gospel of John.* "Relieff"; Publications edited by the Department to Religious Studies, University of Trondheim, 9. Trondheim: Tapir Academic Publishers, 1983.

Borgen, Peder. *Early Christianity and Hellenistic Judaism.* Edinburgh: T&T Clark, 1996.

Borgen, Peder. *The Gospel of John: More Light from Philo, Paul and Archaeology: The Scriptures, Tradition, Exposition, Settings, Meaning.* NovTSup, 154. Leiden, Boston: Brill, 2014.

Borgen, Peder. 'John and the Synoptics in the Passion Narrative'. *NTS* 5 (1958–59): 246–59. Reprinted in Peder Borgen, *Logos Was the True Light*, 67–80; Peder Borgen, *The Gospel of John*, 103–19.

Borgen, Peder. 'The Use of Tradition in John 12:44–50'. *NTS* 26 (1979–80): 18–35. Reprinted in Peder Borgen, *Logos Was the True Light*, 49–66.

Borgen, Peder. 'John and the Synoptics'. In *The Interrelations of the Gospels: A Symposium Led by M.-É. Boismard – W.R. Farmer – F. Neirynck, Jerusalem 1984*, edited by David L. Dungan, 408–37. BETL, 95. Leuven: Leuven University Press and Peeters, 1990. Reprinted in Peder Borgen, *Early Christianity and Hellenistic Judaism*, 121–56 (156–57: 'Added Note'); Peder Borgen, *The Gospel of John*, 121–46 (138–39: 'Additional Note on

John 5:9'; 146: 'Added Note'); 'John and the Synoptics: Can Paul Offer Help? [Repr. of the section on 5:1–18], in *Tradition and Interpretation in the New Testament: Essays in Honour of E. Earle Ellis*, edited by Gerald F. Hawthorne and Otto Betz, 80–94. Grand Rapids, MI: Wm. B. Eerdmans; Tübingen, Mohr Siebeck, 1987.

Borgen, Peder. 'John and the Synoptics: A Reply'. In *The Interrelations of the Gospels: A Symposium Led by M.-É. Boismard – W.R. Farmer – F. Neirynck, Jerusalem 1984*, edited by David L. Dungan, 451–58. BETL, 95. Leuven: Leuven University Press and Peeters, 1990. Reprinted in Peder Borgen, *Early Christianity and Hellenistic Judaism*, 174–82.

Borgen, Peder. 'The Independence of the Gospel of John: Some Observations'. In *The Four Gospels, 1992: Festschrift Frans Neirynck*, edited by Frans Van Segbroeck, Christopher M. Tuckett, Gilbert Van Belle and Joseph Verheyden, 3:1815–33. BETL, 100; 3 vols. Leuven: Leuven University Press and Peeters, 1992. Reprinted in Peder Borgen, *The Gospel of John*, 147–64.

Borgen, Peder. 'The Sabbath Controversy in John 5:1–18 and Analogous Controversy Reflected in Philo's Writings'. In Peder Borgen, *Early Christianity and Hellenistic Judaism*, 105–20. Edinburgh: T&T Clark, 1996.

Borgen, Peder. 'Review of M. Labahn, *Offenbarung in Zeichen und Wort*'. *JTS* 53 (2002): 218–19.

Borgen, Peder. 'The Scriptures and the Words and Works of Jesus'. In *What We Have Heard from the Beginning: The Past, Present and Future of Johannine Studies*, edited by Tom Thatcher, 39–58. Waco, TX: Baylor University Press, 2007. Reprinted in Peder Borgen, *The Gospel of John*, 3–22.

Boring, M. E. 'Markan Christology: God Language for Jesus?'. *NTS* 45 (1999): 451–71.

Borrell, Agusti. *The Good News of Peter's Denial: A Narrative and Rhetorical Reading of Mark 14:54, 66–72*. Atlanta, GA: Scholars Press, 1998.

Bosenius, Bärbel. *Der literarische Raum im Markusevangelium*. WMANT, 140; Neukirchen-Vluyn: Neukirchener Verlagsgesellschaft, 2015.

Bower, Gordon H. and Randolph K. Cirilo. 'Cognitive Psychology and Text Processing'. In *Handbook of Discourse Analysis Vol. 1: Disciplines of Discourse*, edited by Teun A. Van Dijk, 71–105. London: Academic Press, 1985.

Bowersock, Glen W. *Fiction as History: Nero to Julian*. Berkeley, CA: University of California Press, 1994.

Brant, Jo-Ann A. *Dialogue and Drama: Elements of Greek Tragedy in the Fourth Gospel*. Peabody, MA: Hendrickson, 2004.

Brant, Jo-Ann A. *John*. Paideia. Grand Rapids, MI: Baker Academic, 2011.

Bremond, Claude. *Logique du récit*. Poétique. Paris: Seuil, 1973.

Breytenbach, Cilliers. *Nachfolge und Zukunftserwartung nach Markus: Eine methodenkritische Studie*. AThANT, 71. Zürich: Theologischer Verlag Zürich, 1984.

Breytenbach, Cilliers. 'MNHMONEUEIN: Das "Sich-erinnern" in der urchristlichen Überlieferung – Die Bethanienepisode (Mk 14,3–9/Jn 12,1–8) als Beispiel'. In *John and the Synoptics*, edited by Adelbert Denaux, 548–57. BETL, 101. Leuven: Leuven University Press and Peeters, 1992.

Breytenbach, Cilliers. 'Die Vorschriften des Mose im Markusevangelium: Erwägungen zur Komposition von Mk 7,9–13; 10,2–9 und 12,18–27', *ZNW* 97 (2006): 22–43.

Brodie, Thomas. *The Quest for the Origin of John's Gospel: A Source-Oriented Approach*. Oxford: Oxford University Press, 1993.

Brooke, George J. 'Rewritten Bible'. In *Encyclopaedia of the Dead Sea Scrolls*, edited by Lawrence H. Schiffman and James C. VanderKam, 777–80. Oxford: Oxford University Press, 2000.

Brooke, George J. 'Memory, Cultural Memory, and Rewriting Scripture'. In *Reading the Dead Sea Scrolls: Essays in Method,* 51–65. Atlanta, GA: Society of Biblical Literature, 2013.

Brooke, George J. 'Hypertextuality and the "Parabiblical" Dead Sea Scrolls'. In *Reading the Dead Sea Scrolls: Essays in Method,* 67–84. Atlanta, GA: Society of Biblical Literature, 2013.

Brown, Raymond E. *The Gospel According to John.* 2 vols. Anchor Bible, 29–29A. Garden City, NY: Doubleday, 1966, 1970.

Brown, Raymond E. *The Community of the Beloved Disciple.* New York: Paulist Press, 1979.

Brown, Raymond E. 'Incidents that are Units in the Synoptic Gospels but Dispersed in St John'. *CBQ* 23 (1961): 143–60.

Brown, Raymond E. 'John and the Synoptic Gospels: A Comparison'. In Raymond E. Brown, *New Testament Essays,* 246–71. Garden City, NY: Doubleday, 1965.

Bruce, F. F. *The Gospel of John,* Grand Rapids, MI: Wm. B. Eerdmans, 1983.

Bruner, Frederick D. *The Gospel of John: A Commentary.* Grand Rapids, MI: Wm. B. Eerdmans, 2012.

Buch-Hansen, Gitte. 'The Emotional Jesus: Anti-Stoicism in the Fourth Gospel?' In *Stoicism in Early Christianity,* edited by Tuomas Rasimus, Troels Engberg-Pedersen, and Ismo Dunderberg, 93–114. Grand Rapids, MI: Baker Academic, 2010.

Bultmann, Rudolf. *Das Evangelium des Johannes.* KEK, 2. Göttingen: Vandenhoeck und Ruprecht, 21st edn. 1986. ET: *The Gospel of John: A Commentary,* trans. George R. Beasley-Murray. Oxford: Blackwell; Philadelphia, PA: Westminster 1971. Reprinted in *The Gospel of John. A Commentary.* Eugene, OR: Wipf & Stock, 2014.

Bultmann, Rudolf. art. 'Johannesevangelium'. In *Religion in Geschichte und Gegenwart,* edited by Kurt Galling, 3:845–46. 3rd edn. Tübingen: Mohr Siebeck, 1959.

Burge, Gary M. *The Anointed Community: The Holy Spirit in the Johannine Tradition.* Grand Rapids, MI: Wm. B. Eerdmans, 1987.

Burridge, Richard A. *What are the Gospels? A Comparison with Graeco-Roman Biography.* SNTSMS, 70. Cambridge: Cambridge University Press, 1992.

Busse, Ulrich. 'Joh 14,31 und sein Kontext'. *ETL* 94 (2018): 27–75.

Campbell, Jonathan G. 'Rewritten Bible: A Terminological Reassessment'. In *Rewritten Bible after Fifty Years: Texts, Terms, or Techniques?,* edited by József Zsengellér, 49–81. SuppJSJ, 166. Leiden: Brill, 2014.

Charlesworth, James H. 'The Historical Jesus in the Fourth Gospel: A Paradigm Shift?'. *JSHJ* 8 (2010): 3–46.

Clay, Diskin. 'Lucian of Samosata: Four Philosophical Lives (Nigrinus, Demonax, Peregrinus, Alexander Pseudomantis)'. In *ANRW* 36.5, edited by Wolfgang Haase, 3406–48. Berlin: de Gruyter, 1992.

Coakley, James F. 'The Anointing at Bethany and the Priority of John'. *JBL* 107 (1988): 241–56.

Coleman, Kathleen M. 'Fatal Charades: Roman Executions Staged as Mythological Enactments'. *JRS* 80 (1990): 44–73.

Collins, John J. 'Changing Scripture'. In *Changes in Scripture: Rewriting and Interpreting Authoritative Traditions in the Second Temple Period,* edited by Hanne von Weissenberg, Juha Pakkala and Marko Marttila, 23–45. BZAW, 419. Göttingen: de Gruyter, 2011.

Conway, Colleen M. *Behold the Man: Jesus and Greco-Roman Masculinity.* Oxford: Oxford University Press, 2008.

Conway, Colleen M. '"Behold the Man!" Masculine Christology and the Fourth Gospel.' In *New Testament Masculinities*, edited by Stephen D. Moore and Janice Capel Anderson, 163–80. SBL Semeia Studies, 45. Atlanta, GA: Society of Biblical Literature, 2003.

Conzelmann, Hans. 'Present and Future in the Synoptic Tradition', *Journal for Theology and the Church* 5 (1968): 26–44.

Coser, Lewis A. *'On Collective Memory' by Maurice Halbwachs*, edited and translated by Lewis A. Coser. Chicago, IL: University of Chicago Press, 1992.

Craig, William L. 'The Disciples' Inspection of the Empty Tomb (Lk 24,12.24; Jn 20,2–10).' In *John and the Synoptics*, edited by Adelbert Denaux, 614–19. BETL, 101. Leuven: Leuven University Press and Peeters, 1992.

Crawford, Sidnie White. *Rewriting Scripture in Second Temple Times*. Grand Rapids, MI: Wm. B. Eerdmans, 2008.

Cullmann, Oscar. *The Christology of the New Testament*. Rev. ed., trans. Shirley C. Guthrie and Charles A. M. Hall. Philadelphia, PA: Westminster, 1963.

Culpepper, R. Alan. *Anatomy of the Fourth Gospel: A Study in Literary Design*. Philadelphia, PA: Fortress, 1983.

Culpepper, R. Alan. *The Gospel and Letters of John* (Interpreting Biblical Texts; Nashville, TN: Abingdon, 1998).

Culpepper, R. Alan. 'The Weave of the Tapestry: Character and Theme in John'. In *Characters and Characterization in the Gospel of John*, edited by Christopher W. Skinner, 18–35. LNTS, 461. London: T&T Clark, 2013.

Culpepper, R. Alan, and Jörg Frey (eds). *The Opening of John's Narrative (John 1:19–2:22): Historical, Literary, and Theological Readings from the Colloquium Ioanneum 2015 in Ephesus*. WUNT, 385. Tübingen: Mohr Siebeck, 2017.

Cuvillier, Élian. 'Die "Kreuzestheologie" als Leseschlüssel zum Markusevangelium'. In *Kreuzestheologie im Neuen Testament*, edited by Andreas Dettwiler and Jean Zumstein, 107–50. WUNT, 151. Tübingen: Mohr Siebeck, 2002.

Dahl, Nils. 'Anamnesis: Memory and Commemoration in Early Christianity'. In Nils Dahl, *Jesus in the Memory of the Early Church*, 11–29. Minneapolis, MN: Augsburg, 1976.

Dauer, Anton. *Die Passionsgeschichte im Johannesevangelium: Eine traditionsgeschichtliche und theologische Untersuchung zu Joh 18,1–19,30*. SANT, 30. München: Kösel-Verlag, 1972.

Dauer, Anton. *Johannes und Lukas: Untersuchungen zu den johanneisch-lukanischen Parallelperikopen Joh 4,46–54/Lk 7,1–10 – Joh 12,1–8/Lk 7,36–50; 10,38–42 – Joh 20,19–29/Lk 24,36–49*. FzB, 50. Würzburg: Echter Verlag, 1984.

Davidsen, Ole. *The Narrative Jesus: A Semiotic Reading of Mark's Gospel*. Aarhus: Aarhus University Press, 1993.

Debel, Hans. 'Anchoring Revelations in the Authority of Sinai: A Comparison of the Rewritings of "Scripture" in *Jubilees* and in the P Stratum of Exodus'. *JSJ* 45 (2014): 471–92.

Demke, Christoph. 'Das Evangelium der Dialoge: Hermeneutische und methodologische Beobachtungen zur Interpretation des Johannes-evangeliums', *ZThK* 97 (2000): 164–82.

Denaux, Adelbert (ed.), *John and the Synoptics*. BETL, 101. Leuven: Leuven University Press and Peeters, 1992.

Derrenbacker, Robert A. *Ancient Compositional Practices and the Synoptic Problem*. BETL, 186. Leuven: Leuven University Press and Peeters, 2005.

Derrenbacker, Robert A. 'The "External and Psychological Conditions under which the Synoptic Gospels were Written": Ancient Compositional Practices and the Synoptic

Problem'. In *New Studies in the Synoptic Problem: Oxford Conference, April 2008: Essays in Honour of Christopher M. Tuckett*, edited by Paul Foster, Andrew Gregory, John S. Kloppenborg and Joseph Verheyden, 435–57. BETL, 239. Leuven: Leuven University Press and Peeters, 2011.

De Silva, David A. *4 Maccabees*. Sheffield: Sheffield Academic Press, 1998.

De Silva, David A. *4 Maccabees: Introduction and Commentary on the Greek Text in Codex Sinaiticus*. Septuagint Commentary Series. Leiden: Brill, 2006.

De Temmerman, Koen and Kristoffel Deoen (eds), *Writing Biography in Greece and Rome: Narrative Technique and Fictionalization*. Cambridge: Cambridge University Press, 2016.

Dewey, Joanna. *Markan Public Debate: Literary Technique, Concentric Structure and Theology in Mark 2:1–3:6*. SBLDS, 48. Chico, CA: Scholars Press, 1980.

Dibelius, Martin. *From Tradition to Gospel*. London: Nicholson and Watson, 1934; New York: Scribner, 1965; repr. Cambridge: James Clarke, 1971.

Dodd, C. H. *The Interpretation of the Fourth Gospel*. Cambridge: Cambridge University Press, 1953.

Dodd, C. H. *Historical Tradition in the Fourth Gospel*. Cambridge: Cambridge University Press, 1963.

Donahue, John R. *'Are you the Christ?' The Trial Narrative in the Gospel of Mark*. SBLDS, 10. Missoula, MT: Scholars, 1973.

Döring, Klaus. *Exemplum Socratis: Studien zur Sokratesnachwirkung in der kynisch-stoischen Popularphilosophie der frühen Kaiserzeit und im frühen Christentum*. Hermes Einzelschriften, 42. Wiesbaden: Steiner, 1979.

Dormeyer, Detlev. *Das Markusevangelium als Idealbiographie von Jesus Christus, dem Nazarener*. 2nd edn. SBB, 43. Stuttgart: Katholisches Bibelwerk, 2002.

Dover, K. J. (ed.). *Plato, Symposium*. Cambridge: Cambridge University, 1980.

Downing, F. Gerald. 'Redaction Criticism: Josephus' *Antiquities* and the Synoptic Gospels I and II'. *JSNT* 8 (1980): 46–65; 9 (1980): 29–48.

Downing, F. Gerald. 'Compositional Conventions and the Synoptic Problem'. *JBL* 107 (1988): 69–85.

Downing, F. Gerald. 'Writers' Use or Abuse of Written Sources'. In *New Studies in the Synoptic Problem: Oxford Conference, April 2008: Essays in Honour of Christopher M. Tuckett*, edited by Paul Foster, Andrew Gregory, John S. Kloppenborg and Joseph Verheyden, 523–48. BETL, 239. Leuven: Leuven University Press and Peeters, 2011.

Dronsch, Kristina. *Bedeutung als Grundbegriff neutestamentlicher Wissenschaft: Texttheoretische und semiotische Entwürfe zur Kritik der Semantik dargelegt anhand einer Analyse zu akouein in Mk 4*. NET, 15. Tübingen: Francke, 2010.

Duke, Paul D. *Irony in the Fourth Gospel*. Atlanta, GA: John Knox Press, 1985.

Dunderberg, Ismo. *Johannes und die Synoptiker: Studien zu Joh 1–9*. AASF Dissertationes Humanarum Litterarum, 69. Helsinki: Suomalainen Tiedeakatemia, 1994.

Dunderberg, Ismo. 'Zur Literarkritik von Joh 12,1–11'. In *John and the Synoptics*, edited by Adelbert Denaux, 3–62. BETL, 101. Leuven: Leuven University Press and Peeters, 1992.

Dungan, David L. (ed.). *The Interrelations of the Gospels: A Symposium Led by M.-É. Boismard – W. R. Farmer – F. Neirynck, Jerusalem 1984*. BETL, 95. Leuven: Leuven University Press and Peeters, 1990.

Dunn, James D. G. 'John's Gospel and the Oral Gospel Tradition'. In *Jesus and the Oral Gospel Tradition*, edited by Henry Wansbrough, 351–79. JSNTSup, 64. Sheffield: JSOT, 1991, 351–79. Reprinted in *The Fourth Gospel in First-Century Media Culture*, edited by Anthony Le Donne and Tom Thatcher, 157–85. LNTS, 426. London: T&T Clark, 2011.

Dunn, James D. G. 'John and the Synoptics as a Theological Question'. In *Exploring the Gospel of John: In Honor of D. Moody Smith*, edited by R. Alan Culpepper and C. Clifton Black, 301–13. Louisville, KY: Westminster John Knox, 1996.
Easterling, Patricia E. 'From Repertoire to Canon'. In *The Cambridge Companion to Greek Tragedy*, edited by Patricia E. Easterling, 211–27. Cambridge: Cambridge University Press, 1997.
Ebner, Martin. 'Kreuzestheologie im Markusevangelium'. In *Kreuzestheologie im Neuen Testament*, edited by Andreas Dettwiler and Jean Zumstein, 151–68. WUNT, 151. Tübingen: Mohr Siebeck, 2002.
Edwards, Ruth B. *Discovering John: Content, Interpretation, Reception*. 2nd edn. London: SPCK, 2014.
Ehlers, Widu Wolfgang (ed.). *La Biographie antique*. Fondation Hardt. Entretiens, 44. Genève: Librairie Droz, 1998.
Engberg-Pedersen, Troels. *John and Philosophy: A New Reading of the Fourth Gospel*. Oxford: Oxford University Press, 2017.
Engberg-Pedersen, Troels. 'The Past Is a Foreign Country: On the Shape and Purposes of Comparison in New Testament Scholarship'. In *The New Testament in Comparison: Validity, Method, and Purpose in Comparing Traditions*, edited by John M. G. Barclay and Benjamin G. White, 41–61. LNTS, 600. London: T&T Clark, 2020.
Epstein, Richard A. 'Common Law, Labor Law, and Reality: A Rejoinder to Professors Getman and Kohler'. *Yale Law Journal* 92 (1983): 1435–41.
Estes, Douglas. *The Questions of Jesus in John: Logic, Rhetoric and Persuasive Discourse*. BIS, 115. Leiden: Brill, 2013.
Estes, Douglas and Ruth Sheridan (eds). *How John Works: Storytelling in the Fourth Gospel*. RBS, 86. Atlanta, GA: Society of Biblical Literature, 2016.
Evans, Craig A. 'The Function of Isaiah 6:9-10 in Mark and John'. *NovT* 24 (1982): 124–38.
Eve, Eric. *Writing the Gospels: Composition and Memory*. London: SPCK, 2016.
Feldman, Louis H. *Josephus's Interpretation of the Bible*. Berkeley, CA: University of California Press, 1998.
Feldman, Louis H. 'Josephus' Portrait of Moses'. *JQR* 82 (1992): 285–328; 83 (1993): 7–50, 301–30.
Feldman, Louis H. 'The Influence of the Greek Tragedians on Josephus'. In *Hellenic and Jewish Arts: Interaction, Tradition and Renewal*, edited by A. Ovadiah, 51–80. Tel Aviv: Ramot Publ. House, Tel Aviv University, 1998.
Fischbach, Stephanie M. *Totenerweckungen: Zur Geschichte einer Gattung*. FzB, 69. Würzburg: Echter, 1992.
Fleischman, Paul. *Glass Slipper, Gold Sandal: A World-Wide Cinderella*. New York: Henry Holt, 2007.
Fock, Otto. *Der Sozinianismus: Nach seiner Stellung in der Gesamtentwicklung des christlichen Geistes, nach seinem historischen Verlauf und nach seinem Lehrbegriff dargestellt*. Kiel: Carl Schröder Comp., 1847; Neudruck Aalen: Scientia, 1970.
Fornara, Charles W. *The Nature of History in Ancient Greece and Rome*. Berkeley, CA: University of California Press, 1983.
Fortna, Robert T. *The Gospel of Signs: A Reconstruction of the Narrative Source Underlying the Fourth Gospel*. SNTSMS, 11. Cambridge: Cambridge University Press, 1970.
Fortna, Robert T. *The Fourth Gospel and Its Predecessor: From Narrative Source to Present Gospel*. Studies in the New Testament and its World. Philadelphia, PA: Fortress, 1988; Edinburgh: T&T Clark, 1989.

Fortna, Robert T. 'The Gospel of John and the Signs Gospel'. In *What We Have Heard from the Beginning: The Past, Present and Future of Johannine Studies*, edited by Tom Thatcher, 149–58. Waco, TX: Baylor University Press, 2007.

Foster, Paul. 'Memory, Orality, and the Fourth Gospel'. *JSHJ* 12 (2014): 165–83.

Foucault, Michel. 'Counter-Memory: The Philosophy of Difference'. In *Language, Counter-Memory, Practice: Selected Essays and Interviews*, edited by D. F. Bouchard and S. Simon, 113–96. Ithaca, NY: Cornell University Press, 1977.

France, Richard T. *The Gospel of Mark: A Commentary on the Greek Text*. NIGTC. Grand Rapids, MI: Wm. B. Eerdmans, 2002.

Freed, E. D. 'Jn 1,19–27 in Light of Related Passages in John, the Synoptics and Acts'. In *The Four Gospels, 1992: Festschrift Frans Neirynck*, edited by Frans Van Segbroeck, Christopher M. Tuckett, Gilbert Van Belle and Joseph Verheyden, 3:1943–61. BETL, 100; 3 vols. Leuven: Leuven University Press and Peeters, 1992.

Frey, Jörg. *Die johanneische Eschatologie, vol. 1: Ihre Probleme im Spiegel der Forschung seit Reimarus*. WUNT, 96. Tübingen: Mohr Siebeck, 1997.

Frey, Jörg. *Die johanneische Eschatologie, vol. 3: Die eschatologische Verkündigung in den johanneischen Texten*. WUNT, 117; Tübingen: Mohr Siebeck, 2000.

Frey, Jörg. *Die Herrlichkeit des Gekreuzigten: Studien zu den johanneischen Schriften I*, edited by Juliane Schlegel. WUNT, 307. Tübingen: Mohr Siebeck, 2013.

Frey, Jörg. *Theology and History in the Fourth Gospel: Tradition and Narration*. Waco, TX: Baylor University Press, 2018.

Frey, Jörg. *The Glory of the Crucified One: Christology and Theology in the Gospel of John*. Trans. Wayne Coppins and Christoph Heilig. BMSEC, 6. Waco, TX: Baylor University Press, 2018.

Frey, Jörg. 'Das vierte Evangelium auf dem Hintergrund der älteren Evangelientradition: Zum Problem: Johannes und die Synoptiker'. In *Johannesevangelium – Mitte oder Rand des Kanons? Neue Standortbestimmungen*, edited by Thomas Söding, 60–118. Quaestiones Disputatae, 203. Freiburg: Herder, 2003. Reprinted in Jörg Frey, *Die Herrlichkeit des Gekreuzigten*, 239–94.

Frey, Jörg. 'Continuity and Discontinuity between "Jesus" and "Christ": The Possibilities of an Implicit Christology', *RCatT* 36 (2011): 69–98.

Frey, Jörg. 'New Testament Eschatology – an Introduction: Classical Issues, Disputed Themes, and Current Perspectives'. In *Eschatology of the New Testament and Some Related Documents*, edited by Jan G. van der Watt, 6–19. WUNT, 2/315. Tübingen: Mohr Siebeck, 2011.

Frey, Jörg. 'Johannine Christology and Eschatology'. In *Beyond Bultmann: Reckoning a New Testament Theology*, edited by Bruce W. Longenecker and Mikeal C. Parsons, 101–32. Waco, TX: Baylor University Press, 2014.

Frey, Jörg. 'Jesus und Pilatus: Der wahre König und der Repräsentant des Kaisers im Johannesevangelium'. In *Christ and the Emperor: The Gospel Evidence*, edited by Gilbert Van Belle and Joseph Verheyden, 337–93. BTS, 20. Leuven: Leuven University Presss and Peeters, 2014.

Frey, Jörg. 'Zu Hintergrund und Funktion des johanneischen Dualismus'. In Frey, Jörg. *Die Herrlichkeit des Gekreuzigten*, 409–82.

Frey, Jörg. 'Die "theologia crucifixi" des Johannesevangeliums'. In Jörg Frey, *Die Herrlichkeit des Gekreuzigten*, 485–554.

Frey, Jörg. 'Edler Tod – wirksamer Tod – stellvertretender Tod – heilvoller Tod: Zur narrativen und theologischen Deutung des Todes Jesu im Johannesevangelium'. In Jörg Frey, *Die Herrlichkeit des Gekreuzigten*, 555–85.

Frey, Jörg. 'Eschatology in the Johannine Circle'. In Jörg Frey, *Die Herrlichkeit des Gekreuzigten*, 663–98.
Frey, Jörg. 'From the *Sēmeia* Narratives to the Gospel as a Significant Narrative: On Genre-Bending in the Johannine Miracle Stories'. In *The Gospel of John as Genre Mosaic*, edited by Kasper Bro Larsen, 209–32. SANt, 3. Göttingen: Vandenhoeck & Ruprecht, 2015.
Frey, Jörg. 'From the "Kingdom of God" to "Eternal Life": The Transformation of Theological Language in the Fourth Gospel'. In *John, Jesus, and History*, Vol. 3: *Glimpses of Jesus through the Johannine Lens*, edited by Paul Anderson, Felix Just, S.J. and Tom Thatcher, 439–58. ECL, 18. Atlanta, GA: Society of Biblical Literature, 2016.
Frey, Jörg. 'Glauben und Lieben im Johannesevangelium'. In *Glaube, Liebe, Gespräch: Neue Perspektiven johanneischer Ethik*, edited by Christina Hoegen-Rohls and Uta Poplutz, 1–54. BThS, 178. Göttingen: Vandenhoeck & Ruprecht, 2018.
Frey, Jörg. 'The Gospel of John as a Narrative Memory of Jesus'. In *Memory and Memories in Early Christianity*, ed. Simon Butticaz and Enrico Norelli, 261–84. WUNT, 398. Tübingen: Mohr Siebeck, 2018.
Frey, Jörg. 'Johannine Dualism: Reflections on its Background and Function'. In Jörg Frey, *The Glory of the Crucified One*, 101–67.
Frey, Jörg. 'The Glory of the Crucified One'. In Jörg Frey, *The Glory of the Crucified One*, 237–58.
Frey, Jörg. 'Baptism in the Fourth Gospel, and Jesus and John as Baptizers: Historical and Theological Reflections on John 3:22–30'. In *Expressions of the Johannine Kerygma in John 2:23–5:18: Historical, Literary, and Theological Readings from the Colloquium Ioanneum 2017 in Jerusalem,* edited by R. Alan Culpepper and Jörg Frey, 87–115. WUNT, 423; Tübingen: Mohr Siebeck, 2019.
Freyne, Sean. 'Locality and Doctrine: Mark and John Revisited'. In *Galilee and Gospel: Collected Essays*, edited by Sean Freyne, 287–98. WUNT, 125. Tübingen: Mohr Siebeck, 2000.
Friedlieb, Philipp Heinrich. *Eschatologia seu Florilegium theologicum exhibens locorum de morte, resurrectione mortuorum, extremo iudicio, consummatio seculi, inferno seu morte aeterna et denique vita aeterna*. 1644
Fyfe, Hamilton (tr.). *Aristotle: Poetics, Longinus: On the Sublime; Demetrius: On Style*. LCL. Cambridge: Harvard University, 1973.
Gardner-Smith, Percival. *Saint John and the Synoptic Gospels*. Cambridge: Cambridge University Press, 1938.
Garrett, Susan R. *The Temptations of Jesus in Mark's Gospel*. Grand Rapids, MI: Wm. B. Eerdmans, 1998.
Genette, Gérard. *Palimpsestes: La littérature au second degré*. Collection Poétique. Paris: Seuil, 1982; ET *Palimpsests: Literature in the Second Degree*, translated by Channa Newman and Claude Doubinsky. Stages, 8. Lincoln, NE: University of Nebraska Press, 1982; GT *Palimpseste: Die Literatur auf zweiter Stufe*, trans. Wolfram Bayer and Dieter Hornig. Edition Suhrkamp: Aesthetica, 1683. Frankfurt am Main: Suhrkamp, 1993.
Genette, Gérard. *Seuils*. Collection Poétique. Paris: Seuil, 1987.
Gensburger, Sarah. 'Halbwachs' Studies in Collective Memory: A Founding Text for "Memory Studies"?' *Journal of Classical Sociology* 16.4 (2016): 396–413.
Georgia, Allan T. 'Translating the Triumph: Reading Mark's Crucifixion Narrative against a Roman Ritual of Power'. *JSNT* 36 (2013): 17–38.
Giblin, Charles H. 'Suggestion, Negative Response, and Positive Action in St John's Portrayal of Jesus (John 2.1-11; 4.46-50; 7.2-14; 11.1-44)'. *NTS* 26 (1980): 197–211.

Gilbert, M. 'Wisdom Literature'. In *Jewish Writings of the Second Temple Period: Apocrypha, Pseudepigrapha, Qumran Sectarian Writings, Philo, Josephus*, edited by Michael E. Stone, 283–324. CRINT, II/2. Assen: van Gorcum, 1984.

Gnilka, Joachim. *Das Evangelium nach Markus*. 2 vols. EKKNT, II/1–2. Zürich: Benziger Verlag; Neukirchen-Vluyn: Neukirchener Verlag, 1978; 5th edn, 1999.

Goodacre, Mark. *Thomas and the Gospels: The Case for Thomas's Familiarity with the Synoptics*, Grand Rapids, MI: Wm. B. Eerdmans, 2012; *Thomas and the Gospels: The Making of an Apocryphal Text*. London: SPCK, 2012.

Goodacre, Mark. 'The Synoptic Problem: John the Baptist and Jesus'. In *Method and Meaning: Essays on New Testament Interpretation in Honor of Harold W. Attridge*, edited by Andrew B. McGowan and Kent Harold Richards, 177–92. RBS, 67. Atlanta, GA: Society of Biblical Literature Press, 2011.

Goodenough, Erwin R. 'John a Primitive Gospel'. *JBL* 64 (1945): 145–82.

Goulder, Michael D. *Luke: A New Paradigm*. JSNTSup, 20. Sheffield: Sheffield Academic Press, 1989.

Graham, William A. *Beyond the Written Word: Oral Aspects of Scripture in the History of Religion*. Cambridge: Cambridge University Press, 1987.

Gregory, Andrew. 'What is Literary Dependence?'. In *New Studies in the Synoptic Problem: Oxford Conference, April 2008: Essays in Honour of Christopher M. Tuckett*, edited by Paul Foster, Andrew Gregory, John S. Kloppenborg and Joseph Verheyden, 87–114. BETL, 239. Leuven: Leuven University Press and Peeters, 2011.

Gould, Ezra P. *A Critical and Exegetical Commentary on the Gospel According to St Mark*. Edinburgh: T&T Clark, 1896.

Guelich, Robert A. 'The Gospel Genre'. In *Das Evangelium und die Evangelien: Vorträge vom Tübinger Symposium 1982*, edited by Peter Stuhlmacher, 183–220. WUNT, 28. Tübingen: Mohr Siebeck, 1983.

Guttenberger, Gudrun. *Die Gottesvorstellung im Markusevangelium*. BZNW, 123. Berlin: de Gruyter, 2004.

Haenchen, Ernst. *Das Johannesevangelium*, ed. Ulrich Busse. Tübingen: Mohr Siebeck, 1980; ET: *A Commentary on the Gospel of John*, trans. Robert W. Funk, 2 vols. Hermeneia. Philadelphia, PA: Fortress, 1984.

Halbwachs, Maurice. *The Social Frameworks of Memory*. In *On Collective Memory*, edited and translated by Lewis A. Coser. Chicago, IL: University of Chicago Press, 1992.

Harb, Gertraud. *Die eschatologische Rede des Spruchevangeliums Q: Redaktions- und Traditionsgeschichtliche Studien zu Q 17,23–37*. BTS, 19. Leuven: Leuven University Press and Peeters, 2014.

Harrington, Daniel J. 'Palestinian Adaptations of Biblical Narratives and Prophecies: The Bible Rewritten (Narratives)'. In *Early Judaism and its Modern Interpreters*, edited by Robert A. Kraft and George W.E. Nickelsburg, 239–47. Minneapolis, MN: Fortress, 1986.

Harvey, Anthony E. *Jesus on Trial: A Study on the Fourth Gospel*. London: SPCK, 1976.

Hays, Richard B. *The Moral Vision of the New Testament: A Contemporary Introduction to New Testament Ethics*. San Francisco, CA: Harper Collins, 1996.

Hays, Richard B. *Echoes of Scripture in the Gospels*. Waco, TX: Baylor University Press, 2016.

Heilmann, Jan. *Lesen in Antike und frühem Christentum: Kulturgeschichtliche, philologische sowie kognitionswissenschaftliche Perspektiven und deren Bedeutung für die neutestamentliche Exegese*. Habilitationsschrift, Ruhr-Universität Bochum, 2019.

Hengel, Martin. 'The Gospel of Mark: Time of Origin and Situation'. In Martin Hengel, *Studies in the Gospel of Mark*, trans. by John Bowden, 1–30. Minneapolis, MN: Fortress, 1985.

Henten, Jan Willem van. *The Maccabean Martyrs as Saviours of the Jewish People: A Study of 2 and 4 Maccabees*. JSJSupp, 57. Leiden: Brill, 1997.

Hjelde, Sigurd. *Das Eschaton und die Eschata: Eine Studie über Sprachgebrauch und Sprachverwirrung in protestantischer Theologie von der Orthodoxie bis zur Gegenwart*. Beiträge zur evangelischen Theologie, 102. München: Kaiser, 1987.

Hobi, Viktor. 'Kurze Einführung in die Grundlagen der Gedächtnispsychologie'. In *Vergangenheit in mündlicher Überlieferung*, edited by Jürgen von Ungern-Sternberg and Hansjörg Reinau, 9–33. Colloquium Rauricum, 1. Stuttgart: B. G. Teubner, 1988.

Hofrichter, Peter L. *Modell und Vorlage der Synoptiker – Das vorredaktionelle 'Johannesevangelium'*. TTS, 6. Hildesheim: Olms, 1997.

Hofrichter, Peter L. *Für und Wider die Priorität des Johannesevangeliums*. TTS, 9. Hildesheim: Olms, 2002.

Hoegen-Rohls, Christina. *Der nachösterliche Johannes: Die Abschiedsreden als hermeneutischer Schlüssel zum vierten Evangelium*. WUNT, 2/84; Tübingen: Mohr Siebeck, 1996.

Hoegen-Rohls, Christina. 'Leben und Ewigkeit: Der biblische Vorstellungskreis III: Johannes'. In *Das Leben: Historisch-systematische Studien zur Geschichte eines Begriffs, Vol. 1*, edited by Petra Bahr and Stephan Schaede, 129–52. Tübingen: Mohr Siebeck, 2009.

Høgenhaven, Jesper. 'Fortschreibung und Kanonisierung in der Bibliothek von Qumran: Bemerkungen mit besonderem Hinblick auf Genesis-Kommentar A (4Q252)'. In *Rewriting and Reception in and of the Bible*, edited by Jesper Høgenhaven, Jesper Tang Nielsen and Heike Omerzu, 11–31. WUNT, 396. Tübingen: Mohr Siebeck, 2018.

Hooker, Morna D. *The Gospel According to Saint Mark*. Black's New Testament Commentaries. London: A&C Black, 1991.

Hooker, Morna D. 'The Johannine Prologue and the Messianic Secret', *NTS* 21 (1974): 40–58.

Horn, Friedrich Wilhelm. 'Ethik des Neuen Testaments 1982–1992', *ThR* 60 (1995): 32–86.

Horn, Friedrich Wilhelm. 'Ethik des Neuen Testaments 1993–2009: Teil I', *ThR* 76 (2011): 1–36.

Horn, Friedrich Wilhelm. 'Ethik des Neuen Testaments 1993–2009: Teil II', *ThR* 76 (2011): 180–221.

Hornig, Gottfried. *Die Anfänge der historisch-kritischen Theologie: Johann Salomo Semlers Schriftverständnis und seine Stellung zu Luther*. Forschungen zur Systematischen Theologie und Religionsphilosophie, 8. Göttingen: Vandenhoeck & Ruprecht, 1961.

Hoskyns, Edwyn Clement. *The Fourth Gospel*, edited by Francis Noel Davey. 2nd rev. edn. London: Faber and Faber, 1947; repr. 1967.

Huizenga, Leroy A. *The New Isaac: Tradition and Intertextuality in the Gospel of Matthew*. NovTSup, 131. Brill: Leiden, 2009.

Huizenga, Leroy A. 'Obedience unto Death: The Matthean Gethsemane and Arrest Sequence and the Aqedah'. *CBQ* 71 (2009): 507–26.

Hunt, Steven A. *Rewriting the Feeding of Five Thousand: John 6.1–15 as a Test Case for Johannine Dependence on the Synoptic Gospels*. Studies in Biblical Literature, 125. New York: Peter Lang, 2011.

Hunt, Steven A., D. Francois Tolmie and Ruben Zimmermann (eds). *Character Studies in the Fourth Gospel: Narrative Approaches to Seventy Figures in John*. Grand Rapids, MI: Wm. B. Eerdmans, 2016.

Hurtado, Larry W. *Lord Jesus Christ: Devotion to Jesus in Earliest Christianity*. Grand Rapids, MI: Wm. B. Eerdmans, 2005.

Jay, Jeff. *The Tragic in Mark: A Literary-Historical Interpretation*. Hermeneutische Untersuchungen zur Theologie, 66. Tübingen: Mohr Siebeck, 2014.

Jennings, Mark. 'The Fourth Gospel's Reversal of Mark in John 13,31–14,3'. *Bib* 94 (2013): 210–36.

Kähler, Martin. *Der sogenannte historische Jesus und der geschichtliche, biblische Christus*, edited by Ernst Wolf. Theologische Bücherei, 2. 2nd edition. München: Chr. Kaiser Verlag, 1956. ET: *The So-Called Historical Jesus and the Historic Biblical Christ*. trans. Carl E. Braaten; Philadelphia, PA: Fortress, 1964.

Käsemann, Ernst. *Jesu letzter Wille nach Johannes 17*. Tübingen: Mohr Siebeck, 1966; repr. 2nd unrevised edn, 1967.

Keener, Craig S. *The Gospel of John: A Commentary*. 2 vols. Grand Rapids, MI: Baker Academic, 2003.

Keith, Chris. *The Gospel as Manuscript: An Early History of the Jesus Tradition as Material Artifact*, New York: Oxford University Press, 2020.

Keith, Chris. 'Memory and Authenticity: Jesus Tradition and What Really Happened'. *ZNW* 102 (2011): 155–77.

Keith, Chris. 'Social Memory Theory and Gospels Scholarship: The First Decade (Part One)'. *Early Christianity* 6.3 (2015): 354–76.

Keith, Chris. 'Social Memory Theory and Gospels Scholarship: The First Decade (Part Two)'. *Early Christianity* 6.4 (2015): 517–42.

Keith, Chris. 'The Competitive Textualization of the Jesus Tradition in John 20:30–31 and 21:24–25'. *CBQ* 78 (2016): 321–37.

Keith, Chris. 'Jesus the Galilean in the Gospel of John: The Significance of Earthly Origins in the Fourth Gospel'. In *Portraits of Jesus in the Gospel of John: A Christological Spectrum*, edited by Craig Koester, 45–59. Library of New Testament Studies, 589. London: Bloomsbury T&T Clark, 2018.

Kelber, Werner H. *The Oral and the Written Gospel: The Hermeneutics of Speaking and Writing in the Synoptic Tradition, Mark, Paul, and Q*. Philadelphia, PA: Fortress, 1983.

Kelber, Werner H. (ed.), *The Passion in Mark: Studies on Mark 14–16*. Philadelphia, PA: Fortress, 1976.

Kertelge, Karl. *Die Wunder Jesu im Markusevangelium: Eine redaktionsgeschichtliche Untersuchung*. StANT, 23. München: Kösel, 1970.

Kierspel, Lars. *The Jews and the World in the Fourth Gospel: Parallelism, Function, and Context*. WUNT, 2/220. Tübingen: Mohr Siebeck, 2006.

Kiilunen, Jarmo. *Die Vollmacht im Widerstreit: Untersuchungen zum Werdegang von Mk 2,1–3,6*. AASF.DHL, 40. Helsinki: Suomalainen Tiedeakatemi, 1985.

Kirk, Alan. 'Memory and Media: Towards a New History of the Jesus Tradition'. In *Memory and the Jesus Tradition*, 1–8. Reception of Jesus in the First Three Centuries, 2. London: Bloomsbury T&T Clark, 2018.

Kirk, Alan and Tom Thatcher. 'Jesus Tradition as Social Memory'. In *Memory, Tradition, and Text: Uses of the Past in Early Christianity*. 25–42. Semeia Studies, 52. Atlanta, GA: Society of Biblical Literature, 2005.

Klauck, Hans-Josef. 'Geschrieben, erfüllt, vollendet: Die Schriftzitate in der Johannespassion'. In *Israel und seine Heilstraditionen im Johannesevangelium: Festgabe für Johannes Beutler SJ zum 70. Geburtstag*, edited by Michael Labahn, Klaus Scholtissek and Angelika Strotmann, 140–57. Paderborn: Schöningh, 2004.

Klauck, Hans-Josef. *Vorspiel im Himmel? Erzähltechnik und Theologie im Markusprolog.* BthS, 32. Neukirchen-Vluyn: Neukirchener Verlagsgesellschaft, 1997.

Klein, Christian and Matías Martínez. *Wirklichkeitserzählungen: Felder, Formen und Funktionen nicht-literarischen Erzählens.* Stuttgart/Weimar: Metzler, 2009.

Kloppenborg, John S. 'Variation in the Reproduction of the Double Tradition and an Oral Q?'. *ETL* 83 (2007): 49–79.

Kloppenborg, John S. 'The Reception of the Jesus Tradition in James'. In *The Catholic Epistles and Apostolic Tradition: A New Perspective on James to Jude,* edited by Karl-Wilhelm Niebuhr and Robert W. Wall, 71–100. Waco, TX: Baylor University Press, 2009.

Knöppler, Thomas. *Die theologia crucis des Johannesevangeliums: Das Verständnis des Todes Jesu im Rahmen der johanneischen Inkarnations- und Erhöhungschristologie.* WMANT, 69. Neukirchen-Vluyn: Neukirchener Verlag, 1994.

Koch, Dietrich-Alex. *Die Bedeutung der Wundererzählungen für die Christologie des Markusevangeliums.* BZNW, 42. Berlin: de Gruyter, 1985.

Koch, Dietrich-Alex. 'Der Täufer als Zeuge des Offenbarers: Das Täuferbild von Joh 1,19–34 auf dem Hintergrund von Mk 1,2–11'. In *The Four Gospels, 1992: Festschrift Frans Neirynck,* edited by Frans Van Segbroeck, Christopher M. Tuckett, Gilbert Van Belle and Joseph Verheyden, 3:1963–84. BETL, 100; 3 vols. Leuven: Leuven University Press and Peeters, 1992.

Koester, Craig R. *Symbolism in the Fourth Gospel: Meaning, Mystery, Community.* 2nd edn. Minneapolis, MN: Augsburg Fortress, 2003.

Koester, Helmut. *Ancient Christian Gospels: Their History and Development.* Philadelphia, PA: Trinity Press International; London: SCM, 1990.

Kokolakis, M. 'Lucian and the Tragic Performances in his Time'. *Platon* 12 (1960): 67–106.

Konings, Johan. 'The Dialogue of Jesus, Philip and Andrew in John 6,5–9'. In *John and the Synoptics,* edited by Adelbert Denaux, 523–34. BETL, 101. Leuven: Leuven University Press and Peeters, 1992.

Kooten, George van. 'The Last Days of Socrates and Christ: *Euthyphro, Apology, Crito,* and *Phaedo* Read in Counterpoint with John's Gospel'. In *Religio-Philosophical Discourses in the Mediterranean World: From Plato, through Jesus, to Late Antiquity,* edited by Anders Klostergaard Petersen and George van Kooten, 219–43. Ancient Philosophy & Religion, 1. Leiden: Brill, 2017.

Kuhn, Heinz-Wolfgang. *Ältere Sammlungen im Markusevangelium.* StUNT, 8. Göttingen: Vandenhoeck & Ruprecht, 1971.

Kümmel, Werner G. *Introduction to the New Testament.* Rev. ed., Nashville, TN: Abingdon, 1975.

Labahn, Michael. *Jesus als Lebensspender: Untersuchungen zu einer Geschichte der johanneischen Tradition anhand ihrer Wundergeschichten.* BZNW, 98. Berlin: de Gruyter, 1999.

Labahn, Michael. *Offenbarung in Zeichen und Wort: Untersuchungen zur Vorgeschichte von Joh 6,1–25a und seiner Rezeption in der Brotrede.* WUNT, 2/117. Tübingen: Mohr Siebeck, 2000.

Labahn, Michael. *Ausgewählte Studien zum Johannesevangelium: Selected Studies in the Gospel of John: 1998–2013,* edited by Antje Labahn, with an Introduction by Gilbert Van Belle. Biblical Tools and Studies, 28. Leuven: Peeters, 2017.

Labahn, Michael. 'Eine Spurensuche anhand von Joh 5,1–18: Bemerkungen zu Wachstum und Wandel der Heilung eines Lahmen'. *NTS* 44 (1988): 159–79. Reprinted in Michael Labahn, *Ausgewählte Studien,* 391–411.

Labahn, Michael. Review of 'D. M. Smith, *John among the Gospels*, 2nd edn'. *TLZ* 129 (2004): 289–91.
Labahn, Michael. 'Living Word(s) and the Bread of Life'. In *What We Have Heard from the Beginning: The Past, Present and Future of Johannine Studies*, edited by Tom Thatcher, 59–62. Waco, TX: Baylor University Press, 2007. Reprinted in Peder Borgen, *The Gospel of John*, 23–6 (followed by 'Reflections by the Author', 26–27).
Labahn, Michael. 'Die Macht des Gedächtnisses: Überlegungen zu Möglichkeit und Grenzen des Einflusses hebräischer Texttradition auf die Johannesapokalypse'. In *Von der Septuaginta zum Neuen Testament: Textgeschichtliche Erörterungen*, edited by Martin Karrer, Siegfried Kreuzer and Marcus Sigismund, 385–416. ANTF, 43. Berlin: de Gruyter, 2010.
Labahn, Michael. '"It's Only Love" – Is That All? Limits and Potentials of Johannine "Ethic": A Critical Evaluation of Research'. In *Rethinking the Ethics of John: 'Implicit Ethics' in the Johannine Writings*, edited by Jan G. van der Watt and Ruben Zimmermann, 3–43. WUNT, 291. Tübingen: Mohr Siebeck, 2012.
Labahn, Michael. 'Die Gabe des Lebens und kaiserliche Wohltaten – ein unvermeidlicher Gegensatz: Der Jesus des vierten Evangeliums als Wundertäter und der römische Kaiser'. In *Christ and the Emperor: The Gospel Evidence*, edited by Gilbert Van Belle and Joseph Verheyden, 249–77. BiTS, 20. Leuven: Leuven University Press and Peeters, 2014.
Labahn, Michael. '"Secondary Orality" in the Gospel of John: A "Post-Gutenberg" Paradigm for Understanding the Relationship between Written Gospel Texts'. In *The Origins of John's Gospel*, edited by Stanley E. Porter and Hughson T. Ong, 53–80. Johannine Studies, 2. Leiden: Brill, 2016.
Labahn, Michael. 'Bedeutung und Frucht des Todes Jesu im Spiegel des johanneischen Erzählaufbaus'. In Michael Labahn, *Ausgewählte Studien zum Johannesevangelium*, 361–87.
Labahn, Michael. 'Eine Spurensuche anhand von Joh 5.1–18: Bemerkungen zu Wachstum und Wandel der Heilung eines Lahmen'. In Michael Labahn, *Ausgewählte Studien zum Johannesevangelium*, 391–411.
Labahn, Michael. 'Secondary Orality'. In *The Dictionary of the Bible in Ancient Media*, edited by Tom Thatcher, Chris Keith, Raymond F. Person and Elsie Stern, 263–64. London: T&T Clark, 2017.
Labahn, Michael. 'A Narrow Gate to the Johannine Gospel? Re-Thinking the Relationship Between the Johannine Prologue (John 1:1–18) and the Gospel of John in Terms of the Theories of Paratext and of "Discourse Universe"'. In *Johannine Christology*, edited by Stanley E. Porter and Andrew W. Pitts. Johannine Studies, 3. Leiden: Brill, forthcoming.
Labahn, Michael and Manfred Lang. 'Johannes und die Synoptiker: Positionen und Impulse seit 1990'. In *Kontexte des Johannesevangeliums: Das vierte Evangelium in religions- und traditionsgeschichtlicher Perspektive*, edited by Jörg Frey and Udo Schnelle, 443–515. WUNT, 175. Tübingen: Mohr Siebeck, 2004. Reprinted in Michael Labahn, *Ausgewählte Studien zum Johannesevangelium*, 57–61.
de Lacy, Philip. 'Biography and Tragedy in Plutarch'. *AJP* 73 (1952): 159–71.
Lagrange, M.-J. *Évangile selon Saint Jean*. Etudes biblique. Paris: J. Gabalda, 1925.
Lamb, W. R. M. (tr.). *Plato in Twelve Volumes, Vol. 9*. LCL. Cambridge: Harvard University Press, 1925.
Landis, Stephan. *Das Verhältnis des Johannesevangeliums zu den Synoptikern: Am Beispiel von Mt 8,5–13, Lk 7,1–10, Joh 4,46–54*. BZNW, 74. Berlin: de Gruyter, 1992.

Lang, Manfred. *Johannes und die Synoptiker: Eine redaktionsgeschichtliche Analyse von Joh 18-19 vor dem markinischen und lukanischen Hintergrund.* FRLANT, 182. Göttingen: Vandenhoeck & Ruprecht, 1999.
Lang, Manfred. 'Andersheit und Musterwissen: Beobachtungen zum Verhältnis Johannes und die Synoptiker anhand von Johannes 6,1-71'. In *Studies in the Gospel of John and Its Christology: Festschrift Gilbert Van Belle,* edited by Joseph Verheyden, Geert Van Oyen, Michael Labahn, Reimund Bieringer, 189-204. BETL, 265. Leuven, Paris, Walpole: Leuven University Press and Peeters, 2014.
Larsen, Kasper Bro. *Recognizing the Stranger: Recognition Scenes in the Gospel of John.* BIS, 93. Leiden: Brill, 2008.
Larsen, Kasper Bro. 'Narrative Docetism: Christology and Storytelling in the Gospel of John'. In *The Gospel of John and Christian Theology,* edited by Richard Bauckham and Carl Mosser, 346-55. Grand Rapids, MI: Wm. B. Eerdmans, 2007.
Larsen, Matthew D. C. *Gospels Before the Book.* New York: Oxford University Press, 2018.
Le Donne, Anthony and Tom Thatcher (eds). *The Fourth Gospel in First-Century Media Culture.* LNTS, 426. London: T&T Clark International, 2011.
Leonhardt-Balzer, Jutta. 'Review of P. Borgen, *The Gospel of John*'. *JSNT* 37.5 (2015): 56.
Licona, Michael R. *Why Are There Differences in the Gospels? What We Can Learn from Ancient Biography.* Oxford: Oxford University Press, 2017.
Lightfoot, Robert H. *St John's Gospel: A Commentary.* Oxford: Oxford University Press, 1956.
Lincoln, Andrew T. *Truth on Trial: The Lawsuit Motif in John's Gospel.* Peabody, MA: Hendrickson, 2000.
Lincoln, Andrew T. *The Gospel According to St John.* BNTC, 4. London: Continuum, 2005.
Lindars, Barnabas. 'The Composition of John XX', *NTS* 7 (1960-61): 142-47. Reprinted in Barnabas Lindars, *Essays on John,* edited by Christopher M. Tuckett, 1-8. Studiorum Novi Testamenti Auxilia, 17. Leuven: Leuven University Press and Peeters, 1992.
Lindars, Barnabas. 'Capernaum Revisited: Jn 4,46-53 and the Synoptics'. In *The Four Gospels, 1992: Festschrift Frans Neirynck,* edited by Frans Van Segbroeck, Christopher M. Tuckett, Gilbert Van Belle, and Joseph Verheyden, 3:1985-2000. BETL, 100; 3 vols. Leuven: Leuven University Press and Peeters, 1992.
Lohmeyer, Ernst. *Das Evangelium des Markus.* 16th edn; KEK, I/2. Göttingen: Vandenhoeck & Ruprecht, 1963.
Lührmann, Dieter. *Das Markusevangelium.* HNT, 3. Tübingen: Mohr Siebeck, 1987.
Lührmann, Dieter. 'Die Pharisäer und die Schriftgelehrten im Markusevangelium', *ZNW* 78 (1987): 169-85.
Luther, Susanne. *Die Authentifizierung der Vergangenheit: Literarische Geschichtsdarstellung im Johannesevangelium.* WUNT. Tübingen: Mohr Siebeck, 2021.
Luther, Susanne. 'The Authentication of the Past: Narrative Representations of History in the Gospel of John'. *JSNT* (2020): forthcoming.
MacDonald, Dennis R. *My Turn: A Critique of Critics of "Mimesis Criticism".* The Institute for Antiquity and Christianity Occasional Papers, 53. Claremont, CA: Institute for Antiquity and Christianity, 2009.
MacDonald, Dennis R. *The Dionysian Gospel: The Fourth Gospel and Euripides.* Minneapolis, MN: Fortress, 2017.
Mackay, Ian D. *John's Relationship with Mark: An Analysis of John 6 in the Light of Mark 6-8.* WUNT, 2/182. Tübingen: Mohr Siebeck, 2004.
MacGregor, George H. C. *The Gospel of John.* London: Hodder and Stoughton, 1928.
Marcus, Joel. *Mark 1-8: A New Translation with Introduction and Commentary,* The Anchor Bible, 27. New York: Doubleday, 2000.

Marcus, Joel. *Mark 9–16. A New Translation with Introduction and Commentary*. The Anchor Bible, 27A. New York: Doubleday, 2000.
Marincola, John. 'Speeches in Classical Historiography'. In *A Companion to Greek and Roman Historiography*, edited by John Marincola, 118–32. Oxford: Blackwell, 2007.
Martyn, J. Louis. *History and Theology in the Fourth Gospel*. New York: Harper & Row, 1968.
Marxsen, Willi. *Mark the Evangelist: Studies on the Redaction History of the Gospel*. Translated by James Boyce, et al. Nashville, TN: Abingdon, 1969.
Mason, Steve. 'Josephus and His Twenty-Two Book Canon'. In *The Canon Debate*, edited by Lee Martin McDonald and James A. Sanders, 110–27. Peabody, MA: Hendrickson, 2002.
Matera, Frank J. *The Kingship of Jesus: Composition and Theology in Mark 15*. Chico, CA: Scholars Press, 1982.
Matson, Mark A. *In Dialogue with Another Gospel? The Influence of the Fourth Gospel on the Passion Narrative of the Gospel of Luke*. SBLDS, 178. Atlanta, GA: Society of Biblical Literature, 2001.
Maynard, Athur H. 'ΤΙ ΕΜΟΙ ΚΑΙ ΣΟΙ'. *NTS* 31 (1985): 582–86.
McHugh, John F. *John 1–4*. ICC. London: T&T Clark, 2009.
McLaren, James S. *Power and Politics in Palestine: The Jews and the Governing of their Land, 100 BC–70 AD*. Sheffield: JSOT Press, 1991.
Mead, David W. *The Literary Devices in John's Gospel*. Revised and expanded edition. Eugene, OR: Wipf & Stock, 2018.
Meeks, Wayne A. *The Prophet-King: Moses Traditions and the Johannine Christology*. NovTSup, 14. Leiden: Brill, 1967.
Meeks, Wayne A. *The First Urban Christians: The Social World of the Apostle Paul*. New Haven, CT: Yale University Press, 1983.
Meeks, Wayne A. *The Origins of Christian Morality: The First Two Centuries*. New Haven, CT: Yale University Press, 1993.
Meeks, Wayne A. 'Galilee and Judea in the Fourth Gospel'. *JBL* 85 (1966): 159–69.
Meiser, Martin. *Die Reaktion des Volkes auf Jesus: Eine redaktionskritische Untersuchung zu den synoptischen Evangelien*. BZNW, 96. Berlin: de Gruyter, 1998.
Metzger, Bruce. *A Textual Commentary on the Greek New Testament*. 2nd edn. Reprint. Stuttgart: Deutsche Bibelgesellschaft, 2000.
Metzner, Rainer. *Das Verständnis von Sünde im Johannesevangelium*. WUNT, 122. Tübingen: Mohr Siebeck, 2000.
Michaels, J. Ramsey. *The Gospel of John*. NICNT. Grand Rapids, MI: Wm. B. Eerdmans, 2010.
Miller, Susan. '"Among You Stands One Whom You Do Not Know" (John 1:26): The Use of the Tradition of the Hidden Messiah in John's Gospel'. In *The Ways That Often Parted: Essays in Honor of Joel Marcus*, edited by Lori Baron, Jill Hicks-Keeton, and Matthew Thiessen, 243–63. Atlanta, GA: Society of Biblical Literature, 2018.
Mills, Margaret A. 'Domains of Folkloristic Concern: The Interpretation of Scriptures'. In *Text and Tradition: The Hebrew Bible and Folklore*, edited by Susan Niditch, 231–41. Semeia Studies, 32. Atlanta, GA: Scholars Press, 1990.
Mohr, Till Arend. *Markus- und Johannespassion: Redaktions- und traditionsgeschichtliche Untersuchung der markinischen und johanneischen* Passionstradition. AThANT, 70. Zürich: Theologischer Verlag, 1982.
Moloney, Francis J. *The Gospel of John*. SP, 4. Collegeville, MN: Liturgical Press, 1998.

Moloney, Francis J. 'The First Days of Jesus and the Role of the Disciples: A Study of John 1:19-51'. In Francis J. Moloney, *Johannine Studies 1975-2017*, 307-30. WUNT, 372. Tübingen: Mohr Siebeck, 2017.
Moltmann, Jürgen. *The Crucified God*. 40th Anniversary edition. Minneapolis, MN: Fortress, 2015.
Morris, Leon. *Jesus Is the Christ: Studies in the Theology of John*. Grand Rapids, MI: Wm. B. Eerdmans, 1989.
Moser, Marion. *Schriftdiskurse im Johannesevangelium: Eine narrative-intertextuelle Analyse am Paradigma von Joh 4 und Joh 7*. WUNT, 2/380. Tübingen: Mohr Siebeck, 2014.
Mossman, Judith M. 'Tragedy and Epic in Plutarch's *Alexander*'. In *Essays on Plutarch's Lives*, edited by Barbara Scardigli, 209-28. Oxford: Clarendon Press, 1995.
Mroczek, Eva. *The Literary Imagination in Jewish Antiquity*. New York: Oxford University Press, 2016.
Müller, Christoph G. 'Διήγησις nach Lukas: Zwischen historiographischem Anspruch und biographischem Erzählen'. In *Historiographie und Biographie im Neuen Testament und seiner Umwelt*, edited by Thomas Schmeller, 95-126. NTOA/StUNT, 69. Göttingen: Vandenhoeck & Ruprecht, 2009.
Müller, Mogens. 'The New Testament Gospels as Biblical Rewritings: On the Question of Referentiality'. *Studia Theologica* 68 (2014): 21-40.
Müller, Mogens and Jesper Tang Nielsen. *Luke's Literary Creativity*. LNTS, 550. London: T&T Clark, 2016.
Murnaghan, Sheila. *Disguise and Recognition in the Odyssey*. Princeton, NJ: Princeton University Press, 1987.
Myers, Alicia D. 'Prosopopoetics and Conflict: Speech and Expectations in John 8'. *Biblica* 92 (2011): 580-96.
Myers, Alicia D. 'Discerning Characters: *Parresia, Paroimia*, and Jesus's Rhetoric in John 10:1-21'. In *Come and Read: Interpretive Approaches to the Gospel of John*, edited by Alicia D. Myers and Lindsey S. Jodrey, 125-37. Lanham, MD: Fortress Academic, 2020.
Myllykoski, Matti. *Die letzten Tagen Jesu: Markus und Johannes, ihre Traditionen und die historische Frage*. 2 vols. Annales Academiae Scientiarum Fennicae Series B. 256/272. Helsinki: Suomalainen Tiedeakatemia 1991/1994.
Najman, Hindy. *Seconding Sinai: The Development of Mosaic Discourse in Second Temple Judaism*. SuppJSJ, 77. Leiden: Brill, 2003.
Najman, Hindy. 'Interpretation as Primordial Writing: *Jubilees* and Its Authority Conferring Strategies'. *JSJ* 30 (1999): 379-410.
Neirynck, Frans. *Evangelica II: 1982-1991: Collected Essays*, edited by Frans Van Segbroeck. BETL, 99. Leuven: Leuven University Press and Peeters, 1991.
Neirynck, Frans. 'The Signs Source in the Fourth Gospel: A Critique of the Hypothesis', ET of 'De semeia-bron in het vierde Evangelie: Kritiek von een hypothese', *Academiae Analecta* (1983): 1-28; in Frans Neirynck, *Evangelica II*, 651-78.
Neirynck, Frans. 'John and the Synoptics: The Empty Tomb Stories'. *NTS* 30 (1984): 161-87. Reprinted in Frans Neirynck, *Evangelica II*, 571-97.
Neirynck, Frans. 'John 4,46-54: Signs Source and/or Synoptic Gospels'. *ETL* 60 (1984): 367-75. Reprinted in Frans Neirynck, *Evangelica II*, 679-88.
Neirynck, Frans. 'John and the Synoptics: Response to P. Borgen'. In *The Interrelations of the Gospels: A Symposium Led by M.-É. Boismard - W.R. Farmer - F. Neirynck, Jerusalem 1984*, edited by David L. Dungan, 438-50. BETL, 95. Leuven: Leuven University Press and Peeters, 1990. Reprinted in Frans Neirynck, *Evangelica II*, 699-711 (711-12: 'Additional Note').

Neirynck, Frans. 'John 5,1-18 and the Gospel of Mark'. In Frans Neirynck, *Evangelica II*, edited by Frans Van Segbroeck, 699-712. BETL, 99. Leuven: Leuven University Press and Peeters, 1991.

Neirynck, Frans. 'John and the Synoptics 1975-1990'. In *John and the Synoptics*, edited by Adelbert Denaux, 3-62. BETL, 101. Leuven: Leuven University Press and Peeters, 1992. Reprinted in Frans Neirynck, *Evangelica III: 1995-2000: Collected Essays*, 3-64. BETL, 150. Leuven: Leuven University Press, 2001.

Neirynck, Frans, in collaboration with Joël Delobel, Thierry Snoy, Gilbert Van Belle and Frans Van Segbroeck. 'L'Évangile de Jean: Examen critique de M.-É. Boismard et Arnaud Lamouille'. *ETL* 53 (1977) 363-478. Reprinted in *Jean et les Synoptiques: Examen critique de l'exégèse de M.-É. Boismard*, 3-120. BETL, 49. Leuven: University Press, 1979.

Neyrey, Jerome H. 'The "Noble Shepherd" in John 10: Cultural and Rhetorical Background'. *JBL* 120 (2001): 267-91.

Nickelsburg, George W. E. 'The Bible Rewritten and Expanded'. In *Jewish Writings of the Second Temple Period: Apocrypha, Pseudepigrapha, Qumran Sectarian Writings, Philo, Josephus*, edited by Michael E. Stone, 89-156. CRINT, II/2. Assen: van Gorcum, 1984.

Nicol, W. *The Semeia in the Fourth Gospel: Tradition and Redaction*. NovTSup, 32. Leiden: Brill, 1972.

North, Wendy E. S. *A Journey Round John: Tradition, Interpretation and Context in the Fourth Gospel*. LNTS, 534. London: Bloomsbury T&T Clark, 2015.

North, Wendy E. S. 'John for Readers of Mark? A Response to Richard Bauckham's Proposal'. *JSNT* 25 (2003): 449-68.

North, Wendy E. S. '"Lord, if you had been here..." (John 11.21): The Absence of Jesus and Strategies of Consolation in the Fourth Gospel'. *JSNT* 36 (2013): 39-52. Reprinted in Wendy E.S. North, *A Journey Round John*, 193-206.

North, Wendy E. S. 'Points and Stars: John and the Synoptics'. In *John, Jesus, and History*, Vol. 3: *Glimpses of Jesus through the Johannine Lens*, edited by Paul Anderson, Felix Just, S.J. and Tom Thatcher, 119-32. ECL, 18; Atlanta, GA: Society of Biblical Literature, 2016. Reprinted in Wendy E.S. North, *A Journey Round John*, 207-19.

O'Day, Gail R. 'The Johannine Literature' in *The New Testament Today*, edited by Mark Allan Powell, 70-85. Louisville, KY: Westminister John Knox, 1999.

O'Day, Gail R. '"I have said these things to you...": The Unsettled Place of Jesus' Discourses in Literary Approaches to the Fourth Gospel'. In *Word, Theology and Community in John*, edited by John Painter, R. Alan Culpepper and Fernando F. Segovia, 143-54. St. Louis, MO: Chalice Press, 2002.

Omerzu, Heike. 'Das Petrusevangelium als "rewritten Gospel"? Eine forschungsgeschichtliche Erörterung der Rezeption der Kategorie "rewritten Bible" in Bezug auf frühchristliche Texte'. In *Rewriting and Reception in and of the Bible*, edited by Jesper Høgenhaven, Jesper Tang Nielsen and Heike Omerzu, 235-51. WUNT, 396. Tübingen: Mohr Siebeck, 2018.

Ong, Walter J. *Orality and Literacy: The Technologizing of the World*. Reprint. New Accents. London: Routledge, 2007.

Ottillinger, Angelika, *Vorläufer, Vorbild oder Zeuge? Zum Wandel des Taüferbildes im Johannesevangelium*, Dissertationen: Theologische Reihe, 45. St. Ottilien: EOS Verlag, 1991.

Painter, John. 'Tradition and Interpretation in John 6'. *NTS* 35 (1989): 421-50.

Parsenios, George L. *Departure and Consolation: The Johannine Farewell Discourses in Light of Greco-Roman Literature*. NT.S, 117. Leiden: Brill, 2005.

Parsenios, George L. *Rhetoric and Drama in the Johannine Lawsuit Motif*. WUNT, 258. Tübingen: Mohr Siebeck, 2010.
Parsenios, George L. 'The Silent Spaces between Narrative and Drama: Mimesis and Diegesis in the Fourth Gospel'. In *The Gospel of John as Genre Mosaic*, edited by Kasper Bro Larsen, 85–97. SANt, 3. Göttingen: Vandenhoeck & Ruprecht, 2015.
Pausch, Dennis. *Stimmen der Geschichte: Funktionen von Reden in der antiken Historiographie*. Berlin/New York: de Gruyter, 2010.
Penwell, Stewart. *Jesus the Samaritan: Ethnic Labeling in the Gospel of John*. BIS, 170. Leiden: Brill, 2019.
Pesch, Rudolf. *Das Markusevangelium, I. Teil: Einleitung und Kommentar zu Kap.1,1–8,26*. HThK, II/1. Freiburg: Herder, 1976; 4th edn, 1984; 5th edn, 1989.
Petersen, Anders Klostergaard. 'Rewritten Bible as a Borderline Phenomenon – Genre, Textual Strategy, or Canonical Anachronism?'. In *Flores Florentino: Dead Sea Scrolls and Other Early Jewish Studies in Honour of Florentino García Martínez*, edited by Anthony Hilhorst, Émile Puech and Eibert Tigchelaar, 285–306. SuppJSJ, 122. Leiden: Brill, 2007.
Petersen, Anders Klostergaard. 'The Riverrun of Rewriting Scripture: From Textual Cannibalism to Scriptural Completion'. *JSJ* 43 (2012): 475–96.
Petersen, Anders Klostergaard. 'Textual Fidelity, Elaboration, Supersession or Encroachment? Typological Reflections on the Phenomenon of Rewritten Scripture'. In *Rewritten Bible after Fifty Years: Texts, Terms, or Techniques? A Last Dialogue with Geza Vermes*, edited by József Zsengellér, 13–48. SuppJSJ, 166. Leiden: Brill, 2014.
Petersen, Anders Klostergaard. 'Generic Docetism: From the Synoptic Narrative Gospels to the Johannine Discursive Gospel'. In *The Gospel of John as Genre Mosaic*, edited by Kasper Bro Larsen, 99–124. SANt, 3. Göttingen: Vandenhoeck & Ruprecht, 2015.
Petersen, Norman R. 'When Is the End Not the End? Literary Reflections on the Ending of Mark's Narrative'. *Interpretation* 34 (1980): 151–66.
Petridou, Georgia. *Divine Epiphany in Greek Literature and Culture*. Oxford: Oxford University Press, 2015.
Poplutz, Uta. 'Die Wundererzählungen im Johannesevangelium: Hinführung'. In Ruben Zimmermann et al. (eds), *Kompendium der frühchristlichen Wundererzählungen. Band 1: Die Wunder Jesu*, 659–67. Gütersloh: Gütersloher Verlagshaus, 2013.
Porter, Stanley E. *John, His Gospel and Jesus: In Pursuit of the Johannine Voice*. Grand Rapids, MI: Wm. B. Eerdmans, 2015.
Price, Jonathan. 'Drama and History in Josephus'. *Scripta Classica Israelica* 21 (2002): 97–111.
Rahmsdorf, Olivia L., *Zeit und Ethik im Johannesevangelium: Theoretische, methodische und exegetische Annäherungen an die Gunst der Stunde*. WUNT, 2/488. Tübingen: Mohr Siebeck, 2019.
Reinhartz, Adele. '"And the Word Was God": John's Christology and Jesus's Discourses in Jewish Context'. In *Reading the Gospel of John's Christology as Jewish Messianism: Royal, Prophetic, and Divine Messiahs*, edited by Benjamin Reynolds and Gabriele Boccaccini, 69–91. Leiden: Brill, 2018.
Reinhartz, Adele. 'The Jews of the Fourth Gospel'. In *The Oxford Handbook of Johannine Studies*, edited by Judith M. Lieu and Martinus C. de Boer, 123–37. Oxford: Oxford University Press, 2018.
Rajak, Tessa. 'Dying for the Law: The Martyr's Portrait in Jewish-Greek Literature'. In *Portraits: Biographical Representation in the Greek and Latin Literature of the Roman*

Empire, edited by M. J. Edwards and Simon Swain, 39–67. Oxford: Clarendon Press, 1997.
Reinbold, Wolfgang. *Der älteste Bericht über den Tod Jesu: Literarische Analyse und historische Kritik der Passionsdarstellungen der Evangelien*. BZNW, 69. Berlin: de Gruyter, 1994.
Revell, Chelsea N. and Steven A. Hunt. 'The Co-Crucified Men: Shadows by His Cross'. In *Character Studies in the Fourth Gospel: Narrative Approaches to Seventy Figures in John*, edited by Steven A. Hunt, D. Francois Tolmie and Ruben Zimmermann, 607–17. Grand Rapids, MI: Wm. B. Eerdmans, 2016.
Riniker, Christian. 'Jean 6,1–21 et les évangiles synoptiques'. In *La Communauté johannique et son histoire: La trajectoire de l'évangile de Jean aux deux premiers siècles*, edited by Jean-Daniel Kaestli, Jean-Michel Poffet and Jean Zumstein, 41–52. MoBi, 20. Genève: Labor et Fides, 1990.
Robinson, John A. T. *The Priority of John*, edited by J. F. Coakley. London: SCM, 1985; Oak Park, IL: Meyer-Stone, 1987.
Rosati, Gianpiero. 'Trimalchio on Stage'. In *Oxford Readings in the Roman Novel*, edited by S. J. Harrison, 85–104. Oxford: Oxford University Press, 1999.
Rowe, C. Kavin. *Early Narrative Christology: The Lord in the Gospel of Luke*. Grand Rapids, MI: Baker Academic, 2009.
Ruckstuhl, Eugen. 'Die Speisung des Volkes durch Jesus und die Seeüberfahrt der Jünger nach Joh 6,1–25 im Vergleich zu den synoptischen Parallelen'. In *The Four Gospels, 1992: Festschrift Frans Neirynck*, edited by Frans Van Segbroeck, Christopher M. Tuckett, Gilbert Van Belle and Joseph Verheyden, 3:2001–19. BETL, 100; 3 vols. Leuven: Leuven University Press and Peeters, 1992.
Runia, David. *Philo of Alexandria: On the Creation of the Cosmos According to Moses*. Philo of Alexandria Commentary Series, 1. Leiden: Brill, 2002.
Sabbe, Maurits. *Studia Neotestamentica: Collected Essays*. BETL, 98. Leuven: Leuven University Press and Peeters, 1991.
Sabbe, Maurits. 'The Cleansing of the Temple and the Temple Logion', *CBG* 2 (1956): 289–99, 466–80. Reprinted in Maurits Sabbe, *Studia Neotestamentica*, 331–54.
Sabbe, Maurits. 'The Arrest of Jesus in Jn 18,1–11 and Its Relation to the Synoptic Gospels: A Critical Evaluation of A. Dauer's Hypothesis'. In *L'Évangile de Jean: Sources, redaction, théologie*, ed. Marinus de Jonge, 203–34. BETL, 44. Leuven: University Press, 1977.
Sabbe, Maurits. 'The Footwashing in Jn 13 and its Relation to the Synoptic Gospels'. *ETL* 58 (1982): 279–308. Reprinted in Maurits Sabbe, *Studia Neotestamentica*, 409–41.
Sabbe, Maurits. 'The Trial of Jesus before Pilate in John and Its Relation to the Synoptic Gospels'. In *John and the Synoptics*, edited by Adelbert Denaux, 341–85. BETL, 101. Leuven: Leuven University Press and Peeters, 1992. Reprinted in Maurits Sabbe, *Studia Neotestamentica*, 467–513.
Sabbe, Maurits. 'The Johannine Account of the Death of Jesus and Its Synoptic Parallels (Jn 19,16b–42)'. *ETL* 70 (1994): 34–64.
Sandnes, Karl Olav. *Early Christian Discourses on Jesus' Prayer at Gethsemane: Courageous, Committed, Cowardly?* NovTSup, 166. Brill: Leiden, 2016.
Sandy, Gerald N. 'Scaenica Petroniana', *TAPA* 104 (1974): 329–46.
Scardino, Carlo. *Gestaltung und Funktion der Reden bei Herodot und Thukydides*. Beiträge zur Altertumskunde, 250. Berlin: de Gruyter, 2007.

Schenke, Ludger. *Die Wundererzählungen des Markusevangeliums*. SBB, 5. Stuttgart: Katholisches Bibelwerk, 1974.
Schenke, Ludger. *Johannes: Kommentar*. Düsseldorf: Patmos, 1998.
Schenke, Ludger. *Das Markusevangelium. Literarische Eigenart – Text und Kommentierung*. Stuttgart: Kohlhammer, 2005.
Schleritt, Frank. *Der vorjohanneische Passionsbericht: Eine historisch-kritische und theologische Untersuchung zu Joh 2,13–22; 11,47–14,31 und 18,1–20,29*. BZNW, 154. Berlin: de Gruyter, 2007.
Schmidt, Karl Ludwig. 'Die literarische Eigenart der Leidensgeschichte Jesu'. *Die Christliche Welt* 32 (1918): 114–16. Reprinted in *Redaktion und Theologie des Passionsberichtes nach den Synoptikern*, edited by Meinrad Limbeck, 17–20. Wege der Forschung, 481. Darmstadt: Wissenschaftliche Buchgesellschaft, 1981.
Schmidt, Thomas E. 'Mark 15.6–32: The Crucifixion Narrative and the Roman Triumphal Procession'. *NTS* 41 (1995): 1–18.
Schnackenburg, Rudolf. *Das Johannesevangelium*, 4 vols. HThKNT, 4,1–4. Freiburg: Herder, 1965–84); ET: *The Gospel According to St. John*, trans. Kevin Smyth, 3 vols. London: Burns & Oates; New York: Crossroad, 1968–82.
Schnelle, Udo. *The History and Theology of the New Testament Writings*, translated by M. Eugene Boring. Minneapolis, MN: Fortress; London: SCM, 1998.
Schnelle, Udo. *Einleitung in das Neue Testament*. UTB, 1830. Göttingen: Vandenhoeck & Ruprecht, 3rd edn, 1999; 9th edn, 2017.
Schnelle, Udo. *Einführung in die neutestamentliche Exegese*. 6th edn. Göttingen: Vandenhoeck & Ruprecht, 2005.
Schnelle, Udo. *Theologie des Neuen Testaments*. UTB, 2917. Göttingen: Vandenhoeck & Ruprecht, 2007; 3rd edn. 2016.
Schnelle, Udo. *Das Evangelium nach Johannes*. ThKNT, 4. Leipzig: Evangelische Verlagsanstalt, 3rd edn, 2004; 5th edn, 2016.
Schnelle, Udo. 'Johannes und die Synoptiker'. In *The Four Gospels 1992: Festschrift Frans Neirynck*, edited by Frans Van Segbroeck, Christopher M. Tuckett, Gilbert Van Belle and Joseph Verheyden, 3:1799–814. BETL, 100; 3 vols. Leuven: Leuven University Press and Peeters, 1992.
Schnelle, Udo. 'Die Tempelreinigung und die Christologie des Johannesevangeliums'. *NTS* 42 (1996): 359–73.
Schnelle, Udo. 'Die Juden im Johannesevangelium'. In *Gedenkt an das Wort: Festschrift für Werner Vogler zum 65. Geburtstag*, edited by Christoph Kähler and Martina Böhm, 217–30. Leipzig: Evangelische Verlagsanstalt, 1999.
Schnelle, Udo. 'Markinische und johanneische Kreuzestheologie'. In *The Death of Jesus in the Fourth Gospel*, edited by Gilbert van Belle, 233–58. BETL, 200. Leuven: Leuven University Press and Peeters, 2007.
Scholtissek, Klaus. 'Der Sohn Gottes für das Reich Gottes: Zur Verbindung von Christologie und Eschatologie bei Markus'. In *Der Evangelist als Theologe: Studien zum Markusevangelium*, edited by Thomas Söding, 63–90. SBS, 163. Stuttgart: Katholisches Bibelwerk, 1995.
Scholtissek, Klaus. 'Mündiger Glaube: Zur Architektur und Pragmatik johanneischer Begegnungsgeschichten: Joh 5 und Joh 9'. In *Paulus und Johannes: Exegetische Studien zur paulinischen und johanneischen Theologie und Literatur*, edited by Dieter Sänger and Ulrich Mell, 75–105. WUNT, 198. Tübingen: Mohr Siebeck, 2006.

Schröter, Jens. *From Jesus to the New Testament: Early Christian Theology and the Origin of the New Testament Canon*, trans. Wayne C. Coppins. Studies in Early Christianity. Waco, TX: Baylor University Press, 2013.

Schröter, Jens. 'The Criteria of Authenticity in Jesus Research and Historiographical Method'. In *Jesus, Criteria, and the Demise of Authenticity*, edited by Chris Keith and Anthony Le Donne, 49–70. London: T&T Clark, 2012.

Schulz, Siegfried. *Neutestamentliche Ethik*. Zürich: Theologischer Verlag, 1987.

Schwartz, Barry. *Abraham Lincoln and the Forge of National Memory*. Chicago, IL: University of Chicago Press, 2000.

Schwartz, Barry. 'Christian Origins: Historical Truth and Social Memory'. In *Memory, Tradition, and Text: Uses of the Past in Early Christianity*, edited by Alan Kirk and Tom Thatcher, 43–56. Semeia Studies, 52. Atlanta, GA: Society of Biblical Literature, 2005.

Schwartz, Barry. 'What Difference Does the Medium Make?'. In *The Fourth Gospel in First-Century Media Culture*, edited by Anthony Le Donne and Tom Thatcher, 225–38. European Studies on Christian Origins/Library of New Testament Studies, 426. London: T&T Clark, 2011.

Schwartz, Barry. 'Where There's Smoke, There's Fire: Memory and History'. In *Memory and Identity in Ancient Judaism and Early Christianity: A Conversation with Barry Schwartz*, edited by Tom Thatcher, 7–37. Semeia Studies, 78. Atlanta, GA: Society of Biblical Literature, 2014.

Schweibert, Jonathan. 'Jesus's Question to Pilate in Mark 15:2', *JBL* 136 (2017): 937–47.

Schweitzer, Albert. *Von Reimarus bis Wrede: Eine Geschichte der Leben-Jesu-Forschung*. Tübingen: Mohr Siebeck, 1906.

Schweitzer, Albert. *Geschichte der Leben-Jesu-Forschung. Zweite, neu bearbeitete und vermehrte Auflage*. Tübingen: Mohr Siebeck, 1913.

Schweitzer, Albert. *The Quest of the Historical Jesus*, ed. John Bowden. Minneapolis, MN: Fortress, 2001.

Schwemer, Anna Maria. 'Gott als König und seine Königsherrschaft in den Sabbatliedern aus Qumran'. In *Königsherrschaft Gottes und himmlischer Kult im Judentum, Urchristentum und in der hellenistischen Welt*, edited by Martin Hengel and Anna Maria Schwemer, 45–118. WUNT, 55. Tübingen: Mohr Siebeck, 1991.

Scornaienchi, Lorenzo. *Der umstrittene Jesus und seine Apologie: Die Streitgespräche im Markusevangelium*. NTOA/StUNT, 110. Göttingen: Vandenhoeck & Ruprecht, 2016.

Segal, Michael. 'Between Bible and Rewritten Bible'. In *Biblical Interpretation at Qumran*, edited by Matthias Henze, 10–28. Grand Rapids, MI: Wm. B. Eerdmans, 2005.

Senior, Donald. *The Passion of Jesus in the Gospel of John*. Collegeville, MN: Liturgical Press, 1991.

Sevrin, Jean Marie, 'Jésus et le sabbat dans le quatrième évangile'. In *La Foi dans l'un et l'autre Testament*, edited by Camille Focant, 226–42. LD, 168. Paris: Éditions du Cerf, 1997. Reprinted in Jean Marie Sevrin, *Le Quatrième évangile: Recueil d'études*, edited by Gilbert Van Belle, 183–96 BETL, 281. Leuven: Leuven University Press and Peeters, 2016.

Shin, Sookgoo. *Ethics in the Gospel of John: Discipleship as Moral Progress*. BIS, 168. Leiden: Brill, 2019.

Siegert, Folker. *Der Erstentwurf des Johannes: Das ursprüngliche, judenchristliche Johannesevangelium in deutscher Übersetzung vorgestellt, nebst Nachrichten über Verfasser und zwei Briefen von ihm (2./3. Joh.)*. Münsteraner Judaistische Studien: Wissenschaftliche Beiträge zur christlich-jüdischen Begegnung, 16. Münster: LIT, 2004.

Siegert, Folker. *Das Evangelium des Johannes in seiner ursprünglichen Gestalt: Wiederherstellung und Kommentar.* Schriften des Institutum Judaicum Delitzschianum, 7. Göttingen: Vandenhoeck & Ruprecht, 2007.
Siegert, Folker and Siegfried Bergler, *Synopse der vorkanonischen Jesusüberlieferungen: Zeichenquelle und Passionsbericht, die Logienquelle und der Grundbestand des Markusevangeliums in deutscher Übersetzung gegenübergestellt von Folker Siegert: Rekonstruktion der Zeichenquelle von Siegfried Bergler.* Schriften des Institutum Judaicum Delitzschianum, 8/1. Göttingen: Vandenhoeck & Ruprecht, 2010.
Siegman, Edward F. 'St. John's Use of the Synoptic Material'. *CBQ* 30 (1968): 183–98.
Sim, David C. 'Matthew's Use of Mark: Did Matthew Intend to Supplement or to Replace His Primary Source?'. *NTS* 57 (2011): 176–92.
Simons, Eduard. *Hat der dritte Evangelist den kanonischen Matthäus benutzt?* Bonn: Georgi, 1880.
Smith, Dwight Moody. *Johannine Christianity: Essays on its Setting, Sources, and Theology.* Columbia: University of South Carolina Press, 1984.
Smith, Dwight Moody. *John.* Abingdon New Testament Commentaries. Nashville: Abingdon, 1999.
Smith, Dwight Moody. *John among the Gospels.* Minneapolis, MN: Fortress, 1992; 2nd edn. Columbia, S.C.: University of South Carolina Press, 2001.
Smith, Dwight Moody. 'The Problem of John and the Synoptics in Light of the Relation between Apocryphal and Canonical Gospels'. In *John and the Synoptics*, edited by Adelbert Denaux, 147–62. BETL, 101. Leuven: Leuven University Press and Peeters, 1992.
Soards, Marion L. 'Appendix IX: The Question of a Pre-Markan Passion Narrative'. In Raymond E. Brown, *The Death of the Messiah.* New York: Doubleday, 1994, 1492–524.
Söding, Thomas. 'Das Liebesgebot bei Paulus und Markus: Ein literarischer und theologischer Vergleich'. In *Paul and Mark. Comparative Essays Part I: Two Authors at the Beginnings of Christianity*, edited by Oda Wischmeyer, David C. Sim, and Ian J. Elmer, 465–503. BZNW, 198; Berlin/Boston: de Gruyter, 2014.
Sonnabend, Holger. *Geschichte der antiken Biographie: Von Isokrates bis zur Historia Augusta.* Stuttgart, Weimar: J. B. Metzler, 2002.
Starr, James M. and Troels Engberg-Pedersen (eds). *Early Christian Paraenesis in Context.* BZNW, 125. Berlin: de Gruyter, 2004.
Stein, Robert H. 'The Matthew-Luke Agreements against Mark: Insight from John', *CBQ* 54 (1992): 482–502.
Sterling, Greg. '*Mors philosophi*: The Death of Jesus in Luke'. *HTR* 94 (2001): 383–402.
Straub, Esther. 'Der Irdische als der Auferstandene: Kritische Theologie bei Johannes ohne ein Wort vom Kreuz'. In *Kreuzestheologie im Neuen Testament*, edited by Andreas Dettwiler and Jean Zumstein, 239–64. WUNT, 151. Tübingen: Mohr Siebeck, 2002.
Stibbe, Mark W. G. 'The Elusive Christ: A New Reading of the Fourth Gospel'. *JSNT* 44 (1991): 19–37.
Streeter, Burnett H. *The Four Gospels: A Study of Origins.* London: MacMillan, 1964.
Stuhlmacher, Peter. *Das paulinische Evangelium: I. Vorgeschichte.* FRLANT, 95. Göttingen: Vandenhoeck & Ruprecht, 1968.
Syreeni, Kari. *Becoming John: The Making of a Passion Gospel.* LNTS, 590. London: T&T Clark, 2018.
Taylor, Vincent. *The Gospel According to St. Mark: The Greek Text with Introduction, Notes, and Indexes*, 2nd edn. Grand Rapids, MI: Baker, 1966.

Thatcher, Tom (ed.), *What We Have Heard from the Beginning: The Past, Present, and Future of Johannine Studies*. Waco, TX: Baylor University Press, 2007.
Thatcher, Tom. 'The New Current through John: The Old "New Look" and the New Critical Orthodoxy'. In *New Currents through John: A Global Perspective*, edited by Francisco Lozada Jr. and Tom Thatcher, 1–26. Resources for Biblical Study, 54. Atlanta, GA: Society of Biblical Literature, 2006.
Thatcher, Tom and Stephen D. Moore (eds). *Anatomies of Narrative Criticism: The Past, Present and Future of the Fourth Gospel as Literature*. RBS, 55. Atlanta, GA: Society of Biblical Literature, 2008.
Theissen, Gerd. *Die Entstehung des Neuen Testaments als literaturgeschichtliches Problem*. Schriften der Philosophisch-historischen Klasse der Heidelberger Akademie der Wissenschaften, 40. Heidelberg: Winter, 2007.
Theobald, Michael. *Herrenworte im Johannesevangelium*. HBS, 34. Freiburg im Breisgau: Herder, 2002.
Theobald, Michael. *Das Evangelium nach Johannes: Kapitel 1–12*. Regensburger Neues Testament. Regensburg: Friedrich Pustet, 2009.
Theobald, Michael. '"Johannes" im Gespräch – mit wem und worüber?'. In *Studien zum Corpus Iohanneum*, edited by Michael Theobald, 193–203. WUNT, 267. Tübingen: Mohr Siebeck, 2010.
Theobald, Michael. '"Steh auf!" – Erweckung zum Leben hier und jetzt (Die Heilung eines Gelämten): Joh 5,1–18'. In Ruben Zimmermann et al. (eds), *Kompendium der frühchristlichen Wundererzählungen. Band 1: Die Wunder Jesu*, 690–704. Gütersloh: Gütersloher Verlagshaus, 2013.
Theobald, Michael. 'Johannine Dominical Sayings as Metatexts of Synoptic Sayings of Jesus: Reflections on a New Category within Reception History'. In *John, Jesus, and History*, Vol. 3: *Glimpses of Jesus through the Johannine Lens*, edited by Paul Anderson, Felix Just, S.J. and Tom Thatcher, 383–405. ECL, 18. Atlanta, GA: Society of Biblical Literature, 2016.
Thompson, Marianne M. *John: A Commentary*. New Testament Library. Louisville, KY: Westminster John Knox, 2015.
Thorsteinsson, Runar. M. *Jesus as Philosopher: The Moral Sage in the Synoptic Gospels*. Oxford: Oxford University Press, 2018.
Thyen, Hartwig. *Das Johannesevangelium*. HNT, 6. Tübingen: Mohr Siebeck, 2005; 2nd edn, 2015.
Thyen, Hartwig. 'Johannes und die Synoptiker: Auf der Suche nach einem neuen Paradigma zur Beschreibung ihrer Beziehungen anhand von Beobachtungen an Passions- und Ostererzählungen'. In *John and the Synoptics*, edited by Adelbert Denaux, 81–107. BETL, 101. Leuven: Leuven University Press and Peeters, 1992.
Thyen, Hartwig. 'Die Erzählung von den bethanischen Geschwistern (Joh 11,1–12,19) als "Palimpsest" über synoptischen Texten'. In *The Four Gospels, 1992: Festschrift Frans Neirynck*, edited by Frans Van Segbroeck, Christopher M. Tuckett, Gilbert Van Belle and Joseph Verheyden, 3:2021–50. BETL, 100; 3 vols. Leuven: Leuven University Press and Peeters, 1992. Reprinted in Hartwig Thyen, *Studien zum Corpus Iohanneum*, 182–212. WUNT, 214. Tübingen: Mohr Siebeck, 2007.
du Toit, David S. *Der abwesende Herr: Strategien im Markusevangelium zur Bewältigung der Abwesenheit des Auferstandenen*. WMANT, 111. Neukirchen-Vluyn: Neukirchener Verlag, 2006.
Trocmé, Étienne. 'Jean et les Synoptiques: L'example de Jn 1:15–34'. In *The Four Gospels, 1992: Festschrift Frans Neirynck*, edited by Frans Van Segbroeck, Christopher M.

Tuckett, Gilbert Van Belle, and Joseph Verheyden, 3: 1935–41. BETL, 100; 3 vols. Leuven: Leuven University Press and Peeters, 1992.
Ueberschaer, Nadine. *Theologie des Lebens: Glaube und Leben bei Paulus und Johannes – ein theologisch-konzeptioneller Vergleich*. WUNT, 389. Tübingen: Mohr Siebeck, 2017.
Ulrich, Eugene. 'The Notion and Definition of Canon'. In *The Canon Debate*, edited by Lee Martin McDonald and James A. Sanders, 21–35. Peabody, MA: Hendrickson, 2002.
Umoh, Camilus. *The Plot to Kill Jesus: A Contextual Study of John 11.47–53*. EHS, 23/696. Frankfurt: Lang, 2000.
Van Belle, Gilbert. *The Signs Source in the Fourth Gospel: Historical Survey and Critical Evaluation of the Semeia Hypothesis*. BETL, 116. Leuven: Leuven University Press and Peeters, 1994.
Van Belle, Gilbert. 'Style Criticism and the Fourth Gospel'. In *One Text, a Thousand Methods: Studies in Memory of Sjef van Tilborg*, edited by P. Chatelion Counet and Ulrich Berges, 291–316. BIS, 71. Boston: Brill, 2005.
Van Belle, Gilbert. 'Tradition, Exegetical Formation, and the Leuven Hypothesis'. In *What We Have Heard from the Beginning: The Past, Present and Future of Johannine Studies*, edited by Tom Thatcher, 325–37. Waco, TX: Baylor University Press, 2007.
Van Belle, Gilbert. 'In Memoriam Frans Neirynck (1927–2012)'. *ETL* 89 (2013): 116–57.
Van Belle, Gilbert (ed.). *In Memoriam Maurits Sabbe*. Annua Nuntia Lovaniensia, 50. Leuven: Leuven University Press and Peeters, 2004.
Van Belle, Gilbert, and David R. M. Godecharle. 'C. H. Dodd on John 13:16 (and 15:20): St. John's Knowledge of Matthew Revisited'. In *Engaging with C. H. Dodd on the Gospel of John: Sixty Years of Tradition and Interpretation*, edited by Tom Thatcher and Catrin H. Williams, 86–106. Cambridge: Cambridge University Press, 2013.
Vander Waerdt, Paul A. (ed.). *The Socratic Movement*. Ithaca, NY: Cornell University Press, 1994.
Van Iersel, Bas. *Markus: Kommentar*. Düsseldorf: Patmos, 1993.
Van Segbroeck, Frans. 'Theologie als kreative Sinnbildung: Johannes als Weiterbildung von Paulus und Markus'. In *Johannesevangelium – Mitte oder Rand des Kanons? Neue Standortbestimmungen*, edited by Thomas Söding, 119–45. Quaestiones Disputatae, 203. Freiburg: Herder, 2003.
Verheyden, Joseph. 'P. Gardner-Smith and "The Turn of the Tide"'. In *John and the Synoptics*, edited by Adelbert Denaux, 423–52. BETL, 101. Leuven: Leuven University Press and Peeters, 1992.
Vermes, Geza. *Scripture and Tradition in Judaism: Haggadic Studies*. Leiden: Brill, 1961; 2nd rev. edn. 1973.
Voerster, Willem S. 'Literary Reflections on Mark 13.5–37: A Narrated Speech of Jesus'. In *The Interpretation of Mark*, edited by William R. Telford, 269–88. Edinburgh: T&T Clark, 1995.
von Wahlde, Urban C. *The Gospel and Letters of John*, 3 vols. Eerdmans Critical Commentary. Grand Rapids, MI: Wm. B. Eerdmans, 2010.
von Wahlde, Urban C. 'The Gospel of John and Archaeology'. In *Jesus and Archaeology*, edited by James H. Charlesworth, 523–86. Grand Rapids, MI: Wm. B. Eerdmans, 2006.
Voorwinde, Stephen. *Jesus' Emotions in the Fourth Gospel: Human or Divine?* LNTS, 284. London: T&T Clark, 2005.
Vouga, François. 'Le quatrième évangile comme interprète de la tradition synoptique: Jean 6'. In *John and the Synoptics*, edited by Adelbert Denaux, 261–79. BETL, 101. Leuven: Leuven University Press and Peeters, 1992.
Walbank, F. W. 'History and Tragedy'. *Historia* 9 (1960): 216–34.

Watt, Jan G. van der, R. Alan Culpepper and Udo Schnelle (Eds). *The Prologue of the Gospel of John: Its Literary, Theological, and Philosophical Contexts. Papers Read at the Colloquium Ioanneum 2013.* WUNT, 359. Tübingen: Mohr Siebeck, 2016.
Weder, Hans. 'Die Asymmetrie des Rettenden: Überlegungen zu Joh 3,14–21 im Rahmen johanneischer Theologie'. In *Einblicke ins Evangelium: Exegetische Beiträge zur neutestamentlichen Hermeneutik*, edited by Hans Weder, 435–65. Göttingen: Vandenhoeck & Ruprecht, 1992.
Weissenberg, Hanne von, and Juha Pakkala and Marko Marttila. 'Introducing Changes in Scripture'. In *Changes in Scripture: Rewriting and Interpreting Authoritative Traditions in the Second Temple Period*, 3–20. BZAW, 419. Göttingen: de Gruyter, 2011.
Wengst, Klaus. *Das Johannesevangelium: 2. Teilband: Kapitel 11–21.* TKNT, 4,2. Stuttgart: Kohlhammer, 2001.
Westcott, Brook Foss. *The Revelation of the Father: Short Lectures on the Titles of the Lord in the Gospel of St John.* London: Macmillan and Co, 1884.
Westcott, Brook Foss. *The Gospel According to St John.* London: John Murray, 1902.
Williams, Catrin H. *I Am He: The Interpretation of 'Anî Hû' in Jewish and Early Christian Literature.* WUNT, 2/113. Tübingen: Mohr Siebeck, 2000.
Williams, Catrin H. 'John (the Baptist): The Witness on the Threshold'. In *Character Studies in the Fourth Gospel: Narrative Approaches to Seventy Figures in John*, edited by Steven A. Hunt, D. Francois Tolmie, and Ruben Zimmermann, 46–60. WUNT, 314. Tübingen: Mohr Siebeck, 2013; Grand Rapids, MI: Wm. B. Eerdmans, 2016.
Williams, Catrin H. 'The Voice in the Wilderness and the Way of the Lord: A Scriptural Frame for John's Witness to Jesus'. In *The Opening of John's Narrative (John 1:19–2:22): Historical, Literary, and Theological Readings from the Colloquium Ioanneum 2015 in Ephesus*, edited by R. Alan Culpepper and Jörg Frey, 39–57. WUNT, 385. Tübingen: Mohr Siebeck, 2017.
Williams, Catrin H. 'John, Judaism, and "Searching the Scriptures"'. In *John and Judaism: A Contested Relationship in Context*, edited by R. Alan Culpepper and Paul N. Anderson, 77–100. RBS, 87. Atlanta, GA: Society of Biblical Literature, 2017.
Williams, Catrin H. 'Jesus the Prophet: Crossing the Boundaries of Prophetic Beliefs and Expectations in the Gospel of John'. In *Portraits of Jesus in the Gospel of John: A Christological Spectrum*, edited by Craig Koester, 91–107. LNTS, 589. London: T&T Clark, 2018.
Williams, Catrin H. and Christopher Rowland (Eds). *John's Gospel and Intimations of Apocalyptic.* London: Bloomsbury, 2013.
Windisch, Hans. *Johannes und die Synoptiker: Wollte der vierte Evangelist die älteren Evangelien ergänzen oder ersetzen?* UNT, 12. Leipzig: Hinrichs, 1926.
Wink, Walter. *John the Baptist in the Gospel Tradition.* SNTSMS, 7. Cambridge: Cambridge University Press, 1968.
Wischmeyer, Oda. *Liebe als Agape: Das frühchristliche Konzept und der moderne Diskurs.* Tübingen: Mohr Siebeck, 2015.
Wischmeyer, Oda. 'Gut und Böse: Antithetisches Denken im Neuen Testament und bei Jesus Sirach'. In *Treasures of Wisdom: Studies in Ben Sira and the Book of Wisdom: FS M. Gilbert S.J.*, edited by Núria Calduch-Benages and Jacques Vermeylen, 129–36. BETL, 143. Leuven: Leuven University Press and Peeters, 1999.
Wischmeyer, Oda. 'Zwischen Gut und Böse: Teufel, Dämonen, das Böse und der Kosmos im Jakobusbrief'. In *Das Böse, der Teufel und Dämonen – Evil, the Devil, and Demons*, edited by Jan Dochhorn, Susanne Rudnig-Zelt and Benjamin Wold, 153–68. WUNT, 2/412. Tübingen: Mohr Siebeck, 2016.

Witherington III, Ben. *The Gospel of Mark: A Socio-Rhetorical Commentary*. Grand Rapids, MI: Wm. B. Eerdmans, 2001.
Wördemann, Dirk, 2002. *Das Charakterbild im bíos nach Plutarch und das Christusbild im Evangelium nach Markus*. Studien zur Geschichte und Kultur des Altertums, 1/19. Paderborn: Schöningh, 2002.
Wrede, D. W. (William). *Das Messiasgeheimnis in den Evangelien: Zugleich ein Beitrag zum Verständnis des Markusevangeliums*, Göttingen: Vandenhoeck & Ruprecht, 1901; ET. *The Messianic Secret*. Cambridge: James Clarke and Co, 1971.
Wrede, D. W. (William). *Charakter und Tendenz des Johannesevangeliums*. Sammlung gemeinverständlicher Vorträge und Schriften aus dem Gebiet der Theologie und Religionsgeschichte 37. Tübingen: Mohr, 1903.
Yarbro Collins, Adela. *Mark: A Commentary*. Hermeneia. Minneapolis, MN: Fortress, 2007.
Yarbro Collins, Adela. 'From Noble Death to Crucified Messiah'. *NTS* 40 (1994): 481–503.
Young, David M. and Michael Strickland, *The Rhetoric of Jesus in the Gospel of Mark*. Minneapolis: Fortress, 2017.
Young, Frances M. 'John and the Synoptics: An Historical Problem or a Theological Opportunity?' *Louvain Studies* 33 (2008): 208–20.
Zahn, Molly M. *Rethinking Rewritten Scripture: Composition and Exegesis in the 4QReworked Pentateuch Manuscripts*. STDJ, 95. Leiden: Brill, 2011.
Zahn, Molly M. 'Rewritten Scripture'. In *The Oxford Handbook of the Dead Sea Scrolls*, edited by Timothy H. Lim and John J. Collins, 323–36. Oxford: Oxford University Press, 2010.
Zahn, Molly M. 'Talking about Rewritten Texts: Some Reflections on Terminology'. In *Changes in Scripture: Rewriting and Interpreting Authoritative Traditions in the Second Temple Period*, edited by Hanne von Weissenberg, Juha Pakkala and Marko Marttila, 93–119. BZAW, 419. Göttingen: de Gruyter, 2011.
Zahn, Molly M. 'Genre and Rewritten Scripture: A Reassessment'. *JBL* 131 (2012): 271–88.
Zhang, Tong and Barry Schwartz. 'Confucius and the Cultural Revolution: A Study in Collective Memory'. *International Journal of Politics, Culture, and Society* 11.2 (1997): 182–212.
Zanetto, G. 'Plutarch's Dialogues as Comic Dramas'. In *Rhetorical Theory and Praxis in Plutarch: Acta of the IVth International Congress of the International Plutarch Society, Leuven, July 3-6, 1996*, edited by L. Van der Stock, 533–41. Collection d'Etudes Classiques, 11. Leuven: Leuven University Press and Peeters, 2000.
Zimmermann, Ruben. 'Symbolic Communication between John and His Reader: The Garden Symbolism in John 19–20'. In *Anatomies of Narrative Criticism: The Past, Present and Future of the Fourth Gospel as Literature*, edited by Tom Thatcher and Stephen D. Moore, 221–35. Atlanta, GA: Society of Biblical Literature, 2008.
Zimmermann, Ruben. 'Narrative Ethik im Johannesevangelium am Beispiel der Lazarus-Perikope Joh 11'. In *Narrativität und Theologie im Johannesevangelium*, edited by Jörg Frey and Uta Poplutz, 133–70. BThSt, 130. Neukirchen-Vluyn: Neukirchener Verlag, 2012.
Zimmermann, Ruben. 'Frühchristliche Wundererzählungen – Eine Hinführung'. In Ruben Zimmermann et al. (eds), *Kompendium der frühchristlichen Wundererzählungen. Band 1: Die Wunder Jesu*, 5–67. Gütersloh: Gütersloher Verlagshaus, 2013.
Zimmermann, Ruben et al. (eds), *Kompendium der frühchristlichen Wundererzählungen. Band 1: Die Wunder Jesu*. Gütersloh: Gütersloher Verlagshaus, 2013.
Zumstein, Jean. *Kreative Erinnerung: Relecture und Auslegung im Johannesevangelium*. 2nd edn. AThANT, 84. Zürich: TVZ, 2004.

Zumstein, Jean. *L'Évangile selon Saint Jean*, 2 vols. CNT, IV. Genève: Labor et Fides, 2007, 2014; 2nd edn, 2016.

Zumstein, Jean. *Das Johannesevangelium*. KEK, 3. Göttingen: Vandenhoeck & Ruprecht, 2016.

Zumstein, Jean. 'Ein gewachsenes Evangelium: Der Relecture-Prozess bei Johannes'. In *Johannesevangelium – Mitte oder Rand des Kanons? Neue Standortbestimmungen*, edited by Thomas Söding, 9–37. Quaestiones Disputatae, 203. Freiburg: Herder, 2003.

Zumstein, Jean. 'Intratextuality and Intertextuality in the Gospel of John'. In *Anatomies of Narrative Criticism: The Past, Present and Future of the Fourth Gospel as Literature*, edited by Tom Thatcher and Stephen D. Moore, 121–35. Atlanta, GA: Society of Biblical Literature, 2008.

Zumstein, Jean. '"Ich bin das Brot des Lebens": Wiederholung und Variation eines johanneischen Ego-Eimi-Wortes in Joh 6'. In *Repetitions and Variations in the Fourth Gospel: Style, Text, Interpretation*, edited by Gilbert van Belle, Michael Labahn and Petrus Maritz, 435–52. BETL, 223. Leuven: Leuven University Press and Peeters, 2009.

Zumstein, Jean. '"Und wir wissen, dass sein Zeugnis wahr ist": Fiktion und Geschichte in der johanneischen Vita Jesu'. In *Wahrheit und Geschichte: Exegetische und hermeneutische Studien zu einer dialektischen Konstellation*, edited by Eva Ebel and Samuel Vollenweider, 33–52. AThANT, 102. Zürich: Theologischer Verlag, 2012.

Zumstein, Jean. 'Au seuil de la passion (Jean 12)'. In *Studies in the Gospel of John, and its Christology: Festschrift Gilbert Van Belle*, edited by Joseph Verheyden, Gilbert van Oyen, Michael Labahn and Reimund Bieringer, 275–88. BETL, 265. Leuven, Paris, Walpole: Peeters, 2014.

Zumstein, Jean. 'Story, Plot, and History in the Johannine Passion Narrative'. In *John, Jesus, and History*, Vol. 3: *Glimpses of Jesus through the Johannine Lens*, edited by Paul Anderson, Felix Just, S.J., and Tom Thatcher, 109–18. ECL, 18. Atlanta, GA: Society of Biblical Literature, 2016.

Zumstein, Jean. 'Johannes 2:13–22 im Plot und in der Theologie des vierten Evangeliums'. In *The Opening of John's Narrative (John 1:19–2:22)*, edited by R. Alan Culpepper and Jörg Frey, 275–87. WUNT, 385. Tübingen: Mohr Siebeck, 2017.

Index of Ancient Sources

HEBREW BIBLE

Genesis
Genesis 1.1   111, 118
Genesis 1–3   60
Genesis 3   220
Genesis 10.8–12   60
Genesis 12.1–5   217
Genesis 12–50   60
Genesis 22   132, 220

Exodus
Exodus 1.27, 29   62
Exodus 2.1   62
Exodus 2.11–15   227
Exodus 3–13   60
Exodus 3.4   217–18
Exodus 3.14   69, 73
Exodus 12   132
Exodus 12.22   133
Exodus 12.27   133
Exodus 12.46   133
Exodus 13.3   133
Exodus 13.14   133
Exodus 20   53
Exodus 24.12–18   62
Exodus 29   132
Exodus 32.15–20   227
Exodus 34.5–6   70
Exodus 34.6   134

Leviticus
Leviticus 16   132
Leviticus 19.18   189, 191, 193, 196, 197, 199, 200, 201

Numbers
Numbers 9.12   133
Numbers 11.1–9   220
Numbers 11.4   226

Numbers 11.31–35   220

Deuteronomy
Deuteronomy 5   53
Deuteronomy 6.4   201
Deuteronomy 6.5   199
Deuteronomy 31–34   227
Deuteronomy 32.39   69, 71

1 Samuel
1 Samuel   60
1 Samuel 3   218

2 Samuel
2 Samuel 7.1–2   40
2 Samuel 11.1   40

1 Kings
1 Kings 17.17–24   97
3 Kingdoms 19.11 LXX   70

2 Kings
2 Kings 4.18–37   97
2 Kings 13.20–21   97

Job
Job 9.8   70

Psalms
Psalm 6.5   28
Psalm 22   219
Psalm 29.3   68
Psalm 41 LXX   227
Psalm 41.6   226
Psalm 41.7   226
Psalm 42.5   226
Psalm 46.3   68
Psalm 65.8   68
Psalm 69.10   225
Psalm 77.19   70

Isaiah
Isaiah 6   218
Isaiah 6.9–10   16, 21
Isaiah 6.10   87
Isaiah 9.1   48
Isaiah 40   134
Isaiah 40.3   21, 109, 115, 126, 127, 173, 217
Isaiah 43.16   70
Isaiah 41.4   69
Isaiah 43.10–11   69
Isaiah 47.8, 10   69
Isaiah 51.9–10   70
Isaiah 52.7   173
Isaiah 53   132
Isaiah 53.1   87
Isaiah 61.6   173

Jeremiah
Jeremiah 11   132

Ezekiel
Ezekiel 1.28   255

Daniel
Daniel 7.14   182
Daniel 10.9   255

Habakkuk
Habakkuk 3.15   70

Malachi
Malachi 3.1   109, 115, 173, 217

APOCRYPHA

1 Maccabees
1 Maccabees 1–13   56–57

2 Maccabees
2 Maccabees   57, 61, 222
2 Maccabees 2.32   61
2 Maccabees 3–7   61
2 Maccabees 3.1–3   61
2 Maccabees 3.1–6.17   61
2 Maccabees 3.4–40   61
2 Maccabees 3.6   61
2 Maccabees 4.7–17   61
2 Maccabees 5.1–26   61
2 Maccabees 6.1–11   61
2 Maccabees 6.18–31   61, 220
2 Maccabees 6.19–20   222
2 Maccabees 6.21–23   220
2 Maccabees 6.27–28   222
2 Maccabees 7   220
2 Maccabees 7.1–41   61
2 Maccabees 7.24   220

Sirach/Ecclesiasticus
Sir. 24.5–6   70

PSEUDEPIGRAPHA

1 Enoch
1 Enoch 6–11   55

4 Ezra
4 Ezra 9.38–10.4   97

Jubilees
Jubilees 1.1–4   62
Jubilees 1.27   62
Jubilees 2.1   62
Jubilees 2.24   62, 63
Jubilees 6.22   63
Jubilees 11–12   60
Jubilees 20–22   60
Jubilees 30.21   63
Jubilees 50.6   63

4 Maccabees
4 Maccabees   57, 60–1, 220
4 Maccabees 1.1–12   62
4 Maccabees 1.1–19   220
4 Maccabees 1.13–3.18   62
4 Maccabees 3.19   61
4 Maccabees 3.20–21   61
4 Maccabees 4.1–14   61
4 Maccabees 4.15–20   61
4 Maccabees 4.21–23   61
4 Maccabees 4.24–26   61
4 Maccabees 5.1–7.23   61
4 Maccabees 7.23   62
4 Maccabees 8.1–17.6   61

DEAD SEA SCROLLS
Genesis Apocryphon 21.23–22.34   60

Damascus Document 16.3-4 56

Temple Scroll 56.20-21 63
Temple Scroll 56.22-23 63

4Q225-28 56

OTHER EARLY JEWISH LITERATURE

Josephus, Antiquities
Antiquities 1-11 53, 54, 57, 63
Antiquities 2.254 227
Antiquities 3.90-92 53
Antiquities 3.95-102 227
Antiquities 4.189 227
Antiquities 4.322 227
Antiquities 4.328-29 227
Antiquities 4.49 227
Antiquities 12-13 56, 56-7
Antiquities 12.241-13.214 56-7

Philo
Legat. 278 42

Migration of Abraham 156 226

On the Creation of the World 2.12 73

On the Embassy to Gaius 278 42

On the Life of Moses 1.25 226
On the Life of Moses 1.26, 226
On the Life of Moses 1.29 226
On the Life of Moses 1.32 226
On the Life of Moses 1.40 226
On the Life of Moses 1.44 226
On the Life of Moses 1.48 226
On the Life of Moses 1.153 226
On the Life of Moses 1.162 226

On the Special Laws 3.129 226
On the Special Laws 3.134-35 226

That Every Good Person Is Free 18-19 222
That Every Good Person Is Free 20 222
That Every Good Person Is Free 21 222
That Every Good Person Is Free 25 223
That Every Good Person Is Free 46 223
That Every Good Person Is Free 61 223
That Every Good Person Is Free 109 222
That Every Good Person Is Free 111 219
That Every Good Person Is Free 154 223

NEW TESTAMENT AND OTHER EARLY CHRISTIAN LITERATURE

Gospel of Matthew
Matthew 1.18-2.1 33
Matthew 2.1-8 167
Matthew 3.1-17 10
Matthew 3.3 126
Matthew 3.11 11, 131
Matthew 3.17 11
Matthew 4.8-9 221
Matthew 4.11 221
Matthew 4.13-17 10
Matthew 4.18-22 10
Matthew 5.33-36 131
Matthew 8.5-13 10
Matthew 8.18 10
Matthew 9.1-17 159
Matthew 9.6-8 10
Matthew 9.18 95
Matthew 9.23-26 11
Matthew 10.22 12
Matthew 10.24 12
Matthew 10.40 12
Matthew 11.27 12
Matthew 12.1 167
Matthew 12.1-8 154, 155, 156, 157, 158, 159, 162
Matthew 12.2 160, 167
Matthew 12.2-8 167
Matthew 12.5-7 154, 159
Matthew 12.8 167
Matthew 12.9 159
Matthew 12.11-12 159
Matthew 12.38-39 10

Matthew 13.54   42
Matthew 13.55   12
Matthew 13.57   12, 41
Matthew 14.13–21   10
Matthew 14.22–33   10, 80
Matthew 14.27   12
Matthew 15.10–11   81
Matthew 15.29   17
Matthew 16.1–4   10
Matthew 16.13–20   10
Matthew 16.16   12
Matthew 16.17   12
Matthew 16.21   12, 225
Matthew 16.25   12
Matthew 17.5   12
Matthew 17.12   225
Matthew 17.13   34
Matthew 17.20   80
Matthew 18.3   12
Matthew 18.18   12
Matthew 21.1–9   11
Matthew 21.12–13   10
Matthew 21.16   80
Matthew 21.22   12
Matthew 24–25   179
Matthew 24.9   12
Matthew 26.3–4   12
Matthew 26.6–13   11, 81, 94, 95
Matthew 26.21   79
Matthew 26.21–23   12
Matthew 26.30–35   12
Matthew 26.31   12
Matthew 26.36–46   215
Matthew 26.38   12
Matthew 26.39   224
Matthew 26.45   224
Matthew 26.46   12, 225
Matthew 26.47–56   11
Matthew 26.57   259
Matthew 26.61   12
Matthew 26.69–75   11
Matthew 27.15–23   11
Matthew 27.27–29   80
Matthew 27.27–31   11
Matthew 27.31–37   11
Matthew 27.40   12
Matthew 27.55–56   11
Matthew 27.57–60   11
Matthew 28.1–8   11

Matthew 28.15   78
Matthew 28.17   83

Gospel of Mark
Mark 1   7, 16, 21
Mark 1.1   4, 91, 105, 114, 116, 118
Mark 1.1–3   4, 101–5, 108–11, 137, 139
Mark 1.1–4   173
Mark 1.1–8   125
Mark 1.1–10.52   85
Mark 1.1–14   137, 139–40
Mark 1.1–14.43   85
Mark 1.1–15   118
Mark 1.1–22   4, 115–16
Mark 1.2–3   21, 108, 109, 112, 114, 115
Mark 1.2–8   4, 123, 132, 134
Mark 1.2–11   10
Mark 1.3   68, 126, 139, 217
Mark 1.4   112, 114, 125, 128, 130, 137, 139
Mark 1.4–6   137, 139, 143
Mark 1.4–8   4, 111, 114, 115, 139
Mark 1.4–11   136
Mark 1.4–13   109
Mark 1.5   114, 121, 125, 130
Mark 1.6   114, 125, 137
Mark 1.7   11, 113, 130
Mark 1.7–8   125–6, 137, 140, 142
Mark 1.8   11, 113, 126, 132
Mark 1.9   42, 126, 137, 144
Mark 1.9–11   109, 115, 140, 142, 144, 218, 253
Mark 1.11   11, 116, 118, 232
Mark 1.12   171
Mark 1.12–13   109, 115, 116, 218
Mark 1.13   218
Mark 1.14   35, 37, 137, 140
Mark 1.14–15   10, 91, 99, 173–5, 261
Mark 1.15   110, 116, 173, 175, 183
Mark 1.16–20   10, 115
Mark 1.17   116, 176
Mark 1.21   115
Mark 1.21–22   115, 117
Mark 1.22   115, 233
Mark 1.23   115
Mark 1.27   75, 233
Mark 1.34   12
Mark 1.35–45   218

Mark 1.38 218
Mark 2.1 42, 236
Mark 2.1–3 244
Mark 2.1–3.6 85, 154, 155, 156–60, 162, 233, 234, 235, 236, 240, 241, 243, 244–5, 246
Mark 2.1–12 5, 155, 157, 159, 160, 168, 233, 240, 243, 246
Mark 2.3 167
Mark 2.5 167
Mark 2.6–7 244
Mark 2.7 75, 154, 158, 167, 240, 241, 243, 244
Mark 2.9 154, 155–6, 162, 167, 168
Mark 2.10 235
Mark 2.11 10, 155, 163, 167, 168
Mark 2.11–12 168
Mark 2.12 10, 155, 167, 268
Mark 2.13–17 233
Mark 2.16 233, 234
Mark 2.18 233, 234
Mark 2.18–20 140
Mark 2.18–22 137, 140–1, 176, 233
Mark 2.19–20 234
Mark 2.23 167, 168, 234
Mark 2.23–28 154, 155, 156, 157, 162, 167, 233
Mark 2.23–3.6 159, 160
Mark 2.24 168, 167, 233
Mark 2.27 167, 234
Mark 2.28 234
Mark 3.1 159
Mark 3.1–6 155, 156, 168, 230, 233
Mark 3.2 168, 234, 240, 241
Mark 3.2–4 233
Mark 3.4 168, 198, 234
Mark 3.5 234
Mark 3.6 156, 157, 168, 231, 232–6, 240, 241, 242, 243, 244
Mark 3.13–19 218
Mark 3.20 42
Mark 3.20–21 218
Mark 3.20–35 218, 221
Mark 3.21 42
Mark 3.22 236
Mark 3.31 42
Mark 3.31–32 218
Mark 3.33–35 218
Mark 4 91, 208, 213

Mark 4.1–2 205
Mark 4.1–34 204, 205
Mark 4.9 205, 208
Mark 4.10 205, 208
Mark 4.10–12 87, 205
Mark 4.11 175, 176, 205, 208
Mark 4.11–13 87
Mark 4.12 12, 16
Mark 4.13 205, 208
Mark 4.13–20 205
Mark 4.21 205, 208
Mark 4.21–23 205
Mark 4.24 205, 208
Mark 4.24–25 205
Mark 4.26 175, 205, 208
Mark 4.26–29 175, 205
Mark 4.30 175, 205, 208
Mark 4.30–32 205
Mark 4.32–42 215
Mark 4.33–34 205, 215
Mark 4.35–41 68
Mark 4.41 75
Mark 5.11 60
Mark 5.21 95
Mark 5.21–43 96
Mark 5.21ff. 97, 98
Mark 5.23 97
Mark 5.25 97
Mark 5.30 68
Mark 5.35ff 97
Mark 5.35–43 11
Mark 6 42, 244
Mark 6.1–6 41, 42
Mark 6.2–3 75
Mark 6.3 12, 236
Mark 6.4 12, 32, 41, 42, 46–8
Mark 6.7–9 190
Mark 6.14 128, 137
Mark 6.14–16 137
Mark 6.14–29 137, 254
Mark 6.17–29 137
Mark 6.24 128
Mark 6.29 137
Mark 6.32–44 10
Mark 6.37 16, 21, 60
Mark 6.38 21, 80
Mark 6.39 21
Mark 6.42 21
Mark 6.45–52 10, 70, 80

Mark 6.50   12, 60, 69, 70, 80
Mark 6.53–54   10
Mark 7.14–15   81
Mark 7.14–16   190
Mark 7.17–23   190
Mark 7.22   199
Mark 8.11–13   10
Mark 8.17–18   21
Mark 8.22   254
Mark 8.22–26   10
Mark 8.22–10.52   254
Mark 8.27   67, 217, 218, 236
Mark 8.27–29   141
Mark 8.27–30   10
Mark 8.27–33   17
Mark 8.27–10.45   218
Mark 8.27–10.52   236
Mark 8.28   137
Mark 8.29   75
Mark 8.31   12, 19, 91, 218, 225, 231, 232
Mark 8.32–33   96
Mark 8.33   218
Mark 8.34–37   190
Mark 8.34–38   201, 254
Mark 8.35   12
Mark 9.1   12, 28, 99, 175, 178
Mark 9.1–10   175
Mark 9.7   232
Mark 9.9–10   88
Mark 9.11–13   130, 137, 142
Mark 9.12   225
Mark 9.13   34, 137
Mark 9.19   80
Mark 9.31   19, 232
Mark 9.33   42
Mark 9.33–34   217
Mark 9.33–37   190
Mark 9.37   12
Mark 9.43   184
Mark 9.45   184
Mark 9.47   175, 184
Mark 10.1–12   190
Mark 10.2–9   190
Mark 10.13–15   190
Mark 10.14–15   175
Mark 10.15   12
Mark 10.17–22   189, 254
Mark 10.17–31   190

Mark 10.23–25   175
Mark 10.23–27   190
Mark 10.23–30   254
Mark 10.24   80
Mark 10.28–31   190
Mark 10.32–34   232
Mark 10.33–34   19
Mark 10.35–45   190
Mark 10.38–39   176
Mark 10.40   68
Mark 10.41–45   201
Mark 10.42–45   254
Mark 10.45   175, 218, 231
Mark 10.52   217
Mark 11.1–10   11
Mark 11.1–11   85
Mark 11–15   236
Mark 11.1–12.44   235
Mark 11.1–16.8   85
Mark 11.8   236
Mark 11.10   221
Mark 11.11–21   33
Mark 11.15–17   10, 26
Mark 11.18   168, 230, 232–6, 235, 241, 242, 243, 245, 246, 258
Mark 11.24   12, 19
Mark 11.27–33   26, 263
Mark 11.29–33   137
Mark 11.30   137
Mark 11.32   137
Mark 11.50   243
Mark 12   199, 200, 201
Mark 12.1–9, 10–12   235
Mark 12.12   168, 245, 258
Mark 12.13   235
Mark 12.13–17   190, 263
Mark 12.14   217, 190
Mark 12.28–34   189, 191, 192, 193
Mark 12.31   189, 197, 200
Mark 12.33   189, 197
Mark 12.34   175, 190
Mark 12.35   173
Mark 12.35–37   142
Mark 12.38–40   191
Mark 12.41–44   191, 193
Mark 13   91, 174, 176–9, 180, 181, 208, 213
Mark 13.1–2   206
Mark 13.1–37   205–6

Mark 13.2   177
Mark 13.4–8   179
Mark 13.5   206
Mark 13.5–37   204, 206
Mark 13.6   69, 70, 177
Mark 13.6–7   180
Mark 13.7   178
Mark 13.9   177
Mark 13.9–11   257
Mark 13.10   177, 178
Mark 13.12   177
Mark 13.13   12, 97, 177
Mark 13.14   36, 177
Mark 13.14–20   179
Mark 13.20   178
Mark 13.21–23   177
Mark 13.22–23   180
Mark 13.24–27   179
Mark 13.26   179
Mark 13.26–27   178
Mark 13.29   178
Mark 13.30   178
Mark 13.32   68, 178
Mark 13.33   97
Mark 13.34–37   176
Mark 13.35   178
Mark 14   82, 98
Mark 14–15   75, 91
Mark 14–16   252
Mark 14.1   168, 241, 245
Mark 14.1–2   258
Mark 14.3   60, 82
Mark 14.3–9   11, 81, 94, 95
Mark 14.4   82
Mark 14.5   60, 82, 83
Mark 14.6   82, 83
Mark 14.6–7   82
Mark 14.7   82, 83, 191, 192
Mark 14.8   82
Mark 14.9   175
Mark 14.10–11   83
Mark 14.12–25   12, 33
Mark 14.16–72   193
Mark 14.18   79
Mark 14.18–21   12
Mark 14.22–25   153
Mark 14.25   175
Mark 14.26–31   12
Mark 14.27   12

Mark 14.28   105, 106
Mark 14.32–42   27–8, 218, 219
Mark 14.33   123
Mark 14.34   12, 28, 123
Mark 14.35   12, 16, 33, 123, 124, 180, 224
Mark 14.36   28, 124, 219, 224
Mark 14.38   176
Mark 14.39   124
Mark 14.41   12, 16
Mark 14.41–43   123
Mark 14.42   12, 16, 225
Mark 14.43–16.8   85
Mark 14.43–50   11
Mark 14.43–52   85
Mark 14.47   83
Mark 14.49   260
Mark 14.53–15.20   256–8
Mark 14.54   257, 261
Mark 14.55   258
Mark 14.56–59   258
Mark 14.58   12, 26
Mark 14.60–61   256
Mark 14.61–62   174, 258
Mark 14.62   69, 182, 254, 256, 260
Mark 14.64   158, 230, 256
Mark 14.65   257
Mark 14.66   261
Mark 14.66–72   11, 191, 192, 195
Mark 14.67   261
Mark 14.71   257
Mark 15   80
Mark 15–16   232
Mark 15.1   258
Mark 15.1–5   263
Mark 15.2   257, 263
Mark 15.2–5   11
Mark 15.5   257, 264
Mark 15.6   257
Mark 15.6–14   11
Mark 15.7   257
Mark 15.8   257
Mark 15.9–15   265
Mark 15.10   254, 258
Mark 15.13   263
Mark 15.13–15   258
Mark 15.15   257
Mark 15.16   80
Mark 15.16–18   80

Mark 15.16–20   11
Mark 15.17   80, 264
Mark 15.18   80, 81, 264
Mark 15.20   12
Mark 15.20–26   11
Mark 15.21   33, 124, 256
Mark 15.25–39   33
Mark 15.26   91
Mark 15.27   254
Mark 15.29   12, 26
Mark 15.31   258
Mark 15.31–32   218
Mark 15.33   254
Mark 15.34   219
Mark 15.37   254
Mark 15.38–39   254
Mark 15.39   76, 232
Mark 15.40–41   11
Mark 15.42–46   11
Mark 16.1–8   11
Mark 16.6–7   175
Mark 16.7   106, 176
Mark 16.7–8   4, 101, 105–6
Mark 16.8   106
Mark 16.9–10   21
Mark 16.9–20   85
Mark 16.11–13   21
Mark 16.14   21
Mark 16.16–20   21

Gospel of Luke
Luke 1.1–4   64, 91
Luke 1.2   78
Luke 1.5   91
Luke 1.26–2.40   33
Luke 2.1   91
Luke 3.1   91
Luke 3.2   257
Luke 3.2–22   10
Luke 3.4   126
Luke 3.22   11
Luke 4.1–13   221
Luke 4.14–15   10
Luke 4.5–7   221
Luke 4.16   42
Luke 4.16–30   83
Luke 4.22   12
Luke 4.24   12, 41, 42
Luke 5.1–11   10, 11

Luke 5.6   33
Luke 5.24   10
Luke 5.25   10
Luke 6.5   167
Luke 6.14   12
Luke 6.20ff.   91
Luke 6.40   12
Luke 7.1–10   10
Luke 7.11–17   11, 95
Luke 7.36–50   11, 82, 95
Luke 7.38   83
Luke 8.49–56   11
Luke 9.10–17   10
Luke 9.18–21   10
Luke 9.22   11, 225
Luke 9.24   12
Luke 9.27   99
Luke 9.35   12
Luke 9.48   12
Luke 10.16   12
Luke 10.22   12
Luke 10.38–39   12
Luke 10.38–42   95
Luke 11.2   19
Luke 11.16   10
Luke 11.29   10
Luke 12.8–9   182
Luke 12.54–56   10
Luke 13.10–17   154, 155, 156, 157, 158, 162, 167
Luke 14.34–35   10
Luke 16.16   91
Luke 16.19–31   95
Luke 17.25   225
Luke 18.17   12
Luke 19.28–40   11
Luke 19.45–46   10
Luke 21.17   12
Luke 22   98
Luke 22.15   225
Luke 22.21   12
Luke 22.26   12
Luke 22.31–34   12
Luke 22.39–46   215
Luke 22.42   12, 224
Luke 22.47–53   11
Luke 22.49   12
Luke 22.53   224
Luke 22.56–62   11

Luke 22.58   261
Luke 23.3   11
Luke 23.17–23   11
Luke 23.12   264
Luke 23.22   264
Luke 23.33–34   11
Luke 23.49   11
Luke 23.50–54   11
Luke 24.1–8   11
Luke 24.5–8   88
Luke 24.12   11
Luke 24.26   225
Luke 24.46   225
Luke 24.36–49   11
Luke 24.37   83

Gospel of John
John 1   16, 60
John 1.1   4, 68, 102, 104, 105, 217
John 1.1–2   182
John 1.1–5   4, 101–5, 108–11, 114, 118
John 1.1–12.11   85
John 1.1–14   118, 217
John 1.1–17.26   85
John 1.1–18   116, 118, 125
John 1.1–37   137
John 1.1–51   4, 115–16
John 1.4–9   48
John 1.6–8   118, 138, 139, 140, 145
John 1.7   4, 114, 120, 130, 138, 217
John 1.7–8   137
John 1.9   237
John 1.10   130, 237
John 1.10–11   121, 133
John 1.11   45, 237
John 1.12   60, 133, 237
John 1.14   107, 119, 134, 189, 217
John 1.16   119
John 1.18   68, 72, 116, 121, 125
John 1.19   92, 112
John 1.19–21   138
John 1.19–23   118
John 1.19–26   4
John 1.19–34   4, 125–30, 130–4
John 1.20   113, 126, 131, 139, 141
John 1.20–21   141, 142
John 1.21   126
John 1.22   126
John 1.23   21, 114

John 1.24–34   34
John 1.27   11, 126, 131, 138, 140
John 1.29   115, 116, 127, 129, 130, 132, 133, 134, 139, 143, 146, 255, 265
John 1.29–31   115
John 1.29–34   138, 140, 141, 142, 143, 144, 145
John 1.32–33   64, 145
John 1.33   127, 130, 143, 144
John 1.34   11, 115, 116, 139, 143, 146, 189
John 1.35–37   138
John 1.35–42   10, 115
John 1.35–51   115
John 1.36   115, 116, 255
John 1.38   116–17
John 1.40   15
John 1.40–41   137
John 1.41   182
John 1.43–51   115
John 1.45   44, 125, 182
John 1.49   182, 263
John 1.51   117, 119, 182, 259
John 2.1   115
John 2.1–12   85, 125
John 2.4   12, 123, 179, 222, 255
John 2.11   17, 21, 44, 243
John 2.13   45, 133
John 2.14–22   10
John 2.13–22   26, 33, 85, 153, 237, 255, 260
John 2.17   225, 267
John 2.18   43, 137
John 2.19–22   85
John 2.22   88
John 2.23   132–3
John 2.23–25   43, 44, 45
John 2.24–25   44, 45
John 3   183, 197, 213
John 3.1–21   195, 204, 206, 207
John 3.2–3   181
John 3.4   141
John 3.5   141, 144, 183
John 3.5–8   144
John 3.8   141
John 3.12   182
John 3.13   182
John 3.14   19, 256
John 3.14–15   19

John 3.15   21, 184
John 3.16   121, 133, 184, 225, 236, 241, 243
John 3.17–21   195
John 3.18   179, 182, 183
John 3.19–21   48
John 3.21–22   19
John 3.22–30   128
John 3.22–36   140, 141, 142, 144, 145
John 3.23   128
John 3.23–36   137, 138
John 3.24   15, 64, 140, 171, 261
John 3.25   128
John 3.25–26   140
John 3.26   128, 138
John 3.27–36   140, 141, 142, 145
John 3.28   138, 141, 144
John 3.28–30   146
John 3.29–30   140
John 3.31   141, 142, 144
John 3.31–34   142
John 3.31–36   141
John 3.34   141
John 3.35–36   141
John 3.36   141, 179, 183, 184, 225
John 4   23, 130
John 4.1   137, 138
John 4.1–42   195, 204, 206, 207
John 4.3   45
John 4.4   45
John 4.9   45, 68
John 4.21   179
John 4.23   179–80
John 4.26   71, 126
John 4.34   221
John 4.40   45
John 4.40–43   46
John 4.41–42   44
John 4.42   236
John 4.43   42
John 4.43–44   41, 42, 44, 45
John 4.43–45   45
John 4.43–46   10
John 4.43–53   195
John 4.44   12, 32, 41, 42, 43, 44, 45, 46–8
John 4.45   42, 43, 44, 45, 46
John 4.46–5.9   240
John 4.46–54   10
John 4.47   43, 45
John 4.48   43, 44
John 4.49   43
John 4.54   17, 21, 44, 45
John 5   165, 243
John 5–6   60
John 5.1–9   155, 160, 161, 167, 168, 240, 241, 246
John 5.1–18   5, 152–62, 167–8, 230, 231
John 5.45–46   21
John 5.6   167
John 5.8   60, 154, 155–6, 162, 167, 168
John 5.9   167, 168, 238
John 5.9–18   162
John 5.10   160, 167, 168
John 5.10–15   238
John 5.10–18   157
John 5.11   167
John 5.12   155, 167, 168
John 5.14   167, 243
John 5.14–15   19
John 5.16   154, 156, 157, 167, 234, 237, 238, 241, 243, 248
John 5.16–18   241
John 5.17   158, 160–1, 167, 168, 238, 244
John 5.17–18   240
John 5.17–30   238
John 5.18   154, 157, 158, 161, 168, 231, 236, 237–9, 240, 241, 242, 243, 244, 245, 246
John 5.19   160, 207
John 5.19–30   182
John 5.19–47   204, 207
John 5.21–23   182
John 5.23   12
John 5.24   179, 182, 183
John 5.24–25   184
John 5.25   179–80, 181
John 5.26   183
John 5.26–27   182
John 5.27   181
John 5.28   179
John 5.28–29   181
John 5.29   194, 195, 198
John 5.30   221
John 5.33   138, 141, 145, 147
John 5.33–34   142, 146

John 5.33–36   138
John 5.33–37   137, 138, 145, 146, 147
John 5.34   138
John 5.34–35   138
John 5.35   34
John 5.36   34
John 5.37   121
John 5.41   222
John 6   20
John 6.1–15   10
John 6.1–16   149
John 6.3   16–17
John 6.4   132–3
John 6.5–58   153
John 6.6   221
John 6.7   16, 21, 60, 221
John 6.9   21
John 6.10   21
John 6.12   243
John 6.13   222
John 6.14   27
John 6.14–15   10, 27
John 6.16–21   10, 80
John 6.20   12, 60, 70, 71, 80, 123
John 6.22–25   10
John 6.22–29   27
John 6.22–59   204, 206, 207
John 6.26   10, 21
John 6.29   133
John 6.30–32   43
John 6.32   21
John 6.35   71, 111
John 6.38   221
John 6.39   241
John 6.41   71
John 6.42   12, 44, 68, 125
John 6.46   121
John 6.47   183
John 6.48   71
John 6.51   111
John 6.51–58   153, 154
John 6.52–58   27, 255, 265
John 6.52–59   28
John 6.59   260
John 6.62   182
John 6.66–71   10, 17, 64
John 6.67–71   64
John 7.1   64, 157, 239
John 7.1–10   221, 223

John 7.1–13   51
John 7.1–52   204, 206, 207
John 7.4   260
John 7.6   242
John 7.6–8   223
John 7.8   242
John 7.10   223
John 7.10–11   87
John 7.14   260, 263
John 7.16   263
John 7.19   157, 194, 195
John 7.19–20   157, 239
John 7.19–24   166
John 7.20   157, 168
John 7.23   238
John 7.25   157, 239
John 7.25–27   207
John 7.25–31   87
John 7.26   260
John 7.28–29   264
John 7.30   179, 239, 242, 255
John 7.32   239
John 7.37–39   146
John 7.38–39   132
John 7.41   44
John 7.42   33, 48–9, 125
John 7.44   239
John 7.53–8.11   85, 155
John 8.1–11   194, 195
John 8.3   199
John 8.11   167
John 8.12   48, 71, 111, 126
John 8.12–59   204, 206, 207
John 8.14   264
John 8.20   179, 242, 255
John 8.23   263
John 8.24   71
John 8.25   71
John 8.28   71, 256
John 8.37   157, 239
John 8.40   157, 239
John 8.41   199
John 8.48   45
John 8.50   222
John 8.51–52   183
John 8.54   222
John 8.58   71, 72, 74
John 8.59   72, 87, 239
John 9   130

John 9.1–41   160, 195
John 9.2–3   196
John 9.5   48, 71
John 9.22   131
John 9.24   131
John 9.29   264
John 9.31   221
John 10.1   264
John 10.1–21   204, 207
John 10.6–7   206
John 10.7   71
John 10.9   71
John 10.10   164, 243
John 10.11   71, 231
John 10.14   71
John 10.15   12
John 10.17   222
John 10.17–18   255
John 10.18   222, 223
John 10.22–30   260
John 10.24   260
John 10.24–27   86
John 10.28   241, 243
John 10.30   68, 239, 241
John 10.31–39   239
John 10.33   158, 199, 238, 241, 244
John 10.36   158, 199, 238, 241, 244
John 10.40–42   137, 138, 145, 146
John 11   4, 44, 95
John 11.1–44/57   93–9
John 11.2   15, 83, 94
John 11.3   223, 225
John 11.4   96
John 11.5   225
John 11.7   223
John 11.8   239
John 11.9–10   48
John 11.12–19   221
John 11.14   96
John 11.18   258
John 11.21   97, 223
John 11.25   71, 111, 126, 183
John 11.25–26   94, 97, 182, 184
John 11.27   12
John 11.32   96
John 11.33   225
John 11.33–35   225
John 11.35   68
John 11.36   225

John 11.38–44   94
John 11.40   121
John 11.42   44
John 11.47   12, 44, 92, 242, 259
John 11.47–53   230, 236–9, 239, 241, 242, 243, 244, 245, 246, 248, 255
John 11.48   128, 133
John 11.50   243
John 11.53   12, 94, 157, 237, 239, 242, 244, 245, 260
John 11.53–54   223
John 11.54   260
John 11.55–56   133
John 12   94, 123, 133
John 12.1   133
John 12.1–8   15, 81, 194
John 12.1–11   195
John 12.3   60
John 12.5   60
John 12.12–21.25   85
John 12.15   12, 243
John 12.16   88, 267
John 12.19   128
John 12.20–36   239
John 12.23   16, 123, 179, 224, 242, 255
John 12.23–50   204, 206, 207
John 12.26   184
John 12.27   12, 16, 33, 64, 124, 225, 242, 255
John 12.27–28   27–8, 171, 179, 224, 242
John 12.27–35   239
John 12.28   215
John 12.28–30   12
John 12.31–32   256
John 12.33   256
John 12.35–36   48
John 12.36   87
John 12.36–37   87
John 12.37–43   87
John 12.38–41   12
John 12.40   16
John 12.42   131
John 12.43   222
John 12.44–45   153
John 12.44–50   153
John 12.45   121
John 12.46   48
John 12.46–50   153

John 12.47 236	John 15.1 71, 126
John 12.49 196	John 15.9 225
John 12.50 196	John 15.9–17 194, 197
John 13 98, 201	John 15.13 231, 225, 255
John 13–17 85, 189, 191, 239	John 15.19 263
John 13.1 12, 133, 201, 224, 225, 242, 255	John 15.20 157
John 13.1–11 12	John 15.24 121
John 13.1–17.26 116	John 15.27 105
John 13.1–20 194	John 16 156–7
John 13.7 267	John 16.2 157
John 13.12–20 196	John 16.4 105
John 13.14 21	John 16.6 226
John 13.15 220	John 16.8–11 195, 196
John 13.16 12	John 16.10 184
John 13.19 126	John 16.16 98
John 13.20 12, 225	John 16.16–19 179, 181, 184, 185
John 13.21 79, 225	John 16.20–21 226
John 13.21–30 12	John 16.20–22 179, 226
John 13.27 215	John 16.22 184
John 13.31 214	John 16.23 12
John 13.31–16.33 28, 116, 204, 206, 207	John 16.23–24 19
John 13.34 124, 194, 196, 200	John 16.24 184
John 13.34–35 193	John 16.26–27 19
John 13.35 201	John 16.32 12
John 13.36–38 12	John 16.33 124, 184, 255, 256
John 13.38 261	John 17 28
John 14–16 98	John 17.1 207, 224, 242
John 14.1 225	John 17.1–2 265
John 14.2–3 179, 181, 185	John 17.1–26 204, 207
John 14.3 184	John 17.4 221
John 14.6 71, 111, 126, 195, 214, 263	John 17.8 264
John 14.7–9 68, 121	John 17.12 241, 243
John 14.10 239	John 17.14 263
John 14.13–14 12, 19	John 17.16 263
John 14.15–21 194, 197	John 17.17 265
John 14.16–7 184	John 17.20 107, 117
John 14.17 121	John 17.21 116
John 14.18 181, 184	John 17.23 225
John 14.19 181, 184	John 17.24 181, 184, 185
John 14.23 225	John 18 123, 156
John 14.26 107	John 18–19 94, 252
John 14.27 124, 184, 225	John 18.1 180
John 14.28 68	John 18.1–12 123
John 14.30 225, 255, 256	John 18.1–14 85
John 14.31 12, 16, 180, 225, 255	John 18.1–21.25 85
John 15 4	John 18.2 266
John 15–17 20	John 18.3–12 11
	John 18.4 124
	John 18.4–8 215

John 18.5   71, 125, 126
John 18.6   71, 124, 126
John 18.7   124, 125, 126
John 18.7–8   44
John 18.8   71
John 18.9   241
John 18.10–11   163
John 18.11   124, 171, 224
John 18.12–27   259–62
John 18.13   261
John 18.13–19.25   215
John 18.14   242, 261
John 18.20   21, 260
John 18.24   260, 261
John 18.24–28   64
John 18.25   261
John 18.25–27   11, 195
John 18.26   163
John 18.28   133, 261
John 18.28–19.16   262–6
John 18.28–32   262
John 18.29–38   11
John 18.32   262
John 18.31   133
John 18.33   263
John 18.36–37   183
John 18.37–38   263
John 18.38–40   263
John 18.39–40   11
John 18.40   263
John 19.1–3   11, 68, 80, 81, 264
John 19.2   264
John 19.2–3   81
John 19.3   264
John 19.5   81
John 19.7   244
John 19.11   222
John 19.14   33, 133, 231
John 19.15   134
John 19.17   33, 124, 215
John 19.19   44, 125
John 19.19–22   256
John 19.19–23   134
John 19.24–27   11
John 19.25–27   125
John 19.28   216
John 19.26   225
John 19.26–27   256
John 19.28   216

John 19.29   133
John 19.30   216, 256
John 19.31   33, 133, 163
John 19.33   133
John 19.34   132
John 19.38   163
John 19.38–42   51
John 19.40–42   163
John 19.42   33
John 20.1–10   11
John 20.1–18   161
John 20.17   222
John 20.19–20   11
John 20.22   132
John 20.23   12, 134
John 20.24–28   83
John 20.25   76
John 20.27   76
John 20.28   68, 76
John 20.29   76
John 20.30   107
John 20.30–31   44, 64, 98
John 20.31   64, 67, 107, 183
John 21   20, 151
John 21.1–19   11
John 21.7   225
John 21.11   33
John 21.15–19   261
John 21.17   226
John 21.20   225
John 21.22   19, 28, 181
John 21.23   12, 29
John 21.22–23   185
John 21.24–25   64, 171
John 21.25   64, 78, 85

Book of Acts
Acts 1.8   91
Acts 9.25–26   83
Acts 9.36–42   95
Acts 20.7–12   95

Romans
Romans 2.7   184
Romans 5.21   184
Romans 6.3–8   184
Romans 6.8   184
Romans 6.22–23   184
Romans 7.7   190

Romans 8.2   184
Romans 8.6   184
Romans 8.10   184
Romans 14.7–9   184

1 Corinthians
1 Corinthians 5.7–8   265
1 Corinthians 10.1–4   153
1 Corinthians 10.3–4, 16, 17, 21   153
1 Corinthians 10.16–17, 21   153
1 Corinthians 10.21   160
1 Corinthians 11.23–29   153, 160
1 Corinthians 11.27–34   153, 160
1 Corinthians 15.45   184

2 Corinthians
2 Corinthians 4.10–12   184
2 Corinthians 5.14–15   184

Galatians
Galatians 2.20   184
Galatians 4.4   173
Galatians 5.25   184
Galatians 6.8   184

1 Thessalonians
1 Thessalonians 4.13   97
1 Thessalonians 4.13–18   181
1 Thessalonians 4.14   184
1 Thessalonians 4.16–17   181
1 Thessalonians 5.2   97

Hebrews
Hebrews 2.18   217
Hebrews 4.15   217
Hebrews 5.7   217
Hebrews 11.14   42

1 John
1 John 2.18–19   185
1 John 2.18–22   180
1 John 2.8, 17   180
1 John 3.14   183
1 John 4.1–3   180
1 John 4.17   181
1 John 5.12–13   183

2 John
2 John 7–8   180

1 Peter
1 Peter 1.19   265

2 Peter
2 Peter 3.8–9   97

Gospel of Peter
Gospel of Peter 5.7   265

Gospel of Thomas
Gospel of Thomas 31   41

Eusebius
Ecclesiastical History 2.15.1   36
Ecclesiastical History 3.39.15   36
Ecclesiastical History 6.14.6
Ecclesiastical History 6.14.7   13, 24, 251

Justin Martyr
1 Apology 35   265
1 Apology 67.3–4   36

Irenaeus
Against Heresies 3.11.8   36

Origen
Commentary on John 1.6   68

Contra Celsus 2.24   217, 227
Contra Celsus 2.9   217
Contra Celsus 2.38   217
Contra Celsus 2.47   217
Contra Celsus 2.70   260
Contra Celsus10.3   217
Contra Celsus10.10   217

CLASSICAL LITERATURE

Apuleius
Florida 19   97
Metaphysics 2.21–30   97

Aristotle
Poetics 11.4   74
Poetics 11.5–6   74
Poetics 16.4   74

Cicero
Tusculan Disputations 1.74   219

Diogenes Laertius
Lives of Eminent Philosophers
   7.116   226
Lives of Eminent Philosophers
   7.117   225
Lives of Eminent Philosophers
   7.118   226
Lives of Eminent Philosophers
   7.119   228
Lives of Eminent Philosophers
   7.120   222
Lives of Eminent Philosophers
   7.121–22   222

Epictetus
Diatribes 3.26   219
Diatribes 3.26.39   222
Diatribes 3.39   219, 222
Diatribes 4.1.160–66   220
Diatribes 4.7.3–4   219
Diatribes 4.7.17–18   222
Diatribes 4.7.19–20   221
Diatribes 4.7.30–32   220

Iamblichus
Iamblichus 2.700   97

Philostratus
Lives 4.45   97

Plato
Apology 29d   219–20
Apology 30a   222
Apology 33b   260
Apology 33c   222
Apology 34b–d   220, 224
Apology 35c   224
Apology 35d   220, 222
Apology 38d   220
Apology 38e   224
Apology 39b   222
Apology 40a–b   222
Apology 41d   220, 222

Crito 44b–46a   220
Crito 46b   223
Crito 54e   220, 221, 222

Phaedo 67e   219

Timaeus 27d–28a   73

Plutarch
Life of Alexander 1.3   267

On Moral Virtue 449b   225

Quintilian
Institutes of Oratory 1.9.2   52

Seneca
Epistles 24.4   220
Epistles 70.8–9   220
Epistles 85.38–39   224
Epistles 104.27   219
Epistles 104.28   225
Epistles 120.21–22   216

Consolation to Polybius 18.5–7
   226

Xenophon
Memorabilia 1.1.1–1.2.64   219

General Index

Aaron 226
Abraham 60, 71, 72, 220
adultery 195
agrarian parables 21
Alexander, Philip 54
amplification and displacement 26, 27
anamnesis 107
ancient biographical genre 230, 252, 253, 267
ancient historiography 4, 6, 29, 91–9, 210, 211, 212–13
Anderson, Paul 20, 21
Andrew 15, 205
Annas 259, 260, 261
annihilation 241
anointing 4, 11, 15, 81–4, 95, 194, 195
antichrist 180
apocalyptic speech, in Mark 213
apocalyptic tradition, John and 179, 181
apocalyptic woes 21, 177, 178
apocalypticism 172
Apology 219, 224
Aristotle 74
arrest scene, John 124
Attridge, Harold W. vii, 2–3, 102, 103 (*see also* chapter 2)
audience of Jesus, insiders and outsiders 86–7
authentication, literary strategies of 211
authenticity, construction of 6
authority
    of Jesus 182, 233, 234, 236, 244
    rewriting and issues of 62–5
    of the scribes 192, 193, 233
autonomous persons 222
autonomy, divine (of Jesus) 222, 223

Bacchae 15
baptism(s)
    of believers 144, 145
    gaining eternal life and 141

    of Jesus 115, 116, 132, 140, 141, 143–6, 232
    of John the Baptist 142, 143
    the *pneuma* in 5
    in the river Jordan 112
    sin and 139, 140
Barabbas 257, 262, 263–4
Barrett, C.K. 14, 132
Bathsheba 40
Bauckham, Richard 15, 69, 70, 72
Becker, Eve-Marie vii, 4, 101, 104, 210
    (*see also* chapter 1; chapter 8)
Becker, Jürgen 23, 95, 162, 229
beginnings
    of the Gospels of Mark and John 4, 101–5, 108–11, 111–17, 173
    importance of in the gospel genre 102, 117
being/becoming 72–3
believers
    baptism of 144, 145
    gaining eternal life 141, 183
    God, the Logos and 116
    post-Easter 117
Bellum Judaicum 75
Beloved Disciple
    death of as an example to others 255
    in the final edition of John 20
    intimate closeness to Jesus 171
    Jesus sharing his last moments with 256
    as one of Jesus' witnesses/death of 28–9
Bergler, Siegfried 17
Bethany 82, 194, 223
Bethesda 152, 165, 166
Beutler, Johannes 161
bi-optic sources 20
Bible (New Testament) (*see also* Hebrew Bible)
    eschatology and 172
    ethics and 193, 194
    Nestle-Aland 114, 145

New Testament studies 31
  rewritten 3, 54–6, 60
  Biblical Antiquities 54, 60
blasphemy
  Jesus accused of 233, 234–5, 238, 241, 244, 248, 256, 265–6
  motif of 158
Boismard, Marie-Émile 156
boldness 260
Bond, Helen K. vii, 7 (*see also* chapter 1; chapter 18)
Borgen, Peder 5, 152–3, 154–5, 156–63, 165, 166, 167
Boring, M. E. 68
Bosenius, Bärbel 108–9, 110, 111, 112
Bread from Heaven 152–3
bread miracle 149
Bread of Life discourse 204, 206
Breytenbach, Cilliers 247
Brooke, George 57
Brown, Raymond 13, 43, 69
Bruner, Frederick Dale 132
Buch-Hansen, Gitte 226
Bultmann, Rudolf 17, 18, 23, 92, 193
burning bush 227

Caesar, Pilate's loyalty to 265
Caesarea Philippi 221
Caiaphas 239, 242, 259, 261
call of the Twelve 21
Capernaum 42, 44, 115, 117
Celsus 217, 260
charity, and poverty 191
Christ
  Jesus as 103, 191
  Parousia of 181
Christian literature, ethical stereotypes in 199
Christianity
  early Christian communities 191, 192
  early, concept of critical inheritance and 38
Christology
  eschatology and 172, 176, 182–4, 185
  ethical texts and 188–9
  of John 6, 98, 160–1, 171, 236, 241
  of Mark 232
  philosophical 228
Chronicles 60

chronotopes 91
church, the synagogue and 160, 165
Clement of Alexandria 24, 36, 251
commandments
  Decalogue 53, 192
  the greatest commandment 191, 192
  honouring one's parents 190, 192
  keeping the commandments of Christ 194
  new commandment of love 189, 194, 196, 197, 199, 200
community finances, the proper handling of 195
comparison
  genealogical 5
  heuristic 5, 135–6, 142
  parallel 5, 135–7
  of speeches or discourses in Mark and John 205–7
  study of 6, 198
  textual 150–1
Confucius 37–8, 39
controversy stories, literary device of 189
Conzelmann, Hans 88
counter-memory 98
critical inheritance 3, 31, 36–41, 41–6, 47–8
criticism
  form criticism 2, 78, 97
  literary criticism 29, 200
  modern biblical 7
  motif criticism 198, 200
  tradition criticism 198, 199, 200
Crito 219, 220, 221, 222, 223
cross
  the carrying of the 33, 124, 256
  as the final confrontation with the powers of Satan 255
  theology of the 231, 232
crown of thorns 80–1, 264
crucifixion 134, 236, 254
culture(s)
  cultural reception of Jesus 38–9
  cultural settings 40
  media culture 165–6
  oral 245, 246–7
  study of *Motivgeschichte* and 198
  written communication culture 246
cup, the 16, 224

General Index

Dahl, Nils 68
Daniel 255
darkness/light imagery 261
Dauer, Anton 18, 161, 162–3
David, sin with Bathsheba 40
Dead Sea Scrolls 55
death of Jesus
   burial of 51
   the divine necessity of 231, 242
   Jesus' mission and 28
   in John 7, 28, 116, 118, 231, 237, 240, 255–6
   in Mark 7, 28, 231, 232, 240, 253–4
   role of in the plot 231
Decalogue 53, 192
delay, motif of 96–8
Denaux, Adelbert 14
derived texts 3, 25
Diatessaron 1
Dibelius, Martin 18, 194
diegetic transformation 26
Dio Chrysostom 219
Diogenes Laertius 222, 225, 226, 228
disasters, wars/earthquakes/famines 177
disciples
   Beloved Disciple. *See* Beloved Disciple
   the calling of 115, 116–17
   disciples' unbelief 21
   as Jesus' new spiritual family 218
   of John the Baptist 129
   of John the Baptist/Jesus 140
   new understanding of honour and 254
   reunification of with Jesus 181, 184
   specific rules pertaining to 189
discipleship
   characterized by humility and service 6
   concept of 193
   ethics of 189, 190
   Mark and 189, 200
   in Mark and John 3, 189, 201
   meaning of 192
discourses, of John 204, 206, 207, 213
divine will 109, 231
divinity, of Jesus 67–76
divorce 190, 192, 194
Dodd, C.H. 13, 23, 33, 77–8, 89, 159, 251
dramatic models, influence of 74–5, 76
Dunderberg, Ismo 15, 150

Easterling, Patricia E. 74
education, in textual techniques 52
Eleazar 62, 220, 222
Elijah 70
   John the Baptist as 34, 108, 126, 137, 141–2
emotions
   Jesus as moved by 6, 226, 227
   rational 225
   unselfish and philanthropic 226
end of the world 178
Engberg-Pedersen, Troels vii–viii, 5 (*see also* chapter 11)
Epictetus 219, 221, 222
eschatology
   Christology and 172, 176, 182–4, 185
   eschatological salvation 172
   field of 169
   of Jesus 169–70
   in the Johannine circle/John 5–6, 170, 178–84, 185–6
   in Mark 5–6, 170, 172–8, 185–6
   of the Synoptic Gospels 178, 179
   term 172
eternal life
   baptism and the gaining of 141
   believers gaining 141, 183
   in John 16
   Kingdom of God replaced by 21, 185–6
   made available in the presence of Jesus 178–84
ethics
   christologically-based 189, 201
   of discipleship 189, 190
   ethical concept of love 201
   ethical issues found in the Torah 195
   ethical stereotypes 199
   ethical texts 187–8, 188–9, 190–3, 193–8
   the foundations of 200
   Jesus and 189, 195, 196
   Markan and Johannine 6, 187, 189, 190–3, 193–8
   the Synoptic Gospels and 195
Eucharist 21, 28, 153, 154, 255
Euripides 15
Eusebius 36
everlasting life 175
Every Good Man is Free 219, 222, 223

evil powers, removal or defeat of 174
exegesis, patristic 1
exorcisms 21, 255
eyewitnesses, theme of 20 (*see also* witnessing)
Ezekiel, Book of 255
Ezekiel the Tragedian 55

faith, judgement and 195
faithlessness (towards Jesus), as sin 195
familiarity, theory of 32
family, of Jesus 218, 221
Farewell Discourses 116, 180, 184, 195, 204, 207, 255
fasting 233, 234
feeding of 5,000 16, 20, 21
fig tree, parable 178
footwashing 3, 98, 196, 201
forgiveness of sins 155–6, 234, 241, 243, 244, 245
form-critical connections 159
form criticism 2, 78, 97
forms, realm of the 72
Fortna, Robert 17, 18, 161
Foucault, Michel 98
Fowler, Alastair 75
Frey, Jörg viii, 5–6, 14, 16, 68, 150, 193, 194 (*see also* chapter 13)
future-oriented aspects, in John 5–6, 179, 181, 184

Galilee 42, 43, 44, 45, 46, 47, 48, 106, 117, 235, 253, 260
Garden of Eden myth 220
garden scene 123
Gardner-Smith, Percival 3, 13, 14, 32–3, 33–6, 39, 40, 47, 51, 149, 251
genealogical perspective 5, 136
Genesis 132, 256
Genesis Apocryphon 54, 55, 56, 58, 60
Genette, Gérard 15, 25, 199
genre(s)
    ancient biographical 230, 252, 253, 267
    genre bending 103, 114
    genre of revelatory literature 99
    gospel genre. *See* gospel genre
    historical genre 230
    kerygmatic genre 104, 117
    mode and 75
    narrative genre 239
    as a tool of literary criticism 200
    tragic genre 75
Geschichtsdeutung 103
Gethsemane
    in John 27–8, 171
    in Mark 16, 27–8, 171, 179
    process of transformation and 3
    temptation of Jesus and 116, 215, 218, 219, 221, 223–5, 227, 228
Gnilka, Joachim 158
God
    in charge of history 178
    defeating/destroying sin 133, 139
    dominion of 174, 175
    forgiveness of sins and 244
    Jesus as 69, 118
    Kingdom of God. *See* Kingdom of God
    the Logos and 116, 117, 118
    rejection of God's offer of salvation 237
    the revelation of 122
    victory over Satan 255
    as the Word 72, 102, 103–4, 110, 117
good and evil 194, 195, 198–9
Good Shepherd discourse 204, 263–4
Goodacre, Mark viii, 4 (*see also* chapter 7)
gospel genre
    beginnings in the 102, 117
    biographical or historical gospel 248
    invention of 210
    John's development of 114, 119, 214
    kerygmatic character of 104, 117
    Luke adoption/development of 92
    Mark and John's use of 229–30
    Mark as the inventor of 91–2, 114
    narrative plot within 242
Gospel of John (*see also* Index of Ancient Sources)
    agreement with Mark 40–1
    aiming to replace Mark 65
    anointing story 4, 81–4, 95, 194, 195
    apocalyptic tradition and 179, 181
    appropriation of Mark 61
    arrest scene 124
    beginnings of the 4, 101–5, 108–11, 111–17
    being/becoming and 73
    the birth of Jesus and 33

General Index 319

Christology of 6, 98, 160-1, 171, 236, 241
critical inheritance of Mark 47-8
date for the composition of 34, 35
death of Jesus 7, 28, 116, 118, 231, 237, 240, 255-6
the decision to kill Jesus and 242-3, 244, 245, 248
the dependence of the gospel 5, 13-17, 20, 34, 59, 161, 233
dependence or independence in John 5.1-18? 152-62
developing/expanding material from Mark 3-4, 67-76
disagreement with/independence from the Synoptic Gospels 33-6
disagreement with Mark 32, 33-6, 40-6, 47, 48
discourses of 204, 206, 207, 213
divine identity in 67-76
dramatic recognition 74
editions of 20, 21
emotional Jesus of 226
eschatology in 5-6, 170, 178-84, 185-6
eternal life in 16
ethical concept of discipleship and 189
ethical texts in 193-8
ethics and 6, 187, 197
Eucharist traditions in 153
as a factual text with a claim to historical referentiality 211
Farewell Discourses 116, 180, 184, 195, 204, 207, 255
form, narrative structure and audience of the speeches 205-7
as a fourth Synoptic Gospel 81-4
future-oriented aspects in 5-6, 179, 181, 184
Gethsemane in 27-8, 171
the haul of fish 33
the hermeneutical key: the resurrection 88
history and 93, 98-9
the hour is coming, and now it is 179-80
as the hypertext 24
independence from the Synoptics 77, 170-1
the independence of the gospel 13, 47

as independent but sharing common sources 17-18, 253
as an indirect literary recipient of Mark 244
intertextuality and 95
is there a hermeneutical pendant in? 105-7
Jesus' hometown 41-6
Jesus' identity and mission and 64-5, 67, 68, 74, 86
Jesus, teaching of 205
Jesus' words and 213
Jewish interpretative methods and 54
John 11 as the turning point of the narrative 93-9
John the Baptist and 34, 114, 125-30, 135-7, 137-8, 138-45, 145-7
John's development of the gospel genre 114, 119, 214
Kingdom of God and 104, 116, 141, 183
knowing/using Mark 2-3, 14, 35-6, 46, 51, 53, 95, 170-1, 244, 253
Lazarus 97-8
in light of ancient historiography 92-4
literary dependence on Mark 246, 248-9
love and 197, 198
Luke and 16, 95, 98, 99
Matthew and 81
methods/criteria used to determine dependence/independence of 150-1
narrative strategy/outline of 92, 93, 96, 98, 99, 112, 240
oral or written tradition? 160-1
oral traditions and 18, 19-21, 51, 245
Passion narrative 17-18, 20, 27-8, 84-5, 215-16, 223, 252, 255, 266-7
Plato/Philo and 73, 74
the plot to kill Jesus and 230-1, 236-9, 241-2
prologue 237, 255
the prophet without honour 41-2
recognition (*anagnôrisis*) and 76
relationship with Mark 57-8
as a relecture of Mark 5, 23-9, 122
resurrection narrative 97

rewriting in a philosophical mode 227, 228
rewriting of Mark 5, 54, 57–65, 123–4, 134, 217, 221–2
signs-based faith and 43–4
speech-compositions in 6, 203–4, 210, 213–14
the Synoptic Gospels and 9–11, 15, 16, 46–7, 51, 68, 78–81, 84, 89, 92–3, 95, 96, 98, 149–50, 170–1, 208
temptation scene in 216, 217, 221–2, 223, 225, 227
time and 94, 96–9
the transcendence of history/time in John 11 98–9
transforming Mark 117–19, 138–45
transforming the passion narrative into an action narrative 216
two-level narrative of 119
use of sources and traditions in 17–18, 207–9, 253
Gospel of Luke (*see also* Index of Ancient Sources)
anointing 82, 83, 84
burial of Jesus and 51
gospel genre and 92
the haul of fish 33
infancy narrative 33
Jesus narratives 189
John and 16, 95, 98, 99
in light of ancient historiography 91–4
Mark and 2, 52–3, 91, 125
Passion narrative 219
the prophet without honour 41
temple incident 26
temptation scene in 223
tradition and sources and 209
Gospel of Mark (*see also* Index of Ancient Sources)
abrupt end of 106
acceptance of his Gospel not yet being fixed in the Church 35
anointing 83
apocalyptic speech in 213
authoritative status of 36
beginnings of the 4, 101–5, 108–11, 111–17, 173
burial of Jesus and 51
Christology of 232

'corrections' of 21
'cup' petition 224
death of Jesus 7, 28, 231, 232, 240, 253–4
the decision to kill Jesus and 241, 248
as a derived text 25
discipleship and 189, 200, 201
divine identity in 67–76
dramatic recognition 74
editing of by Matthew and Luke 2
eschatological concepts in 5–6, 170, 172–9, 185–6
ethical concept of discipleship and 189
ethical texts in 190–3
ethics and 6, 187, 191–2, 193–8
form, narrative structure and audience of the speeches 205–7
garden scene 123
Gethsemane in 16, 27–8, 171, 179
gospel genre and 91–2, 114, 229–30
as the hypotext 24
as independent but sharing common sources 17–18, 253
Jesus' hometown 41–6
Jesus' identity and 67, 68, 74
Johannine 'relecture' of 5, 23–9, 122
John knowing/using 2–3, 14, 35–6, 46, 51, 53, 95, 170–1, 244, 253
John the Baptist and 34, 114, 125, 128, 130, 132, 137, 139–41, 147
John the Baptist – comparison with John 135–7
Kingdom of God and 16, 104, 110, 116, 172, 174, 175, 176, 183, 190
in light of ancient historiography 91–4
literary dynamics of 21
literary elements in 91
Luke and 2, 52–3, 91, 125
Matthew and 2, 52–3, 63, 125
memory elements in 245
motif of delay in 96–7
narrative plot of 112, 232
oral traditions and 18, 19–21, 51, 245
Passion narrative 17–18, 20, 84–5, 232, 252–3, 266
the plot to kill Jesus and 230–1, 232–6, 241–2, 243, 245, 246–8
as a pre-historiographical author 210–11

General Index 321

the prophet without honour 41–2
recognition (*anagnôrisis*) and 75–6
Simon of Cyrene 124
speech-compositions in 6, 203–4, 213–14
the summary at the beginning of Jesus' ministry 173–5
technique of 'sandwiching' 97
temptation scene in 216, 217–19, 223–5, 227
Thomas and 21
trial narratives 256–8
as an 'unfinished' text 21–2
use of sources and traditions in 207–9
Gospel of Matthew (see also Index of Ancient Sources)
   anointing 83
   infancy narrative 33
   John and 81
   John the Baptist and 34
   Mark and 2, 52–3, 63, 125
   the prophet without honour 41
   Temple incident 26
   temptation scene in 223
Gospel of Peter 265
Gospel of Thomas
   identity of Jesus and 68, 76
   Jesus and 40
   Mark and 21
   the prophet without honour 41
Gospel writing, as a substitute for Jesus 176
Gospels studies, critical inheritance and 39–40
great tribulation 177–8
Greco-Roman literature 75, 97
Greco-Roman philosophical tradition 216, 225
Greek drama 67
Greek philosophy 67, 72
Greek tragedy, influence of 74–5

Haenchen, Ernst 13
Halbwachs, Maurice 36–7
Hays, Richard B. 192
healing
   the forgiveness of sins and 243
   healing activity of Jesus 157
   healing miracles 244

healing stories 155–6, 165
   of the man born blind 195, 196
   miracle at the pool of Bethesda 152, 165, 166
   of a paralytic 233, 234, 238, 240, 243, 245
   of the sick 253–4
heaven 104
Torah 6, 63, 189, 192, 195, 201, 220
Herod 35, 125, 235, 254
Herodians 235
Herodotus 75
heuristic comparison 5, 135–6, 142
High Priest 256, 257, 258, 259, 260–1, 262
history
   ancient historiography 4, 6, 29, 91–9, 210, 211, 212–13
   God in charge of 178
   historical accounts, enriching with speeches 212
   historical-critical perspective 191
   historical genre 230
   historical research 29
   historiographical claim of Mark/John 210–13
   John and 93, 98–9
   of research 9–22
   Synoptic approach to history-writing 4
   tradition history 23–4, 165
History of the Peloponnesian War 212
Hoegen-Rohls, Christina viii, 4 (*see also* chapter 9)
Hofrichter, Peter 16
Holy Spirit 129, 132 (*see also* Paraclete)
Homer 218
hometown, of Jesus 41–6
honour, new understanding of 254
honouring one's parents, commandment 190, 192
hope, eschatological 177
Hoskyns, Edwin 14
hour, the 33, 171, 179, 180, 224, 242, 255
Hunt, Steven A. viii, 4–5 (*see also* chapter 10)
Hurtado, Larry W. 67
hymn prologues 116, 118
hypertextuality
   defined 25

examples of 26–9
the relationship between John and Mark and 3, 25, 29, 199
rereading and 15
hypotexts/hypertexts 24, 25, 28, 29
hyssop 133

identity(ies)
of Christ 27
and dignity of Jesus 182, 183
divine identity in Mark and John 67–76
of Jesus 64–5, 86, 88, 129, 141, 256–7, 260, 262
of John the Baptist 125–30, 140, 142, 145
Iliad 218
imagery, darkness/light 261
incomprehension, motif of 95–6
independence, theory of 2, 33, 34
inherited tradition 3
insiders and outsiders 86–7
interdependence, oral traditions and 20–1
interfluentiality 21
interpretative frames, of rewritten texts 62
'Interrelations of the Gospels' Symposium 152–5
intertextuality
defined 25
John, the Synoptic Gospels and 95, 208
recent scholarship 14, 21
the relationship between Mark and John and 29, 199–200
textual comparisons and 151
theory of 24–6
tool of 198
intratextuality 132
invented traditions 199
Ioudaioi 241
Irenaeus 36
Isaac, Abraham's binding of 220
Isaiah 108, 109, 113, 132
Israel, restoration of 174
Israel's journey through the wilderness 220

Jairus' daughter 97
James 205

Jay, Jeff 75
Jeremiah 132
Jerusalem 43, 44, 45, 46, 47, 85, 112, 125, 127, 128
Jerusalem aristocracy 242, 245, 248
Jerusalem Council 83
Jerusalem Symposium (1984) 5, 152–5
Jesus
accusations of blasphemy 233, 234–5, 238, 241, 244, 248, 256, 265–6
anointing of by Mary of Bethany 15 (*see also* anointing)
apparent violation of the Sabbath 157, 158, 159 (*see also* Sabbath)
as the authoritative teacher of Torah 6, 189, 192, 201
authority of 182, 233, 234, 236, 244
baptism of 115, 116, 132, 140, 141, 143–6, 232
the Beloved Disciple and 171, 256
birth of 33
burial of 51
carrying the cross 33
changing images of 38–9
as Christ, the Son of God 103, 191
cleansing of the temple. See temple incident
coming of 185
the crucifixion 134, 236, 254
cultural reception of 38–9
death of. See death of Jesus
the decision to kill 235, 239, 241, 242, 243, 244, 245, 248, 249
dining with his disciples 21
divine autonomy of 222, 223
divinity of 67–76
early Jesus movement 172
as the Elect and Son of God 5
an emotional 6, 226, 227
eschatology of 169–70
ethics and 189, 195, 196
family of 218, 221
Farewell Discourses 116, 180, 184, 195, 204, 207, 255
flogged and mocked by the soldiers 264, 266
formal agreement to kill Jesus 240
as God 69, 118
healing activity of. See healing

as a hidden Messiah 86, 87
his disciples and 21, 140, 181, 184, 192, 218
hometown of 41–6
identity and dignity of 182, 183
identity and mission of 64–5, 68, 74, 86–7
identity (divine) in Mark and John 67–76
identity of 88, 129, 141, 256–7, 260, 262
in John 4, 6, 122
John the Baptist and 16, 137, 138, 140–1, 142, 145–6, 147, 171
judgement/eternal life made available in the presence of 178–84
as King of the Jews 257, 262, 263, 264
as the Lamb of God 133, 139, 143
last meal of 28
the law and 189, 192
love concept of 189
in Mark 6, 200
as the Messiah 86, 87, 107, 172, 174, 182, 189
motivation of 217–18
Parousia of 179, 185
Passion of. *See* Passion narrative
performance of signs 44
persecution of 156, 157, 158, 238, 241, 243
the plot to kill 6–7, 156, 157, 158, 230–1, 232–9, 240, 241–2, 243, 245, 246–8
Prayer of Jesus 204
prediction of his death 225, 240
proclamation of 173, 174, 175, 176
reception in Galilee 43, 44
rejection of 45, 46, 47
return of 181
role and mission of 213
Sabbath controversies. See Sabbath controversies
the scribes and 193, 244
self presentation of 196
as the Son of God 5, 103, 107, 116, 118, 143, 182, 189, 191, 218, 253
as Son of Man 182
speech of 205–7
stoning of 72
suffering of 236

taking away the sin of the world 134, 139, 143
teaching of 205
temptation of 6, 116, 215, 218, 219, 221, 223–5, 227, 228
tested by God 217
Thomas and 40
trial scenes 7, 256–8, 259–66
as a witness to the truth 263
as the Word 72, 73, 107, 116, 255
Jesus as Lebensspender 164
Jesus through the Centuries 38–9
Jewish Antiquities 53
Jewish Scriptures (*see also* Index of Ancient Sources)
rewriting of 53–4
temptation and 220
Jewish texts, rewritten 3, 56–7, 58
Jews, persecution of Jesus 156, 158
Johannes und die Synoptiker 163–4
John among the Gospels 152, 163
'John and the Synoptics in the Passion Narrative' 152, 153
'John, Jesus, and History' project 20
John the Baptist
baptising of Jesus 115, 116, 140, 142, 143
baptism of 142, 143
disciples of 129, 140
as Elijah 34, 108, 126, 137, 141–3
the historical beginning of the good news and 103, 104
identity and ministry of 125–30
identity of 140, 142, 145
imprisonment of 15, 140
Jesus and 16, 137, 138, 140–1, 142, 145–6, 147, 171
John and 34, 114, 125–30, 135–7, 137–8, 138–45, 145–7
the light and 138, 145
Mark and 34, 114, 125, 128, 130, 132, 137, 139–41, 147
in Mark and John 4, 5, 34, 111–14, 115, 118, 123, 147
in Matthew 34
as a model (*Vorbild*) 137, 147
as a predecessor 137, 141
role of 140
voice and 139

why he baptised 142–3
as a witness 5, 137, 138, 139, 140, 142, 143, 144, 145, 146, 147 (*see also* John the Witness)
'John (the Baptist): The Witness on the Threshold' 136
John the Witness 114, 118, 129 (*see also* John the Baptist)
John 'the Witness/Confessor 130–4 (*see also* John the Baptist)
Jordan (river) 112, 140
Joseph of Arimathea 51
Josephus 53, 54, 56–7, 63, 75, 220, 226–7, 227–8
Jubilees 54, 55, 56, 58, 60, 62, 63
Judaea 104
Judaism
the Jewish ethos 189
late Second Temple 3, 54, 55, 61, 63, 65
rewriting in ancient Judaism 53–7, 63, 65
Second Temple Judaism 38, 172
Judas 79, 83, 195
Judea 43, 44, 45, 47, 112
judgement 178–84, 195, 196, 262
Judges, the period of the 60
justice 195
Justin Martyr 36

Kähler, Martin 84, 86, 232
Käsemann, Ernst 193
Keith, Chris viii–ix, 3 (*see also* chapter 4)
Kelber, Werner 246
kephalaia 4, 114–17
kerygmatic genre 104, 117
King of the Jews, Jesus as 257, 262, 263, 264
Kingdom of God
Jesus as the Messiah who announces 189
John and 104, 116, 141, 183
in Mark 16, 104, 110, 116, 172, 174, 175, 176, 183, 190
replaced with eternal life 21, 185–6
Kings, Books of 60
kingship, theme of 7, 254
Kirk, Alan 165
Klauck, Hans-Josef 108, 109, 110
knowledge, of a prior tradition 3

Koester, Helmut 13
Konings, Johan 150
Konventikelethik 193, 197

Labahn, Michael ix, 6–7, 14, 163, 164, 165, 187–8, 194 (*see also* chapter 17)
Lagrange, M.-J. 46
Lamb of God 133, 139, 143, 264
Lang, Manfred 14, 18, 163–4
language/literary-based approach, to Johannine ethics 194
language, the influence of classical 67–76
Larsen, Kasper Bro ix, 6, 76 (*see also* chapter 16)
Larsen, Matthew 21–2
last judgement, as a new ethical idea 195
last meal, of Jesus 28
law(s)
Jesus as teacher of the Law 192
Jesus' interpretation of the ethos of the 189
of Moses 192
Lazarus 44, 95, 96, 97–8, 223, 225, 239
leadership 190, 192
Letter of Aristeas 53, 56
Letter to the Hebrews 217
Leuven school 5, 149, 161, 162–3
Leviticus 132
life
conceptualizations of 184
made present 182–4
Life-Giving Spirit, discourse on the 204
light
John the Baptist and 138, 145
Light of the World Discourse 204
Logos as the 118
metaphor of 111
Lindars, Barnabas 20
literary causality 46
literary criticism 29, 200
literary dependence
direct 247
of Jewish Scriptures 54
between John and Mark 246, 248–9
the speeches in Mark and John and 214
theory of 23, 208
literary device, of controversy stories 189

literary dynamics, of Mark 21
literary elements, in Mark 91
literary form 158–9
literary genres, of the ethical texts 193 (*see also* genre(s))
literary independence
　from the Synoptic Gospels 23
　theory of 208
literary/language-based approach, to Johannine ethics 194
literary motifs 198
literary relationship, (indirect oral) between Mark and John 243
literary strategies 6, 211
literature (*see also* genre(s))
　ancient biography 230, 252, 253, 267
　classical 3
　early Christian literature that is 'revelatory' 4
　early Christian writings 246
　Greco-Roman 75, 97
　the influence of classical 67–76
　recognition scene in ancient 76
　Roman Empire 74
　tragic genre 75
Literaturgeschichte 200
Logos
　as the Creator 111, 118
　God and the 116, 117, 118
　as the light 118
　origin of the 103, 104, 114 (*see also* Word, the)
　the philosophical autonomy of the 222–3
Lohmeyer, Ernst 108, 109, 110
Louvain school 14, 17
love
　different aspects of 201
　ethical concept of 201
　mutual love and service 196–7, 198, 200
　new commandment of love 189, 194, 196, 197, 199, 200
　of one's neighbour 193, 197, 200
Lucian 75
Luke-Acts 92
Luther, Martin 203
Luther, Susanne ix, 6 (see also chapter 15)
LXX (Septuagint) 71, 72

Maccabees 1 62
Maccabees 2 57, 61, 222
Maccabees 4 3, 57, 60, 61, 62, 220
MacDonald, Dennis R. 15, 122
Mackay, Ian D. 20
manna 153
Marcus, Joel 70
Martyn, J. Louis 160, 179
martyrdoms, *4 Maccabees* 61, 62
Mary Magdalene 21, 83, 84, 222
media culture 165–6
memory
　collective 37, 38
　components or triggers of 248
　counter-memory 98
　early Christian 99
　group 37
　human 247–8
　memory elements in Mark 245
　oral 7, 248, 249
　social memory theory. See social memory theory
Messiah(s)
　false Messiahs or prophets 177, 178
　Jesus as the 86, 87, 107, 172, 174, 182, 189
　messianic woes 177
　revelation of the hidden 86–8
　messianic period 178
　Messianic secret, reversal of 21
Messianic Secret 86
metaphorical transfers 27
metatextuality 25
miracles (*see also* individual miracles)
　five non-Markan 21
　miracle of the loaves 3, 27
　miracle stories 98, 165
　miracle tradition 164
　as revelatory 'signs' 21
missionaries, ascetic ethos and lifestyle of 192
misunderstanding, motif of 95–6, 231
mockery, of Jesus 264, 266
mode, genre and 75
model (*Vorbild*), John the Baptist as 137, 147
Mohr, Till Arend 18
moral values 199
Moses 62, 63, 73, 192, 220, 226–7, 227–8

Motivgeschichte 198, 200
Müller, Mogens 58
Myllykoski, Matti 18

nachösterliche(r) Anamnese 93
narrative(s)
   action narrative 215–16, 223
   biographical narrative of Jesus' life 230
   Christ narratives 200
   epiphany narratives 27
   Gethsemane narrative 171
   infancy narrative 33
   Jesus narratives 64, 189, 200
   Mark and John as factual narratives 211
   narrative complexity of John 96
   narrative disagreements 34–5
   narrative genre 239
   narrative mode 26
   narrative outline of Mark 91
   narrative patterns 4
   narrative plot 112, 232, 239, 242
   narrative strategy of John 92, 93, 96, 98, 99, 112, 240
   the Passion narrative. See Passion narrative
   point of view guiding 26
   resurrection narratives 96–7, 98
   speeches and 213
   tragic 4, 67
   two-level narrative of John 119
   where do the narratives of Mark and John begin? 111–14
Nazareth 42, 46, 47
Neirynck, Frans 5, 14, 150, 152, 153–5, 156, 157–63, 164, 166, 168
Nestle-Aland 114, 145
New Birth, discourse on 204, 206
New Testament. See Bible (New Testament)
Nicodemus 51, 183, 195, 197, 206, 207, 213
Nicol, W. 17
Novum Testamentum Graece 101

Oedipus Rex 74
Of Freedom from Fear 221
Offenbarung in Zeichen und Wort 165
On the Creation of the World 73
Ong, Walter 246

oral culture 245, 246–7
oral dependence 247
oral 'interfluentiality' 21
oral literary relationship, between Mark and John 243
oral memory 7, 248, 249
oral traditions
   the Christian faith and the Gospel story and 78
   common 3, 19
   the decision to kill Jesus and 249
   interdependence and 20–1
   John and 51, 160–1
   and the Leuven approach 162–3
   Mark, John and 18, 19–21, 51, 245
   media culture and 165
   as the primary source 153
   re-oralization 7, 246–8, 249
   recent research on 5
   secondary orality 7, 20, 163–5, 232, 246, 247, 248, 249
Origen 68, 217, 227, 260

Pancaro, Severino 160
Papias 36, 164
parable of the cornerstone 235
parable of the fig tree 178
parable of the vineyard 235
parable theory 175
parables of the 'automatically' growing seed/mustard seed 175
Paraclete 107, 116, 267 (see also Holy Spirit)
parallel comparison 5, 135–6
parallel traditions model 78
parallelism, deep 135
paratextuality 25
parenesis, the concept of 198
parents, obligations towards 190, 192
Parousia
   of Christ 181
   the delay of the 97, 98, 99
   expectation of an imminent 169
   expectation of the 181, 186
   hope for the 184
   of Jesus 179, 185
   of the Son of Man 178, 185
Parsenios, George ix–x, 3–4 (*see also* chapter 6)

Passion narrative
   with an extended introduction 84–5
   in John 84–5, 163, 252, 255, 266–7
   John's transformation of 27–8, 215–16, 223
   in Luke 219
   in Mark 17–18, 20, 84–5, 232, 252–3, 266
   the Passover motif and 133
   the 'Signs Gospel' and 18
   similarities between John and Mark 17–18, 20
passions
   mastery over the 225
   Stoic theory of the 226
Passover lambs 133, 231, 265
Passover motif 132–3
past, the 37, 38, 39, 40
patristic exegesis 1
Paul, Saint 153, 184, 195
Pelikan, Jaroslav 38–9
Pentateuch 54, 62, 63
persecution(s)
   and accusations 177
   of Jesus 156, 157, 238, 241, 243
Pesch, R. 159
Peter, apostle
   attacking one of the arresting party 124
   cutting off the ear of the High Priest's slave 224
   denials of 257, 259, 261, 262
   Jesus rebuking 171
   Jesus' teaching of 205
   John and 195
   the personal vices of cowardice/denial and 191
   temptation of Jesus and 218
Petersen, Norman 106
Pharisees 235, 236, 239, 242, 245, 248
Philo 67, 73, 220, 222, 223, 226, 227–8
philosophical revisions 216
philosophical tradition, Greco-Roman 216, 225
philosophy, Greek 67, 72
Pilate 124, 134, 183, 222, 254, 256–7, 258, 261, 262, 263, 264–6
Plato 3, 67, 72, 73, 219, 222
play (*Spiel*) 24
Plutarch 75, 267

pneuma, role of 5
Poetics 74
politics
   the decision to kill Jesus and 235, 239
   period of political crisis 176
   public-political context 240
Polybius 75
poor widow, paradigm of the 191
post-Easter period 176, 182, 183, 184
post-Guttenberg paradigm 246, 247
poverty
   and charity 191
   missionaries and 192
   virtue of supporting the poor 195
power, cosmic theme of 262
praetorium 262, 264
pre-texts 24
predecessor (*Vorläufer*), John the Baptist as 137, 147
priests 242, 262
proclamation(s)
   of Jesus 173, 174, 175, 176
   of the kingdom 177
   post-Easter 176
prophet without honour 41–2, 43
prophets, false 177, 178
prosopopoiia 207
Pseudo-Philo 54, 60
public-political context 240
purity 192

quantitative transformation 25–6

re-oralization 7, 246–8
recognition (*anagnôrisis*) 4, 74, 75–6
redactional elements, of the Synoptic Gospels 16–17
Reinbold, Wolfgang 18
relationships
   between John and Mark 1, 2, 7, 9, 22, 23n.5, 57–8
   between John and Mark as hypertextuality 3, 25, 29, 199
   between Matthew, Mark and Luke 1
   Synoptic 1
   trans-textual 25
relecture, of Mark by John 5, 23–9, 122
remembering 88
repenting 175

research
  historical 29
  John and Mark in the history of 9–22
  Western bias in 38
resurrection and the life 183
resurrection, John and the 88
resurrection narratives 96–7, 98
resurrection of the dead 172, 181
Revelation, Book of 132
revelation of God 122
revelation of the hidden Messiah 86–8
revelatory literature, genre of 99
revisions, philosophical 216
revivification stories 97
rewriting
  in ancient Judaism 53–7, 63, 65
  of authoritative texts 52
  interpretative frames 62
  issues of authority and 62–5
  of Jewish texts 3, 56–7, 58
  John and 5, 54, 57–65, 123–4, 134, 217, 221–2, 227, 228
  literal or physical replacement/ functional replacement 63
  preservation of outline and 'rewriting' of content 59–61
  the rewritten Bible 3, 54–6, 60
  rewritten Scripture 54–6
  of sources 53
  the term 'rewriting' 58–9
  textual strategies 55
"rise, take up your bed (pallet) and walk" 155, 156
Robinson, John A. T. 16
Roman Empire, prose literature of the 74
Runesson, Anders 101

Sabbath controversies 154, 155, 156, 157–9, 160, 233, 234–5, 237–8, 244
Sabbath healings 7, 230, 234, 240, 241, 242, 243, 248
Sabbe, Maurits 14, 150, 161
Saint John and the Synoptic Gospels 32–3, 51
salvation
  eschatological 172, 185
  eternal life and 183
  rejection of God's offer of 237
  the rich and 175

Samaria, Sychar 44–5, 46
Samaritan woman 71, 130, 195, 196, 206, 207
Samuel, Books of 60
Sanhedrin, the 239, 242, 255, 259
Satan
  God's victory over 255
  temptation of Jesus by 6, 116, 215, 216, 217–19, 221, 223–5, 227, 228
sayings, absolute 'I am' sayings 71
sayings of the Lord (*Herrenworte*) 28
sayings parallels 11–12
Scheritt, Frank 18
Schmidt, Karl Ludwig 18
Schnackenburg, Rudolf 13, 158
Schnelle, Udo 9, 14, 163, 164, 194, 200, 229
Schwartz, Barry 37–40
Schwiebert, Jonathan 263
scribes
  accusing Jesus of claiming God's authority 244
  authority of 192, 193, 233
  moral critique of the 191
Scripture, rewritten 54–6
Scriptures of Israel 173
Second Temple Judaism 3, 38, 54, 55, 61, 63, 65, 172
secondary orality 7, 20, 163–5, 232, 246, 247, 248, 249
secrecy, misinterpretation of 260
Selong, Gabriel 150
Semeia-source (SQ) 95
Seneca 216, 219, 220
Senior, Donald 264
Sevrin, Jean-Marie 166
shepherd imagery 102
Shin, Sookgoo 194, 195–6, 197
Siegert, Folker 17
signs-based faith, John and 43–4
signs, forcing the Sanhedrin to take action 242
Signs Gospel 3, 18
signs sources 17, 161
Simon of Cyrene 33, 124
Sinai, Mount 62
sin(s)
  baptism and 139, 140
  faithlessness (towards Jesus) as 195

forgiveness of 155–6, 234, 241, 243, 244, 245
God defeating/destroying 133, 139
Jesus taking away the sin of the world 134, 139, 143
judgement and 196
as a new ethical idea 195
Smith, Dwight Moody 9, 13, 32–3, 152, 163, 164, 253
social frameworks 37
social memory theory, critical inheritance 3, 31–2, 36–41, 48
Society of Biblical Literature 20
Socinianism 104–5
Socrates 219–21, 222, 224, 260
Söding, Thomas 199
Son of God, Jesus as the 5, 103, 107, 116, 118, 143, 182, 189, 191, 218, 253
Son of Man
  Jesus as 182
  in John and Mark 19, 179
  Parousia of 178, 185
sources
  bi-optic 20
  Bultmann's source analysis 18
  direct/indirect 59
  John and Mark sharing 17–18, 253
  Mark as the hypotext 24
  oral traditions 153 (*see also* oral traditions)
  reconfiguration of 52
  rewriting of 53
  Semeia-source (SQ) 95
  Signs Gospel 3, 18
  signs sources 17, 161
  Synoptic Gospels as a 23
  two-source theory 25, 77, 153
  use of in Mark and John 207–9
  used by ancient authors 2
Sozzini, Lelio and Fausto 104
spatiality 91, 92
speech-compositions
  form, narrative structure and audience of the speeches 205–7
  the historiographical claim of Mark/John and 210
  in Mark and John 6, 203–4, 210, 213–14
  use of sources and traditions in Mark and John 17–18, 207–9, 253

speech(es)
  in ancient historiography 212–13
  function of 213
  in the Gospels 203
  literary strategies of 6
  role and mission of Jesus and 213
  speech of Jesus 205–7
stereotypes
  ancient gender 216
  ethical 199
Stoics 216, 222, 225, 226
structure, of Mark and John 16, 21
stylistic transformation 25
suffering, of Jesus 236
Sychar, Samaria 44–5, 46
synagogal punishments 177
synagogue, the church and 160, 165
Synoptic Gospels
  eschatology of the 178, 179
  ethical issues found in the 195
  John and the 9–11, 15, 16, 46–7, 51, 68, 78–81, 84, 89, 92–3, 95, 96, 98, 149–50, 208
  John as a fourth Synoptic Gospel 81–4
  John's disagreement with/independence from the 33–6, 77, 170–1
  John's literary familiarity with 4
  redactional elements of 16–17
  as a source 23
  speech in 203
  Synoptic narrative parallels 10–12
  Synoptic problem 1
  Synoptic relationships 2
  two-source hypothesis for 25
Synoptic tradition
  Johannine reinterpretation of 26
  sayings of the Lord (Herrenworte) as metatexts of 28

Tannehill, Robert C. 192
Tatian 1
taxes 190, 192, 235
Taylor, Vincent 18
teaching, of Jesus 205
temple incident
  conflict with opponents and 237
  hypertextuality and 26–7

the intention to kill him and 236
placement of 33, 85, 245, 255
process of transformation and 3
Temple Scroll 55, 63
temptation
  of Jesus by Satan 6, 116, 215, 216, 217–19, 221, 223–5, 227, 228
  Jewish Scriptures and 220
  Johannine rewriting of Markan temptation scenes 216, 217, 221–2, 223–5, 227
  scene in Gethsemane 215, 218, 219, 221, 223–5, 227, 228
  the Socratic philosopher in 219–21
'The Temptation of Jesus' 217–18
tests of volition 217, 218
texts
  authoritative status of 62–5
  availability of written texts 247
  derived texts 3, 25
  ethical texts 187–8, 188–9, 190–3
  the renewed verbalization of a 247
  rewriting Jewish 3, 56–7, 58
textual comparisons 150–1
textual strategies, rewriting 55
textual techniques, education in 52
Thatcher, Tom 32, 165
Theobald, Michael 19, 23, 28
Thucydides 75, 212
Thyen, Hartwig 14, 15, 24, 46, 48, 95
Timaeus 73
time
  of fulfilment 174
  John and 94, 96–9
  measured and set by God 173
  the past 37, 38, 39, 40
  post-Easter period and 176
Titania Hotel, Athens, Greece (conference) 1–2
Torah
  acting according to the 195
  ancient Jewish and early Christian discourse on 192
  ethical issues found in the 195
  Jesus as the authoritative teacher of 6, 189, 192, 201
  reason taught by Torah conquers the passions 220
  the *Temple Scroll* and 63

tradition criticism 198, 199, 200
tradition history 23–4, 165
'Tradition Received and Handed on: A Paraphrasing Commentary Attached' 154
tradition, transmitted 160
traditions and sources, use of in Mark, Luke and John 207–9
traditions, invented 199
Traditionsgeschichte 198, 199, 200
tragic genre 75
tragic narrative 4, 67
Transfiguration story 88
transformation(s)
  diegetic 26
  literary and theological 29
  process of 3
  stylistic/quantitative 25–6
  of the traditions 29
transmitted tradition 160
trial scenes 7, 256–8, 259–62, 262–6
tribulations within the community 185
triumph, theme of 7
Triumphal Entry 85
200 denarii 21
two-source theory 25, 77, 153

Ueberschaer, Nadine 184
universal tribulation 179

values, moral 199
Van Belle, Gilbert x, 5, 17 (*see also* chapter 12)
vices 190, 191, 192, 199, 226
virtue, of supporting the poor 195
virtues, vices and 192
virtuous lament 226
voice, John the Baptist and 139
Vorbild (model), John the Baptist as 137, 147
Vorläufer (predecessor), John the Baptist as 137, 147

Wahlde, Urban von 15
walking on water 3, 27, 69, 70, 71, 80
washing of feet 28, 194
Water of Life discourse 204, 206
water, the Holy Spirit and 132
Watt, Jan G. van der 194

wedding in Cana 222–3, 227
well, the 153
Williams, Catrin H. x, 3, 43–4, 70, 136, 138, 145 (*see also* chapter 1; chapter 5)
Windisch, Hans 13, 21
Wischmeyer, Oda x, 6 (*see also* chapter 14)
witness, John the Baptist as 5, 137, 138, 139, 140, 142, 143, 144, 145, 146, 147
witness, the Beloved Disciple as 28–9
witnessing
  Jesus as a witness to the truth 263
  theme of 16
Word, the
  God as 72, 102, 103–4, 110, 117
  Jesus as 72, 73, 107, 116, 255
  the pre-existence of 131

Words on the Glorification of the Son 204, 207
Wrede, William 86, 92
written texts, availability of 247

Xenophon 219

Yahweh 69, 71, 72
Yarbro Collins, Adela 20, 70, 193

Zahn, Molly 56, 63
Zeuge (witness), John the Baptist as. *See* witness, John the Baptist as
Zhang, Tong 37–40
Zimmermann, Ruben 194
Zumstein, Jean x, 3, 14–15, 48, 93, 166, 193, 195, 199, 200 (*see also* chapter 3)

www.ingramcontent.com/pod-product-compliance
Ingram Content Group UK Ltd.
Pitfield, Milton Keynes, MK11 3LW, UK
UKHW021904220326
469204UK00008B/177